AS Law

Visit the *AS Law*, third edition, Companion Website at **www.pearsoned.co.uk/elliottquinn** to find valuable **student** learning material including:

- Extra quizzes and exercises
- Templates of the interactive exercises in the book
- An online glossary to explain key terms
- Extensive links to valuable resources on the web
- Regular updates on major legal changes affecting the book

Third Edition

AS Law

Catherine Elliott and
Frances Quinn

PEARSON
Longman

Harlow, England • London • New York • Boston • San Francisco • Toronto
Sydney • Tokyo • Singapore • Hong Kong • Seoul • Taipei • New Delhi
Cape Town • Madrid • Mexico City • Amsterdam • Munich • Paris • Milan

Pearson Education Limited

Edinburgh Gate
Harlow
Essex CM20 2JE
England

and Associated Companies throughout the world

Visit us on the World Wide Web at:
www.pearsoned.co.uk

First published in 2002
Second edition published 2004
Third edition published 2006

ISBN-10 1-405-83618-0
ISBN-13 978-1-4058-3618-0

British Library Cataloguing-in-Publication Data
A catalogue record for this book is available from the British Library

Library of Congress Cataloging-in-Publication Data
A catalog record for this book is available from the Library of Congress

10 9 8 7 6 5 4 3 2 1
10 09 08 07 06

Typeset in 10/13pt Palatino by 35
Printed by Ashford Colour Press Ltd, Gosport

The publisher's policy is to use paper manufactured from sustainable forests.

Brief contents

Contents

Contents

Supporting resources
Visit **www.pearsoned.co.uk/elliottquinn** to find valuable online resources

Companion Website for students
- Extra quizzes and exercises
- Templates of the interactive exercises in the book
- An online glossary to explain key terms
- Extensive links to valuable resources on the web
- Regular updates on major legal changes affecting the book

For instructors
- Lesson plans
- Additional problems and questions which can be set as student assignments

For more information please contact your local Pearson Education sales representative or visit **www.pearsoned.co.uk/elliottquinn**

Guided Tour

Task boxes provide activities that can be carried out to help you to explore the subject.

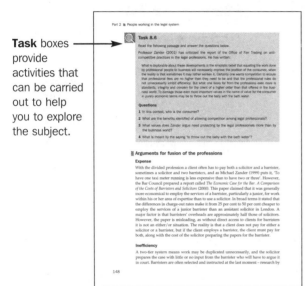

Quick quizzes allow you to test your knowledge and understanding of the law, and Know your terms boxes help you to understand and remember technical legal terms.

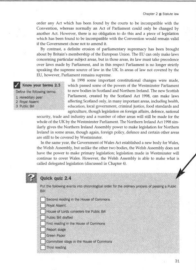

Exam question and answer guides, placed at the end of each chapter, aid your exam preparations and provide useful advice on answering exam questions.

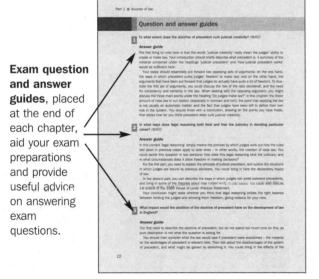

Chapter summaries provide you with an outline of the main topic areas covered in the chapter to ensure that you have covered all the essential points.

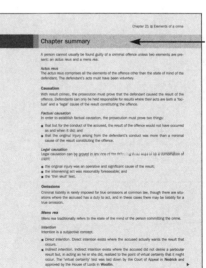

Guided Tour

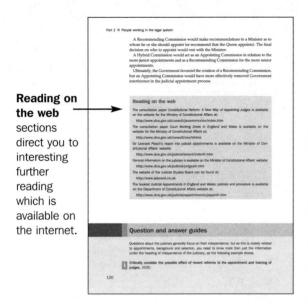

Reading on the web sections direct you to interesting further reading which is available on the internet.

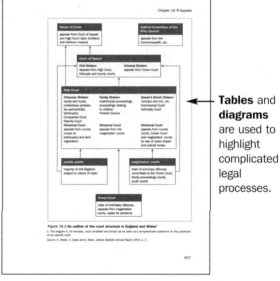

Tables and **diagrams** are used to highlight complicated legal processes.

Real **forms** are used to bring the subject to life, and highlight how the law operates in practice.

Accompanied by a **Companion Website**, including regular updates on major legal changes affecting the book, links to valuable web resources, an online glossary to explain key terms and extra quizzes and exercises.

Preface

This book provides a fresh approach to the study of AS level law. It builds on the strengths of previous books written by the authors by offering a clear explanation of the law in plain English. It also includes certain features to provide extra help and stimulation for the student, including:

- **Know your terms** boxes to help students understand and remember some of the technical legal vocabulary that they need to know. There is also a detailed glossary at the back of the book.
- **Tasks** providing possible activities that can be carried out easily to help the student explore the subject further.
- **Quick quizzes** at key stages in each chapter, to give students an opportunity to test their knowledge and understanding of the law.
- **Reading on the web** sections at the end of each chapter. These provide references to interesting material that has been referred to in the chapter and which is available free on the Internet.
- **Exam questions and answer guidelines** at the end of each chapter to assist students in preparing for their assessments.
- **Chapter summaries** at the end of each chapter providing a quick and easy outline of the material covered.

All the chapters are structured so that the material is in a systematic order for the purposes of both learning and revision, and clear subheadings make specific points easy to locate. There is also an appendix at the end of the book which gives useful general advice on answering exam questions in law.

The book caters for the specifications of all the examination boards offering AS law: the Assessment and Qualifications Alliance (AQA), the Oxford, Cambridge and RSA Examinations (OCR) and the Welsh Joint Education Committee (WJEC). A chart is provided on pp. xvii–xviii illustrating which chapters are required for each module of the examination boards.

This book is part of a series that has been written by the same authors. The other books in the series which will be of use to students when they progress to A2 level law and the study of law at university are *Criminal Law*, *Contract Law* and *Tort Law*.

We have endeavoured to state the law as at 1 January 2006.

Catherine Elliott
Frances Quinn
London, 2006

Acknowledgements

We are grateful to the following for permission to reproduce copyright material:

Figures 1.1, 5.1, 6.3, 7.2, 9.1, 9.2, 12.1, 12.2, 15.1 and 16.1 photographs © EMPICS; Figure 2.1 from Criminal Defence Service (Advice and Assistance) Act 2001, p. c.4., Crown copyright material is reproduced under Class Licence Number C01W0000039 with the permission of the Controller of HMSO and the Queen's Printer for Scotland; Figure 2.2 photograph reproduced with permission of the House of Commons Information Office; Figure 6.1 from *News of the World*, London, 23 July 2000, © News International Newspapers Limited, 27 July 2000, reproduced with permission; Figure 6.2 photograph © Rex Features Ltd.; Figures 7.1, 10.1, 17.3, 19.1 and 19.2 redrawn from *Judicial Statistics Annual Report 2004*, Crown copyright material is reproduced under Class Licence Number C01W0000039 with the permission of the Controller of HMSO and the Queen's Printer for Scotland; Figure 8.1 redrawn from *Fact Sheet 2: Women in the Profession*, www.lawsociety.org.uk, reprinted by permission of The Law Society; Table 8.1 from the *Annual Report of the Legal Services Ombudsman for England and Wales 2004/2005*, Crown copyright material is reproduced under Class Licence Number C01W0000039 with the permission of the Controller of HMSO and the Queen's Printer for Scotland; Figure 8.2 photograph by permission of the Masters of the Bench of The Honourable Society of Gray's Inn; Figure 8.3 redrawn from the *Annual Report of the Legal Services Ombudsman for England and Wales 2004/2005*, Crown copyright material is reproduced under Class Licence Number C01W0000039 with the permission of the Controller of HMSO and the Queen's Printer for Scotland; Figure 8.4 redrawn from *Fact Sheet 3: Solicitors from minority ethnic groups*, www.lawsociety.org.uk, reprinted by permission of The Law Society; Figure 8.5 by kind permission of The Law Society; Tables 10.1 and 10.2 from *The Judiciary in the Magistrates' Courts*, Home Office RDS Occasional Paper No. 66, Crown copyright material is reproduced under Class Licence Number C01W0000039 with the permission of the Controller of HMSO and the Queen's Printer for Scotland (Morgan, R. and Russell, N. 2000); Figure 10.2 from *AQA General Certificate of Education Law Teachers' Guide 2001/2*, designed by F. Mahar and M. J. Duffy, reprinted by permission of Fareen Mahar; Figures 10.3, 13.3 and 13.4 redrawn from *Crown Prosecution Service Annual Report 2004–2005*, Crown copyright material is reproduced under Class Licence Number C01W0000039 with the permission of the Controller of HMSO and the Queen's Printer for Scotland; Figure 11.1 reprinted by permission of Legal Services Commission; Figures 12.3 and 13.5 redrawn from *Crime in England and Wales 2002/2003, Supplementary Vol. 2: Crime, disorder and the criminal justice system and public attitudes and perceptions*, Crown copyright material is reproduced under

Class Licence Number C01W0000039 with the permission of the Controller of HMSO and the Queen's Printer for Scotland; Figures 12.4, 13.1, 14.1, 15.2, 15.3, 15.4, 16.2 and 16.4 redrawn from *Criminal Statistics England and Wales 2001*, Crown copyright material is reproduced under Class Licence Number C01W0000039 with the permission of the Controller of HMSO and the Queen's Printer for Scotland (Home Office 2002); Figure 12.11 redrawn from *The Crown Prosecution Service Annual Report 2000–2001*, Crown copyright material is reproduced under Class Licence Number C01W0000039 with the permission of the Controller of HMSO and the Queen's Printer for Scotland; Figure 14.2 photograph Mercury Press Agency; Figure 14.3 redrawn from *Crown Prosecution Service Annual Report 2002–2003*, Crown copyright material is reproduced under Class Licence Number C01W0000039 with the permission of the Controller of HMSO and the Queen's Printer for Scotland; Table 16.1 from *Criminal Statistics England and Wales 2001*, Crown copyright material is reproduced under Class Licence Number C01W0000039 with the permission of the Controller of HMSO and the Queen's Printer for Scotland (Home Office 2002); Figure 16.3 photograph John Edward Linden/Arcaid; Figure 17.2 from Claim Form from Court Service website at www.mcsi.gov.uk, Crown copyright material is reproduced under Class Licence Number C01W0000039 with the permission of the Controller of HMSO and the Queen's Printer for Scotland; Figures 17.4, 17.5, 17.6, 17.7 and 17.8 redrawn from *Civil Justice Reform Evaluation Further Findings*, Crown copyright material is reproduced under Class Licence Number C01W0000039 with the permission of the Controller of HMSO and the Queen's Printer for Scotland (Department for Constitutional Affairs 2002); Figure 18.1 redrawn from *Judicial Statistics Annual Report 2002*, Crown copyright material is reproduced under Class Licence Number C01W0000039 with the permission of the Controller of HMSO and the Queen's Printer for Scotland (Dibdin, K. *et al.*, eds); Figure 18.4 redrawn from *Annual Report 2004–2005*, Crown copyright material is reproduced under Class Licence Number C01W0000039 with the permission of the Controller of HMSO and the Queen's Printer for Scotland (Criminal Cases Review Commission 2005); Figure 19.3 photograph Criminal Cases Review Commission; Figure 20.1 Association of British Travel Agents; Figures 23.1 and 23.5 redrawn from *Crime in England and Wales 2004/05*, Crown copyright material is reproduced under Class Licence Number C01W0000039 with the permission of the Controller of HMSO and the Queen's Printer for Scotland; Table 23.1 adapted from *Crime in England and Wales 2001/2002: Supplementary Volume*, reprinted by permission of Home Office, © Crown Copyright 2003 (Flood-Page, C. and Taylor, J., eds. 2003); Figure 23.3 redrawn from *Crime in England and Wales 2001/2002: Supplementary Volume*, reprinted by permission of Home Office, © Crown Copyright 2003 (Flood-Page, C. and Taylor, J., eds. 2003).

We are grateful to the following examination boards for permission to reproduce questions that have appeared in their examination papers:

Assessment and Qualifications Alliance (AQA)
London Qualifications Limited trading as Edexcel
Oxford Cambridge and RSA Examinations Board (OCR)
Welsh Joint Education Committee (WJEC)

The examination boards are not responsible for any suggested answers to the questions.

We are also grateful to Guardian Newspapers Limited for an extract from 'Meddle at your peril', by Anthony Lester, published in *The Observer*, 14 August 2005; News International Syndication for extracts from 'Wigs in court: it's time for this horseplay to stop', by David Pannick, published in *The Times*, 27 May 2003; 'Tagging is harder than prison because I have to make an effort every day', by Dick Whitfield, published in *The Times*, 11 March 2003; and 'Grim facts of domestic violence', by Marilyn Stowe published in *The Times*, 1 July 2003; and HMSO for an extract from the Home Office consultation paper *Violence: Reforming the Offences Against the Person Act 1861*.

In some instances we have been unable to trace the owners of copyright material, and we would appreciate any information that would enable us to do so.

Table of chapters required for examination boards

AQA Examination Board

AS Module 1: Law making

Chapter 1   Case law
Chapter 2   Statute law
Chapter 3   Statutory interpretation
Chapter 4   Delegated legislation
Chapter 5   European law
Chapter 6   Law reform

AS Module 2: Dispute solving

Chapter 7   The judiciary
Chapter 8   The legal professions
Chapter 9   The jury system
Chapter 10   Magistrates
Chapter 11   Paying for legal services
Chapter 12   The police
Chapter 13   The criminal trial process

Chapter 14   Young offenders
Chapter 17   The civil justice system
Chapter 18   Tribunals
Chapter 19   Appeals
Chapter 20   Alternative methods of dispute resolution

AS Module 3: The concept of liability

Chapter 15   Sentencing
Chapter 21   Elements of a crime
Chapter 22   Strict liability in criminal law
Chapter 23   Non-fatal offences against the person
Chapter 24   Negligence
Chapter 25   Remedies for torts

A2 Module 6: Concepts of law

On companion website.

OCR Examination Board

AS Unit 1: English Legal System

Chapter 7   Judges
Chapter 8   Legal professions
Chapter 9   The jury system
Chapter 10   Magistrates
Chapter 11   Paying for legal services
Chapter 12   The police
Chapter 13   The criminal trial process
Chapter 14   Young offenders
Chapter 15   Sentencing
Chapter 16   Sentencing young offenders
Chapter 17   The civil justice system

Chapter 19   Appeals
Chapter 20   Alternative methods of dispute resolution

AS Unit 2: Sources of law

Chapter 1   Case law
Chapter 2   Statute law
Chapter 3   Statutory interpretation
Chapter 4   Delegated legislation
Chapter 5   European law
Chapter 6   Law reform

Table of chapters required for examination boards

WJEC Examination Board

Module: Legal concepts, sources and methodology
Chapter 1 Case law
Chapter 2 Statute law
Chapter 3 Statutory interpretation
Chapter 4 Delegated legislation
Chapter 5 European law
Chapter 6 Law reform

Module: Machinery of justice
Chapter 9 The jury system
Chapter 11 Paying for legal services

Chapter 12 The police
Chapter 13 The criminal trial process
Chapter 14 Young offenders
Chapter 17 The civil justice system
Chapter 18 Tribunals
Chapter 19 Appeal courts
Chapter 20 Alternative dispute resolution

Module: Personnel
Chapter 7 The judiciary
Chapter 8 The legal professions
Chapter 10 Magistrates

Table of cases

Table of legislation

Table of Statutory Instruments

PART 1

Sources of law

English law stems from four main sources, though these vary a great deal in importance. The basis of our law today is case law, a mass of judge-made decisions which lay down rules to be followed in future court cases. For many centuries it was the main form of law and it is still very important today. However, the most important source of law, in the sense that it prevails over most of the others, are Acts of Parliament. Delegated legislation is made by the administration rather than the legislature, and lays down detailed rules to implement the broader provisions of Acts of Parliament.

An increasingly important source of law is the legislation of the European Union, which is the only type of law that can take precedence over Acts of Parliament in the UK.

Part 1 concludes with a discussion of the process of law reform, whereby these sources of law can be changed to reflect the changes taking place in society.

AQA Examination Board

Chapters 1–6 cover AS module 1: Law making

OCR Examination Board

Chapters 1–6 cover the Sources of law module

WJEC Examination Board

Chapters 1–6 cover the Legal concepts, sources and methodology module

---

Chapter 1

Case law

Judicial precedent

Case law comes from the decisions made by judges in the cases before them. In deciding a case, there are two basic tasks; first, establishing what the facts are, meaning what actually happened; and secondly, how the law applies to those facts. It is the second task that can make case law. Once a decision has been made on how the law applies to a particular set of facts, similar facts in later cases should be treated in the same way. This is known as the principle of *stare decisis* which is a Latin term meaning 'let the decision stand'. This is obviously fairer than allowing each judge to interpret the law differently, and also provides predictability, which makes it easier for people to live within the law.

English judgments are frequently quite long, containing quite a lot of comment which is not strictly relevant to the case, as well as an explanation of the legal principles on which the judge has made a decision. The explanation of the legal principles on which the decision is made is called the *ratio decidendi* – Latin for the 'reason for deciding'. It is this part of the judgment, known as binding precedent, which forms case law.

All the parts of the judgment which do not form part of the *ratio decidendi* of the case are called *obiter dicta* – which is Latin for 'things said by the way'. These are often discussions of hypothetical situations: for example, the judge might say 'Jones did this, but if she had done that, my decision would have been . . .'. None of the *obiter dicta* forms part of the case law, though judges in later cases may be influenced by it, and it is said to be a persuasive precedent.

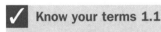 **Know your terms 1.1**

Define these Latin terms:

1 *Stare decisis*
2 *Ratio decidendi*
3 *Obiter dicta*

In deciding a case, a judge must follow any decision that has been made by a higher court in a case with similar facts. The rules concerning which courts are bound by which are known as the rules of judicial precedent, or *stare decisis*. As well as being bound by the decisions of courts above them, some courts must also follow their own previous decisions; they are said to be bound by themselves.

The history of common law

Before the Norman Conquest in 1066, different areas of England were governed by different systems of law. When William the Conqueror gained the English throne in

1066, he established a strong central government and began to standardize the law. Representatives of the king were sent out to the countryside to check the local administration, and were given the job of adjudicating in local disputes, according to local law.

When these 'itinerant justices' returned to Westminster, they were able to discuss the various customs of different parts of the country and, by a process of sifting, reject unreasonable ones and accept those that seemed rational, to form a consistent body of rules. During this process – which went on for around two centuries – the principle of *stare decisis* grew up. Whenever a new problem of law came to be decided, the decision formed a rule to be followed in all similar cases, making the law more predictable.

The result of all this was that by about 1250 a 'common law' had been produced, that ruled the whole country, could be applied consistently and could be used to predict what the courts might decide in a particular case. It contained many of what are now basic points of English law – the fact that murder is a crime, for example.

The English common law system was exported around the world wherever British influence dominated during the colonial period. These countries, including the USA and many Commonwealth countries, are described as having common law systems. They are often contrasted with civil law systems which can be found in continental Europe and countries over which Europe has had influence. The best known civil law system is the French legal system whose civil code has been highly influential.

Equity

The common law became increasingly rigid and only offered one remedy, damages, which was not always an adequate solution to every problem. Many people were unable to seek redress for wrongs through the common law courts. Some of these people petitioned the king, who was thought of as the 'fountain of justice'. These petitions were commonly passed to the Chancellor, the king's chief minister, as the king did not want to spend time considering them. Litigants appeared before the Chancellor, who would question them, and then deliver a verdict based on his own moral view of the question. Because the Court followed no binding rules, relying entirely on the Chancellor's view of right and wrong, it could enforce rights not recognized by the common law, which, restricted by the concept of *stare decisis*, was failing to adapt to new circumstances. This type of justice came to be known as equity.

By the nineteenth century equity had become a body of law with established cases, rather than an arbitrary exercise of conscience. Today equity is still a separate body of rules, distinct from the common law rules, but it is applied in the same courts as the common law. Where there is a conflict between the two, equity prevails.

Case names

Each legal case that is taken to court is given a name. The name of the case is usually based on the family name of the parties involved. In essays, the name of the case should normally be put into italics or underlined, though in this book we have chosen to put them in bold.

If Ms Smith steals Mr Brown's car then a criminal action is likely to be brought by the state against her. The written name of the case would then be **R** *v* **Smith**. The letter 'R' stands for the Latin *Rex* (King) or *Regina* (Queen) depending on whether there was a king or queen in office at the time of the decision. Sometimes the full Latin terms are used rather than the simple abbreviation R, so that the case **R** *v* **Smith** if brought now while Queen Elizabeth is in office could also be called **Regina** *v* **Smith**.

The 'v' separating the two parties' names is short for 'versus' (against), in the same way as one might write Manchester Football Club *v* Arsenal Football Club when the two teams are going to play a match against each other. When speaking, instead of saying 'R versus Smith' one should really say 'The Crown against Smith'.

In civil law, if Mr Brown is in a neighbour dispute with Ms Smith and decides to bring an action against Ms Smith, the name of the case will be **Brown** *v* **Smith**.

The hierarchy of the courts

The European Court of Justice

Decisions of the European Court of Justice (ECJ) are binding on all English courts. It appears not to be bound by its own decisions.

The House of Lords

Apart from cases concerning European law, this is the highest appeal court on civil and criminal matters, and all other English courts are bound by it. It was traditionally bound by its own decisions, but in 1966, the Lord Chancellor issued a practice statement saying that the House of Lords was no longer bound by its previous decisions. In practice the House of Lords only rarely overrules one of its earlier decisions. This reluctance to do so is illustrated by the case of **R** *v* **Kansal (No. 2)** (2001). In that case the House of Lords held that it had probably got the law wrong in its earlier decision of **R** *v* **Lambert** (2001). The latter case had ruled that the Human Rights Act 1998 would not have retrospective effect in relation to appeals heard by the House of Lords after the Act came into force, but which had been decided by the lower courts before the Act came into force. Despite the fact that the majority thought the earlier judgment of **Lambert** was wrong, the House decided in **Kansal** to follow it. This was because **Lambert** was a recent decision, it represented a possible interpretation of the statute which was not unworkable and it only concerned a temporary transitional period.

There are, however, a range of cases where the House of Lords has been prepared to apply the 1966 practice statement. For example, in **R** *v* **R** (1991) it held that rape within marriage is a crime, overturning a legal principle that had stood for centuries.

In **Authur JS Hall & Co** *v* **Simons** (2000), the House of Lords refused to follow the earlier case of **Rondel** *v* **Worsley** (1969), which had given barristers immunity against claims for negligence in their presentation of cases.

In **R** *v* **G and another** (2003) the House of Lords overruled an established criminal case of **R** *v* **Caldwell** (1981). Under **R** *v* **Caldwell** the House had been prepared to convict people for criminal offences where the prosecution had not proved that the defendant personally had intended or seen the risk of causing the relevant harm, but had simply shown that a reasonable person would have had this state of mind on the facts. This was particularly harsh where the actual defendant was incapable of seeing the risk of harm, because, for example, they were very young or of low intelligence. **Caldwell** had been heavily criticized by academics over the years, but when the House of Lords originally reconsidered the matter in 1990 in **R** *v* **Reid**, it confirmed its original decision. However, when the matter again came to the House of Lords in 2003, the House dramatically admitted that it had got the law wrong. It stated:

> The surest test of a new legal rule is not whether it satisfies a team of logicians but how it performs in the real world. With the benefit of hindsight the verdict must be that the rule laid down by the majority in **Caldwell** failed this test. It was severely criticised by academic lawyers of distinction. It did not command respect among practitioners and judges. Jurors found it difficult to understand; it also sometimes offended their sense of justice. Experience suggests that in **Caldwell** the law took a wrong turn.

An important case is **In Re Pinochet** (1998), where the House of Lords stated that it had the power to reopen an appeal where one of the parties has been subjected to an unfair procedure. The case was part of the litigation concerning General Augusto Pinochet, the former Chilean president. The Lords reopened the appeal because one of the Law Lords who heard the original appeal, Lord Hoffmann, was connected with the human rights organization Amnesty International, which had been a party to the appeal. This meant that there was a possibility of bias and so the proceedings could be viewed as unfair. The Lords stressed, however, that there was no question of them being able to reopen an appeal because the decision made originally was thought to be wrong; the Pinochet appeal was reopened because it could be said that there had not been a fair hearing, and not because the decision reached was wrong (although at the second hearing of the appeal, the Lords did in fact come to a slightly different decision).

The Government intends to abolish the House of Lords and replace it with a Supreme Court. This reform is contained in the Constitutional Reform Act 2005 and is discussed at p. 408.

Task 1.2

Visit the House of Lords' judicial business website at:

http://www.publications.parliament.uk/pa/ld/ldjudinf.htm

Find the judgment **In Re Pinochet** (1999). Who were the judges in that case?

Figure 1.1 Demonstrators in favour of the deportation of the former Chilean President Augusto Pinochet

Source: © EMPICS.

Privy Council

The Privy Council was established by the Judicial Committee Act 1833. It is the final appeal court for many Commonwealth countries. The Privy Council currently has jurisdiction to hear devolution cases relating to the powers of the devolved legislative and executive authorities in Scotland, Northern Ireland and Wales. Once the Supreme Court has been established, this domestic jurisdiction will be transferred to the new court. Its cases do not bind English courts, but they have strong persuasive authority because of the seniority of the judges who sit in the Privy Council.

The Court of Appeal

This is split into Civil and Criminal Divisions; they do not bind each other. Both divisions are bound by the House of Lords.

The Civil Division is usually bound by its own previous decisions, but there are four exceptions to this where:

1 the previous decision was made in ignorance of a relevant law (it is said to have been made *per incuriam*);
2 there are two previous conflicting decisions;
3 there is a later, conflicting House of Lords' decision;

4 a proposition of law was assumed to exist by an earlier court and was not subject to argument or consideration by that court.

The first three of these exceptions were laid down in **Young** *v* **Bristol Aeroplane Co. Ltd** (1944). The fourth was added by **R** *v* **Brent London Borough Housing Benefit Review Board, ex parte Khadim** (2001).

In the Criminal Division, the results of cases heard may decide whether or not an individual goes to prison, so the Criminal Division takes a more flexible approach to its previous decisions and does not follow them where doing so could cause injustice.

Lord Denning would have liked the Court of Appeal to have had the power to overrule its own previous decisions wherever it felt it had got the law wrong, in the same way as the House of Lords has this power following the Practice Statement of 1966. He put forward this view in **Davis** *v* **Johnson** (1979). The Court of Appeal has not been prepared to take this stance, and Lord Simon was of the view that any such change to the rules of precedent concerning the Court of Appeal would require an Act of Parliament (**Miliangos** *v* **George Frank (Textiles) Ltd** (1976)).

The High Court

This court is divided between the Divisional Courts and the ordinary High Court. All are bound by the Court of Appeal and the House of Lords.

The Divisional Courts are the Queen's Bench Division, which deals with criminal appeals and judicial review, the Chancery Division and the Family Division, which both deal with civil appeals. The two civil Divisional Courts are bound by their previous decisions, but the Divisional Court of the Queen's Bench is more flexible about this, for the same reason as the Criminal Division of the Court of Appeal. The Divisional Courts bind the ordinary High Court.

The ordinary High Court is not bound by its own previous decisions. It can produce precedents for courts below it, but these are of a lower status than those produced by the Court of Appeal or the House of Lords.

The Crown Court

The Crown Court is bound by all the courts above it. Its decisions do not form binding precedents, though when High Court judges sit in the Crown Court, their judgments form persuasive precedents, which must be given serious consideration in subsequent cases, though it is not obligatory to follow them. Since the Crown Court cannot form binding precedents, it is obviously not bound by its own decisions.

Magistrates' and county courts

These are called the inferior courts. They are bound by the High Court, Court of Appeal and House of Lords. Their own decisions are not reported, and cannot produce binding precedents, or even persuasive ones; like the Crown Court, they are therefore not bound by their own decisions.

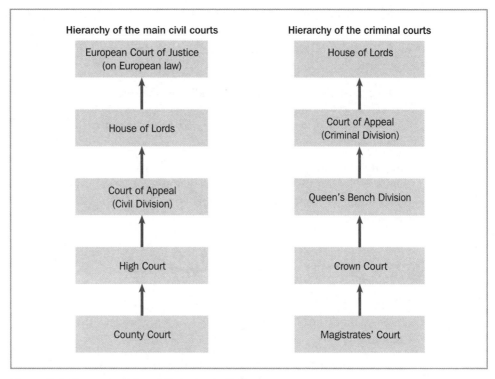

Figure 1.2 The routes for civil and criminal cases

European Court of Human Rights

The European Court of Human Rights (ECtHR) is an international court based in Strasbourg. It hears cases alleging that there has been a breach of the European Convention on Human Rights. This court does not fit neatly within the hierarchy of the courts. Under s. 2 of the Human Rights Act 1998 an English court is required to 'take account of' the cases decided by the ECtHR, though its decisions do not bind the English courts. In practice, when considering a Convention right, the domestic courts try to follow the same interpretation as that given by the ECtHR. In **R (Alconbury)** *v* **Secretary of State for the Environment, Transport and the Regions** (2001) the House of Lords said:

> In the absence of some special circumstances it seems to me the court should follow any clear and constant jurisprudence of the European Court of Human Rights. If it does not do so there is at least a possibility the case will go to that court which is likely in the ordinary case to follow its own constant jurisprudence.

Despite this, the House of Lords has refused to follow an earlier decision of the ECtHR. In **Morris** *v* **UK** (2002) the European Court of Human Rights ruled that the courts martial system (which is the courts system used by the army) breached the European Court of Human Rights as it did not guarantee a fair trial within the meaning of Art. 6 of the European Convention. Subsequently, in **Boyd** *v* **The Army Prosecuting Authority** (2002) three soldiers who had been convicted of assault by a court martial argued before the House of Lords that the court martial had violated their right to a fair trial under the Convention. Surprisingly, the argument was rejected and the House of Lords refused to follow the decision of the ECtHR of **Morris** *v* **UK**. It stated:

> While the decision in **Morris** is not binding on the House, it is of course a matter which the House must take into account (s. 2(1)(a) of the Human Rights Act 1998) and which demands careful attention, not least because it is a recent expression of the European Court's view on these matters.

The House considered that the European Court was given 'rather less information than the House' about the courts martial system, and in the light of this additional information it concluded that there had been no violation of the European Convention.

How judicial precedent works

When faced with a case on which there appears to be a relevant earlier decision, either by that court (if bound by itself), or a higher one, the judges can do any of the following:

Follow. If the facts are sufficiently similar, the precedent set by the earlier case is followed, and the law applied in the same way to produce a decision.

Distinguish. Where the facts of the case before the judge are significantly different from those of the earlier one, then the judge distinguishes the two cases and need not follow the earlier one.

Overrule. Where the earlier decision was made in a lower court, the judges can overrule that earlier decision if they disagree with the lower court's statement of the law. The outcome of the earlier decision remains the same, but will not be followed.

Reverse. If the decision of a lower court is appealed to a higher one, the higher court may change it if they feel the lower court has wrongly interpreted the law. Clearly when a decision is reversed, the higher court is usually also overruling the lower court's statement of the law.

In practice the process is rather more complicated than this, since decisions are not always made on the basis of only one previous case; there are usually several different cases offered in support of each side's view of the question.

How do judges really decide cases?

The independence of the judiciary was ensured by the Act of Settlement 1700, which transferred the power to sack judges from the Crown to Parliament. Consequently, judges should theoretically make their decisions based purely on the logical deductions of precedent, uninfluenced by political or career considerations.

The eighteenth-century legal commentator, William Blackstone, introduced the declaratory theory of law, stating that judges do not make law, but merely, by the rules of precedent, discover and declare the law that has always been. He thought there was always one right answer to a legal question, to be deduced from an objective study of precedent.

Today, however, this position is considered somewhat unrealistic. If the operation of precedent is the precise science Blackstone suggests, a large majority of cases in the higher courts would never come to court at all. The lawyers concerned could simply look up the relevant case law and predict what the decision would be, then advise whichever of the clients would be bound to lose not to bother bringing or fighting the case. In civil litigation no good lawyer would advise a client to bring or defend a case that they had no chance of winning. Evidence that more than one solution is possible is provided by reading a judgment of the Court of Appeal, argued as though it were the only possible decision in the light of the cases that had gone before, and then discover that this apparently inevitable decision has promptly been reversed by the House of Lords.

In practice, then, judges' decisions may not be as neutral as Blackstone's declaratory theory suggests: they have to make choices which are by no means spelt out by precedents. Yet, rather than openly stating that they are choosing between two or more equally relevant precedents, the courts find ways to avoid awkward ones, which give the impression that the precedents they do choose to follow are the only ones that could possibly apply. In theory, only the House of Lords, which can overrule its own decisions as well as those of other courts, can depart from precedent: all the other courts must follow the precedent that applies in a particular case, however much they dislike it. In fact, there are a number of ways in which judges may avoid awkward precedents that at first sight might appear binding. In particular, the courts may distinguish an earlier case by saying that its facts are different in some significant way. Since the facts are unlikely to be identical, this is the simplest way to avoid an awkward precedent, and the courts have made some extremely narrow distinctions in this way. Or the court may give the precedent a very narrow *ratio decidendi*.

There is considerable room for manoeuvre within the doctrine of precedent, so what factors guide judicial decisions, and to what extent? The following are some of the answers that have been suggested.

 Quick quiz 1.3

1 What are the four main sources of English law?

2 In what year did the House of Lords declare that it was no longer bound by its previous decisions?

3 What are the four situations where the Court of Appeal Civil Division is not bound by its own decisions?

4 Which of the following courts can create a binding precedent: the High Court, Crown Court, magistrates' court and county court?

Dworkin: a seamless web of principles

Ronald Dworkin argues that judges have no real discretion in making case law. He sees law as a seamless web of principles, which supply a right answer – and only one – to every possible problem. Dworkin reasons that although stated legal rules may 'run out' (in the sense of not being directly applicable to a new case) legal principles never do, and therefore judges never need to use their own discretion.

In his book *Law's Empire* (1986), Professor Dworkin claims that judges first look at previous cases, and from those deduce which principles could be said to apply to the case before them. Then they consult their own sense of justice as to which apply, and also consider what the community's view of justice dictates. Where the judge's view and that of the community coincide, there is no problem, but if they conflict, the judges then ask themselves whether or not it would be fair to impose their own sense of justice over that of the community. Dworkin calls this the interpretive approach, and although it may appear to involve a series of choices, he considers that the legal principles underlying the decisions mean that in the end only one result could possibly surface from any one case.

Dworkin's approach has been heavily criticized as being unrealistic: opponents believe that judges do not consider principles of justice but take a much more pragmatic approach, looking at the facts of the case, not the principles.

Critical theorists: precedent as legitimation

Critical legal theorists, such as David Kairys (1998), take a quite different view. They argue that judges have considerable freedom within the doctrine of precedent. Kairys suggests that there is no such thing as legal reasoning, in the sense of a logical, neutral method of determining rules and results from what has gone before. He states that judicial decisions are actually based on 'a complex mixture of social, political, institutional, experiential and personal factors', and are simply legitimated, or justified, by reference to previous cases. The law provides 'a wide and conflicting variety' of such justifications 'from which courts pick and choose'.

The process is not necessarily as cynical as it sounds. Kairys points out that he is not saying that judges actually make the decision and then consider which precedents they can pick to justify it; rather their own beliefs and prejudices naturally lead them to give more weight to precedents which support those views. Nevertheless, for critical legal theorists, all such decisions can be seen as reflecting social and political judgements, rather than objective, purely logical deductions.

Critical theory argues that the neutral appearance of so-called 'legal reasoning' disguises the true nature of legal decisions which, by the choices made, uphold existing power relations within society, tending to favour, for example, employers over employees, property owners over those without, men over women, and rich developed countries over poor undeveloped ones.

Griffith: political choices

In similar vein, Griffith (1997) argues that judges make their decisions based on what they see as the public interest, but that their view of this interest is coloured by their background and their position in society. He suggests that the narrow social background – usually public school and Oxbridge – of the highest judges (see p. 115), combined with their position as part of established authority, leads them to believe that it is in the public interest that the established order should be maintained: in other words, that those who are in charge – whether of the country or, for example, in the workplace – should stay in charge, and that traditional values should be maintained. This leads them to 'a tenderness for private property and dislike of trade unions, strong adherence to the maintenance of order, distaste for minority opinions, demonstrations and protests, the avoidance of conflict with Government policy even where it is manifestly oppressive of the most vulnerable, support of governmental secrecy, concern for the preservation of the moral and social behaviour [to which they are] accustomed'.

As Griffith points out, the judges' view of public interest assumes that the interests of all the members of society are roughly the same, ignoring the fact that within society, different groups – employers and employees, men and women, rich and poor – may have interests which are diametrically opposed. What appears to be acting in the public interest will usually mean in the interest of one group over another, and therefore cannot be seen as neutral.

Waldron: political choices, but why not?

In his book, *The Law* (1989), Waldron agrees that judges do exercise discretion, and that they are influenced in those choices by political and ideological considerations, but argues that this is not necessarily a bad thing. He contends that while it would be wrong for judges to be biased towards one side in a case, or to make decisions based on political factors in the hope of promotion, it is unrealistic to expect a judge to be 'a political neuter – emasculated of all values and principled commitments'.

Waldron points out that to be a judge at all means a commitment to the values surrounding the legal system: recognition of Parliament as supreme, the importance of precedent, fairness, certainty, the public interest. He argues that this itself is a political choice, and further choices are made when judges have to balance these values against one another where they conflict. The responsible thing to do, according to Waldron, is to think through such conflicts in advance, and to decide which might generally be expected to give way to which. These will inevitably be political and ideological decisions. Waldron argues that since such decisions have to be made 'the thing to do is not to try to hide them, but to be as explicit as possible'. Rather than hiding such judgments behind 'smokescreens of legal mystery . . . if judges have developed particular theories of morals, politics and society, they should say so up front, and incorporate them explicitly into their decision-making'.

Waldron suggests that where judges feel uncomfortable about doing this, it may be a useful indication that they should re-examine their bias, and see whether it is an appropriate consideration by which they are to be influenced. In addition, if the public know the reasoning behind judicial decisions 'we can evaluate them and see whether we want to rely on reasons like that for the future'.

Some support for Waldron's analysis can be found in Lord Hoffmann's judgment in **Arthur J S Hall** *v* **Simons** (2000). In that case the House of Lords dramatically removed the established immunity of barristers from liability in negligence for court work. In reaching his decision Lord Hoffmann stated:

> I hope that I will not be thought ungrateful if I do not encumber this speech with citations. The question of what the public interest now requires depends upon the strength of the arguments rather than the weight of authority.

Quick quiz 1.4

1 What is the difference between a court overruling a previous decision and a court reversing a previous decision?

2 What is the name of Professor Dworkin's influential book?

3 What school of thought is David Kairys associated with?

4 Which legal writer is traditionally associated with the declaratory theory of law?

Do judges make law?

Although judges have traditionally seen themselves as declaring or finding rather than creating law, and frequently state that making law is the prerogative of Parliament, there are several areas in which they clearly do make law.

Historically, a great deal of our law is and always has been case law, made by judicial decisions. Contract and tort law are still largely judge made, and many of the most important developments – for example, the development of negligence as a tort – have had profound effects. Even though statutes have later been passed on these subjects, and occasionally Parliament has attempted to embody whole areas of common law in statutory form, these still embody the original principles created by the judges.

The application of law, whether case law or statute, to a particular case is not usually an automatic matter. Terminology may be vague or ambiguous, new developments in social life have to be accommodated, and the procedure requires interpretation as well as application. As we have suggested, judicial precedent does not always make a particular decision obvious and obligatory – there may be conflicting precedents, their implications may be unclear, and there are ways of getting round a precedent that would otherwise produce an undesirable decision. If it is accepted that Blackstone's declaratory theory does not apply in practice, then clearly the judges do make law, rather than explaining the law that is already there. The theories advanced by Kairys, Griffith and Waldron all accept that judges do have discretion, and therefore they do to some extent make law.

Where precedents do not spell out what should be done in a case before them, judges nevertheless have to make a decision. They cannot simply say that the law is not clear and refuse to decide the case. In **Airedale NHS Trust** *v* **Bland** (1993) the House of Lords considered the fate of Tony Bland, the football supporter left in a coma after the Hillsborough stadium disaster. The court had to decide whether it was lawful to stop supplying the drugs and artificial feeding that were keeping Mr Bland alive, even though it was known that doing so would mean his death soon afterwards. Several Law Lords made it plain that they felt that cases raising 'wholly new moral and social issues' should be decided by Parliament, the judges' role being to 'apply the principles which society, through the democratic process, adopts, not to impose their standards on society'. Nevertheless, the courts had no option but to make a decision one way or the other, and they decided that the action was lawful in the circumstances, because it was in the patient's best interests.

The House of Lords has explained its approach to judicial law-making in the case of **C** *v* **DPP** (1995), which raised the issue of children's liability for crime. Under common law a defendant aged between 10 and 14 could be liable for a crime only if the prosecution could prove that the child knew that what he or she did was seriously wrong. On appeal from the magistrates' court, the Divisional Court held that the defence was outdated and should no longer exist in law. An appeal was brought before the House of Lords, arguing that the Divisional Court was bound by precedent and not able to change the law in this way. The House of Lords agreed, and went on to consider whether it should change the law itself (as the 1966 Practice Statement clearly allowed it could do), but decided that this was not an appropriate case for judicial law-making. Explaining this decision, Lord Lowry suggested five factors were important:

■ where the solution to a dilemma was doubtful, judges should be wary of imposing their own answer;

■ judges should be cautious about addressing areas where Parliament had rejected opportunities of clearing up a known difficulty, or had passed legislation without doing so;

■ areas of social policy over which there was dispute were least likely to be suitable for judicial law-making;

■ fundamental legal doctrines should not be lightly set aside;

■ judges should not change the law unless they can be sure that doing so is likely to achieve finality and certainty on the issue.

This guidance suggests that the judges should take quite a cautious approach to changing the law. In practice, however, the judges do not always seem to be following these guidelines. For example, in an important criminal case of **R** *v* **Dica** (2004) the Court of Appeal overruled an earlier case of **R** *v* **Clarence** (1888) and held that criminal liability could be imposed on a defendant for recklessly infecting another person with AIDS. This change in the law was made despite the fact that the Home Office had earlier decided that legislation should not be introduced which would have imposed liability in this situation (*Violence: Reforming the Offences Against the Person Act 1861* (1998)). The Home Office had observed that 'this issue had ramifications going beyond the criminal law into wider considerations of social and public health policy'.

When should judges make law?

Again, this is a subject about which there are different views, not least among the judiciary, and the following are some of the approaches which have been suggested.

Adapting to social change

A survey has been carried out by an academic, Paterson, of 19 Law Lords active between 1967 and 1973. This survey found that at least 12 Law Lords thought that they had a duty to develop the common law in response to changing social conditions. A case where the judges did eventually show themselves willing to change the law in the light of social change is **Fitzpatrick *v* Sterling Housing Association Ltd** (2000). The case concerned a homosexual man, Mr Fitzpatrick, who had lived with his partner, Mr Thompson, for 18 years, nursing and caring for him after Mr Thompson suffered an accident which caused irreversible brain damage and severe paralysis. Mr Thompson was the tenant of the flat in which they lived and, when he died in 1994, Mr Fitzpatrick applied to take over the tenancy, which gave the tenant certain protections under the Rent Acts. The landlords refused. The legislation states that when a statutory tenant dies, the tenancy can be taken over by a spouse, a person living with the ex-tenant as wife or husband, or a member of the family who was living with the tenant. Mr Fitzpatrick's case sought to establish that he was a member of Mr Thompson's family, by virtue of their close and loving relationship.

The Court of Appeal rejected the claim while acknowledging that discrimination against same-sex partners was out of step with modern society. The House of Lords allowed the appeal, finding that a same-sex partner could establish the necessary familial link for the purposes of the legislation.

Consensus law-making

Lord Devlin has distinguished between activist law-making and dynamic law-making. He saw new ideas within society as going through a long process of acceptance. At first society will be divided about them, and there will be controversy, but eventually such ideas may come to be accepted by most members of society, or most members will at least become prepared to put up with them. At this second stage we can say there is a consensus. This process can be seen in the way that views changed towards the end of the last century on subjects such as homosexuality and sex before marriage.

Law-making which takes one side or another while an issue is still controversial is what Devlin called dynamic law-making, and he believed judges should not take part in it because it endangered their reputation for independence and impartiality. Their role is in activist law-making, concerning areas where there is a consensus. The problem with Devlin's view is that in practice the judges sometimes have no choice but to embark on dynamic law-making. In **Gillick** *v* **West Norfolk and Wisbech Area Health Authority** (1985), the House of Lords was asked to consider whether a girl under 16 needed her parents' consent before she could be given contraceptive services. It was an issue on which there was by no means a consensus, with one side claiming that teenage pregnancies would increase if the courts ruled that parental consent was necessary, and the other claiming that the judges would be encouraging under-age sex if they did not. The House of Lords held, by a majority of three to two, that a girl under 16 did not have to have parental consent if she was mature enough to make up her own mind. But the decision did not end the controversy, and it was widely suggested that the judges were not the right people to make the choice. However, since Parliament had given no lead, they had no option but to make a decision one way or the other, and were therefore forced to indulge in what Devlin would call dynamic law-making.

Respecting Parliament

Some commentators feel that the judiciary's current approach is tending to go too far, and straying outside its constitutional place. Writing in the *New Law Journal* in 1999 Francis Bennion has criticized what he called the 'growing appetite of some judges for changing the law themselves, rather than waiting for Parliament to do it'. Bennion cites two cases as examples of this. The first, **Kleinwort Benson Ltd** *v* **Lincoln City Council** (1998), concerns contract law, and, in particular, a long-standing rule, originating from case law, that where someone made a payment as a result of a mistake about the law, they did not have the right to get the money back. The rule had existed for nearly two centuries, and been much criticized in recent years – so much so that a previous Lord Chancellor had asked the Law Commission to consider whether it should be amended by legislation, and they had concluded that it should. This would normally be taken by the courts as a signal that they should leave the issue alone and wait for Parliament to act, but in this case the Lords decided to change the rule. In doing so, Lord Keith expressed the view that 'a robust view of judicial development of the law' was desirable. Bennion argues that in making this decision, the Lords were usurping the authority which constitutionally belongs to Parliament.

The second case Bennion criticizes is **DPP** *v* **Jones** (1999), which concerned a demonstration on the road near Stonehenge. In that case the Lords looked at another long-held rule, that the public have a right to use the highway for 'passing and repassing' (in other words, walking along the road), and for uses which are related to that, but that there is no right to use the highway in other ways, such as demonstrating or picketing. In **Jones**, the House of Lords stated that this rule placed unrealistic and unwarranted restrictions on everyday activities, and that the highway is a public place that the public has a right to enjoy for any reasonable purpose. This decision clearly has major implications for the powers of the police to break up demonstrations and pickets.

Bennion argues that in making decisions like these, the judiciary is taking powers to which it is not constitutionally entitled, and that judges should not extend their law-making role into such controversial areas.

Task 1.5

Read the Practice Statement that was issued by the House of Lords in 1966 stating that it was no longer bound by its previous decisions, and then answer the questions below.

Their Lordships regard the use of precedent as an indispensable foundation upon which to decide what is the law and its application to individual cases. It provides at least some degree of certainty upon which individuals can rely in the conduct of their affairs, as well as a basis for orderly development of legal rules.

Their Lordships nevertheless recognize that the rigid adherence to precedent may lead to injustice in a particular case and also unduly restrict the proper development of the law. They propose, therefore, to modify their present practice and while treating former decisions of this House as normally binding, to depart from a previous decision when it appears right to do so.

In this connection they will bear in mind the danger of disturbing retrospectively the basis on which contracts, settlement of property and fiscal arrangements have been entered into and also the especial need for certainty as to the criminal law.

This announcement is not intended to affect the use of precedent elsewhere than in the House.

Questions

1 Define the term 'retrospectively'.

2 What did the House of Lords consider to be the advantages of the doctrine of judicial precedent?

3 What disadvantages did they recognize exist in the strict application of the rules of judicial precedent?

4 In which areas of law did their Lordships state that they would be less willing to change their previous decisions?

Advantages of binding precedent

Certainty

Judicial precedent means litigants can assume that like cases will be treated alike, rather than judges making their own random decisions, which nobody could predict. This helps people plan their affairs.

Detailed practical rules

Case law is a response to real situations, as opposed to statutes, which may be more heavily based on theory and logic. Case law shows the detailed application of the law to various circumstances, and thus gives more information than statute.

Free market in legal ideas

The right-wing philosopher Hayek (1982) has argued that there should be as little legislation as possible, with case law becoming the main source of law. He sees case law as developing in line with market forces; if the *ratio* of a case is seen not to work, it will be abandoned, if it works it will be followed. In this way the law can develop in response to demand. Hayek sees statute law as imposed by social planners, forcing their views on society whether they like it or not, and threatening the liberty of the individual.

Flexibility

Law needs to be flexible to meet the needs of a changing society, and case law can make changes far more quickly than Parliament. The most obvious signs of this are the radical changes the House of Lords has made in the field of criminal law, since announcing in 1966 that it would no longer be bound by its own decisions.

Disadvantages of binding precedent

Complexity and volume

There are hundreds of thousands of decided cases, comprising several thousand volumes of law reports, and more are added all the time. Judgments themselves are long, with many judges making no attempt at readability, and the *ratio decidendi* of a case may be buried in a sea of irrelevant material. This can make it very difficult to pinpoint appropriate principles.

Rigidity

The rules of judicial precedent mean that judges should follow a binding precedent even where they think it is bad law, or inappropriate. This can mean that bad judicial decisions are perpetuated for a long time before they come before a court high enough to have the power to overrule them.

Illogical distinctions

The fact that binding precedents must be followed unless the facts of the case are significantly different can lead to judges making minute distinctions between the facts of a previous case and the case before them, so that they can distinguish a precedent which they consider inappropriate. This in turn leads to a mass of cases all establishing different precedents in very similar circumstances, and further complicates the law.

Unpredictability

The advantages of certainty can be lost if too many of the kind of illogical distinctions referred to above are made, and it may be impossible to work out which precedents will be applied to a new case.

Dependence on chance

Case law changes only in response to those cases brought before it, so important changes may not be made unless someone has the money and determination to push a case far enough through the appeal system to allow a new precedent to be created.

Unsystematic progression

Case law develops according to the facts of each case and so does not provide a comprehensive code. A whole series of rules can be built on one case, and if this is overruled the whole structure can collapse.

Lack of research

When making case law the judges are only presented with the facts of the case and the legal arguments, and their task is to decide on the outcome of that particular dispute. Technically, they are not concerned with the social and economic implications of their decisions, and so they cannot commission research or consult experts as to these implications, as Parliament can when changing the law. In the USA litigants are allowed to present written arguments containing socio-economic material.

Retrospective effect

Changes made by case law apply to events which happened before the case came to court, unlike legislation, which usually only applies to events after it comes into force. This may be considered unfair, since if a case changes the law, the parties concerned in that case could not have known what the law was before they acted. US courts sometimes get round the problems by deciding the case before them according to the old law, while declaring that in future the new law will prevail: or they may determine with what degree of retroactivity a new rule is to be enforced.

In **SW v United Kingdom** (1995), two men, who had been convicted of the rape and attempted rape of their wives, brought a case before the European Court of Human Rights, alleging that their convictions violated Art. 7 of the European Convention on Human Rights, which provides that criminal laws should not have retrospective effect. The men argued that when the incidents which gave rise to their convictions happened, it was not a crime for a man to force his wife to have sex; it only became a crime after the decision in **R** *v* **R** (1991) (see p. 82). The Court dismissed the men's argument: Art. 7 did not prevent the courts from clarifying the principles of criminal liability, provided the developments could be clearly foreseen. In this case, there had been mounting criticism of the previous law, and a series of cases which had chipped away at the marital rape exemption, before the **R** *v* **R** decision.

The same issue again came before the courts in **R** *v* **C** (2004). In that case the defendant was convicted in 2002 of raping his wife in 1970. On appeal, he argued that this conviction breached Art. 7 of the European Convention and tried to distinguish the earlier case of **SW** *v* **United Kingdom** (1995). He said that while in **SW** *v* **United Kingdom** the defendant could have foreseen in 1989 when he committed his offence that his conduct would be regarded as criminal, this was not the case in 1970. This argument was rejected by the Court of Appeal. It claimed, rather unconvincingly, that a husband in 1970 could have anticipated this development in the law. In fact, the leading textbooks at the time clearly stated that husbands were not liable for raping their wives.

Undemocratic

Lord Scarman pointed out in **Stock** *v* **Jones** (1978) that a judge cannot match the experience and vision of the legislator; and that unlike the legislator a judge is not answerable to the people. Theories, like Griffith's (1997), which suggest that precedent can actually give judges a good deal of discretion, and allow them to decide cases on grounds of political and social policy, raise the question of whether judges, who are unelected, should have such freedom.

Reading on the web

The House of Lords' recent judgments are available on the House of Lords' judicial business website at:

http://www.publications.parliament.uk/pa/ld/ldjudinf.htm

Some important judgments are published on the Court Service website at:

http://www.hmcourts-service.gov.uk/

Question and answer guides

 1 **To what extent does the doctrine of precedent curb judicial creativity?** *(WJEC)*

Answer guide

The first thing to note here is that the words 'judicial creativity' really mean the judges' ability to create or make law. Your introduction should briefly describe what precedent is. A summary of the material contained under the headings 'judicial precedent' and 'how judicial precedent works' would be sufficient here.

Your essay should essentially put forward two opposing sets of arguments: on the one hand, the ways in which precedent curbs judges' freedom to make law; and on the other hand, the arguments that have been put forward that judges do actually have quite a bit of freedom. To illustrate the first set of arguments, you could discuss the role of the *ratio decidendi*, and the need for consistency and certainty in the law. When dealing with the opposing argument, you might discuss the three main points under the heading 'Do judges make law?' in this chapter: the sheer amount of case law in our system (especially in contract and tort); the point that applying the law is not usually an automatic matter; and the fact that judges have been left to define their own role in the system. You should finish with a conclusion, drawing on the points you have made, that states how far you think precedent does curb judicial creativity.

2 **In what ways does legal reasoning both bind and free the judiciary in deciding particular cases?** *(WJEC)*

Answer guide

In this context 'legal reasoning' simply means the process by which judges work out how the rules laid down in previous cases apply to later ones – in other words, the creation of case law. You could tackle this question in two sections: how does this legal reasoning bind the judiciary; and in what circumstances does it allow freedom in making decisions?

For the first part, you need to explain the principle of judicial precedent, and outline the situations in which judges are bound by previous decisions. You could bring in here the declaratory theory of law.

In the second part, you can describe the ways in which judges can avoid awkward precedents, and bring in some of the theories about how judges really decide cases. You could also discuss the effects of the 1966 House of Lords' Practice Statement.

Your conclusion might state whether you think that legal reasoning strikes the right balance between binding the judges and allowing them freedom, giving reasons for your view.

3 **What impact would the abolition of the doctrine of precedent have on the development of law in England?**

Answer guide

You first need to describe the doctrine of precedent, but do not spend too much time on this, as pure description is not what the question is asking for.

You should then consider what the law would lose if precedent were abandoned – the material on the advantages of precedent is relevant here. Then talk about the disadvantages of the system of precedent, and what might be gained by abolishing it. You could bring in the effects of the

1966 House of Lords' Practice Statement as an example of the relaxation of precedent, and talk about whether you feel it has benefited the law or not, mentioning appropriate cases.

You might mention innovations which would lessen the role of precedent, such as codification, and say whether you feel they would be desirable and why.

Your conclusion could state whether or not you feel precedent serves a useful role, and outline any changes which you feel should be made to its operation.

 4 **To what extent does the doctrine of precedent allow judges to make law?**

Answer guide

Here again, you need to start by defining judicial precedent. You can then go on to describe the ways in which it prevents judges from making new law, and the declaratory theory. Follow this with a discussion of the ways in which judges can avoid awkward precedents, and whether this means that they make law. You might use some examples of judges making law, such as **R** v **R**. You can use the material on how judges really decide cases, and on whether judges make law, to debate how far judges are allowed by precedent to make law. You should make the point that theorists such as Kairys and Griffith who argue that precedent allows a great deal of discretion are arguing that judges do make law. You might also introduce some of the ideas about when judges ought to make law.

As a conclusion, you could suggest whether the present system strikes the right balance in the extent to which it allows judges to make law, giving reasons for your views and suggesting any changes you think should be made.

Chapter summary

Judicial precedent

In deciding a case, a judge must follow any decision that has been made by a higher court in a case with similar facts. Judges are only bound by the part of the judgment that forms the legal principle that was the basis of the earlier decision, known as the *ratio decidendi*. The rest of the judgment is known as *obiter dicta* and is not binding.

The hierarchy of the courts

The European Court of Justice is the highest authority on European law, in other matters the House of Lords is the highest court in the UK. Following the 1966 Practice Direction, the House of Lords is not bound by its previous decisions.

How do judges really decide cases?

According to the traditional declaratory theory laid down by William Blackstone, judges do not make law but merely discover and declare the law that has always been. Ronald Dworkin also accepts that the judges have no real discretion in making case law, but he bases this view on his concept that law is a seamless web of principles.

Very different views have been put forward by other academics. Critical theorists argue that judicial decisions are actually influenced by social, political and personal factors and that the doctrine of judicial precedent is merely used to legitimate the judges' decisions. Griffith also ▶

thinks that judges are influenced by their personal background. Waldron accepts that judges make political choices but sees no fundamental problem with this.

When should judges make law?

There is no doubt that on occasion judges make law. There is some debate as to when judges ought to make law. When judges make law they can adapt it to social change, but Francis Bennion has highlighted the danger that if the courts are too willing to make law, they undermine the position of Parliament.

Advantages of binding precedent

The doctrine of judicial precedent provides:

■ certainty
■ detailed practical rules
■ a free market in legal ideas, and
■ flexibility.

Disadvantages of binding precedent

Case law has been criticized because of its:

■ complexity and volume
■ rigidity
■ illogical distinctions
■ unpredictability
■ dependence on chance
■ retrospective effect, and
■ undemocratic character.

Chapter 2   Statute law

Statutes are made by Parliament, which consists of the House of Commons, the House of Lords and the monarch. Following the House of Lords Act 1999 and the Royal Commission for the Reform of the House of Lords which reported in 2000, membership of the House of Lords is currently undergoing a major reform to remove the role of the hereditary peers.

In Britain, Parliament is sovereign, which has traditionally meant that the law it makes takes precedence over that from any other source, though as we shall see, membership of the European Union has compromised this principle. European law aside, Parliament can make or cancel any law it chooses, and the courts must enforce it. In other countries, such as the USA, the courts can refuse to apply legislation on the basis that it is unconstitutional.

Making an Act of Parliament

Bills

All statutes begin as a Bill, which is a proposal for a piece of legislation. There are three types of Bill:

Public Bills. These are prepared by the Cabinet and change the general law of the whole country. They are often preceded by a Green Paper, a consultation document putting forward tentative proposals, which interested parties may consult and give their views on.

Private Members' Bills. These are prepared by an individual backbench MP (someone who is not a member of the Cabinet). MPs wanting to put forward a Bill have to enter a ballot to win the right to do so, and then persuade the Government to allow enough parliamentary time for the Bill to go through. Consequently, very few such Bills become Acts, and they tend to function more as a way of drawing attention to particular issues. Some, however, have made important contributions to legislation, an example being the 1967 Abortion Act, which stemmed from a Private Member's Bill put forward by David Steel.

Criminal Defence Service (Advice and Assistance) Act 2001

2001 CHAPTER 4

An Act to clarify the extent of the duty of the Legal Services Commission under section 13(1) of the Access to Justice Act 1999.   [10th April 2001]

B E IT ENACTED by the Queen's most Excellent Majesty, by and with the advice and consent of the Lords Spiritual and Temporal, and Commons, in this present Parliament assembled, and by the authority of the same, as follows: —

1   Extent of duty to fund advice and assistance

(1)   Subsection (1) of section 13 of the Access to Justice Act 1999 (c. 22) (duty of Legal Services Commission to fund advice and assistance as part of Criminal Defence Service) shall be treated as having been enacted with the substitution of the following for paragraph (b) and the words after it—

"(b)   in prescribed circumstances, for individuals who—

(i)   are not within paragraph (a) but are involved in investigations which may lead to criminal proceedings,

(ii)   are before a court or other body in such proceedings, or

(iii)   have been the subject of such proceedings;

and the assistance which the Commission may consider appropriate includes assistance in the form of advocacy."

(2)   Regulations under subsection (1) of section 13 (as amended above) may include provision treating them as having come into force at the same time as that subsection.

2   Short title

This Act may be cited as the Criminal Defence Service (Advice and Assistance) Act 2001.

Figure 2.1 Criminal Defence Service (Advice and Assistance) Act 2001

Source: © Crown Copyright 2001.

Private Bills. These are usually proposed by a local authority, public corporation or large public company, and usually only affect that sponsor. An example might be a local authority seeking the right to build a bridge or road.

The actual preparation of Bills is done by expert draftsmen known as Parliamentary Counsel.

Task 2.1

Public Bills that are currently being considered by Parliament are available at:

http://www.parliament.the-stationery-office.co.uk/pa/pabills.htm

Visit this website and find a Public Bill that is before Parliament.

First reading

The title of the prepared Bill is read to the House of Commons. This is called the first reading, and acts as a notification of the proposed measure.

Second reading

At the second reading, the proposals are debated fully, and may be amended, and members vote on whether the legislation should proceed. In practice, the whip system (party officials whose job is to make sure MPs vote with their party) means that a government with a reasonable majority can almost always get its legislation through at this and subsequent stages.

Committee stage

The Bill is then referred to a committee of the House of Commons for detailed examination, bearing in mind the points made during the debate. At this point further amendments to the Bill may be made.

Report stage

The committee then reports back to the House, and any proposed amendments are debated and voted upon.

Third reading

The Bill is re-presented to the House. There may be a short debate, and a vote on whether to accept or reject the legislation as it stands.

▮ House of Lords

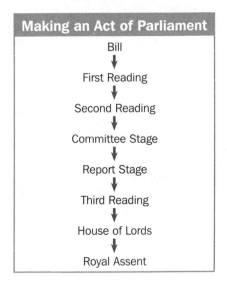

Making an Act of Parliament

Bill
↓
First Reading
↓
Second Reading
↓
Committee Stage
↓
Report Stage
↓
Third Reading
↓
House of Lords
↓
Royal Assent

The Bill then goes to the House of Lords, where it goes through a similar process of three readings. If the House of Lords alters anything, the Bill returns to the Commons for further consideration. The Commons then responds with agreement, reasons for disagreement, or proposals for alternative changes.

At one time legislation could not be passed without the agreement of both Houses, which meant that the unelected House of Lords could block legislation put forward by the elected House of Commons. The Parliament Acts of 1911 and 1949 lay down special procedures by which proposed legislation can go for Royal Assent without the approval of the House of Lords after specified periods of time. These procedures are only rarely used, because the House of Lords usually drops objections that are resisted by the Commons, though their use has increased in recent years.

Four Acts of Parliament have been passed to date relying on the Parliament Act 1949:

- War Crimes Act 1991
- European Parliamentary Elections Act 1999
- Sexual Offences (Amendment) Act 2000
- Hunting Act 2004.

It is of particular note that the procedures were used to pass the controversial Hunting Act 2004. This Act bans hunting wild animals with dogs and a form of hunting known as hare coursing. It was passed despite the House of Lords' opposition, by using the Parliament Act 1949. Members of the pressure group Countryside Alliance brought a legal challenge to the Act in **R (Jackson and others)** *v* **Attorney General** (2005). They argued that the Parliament Act 1949 was itself unlawful and that therefore the Hunting Act, which was passed relying on the procedures it laid down, was also unlawful. The initial Act of 1911 had required a two year delay between the first vote in the House of Commons and reliance on the special procedures in the Act. The 1949 Act reduced this delay to one year and was itself passed using the special procedures in the 1911 Act. The Countryside Alliance claimed that the 1949 Act was unlawful because it had been passed relying on the procedures laid down in the 1911 Act, when the 1911 Act was not drafted to allow its procedures to be used to amend itself. This argument was rejected by the courts. The Law Lords stated that the 1911 and 1949 Acts could not be used to enact major constitutional reforms, such as the abolition of the House of Lords. Since the 1949 Act was simply reducing the House of Lords' delaying power from two years to one, this did not amount to a major constitutional reform and so the 1949 Act was lawful and so also, therefore, was the Hunting Act.

Task 2.2

Recent legislation is published on Her Majesty's Stationery Office website. Visit this site at:

http://www.opsi.gov.uk/acts.htm

Find s. 46 of the Criminal Justice and Court Services Act 2000. What is the definition of an exclusion order?

Explanatory notes provide guidance as to the implications of new legislation. These are available at:

http://www.opsi.gov.uk/legislation/uk-expa.htm

Find the explanatory notes that accompany the Criminal Justice and Court Services Act 2000. What guidance is given in relation to s. 46?

Royal Assent

In the vast majority of cases, agreement between the Lords and Commons is reached, and the Bill is then presented for Royal Assent. Technically, the Queen must give her consent to all legislation before it can become law, but in practice that consent is never refused.

The Bill is then an Act of Parliament, and becomes law, though most do not take effect from the moment the Queen gives her consent, but on a specified date in the near future.

In the case of legislation about which there is no controversy, the procedure may be simplified, with the first three readings in the Lords, then three in the Commons, with the Bill passing back to the Lords only if there is disagreement. Private Bills technically go through the above procedure, and are examined to make sure that adequate warning has been given to anyone affected by the provisions, but there is little debate on them. Consolidating Acts, which simply bring together all the existing law on one topic, also go through an accelerated procedure, with no debate, because they do not change the law; codification bills on the other hand, go through the normal process (see p. 83).

The supremacy of Parliament

The supremacy of Parliament (also known as the 'sovereignty of Parliament') is a fundamental principle of our constitution. This means that Parliament is the highest source of English law; so long as a law has been passed according to the rules of parliamentary procedure, it must be applied by the courts. So if, for example, Parliament had passed a law stating that all newborn boys had to be killed, or that all dog owners had to keep a cat as well, there might well be an enormous public outcry, but the laws would still be valid and the courts would, in theory at least, be obliged to uphold them. The reasoning behind this approach is that Parliament, unlike the judiciary, is democratically elected, and therefore ought to have the upper hand when making the laws that every citizen has to live by.

Figure 2.2 Houses of Parliament
Source: © Copyright 2002 Parliamentary Education Unit (House of Commons).

This approach is unusual in democratic countries. Most comparable nations have what is known as a Bill of Rights. This is a statement of the basic rights which citizens can expect to have protected from state interference and takes precedence over other laws. The courts are able to refuse to apply legislation which infringes any of the rights protected by it.

Britain does not have a Bill of Rights but under the Human Rights Act 1998 the European Convention on Human Rights has been incorporated into domestic law. But the Act does not give the Convention superiority over English law. It requires that wherever possible, legislation should be interpreted in line with the principles of the Convention, but it does not allow the courts to override statutes that are incompatible with it, nor does it prevent Parliament from making laws that are in conflict with it.

Section 19 of the Act requires that when new legislation is made, a Government Minister must make a statement before the second reading of the Bill in either House of Parliament, saying either that in their view the provisions of the Bill are compatible with the Convention, or that even if they are not, the Government wishes to proceed with the Bill anyway. Although the implication is obviously that, in most cases, Ministers will be able to say that a Bill conforms with the Convention, the Act's provision for the alternative statement confirms that parliamentary supremacy is not intended to be overridden. The Act does make one impact on parliamentary supremacy, though a small one: s. 10 allows a minister of the Crown to amend by order any Act which has been found by the courts to be incompatible with the Convention, whereas normally an Act of Parliament could only be changed by another Act. However, there is no obligation to do this and a piece of legislation which has been found to be incompatible with the Convention would remain valid if the Government chose not to amend it.

By contrast, a definite erosion of parliamentary supremacy has been brought about by Britain's membership of the European Union. The EU can only make laws concerning particular subject areas, but in those areas, its law must take precedence over laws made by Parliament, and in this respect Parliament is no longer strictly speaking the supreme source of law in the UK. In areas of law not covered by the EU, however, Parliament remains supreme.

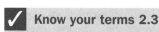 **Know your terms 2.3**

Define the following terms:

1 Hereditary peer
2 Royal Assent
3 Public Bill

In 1998 some important constitutional changes were made, which passed some of the powers of the Westminster Parliament to new bodies in Scotland and Northern Ireland. The new Scottish Parliament, created by the Scotland Act 1998, can make laws affecting Scotland only, in many important areas, including health, education, local government, criminal justice, food standards and agriculture, though legislation on foreign affairs, defence, national security, trade and industry and a number of other areas will still be made for the whole of the UK by the Westminster Parliament. The Northern Ireland Act 1998 similarly gives the Northern Ireland Assembly power to make legislation for Northern Ireland in some areas, though again, foreign policy, defence and certain other areas are still to be covered by Westminster.

In the same year, the Government of Wales Act established a new body for Wales, the Welsh Assembly, but unlike the other two bodies, the Welsh Assembly does not have the power to make primary legislation; legislation made in Westminster will continue to cover Wales. However, the Welsh Assembly is able to make what is called delegated legislation (discussed in Chapter 4).

? Quick quiz 2.4

Put the following events into chronological order for the ordinary process of passing a Public Bill:

☐ Second reading in the House of Commons
☐ Royal Assent
☐ House of Lords considers the Public Bill
☐ Public Bill drafted
☐ First reading in the House of Commons
☐ Report stage
☐ Green Paper
☐ Committee stage in the House of Commons
☐ Third reading

Task 2.5

Read the following article and then answer the questions that follow:

Many of the measures announced by Tony Blair to tackle terrorism in the wake of the London suicide bombings could and should have been taken long ago. Announcing plans for new legislation and more extensive use of existing powers to deport those who advocate terrorism, the Prime Minister twice said 'the rules of the game' are changing. By this, he seemed to mean the 'rules' within international human rights law and the Human Rights Act needed changing. That impression was strengthened when the Lord Chancellor, Lord Falconer, warned that British judges might have to be instructed by Act of Parliament on how to interpret and apply article 3 of the European Convention on Human Rights (prohibiting torture) more restrictively than the European Court of Human Rights.

Our courts need no instruction from government or parliament about how to interpret and apply the Human Rights Act. Contrary to the intemperate and ignorant attacks on the judiciary by Michael Howard, they have not been guilty of 'aggressive judicial activism', 'thwarting the will of parliament'. Our courts are in a weaker position than those of the rest of Europe and the common-law world. In deference to parliamentary sovereignty, they cannot strike down Acts of Parliament, but can only give declarations of incompatibility, leaving it to ministers and parliament to decide what to do. British courts have interpreted and applied the Human Rights Act wisely, without encroaching on the executive and legislative branches of government.

Source: Adapted from an article by Anthony Lester in *The Observer*, 14 August 2005.

1 Why is Art. 3 of the European Convention important?

2 Who is Michael Howard?

3 Why are our judges in a weaker position than their European counterparts?

4 Who do you think should have the most power, the judges or Parliament?

Reading on the web

Copies of Public Bills currently being considered by Parliament can be found at:

http://www.parliament.the-stationery-office.co.uk/pa/pabills.htm

Copies of recent legislation can be found at:

http://www.opsi.gov.uk/acts.htm

Useful explanatory notes prepared by the Government to explain the implications of recent legislation can be found at:

http://www.opsi.gov.uk/legislation/uk-expa.htm

Answering questions

Examination questions in this field tend to be linked to the issue of statutory interpretation and will therefore be considered at the end of the next chapter.

Chapter summary

Introduction

Statutes are made by Parliament, which consists of the House of Commons, the House of Lords and the Monarch.

Making an Act of Parliament

All statutes begin as a Bill. There are three types of Bill:

- Public Bills
- Private Members' Bills, and
- Private Bills.

The legislative process usually starts in the House of Commons and proceeds as follows:

- First reading
- Second reading
- Committee stage
- Report stage
- Third reading
- House of Lords
- Royal Assent.

Role of the House of Lords

The Parliament Acts of 1911 and 1949 lay down special procedures by which proposed legislation can go for Royal Assent without the approval of the House of Lords after specified periods of time. These procedures are only rarely used, because the House of Lords usually drops objections that are resisted by the Commons, though their use has increased in recent years.

The supremacy of Parliament

This means that Parliament is the highest source of English law, and statutes must be applied by the courts. Britain does not have a Bill of Rights which could restrict Parliament's powers to make laws. The Human Rights Act 1998 incorporated the European Convention on Human Rights but this does not give the Convention superiority over English law. Statutes which breach the Convention must still be applied by the courts.

One limit on parliamentary supremacy is now European law. As part of a process of devolution, Parliament has chosen to give legislative powers to the Scottish Parliament and the Northern Ireland Assembly. In theory, Parliament could take back these legislative powers and therefore remains supreme.

Chapter 3 Statutory interpretation

Introduction

Although Parliament makes legislation, it is left to the courts to apply it. The general public imagines that this is simply a case of looking up the relevant law and ruling accordingly, but the reality is not so simple. Despite the fact that Acts of Parliament are carefully written by expert draftsmen, there are many occasions on which the courts find that the implications of a statute for the case before them are not at all clear.

Where the meaning of a statute is uncertain, the job of the courts – in theory at least – is to discover how Parliament intended the law to apply and put that into practice. This is because, as you know, in our constitution, Parliament is the supreme source of law (excluding European law, which will be discussed later), and therefore the judiciary's constitutional role is to put into practice what it thinks Parliament actually intended when Parliament made a particular law, rather than simply what the judges themselves might think is the best interpretation in the case before them. However, as we shall see, the practice is not always as straightforward as the constitutional theory suggests.

What is parliamentary intention?

The idea of parliamentary intention is a very slippery concept in practice. Is it the intention of every individual Member of Parliament at the time the law was passed? Obviously not, since not every member will have voted for the legislation or even necessarily been present when it was passed. The intention of all those who did support a particular piece of legislation is no easier to assess; it is not feasible to conduct a questionnaire every time a legislative provision is found to be unclear.

Lord Reid has pointed out that when judges say they are looking for the intention of Parliament, what they really mean is that they are looking for 'the meaning of the words that Parliament used. We are seeking not what Parliament meant, but the true meaning of the words they used.'

Statutory interpretation and case law

Once the courts have interpreted a statute, or a section of one, that interpretation becomes part of case law in just the same way as any other judicial decision, and subject to the same rules of precedent. A higher court may decide that the interpretation is wrong, and reverse the decision if it is appealed, or overrule it in a later case, but unless and until this happens, lower courts must interpret the statute in the same way.

Rules of interpretation

Parliament has given the courts some sources of guidance on statutory interpretation. The Interpretation Act 1978 provides certain standard definitions of common provisions, such as the rule that the singular includes the plural and 'he' includes 'she', while interpretation sections at the end of most modern Acts define some of the words used within them – the Police and Criminal Evidence Act 1984 contains such a section. A further source of help has been provided since the beginning of 1999: all Bills passed since that date are the subject of special explanatory notes, which are made public. These detail the background to the legislation and explain the effects particular provisions are intended to have.

Apart from this assistance, it has been left to the courts to decide what method to use to interpret statutes, and three basic approaches have developed, in conjunction with certain aids to interpretation.

The literal rule

This rule gives all the words in a statute their ordinary and natural meaning, on the principle that the best way to interpret the will of Parliament is to follow the literal meaning of the words it has used. Under this rule, the literal meaning must be followed, even if the result is absurd.

Table 3.1 **The three rules of statutory interpretation**

Literal rule	The words are given their ordinary and natural meaning.
Golden rule	If the literal rule gives an absurd result that Parliament cannot have intended, then the judge can substitute a reasonable meaning in the light of the statute as a whole.
Mischief rule	This rule was laid down in **Heydon's Case**. Judges should consider three factors: ■ what the problem was before the statute was passed; ■ what problem, or 'mischief', the statute was trying to remedy; ■ what remedy Parliament was trying to provide. The judge should then interpret the statute in such a way as to put a stop to the problem that Parliament was addressing.

Advantages of the literal rule

The literal rule respects parliamentary sovereignty, giving the courts a restricted role and leaving law-making to those elected for the job.

Disadvantages of the literal rule

Where use of the literal rule does lead to an absurd or obviously unjust conclusion, it can hardly be said to be enacting the will of Parliament, since Parliament is unlikely to have intended absurdity and injustice.

Examples of the literal rule

Whitely v **Chapell** (1868). A statute aimed at preventing electoral malpractice made it an offence to impersonate 'any person entitled to vote' at an election. The accused was acquitted because he impersonated a dead person and a dead person was clearly not entitled to vote!

Fisher v **Bell** (1961). After several violent incidents in which the weapon used was a flick-knife, Parliament decided that these knives should be banned. The Restriction of Offensive Weapons Act 1959 consequently made it an offence to 'sell or offer for sale' any flick-knife. The defendant had flick-knives in his shop window and was charged with offering these for sale. The court held that 'offers for sale' must be given its ordinary meaning in law, and that in contract law this was not an offer for sale but only an invitation to people to make an offer to buy. The defendant was therefore not guilty of a crime under the Act, despite the fact that this was obviously just the sort of behaviour the Act was set up to prevent.

In addition, the literal rule is useless where the answer to a problem simply cannot be found in the words of the statute.

The Law Commission in 1969 pointed out that interpretation based only on literal meanings 'assumes unattainable perfection in draftsmanship'; even the most talented and experienced draftsmen cannot predict every situation to which legislation may have to be applied. The same word may mean different things to different people, and words also shift their meanings over time.

The golden rule

This provides that if the literal rule gives an absurd result, which Parliament could not have intended, then (and only then) the judge can substitute a reasonable meaning in the light of the statute as a whole.

Advantages of the golden rule

The golden rule can prevent the absurdity and injustice caused by the literal rule, and help the courts put into practice what Parliament really means.

Disadvantages of the golden rule

The Law Commission noted in 1969 that the 'rule' provided no clear meaning of an 'absurd result'. As in practice that was judged by reference to whether a particular interpretation was irreconcilable with the general policy of the legislature, the golden rule turns out to be a less explicit form of the mischief rule (discussed below).

Examples of the golden rule

R v **Allen** (1872). Section 57 of the Offences Against the Person Act 1861 stated that 'Whosoever being married shall marry any other person during the life of the former husband or wife . . . shall be guilty of bigamy.' It was pointed out that it was impossible for a person already married to 'marry' someone else – he or she might go through a marriage ceremony, but would not actually be married; using the literal rule would make the statute useless. The court therefore held that 'shall marry' should be interpreted to mean 'shall go through a marriage ceremony'.

Adler v **George** (1964). The defendant was charged under s. 3 of the Official Secrets Act 1920, with obstructing a member of the armed forces 'in the vicinity of any prohibited place'. He argued that the natural meaning of 'in the vicinity of' meant near to, whereas the obstruction had actually occurred in the prohibited place itself, an air force station. The court held that while in many circumstances 'in the vicinity' could indeed only be interpreted as meaning near to, in this context it was reasonable to construe it as including being within the prohibited place.

Inco Europe Ltd v **First Choice Distribution** (2000). The House of Lords stated that words could be added to a statute by the judge to give effect to Parliament's intention where an obvious error had been made in drafting a statute.

The mischief rule

This rule was laid down in **Heydon's Case** in the sixteenth century, and provides that judges should consider three factors:

- what the law was before the statute was passed;
- what problem, or 'mischief', the statute was trying to remedy;
- what remedy Parliament was trying to provide.

Examples of the mischief rule

Smith v **Hughes** (1960). The Street Offences Act 1958 made it a criminal offence for a prostitute to solicit potential customers in a street or public place. In this case, the prostitute was not actually in the street, but was sitting in a house, on the first floor, and tapping on the window to attract the attention of the men walking by. The judge decided that the aim of the Act was to enable people to walk along the street without being solicited, and since the soliciting in question was aimed at people in the street, even though the prostitute was not in the street herself, the Act should be interpreted to include this activity.

Elliott v **Grey** (1960). The Road Traffic Act 1930 provided that it was an offence for an uninsured car to be 'used on the road'. The car in this case was not being used on the road, but jacked up, with its battery removed, but the court held that as it was nevertheless a hazard of the type which the statute was designed to prevent, it was covered by the phrase 'used on the road'.

The judge should then interpret the statute in such a way as to put a stop to the problem that Parliament was addressing.

Advantages of the mischief rule

The mischief rule helps avoid absurdity and injustice, and promotes flexibility. It was described by the Law Commission in 1969 as a 'rather more satisfactory approach' than the other two established rules.

Disadvantages of the mischief rule

Heydon's Case was the product of a time when statutes were a minor source of law, compared to the common law. Drafting was by no means as exact a process as it is today, and the supremacy of Parliament was not really established. At that time too, statutes tended to include a lengthy preamble, which more or less spelt out the 'mischief' with which the Act was intended to deal. Judges of the time were very well qualified to decide what the previous law was and what problems a statute was intended to remedy, since they had usually drafted statutes on behalf of the king, and Parliament only rubber-stamped them. Such a rule may be less appropriate now that the legislative situation is so different.

Quick quiz 3.1

Complete the following table by giving one case to illustrate each of the rules of interpretation.

Literal rule	
Golden rule	
Mischief rule	

Aids to interpretation

Whichever approach the judges take to statutory interpretation, they have at their disposal a range of material to help. Some of these aids may be found within the piece of legislation itself, or in certain rules of language commonly applied in statutory texts – these are called internal aids. Others, outside the piece of legislation, are called external aids.

Internal aids

The literary rule and the golden rule both direct the judge to internal aids, though they are taken into account whatever the approach applied.

The statute itself

To decide what a provision of the Act means the judge may draw a comparison with provisions elsewhere in the statute. Clues may also be provided by the long title of the Act or the subheadings within it.

Rules of language

Developed by lawyers over time, these rules are really little more than common sense, despite their intimidating names. As with the rules of interpretation, they are not always precisely applied. Examples include:

Ejusdem generis. General words which follow specific ones are taken to include only things of the same kind. For example, if an Act used the phrase 'dogs, cats and other animals', the phrase 'and other animals' would probably include other domestic animals, but not wild ones.

Expressio unius est exclusio alterius. Express mention of one thing implies the exclusion of another. If an Act specifically mentioned 'Persian cats', the term would not include other breeds of cat.

Noscitur a sociis. A word draws meaning from the other words around it. If a statute mentioned 'cats, kittens and food', it would be reasonable to assume that 'food' meant cat food, and dog food was not covered by the relevant provision.

Presumptions

The courts assume that certain points are implied in all legislation. These presumptions include the following:

- statutes do not change the common law;
- the legislature does not intend to remove any matters from the jurisdiction of the courts;
- existing rights are not to be interfered with;
- laws which create crimes should be interpreted in favour of the citizen where there is ambiguity;
- legislation does not operate retrospectively: its provisions operate from the day it comes into force, and are not backdated.

It is always open to Parliament to go against these presumptions if it sees fit – for example, the European Communities Act 1972 makes it clear that some of its provisions are to be applied retrospectively. But unless the wording of a statute makes it absolutely clear that Parliament has chosen to go against one or more of the presumptions, the courts can assume that the presumptions apply.

External aids

The mischief rule directs the judge to external aids, including the following:

Historical setting

A judge may consider the historical setting of the provision that is being interpreted, as well as other statutes dealing with the same subjects.

Dictionaries and textbooks

These may be consulted to find the meaning of a word, or to gather information about the views of legal academics on a point of law.

Explanatory notes

Acts passed since the beginning of 1999 are provided with explanatory notes, published at the same time as the Act.

Reports

Legislation may be preceded by a report of a Royal Commission, the Law Commission or some other official advisory committee (see pp. 86–89). The House of Lords stated in **Black Clawson International Ltd** (1975) that official reports may be considered as evidence of the pre-existing state of the law and the mischief that the legislation was intended to deal with.

The Human Rights Act 1998

This Act incorporates into UK law the European Convention on Human Rights, which is an international treaty signed by most democratic countries, and designed to protect basic human rights. In many countries, the Convention has been incorporated into national law as a Bill of Rights, which means that the courts can overrule domestic legislation which is in conflict with it. This is not the case in the UK. Instead, s. 3(1) of the Human Rights Act requires that: 'So far as it is possible to do so, primary and subordinate legislation must be read and given effect in a way which is compatible with the Convention rights.' This means essentially that where a statutory provision can be interpreted in more than one way, the interpretation which is compatible with the European Convention should be the one chosen. Section 2 further requires that in deciding any question which arises in connection with a right protected by the Convention, the courts should take into account any relevant judgments made by the European Court of Human Rights. If it is impossible to find an interpretation which is compatible with the Convention, the court concerned can make a declaration of incompatibility. This does not affect the validity of the statute in question, but it is designed to draw attention to the conflict so that the Government can change the law to bring it in line with the Convention (although the Act does not oblige the Government to do this). There is a special 'fast track' procedure by which a Minister can make the necessary changes.

To clarify interpretation, when new legislation is made, the relevant Bill must carry a statement from the relevant Minister, saying either that its provisions are compatible with the Convention, or that even if they are not, the Government wishes to go ahead with the legislation anyway. In the latter case, the Government would be specifically saying that the legislation must override Convention rights if there is a clash, but clearly any government intent on passing such legislation would be likely to face considerable opposition and so would have to have a very good reason, in the eyes of the public, for doing so.

Hansard

This is the official daily report of parliamentary debates, and therefore a record of what was said during the introduction of legislation. For over 100 years, the judiciary held that such documents could not be consulted for the purpose of statutory interpretation. During his career Lord Denning made strenuous efforts to do away with this rule, and in **Davis** *v* **Johnson** (1978) justified his interpretation of a piece of legislation by reference to the parliamentary debates during its introduction. The House of Lords, however, rebuked him for doing so, and maintained that the rule should stand.

In 1993, the case of **Pepper** *v* **Hart** overturned the rule against consulting *Hansard*, and such consultation is clearly now allowed. The case was between teachers at a fee-paying school (Malvern College) and the Inland Revenue, and concerned the tax which employees should have to pay on perks (benefits related to their job). Malvern College allowed its teachers to send their sons there for one-fifth of the usual fee, if places were available. Tax law requires employees to pay tax on perks, and the amount of tax is based on the cost to the employer of providing the benefit, which is usually taken to mean any extra cost that the employer would not otherwise incur. The amount paid by Malvern teachers for their sons' places covered the extra cost to the school of having the child there (in books, food and so on), but did not cover the school's fixed costs, for paying teachers, maintaining buildings and so on, which would have been the same whether the teachers' children were there or not. Therefore the perk cost the school little or nothing, and so the teachers maintained that they should not have to pay tax on it. The Inland Revenue disagreed, arguing that the perk should be taxed on the basis of the amount it saved the teachers on the real cost of sending their children to the school.

The reason why the issue of consulting parliamentary debates arose was that during the passing of the Finance Act 1976 which laid down the tax rules in question, the then Secretary to the Treasury, Robert Sheldon, had specifically mentioned the kind of situation that arose in **Pepper** *v* **Hart**. He had stated that where the cost to an employer of a perk was minimal, employees should not have to pay tax on the full cost of it. The question was, could the judges take into account what the Minister had said? The House of Lords convened a special court of seven judges, which decided that they could look at *Hansard* to see what the Minister had said, and that his remarks could be used to decide what Parliament had intended.

The decision in **Pepper** *v* **Hart** was confirmed in **Three Rivers District Council** *v* **Bank of England (No. 2)** (1996), which concerned the correct interpretation of legislation passed in order to fulfil obligations arising from an EC directive. Although the legislation was not itself ambiguous, the claimants stated that, if interpreted in the light of the information contained in *Hansard*, the legislation imposed certain duties on the defendants, which were not obvious from the legislation itself. The defendants argued that *Hansard* could only be consulted where legislation contained ambiguity, but the court disagreed, stating that where legislation was passed in order to give effect to international obligations, it was important to make sure that it did so, and consulting legislative materials was one way of helping to ensure this. The result would appear to be that *Hansard* can be consulted not just to explain ambiguous phrases, but to throw light on the general purpose of legislation.

In **R *v* Secretary of State for the Environment, Transport and the Regions, ex parte Spath Holme Ltd** (2001) the House of Lords gave a restrictive interpretation of the application of **Pepper *v* Hart**. The applicant was a company that was the landlord of certain properties. It sought judicial review of the Rent Acts (Maximum Fair Rent) Order 1999, made by the Secretary of State under s. 31 of the Landlord and Tenant Act 1985. The applicant company contended that the 1999 Order was unlawful as the Secretary of State had made it to alleviate the impact of rent increases on certain categories of tenants, when a reading of *Hansard* showed that Parliament's intention was that such orders would only be made to reduce the impact of inflation. On the use of *Hansard* to interpret the intention of Parliament, the House of Lords pointed out that the case of **Pepper *v* Hart** was concerned with the meaning of an expression used in a statute ('the cost of a benefit'). The Minister had given a statement on the meaning of that expression. By contrast, the present case was concerned with a matter of policy, and in particular the meaning of a statutory power rather than a statutory expression. Only if a Minister were, improbably, to give a categorical assurance to Parliament that a power would not be used in a given situation would a parliamentary statement on the scope of a power be admissible.

In **Wilson *v* Secretary of State for Trade and Industry** (2003) the House of Lords again gave a restrictive interpretation to **Pepper *v* Hart**. It held that only statements in *Hansard* made by a Minister or other promoter of legislation could be looked at by the court, other statements recorded in *Hansard* had to be ignored.

Under the British constitution, Parliament and the courts have separate roles. Parliament enacts legislation, the courts interpret and apply it. Due to the principle of the separation of powers (see p. 103), neither institution should stray into the other's domain. Thus, Art. 9 of the Bill of Rights 1689 provides that 'the freedom of speech and debates or proceedings in Parliament ought not to be impeached or questioned in any court or place out of Parliament'. In **Wilson *v* Secretary of State for Trade and Industry** (2003) the House of Lords emphasized the importance of the courts not straying into Parliament's constitutional role. It concluded from this that *Hansard* could only be used to interpret the meaning of words in legislation; it could not be used to discover the reasons for the legislation. The Court of Appeal in **Wilson** had used *Hansard* to look at the parliamentary debates concerning a particular Act. It was not trying to discover the meaning of words, as their meaning was not in doubt, but to discover the reason which led Parliament to think that it was necessary to pass the Act. The House of Lords held that the Court of Appeal had been wrong to do this. Referring to *Hansard* simply to check the meaning of enacted words supported the principle of parliamentary sovereignty (see p. 29). Referring to *Hansard* to discover the reasoning of Parliament, where there was no ambiguity as to the meaning of the words, would go against the sovereignty of Parliament.

The Human Rights Act 1998 requires the courts to exercise a new role in respect of Acts of Parliament. This new role is fundamentally different from interpreting and applying legislation. The courts are now required to determine whether the legislation violates a right laid down in the European Convention on Human Rights. If the

Act does violate the Convention, the courts have to issue a declaration of incompatibility. In order to determine this question, the House of Lords stated in **Wilson** that the courts can only refer to *Hansard* for background information, such as the social policy aim of the Act. Poor reasoning in the course of parliamentary debate was not a matter which could count against the legislation when determining the question of compatibility.

Although it is now clear that *Hansard* can be referred to in order to find evidence of parliamentary intention, there is still much debate as to how useful it is, and whether it can provide good evidence of what Parliament intended. The following are some of the arguments for use of this source:

Usefulness. Lord Denning argued in **Davis** *v* **Johnson** (1978) that to ignore the parliamentary debates would be to 'grope in the dark for the meaning of an Act without switching on the light'. When such an obvious source of enlightenment was available, it was ridiculous to ignore it.

Media reports. Parliamentary proceedings are reported in newspapers and on radio and television. Since judges are as exposed to these as anyone else, it seems ridiculous to blinker themselves in court, or to pretend that they are blinkered.

The arguments against the use of this source are:

Lack of clarity. The House of Lords, admonishing Lord Denning for his behaviour in **Davis** *v* **Johnson**, and directing that parliamentary debates were not to be consulted, stated that the evidence provided by the parliamentary debates might not be reliable; what was said in the cut and thrust of public debate was not 'conducive to a clear and unbiased explanation of the meaning of statutory language'.

Time and expense. Their Lordships also suggested that if debates were to be used, there was a danger that the lawyers arguing a case would devote too much time and attention to ministerial statements and so on, at the expense of considering the language used in the Act itself.

> It would add greatly to the time and expense involved in preparing cases involving the construction of a statute if counsel were expected to read all the debates in *Hansard*, and it would often be impracticable for counsel to get access to at least the older reports of debates in select committees in the House of Commons; moreover, in a very large proportion of cases such a search, even if practicable, would throw no light on the question before the court . . .

Parliamentary intention. The nature of parliamentary intention is difficult, if not impossible, to pin down. Parliamentary debates usually reveal the views of only a few members, and even then, those words may need interpretation too.

Lord Steyn, a judge in the House of Lords, has written an article entitled '*Pepper v Hart: A Re-examination*' (2001). In that article he criticizes the way the use of *Hansard* in **Pepper** *v* **Hart** gives pre-eminence to the Government Minister's interpretation of the statute and ignores any dissenting voices by opposition MPs. The Minister only spoke in the House of Commons and the detail of what he said was unlikely to have been known by the House of Lords. He therefore queries how the Minister's statement can be said to reflect the intention of Parliament, which is made up of both Houses. He points to the nature of the parliamentary process:

> The relevant exchanges sometimes take place late at night in nearly empty chambers. Sometimes it is a party political debate with whips on. The questions are often difficult but politician warfare sometimes leaves little time for reflection. These are not ideal conditions for the making of authoritative statements about the meaning of a clause in a Bill. In truth a Minister speaks for the government and not for Parliament. The statements of a Minister are no more than indications of what the Government would like the law to be. In any event, it is not discoverable from the printed record whether individual members of the legislature, let alone a plurality in each chamber, understood and accepted a ministerial explanation of the suggested meaning of the words.

This criticism has been partly tackled by the House of Lords in **Wilson** *v* **Secretary of State for Trade and Industry** (2003). The House stated that the courts must be careful not to treat the ministerial statement as indicative of the intention of Parliament.

> Nor should the courts give a ministerial statement, whether made inside or outside Parliament, determinative weight. It should not be supposed that members necessarily agreed with the Minister's reasoning or his conclusions.

The House emphasized that the will of Parliament is expressed in the language used in its enactments.

Quick quiz 3.2

1 Name the three main rules of statutory interpretation.

2 Give three examples of internal aids to statutory interpretation.

3 Give three examples of external aids to statutory interpretation.

4 What is the legal significance of the House of Lords' decision in **Pepper** *v* **Hart**?

How do judges really interpret statutes?

This question has much in common with the discussion of case law and the operation of precedent (p. 10); in both cases, discussion of rules conceals a certain amount of flexibility. The so-called 'rules of interpretation' are not rules at all, but different approaches. Judges do not methodically apply these rules to every case, and the fact that the rules can conflict with each other and produce different results necessarily implies some choice as to which is used.

Just as with judicial precedent, the idea that statutory interpretation is an almost scientific process that can be used to produce a single right answer is simply nonsense. There is room for more than one interpretation (otherwise the question would never reach the courts) and judges must choose between them. For clear evidence of this, there is no better example than the recent litigation concerning Augusto

Pinochet, the former President of Chile. He had long been accused of crimes against humanity, including torture and murder and conspiracy to torture and to murder. When he made a visit to the UK, the Spanish Government requested his extradition to Spain so that it could put him on trial. This led to a protracted sequence of litigation concerning whether it was legal for Britain to extradite him to Spain, and eventually the question came before the House of Lords. Pinochet's defence argued on the basis of the State Immunity Act 1978, which provides other states with immunity from prosecution in English courts; the Act provides that 'states' includes heads of state. The Lords were therefore asked to decide whether this immunity extended to Pinochet's involvement in the acts he was accused of and, by a majority of three to two, they decided that it did not. Yet when the appeal was reopened (because one of the judges, Lord Hoffmann, was found to have links with Amnesty International, which was a party to the case), this time with seven Law Lords sitting, a different decision was reached. Although the Lords still stated that the General did not have complete immunity, by a majority of six to one, they restricted his liability to those acts which were committed after 1978, when torture committed outside the UK became a crime in the UK. This gave General Pinochet immunity for the vast majority of the torture allegations, and complete immunity for the allegations of murder and conspiracy to murder.

The reasoning behind both the decisions is complex and does not really need to concern us here; the important point to note is that in both hearings, the Lords were interpreting the same statutory provisions, yet they came up with significantly different verdicts. Because of the way it was reopened, the case gives us a rare insight into just how imprecise and unpredictable statutory interpretation can be, and it is hard to resist the implication that if you put any other case involving statutory interpretation before two separate panels of judges, they might well come up with different judgments too.

Given then that judges do have some freedom over questions of statutory interpretation, what influences the decisions they make? As with case law, there are a number of theories.

Dworkin: fitting in with principles

Dworkin (1986) claims that in approaching a case, the job of judges is to develop a theory about how the particular measure they are dealing with fits with the rest of the law as a whole. If there are two possible interpretations of a word or phrase, the judge should favour the one that allows the provision to sit most comfortably with the purpose of the rest of the law and with the principles and ideals of law and legality in general. This should be done, not for any mechanical reason, but because a body of law which is coherent and unified is, just for that reason, a body of law more entitled to the respect and allegiance of its citizens.

Willis: the just result

John Willis's influential article 'Statute Interpretation in a Nutshell' was cynical about the use of the three 'rules'. He points out that a statute is often capable of several different interpretations, each in line with one of the rules. Despite the emphasis placed on literal interpretation, Willis suggests that the courts view all three rules as equally valid. He claims they use whichever rule will produce the result that they themselves believe to be just.

■ Griffith: political choices

As with case law (see p. 13), Griffith (1997) claims that where there is ambiguity, the judges choose the interpretation that best suits their view of policy. An example of this was the 'Fares Fair' case, **Bromley London Borough Council *v* Greater London Council** (1983). The Labour-controlled GLC had enacted a policy – which was part of their election manifesto – to lower the cost of public transport in London, by subsidizing it from the money paid in rates (what we now call Council Tax). This meant higher rates. Conservative-controlled Bromley Council challenged the GLC's right to do this.

The powers of local authorities (which then included the GLC) are defined entirely by statute, and there is an assumption that if a power has not been granted to a local authority by Parliament, then it is not a power the authority is entitled to exercise. The judges' job then was to discover what powers Parliament had granted the GLC, and to determine whether their action on fares and rates was within those powers.

Section 1 of the Transport (London) Act 1969 stated: 'It shall be the general duty of the Greater London Council to develop policies, and to encourage, organize and where appropriate, carry out measures which will promote the provision of integrated, efficient and economic transport facilities and services in Greater London.' The key word here was 'economic', with each side taking a different view of its meaning.

The GLC said 'economic' meant 'cost-effective', in other words, giving good value for money. The GLC stated that good value covered any of the policy goals that transport services could promote: efficient movement of passengers, reduction of pollution and congestion, possibly even social redistribution. Bromley Council, on the other hand, said that 'economic' meant 'breaking even': covering the expenses of its operation out of the fares charged to the passengers and not requiring a subsidy.

It is not difficult to see that both sides had a point – the word 'economic' could cover either meaning, making the literal rule more or less useless. Because of this, Lord Scarman refused to consult a dictionary, stating that 'The dictionary may tell us the several meanings the word can have but the word will always take its specific meaning (or meanings) from its surroundings.' Lord Scarman stressed that those surroundings meant not just the statute as a whole, but also the general duties of the GLC to ratepayers; that duty must coexist with the duty to the users of public transport.

Lord Scarman concluded:

> 'Economic' in s. 1 must, therefore, be construed widely enough to embrace both duties. Accordingly, I conclude that in s. 1(1) of the Act 'economic' covers not only the requirement that transport services be cost-effective but also the requirement that they be provided so as to avoid or diminish the burden on the ratepayers so far as it is practicable to do so.

Griffith has argued that the idea of a 'duty' to ratepayers as explained in the case is entirely judge made, and that the Law Lords' ruling that the interests of transport users had been preferred over those of ratepayers is interfering with the role of elected authorities. He suggests that 'public expenditure can always be criticised on the ground that it is excessive or wrongly directed', but that it is the role of elected bodies to make such decisions, and if the public does not like them 'the remedy lies in their hands at the next election'.

It is certainly odd that when the judges make so much play of the fact that Parliament should legislate because it is elected and accountable, they do not consider themselves bound to respect decisions made in fulfilment of an elected body's manifesto. What the Lords were doing, argues Griffith, was making a choice between two interpretations, based not on any real sense of what Parliament intended, but 'primarily [on] the Law Lords' strong preference for the principles of the market economy with a dislike of heavy subsidisation for social purposes' – in other words, a political choice.

The judiciary would argue against this proposition, but it is certainly difficult to see where any of the 'rules of interpretation' fitted into this case: none of the rules of interpretation or the aids to interpretation forced the judges to favour Bromley Council's interpretation of the law over that of the GLC. They could have chosen either interpretation and still been within the law, so that their choice must have been based on something other than the law.

▌ The purposive approach

Over the past three decades, the judiciary has come to acknowledge that it does have some degree of discretion in interpreting statutes, but there is still considerable debate as to how far it can, and should, take this.

During his judicial career, Lord Denning was in the forefront of moves to establish a more purposive approach, aiming to produce decisions that put into practice the spirit of the law, even if that meant paying less than usual regard to the letter of the law, the actual words of the statute. He felt that the mischief rule could be interpreted broadly, so that it would not just allow the court to look at the history of the case, but it would also allow the court to carry out the intention of Parliament, however imperfectly this might have been expressed in the words used.

Denning stated his view in **Magor and St Mellons** *v* **Newport Corporation** (1952): 'We do not sit here to pull the language of Parliament to pieces and make nonsense of it . . . we sit here to find out the intention of Parliament and carry it out, and we do this better by filling in the gaps and making sense of the enactment than by opening it up to destructive analysis.'

This approach was roundly criticized by the House of Lords, with Lord Simonds describing 'filling in the gaps' as 'a naked usurpation of the judicial function, under the guise of interpretation . . . If a gap is disclosed, the remedy lies in an amending Act.'

Denning's views nevertheless contributed to the growth of a more purposive approach which has gained ground in the last 20 years, with courts seeking to interpret statutes in ways which will promote the general purpose of the legislation. However, the courts still maintain that this cannot be taken too far.

The introduction of the Human Rights Act 1998 is likely to prompt a shift to a purposive interpretation of legislation, as the courts weigh up important issues concerning the rights of the individual against the state, and take into account the judgments of the European Court of Human Rights, which itself takes a purposive approach to interpretation. Some experts have predicted that the House of Lords' role will become increasingly like that of the American Supreme Court, dealing with vital questions for society and the individual, rather than the detailed and technical commercial and taxation matters which form the bulk of its current work.

Quick quiz 3.3

1 If there are two possible interpretations to a word in a statute, what approach does Dworkin think should be taken to its interpretation?

2 Name John Willis's influential article on statutory interpretation.

3 What was the subject matter of **Bromley London Borough Council** v **Greater London Council** (1983)? Why was this case of interest to the legal academic Griffith?

4 What is the purposive approach to statutory interpretation?

Interpretation of European legislation

Under Art. 234 of the Treaty of Rome, the European Court is the supreme tribunal for the interpretation of European Community law. Section 3(1) of the European Communities Act 1972 states that questions as to the validity, meaning or effect of Community legislation are to be decided in accordance with the principles laid down by the European Court.

In the light of these provisions, Lord Denning stated that when interpreting European law, English courts should take the same approach as the European Court would:

> No longer must they examine the words in meticulous detail. No longer must they argue about the precise grammatical sense. They must look to the purpose or intent. To quote the words of the European Court in the **Da Costa** case they must deduce from the wording and the spirit of the Treaty the meaning of the Community rules . . . They must divine the spirit of the Treaty and gain inspiration from it. If they find a gap, they must fill it as best they can. They must do what the framers of the instrument would have done if they had thought about it. So we must do the same. (**Bulmer** v **Bollinger** (1974))

In other words, he was saying that rather than using the literal rule, the courts should apply a broadly interpreted mischief rule – which was, of course, the same approach that he felt should be applied to domestic legislation.

If the English courts are uncertain as to how a piece of European legislation should be interpreted they can, and sometimes must, refer it to the European Court of Justice for interpretation (see p. 69). In such circumstances the case is adjourned, until the European Court directs the English one on how to interpret the European legislation. The English court then reopens the case in England and applies this interpretation.

Effect of EU membership on the interpretation of UK law

Section 2(4) of the European Communities Act 1972 provides that all parliamentary legislation must be construed and applied in accordance with European law. The case of **R *v* Secretary of State for Transport, ex parte Factortame** (1990) makes it clear that the English courts must apply European law which is directly effective even if it conflicts with English law, including statute law (these issues are discussed more fully in Chapter 5).

Reform of statutory interpretation

The problems with statutory interpretation have been recognized for decades, but despite several important reports, little has changed. The Law Commission examined the interpretation of statutes in 1967 and had 'little hesitation in suggesting that this is a field not suitable for codification'. Instead, it proposed certain improvements within the present system:

- More liberal use should be made of internal and external aids.
- In the event of ambiguity, the construction which best promoted the 'general legislative purpose' should be adopted. This could be seen as supporting Denning's approach.

The Renton Committee on the Preparation of Legislation produced its report in 1975, making many proposals for improving the procedure for making and drafting statutes, including the following:

- Acts could begin with a statement of purpose in the same way that older statutes used to have preambles.
- There should be a move towards including less detail in the legislation, introducing the simpler style used in countries such as France.
- More use could be made in statutes of examples showing the courts how an Act was intended to work in particular situations.
- Long, unparagraphed sentences should be avoided.
- Statutes should be arranged to suit the convenience of the ultimate users.
- There should be more consolidation of legislation.

In 1978, Sir David Renton, in a speech entitled 'Failure to Implement the Renton Report', noted that there had been a small increase in the number of draftsmen and increased momentum in the consolidation process, but that Parliament had continued to pass a huge amount of legislation, with no reduction in the amount of detail and scarcely any use of statements of purpose. Fifteen years later, in 1993, a Commission appointed by the Hansard Society for Parliamentary Government reported that little had changed. Having consulted widely, it concluded that there was widespread dissatisfaction with the situation, and suggested that the drafting style adopted should be appropriate for the main end-users of legislation, with the emphasis on clarity, simplicity and certainty. There should be some means of informing citizens, lawyers and the courts about the general purpose behind a particular piece of legislation, and unnecessary detail should be avoided. The Commission suggested that an increase in the number of draftsmen might be necessary to achieve these aims: since its report, four more draftsmen have been recruited, but otherwise there was little response from the previous Government. The current Government, however, has placed a high priority on making the workings of law and government accessible to ordinary people, and the introduction of explanatory notes to Bills passed from 1999 is an important step forward.

Reading on the web

Hansard is available at:

http://www.parliament.uk/hansard/hansard.cfm

Question and answer guides

1 Read the source material below and answer questions **(a)** to **(c)** which follow.

EXERCISE ON STATUTORY INTERPRETATION

Source: DPP v Bull (1994)

Bull was a male prostitute charged with an offence against s. 1(1), Street Offences Act 1959. This section states:

> It shall be an offence for a common prostitute to loiter or solicit in a public street or public place for the purposes of prostitution.

The case was heard in the magistrates' court. The case was dismissed on the ground that the words 'common prostitute' only applied to female prostitutes. The prosecution appealed and the Queen's Bench Divisional Court had to decide whether the words were only meant to apply to women or could also cover male prostitutes.

On appeal the prosecution argued that s. 1(1) of the 1959 Act was ambiguous and drew the court's attention to a number of points:

i Section 1(2) and (3) of the 1959 Act refer respectively to 'a person' and 'anyone'.
ii The phrase in s. 1(1) 'a common prostitute' was capable of including both men and women. The *Oxford English Dictionary* (1989) includes within the possible definition for 'prostitute', 'a man who undertakes male homosexual acts for payment'.
iii Lord Taylor said in an earlier case (**R** v **McFarlane**), 'both the dictionary definitions and the cases show that the crucial feature defining prostitution is the making of an offer of sexual services for a reward'.

iv The Act was introduced as a result of the Report of the Committee on Homosexual Offences and Prostitution (Wolfenden Committee Report).

v The contents of the parliamentary debate on the Bill for the Act were relevant.

The appeal court judge decided that the relevant part of the Wolfenden Committee Report left him in no doubt that the committee was only concerned with the female prostitute and stated:

It is plain that the mischief that the Act was intended to remedy, was a mischief created by women.

Because of this it was held that the Act only applied to female prostitutes.

(Adapted from **DPP** v **Bull** (1994))

Answer *all* parts.

(a) The source makes clear reference to a number of extrinsic (external) aids. Describe these and any other extrinsic aids available in statutory interpretation. [15]

(b) Section 1(1) of the Street Offences Act 1959 states:

It shall be an offence for a common prostitute to loiter or solicit in a public street or public place for the purpose of prostitution.

Using the source and your knowledge of the rules of statutory interpretation discuss whether each of the following could be found guilty of the above offence:

i Gloria (a female) is charged with soliciting in the car park of a pub.
ii Frank (a male) is charged with soliciting outside a nightclub.
iii Sylvia (a female) is charged with soliciting from the third floor balcony of her flat. [15]

(c) The mischief rule was applied in **DPP** v **Bull**. Using the source **and** other cases explain how this rule is applied and discuss the problems that the use of the rule can cause. [30]

[TOTAL: 60]
(OCR)

Answer guide

(a) The material you need to answer this part of the question is contained at pp. 39–44. The external aids referred to in the source are:

■ the *Oxford English Dictionary* (1989);
■ the case of **R** v **McFarlane**;
■ the Report of the Committee on Homosexual Offences and Prostitution (the Wolfenden Committee Report); and
■ parliamentary debate on the Bill which can be found in *Hansard*.

(b)(i) In the light of **DPP** v **Bull**, the section applies to women. Gloria is a woman who was soliciting. The only issue for the court is whether a car park of a pub is a public place. It is likely to be private land, but the public have access to it. An application of the literal rule to this issue of the car park would not clarify the matter. The golden rule should only apply where there is obvious absurdity and there is no obvious absurdity here. Under the mischief rule, we can look at the problem that the Act was trying to remedy, which was to stop men being harassed in public places by female prostitutes. Men could be harassed by prostitutes in ▶

51

car parks, so the car park might be treated as a public place on this basis. Gloria would therefore be guilty of the offence under s. 1(1) of the 1959 Act.

(ii) The facts in this scenario are essentially the same as those in the case of **DPP** v **Bull**. In that case the court found that the offence in s. 1 of the 1959 Act could only be committed by women and therefore Frank is not committing an offence. In reaching this conclusion it applied the mischief rule and made reference to external sources such as *Hansard*. The prosecution in **DPP** v **Bull** had sought to rely on a literal interpretation of the section, but this was rejected by the Divisional Court. If the purposive approach had been applied (discussed on pp. 47–8) then the offence could have been interpreted as applying to both men and women.

(iii) If the literal rule was applied to s. 1 of the 1959 Act, Sylvia would be acquitted as she is not literally in a public street or place. But the case of **Smith** v **Hughes**, discussed on p. 37, is very similar and in that case the court applied the mischief rule. That case found that the aim of the Act was to enable people to walk along the street without being molested or solicited by common prostitutes. As a result, it would not matter that Sylvia was standing on a private balcony, since the effect was still that people in the street were being solicited.

(c) The material required to answer this question is contained at pp. 37–8. The mischief rule in **DPP** v **Bull** gave an unsatisfactory interpretation as it discriminated against women. You could have discussed the problems in identifying Parliament's intention (see pp. 43–4), and considered whether the more modern purposive approach is better (see pp. 47–8).

2 A statute states that 'It is an offence to loiter or solicit in a street for the purposes of prostitution.'

Mary, a known prostitute, sits in a large bay window on the first floor of a house overlooking a busy street. She taps the window to attract the attention of men on the pavement. She invites John upstairs by beckoning and pointing to the door. He accepts her invitation.

Jane, a known prostitute, who is unable to speak, stands on a street corner and waits for men in cars to stop. She is observed getting into a car and handing Peter, the driver, a card which he reads. He then drives off immediately, without Jane.

Have any offences been committed? Discuss the rules of statutory interpretation which guide you to your answer.

Answer guide

You might start your answer by briefly describing the three rules of interpretation, and pointing out that there is no strict procedure dictating which should be applied, even though they can lead to different interpretations of the same statute.

You then need to take each person in turn, starting with Mary. The first thing to note is that it appears the offence can be committed in two ways: by either loitering in the street, or soliciting in the street, each for the purposes of prostitution. Taking a literal approach first, can Mary be said to be loitering in the street or soliciting in the street? Since she is not physically in the street, it seems unlikely that she could be described as loitering there. She is clearly soliciting, but can she be said to be doing so 'in the street'? She may not be in the street, but her soliciting appears to be taking effect in the street, so do you think the term can be interpreted to cover her behaviour? You could then point out that since there appears to be some ambiguity, the golden rule should be applied, allowing you to modify the sense of the words in order to resolve the ambiguity – point out that in a real case, you would want to look at the rest of the statute to help you do this.

If the golden rule is unhelpful, you could apply the mischief rule – again, in real life, you would want to consult the rest of the statute, and probably other materials too, to establish the purpose of the statute, so that you could interpret the provision in line with that purpose. Using this rule, whether Mary had committed an offence would depend on what the purpose of the statute was: if it was to stop men in the street being harassed by prostitutes, you might feel that the provision should be interpreted to make Mary guilty of an offence; alternatively, if, for example, the purpose was to keep prostitution within brothels, you might find that Mary had not committed an offence.

You also need to consider the issue of whether Mary's behaviour is 'for the purposes of prostitution': there does seem to be evidence of this, but on the facts as we have them here, it is only evidence which the jury or magistrates will consider, rather than definite proof.

Moving on to Jane, you can see that on a literal interpretation she is loitering in the street, but is she doing so for the purposes of prostitution? Here again, you might point out that you would need to know more about the facts (particularly what is on the card), but if there is evidence that she is acting for the purposes of prostitution, an offence may have been committed since she is clearly loitering in the street. The statute appears not to require that the accused should both loiter and solicit, so even though soliciting in the normal sense of the word would seem to require some sort of verbal communication, the fact that she has not spoken to the man does not mean she cannot have committed the offence. Since the literal rule does not give rise to ambiguity or absurdity, it appears not to be necessary to apply the golden or mischief rules.

You should conclude by pointing out that to make a firm decision on whether an offence has been committed, you would need to consider both internal and external aids to interpretation. You might also point out that there is a presumption that statutes which impose a criminal penalty should be interpreted in favour of the citizen where there is ambiguity, which might mean that in Mary's case the ambiguity could mean that she has committed no offence.

3 Explain the methods used by judges in interpreting statutes and consider how far judges are concerned to discover the true intentions of Parliament.

Answer guide

A good introduction would explain briefly why judges might need to interpret statutes (see p. 34), and then go on to talk about the importance of parliamentary intention. You need to show you understand why the courts are supposed to look for the intention of Parliament, by discussing the constitutional issue of parliamentary sovereignty, and the fact that judges are not elected. You should also examine the problems of deciding what parliamentary intention actually is, as discussed on p. 34. Having set the issue in its context, you can go on to look at the methods used by judges to attempt to find and apply parliamentary intention: the rules and presumptions, and the internal and external aids. Give examples of these in use if you can, as this shows you understand how they work. Do not forget to discuss the change made by **Pepper** v **Hart**, and the usefulness or otherwise of consulting *Hansard*.

You then need to answer the second part of the question, which essentially asks how far judicial interpretation of statutes is really concerned with applying parliamentary intention, and how far judges can make decisions on other grounds. You need to discuss the idea that a more purposive approach seems to be becoming the norm, mentioning the influence that European law has had in this area; and it would be a good idea to talk about the views of writers such as Griffith, Willis and Dworkin (see pp. 45–6).

Your conclusion might state whether you feel judges currently pay the right degree of attention to what Parliament intends, and why; if not, what reforms could change this?

4 Read the following extract and answer parts (a) to (c) which follow.

EXERCISE ON STATUTORY INTERPRETATION

Pepper v Hart [1993] 1 All ER 42

In this case, heard by seven Law Lords, the House of Lords (the Lord Chancellor dissenting) held that judges could consult *Hansard* to assist them in interpreting a statutory provision. Lord Browne-Wilkinson, who gave the leading judgment, said:

> Statute law consists of the words that Parliament has enacted. It is for the courts to construe those words and it is the court's duty in so doing to give effect to the intention of Parliament in using those words. It is an inescapable fact that, despite all the care taken in passing legislation, some statutory provisions when applied to the circumstances under consideration in any specific case are found to be ambiguous . . . In many, I suspect most, case references to parliamentary materials will not throw any light on the matter. But in a few cases it may emerge that the very question was considered by Parliament in passing the legislation. Why in such a case should the courts blind themselves to a clear indication of what Parliament intended in using those words? . . .
>
> I therefore reach the conclusion . . . that the exclusionary rule should be relaxed so as to permit reference to parliamentary materials where (a) legislation is ambiguous or obscure, or leads to an absurdity; (b) the material relied on consists of one or more statements by a minister or other promoter of the Bill . . . (c) the statements relied on are clear. Further than this, I would not at present go.

(a) What difficulties are faced by judges in finding the 'intention of Parliament'? With reference to the second paragraph of the extract, critically examine the arguments for and against the use of *Hansard* by judges when interpreting statutes.

(b) Briefly explain and evaluate the rules of statutory interpretation.

(c) With reference to the extract, and using the rules set out in your answers to (b), discuss the situation below.

In 1999 the (fictitious) Vehicles in Parks Act was passed in response to a Royal Commission recommendation that vehicles should be banned from public parks in order to ensure safe and unpolluted spaces within towns. In the course of the debate, an opposition MP said, 'It is not the intention of Parliament to ban all vehicles from parks – obviously motorcars and motorcycles may be a danger to children playing in the park, but there is no evidence that other vehicles are likely to cause either accidents or pollution.'

The Act provides that 'any person who knowingly brings any vehicle into a public park shall be guilty of an offence', and the interpretation section defines 'vehicle' as 'any wheeled conveyance designed for the carriage of people or goods'.

Adam, who went into Hightown Park in his motorized wheelchair, was charged under the Act.

Answer guide

(a) Relevant material to answer the first part of this question can be found at p. 43 under the heading 'Parliamentary intention'. To answer the second part of the question, look at p. 43. Make sure that in discussing this material you make reference to the extract as requested to do by the examiner.

(b) The material to answer this question can be found at pp. 35–8. In particular, you need to discuss the literal rule, the golden rule and the mischief rule, intrinsic aids (with particular reference to the language rules and the presumptions) and extrinsic aids (placing the *Hansard* reports as an extrinsic aid). In evaluating these rules you could refer to the specific criticism contained in the aforementioned pages, but also the alternative arguments on how judges really interpret statutes discussed at p. 43. You could also discuss the effect that membership of the European Union has had on statutory interpretation (see p. 49).

(c) The literal rule would lead to a conviction as under its ordinary and natural meaning a motorized wheelchair is a 'vehicle'. There is no ambiguity in the Act so it would not be appropriate to rely on the golden rule. Adam would want the courts to apply the mischief rule in interpreting the statute. In applying this, use of *Hansard* is unlikely to be possible because the words referred to were those of an opposition MP; Lord Browne-Wilkinson stated in **Pepper** v **Hart** that the material relied on 'must consist of one or more statements by a minister or other promoter of the Bill'. However, the Royal Commission Report could be looked at as an external aid to interpretation and reference could be made to the case of **Black Clawson International Ltd** (1975). As this report aimed to create 'safe' spaces in towns it could be argued that the motorized wheelchair should not be included within the statute's provisions as, at the speed it travels, it creates very little danger. It is also likely that the wheelchair has an electric motor which would not add to the problem of pollution.

Chapter summary

Parliamentary intention

In interpreting statutes the courts are looking for the intention of Parliament, but this intention is frequently difficult to find.

Rules of statutory interpretation

There are three rules of statutory interpretation:

- the literal rule
- the golden rule, and
- the mischief rule.

Internal aids to statutory interpretation

Internal aids consist of the statute itself and rules of language.

External aids

These include:

- dictionaries and textbooks
- the explanatory notes
- reports that preceded the legislation
- treaties, and
- *Hansard*, following the decision of **Pepper** v **Hart**.

How do judges really interpret statutes?

Different academics have put forward arguments as to how judges really interpret statutes. John Willis argues that the courts use whichever rule will produce the result that they themselves believe to be just. Griffith thinks that judges interpret statutes in a way that coincides with their political preferences, referring to the case of **Bromley London Borough Council v Greater London Council** to support his arguments.

Interpretation of European legislation

Under Art. 234 of the Treaty of Rome European legislation can be referred to the European Court of Justice for interpretation.

Reform of statutory interpretation

The Renton Committee on the Preparation of Legislation in 1975 recommended reforms of the procedure for making and drafting statutes, but little has changed.

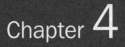

Chapter 4 Delegated legislation

In many cases, the statutes passed by Parliament lay down a basic framework of the law, with creation of the detailed rules delegated to Government departments, local authorities, or public or nationalized bodies; the statute is known as the enabling Act. There are three main forms of delegated legislation:

Statutory instruments. These are made by Government departments.

Bye-laws. These are made by local authorities, public and nationalized bodies. Bye-laws have to be approved by central government.

Orders in Council. These are made by Government in times of emergency. They are drafted by the relevant government department, approved by the Privy Council and signed by the Queen.

On an everyday basis, delegated legislation is an extremely important source of law. The output of delegated legislation far exceeds that of Acts of Parliament, and its provisions include rules that can substantially affect the day-to-day lives of huge numbers of people – safety laws for industry, road traffic regulations, and rules relating to state education, for example.

Task 4.1

Statutory instruments are published on Her Majesty's Stationery Office website at:

http://www.opsi.gov.uk/stat.htm

Go to this website and find the Data Protection Act 1998 (Commencement) Order 2000, number 183. This statutory instrument brought the main provisions of the Data Protection Act 1998 into force.

1 Under which legislative provisions was this piece of delegated legislation made?

2 On what date did these provisions come into force?

Why is delegated legislation necessary?

Delegated legislation is necessary for a number of reasons:

Insufficient parliamentary time. Parliament does not have the time to debate every detailed rule necessary for efficient government.

Speed. It allows rules to be made more quickly than they could by Parliament. Parliament does not sit all the time, and its procedure is slow and cumbersome; delegated legislation often has to be made in response to emergencies and urgent problems.

Technicality of the subject matter. Modern legislation often needs to include detailed, technical provisions – those in building regulations or safety at work rules, for example. MPs do not usually have the technical knowledge required, whereas delegated legislation can use experts who are familiar with the relevant areas.

Need for local knowledge. Local bye-laws in particular can only be made effectively with awareness of the locality. Recognition of the importance of local knowledge can be found with the new devolved assemblies for Scotland, Wales and Northern Ireland. These new democratic bodies have important powers to make delegated legislation.

Flexibility. Statutes require cumbersome procedures for enactment, and can only be revoked or amended by another statute. Delegated legislation, however, can be put into action quickly, and be easily revoked if it proves problematic.

Future needs. Parliament cannot hope to foresee every problem that might arise as a result of a statute, especially concerning areas such as health provision or welfare benefits. Delegated legislation can be put in place as and when such problems arise.

Control of delegated legislation

Because it is not directly made by elected representatives, delegated legislation is subject to the following range of controls, designed to ensure that the power delegated is not abused.

Consultation

Those who make delegated legislation often consult experts within the relevant field, and those bodies who are likely to be affected by it. In the case of road traffic regulations, for example, Ministers are likely to seek the advice of police, motoring organizations, vehicle manufacturers and local authorities before making the rules. Often the relevant statute makes such consultation obligatory and names the bodies who should be consulted. Under the National Insurance Act 1946, for example, draft regulations must be submitted to the National Insurance Advisory Committee, and any Minister proposing to make rules of procedure for a tribunal within a department is required by the Tribunals and Inquiries Act 1971 to consult the Council on Tribunals. In other cases there may be a general statutory requirement for 'such consultation as the minister thinks appropriate with such organizations as appear to him to represent the interest concerned'.

Publication

All delegated legislation is published, and therefore available for public scrutiny.

Supervision by Parliament

There are a number of ways in which Parliament can oversee delegated legislation.

Revocation

Parliamentary sovereignty means that Parliament can at any time revoke a piece of delegated legislation itself, or pass legislation on the same subject as the delegated legislation.

The affirmative resolution procedure

Enabling Acts dealing with subjects of special, often constitutional, importance may require Parliament to vote its approval of the delegated legislation. This is called the affirmative resolution procedure, whereby delegated legislation is laid before one or both Houses (sometimes in draft), and becomes law only if a motion approving it is passed within a specified time (usually 28 or 40 days). Since a vote has to be taken, the procedure means that the Government must find parliamentary time for debate, and opposition parties have an opportunity to raise any objections. In practice, though, it is very rare for the Government not to achieve a majority when such votes are taken.

The negative resolution procedure

Much delegated legislation is put before Parliament for MPs under the negative resolution procedure. Within a specified time (usually 40 days), any member may put down a motion to annul it. An annulment motion put down by a backbencher is not guaranteed to be dealt with, but one put down by the Official Opposition (the party with the second largest number of MPs) usually will be. If, after debate, either House passes an annulment motion, the delegated legislation is cancelled.

Committee supervision

A parliamentary committee watches over the making of delegated legislation, and reports to each House on any delegated legislation which requires special consideration, including any regulations made under an Act that prohibits challenge by the courts, or which seem to make unusual or unexpected use of the powers granted by the enabling Act. However, the Committee may not consider the merits of any piece of delegated legislation.

Questions from MPs

MPs can ask Ministers questions about delegated legislation at question time, or raise them in debates.

The House of Lords

Although the House of Lords cannot veto proposed Acts, the same does not apply to delegated legislation. In 1968 the House of Lords rejected an order imposing sanctions against the Rhodesian Government made under the Southern Rhodesia Act 1965.

▌Control by the courts: judicial review

While the validity of a statute can never be challenged by the courts because of parliamentary sovereignty, delegated legislation can. In a judicial review hearing the courts undertake a review of the process that has been followed in making a decision and can make sure that the public authority had the power to make this decision. Delegated legislation may be challenged on any of the following grounds under the procedure for judicial review.

Procedural *ultra vires*. The term *ultra vires* is Latin and can be translated as 'beyond the powers'. It refers to the situation where a public authority has overstepped its powers. Procedural *ultra vires* occurs where the procedures laid down in the enabling Act for producing delegated legislation have not been followed. In **Agricultural, Horticultural and Forestry Training Board *v* Aylesbury Mushrooms Ltd** (1972), an order was declared invalid because the requirement to consult with interested parties before making it had not been properly complied with.

Substantive *ultra vires*. This is usually based on a claim that the measure under review goes beyond the powers Parliament granted under the enabling Act. In **Commissioners of Customs and Excise *v* Cure and Deeley Ltd** (1962), the powers of the Commissioners to make delegated legislation under the Finance (No. 2) Act 1940 were challenged. The Act empowered them to produce regulations 'for any matter for which provision appears to them necessary for the purpose of giving effect to the Act'. The Commissioners held that this included allowing them to make a regulation giving them the power to determine the amount of tax due where a tax return was submitted late. The High Court invalidated the regulation on the grounds that the Commissioners had given themselves powers far beyond what Parliament had intended; they were empowered only to collect such tax as was due by law, not to decide what amount they thought fit.

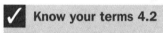

Know your terms 4.2

Define the following terms:

1 Judicial review
2 *Ultra vires*
3 Bye-law
4 Order in Council
5 Enabling Act

R *v* Secretary of State for Social Security, ex parte Joint Council for the Welfare of Immigrants (1996) concerned the Asylum and Immigration Appeals Act 1993 which provided a framework for determining applications for asylum, and for appeals after unsuccessful applications. It allowed asylum seekers to apply for social security benefits while they were waiting for their applications or appeals to be decided, at a cost of over £200 million per year to British taxpayers. This led to concern from some quarters that the provisions might attract those who were simply seeking a better lifestyle than that available in their own countries (often called economic migrants), as opposed to those fleeing persecution, whom the provisions were actually designed to help.

In order to discourage economic migrants, the then Secretary of State for Social Security exercised his powers to make delegated legislation under the Social Security (Contributions and Benefits) Act 1992, and produced regulations which stated that social security benefits would no longer be available to those who sought asylum after they had entered the UK, rather than immediately on entry, or those who had been refused leave to stay here and were awaiting the outcome of appeals against the decision.

The Joint Council for the Welfare of Immigrants challenged the regulations, claiming that they fell outside the powers granted by the 1992 Act. The Court of Appeal upheld the claim, stating that the 1993 Act was clearly intended to give asylum seekers rights which they did not have previously. The effect of the regulations was effectively to take those rights away again, since without access to social security benefits, most asylum seekers would have either to return to the countries from which they had fled, or to live on nothing while their claims were processed. The court ruled that Parliament could not have intended to give the Secretary of State powers to take away the rights it had given in the 1993 Act: this could only be done by a new statute, and therefore the regulations were *ultra vires*.

The decision was a controversial one, because the regulations had themselves been approved by Parliament, and overturning them could be seen as a challenge to the power of the legislature, despite the decision being explained by the court as upholding that power.

Unreasonableness. If rules are manifestly unjust, have been made in bad faith (for example, by someone with a financial interest in their operation) or are otherwise so perverse that no reasonable official could have made them, the courts can declare them invalid.

Quick quiz 4.3

1 Name the three main forms of delegated legislation.

2 Give three reasons why delegated legislation is necessary.

3 Explain what is meant by the affirmative resolution procedure.

4 Name the three grounds on which delegated legislation can be challenged before the courts.

Criticism of delegated legislation

Lack of democratic involvement

This argument is put forward because delegated legislation is usually made by civil servants, rather than elected politicians. This is not seen as a particular problem where the delegated legislation takes the form of detailed administrative rules, since these would clearly take up impossible amounts of parliamentary time otherwise. However, in the last years of the Conservative Government there was increasing concern that delegated legislation was being used to implement important policies.

Overuse

Critics argue that there is too much delegated legislation; this is linked to the point above, as there would be little problem with increasing amounts of delegated legislation if its purpose was merely to flesh out technical detail.

Sub-delegation

Delegated legislation is sometimes made by people other than those who were given the original power to do so.

Lack of control

Despite the above list of controls over delegated legislation, the reality is that effective supervision is difficult. First, publication has only limited benefits, given that the general public are frequently unaware of the existence of delegated legislation, let alone on what grounds it can be challenged and how to go about doing so. This in turn has an effect on the ability of the courts to control delegated legislation, since judicial review relies on individual challenges being brought before the courts. This may not happen until years after a provision is enacted, when it finally affects someone who is prepared and able to challenge it. The obvious result is that legislation which largely affects a class of individuals who are not given to questioning official rules, are unaware of their rights, or who lack the financial resources to go to court, will rarely be challenged.

A further problem is that some enabling Acts confer extremely wide discretionary powers on Ministers; a phrase such as 'the minister may make such regulations as he sees fit for the purpose of bringing the Act into operation' would not be unusual. This means that there is very little room for anything to be considered *ultra vires*, so judicial review is effectively frustrated.

The main method of control over delegated legislation is therefore parliamentary, but this too has its drawbacks. Although the affirmative resolution procedure usually ensures that parliamentary attention is drawn to important delegated legislation, it is rarely possible to prevent such legislation being passed. The Select Committee on the Scrutiny of Delegated Powers makes an important contribution, and has been able to secure changes to a number of important pieces of legislation. However, it too lacks real power, as it is unable to consider the merits of delegated legislation (as opposed to whether the delegated powers have been correctly used) and its reports have no binding effect.

Reading on the web

Statutory instruments are published on Her Majesty's Stationery Office website at:

http://www.opsi.gov.uk/stat.htm

Question and answer guides

1 Why is it necessary to have controls over delegated legislation? Are the present controls satisfactory? *(Oxford)*

Answer guide

Your introduction should explain what delegated legislation is. You should then go on to explain why it needs to be controlled – the main reason being the fact that it is not made by Parliament. Describe the controls that exist, and then go through the problems with those controls. Your conclusion should state whether you feel the controls are adequate, and if not, whether you feel anything could be done to improve them.

2 Read the source material below and answer parts (a), (b) and (c) which follow.

EXERCISE ON DELEGATED LEGISLATION

Source A

Police and Criminal Evidence Act 1984
(1984 c.60)
Section 60
Tape-recording of Interviews

(1) It shall be the duty of the Secretary of State –

. . .

    (b) to make an order requiring the tape-recording of interviews of persons suspected of the commission of criminal offences, or of such descriptions of criminal offences as may be specified in the order . . .

(2) An order under subsection (1) above shall be made by statutory instrument and shall be subject to annulment in pursuance of a resolution of either House of Parliament.

Source B

Statutory Instrument
1991 No. 2687
The Police and Criminal Evidence Act 1984
(Tape-recording of Interview) (No. 1) Order 1991

Made   29th November 1991
Laid before Parliament   6th December 1991
Coming into force   1st January 1992

Now, therefore, in pursuance of the said section 60(1)(b), the Secretary of State hereby orders as follows:

. . .

2. This Order shall apply to interviews of persons suspected of the commission of indictable offences which are held by police officers at police stations in the police areas specified in the schedule to this Order and which commence after midnight on 31st December 1991.

3(1) Subject to paragraph (2) below, interviews to which this Order applies shall be tape-recorded in accordance with the requirements of the code of practice on tape-recording which came into operation on 29th July 1988 . . .

▶

3(2) The duty to tape-record interviews under paragraph (1) above shall not apply to interviews –

(a) where the offence of which a person is suspected is one in respect of which he has been arrested or detained under section 14(1)(a) of the Prevention of Terrorism (Temporary Provisions) Act 1989; . . .

(a) Using Sources A and B to illustrate your answer, compare the legislative process in relation to an Act of Parliament on the one hand and delegated legislation on the other.

(b) What are the advantages and disadvantages of delegated legislation?

(c) Each of the following interviews was conducted by police officers and took place at a police station covered by SI 1991/2687, but none of the interviews was tape-recorded.

(i) On 30 November 1991 Alice was charged with an indictable offence and interviewed;

(ii) Bertie, who was suspected of an indictable offence, was interviewed on 1 April 1998;

(iii) Cedric, detained under s. 14(1)(a) of the Prevention of Terrorism (Temporary Provisions) Act 1989, was interviewed in April 1998.

Discuss interviews (i), (ii) and (iii) with reference to Source B.

Answer guide

(a) For material on the legislative process in relation to an Act of Parliament see p. 25 and for delegated legislation pp. 57–8. You could point out that the Police and Criminal Evidence Act 1984 was an enabling Act which allowed the Secretary of State to make the Statutory Instrument 1991 No. 2687. You could mention that statutory instruments are made by Government departments and contrast this with bye-laws and Orders in Council (p. 57). When explaining the negative resolution procedure (p. 59) you could refer to the fact that the statutory instrument on tape-recording interviews was laid before Parliament on 6 December 1991 and that s. 60(2) of PACE refers to this process.

(b) Material on the advantages of delegated legislation can be found on p. 58 under the heading 'Why is delegated legislation necessary?' Criticisms can be found on pp. 61–62.

(c) (i) As statutory instrument 1991/2687 provides that its provisions only apply to interviews that take place after midnight on 31 December 1991, the police were under no obligation to tape-record Alice's interview.

(ii) Bertie's interview should have been tape-recorded as he was suspected of committing an indictable offence and the interview took place after the provisions of the statutory instrument came into force. You could look at possible remedies, particularly the exclusion of the evidence obtained, which is discussed at p. 253.

(iii) There was no obligation to tape-record Cedric's interview as he had been detained under the Prevention of Terrorism (Temporary Provisions) Act 1989.

 Read the following source material and answer parts (a) to (d) which follow.

EXERCISE ON DELEGATED LEGISLATION

There are three main forms of delegated legislation: statutory instruments, bye-laws, Orders in Council. While the validity of a statute can never be challenged by the courts, delegated legislation can under the procedure for judicial review.

R v Secretary of State for Social Security, ex parte Joint Council for the Welfare of Immigrants (1996) concerned the Asylum and Immigration Appeals Act 1993, which provided a framework for determining applications for asylum. It allowed asylum seekers to apply for social security benefits while they were waiting for their applications to be decided, at a cost of £200 million per year to the British taxpayers. This led to concern that the provisions might attract those who were simply seeking a better lifestyle (often called economic migrants). In order to discourage economic migrants, the Secretary of State for Social Security exercised powers to make delegated legislation under the Social Security (Contributions and Benefits) Act 1992 and produced regulations which stated that social security benefits would no longer be available to those who sought asylum after they had entered the UK, rather than immediately on entry, or those who had been refused leave to stay here and were awaiting the outcome of appeals against the decision.

The Joint Council for the Welfare of Immigrants challenged the regulations, claiming that they fell outside the powers granted by the Social Security (Contributions and Benefits) Act 1992. The Court of Appeal upheld the claim, stating that the Asylum and Immigration Appeals Act 1993 was clearly intended to give asylum seekers rights which they did not have previously. The effect of the regulations was effectively to take those rights away again, since without access to social security benefits, most asylum seekers would either have to return to the countries from where they had fled, or live on nothing while their claims were processed. The court ruled that Parliament could not have intended to give the Secretary of State powers to take away the rights it had given in the 1993 Act: this could only be done in a new statute, and therefore the regulations were *ultra vires*.

Adapted from: *English Legal System*, Catherine Elliott and Frances Quinn, Longman.

(a) Describe and explain the three types of delegated legislation identified in the source (lines 1–2). [28]

(b) Refer to the source (lines 2–3):
  (i) Explain for what reasons delegated legislation can be challenged in the courts;
  (ii) Describe the orders that can be made if that challenge is successful. [24]

(c) With reference to the source and your knowledge of delegated legislation, discuss the main advantages and disadvantages of delegated legislation. [26]

(d) Using the source and other cases, suggest whether the following situations might be subject to challenge in the courts:
  (i) Using powers of discretion given under a statute for applications for asylum the Home Secretary introduces a statutory instrument preventing applications for asylum from any immigrant entering from an Asian, African or Latin American country.
  (ii) An Act allows the Home Secretary to introduce statutory instruments to provide emergency accommodation for asylum seekers after first consulting local authorities and holding meetings with local residents. The Home Secretary, responding to a sudden influx of asylum seekers, erects a camp near to a town without consulting the local council or holding a public meeting. [12]

(OCR)

Answer guide

(a) Relevant material to answer this question can be found at p. 57.

(b) Delegated legislation can be challenged in the courts by legal proceedings known as judicial review. This is discussed at pp. 60–1.

(c) There are three types of order that can be made if the challenge is successful: *certiorari* which quashes the original decision, *mandamus* which orders that a course of conduct must be followed, and prohibition which orders that certain actions must not be carried out.

(d) (i) The statute was for applications for asylum, but the regulations prevent applications from being made, so it may be *ultra vires* for the same reason as the case that is the subject matter of the source material.

(ii) The Minister has not followed the procedure laid down by an Act for the making of statutory instruments. This would therefore appear to be a case of procedural *ultra vires*. The facts of the case are very similar to **Agricultural, Horticultural and Forestry Training Board** v **Aylesbury Mushrooms Ltd** (1972), discussed on p. 60.

Chapter summary

There are three main forms of delegated legislation:

- statutory instruments
- bye-laws, and
- Orders in Council.

Why is delegated legislation necessary?

Delegated legislation is necessary because it saves parliamentary time, constitutes a quick form of legislation, and is suited to technical subject areas or where local knowledge is needed.

Control of delegated legislation

Delegated legislation is controlled through:

- the consultation of experts
- publication of the legislation
- supervision by Parliament, and
- the courts with the judicial review procedure.

Criticism of delegated legislation

Delegated legislation has been criticized due to:

- lack of democratic involvement
- overuse
- sub-delegation, and
- lack of controls.

Chapter 5

European law

The European Union currently comprises 25 western European countries. The original members – France, West Germany, Belgium, Luxembourg, Italy and The Netherlands – founded the community in 1951, when they created the European Coal and Steel Community. Six years later, they signed the Treaties of Rome, creating the European Economic Community (EEC) and the European Atomic Energy Community (Euratom). Following the Nice summit, the EU increased its membership from 15 to 25 in 2004, with most of the new members coming from eastern Europe.

In 1993 the Maastricht Treaty renamed the European Economic Community the European Community. It also created the European Union, which is likely to become the most important body in Europe and so will be the label that we will refer to in this book.

The aims of the European Union

The original aim of the first treaty signed, the Treaty of Paris, was to create political unity within Europe and prevent another world war. The European Coal and Steel Community placed the production of steel and coal in all the Member States under the authority of a single community organization, with the object of indirectly controlling the manufacture of arms and therefore helping to prevent war between member states. Euratom was designed to produce co-operative nuclear research, and the EEC to improve Europe's economic strength.

Task 5.1

Find a newspaper article about the European Union in a quality newspaper that was published this week. Write a summary of the article.

Though all three communities still exist, it is the EEC (now known as the EU) that has the most significance, particularly for law. Its object now is to weld Europe into a single prosperous area by abolishing all restrictions affecting the movement of people, of goods and money between Member States, producing a single market of over 370 million people, available to all producers in the Member States. This, it is hoped, will help Europe to compete economically with Japan and the United States, the Member States being stronger as a block than they could possibly be on their own. Along with these closer economic ties, it is intended that there should be increasing political unity, though there is some disagreement – particularly, though not exclusively, in Britain – as to how far this should go.

The institutions of the European Union

There are four key European institutions: the Commission, the Council, the European Parliament and the European Court of Justice. Of less importance is the European Court of First Instance. Each of these institutions will be considered in turn, and then we look briefly at the reforms being undertaken to prepare the institutions for an enlarged membership of the EU.

The Commission

The Commission is composed of 20 members, called Commissioners, who are each appointed by the Member States, subject to approval by the European Parliament, for five years. They must be nationals of a Member State, and in practice there tend to be two each from the largest states – France, Germany, Italy, Spain and the UK – and one each from the rest. However, the Commissioners do not represent their own countries: they are independent, and their role is to represent the interests of the EU overall. The idea is that the Commission's commitment to furthering EU interests balances the role of the Council, whose members represent national interests.

In addition to its part in making EU legislation (see p. 73), the Commission is responsible for ensuring that Member States uphold EU law, and has powers to investigate breaches by Member States and, where necessary, bring them before the Court of Justice. It also plays an important role in the relationship of the EU with the rest of the world, negotiating trade agreements and the accession of new members, and draws up the annual draft budget for the EU. It is assisted in all these functions by an administrative staff, which has a similar role to that of the civil service in the UK.

The Council

The Council represents the interests of individual Member States. It is the most powerful body in Europe and plays an important role in the passing of legislation. It does not have a permanent membership – in each meeting, the members, one from each country, are chosen according to the subject under discussion (so, for example, a discussion of matters relating to farming would usually be attended by the Minister of Agriculture of each country). Presidency of the Council rotates among the Member States every six months.

Figure 5.1 The European Parliament building, Strasbourg
Source: © EMPICS.

The Council may be questioned by the European Parliament, but the chief control is exercised by national governments controlling their Ministers who attend the Council.

The European Parliament

The Parliament is composed of 626 members (MEPs), who are directly elected in their own countries. Elections are held every five years.

As well as taking part in the legislative process (discussed below) the Parliament has a variety of roles to play in connection with the other institutions. Over the Commission, it exercises a supervisory power. It has a right of veto over the appointment of the Commission as a whole, and can also dismiss the whole Commission by a vote of censure.

The Council is not accountable to Parliament in the same way, and Parliament only has very limited controls over its activities.

The Parliament appoints an Ombudsman, who investigates complaints of maladministration by EU institutions from individuals and MEPs.

The European Court of Justice (ECJ)

The ECJ has the task of supervising the uniform application of EU law throughout the member states, and in so doing it can create case law. It is important not to confuse it with the European Court of Human Rights, which deals with alleged breaches of human rights by countries who are signatories to the European Convention on Human Rights. That court is completely separate, and not an institution of the European Union.

The ECJ, which sits in Luxembourg, has 15 judges, appointed by agreement among Member States for a period of six years (which may be renewed). The judges are assisted by eight Advocates General, who produce opinions on the cases assigned to them, indicating the issues raised and suggesting conclusions. These are not binding, but are nevertheless usually followed by the court. Both judges and Advocates General are chosen from those who are eligible for the highest judicial posts in their own countries.

Most cases are heard in plenary session, that is with all the judges sitting together. Only one judgment will be delivered, giving no indication of the extent of agreement between the judges, and these often consist of fairly brief propositions, from which it can be difficult to discern any *ratio decidendi*. Consequently, lawyers seeking precedents often turn to the opinions written by the Advocates General.

The majority of cases heard by the ECJ are brought by Member States and institutions of the Community, or are referred to it by national courts. It has only limited power to deal with cases brought by individual citizens, and such cases are rarely heard.

The ECJ has two separate functions: a judicial role, deciding cases of dispute; and a supervisory role.

The judicial role of the ECJ

The ECJ hears cases of dispute between parties, which fall into two categories: proceedings against Member States, and proceedings against European institutions.

Proceedings against Member States may be brought by the Commission, or by other member states, and involve alleged breaches of European law by the country in question. For example, in **Re Tachographs: EC Commission** *v* **UK** (1979), the ECJ upheld a complaint against the UK for failing to implement a European regulation making it compulsory for lorries used to carry dangerous goods to be fitted with tachographs (devices used to record the speed and distance travelled, with the aim of preventing lorry drivers from speeding, or for driving for longer than the permitted number of hours). The Commission usually gives the Member State the opportunity to put things right before bringing the case to the ECJ.

Proceedings against European institutions may be brought by Member States, other European institutions and in limited circumstances, by individual citizens or organizations. The procedure can be used to review the legality of regulations, directives or decisions, on the grounds that proper procedures have not been followed, the provisions infringe a Treaty or any rule relating to its application, or powers have been misused. In **United Kingdom** *v* **Council of the European Union** (1996) the UK sought to have the Directive on the 48-hour working week annulled on the basis that it had been unlawfully adopted by the Council. The application was unsuccessful.

Decisions made in these kinds of cases cannot be questioned in UK courts. Member States can be fined for failure to implement a judgment of the European Court.

The supervisory role of the ECJ

Under Art. 234 of the Treaty of Rome any court or tribunal in a Member State may refer a question on European law to the ECJ if it considers that 'a decision on that question is necessary to enable it to give judgment'. The object of this referral system is to make sure that the law is interpreted in the same way throughout Europe.

A reference must be made if the national court is one from which there is no further appeal – so in Britain, the House of Lords must refer such questions, while the lower courts usually have some discretion about whether or not to do so.

Attempts have been made to set down guidelines by which a court can determine when a reference is necessary. In **Bulmer** *v* **Bollinger** (1974), Lord Denning set down guidelines on the points which should be taken into account in considering whether a reference was necessary. He emphasized the cost and delay that a reference could cause, and stated that no reference should be made:

- where it would not be conclusive of the case, and other matters would remain to be decided;
- where there had been a previous ruling on the same point;
- where the court considers that point to be reasonably clear and free from doubt;
- where the facts of the case had not yet been decided.

Unless the point to be decided could be considered 'really difficult and important', said Lord Denning, the court should save the expense and delay of a reference and decide the issue itself.

Denning's view has since been criticized by academics, who point out that it can be cheaper and quicker to refer a point at an early stage, than to drag the case up through the English courts first. In addition, the clear and consistent interpretation of EU law can come to depend on whether individual litigants have the resources to take their cases all the way up to the House of Lords.

Although the judiciary still uses Denning's **Bulmer** guidelines, there now appears to be a greater willingness to refer cases to the ECJ. In **R** *v* **International Stock Exchange, ex parte Else** (1993) Lord Justice Bingham said that if, once the facts have been found, it is clear that an issue of European law is vital to a court's final decision, that court should normally make a reference to the ECJ. English courts should only decide such issues without referral if they have real confidence that they can do so correctly, without the help of the ECJ.

Where a case is submitted, proceedings will be suspended in the national court until the ECJ has given its verdict. This verdict does not tell the national court how to decide the case, but simply explains what European law on the matter is. The national court then has the duty of making its decision in the light of this.

Regardless of which national court submitted the point for consideration, a ruling from the ECJ should be followed by all other courts in the EU.

The court's decisions can be changed only by its own subsequent decision or by an amendment of the Treaty. Decisions of the European Court cannot be questioned in English courts.

An illustration of the use of Art. 234 is the case of **Marshall *v* Southampton and South West Hampshire Area Health Authority** (1986). Miss Marshall, a dietitian, was compulsorily retired by the Authority from her job when she was 62, although she wished to continue to 65. It was the Authority's policy that the normal retiring age for its employees was the age at which state retirement pensions became payable: for women this was 60, though the Authority had waived the rule for two years in Miss Marshall's case. She claimed that the Authority was discriminating against women by adopting a policy that employees should retire at state pension age, hence requiring women to retire before men. This policy appeared to be legal under the relevant English legislation but was argued to be contrary to a Council directive providing for equal treatment of men and women. The national court made a reference to the ECJ asking for directions on the meaning of the directive. The ECJ found that there was a conflict with UK law, and the UK later changed its legislation to conform.

European Court of First Instance

A European Court of First Instance was established in 1988 by the Single European Act inserting Art. 225 into the EC Treaty. The aim was to reduce the workload of the ECJ. It has a very limited jurisdiction, handling primarily internal staff litigation, and appeals on points of law are heard by the ECJ.

Making European legislation

The Council, the Commission and the European Parliament all play a role in making European legislation. A complicated range of different procedures has been developed to make these laws. All legislation starts with a proposal from the Commission and the Council enjoys the most power in the legislative process.

Parliament's legislative role was historically purely advisory, with the Commission and the Council having a much more powerful role in the legislative process. This led to concern over the lack of democracy within Europe, for while Parliament is directly elected by the citizens of Europe, the Commission and Council members are not.

Table 5.1 Membership of the European institutions

Commission	20 Commissioners.
Council	It does not have a permanent membership. For each meeting one Minister is chosen from each country according to the subject of the meeting.
European Parliament	732 Members of the European Parliament (MEPs).
European Court of Justice	25 judges.

The role of the European Parliament in the passing of European legislation has gradually been increased over the years but problems still remain. There are still areas of law on which Parliament does not even have the right to be consulted. Where Parliament is consulted by the Council, it normally has no power to block the legislation, but can merely delay it.

The Council plays an important role in the passing of European legislation. There are three systems of voting in the Council:

- unanimity, where proposals are only passed if all members vote for them;
- simple majority, where proposals only require more votes for than against; and
- qualified majority, which allows each country a specified number of votes (the larger the country, the more votes it has), and provides that a proposal can only be agreed if there are a specified number of votes in its favour. The number is calculated to ensure that larger states cannot force decisions on the smaller ones.

These voting procedures have been controversial, because where unanimity is not required a Member State can be forced to abide by legislation for which it has not voted, and which it believes is against its interests. This is seen as compromising national sovereignty. However, requiring unanimity makes it difficult to get things done quickly (or sometimes at all). Increasingly, only a qualified majority is required.

Types of European legislation

There is a range of different forms of European legislation: treaties, regulations, directives and decisions. In considering the impact of this legislation on UK law a distinction has to be drawn between *direct applicability* and *direct effect*. Direct applicability refers to the fact that treaty articles, regulations and some decisions immediately become part of the law of each Member State. Directives are not directly applicable.

Where European legislation has direct effect it creates individual rights which national courts must protect without any need for implementing legislation in that Member State. In the UK the national courts were given this power under s. 2(1) of the European Communities Act 1972.

There are two types of direct effect: *vertical direct effect* gives individuals rights against governments; and *horizontal direct effect* gives rights against other people and organizations.

Provisions of treaties, regulations and directives only have direct effect if they are clear and unconditional and their implementation requires no further legislation in Member States. These conditions were first laid down in the context of treaties in **Van Gend en Loos** *v* **Nederlandse Tariefcommissie** (1963).

The ability of individuals to rely on Community law before their national courts greatly enhances its effectiveness. National courts can quickly apply directly effective legislation and can draw on a wide range of remedies. Where legislation does not have direct effect, the only method of enforcement available in the past was an action brought by the Commission or a Member State against a Member State before the

European Court of Justice. This process can be slow and provides no direct remedy for the individual.

However, in the 1990s the European Court of Justice recognized the right of individuals to be awarded damages by their national courts for breach of European legislation by a Member State, even where the legislation did not have direct effect. Originally, in **Francovich** *v* **Italy** (1991), this right was applied where directives had not been implemented, but it has been developed to extend to any violation of European law.

Quick quiz 5.2

1 How many countries are members of the European Union?

2 Name the four key institutions of the European Union.

3 Explain the supervisory role of the European Court of Justice.

4 What are the three systems of voting in the Council?

▊ Treaties

These are the highest source of EU law and, as well as laying down the general aims of the European Union, they themselves create some rights and obligations. The existing treaties are the three treaties of Rome that established the framework for Europe (the European Coal and Steel Community Treaty, the Euratom Treaty and the European Community Treaty), the Single European Act, the Treaty on European Union (known as the Maastricht Treaty), and the Treaty of Amsterdam. The article numbers of the European Community Treaty were changed by the Treaty of Amsterdam, as old articles had been repealed and new articles added since it had been originally drafted.

The case of **Van Gend en Loos** (1963) decided that a treaty provision has direct effect if it is unconditional, clear and precise as to the rights or obligations it creates, and leaves Member States no discretion on implementing it. Treaty provisions which are unconditional, clear and precise, and allow no discretion on implementation have both horizontal and vertical direct effect. An example of a directly effective treaty provision is Art. 139 of the EC Treaty. This provides that 'men and women shall receive equal pay for equal work'. In **Macarthys** *v* **Smith** (1979), Art. 139 was held to give a woman in the UK the right to claim the same wages as were paid to the male predecessor in her job, even though she had no such right under the UK equal pay legislation passed in 1970, before the UK joined Europe.

Treaty provisions which are merely statements of intent or policy, rather than establishing clear rights or duties, require detailed legislation to be made before they can be enforced in the Member States.

Regulations

A regulation is the nearest that European law comes to an English Act of Parliament. Regulations apply throughout the EU, usually to people in general, and they become part of the law of each member nation as soon as they come into force, without the need for each country to make its own legislation. Regulations must be applied even if the Member State has already passed legislation which conflicts with them.

Directives

Directives are less precisely worded than regulations, because they aim to set out broad objectives, leaving the Member States to create their own detailed legislation in order to put those objectives into practice (within specified time limits). As a result, it was originally assumed by most Member States that directives could not have direct effect, and would not create individual rights until they had been translated into domestic legislation. However, the European Court of Justice has consistently refused to accept this view, arguing that direct effect is an essential weapon if the EU is to ensure that Member States implement directives.

> ✓ **Know your terms 5.3**
>
> Define the following terms:
> 1 Advocate General
> 2 Veto
> 3 European Commission
> 4 Directive

The case which initially established direct effect for directives was **Van Duyn** *v* **Home Office** (1974). The Home Office had refused Van Duyn permission to enter the UK, because she was a member of a religious group, the Scientologists, which the Government wanted to exclude from the country at the time. Van Duyn argued that her exclusion was contrary to provisions in the Treaty of Rome on freedom of movement. The Government responded by pointing out that the treaty allowed exceptions on public policy grounds, but Van Duyn then relied on a later directive which said that public policy could only be invoked on the basis of personal conduct, and Van Duyn herself had done nothing to justify exclusion. The case was referred to the ECJ, which found that the obligation conferred on the Government was clear and unconditional, and so created enforceable rights.

Directives have vertical direct effect but not horizontal direct effect. This means that they impose obligations on the state and not individuals. A directive with direct effect can be utilized by an individual against the state when the state has failed to implement the directive properly or on time.

The issue of direct effect was important in the high-profile case of **R (Westminster City Council)** *v* **Mayor of London** (2002). Westminster Council had applied for judicial review of the decision to introduce a congestion charge to enter central London. The decision had been taken by the Mayor of London, Ken Livingstone. The High Court rejected the application. Westminster Council had sought to rely on a provision of a directive. The High Court stated that the Council could not do this, as when directives had direct effect they only gave rights to individuals and not to Government institutions.

The ECJ has found a number of ways to widen access where the principle of vertical direct effect applies. First, it has defined 'the state' very broadly to include all public bodies, including local authorities and nationalized industries. This meant, for example, that in **Marshall** *v* **Southampton and Southwest Hampshire Area**

Table 5.2 Impact of European legislation

Impact	Meaning of term
Direct applicability	Legislative provisions immediately become part of the law of each Member State.
Direct effect	Legislation creates individual rights which national courts must protect without any need for implementing legislation in the Member State.
Horizontal direct effect	Legislation gives rights against governments, individuals and private organizations.
Vertical direct effect	Legislation gives rights against governments.
Indirect effect	National courts should interpret national law in accordance with relevant European legislation.

Health Authority (1986), discussed on p. 72, Miss Marshall was able to take advantage of the relevant directive even though she was not suing the Government itself, because her employer was a health authority and therefore considered a public body.

Secondly, in **Von Colson** *v* **Land Nordrhein-Westfalen** (1984), the court introduced the principle of indirect effect, stating that national courts should interpret national law in accordance with relevant directives, whether the national law was designed to implement a directive or not. The principle was confirmed in **Marleasing SA** *v* **La Comercial Internacional de Alimentacion SA** (1990).

Decisions

A decision may be addressed to a state, a person or a company and is binding only on the recipient. Examples include granting, or refusing, export licences to companies from outside the European Union.

Recommendations and opinions

The Council and the Commission may issue recommendations and opinions which, although not to be disregarded, are not binding law.

The future

One view of the influence of UK membership of Europe on our national law was given by Lord Denning, in poetic mood, in **Bulmer** *v* **Bollinger** (1974): 'The Treaty is like an incoming tide. It flows into the estuaries and up the rivers. It cannot be held back.' Lord Scarman, obviously in an equally lyrical frame of mind, commented:

For the moment, to adopt Lord Denning's imagery, the incoming tide has not yet mingled with the home waters of the common law: but it is inconceivable that, like the Rhone and the Arve where those two streams meet at Geneva, they should move on, side by side, one grey with the melted snows and ice of the distant mountains of our legal history, the other clear blue and clean, reflecting modern opinion. If we stay in the Common Market, I would expect to see its principles of legislation and statutory interpretation, and its conception of an activist court whose role is to strengthen and fulfil the purpose of statute law, replace the traditional attitudes of English judges and lawyers to statute law and the current complex style of statutory drafting.

What Lord Scarman was referring to was the difference in approach between the English legal system and those in mainland Europe. When drafting statutes, for example, English law has tended towards tightly written, very precise rules, whereas the continental style is looser, setting out broad principles to be followed. As a result, the continental style of statutory interpretation takes a very purposive approach, paying most attention to putting into practice the spirit of the legislation, and filling in any gaps in the wording if necessary, as opposed to the more literal style traditionally associated with English judges. The ECJ tends to take the continental approach, and it has been suggested that, as time goes on, this will influence our own judges more and more, leading to more creative judicial decision-making, with corresponding changes in the drafting of statutes.

Following the **Factortame** litigation (see p. 49), there was concern that Europe was threatening the sovereignty of the UK Parliament, as the ECJ ruling had caused an Act of Parliament to be set aside. Lord Denning revised his description of European law as like an 'incoming tide' and stated:

> No longer is European law an incoming tide flowing up the estuaries of England. It is now like a tidal wave bringing down our sea walls and flowing inland over our fields and houses – to the dismay of all. (*The Independent*, 16 July 1996)

In **R *v* Secretary of State for Foreign and Commonwealth Affairs, ex parte Rees-Mogg** (1994) an unsuccessful attempt was made to demonstrate that the UK could not legally ratify the Maastricht Treaty. In rejecting this claim, the court pointed out that the Treaty did not involve the abandoning or transferring of powers, so that a government could choose later to denounce the Treaty, or fail to honour its obligations under it.

▌A European Constitution

The European institutions were expected to be modernized to cope with the European Union's expanded membership through the passing of a new European Constitution. However, referendums in the Netherlands and France rejected the Constitution so it is uncertain which reforms will be introduced and when.

The Constitution contained a wide range of provisions. It would have explicitly stated for the first time that EU law had primacy over national law. EU legal instruments would have been re-classified, to establish a clear hierarchy and to distinguish between legislative and administrative acts. Constitutional law would be the highest source of law, amendable only under treaty amendment procedures. European laws and Framework laws would be binding legislative acts (similar to the current regulations and directives), regulations and decisions would be binding administrative acts; and recommendations and opinions would not be binding.

The European Union would have had a stronger political profile through the creation of two new posts: a Commission President and a Minister for Foreign Affairs. The Commission President would have been elected by the European Parliament. The Minister for Foreign Affairs would have been elected by the European Council. The President of the Council of Ministers would no longer have been held for six months, instead a team presidency would have been established consisting of three individuals appointed for 18 months. The number of Commissioners would have been reduced to two-thirds of the number of Member States. Membership of the European Parliament would have been restricted to 750. The European Parliament's legislative role would have been strengthened. The rotating six-monthly presidency of the European Council would have been abolished and replaced by a person appointed for a renewable period of two and a half years.

Within the European Council the emphasis would have been on qualified majority voting, with a view to reducing the current number of national vetoes. The existing system of weighted votes for calculating a qualified majority would have been replaced by a 'double majority' system. This would have required the support of 55 per cent of Member States which also represented at least 65 per cent of the EU population. To prevent two or three large countries blocking a vote, a blocking minority would require at least four Council members.

Part II of the Constitution contained a Charter of Fundamental Rights. This laid down much more extensive rights than those contained in the European Convention on Human Rights, because as well as containing civil and political rights, it contained social and economic rights.

Reading on the web

Access to the homepages of the European institutions can be obtained from the following website:

http://www.europa.eu.int/index_en.htm

European legislation is available at:

http://europa.eu.int/eur-lex/

Question and answer guides

1 Read the source material A and B below and answer parts **(a)** to **(c)** which follow.

EXERCISE ON EUROPEAN LAW

Source A

Council Directive 93/104/EC of 23 November 1993, concerning certain aspects of the organisation of working time.

> The Council of the European Union, having regard to the Treaty establishing the European Community, having regard to the proposal from the Commission, in co-operation with the European Parliament, has adopted this Directive.
>
> *Article 1*
> Purpose and scope
> This Directive shall apply to all sectors of activity, both public and private, with the exception of air, rail, road, sea, inland waterway and lake transport, sea fishing, other work at sea and the activities of doctors in training.
>
> *Article 3*
> Daily rest
> Member States shall take the measures necessary to ensure that every worker is entitled to a minimum daily rest period of 11 consecutive hours per 24-hour day.
>
> *Article 4*
> Breaks
> Member States shall take the measures necessary to ensure that, where the working day is longer than 6 hours, every worker is entitled to a break . . .
>
> *Article 6*
> Maximum weekly working time
> Member States shall take the measures necessary to ensure that, in keeping with the need to protect safety and health of workers, the average working time for each 7-day period, including overtime, does not exceed 48 hours.
>
> Adapted from Council Directive 93/104/EC, 'The Working Time Directive'.

Source B

Directives are the main way in which harmonisation of laws within Member States is reached. However, problems have arisen where Member States have not implemented a directive within the time laid down and the European Court of Justice has, therefore, developed the concept of 'direct effect' to cover directives in certain situations.

(Adapted from: *The English Legal System*, Jacqueline Martin, Hodder & Stoughton, 2000.)

Answer *all* parts.

(a) Briefly describe the law-making functions of the Council of the European Union, the Commission and the European Parliament as mentioned at lines 3–5 of Source A. [15]

(b) Advise each of the following workers whether their rights under the Working Time Directive, as outlined in Source A, are being denied:

▶

(i) Jenny, a trainee doctor, is required to work 14-hour shifts, often without a break.

(ii) Stanley, a supermarket cashier, is required to work a 6-day week of 10 hours per day.

(iii) Tarry has a part-time job in a video store working a 7-hour shift. Her manager does not allow her to have any break. [15]

(c) With reference to Source B, explain how directives, such as the Working Time Directive, become law in Member States and discuss the problems that can arise. [30]

[Total: 60]

(OCR)

Answer guide

(a) The material that you need to answer this part of the question is at p. 73 under the sub-heading 'Making European legislation'. The opening paragraph of the directive refers to the Council adopting the directive, having regard to the proposal from the Commission, in cooperation with the European Parliament. All three bodies play a role in preparing European legislation, and the role of each body will be considered in turn.

(i) **The Council** The Council is the supreme legislative body of the EU. It has the responsibility of developing specific legislation to apply the broad policies contained in the foundation treaties. The Council cannot work on its own initiative, it has to wait for a proposal to be presented to it from the Commission. The other European institutions are then usually consulted, including the European Parliament, before the Council then passes the legislation. You could discuss the three voting systems used by the Council to pass legislation discussed at p. 73.

(ii) **The Commission** The Commission produces the proposals for new legislation, which it then presents to the Council. Council has delegated some of its law-making powers to the Commission.

(iii) **The European Parliament** Surprisingly, the European Parliament does not have the power to make legislation itself. It usually has the right to be consulted on legislation, but can then only delay it being passed, rather than block it altogether.

(b)(i) Article 1 of the Working Time Directive states that it does not apply to trainee doctors. Jenny is not therefore being denied her rights.

(ii) Article 6 of the Working Time Directive is particularly relevant to Stanley. Under this article, workers should work an average of no more than 48 hours a week. Stanley is working an average of 60 hours and therefore his rights are being denied.

(iii) Article 4 of the Directive provides that workers with a working day longer than 6 hours are entitled to a break. Tarry is working 7-hour shifts, so the manager's refusal to give her a break means that Tarry's rights are being denied.

(c) Most of the material you need to answer this question is contained at pp. 75–6, under the heading 'Directives'. In addition, Source B refers to the concept of direct effect and a general explanation of this concept is provided at p. 74. Source B also refers to the fact that problems have arisen where Member States have not implemented a directive within the time laid down; the case of **Francovich** v **Italy** (1992) established that states could be liable to individuals for failure to implement directives (discussed on p. 74).

2 Describe the composition and role of the European Court of Justice, and evaluate its importance with regard to the English legal system. *(Oxford)*

Answer guide

The first part of this question requires a factual description of the ECJ and what it does. You need to talk about the judges, how they are appointed, how they deal with cases and then talk about the two roles of the ECJ, explaining its supervisory and its judicial roles.

For the second part of the question, you need more than just description as the question requires you to 'evaluate' its importance. You should obviously talk about the Art. 234 procedure, and the fact that decisions of the court in these cases provide precedents which the English courts must follow, which effectively means that the House of Lords no longer has the final say on those areas of law in which the EU is involved (but remember to explain that the ECJ is not an appellate court; it does not decide the cases referred to it under Art. 234, but explains the law so that the national court can do so). Point out that as a result of Art. 234 rulings, the government has often had to change statute law – you could talk about **Marshall** as an example of this.

You could also discuss the way in which the ECJ has been instrumental in ensuring that member states abide by EU legislation. An example of this is its approach to directives: the ruling in **Van Duyn** that they could have direct effect; the broad interpretation of 'government' so as to extend vertical direct effect in **Marshall**; the creation of indirect effect in **Von Colson**; and the principles of compensation introduced in **Francovich**.

You might also discuss the fact that the ECJ uses a much more purposive style when interpreting legislation than has been traditional in the English legal system, and the suggestions that this may eventually influence English judges to move in a similar direction.

Chapter summary

Introduction

The European Union currently has 25 members. It was established to create political unity within Europe and to prevent another world war.

The institutions of the European Union

There are four key institutions of the European Union: the Commission, the Council, the European Parliament and the European Court of Justice. The European Court of Justice has two separate functions: a judicial role where it decides cases of dispute and a supervisory role under Art. 234 of the Treaty of Rome.

Making European legislation

The Council, the Commission and the European Parliament all play a role in making European legislation. All legislation starts with a proposal from the Commission, though the Council enjoys the most power in the legislative process. Increasingly, the qualified majority system of voting is being used by the Council in agreeing new legislation.

Types of European legislation

The different forms of European legislation are:

■ treaties
■ regulations
■ directives, and
■ decisions.

The future

The impact of EU legislation on the United Kingdom is likely to increase in the future.

Chapter 6

Law reform

An effective legal system cannot stand still. Both legal procedures and the law itself must adapt to social change if they are to retain the respect of at least most of society, without which they cannot survive. Many laws which were made even as short a time ago as the nineteenth century simply do not fit the way we see society today – until the early part of the twentieth century, for example, married women were legally considered the property of their husbands, while, not much earlier, employees could be imprisoned for breaking their employment contracts.

Most legislation in this country stands until it is repealed – the fact that it may be completely out of date does not mean it technically ceases to apply. The offences of challenging to fight, eavesdropping and being a common scold, for example, which long ago dropped out of use, nevertheless remained on the statute book until they were abolished by the Criminal Law Act 1967. In practice, of course, many such provisions simply cease to be used, but where it becomes clear that the law may be out of step with social conditions, or simply ineffective, there is a range of ways of bringing about change.

Judicial activity

Case law can bring about some reform – one of the most notable recent examples was the decision in **R** *v* **R** (1991), in which the House of Lords declared that a husband who has sexual intercourse with his wife without her consent may be guilty of rape. Before this decision, the law on rape within marriage was based on an assertion by the eighteenth-century jurist Sir Matthew Hale, that 'by marrying a man, a woman consents to sexual intercourse with him, and may not retract that consent'. This position had been found offensive for many years before **R** *v* **R**. In 1976, Parliament considered it during a debate on the Sexual Offences Act, but decided not to make changes at that time, and it was not until 1991 that the Court of Appeal and then the House of Lords held that rape within marriage should be considered an offence.

Lord Keith stated that Hale's assertion reflected the status of women within marriage in his time, but since then both the status of women and the marriage relationship had completely changed. The modern view of husband and wife as equal partners meant that a wife could no longer be considered to have given irrevocable consent to sex with her husband; the common law was capable of evolving to reflect such changes in society, and it was the duty of the court to help it do so.

In practice, however, major reforms like this are rarely produced by the courts, and would not be adequate as the sole agency of reform. Norman Marsh's article 'Law Reform in the United Kingdom' (1971) puts forward a number of reasons for this.

First, as we saw in the chapter on case law, there is no systematic, state-funded process for bringing points of law in need of reform to the higher courts. The courts can only deal with such points as they arise in the cases before them, and this depends on the parties involved having sufficient finance, determination and interest to take their case up through the courts. Consequently, judge-made reform proceeds not on the basis of which areas of law need changes most, but on a haphazard presentation of cases.

Secondly, judges have to decide cases on the basis of the way the issues are presented to them by the parties concerned. They cannot commission research, or consult with interested bodies to find out the possible effects of a decision on individuals and organizations other than those in the case before them – yet their decision will apply to future cases.

Thirdly, judges have to recognize the doctrine of precedent, and for much of the time this prohibits any really radical reforms.

Marsh's fourth point is that reforming decisions by judges have the potential to be unjust to the losing party. Law reforms made by Parliament are prospective – they come into force on a specified date, and we are not usually expected to abide by them until after that date. Judicial decisions, on the other hand, are retrospective, affecting something that happened before the judges decided what the law was. The more reformatory such a decision is, the less the likelihood that the losing party could have abided by the law, even if they wanted to.

Finally, Marsh argues, judges are not elected, and therefore feel they should not make decisions which change the law in areas of great social or moral controversy. They themselves impose limits on their ability to make major changes and will often point out to Parliament the need for it to make reforms, as happened in the **Bland** case concerning the Hillsborough stadium disaster victim (see p. 15).

Reform by Parliament

The majority of law reform is therefore carried out by Parliament. It is done in four ways:

- **Repeal** of old and/or obsolete laws.
- **Creation** of completely new law, or adaptation of existing provisions, to meet new needs. The creation of the offence of insider dealing (where company officials make money by using information gained by virtue of a privileged position) in the Companies Act 1980 was a response to public concern about 'sharp practice' in the City of London.
- **Consolidation.** When a new statute is created, problems with it may become apparent over time, in which case further legislation may be enacted to amend it.

Consolidation brings together successive statutes on a particular subject and puts them into one statute. For example, the legislation in relation to companies was consolidated in 1985.

■ **Codification.** Where a particular area of the law has developed over time to produce a large body of both case law and statute, a new statute may be created to bring together all the rules on that subject (case law and statute) in one place. That statute then becomes the starting point for cases concerning that area of the law, and case law, in time, builds up around it. The Criminal Attempts Act 1981 and the Police and Criminal Evidence Act 1984 are examples of codifying statutes. Codification is thought to be most suitable for areas of law where the principles are well worked out; areas that are still developing, such as tort, are less suitable for codifying.

These types of reform often happen together – the Public Order Act 1986, for example, created new public order offences designed to deal with specific problems of the time, such as football hooliganism, and at the same time, repealed out of date public order offences.

Some significant law reforms have come about as a result of Private Members' Bills (see p. 25) – an example is the 1967 Abortion Act which resulted from a Private Member's Bill put forward by David Steel.

Pressures for reform

The inspiration for reform may come from a variety of sources, alone or in combination. As well as encouraging Parliament to consider particular issues in the first place, they may have an influence during the consultation stage of legislation.

Pressure groups

Groups concerned with particular subjects may press for law reform in those areas – examples include charities such as Shelter, Help the Aged and the Child Poverty Action Group; professional organizations such as the Law Society and the British Medical Association; business representatives such as the Confederation of British Industry. Justice is a pressure group specifically concerned with promoting law reform in general.

Task 6.1

The following organizations are examples of influential pressure groups:

The Campaign for Nuclear Disarmament: http://www.cnduk.org/

Greenpeace: http://www.greenpeace.org/international/

Shelter: http://www.shelter.org.uk/

Select the website of one of them and consider the ways in which they are trying to influence legal developments in this country.

Pressure groups use a variety of tactics, including lobbying MPs, gaining as much publicity as possible for their cause, organizing petitions and encouraging people to write to their own MP and/or relevant Ministers. Some groups are more effective than others: size obviously helps, but sheer persistence and a knack for grabbing headlines can be just as productive – the anti-porn campaigner Mary Whitehouse almost single-handedly pressurized the Government to create the Protection of Children Act 1978, which sought to prevent child pornography. The amount of power wielded by the members of a pressure group is also extremely important – organizations involved with big business tend to be particularly effective in influencing legislation, and there is a growing industry set up purely to help them lobby effectively, for a price. On the other hand, pressure groups made up of ordinary individuals can be very successful, particularly if the issue on which they are campaigning is one which stirs up strong emotion in the general public. A recent example was the Snowdrop Petition, organized after the shooting of sixteen young children and their teacher in Dunblane, Scotland. Despite enormous opposition from shooting clubs, it managed to persuade the previous Government to ban most types of handguns.

Political parties

Some of the most high-profile legislation is that passed in order to implement the Government party's election manifesto, or its general ideology – examples include the privatizations of gas and water and the creation of the Poll Tax by the Conservative Government which began in 1979.

The civil service

Although technically neutral, the civil service nevertheless has a great effect on legislation in general. It may not have party political goals, but various departments will have their own views as to what type of legislation enables them to achieve departmental goals most efficiently – which strategies might help the Home Office control the prison population, for example, or the Department of Health make the NHS more efficient. Ministers rely heavily on senior civil servants for advice and information on the issues of the day, and few would consistently turn down their suggestions.

Treaty obligations

The UK's obligations under the treaties establishing the European Union and the European Convention on Human Rights both influence changes in English law (see Chapter 5 on European law and p. 29 on the incorporation of the European Convention).

Public opinion and media pressure

As well as taking part in campaigns organized by pressure groups, members of the public make their feelings known by writing to their MPs, to Ministers and to newspapers. This is most likely to lead to reform where the ruling party has a small majority. The media can also be a very powerful force for law reform, by highlighting issues of concern. In 1997, media pressure helped secure a judicial inquiry into the racially motivated killing of South London teenager Stephen Lawrence. The inquiry was authorized to look not only at the Lawrence case itself, but at the general issue of how racially motivated killings are investigated.

Public opinion and media pressure interact; the media often claim to reflect public opinion, but they can also whip it up. What appears to be a major epidemic of a particular crime may in fact be no more than a reflection of the fact that once one interesting example of it hits the news, newspapers and broadcasting organizations are more likely to report others. An example of this is the rash of stories during 1993 about parents going on holiday and leaving their children alone, which caught the headlines largely because of a popular film about just such a situation, *Home Alone*. Leaving children alone like this may have been common practice for years, or it may be something done by a tiny minority of parents, but the media's selection of stories gave the impression of a sudden epidemic of parental negligence. In 2000 there was a high-profile campaign by the *News of the World* to 'name and shame' paedophiles. The Government subsequently introduced a limited reform of the law.

Quick quiz 6.2

1 Which court heard the final appeal in **R** v **R** (1991) and what is the *ratio decidendi* of this decision?

2 What are the four main ways in which Parliament can change the law?

3 Give three examples of pressure groups that seek to influence the development of the law.

4 What did you think of the campaign by the *News of the World* to name and shame paedophiles?

Agencies of law reform

Much law reform happens as a direct response to pressure from one or more of the above sources, but there are also a number of agencies set up to consider the need for reform in areas referred to them by the Government. Often problems are referred to them as a result of the kind of pressures listed above – the Royal Commission on Criminal Justice 1993 was set up as a result of public concern and media pressure about high-profile miscarriages of justice, such as the 'Birmingham Six' and the 'Guildford Four'.

The Law Commission

Established in 1965 (along with another for Scotland), the Law Commission is a permanent body, comprising five people drawn from the judiciary, the legal profession

Figure 6.1 *News of the World*: its campaign to name and shame paedophiles

Source: Remember When, The Newspaper Archive. The *News of the World*, London, 23 July 2000. © News International Newspapers Limited, 23 July 2000.

and legal academics. In practice, the chairman tends to be a High Court judge, and the other four members to include a QC experienced in criminal law, a solicitor with experience of land law and equity, and two legal academics. They are assisted by legally qualified civil servants.

Under the Law Commission Act 1965 the Law Commission's task is to:

- codify the law
- remove anomalies in the law
- repeal obsolete and unnecessary legislation
- consolidate the law
- simplify and modernize the law.

The Commission works on reform projects referred to it by the Lord Chancellor or a government department or on projects which the Commission itself has decided would be suitable for its consideration. At any one time the Commission will be engaged on between 20 and 30 projects of law reform.

A typical project will begin with a study of the area of law in question, and an attempt to identify its defects. Foreign legal systems will be examined to see how they deal with similar problems. The Commission normally publishes a consultation paper inviting comments on the subject. The consultation paper describes the present law and its shortcomings and sets out possible options for reform. The Commission's final recommendations are set out in a report which contains a draft Bill where legislation is proposed. It is then essentially for the Government to decide whether it accepts the recommendations and to introduce any necessary Bill in Parliament.

The Criminal Law Revision Committee

The Criminal Law Revision Committee (CLRC) considers reform to the criminal law. It is responsible to the Home Secretary and its membership includes the Director of Public Prosecutions (DPP) as well as judges and academics. The CLRC has not been convened since 1985, though it has never been formally abolished.

Royal Commissions

These are set up to study particular areas of law reform, usually as a result of criticism and concern about the area concerned. They are made up of a wide cross-section of people: most have some expertise in the area concerned, but usually only a minority are legally qualified. The Commissions are supposed to be independent and non-political.

A Royal Commission can commission research, and also take submissions from interested parties. It produces a final report detailing its recommendations, which the Government can then choose to act upon or not. Usually a majority of proposals are acted upon, sometimes in amended form.

Important recent Royal Commissions include the 1981 Royal Commission on Criminal Procedure and the Royal Commission on Criminal Justice, which reported in 1993, and the Royal Commission on reform of the House of Lords which reported in 2000.

Public inquiries

Where a particular problem or incident is causing social concern, the Government may set up a one-off, temporary committee to examine possible options for dealing

Figure 6.2 Victoria Climbie

Source: © Rex Features Ltd.

with it. Major disasters, such as the Hillsborough football stadium disaster, the sinking of the ferry *Herald of Free Enterprise* and the Paddington railway disaster; events such as the Brixton riots during the 1980s; and advances in technology, especially medical technology (such as the ability to fertilize human eggs outside the body and produce 'test-tube babies') may all be investigated by bodies set up especially for the job. In recent years inquiries have been set up following the BSE crisis, the murder of Victoria Climbie (a young girl living away from her parents), and the conviction of the serial killer Harold Shipman. These inquiries usually comprise individuals who are independent of Government, often with expertise in the particular area. Academics are frequent choices, as are judges – Lord Scarman headed the inquiry into the Brixton riots, and Lord Cullen headed the inquiry into the Paddington railway disaster.

Public inquiries consult interested groups, and attempt to reach a consensus between them, conducting their investigation as far as possible in a non-political way. In the case of disasters and other events, they may try to discover the causes, as well as making recommendations on legislation to avoid a repeat.

Other temporary inquiries

From time to time, various government departments set up temporary projects to investigate specific areas of law. One of the most important recent examples is the inquiry by Lord Woolf into the Civil Justice System (p. 350).

Performance of the law reform bodies

The Law Commission

One of the principal tasks of the Commission at its inception was codification, and this programme has not on the whole been a success. The Commission's programme was ambitious: in 1965 it announced that it would begin codifying family, contract, landlord and tenant, and evidence law. Attempts in the first three were abandoned – family in 1970, contract in 1973 and landlord and tenant in 1978. Evidence was never begun.

Task 6.3

Visit the Law Commission's website at:

http://www.lawcom.gov.uk/

The work it undertakes is grouped together according to the area of law. Choose an area of law that you are currently studying or going to study. Find a report that has been prepared by the Law Commission in this field. At the end of the report you will find a summary of the Law Commission's proposals. Summarize three of its recommendations.

The Law Commission is particularly concerned with the Government's failure to codify the criminal law. From 1968 to 1974 the Commission produced a series of working papers, but in 1980 announced that its shortage of resources would not allow it to continue, and appealed for help with the task. The Society of Public Teachers of Law responded, and set up a four-person committee which by 1985 had produced a draft code. But this has never been legislated as law. In most countries criminal law is contained in a single code so that it is accessible to the people against whom it will be applied. The Commission has now embarked upon a programme to produce a series of draft Bills, based on the Code but incorporating appropriate law reform proposals, which will in themselves make substantial improvements in the law. If enacted, these Bills will form a criminal code. But at the moment there is no tangible sign of progress in implementation of any of their major reports dating back to 1993. Decisions of the courts continue to draw attention to defects in the substantive law in areas on which they have already reported. One ray of hope has been the passing of legislation consolidating the sentencing regime, and further impetus for codification has been given by the review of criminal procedure under Lord Justice Auld. In the Government's White Paper *Criminal Justice: the Way Ahead* (2001) it stated that it did intend to codify the criminal law as part of its modernization process.

Zander (1988) suggests the reasons for the failure are 'a mixture of conservatism and a realisation on the part of draftsmen, legislators and even judges that [codification] simply did not fit the English style of lawmaking'. The draftsmen were not keen on the idea that codes would have to be drawn up in a broader manner than was normal for traditional statutes. Legislators were doubtful of the concept of a huge Bill which would attempt to state the law in a vast area such as landlord and tenant. The judges objected to the vision promoted by Lord Scarman, the Commission's first chairman, of the code coming down like an iron curtain making all pre-code law irrelevant. As Zander explains, this appeared to the judges like 'throwing the baby out with the bath water – losing the priceless heritage of the past and wasting the fruits of legislation and litigation on numerous points which would still be relevant to interpret the new code'.

However, opinions are mixed on whether codification would prove to be of very great value even if it ever becomes possible. Supporters say it would provide accessibility, comprehensibility, consistency and certainty. A code allows people to see their rights and liabilities more clearly than a mixture of case law and separate statutes could, and should encourage judges and others who use it to look for and expect to find answers within it. Lord Hailsham has said that a good codification would save a great deal of judicial time and so reduce costs, and the academic Glanville Williams (1983) makes the point that criminal law is not like the law of procedure, meant for lawyers only, but is addressed to all classes of society, and so the greater accessibility and clarity of a code should be particularly welcomed in this area.

Critics say a very detailed codification could make the law too rigid, losing the flexibility of the common law. And if it were insufficiently detailed, as Zander (1999) points out, it would need to be interpreted by the courts, so creating a new body of case law around it, which would defeat the object of codification and make the law neither more accessible nor more certain. It may be that the Law Commission's failure to codify the law signifies a problem with codification, not with the Law Commission.

Instead of proceeding with large-scale codification, the Law Commission has chosen to clarify areas of law piece by piece, with the aim of eventual codification if possible. Family law, in particular, has been significantly reformed in this way, even if the results are, as Zander points out, a 'jumble of disconnected statutes rather than a spanking new code'.

As far as general law reform is concerned, as well as the major family law reforms, the Commission has radically changed contract law by recommending control of exclusion clauses which led to the passing of the Unfair Contract Terms Act 1977. Its report, *Criminal Law: Conspiracy and Criminal Law Reform* (1976), helped shape the Criminal Law Act 1977 and its working paper, *Offences Against Public Order* (1982), was instrumental in creating the Public Order Act 1986. Following its recommendations, the Computer Misuse Act 1990 introduced new criminal offences relating to the misuse of computers; and the Family Law Act 1996 changed the law on domestic violence and divorce.

In recent years, however, there has been a major problem with lack of implementation of Law Commission proposals. By 1999, 102 law reform reports had been implemented, which represented two-thirds of their final reports. There is a better chance of proposals from the Law Commission becoming legislation if the subject concerned comes within the jurisdiction of the Lord Chancellor's Department; there is less chance if they concern other departments, particularly the Home Office. In any case, it has been pointed out that implementation of proposals is not the only benefit of a permanent law reform body. Stephen Cretney (1998) a legal academic who has been a Law Commissioner, suggests that one of its most important contributions has simply been getting law reform under discussion and examination, and drawing attention to the needs of various areas of law.

▌Criminal Law Revision Committee

The Theft Acts 1968 and 1978 are generally thought of as the CLRC's greatest achievement. The legislation effectively codified the previous law in this area, aiming for a fundamental reconsideration of the principles underlying this branch of the law, to be embodied in a modern statute. Unfortunately this was not a complete success; as Smith and Hogan (2002) point out, one offence (that of obtaining a pecuniary advantage by deception) proved so troublesome that it had to be completely reviewed in the 1978 Act, and 'in some other respects cracks are beginning to show through . . . The legislation would benefit from a review'. Reported appeals in the first ten years of the Theft Act were more than double the number made in the ten years before.

The CLRC was also responsible for a report into the criminal justice system, which stated that the system had shifted much too far in favour of defendants' rights. It recommended a string of measures designed to tip the balance back in favour of the prosecution, including abolishing the right to silence, on the grounds that 'it is as much in the public interest that a guilty person should be convicted as that an innocent person should be acquitted'. As Zander points out, this contravenes the traditional belief that it is better that ten guilty people go free than that one innocent one is convicted – the reasoning behind our system's insistence on a suspect being innocent until proven guilty.

The report caused a storm of opposition, not only from civil liberties campaigners but from members of both Houses of Parliament, lawyers and judges, and none of it was implemented. History seems to suggest that the Committee's assessment was badly mistaken. The report was delivered in 1972; two years later, the Birmingham Six were wrongly convicted, followed in 1975 by the Guildford Four and in 1976 by the Maguire Seven. A whole string of other miscarriages of justice also date from this period. It is difficult to see these as the work of a system too heavily weighted towards defendants' rights.

Royal Commissions

These have had mixed success. The 1978 Royal Commission on Civil Liability and Compensation for Personal Injury produced a report that won neither public nor Government support, and few of its proposals were implemented.

The Royal Commission on Criminal Procedure had most of its recommendations implemented by the Police and Criminal Evidence Act 1984 (PACE), but subsequent criticisms of PACE mean this is less of a success than it appears. The Royal Commission stated that the aim behind its proposals was to secure a balance between the rights of individuals suspected of crime, and the need to bring guilty people to justice. PACE has, however, been criticized by the police as leaning too far towards suspects' rights, and by civil liberties campaigners as not leaning far enough.

Perhaps the most successful Royal Commission in recent years has been the Royal Commission on Assizes and Quarter Sessions, which reported in 1969. Its proposals for the reorganization of criminal courts were speedily implemented.

As regards the 1993 Royal Commission on Criminal Justice, this has met with mixed results. Some of its recommendations were introduced in the Criminal Justice and Public Order Act 1994 and the Criminal Appeal Act 1995, which created the Criminal Cases Review Commission (see p. 414) in response to the Commission's criticism of the criminal appeals system. On the other hand, the Government has ignored some of its proposals and has proceeded to introduce changes that the Royal Commission was specifically opposed to, for example the abolition of the right to silence.

Public inquiries and other temporary committees

These rely to a great extent on political will, and the best committees in the world may be ineffective if they propose changes that a government dislikes. Lord Scarman's investigation into the Brixton riots is seen as a particularly effective public inquiry, getting to the root of the problem by going out to ask the people involved what caused it (his Lordship took to the streets of Brixton and was seen on television chatting to residents and cuddling their babies). His proposals produced some of the steps towards police accountability in PACE. But the subsequent inquiry into the case of Stephen Lawrence shows that the progress made was not sufficient. The Law Lord, Lord Hutton, has headed the inquiry into the suicide of Dr David Kelly following the war in Iraq.

The Government has been concerned by the inefficiency and cost of recent public inquiries. For example, the inquiry into Bloody Sunday in Ireland took seven years and is reported to have cost £155 million. The Inquiries Act 2005 has now been passed. The stated aim of the Government in passing this legislation was to modernize procedures, control costs and give more effective powers to those chairing the inquiries. Despite this, the legislation has been criticized and Amnesty International has claimed that any inquiries established under this legislation would be a 'sham' and urged judges to refuse appointments to them. It is worried that the legislation fails to allow adequate public scrutiny and 'undermines the rule of law, the separation of powers and human rights protection'. The Act arguably gives too much

Figure 6.3 Scene outside the Lawrence Inquiry, Elephant and Castle, London
Source: © EMPICS. Photograph Tony Harris.

power to the executive, as the executive will be able to decide whether or not to publish the final report of any inquiry, whether to exclude evidence if this is deemed 'in the public interest', and whether the inquiry or part of it will be held in public or private.

The first inquiry to be set up under this legislation is looking at allegations of state collusion in the murder of Patrick Finucane, who was an outspoken human rights lawyer in Northern Ireland. Amnesty International is concerned that this inquiry will be ineffective because of the limitations of the Inquiries Act 2005.

Task 6.4

The Macpherson Report on the police investigation into the death of the black teenager Stephen Lawrence, along with the Government's action plan in response to this report, is available on the Home Office website **http://www.homeoffice.gov.uk**

Carry out a search of this website and consider how effective you think this public inquiry has been in bringing about reforms to the English legal system.

Quick quiz 6.5

1 In what year was the Law Commission established?

2 How successful has the Law Commission been in its mission to codify the law?

3 What do the initials 'CLRC' stand for?

4 Who chaired the public inquiry into the Brixton riots?

Problems with the law reform agencies

Lack of power

There is no obligation for Government to consult the permanent law reform bodies, or to set up Royal Commissions or other committees when considering major law reforms. Mrs Thatcher set up no Royal Commissions during her terms of office, despite the fact that important and controversial legislation – such as that abolishing the GLC – was being passed.

Political difficulties

Governments also have no obligation to follow recommendations, and perfectly well-thought-out proposals may be rejected on the grounds that they do not fit in with a government's political position. An example was the recommendation of the Law Commission in 1978 that changes be made to the rule that interest is not payable on a contract debt unless the parties agreed otherwise. The idea was supported by the House of Lords in **President of India** *v* **La Pintada Compania Navigacion SA** (1984), but the Government was persuaded not to implement the proposals after lobbying from the business community and consumer organizations.

Even where general suggestions for areas of new legislation are implemented, the detailed proposals may be radically altered. The recommendations of law reform agencies may act as justification for introducing new legislation, yet, as Zander (1999) points out, often when the Bill is published it becomes clear that the carefully constructed proposal put together by the law reform agency 'has been unstitched and a new and different package has been constructed'.

Lack of influence on results

Where proposals are implemented, ideas that are effective in themselves may be weakened if they are insufficiently funded when put into practice – a matter on which law reform bodies can have little or no influence. The 1981 Royal Commission on Criminal Procedure's recommendations were largely implemented in the Police and Criminal Evidence Act 1984, and one of them was that suspects questioned in a police station should have the right to free legal advice, leading to the setting up of the duty solicitor scheme. While the idea of the scheme was seen as a good one, underfunding has brought it close to collapse, and meant that in practice relatively small numbers of suspects actually get advice from qualified, experienced solicitors within a reasonable waiting time. This has clearly frustrated the aims of the Royal Commission's recommendation.

Too much compromise

Royal Commissions and temporary committees have the advantage of drawing members from wide backgrounds, with a good spread of experience and expertise.

95

However, in some cases this can result in proposals that try too hard to represent a compromise. The result can be a lack of political support and little chance of implementation. It is generally agreed that this was the problem with the Pearson Report (1978), the report of the Royal Commission on Civil Liability and Compensation for Personal Injury.

Influence of the legal profession

Where temporary law reform committees have a high proportion of non-lawyers, the result can be more innovative, imaginative ideas than might come from legally trained people who, however open-minded, are within 'the system' and accustomed to seeing the problems in a particular framework. However, this benefit is heavily diluted by the fact that the strong influence of the legal profession on any type of reform can defeat such proposals even before they reach an official report.

An example was the suggestion of the Civil Justice Review in its consultation paper that the county courts and High Court might merge, with some High Court judges being stationed in the provinces to deal with the more complex cases there. Despite a warm welcome from consumer groups and the National Association of Citizens' Advice Bureaux, the proposals were effectively shot down by the outcry from senior judges who were concerned that their status and way of life might be adversely affected, and the Bar, which was worried that it might lose too much work to solicitors. In the event the proposal was not included in the final report.

Waste of expertise

Royal Commissions and temporary committees are disbanded after producing their report, and take no part in the rest of the law-making process. This is in many ways a waste of the expertise they have built up.

Lack of ministerial involvement

There is no single ministry responsible for law reform so that often no Minister makes it his or her priority.

Reading on the web

John Halliday has produced a report on the work of the Law Commission which has been published on the Law Commission's website:

  http://www.dca.gov.uk/majrep/lawcom/halliday.htm

The Law Commission's website is:

  http://www.lawcom.gov.uk/

Question and answer guides

1 'It shall be the duty of the Commissions to take and keep under review all the law with which they are respectively concerned, with a view to its systematic development and reform, including in particular the codification of such law . . .' (s. 3, Law Commission Act 1965). Should the Law Commission concentrate on codification, or are there more suitable ways of reforming the law? *(Oxford)*

Answer guide

You could start by defining what codification is, and mention the plans for codification which the Law Commission had when it was created, and what happened to them. Then go on to discuss the advantages and disadvantages of codification, and whether you feel that the Law Commission should still concentrate on it.

You could then move on to look at the other ways of reforming the law. As well as examining the successful work which the Law Commission has done, you could look at other ways of law reform – such as the way in which public inquiries and temporary committees examine specific problems, using advisers who are not necessarily lawyers, but may have experience in the relevant field. Do you think this is an approach the Law Commission should consider?

Your conclusion should sum up what you think the Commission's priorities should be and why.

2 'The Law Commission has provided an important impetus to the process of law reform in England and Wales.' Discuss. *(WJEC)*

Answer guide

Here you are basically being asked how well the Law Commission has done its job. Your introduction might state what the Commission was set up to do, and then the rest of your essay can consider whether it has fulfilled that function and thereby given an important impetus to law reform.

You might want to consider the successes of the Law Commission first, and then go on to talk about codification, pointing out that the Commission has not provided much of an impetus in this area, but discussing the arguments on whether codification would actually be beneficial anyway. Finish by summing up what you think the Commission's contribution has been.

3 Critically evaluate the role of the law reform bodies. *(Oxford)*

Answer guide

Note that this question can apply not only to the official bodies such as the Law Commission, but also to informal ones such as pressure groups, and you need to discuss both types. It may be a good idea to divide your answer into official and unofficial law reform bodies: taking each in turn, you can describe how they operate and assess their effectiveness, pointing out any problems in the way they work. Don't forget that what is needed is a critical account – just listing the bodies and what they do will get you very few marks. What the examiners want to know is not just what the bodies do, but how well they do it. Your conclusion might generally sum up the effect of these multiple bodies, saying whether, taken together, you feel they do an adequate job in reforming the law.

Chapter summary

The law needs to change to reflect the changes in society. Changes in the law can be made through the process of case law or by Parliament. The four ways in which Parliament can change the law are:

■ repeal
■ creation
■ consolidation, and
■ codification.

Pressures for reform

The inspiration for reform may come from a variety of sources, including:

■ pressure groups
■ political parties
■ the civil service
■ treaty obligations, and
■ public opinion and media pressure.

Agencies of law reform

There are a number of agencies set up to consider the need for reform in areas referred to them by the Government. These agencies are:

■ the Law Commission
■ the Criminal Law Revision Committee
■ Royal Commissions
■ public inquiries, and
■ other temporary inquiries.

The level of success of these agencies has varied considerably. Governments have no obligation to follow their recommendations. Some of the recommendations involve too many compromises, and where lawyers dominate the resulting reforms may be under-ambitious.

PART 2

People working in the legal system

This Part of the book looks at the different people involved in the English legal system. Some of these are in paid employment, such as the professional judges, barristers, solicitors and legal executives. Others are essentially unpaid and include jurors and magistrates.

AQA Examination Board

Chapters 7–10 in this part covers the Dispute solving module 2: Dispute solving

OCR Examination Board

Chapters 7–10 in this part covers the English legal system module

WJEC Examination Board

Chapters 7, 8 and 10 cover the Personnel module

Chapter 9 in this part covers the Machinery of justice module

---

Chapter 7

The judges

Judicial hierarchy

The judges are at the centre of any legal system, as they sit in court and decide the cases. At the head of the judiciary is the President of the Courts of England and Wales. This position was created by the Constitutional Reform Act 2005. Before that Act was passed, the Lord Chancellor had been the head of the judiciary. The new President of the Courts of England and Wales is the president of the Court of Appeal, the High Court, the Crown Court, the county courts and the magistrates' courts. He or she is technically allowed to hear cases in any of these courts, though in practice he or she is only likely to choose to sit in the Court of Appeal. Under s. 7 of the Act, the President's role is to represent the views of the judiciary to Parliament and to Government Ministers. He or she is also responsible for the maintenance of appropriate arrangements for the welfare, training and guidance of the judiciary and for arranging where judges work and their workload.

The most senior judges are the 12 Lords of Appeal in Ordinary, more commonly known as the Law Lords. They currently sit in the House of Lords and the Privy Council. Their role will soon change, as the Government has decided to abolish the House of Lords and replace it with a Supreme Court. The Constitutional Reform Act 2005 contains this reform and the new court is likely to be established in 2008. It is discussed in detail at p. 408.

At the next level down sitting in the Court of Appeal, are 37 judges known as Lord Justices of Appeal and Lady Justices of Appeal. The Criminal Division of the Court of Appeal is presided over by the Lord Chief Justice who, following the Constitutional Reform Act 2005, is also known as the President of the Courts of England and Wales (discussed above). He or she can at the same time act as the Head of Criminal Justice or appoint another Court of Appeal judge to take this role.

The Civil Division of the Court of Appeal is presided over by the Master of the Rolls. There is also a head of civil justice and a head of family justice.

In the High Court, there are 107 full-time judges. As well as sitting in the High Court itself, they hear the most serious criminal cases in the Crown Court. Although – like judges in the Court of Appeal and the House of Lords – High Court judges receive a knighthood, they are referred to as Mr or Mrs Justice Smith (or whatever their surname is), which is written as Smith J.

The next rank down concerns the circuit judge, who travels around the country, sitting in the county courts and also hearing the middle-ranking Crown Court cases.

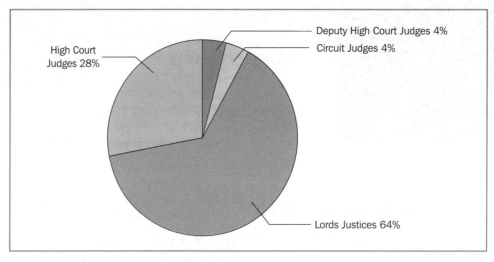

Figure 7.1 Court of Appeal: days sat, 2004

Source: K. Dibdin, A. Sealy and S. Aktar, *Judicial Statistics Annual Report 2004*, p. 131.

The Criminal Justice and Public Order Act 1994 added a further role, allowing them occasionally to sit in the Criminal Division of the Court of Appeal.

The slightly less serious Crown Court criminal cases are heard by district judges, and then there are recorders, who are part-time judges dealing with the least serious Crown Court criminal cases. Recorders are usually still working as barristers or solicitors, and the role is often used as a kind of apprenticeship before becoming a circuit judge. Because of the number of minor cases coming before the Crown Court, there are now assistant recorders as well, and at times retired circuit judges have been called upon to help out. Finally, in larger cities there are district judges (magistrates' courts), who were previously known as stipendiary judges, and are full-time, legally qualified judges working in the magistrates' courts.

In practice, there is some flexibility between the courts so that judges sometimes sit in more senior courts than their status would suggest. This practice is illustrated in Figure 7.1.

Table 7.1 The hierarchy of the judiciary

Judge	Usual court
Lord of Appeal in Ordinary	House of Lords and Privy Council
Lord Chief Justice	Criminal Division of the Court of Appeal
Master of the Rolls	Civil Division of the Court of Appeal
Lord Justice of Appeal	Court of Appeal
High Court judge	High Court and Crown Court
Circuit judge	County court and Crown Court
District judge	County court and Crown Court
District judge (magistrates' court)	Magistrates' court
Recorder	Crown Court

Tribunals are not served by members of the judiciary; cases there are heard by a panel of people who are not legally qualified but have experience in the relevant areas. The chairperson may be a practising lawyer, but this is not always the case.

Moderniser swims into top judge's post

A brainy modernizer who keeps fit by swimming outdoors all year round is to become the new top judge in England and Wales when Lord Woolf retires at the end of September 2005.

Lord Phillips will take over as Lord Chief Justice for England and Wales from 1 October 2005. He will move from the number two post in the judiciary, Master of the Rolls, to the top job. Like Lord Woolf, he is seen as a liberal, while the other candidate who had been tipped for the job, the deputy Chief Justice, Lord Justice Judge, is regarded as more conservative.

The new Lord Chief Justice is less at ease with the media than Lord Woolf, but his friends say he will be equally effective in the top judge's most difficult role, standing up to the executive in defence of the rule of law.

'He's quite a shy, internal person with a very great sense of duty and obligation', said one judge who knows him well. 'He's very jolly with his friends, but finds it quite difficult to have a public persona.'

Source: Adapted from Claire Dyer, *The Guardian*, 18 June 2005.

A reduced role for the Lord Chancellor

The position of Lord Chancellor has existed for over 1,400 years. He (there has never actually been a female Lord Chancellor) has played a central role in the English legal system, but the position is currently being reformed following persistent criticism. This criticism is based on the constitutional doctrine of the separation of powers. Under this doctrine, the power of the state has to be divided between three separate and independent arms: the judiciary (comprising the judges), the legislature (Parliament in the United Kingdom); and the executive (the Government of the day). The idea is that the separate arms of the state should operate independently, so that each one is checked and balanced by the other two, and none becomes all powerful. The doctrine of the separation of powers was first put forward in the eighteenth century by the French political theorist Montesquieu. Montesquieu argued that if all the powers were concentrated in the hands of one group, the result would be tyranny. Therefore, the doctrine requires that individuals should not occupy a position in more than one of the three arms of the state – judiciary, legislature and executive; each should exercise its functions independently of any control or interference from the others; and one arm of the state should not exercise the functions of either of the others.

The Lord Chancellor has had such wide powers, which extended to all three arms of the state, that his existence was a clear breach of the doctrine of the separation of powers. We will look first at his judicial powers. He has been at the head of the whole judiciary, and effectively appointed all the other judges. He has been President of the Supreme Court (the term currently used to describe the High Court, the Crown Court and the Court of Appeal together, though this name will change when the new 'Supreme Court' is established to replace the House of Lords). He has also officially been President of the Chancery Division of the High Court, although in practice the Vice-Chancellor usually performed this role. When the Lord Chancellor sat as a judge, it was in the House of Lords or the Privy Council, but recent Lord Chancellors have only chosen to do this occasionally or not at all.

As regards his political role, the Lord Chancellor has been a Cabinet Minister and Speaker of the House of Lords. Although technically appointed by the Queen, the Lord Chancellor is actually chosen by the Prime Minister and goes out of office when that party loses an election, as well as being eligible for removal by the Prime Minister, just like any other Minister.

In relation to his executive functions, he was at the head of the Lord Chancellor's Department. He had powers to give directions about the business of the courts, and responsibility for the Law Commission and the state funding of legal services. Most controversially, he has had control over judicial appointments. Politically, the most important judicial appointment is that of the Master of the Rolls; as President of the Court of Appeal his or her view on the proper relationship between the executive government and the individual is crucial. The appointment of Lord Donaldson in 1982 was seen as a strongly political appointment and one which the then Prime Minister favoured: he had been a Conservative councillor, and was not promoted during the years of the previous Labour Government, 1974–79. There was some publicity concerning Lord Donaldson's political views at the time of the high profile GCHQ union membership case: **Council of Civil Service Unions *v* Minister for the Civil Service** (1985) and as a result, his Lordship declined to preside over the Court of Appeal when it considered the Government's appeal in that case.

So the position of the Lord Chancellor as a member of the judiciary, the executive and the legislature clearly went against the idea that no individual should be part of all three arms of the state. The conflicting roles of the Lord Chancellor were highlighted in 2001 when the media drew attention to the fact that the Lord Chancellor had been involved in political fundraising. Guests to a dinner he had organized were invited to make donations to the Labour Party and there were concerns that lawyers might seek promotion by giving substantial donations. Legal Action Group, a pressure group, have argued that the various roles of the Lord Chancellor put him in breach of the European Convention on Human Rights.

In June 2003 the Government announced that it intended to abolish the office of Lord Chancellor. At the same time it established a Minister for Constitutional

Table 7.2 Past role of the Lord Chancellor

Branch of Government	Past role of the Lord Chancellor
Legislature	Speaker of the House of Lords
Executive	Government Minister
Judiciary	Judge in the House of Lords and Privy Council. He was also President of the Supreme Court and President of the Chancery Division of the High Court.

Figure 7.2 Lord Falconer, the Minister for Constitutional Affairs

Source: © EMPICS.

Affairs, with significantly fewer powers than his or her predecessor. The new Minister was intended to be a more traditional member of the executive, with no right to sit as a judge, no role in the judicial appointments' process and not the Speaker of the House of Lords. The first person to be appointed Minister for Constitutional Affairs was Lord Falconer.

There was considerable criticism of the hasty way in which this reform was commenced and much of the detail about who would fulfill many of the previous powers of the Lord Chancellor had not been decided before some of the changes were introduced. The new Minister for Constitutional Affairs therefore had to be Lord Chancellor as well and was forced to fulfill some of the old functions of the Lord Chancellor, though he stated he would not choose to sit as a judge in the House of Lords.

The Government introduced to Parliament the Constitutional Reform Bill, which in its original form would have abolished the office of Lord Chancellor and given his powers to a range of individuals including the Minister for Constitutional Affairs. The passage of this Bill through Parliament proved to be complicated. Many people were unhappy with the speed at which these important reforms were being introduced with only a limited consultation process. Following opposition in the House of Lords, the Government agreed to amend the Constitutional Reform Bill. The position of Lord Chancellor was retained, though his or her role was significantly reduced. With the passing of the Constitutional Reform Act 2005, four major changes to the role of the Lord Chancellor have been made. As a result he or she no longer:

■ sits as a judge
■ heads the judiciary
■ takes a central role in the judicial appointments process, nor
■ automatically becomes the speaker of the House.

He or she will remain as the head of a government department (now called the Ministry for Constitutional Affairs), but his or her powers and links to the judges have been removed to satisfy the principle of the separation of powers. At pp. 108–111 we look at how the Lord Chancellor's powers are going to be replaced as regards judicial appointments. A new position of President of the Court of England and Wales has been created by s. 7 of the Constitutional Reform Act 2005. This person is at the head of the judiciary and the Lord Chancellor's judicial functions are transferred to him or her.

As regards the Lord Chancellor's current function as Speaker of the House of Lords, it will be for the House of Lords in its parliamentary capacity to determine who will be the Speaker of the House in future.

In the past, the Lord Chancellor had to be a lawyer, but under s. 2 of the Constitutional Reform Act 2005, the Lord Chancellor must simply appear to the Prime Minister to be qualified 'by experience'. Sub-section 2 states that this experience could have been gained as a Government Minister, a member of either of the Houses of Parliament, a qualified lawyer, a teacher of law in a university or 'other experience that the Prime Minister considers relevant'.

Appointments to the judiciary

The way in which judges are appointed has been radically reformed by provisions in the Constitutional Reform Act 2005 which are expected to take effect in April 2006. In order to evaluate the new appointment procedures, it is useful to understand how judges were appointed before these reforms were introduced. We will therefore look first at the old procedures before looking at the new ones.

The old appointment procedures

Prior to the 2005 Act, the Lord Chancellor played a central role in the appointment of judges. The Lords of Appeal in Ordinary and the Lord Justices of Appeal were appointed by the Queen on the advice of the Prime Minister who in turn was advised by the Lord Chancellor. High Court judges, circuit judges and recorders were appointed by the Queen on the advice of the Lord Chancellor.

Over the years there had been considerable criticism of the way in which judges were appointed and, as a result, changes had been made even before the more radical reforms of the 2005 Act. In the past only barristers could become senior judges. The Courts and Legal Services Act 1990 widened entry to the judiciary, reflecting the changes in rights of audience (see p. 125), and (at least in theory) opening up the higher reaches of the profession to solicitors as well as barristers. The selection process for judges in the High Court involved the Department for Constitutional Affairs gathering information about potential candidates over a period of time by making informal inquiries (known as 'secret soundings') from leading barristers and judges.

The normal procedure for recruiting for a job is to place an advertisement in a newspaper and to allow people to apply. By contrast, until recently, there were no advertisements for judicial office, you simply waited to be invited to the post. Advertisements have more recently been placed for junior and High Court judges, but still not for positions in the Court of Appeal and the House of Lords.

At the Government's request, an inquiry into the system for judicial appointments was undertaken by Sir Leonard Peach, a senior civil servant. His report was published in December 1999. Sir Leonard was generally happy with the quality of the work and the professionalism of the civil servants involved in the appointments process. One of the key recommendations of the report was that a Commissioner for Judicial Appointments should be appointed to provide independent monitoring of the procedures for appointing judges and Queen's Counsel (for an explanation of Queen's Counsel, see p. 132). This recommendation was accepted by the Government and the first Commissioner was appointed in 2001. Sir Leonard Peach did not recommend any changes to the system of secret soundings.

The Law Society, the professional body representing solicitors, considered the limited reforms made following Sir Leonard Peach's report in 1999 'inadequate', particularly as the new Commissioner was merely responsible for monitoring the existing system, rather than having any direct involvement in the appointments process itself.

The three main criticisms of the old system of selecting judges were that it was dominated by politicians, secretive and discriminatory. On the first issue, the Lord Chancellor and the Prime Minister played central roles in this process but they were politicians and could be swayed by political factors in the selection of judges. The Lord Chancellor presented the Prime Minister with a shortlist of two or three names listing them in the order of his or her own preference. Mrs Thatcher is known to have selected Lord Hailsham's second choice on one occasion.

On the second issue, the constitutional reform organization Charter 88, among others, criticized the old selection process for being secretive and lacking clearly defined selection criteria. The process was handled by a small group of civil servants who, although they consulted widely with judges and senior barristers, nevertheless wielded a great deal of power. This process was considered to be unfair because it favoured people who had a good network of contacts, perhaps because of their school and family, rather than focusing on the individual's strength as a future judge. There was also a danger that too much reliance was placed on a collection of anecdotal reports from fellow lawyers, with candidates given no opportunity to challenge damning things said about them.

Since 1999 the Law Society had refused to participate in the secret soundings process. The president of the Law Society described the system as having 'all the elements of an old boys' network', and being inconsistent with an open and objective recruitment process. 'We suspect we were being used to legitimize a system where other peoples' views were more important than ours. It didn't really matter what we thought, it was the views of the senior judiciary and the Bar which counted.' The highest ranking solicitor among the judiciary is a single High Court judge.

The first report of the Commission for Judicial Appointments was published in 2002. The secret soundings system was found to be poorly understood by both the applicants and the people who were consulted. The Lord Chancellor's Department was criticized for the way it administered the 'sifting' process, where officials weeded out weak applicants at an early stage. In addition, the report concluded that the Department's lack of detailed records of how decisions were reached meant it was impossible to determine whether applicants had been fairly assessed.

As regards the third criticism that the old appointments process was discriminatory, a 1997 study commissioned by the Association of Women Barristers is of interest. It found that there was a strong tendency for judges to recommend candidates from their own former chambers. The study looked at appointments to the High Court over a ten-year period (1986–96) and found that of the 104 judges appointed, 70 (67.3 per cent) came from a set of chambers which had at least one ex-member among the judges likely to be consulted. In addition, a strikingly high percentage of appointments came from the same handful of chambers: 28.8 per cent of new judges from chambers which represented 1.8 per cent of the total number of chambers in

England and Wales. The fact that those who advised on appointments were already well established within the system could make it unlikely that they would encourage appointment from a wider base: Lord Bridge, the retired Law Lord, commented in a 1992 television programme that they tend to look for 'chaps like ourselves'. As Helena Kennedy QC has put it, 'the potential for cloning is overwhelming', and the outlook for potential female judges and those from the ethnic minorities not promising.

The process of 'secret soundings' gave real scope for discrimination, with lawyers instinctively falling back on gender and racial stereotypes in concluding whether someone was appropriate for judicial office. For example, individuals were asked whether they thought candidates showed 'decisiveness' and 'authority'. But these are very subjective concepts and Kamlesh Bahl has argued (*The Guardian*, 10 April 1995) that as the judiciary is seen as a male profession, perceptions of judicial characteristics, such as 'authority', are also seen as male characteristics. 'Authority' is dependent more on what others think than on the person's own qualities. Indeed, research published by the Bar Council in 1992 concluded:

> It is unlikely that the judicial appointment system offers equal access to women or fair access to promotion to women judges . . . The system depends on patronage, being noticed and being known. (*Without Prejudice? Sex Equality at the Bar and in the Judiciary*, 1992, para. 48(1))

However, in his book *The Judge*, Lord Devlin says that, while it would be good to open up the legal profession, so that it could get the very best candidates from all walks of life, the nature of the job means that judges will still be the same type of people whether they come from public schools and Oxbridge or not, namely those 'who do not seriously question the status quo'.

In its second annual report published in 2003, the Commission for Judicial Appointments concluded that there was systemic bias in the way that the judiciary and the legal profession operated. This bias prevented women, ethnic minorities and solicitors from applying successfully for judicial office. The Commission was fundamentally unhappy with the appointment process for High Court judges and recommended that it should be stopped immediately because it was 'opaque, out-dated and not demonstrably based on merit'.

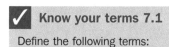

✓ Know your terms 7.1

Define the following terms:

1 Secret soundings
2 Lord Chancellor
3 Master of the Rolls
4 Lord Chief Justice

▌The new appointment procedures

The Government published a consultation paper, *Constitutional Reform: a new way of appointing judges* (2003). While some improvements had been made in recent years to the appointment procedures, the Government concluded that:

> The most fundamental features of the system . . . remain rooted in the past. Incremental changes to the system can only achieve limited results, because the fundamental problem with the current system is that a Government minister, the Lord Chancellor, has sole responsibility for the appointments process and for making or recommending those appointments. However well this has worked in practice, this system no longer commands public confidence, and is increasingly hard to reconcile with the demands of the Human Rights Act.

Following a limited consultation process, the Constitutional Reform Act 2005 was passed containing provisions for the establishment of a new Judicial Appointments Commission. It is hoped that the creation of this body will help to put an end to the breaches of the principle of the separation of powers and reinforce judicial independence.

Under Schedule 12 to the Act, the Commission will have 15 members: six lay members (including the chair), five judges, two legal professionals, a tribunal member and a lay magistrate. The members will be appointed by the Queen on the recommendation of the Lord Chancellor. Candidates must be selected on the basis of merit and be of good character. To be appointed to the House of Lords or the new Supreme Court a person must either have held judicial office for two years or have a right of audience in the senior courts (meaning in this context the High Court, the Crown Court and the Court of Appeal); most will already have been judges in the Court of Appeal. The qualification for appointment to the Court of Appeal is either experience as a judge in the High Court or a right of audience in the High Court for ten years. To be appointed as a High Court judge it is also necessary to have had a right of audience for ten years in the High Court. Circuit judges, recorders or assistant recorders can now be appointed from anyone who has had general rights of audience in the Crown Court or county courts for ten years. Anyone who has been a district judge for at least three years is also eligible for appointment as a circuit judge.

Government lawyers are now allowed to become judges. These lawyers are people employed in the Crown Prosecution Service, Serious Fraud Office and the Government Legal Service. They will be able to sit as civil recorders (part-time judges) and deputy district judges in the magistrates' court, provided their own department is not involved in the case. This is a major development, as such lawyers have a wide range of backgrounds, with women and ethnic minorities well represented and the majority state educated. Their recruitment as junior judges will hopefully make the profession at this level more representative of society.

In performing its functions the Commission must have regard to the need to encourage diversity in the range of persons available for selection for appointments (s. 64). The Minister is able to issue guidance which the Commission must have regard to. This guidance can include directions on increasing diversity in the judiciary.

The Judicial Appointments Commission will evaluate candidates and recommend, on the basis of merit only, one individual for each vacancy. The Minister will not be able to choose someone who has not been recommended to him or her by the Commission. He or she will, however, be able to ask for a candidate who is not initially recommended by the Commission to be reconsidered, and can refuse the appointment of someone recommended and ask for a new name to be put forward. The Minister will have the ability to reject a candidate once, and to ask the Commission to reconsider once. Having rejected once, the Minister must accept whichever subsequent candidate is selected.

There is special provision for the appointment of the Lord Chief Justice, the heads of Division and the Lord Justices of Appeal. The Commission will establish a selection panel of four members, consisting of two senior judges (normally including the Lord Chief Justice) and two lay members of the Commission.

Appointments of Lords Justices and above will continue to be made formally by the Queen on the advice of the Prime Minister, after the Commission has made a recommendation to the Minister.

The new Appointments Commission will not be involved in the appointment of judges to the future Supreme Court. Instead, when there is a vacancy, the Minister will appoint a temporary Commission. This Commission will include the President and Deputy President of the Supreme Court, as well as one member of each of the three judicial appointing bodies of England and Wales, Scotland and Northern Ireland. The temporary Commission will put forward between two and five recommended candidates to the Minister, according to prescribed criteria. The Minister must then consult with the senior judges, the First Minister in Scotland, the National Assembly for Wales, and the First Minister and deputy First Minister in Northern Ireland. The Minister will afterwards notify the name of the selected candidate to the Prime Minister who must recommend this candidate to the Queen for appointment.

The Law Society thinks that a choice of up to five gives too much scope for political interference, and thinks that only one name should be put forward for each job vacancy.

A Judicial Appointments and Conduct Ombudsman will oversee the recruitment process and will have the power to investigate individual complaints about judicial appointments. He or she is expected to start working in April 2006.

Wigs and gowns

Judges are frequently required to wear wigs and gowns when they sit in court. The Government is concerned that their presentation can appear old-fashioned to court users, and has issued a consultation paper which is considering modernizing court clothes.

Training

Although new judges have the benefit of many years' experience as barristers or solicitors, they have traditionally received a surprisingly small amount of training for their new role, limited until recently to a brief training period, organized by the Judicial Studies Board. In the last few years, this has been supplemented in several ways: the advent of the Children Act 1989 has meant that social workers, psychiatrists and paediatricians have shared their expertise with new judges, while concern about the perception of judges as racist, or at best racially unaware, has led to the introduction of training on race issues. The reforms to the civil justice system and the passing of the Human Rights Act 1998 have led to the provision of special training to prepare for these legal reforms.

Pay

Judges are paid large salaries – £150,878 at High Court level – which are not subject to an annual vote in Parliament. The official justification for this is the need to attract an adequate supply of candidates of sufficient calibre for appointment to judicial office, and in fact some top barristers can earn more by staying in practice. One of the attractions for a barrister of becoming a judge is the security of a pensionable position after years of self-employment.

Table 10.3 **Judicial salaries**

Judge	Pay
Lord of Appeal in Ordinary (Law Lord)	£179,431
Lord Chief Justice	£205,242
Master of the Rolls	£185,705
Lord Justice of Appeal	£170,554
High Court judge	£150,878
Circuit judge	£113,121
District judge	£90,760
District judge (magistrates' court)	£90,760

Task 7.2

Read the following newspaper article and answer the questions below.

Wigs in court – it's time for this horseplay to stop

There are more important issues about the future of the legal system than whether lawyers and judges should continue to wear wigs and gowns. But the Lord Chancellor issued a consultation paper inviting us all to express our views. The legal bigwigs should be told by as many people as possible that fancy dress for lawyers is a nonsense that should have been mothballed long ago.

There is no positive case for retaining legal costume. As the consultation paper observes, tradition is no justification since 'our courts are not a tourist attraction'. The suggestion that the wearing of wigs and gowns symbolises the authority of office holders, instils respect for the law, and emphasises the impersonal and disinterested approach of the judge is impossible to sustain.

We are mature enough to understand that legal authority depends on the quality of the justice on offer, not on whether the judge and the lawyers have some horse hair on their head and a piece of cloth on their back. Indeed, it would be a sad reflection on the quality of the legal profession if its ability to command respect really did depend on its clothing.

Many courts of law perform their functions very satisfactorily without imposing a dress code. Neither the magistrates' courts nor employment tribunals require judges and lawyers to dress up for the occasion. The law lords sitting in the highest court of the land wear ordinary business suits. Without any noticeable effect on the quality of the product, judges of the High Court frequently make orders unrobed, indeed occasionally undressed (vice-chancellor Sadwell is said to have granted an injunction during the 1840s while bathing in the Thames).

Those judges and lawyers who argue that the wig and gown provide a welcome measure of anonymity which protects them from the antipathy of defendants and witnesses who may meet them out of court have no right to impose their lack of self-confidence on the rest of us. Anyone who insists on maintaining a disguise is free to wear fake spectacles, a false nose and an imitation moustache during court proceedings.

It is not simply that legal dress has no justification. It is positively damaging to the health of the legal system. The legal profession cannot convince its customers that it understands contemporary concerns and can provide a service for today's community when it looks as if it is still living in the 18th century.

Legal workers of the world unite. We have nothing to lose but our manes.

(Adapted from an article by David Pannick, published in *The Times* on 27 May 2003.)

Questions

1 Does the author of this article favour the wearing of wigs and gowns in court?

2 What are judges' wigs made out of?

3 Do the Law Lords wear wigs and gowns in the House of Lords?

4 Do you think judges should wear wigs and gowns in court?

Quick quiz 7.3

1 In which court does the Lord Chief Justice sit?

2 Who appoints High Court judges?

3 Who appoints Lords of Appeal in Ordinary?

4 Which body is responsible for providing judicial training?

5 What is the doctrine of the separation of powers?

Termination of appointment

There are five ways in which a judge may leave office:

Dismissal. Judges of the High Court and above are covered by the Act of Settlement 1700, which provides that they may only be removed from office by the Queen on the petition of both Houses of Parliament. The machinery for dismissal has been used successfully only once and no judge has been removed by petition of Parliament for many years.

Under the Courts Act 1971, circuit judges and district judges can be dismissed by the Lord Chancellor, if the Lord Chief Justice agrees, for 'inability or misbehaviour'. In fact this has occurred only once since the passing of the Act: Judge Bruce Campbell (a circuit judge) was sacked in 1983 after being convicted of smuggling spirits, cigarettes and tobacco into England in his yacht. 'Misbehaviour' can include a conviction for drink-driving or any offence involving violence, dishonesty or moral turpitude. It would also include any behaviour likely to cause offence, particularly on religious or racial grounds or behaviour that amounted to sexual harassment.

In dismissing a judge, s. 108(1) of the Constitutional Reform Act 2005 provides that the Lord Chancellor will have to comply with any procedures that have been laid down to regulate this process.

In addition to dismissal there is, of course, also the power not to re-appoint those who have been appointed for a limited period only.

Discipline. In practice the mechanisms for disciplining judges who misbehave are more significant than those for dismissal, which is generally a last resort. There was concern in the past that there were no formal disciplinary procedures for judges. Over the years there had been a few judges whose conduct had been frequently criticized, but who had nevertheless remained on the Bench, and the lack of a formal machinery for complaints was seen as protecting incompetent judges. The pressure group Justice had recommended the establishment of a formal disciplinary procedure in its report on the judiciary in 1972. The Constitutional Reform Act 2005 contains provision for the establishment of such procedures. The Act gives the Lord Chancellor and the Lord Chief Justice joint responsibility for judicial discipline. Section 108(3) states:

> The Lord Chief Justice may give a judicial office holder formal advice, or a formal warning or reprimand, for disciplinary purposes (but this section does not restrict what he may do informally or for other purposes or where any advice or warning is not addressed to a particular office holder).

A person can be suspended from judicial office for any period when they are subject to criminal proceedings, have been convicted, are serving a criminal sentence, are subject to disciplinary procedures or where it has been determined under prescribed procedures that a person should not be removed from office, but it appears to the Lord Chief Justice, with the agreement of the Lord Chancellor, that the suspension is necessary for maintaining public confidence in the judiciary. The Judicial Appointments and Conduct Ombudsman will consider complaints about disciplinary cases.

The Judicial Appointments and Conduct Ombudsman will be able to review the handling of complaints about judicial conduct.

As well as the formal procedures discussed above, judges may be criticized in Parliament, or rebuked in the appellate courts, and are often censured in the press. There may be complaints from barristers, solicitors or litigants, made either in court or in private to the judge personally. 'Scurrilous abuse' of a judge may, however, be punished as contempt of court.

Resignation. Serious misbehaviour has on occasion been dealt with not by dismissal, but by the Lord Chancellor suggesting to the judge that he or she should resign.

Retirement. Judges usually retire at 70.

Removal due to infirmity. The Lord Chancellor has the power to remove judges who are disabled by permanent infirmity from the performance of their duties and who are incapacitated from resigning their post.

Independence of the judiciary

In our legal system great importance is attached to the idea that judges should be independent and be seen to be independent. In addition to the common sense view that they should be independent of pressure from the Government and political groups, and in order to decide cases impartially, judicial independence is required by the constitutional doctrine known as the separation of powers (discussed at p. 103).

In the past, the broad role of the Lord Chancellor was seen as both a threat to judicial independence and as the protector of judicial independence. He was a threat because he breached the doctrine of separation of powers, but at the same time as the head of the judiciary, he was responsible for defending judges from Government influence. With the changes in the role of the Lord Chancellor introduced by the Constitutional Reform Act 2005, the Government sought to reassure judges that their independence would still be guaranteed, by introducing a statutory guarantee of the independence of the judiciary. Section 3 states:

> The Lord Chancellor, other Ministers of the Crown and all with responsibility for matters relating to the judiciary or otherwise to the administration of justice must uphold the continued independence of the judiciary.

It also provides that:

> The Lord Chancellor and other Ministers for the Crown must not seek to influence a particular judicial decision through any special access to the judiciary.

Other safeguards of judicial independence include the security of tenure given to judges, which ensures they cannot be removed at the whim of one of the other branches of power; the fact that their salaries are not subject to a parliamentary vote; and the rule that they cannot be sued for anything done while acting in their judicial capacity. Independence in decision making is provided through the fact that judges are only accountable to higher judges in appellate courts.

The importance of the independence of the judiciary can be seen, for example, in judicial review, where the courts can scrutinize the behaviour of the executive, and in some cases declare it illegal. However, there are a number of problems with the idea of the judiciary as independent (see p. 117).

Criticisms of the judiciary

Background, ethnic origin, sex and age

Judges are overwhelmingly white, male and middle- to upper-class, and frequently elderly, leading to accusations that they are unrepresentative of, and distanced from, the majority of society. In 1995, 80 per cent of Lords of Appeal, Heads of Division, Lord Justices of Appeal and High Court judges were educated at Oxford or

Cambridge. Eighty per cent of judges appointed since 1997 were educated at a public school. The narrow background of the judges does mean that they can be frighteningly out of touch with the world in which they are working. One judge, who resigned in 1998, said in three different cases that he had not heard of the footballer Paul Gascoigne, the rock band Oasis and the singer Bruce Springsteen.

In 2004 only 16 per cent of judges were women. There are still no women sitting as judges in the European Court of Justice. The first female judge was appointed to the House of Lords in 2004, Lady Justice Hale. There are only three female judges in the Court of Appeal and seven female High Court judges. Just 3 per cent of court judges in 2004 came from an ethnic minority, with one member of the Court of Appeal coming from an ethnic minority and one High Court judge. By comparison, 8 per cent of the population of England and Wales come from an ethnic minority. Lord Lane, the former Lord Chief Justice, said after his retirement that his regret at being forced off the bench was due, at least partly, to the fact that his colleagues were 'a jolly nice bunch of chaps'. This remark reinforces the view of many that the judiciary is actually a sort of rarefied gentlemen's club.

The age of the full-time judiciary has remained constant over many years with the average age of a judge being 58. With a retirement age of 70, judges are allowed to retire five years later than most other professions. David Pannick has written in his book, *Judges*, that 'a judiciary composed predominantly of senior citizens cannot hope to apply contemporary standards or to understand contemporary concerns'.

Before the Courts and Legal Services Act 1990, judges were almost exclusively selected from practising barristers. Since it is difficult for anyone without a private income to survive the first years of practice, successful barristers have tended to come from reasonably well-to-do families, who are of course more likely to send their sons or daughters to public schools and then to Oxford or Cambridge. Although the background of the Bar is gradually changing, the age at which judges are appointed means that it will be some years before this is reflected in the ranks of the judiciary.

The new opportunities provided for solicitors to join the judiciary, provided by the Courts and Legal Services Act 1990 and the new right of Government lawyers to become junior judges may in time help to alter the traditional judicial background, since there are larger numbers of women, members of the ethnic minorities and those from less privileged backgrounds working as solicitors and Government lawyers than in the barrister profession. Since April 2005 judges below High Court level are able to sit part-time, which may prove attractive to women combining work with childcare responsibilities.

Section 64 of the Constitutional Reform Act 2005 provides that the Judicial Appointments Commission 'must have regard to the need to encourage diversity in the range of persons available for selection for appointments'. The Lord Chancellor can issue guidance for the Commission in order to encourage a range of persons to be available for selection (s. 65). The Government issued a consultation paper, *Increasing Diversity in the Judiciary* (2004). At the launch of this paper, the Minister for Constitutional Affairs stated:

It is a matter of great concern that the judiciary in England and Wales – while held in high regard for its ability, independence and probity, is not representative of the diverse society it serves. A more diverse judiciary is essential if the public's confidence in its judges is to be maintained and strengthened.

We need to find out why people from diverse backgrounds and with disabilities are not applying for judicial appointment in the numbers we might expect and, once we have identified the barriers, we need to do something about removing them. Judicial appointments will continue to be made on merit. But I do not believe that there is any conflict between merit and diversity.

The Minister is considering introducing flexible working hours for judges and changes to age limits in order to try to attract a more diverse range of people to a judicial career. He plans to introduce legislation to widen the pool of lawyers eligible for the judiciary. Eligibility requirements may be amended so that legal executives, patent agents and trademark attorneys can apply to become judges in certain courts. Sixty per cent of legal executives are women, which should help to increase the number of female judges. Eligibility will no longer be based on the number of years candidates have had 'rights of audience', but instead on their number of years' post-qualification legal experience. The latter is a much broader concept but equally reflects a person's experience of the law. The required number of years' experience will also be reduced from seven to five years and ten to seven years, depending on judicial office.

Training

Considering the importance of their work, judges receive very little training, even with recent changes. They may be experienced as lawyers, but the skills needed by a good lawyer are not identical to those required by a good judge.

Problems with judicial independence

While the Constitutional Reform Act 2005 has now given statutory recognition to the independence of the judiciary, there remain a number of threats to judicial independence:

Supremacy of Parliament

Apart from where European law is involved, it is never possible for the courts to question the validity of existing Acts of Parliament. In the United Kingdom all Acts of Parliament are treated as absolutely binding by the courts, until such time as any particular Act is repealed or altered by Parliament itself in another statute or by a Minister under the special fast-track procedure provided for under the Human Rights Act 1998. The judiciary is therefore ultimately subordinate to the will of Parliament.

The House of Lords

Lords of Appeal in Ordinary are also members of more than one arm of the state, since they take part in the legislative business in the House of Lords. However, they tend not to get involved in political controversy or ally themselves with a particular party, confining their contributions to technical questions of a legal nature. The Royal Commission on the House of Lords recommended in 2000 that the basic conventions restricting the role of the Law Lords should be put down in writing. The Government announced in 2003 that it intended to replace the House of Lords with a Supreme Court and the Constitutional Reform Act 2005 contains provisions for the creation of this new court (see p. 408).

Non-judicial work

Judges also get involved in non-judicial areas with political implications, for example, chairing inquiries into Bloody Sunday in Northern Ireland, the Brixton riots or the Zeebrugge ferry disaster. Thus Sir William Macpherson headed the inquiry into the handling of the police investigation of the death of the black teenager Stephen Lawrence, who was murdered in South London. This function can often be seen to undermine the political neutrality of the judiciary. The Hutton inquiry, following the war against Iraq, raised questions about the future role of judges in public inquiries. There was wide public dissatisfiaction with the Hutton report (2003), and a general unease as to how independent the judge and chair, Lord Hutton, had been. As a result the Lord Chief Justice, Lord Woolf, wrote a memo to the House of Commons Public Administration Select Committee expressing concern that Lord Hutton had been used as a political tool by the Government.

Cases with political implications

Although judges generally refrain from airing their political views, they are sometimes forced to make decisions that have political ramifications. Concerns have been expressed that too often such decisions defend the interests of the Government of the day, sometimes at the expense of individual liberties.

Certain cases have borne out this concern. In **McIlkenny** *v* **Chief Constable of the West Midlands** (1980), Lord Denning dismissed allegations of police brutality against the six men accused of the Birmingham pub bombings with the words:

> Just consider the course of events if this action were to go to trial . . . If the six men fail, it will mean that much time and money and worry will have been expended by many people for no good purpose. If the six men win, it will mean that the police were guilty of perjury, that they were guilty of violence and threats, that the confessions were involuntary and were improperly admitted in evidence: and that the convictions were erroneous. That would mean that the Home Secretary would have either to recommend they be pardoned or he would have to remit the case to the Court of Appeal under section 17 of the Criminal Appeal Act 1968. This is such an appalling vista that every sensible person in the land would say: it cannot be right that these actions should go any further. They should be struck out.

In other words, Lord Denning was saying, the allegations should not be addressed, because if proved true, the result would be to bring the legal system into disrepute.

The danger of political bias has been increased with the passing of the Human Rights Act 1998. While judges already decide some politically sensitive cases, their number is likely to increase, with litigation directly accusing government actions and legislation of breaching fundamental human rights. The changing role of the judiciary will be particularly visible in the House of Lords. At the moment it decides about 100 cases a year, which are usually on technical commercial and tax matters. With the implementation of the HRA the House of Lords will move closer to the US Supreme Court, deciding fundamental issues on the rights of the individual against the State. The Government now intends to abolish the House of Lords and replace it with a Supreme Court. The details of this reform have not yet been decided.

Quick quiz 7.4

1 What are the five ways in which a judge may leave office?

2 Who developed the doctrine of the separation of powers?

3 What is the average age of the Law Lords?

4 Can judges question the validity of an Act of Parliament?

Right-wing bias

In addition to its alleged readiness to support the Government of the day, the judiciary has been accused of being particularly biased towards the interests traditionally represented by the right wing of the political spectrum. In his influential book *The Politics of the Judiciary* (1985), Griffith states that: 'in every major social issue which has come before the courts in the last thirty years – concerning industrial relations, political protest, race relations, government secrecy, police powers, moral behaviour – the judges have supported the conventional, settled and established interests'.

Among the cases he cites in support of this theory is **Bromley London Borough Council** *v* **Greater London Council** (1983). In this case the Labour-run GLC had won an election on a promise to cut bus and tube fares by 25 per cent. The move necessitated an increase in the rates levied on the London boroughs, and one of those boroughs, Conservative-controlled Bromley, challenged the GLC's right to do this. The challenge failed in the High Court, but succeeded on appeal. The Court of Appeal judges condemned the fare reduction as 'a crude abuse of power', and quashed the supplementary rate that the GLC had levied on the London boroughs to pay for it. The House of Lords agreed, the Law Lords holding unanimously that the GLC was bound by a statute requiring it to 'promote the provision of integrated, efficient and economic transport facilities and services in Greater London', which they interpreted to mean that the bus and tube system must be run according to 'ordinary business principles' of cost-effectiveness. The decision represented a political defeat for the Labour leaders of the GLC and a victory for the Conservative councillors of Bromley.

Bias against women

In her book *Eve was Framed* (1992), Helena Kennedy argues that the attitude of many judges to women is outdated, and sometimes prejudiced. Kennedy alleges that women are judged according to how well they fit traditional female stereotypes. Because crime is seen as stepping outside the feminine role, women are more severely punished than men, and women who do not fit traditional stereotypes are treated most harshly.

The Judicial Studies Board, responsible for the training of judges, has issued judges with the *Equal Treatment Bench Book*. This advises judges on equal treatment of people in court and the appropriate use of language to avoid causing offence by, for example, being sexist.

Influence of Freemasonry

 Know your terms 7.5

Define the following terms:

1 Executive
2 Freemasonry
3 Law Society
4 Stereotype

Freemasonry is a form of secret society, which does not allow women to join. Among its stated aims is the mutual self-advancement of its members. There has long been concern about the extent of membership among the police as well as the judiciary, on the basis that loyalty to other Masons – who might be parties in a case, or colleagues seeking promotion or other favours – could have a corrupting influence.

In an attempt to introduce greater transparency, a questionnaire was sent in 1998 to all members of the judiciary asking them to declare their 'Masonic status'. Five per cent of those who responded admitted to being Freemasons.

Reform of the judiciary

The appointment process

The judicial appointment process will undoubtedly be better following the reforms introduced by the Constitutional Reform Act 2005. However, there are some weaknesses in those reforms and the Government could have gone much further in removing itself from the appointment process. The pressure group, Civil Liberties, is concerned that the Act only creates an advisory panel for judicial appointments, as the ultimate decision to appoint will still be made by the Government Minister (or effectively the Prime Minister for Court of Appeal and Supreme Court judges).

The Government's consultation paper, *Constitutional Reform: a new way of appointing judges* (2003), considered the creation of three possible types of commission:

■ An Appointing Commission.
■ A Recommending Commission.
■ A Hybrid Commission.

An Appointing Commission would itself make the decision whom to appoint with no involvement of a Minister at any stage. This is similar to the arrangements that exist in some continental European countries.

119

A Recommending Commission would make recommendations to a Minister as to whom he or she should appoint (or recommend that the Queen appoints). The final decision on who to appoint would rest with the Minister.

A Hybrid Commission would act as an Appointing Commission in relation to the more junior appointments and as a Recommending Commission for the more senior appointments.

Ultimately, the Government favoured the creation of a Recommending Commission, but an Appointing Commission would have more effectively removed Government interference in the judicial appointment process.

Reading on the web

The consultation paper *Constitutional Reform: A New Way of Appointing Judges* is available on the website for the Ministry of Constitutional Affairs at:

http://www.dca.gov.uk/consult/jacommission/index.htm

The consultation paper *Court Working Dress in England and Wales* is available on the website for the Ministry of Constitutional Affairs at:

http://www.dca.gov.uk/consult/courtdress

Sir Leonard Peach's report into judicial appointments is available on the Minister of Constitutional Affairs' website:

http://www.dca.gov.uk/judicial/peach/indexfr.htm

General information on the judiciary is available on the Minister of Constitutional Affairs' website:

http://www.dca.gov.uk/judicial/judgesfr.htm

The website of the Judicial Studies Board can be found at:

http://www.jsboard.co.uk

The booklet *Judicial Appointments in England and Wales: policies and procedure* is available on the Department of Constitutional Affairs website at:

http://www.dca.gov.uk/judicial/appointments/jappinfr.htm

Question and answer guides

Questions about the judiciary generally focus on their independence, but as this is closely related to appointments, background and selection, you need to know more than just the information under the heading of independence of the judiciary, as the following example shows.

1 **Critically consider the possible effect of recent reforms to the appointment and training of judges.** *(OCR)*

Answer guide

An answer to this question could be divided into two parts, first looking at judicial appointment and secondly looking at judicial training. As regards judicial appointment, you could explain that there have been for many years a number of perceived problems with the appointment and training of the English judiciary, including the lack of openness about the selection process, the narrow background of the resulting appointees and their perceived biases. Direct reference should be made to Sir Leonard Peach's report which is discussed at p. 106. Explain that a variety of recent reforms have taken place with the aim of addressing these problems. You need to discuss in most detail the changes to the appointment process introduced by the Constitutional Reform Act 2005. You could also list some of the earlier reforms at this point: the creation of a Commissioner for Judicial Appointments; increased training; open advertising for some posts; openness about the selection process; and increased access to the judiciary for solicitors. Do not forget that any reform in the training of solicitors or barristers which widens access to those professions will also eventually have an effect on the composition of the judiciary, just as any limits on access to the professions can be a reason for problems with the narrow background of judges.

You could conclude this part of your essay by evaluating how effective you think these reforms will be in increasing diversity in judicial appointments.

The second part of your essay will be much shorter and will discuss judicial training. This is discussed at p. 111 and p. 117, and no major reforms have been introduced on this subject in recent years.

 'For nearly 300 years, the English judge has been guaranteed his independence.' How far is this true? In your opinion, can the decisions of our judges be regarded as satisfactory to all members of society?

Answer guide

Your introduction should place the reference to 300 years by mentioning the provisions of the Act of Settlement (p. 113). After that the question seems to need answering in two parts: has the English judge been guaranteed independence, and in the light of the answer, can his or her judgments properly be regarded as satisfactory to all members of society?

In the first part, you should look at the factors that are supposed to guarantee the independence of the judiciary. These include the new statutory guarantee contained in the Constitutional Reform Act 2005, security of tenure, separation of powers, and the fact that judicial salaries are not subject to a parliamentary vote and so on (see p. 114). Then go on to examine the problems with independence that suggest it is not guaranteed.

In the second part of your answer, you can give examples of cases where the lack of judicial independence has resulted in decisions that are not satisfactory to certain members of society – again, the material on right-wing and executive bias is useful here.

If you have time you could add that the lack of independence is not the only reason that their decisions are not satisfactory to all members of society, and bring in the material about the background of judges and their alleged bias against women.

Chapter summary

The role of the judges

The judges play a central role under the British Constitution, playing a vital but sensitive role in controlling the exercise of power by the state.

Judicial hierarchy

At the head of the judiciary is the President of the Courts of England and Wales. The most senior judges are the 12 Lords of Appeal in Ordinary. They currently sit in the House of Lords and the Privy Council. At the next level down sitting in the Court of Appeal, are 37 judges known as Lord Justices of Appeal and Lady Justices of Appeal.

A reduced role for the Lord Chancellor

With the passing of the Constitutional Reform Act 2005, four major changes to the role of the Lord Chancellor have been introduced. As a result he or she no longer:

■ sits as a judge
■ heads the judiciary
■ takes a central role in the judicial appointments process, nor
■ automatically becomes the speaker of the House.

He or she will remain as the head of a Government department (now called the Ministry for Constitutional Affairs), but his or her powers and links to the judges have been removed to satisfy the principle of the separation of powers.

Appointing the judges

The way in which judges are appointed has been radically reformed by provisions in the Constitutional Reform Act 2005. The Act contains provisions for the establishment of a new Judicial Appointments Commission. It is hoped that the creation of this body will help to put an end to the breaches of the principle of separation of powers and reinforce judicial independence. Depending on their rank, judges are appointed by the Queen on the advice of the Prime Minister or by the Lord Chancellor.

Training

Training is provided by the Judicial Studies Board.

Termination of appointment

There are five ways in which a judge may leave office:

■ dismissal
■ discipline
■ resignation
■ retirement, or
■ removal due to infirmity.

Independence of the judiciary

In our legal system great importance is attached to the idea that judges should be independent and be seen to be independent. Section 3 of the Constitutional Reform Act 2005 states:

> The Lord Chancellor, other Ministers of the Crown and all with responsibility for matters relating to the judiciary or otherwise to the administration of justice must uphold the continued independence of the judiciary.

Criticisms of the judiciary

Judges are overwhelmingly white, male and middle- to upper-class, and frequently elderly, leading to accusations that they are unrepresentative of the society they serve. The appointments process has been criticized for being dominated by politicians, secretive and discriminatory. Judges receive very little training. There are real concerns that the independence of the judiciary is not sufficiently protected. The academic, Griffith, has accused judges of being biased towards the interests traditionally represented by the right wing of the political spectrum. The lawyer, Helena Kennedy, has argued that the attitude of many judges to women is outdated and sometimes prejudiced. There is also concern that some judges are members of the Freemasons.

Chapter 8

The legal professions

The British legal profession, unlike that of most other countries, includes two separate branches: barristers and solicitors (the term 'lawyer' is a general one which covers both branches). They each do the same type of work – advocacy, which means representing clients in court, and paperwork, including drafting legal documents and giving written advice – but the proportions differ, with barristers generally spending a higher proportion of their time in court.

In addition, some types of work have traditionally been available to only one branch (conveyancing to solicitors, and advocacy in the higher courts to barristers, for example), and barristers are not usually hired directly by clients. A client's first point of contact will usually be a solicitor, who then engages a barrister on their behalf if it proves necessary. As we shall see though, these divisions are beginning to break down.

In the past, the two branches of the profession have been fairly free to arrange their own affairs, but over the last fifteen years this situation has changed significantly, with the Government increasingly passing legislation to control the professions.

As well as barristers and solicitors, an increasingly important profession is that of the legal executives.

Solicitors

There are around 92,000 solicitors. Their governing body is the Law Society, which supervises training and discipline, as well as acting on behalf of the profession as a whole.

Work

For most solicitors, paperwork takes up much of their time. It includes conveyancing (when solicitors deal with the legal aspects of the buying and selling of houses and other property) and drawing up wills and contracts, as well as giving written and oral legal advice. Until 1985, solicitors were the only people allowed to do conveyancing work, but this is no longer the case – people from different occupations can qualify as licensed conveyancers, and the service is often offered by banks and building societies.

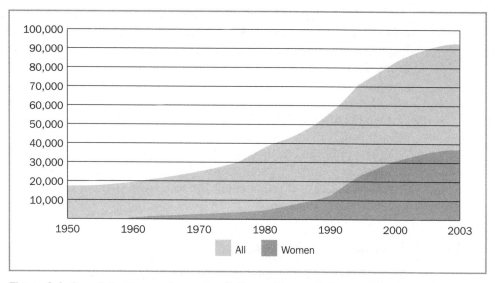

Figure 8.1 Growth in the numbers of solicitors with practising certificates, 1950–2003

Source: Law Society website. *Fact Sheet 2: Women in the profession* (www.lawsociety.org.uk). © The Law Society.

Solicitors have traditionally been able to do advocacy work in the magistrates' court and the county court, but not generally in the higher courts. This situation was changed by the Courts and Legal Services Act 1990 and the Access to Justice Act 1999. These Acts put in place the mechanics for equalizing rights of audience between barristers and solicitors. Now all barristers and solicitors automatically acquire full rights of audience, though they will only be able to exercise these rights on completion of the necessary training. There are currently 1,000 solicitor advocates. Many firms are sending their solicitors on courses, making advocacy training compulsory and designating individuals as in-house advocates. Thus, solicitors are increasingly doing the advocacy work themselves rather than sending it to a barrister. Where Government funding has established fixed fees for work, solicitors are faced with a simple choice: keep the money or give it away. Even those solicitors who do not have full rights of audience can appear in the higher courts for a limited range of proceedings.

Traditionally, an individual solicitor did much less advocacy work than a barrister, but as more solicitors gain the necessary training, this is changing. In any case, solicitors as a group do more advocacy than barristers, simply because 98 per cent of criminal cases are tried in the magistrates' court, where the advocate is usually a solicitor.

Solicitors can, and usually do, form partnerships, with other solicitors. Alternatively, since 2001, they can form a limited liability partnership. Under an ordinary partnership a solicitor can be personally liable (even after retirement) for a claim in negligence against the solicitor firm, even if he or she was not involved in the transaction giving rise to the claim. Under a limited liability partnership a partner's liability is limited to negligence for which he or she was personally responsible.

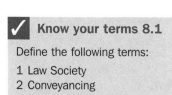

Know your terms 8.1

Define the following terms:

1 Law Society
2 Conveyancing
3 Rights of audience
4 Solicitor advocate

Solicitors work in ordinary offices, with, in general, the same support staff as any office-based business, and have offices all over England and Wales and in all towns. Practices range from huge London-based firms dealing only with large corporations, to small partnerships or individual solicitors, dealing with the conveyancing, wills, divorces and minor crime of a country town. In practice, most law firms are small, with 85 per cent of them having four or fewer partners, and nearly half having only one partner. Some solicitors work in law centres and other advice agencies, Government departments, private industry and education rather than in private practice.

Figures published in the journal *Commercial Lawyer* in September 2000 show that an elite group of 100 City solicitors working in central London are earning more than £1 million per year. But this figure has to be seen in the context of a profession that has over 80,000 members.

Qualifications and training

Almost all solicitors have a university degree, though not necessarily in law. A number of universities introduced an admissions test in 2004, the National Admissions Test for Law, to help select students onto their popular law degrees. Students whose degree is not in law have to take a one-year conversion course leading to the Common Professional Examination (CPE).

The next step, for law graduates and those who have passed the CPE, is a one-year Legal Practice Course, designed to provide practical skills, including advocacy, as well as legal and procedural knowledge. The course costs between £5,000 and £9,000 and the vast majority of students are obliged to fund themselves or rely on loans.

After passing the Legal Practice exams, the prospective solicitor must find a place, usually in a solicitor firm, to serve a two-year apprenticeship under a training contract. There can be intense competition for these places, especially in times of economic difficulty when firms are reluctant to invest in training. Trainee solicitors should receive a minimum salary of £14,720 outside London and £16,450 in London. However, the Law Society, as part of its review of the qualification process, is considering abolishing the guaranteed minimum pay, instead leaving the issue of pay to be determined by the market. The work of a trainee solicitor can be very demanding, and a survey carried out for the Law Society found that a third work more than 50 hours a week.

It is possible to become a solicitor without a degree, by completing the one-year Solicitors First Examination Course, and the Legal Practice Course, and having a five-year training contract. Legal executives (see p. 151) sometimes go on to qualify this way.

Solicitors are required to participate in continuing education throughout their careers. They have to undertake 16 hours of education a year, with the subjects covered depending on each individual's areas of interest or need.

Lord Woolf, an influential judge, has observed that the solicitor profession is becoming 'increasingly polarised' depending on the nature of the work carried out, with lawyers working in City firms earning significantly more than those in high street practices. Specialist LPC courses are now being offered for some City law firms. Lord Woolf has criticized this development, as he fears it could undermine the concept of a single solicitor profession with a single professional qualification.

Complaints

Complaints can be made to the Consumer Complaints Service, to the Legal Services Ombudsman and/or by an action in negligence.

Consumer Complaints Service

Until 1996, complaints about solicitors were handled by the Solicitors Complaints Bureau (SCB). The Bureau was widely criticized for delay and inefficiency, and a report by the National Consumer Council in 1994 suggested that its policy of attempting to conciliate the parties favoured solicitors over complainants, tending in many cases to impose a settlement or dismiss the complaint. The maximum compensation available to complainants was £1,000, and this was criticized as being too low. Another frequent complaint was that the Solicitors Complaints Bureau was not sufficiently independent of the profession, as its powers were merely delegated to it by the Law Society.

Concerned by these criticisms, the Law Society looked into the problems and in 1995 produced a report entitled *Supervision of Solicitors; the next decade*. The report found that the complaints process needed to be more efficient and customer-friendly, with a greater role for non-lawyers so that the process was independent of the profession. Its main recommendation was acted upon in 1996, when the Solicitors Complaints Bureau was replaced by the Office for the Supervision of Solicitors (OSS). This body was renamed the Consumer Complaints Service (CCS) in 2004. Complaints are initially handled by a seven-strong team of solicitors, who sift them into those which can be quickly dealt with on the telephone, those which involve serious allegations of shoddy work, and those which concern serious breaches of professional rules. The aim is to make early, direct contact with complainants, and ensure they are kept informed.

Minor complaints are sent to the firms concerned to deal with, as part of the CCS's aim to encourage law firms to develop better customer care practices. Where complaints remain in the CCS's hands, they are directed to its network of local conciliation points so that, where possible, complainants can be seen face to face.

However, the problems associated with the Solicitors Complaints Bureau remain. The CCS has been repeatedly criticized by the Legal Services Ombudsman (discussed below). In his annual report for 2001/02, the Ombudsman stated he was dissatisfied with the handling of complaints in 32 per cent of the cases referred to him. The report concludes:

> it is apparent that sustained and continuing improvement in the Law Society's complaint-handling activities has not been achieved . . . Sometimes it seems that the OSS create problems for themselves and their customers by neglecting the very basics of complaint handling – like reading the information the complainant sends them.

The CCS has also been criticised by the Consumers' Association magazine *Which?* for not being sufficiently independent of the profession: like the Solicitors

Complaints Bureau, it is run by the Law Society, and its main decision-making committee comprises ten members of the public, and 15 solicitors, including ten who are members of the Law Society Council. The CCS's director also sits on the Law Society's management board. *Which?* suggests that complaints about solicitors should be handled by a completely independent organization.

In 2005, the Law Society was threatened by the Government with a £1 million fine, if it failed to improve its handling of complaints.

The problem of complaints handling was considered in Sir David Clementi's review of the legal professions in 2004. He recommended that an independent Office for Legal Complaints should be established which would handle all consumer complaints against any legal service provider (including solicitors and barristers). It would be supervised by a new Legal Services Board. The Legal Services Complaints Commissioner would be abolished. While the Law Society was happy with this proposal, the Bar Council is concerned that the new body may prove slower and more expensive than the existing arrangements. It commented:

> We have an extremely good record on complaints as confirmed by the Legal Services Ombudsman. We do not want the service provided to the public to be diminished by being sucked into a large bureaucratic Office for Legal complaints.

The Government has, however, accepted Sir David Clementi's recommendation, and the office is expected to be established in January 2006.

Legal Services Ombudsman

The Office of the Legal Services Ombudsman was established in 1990. Its role is to oversee the handling of complaints by the professional regulatory bodies, and offers the final appeal regarding complaints against lawyers. Complainants who are dissatisfied with the way their grievances are handled by the CCS can ask the Legal Services Ombudsman to investigate. The number of cases being accepted for investigation by the Ombudsman is at an all-time high. In 2001/02 the Ombudsman received 1,677 new cases for investigation. If he or she is dissatisfied with the way the relevant professional body has handled the complaint, the Ombudsman can recommend that the relevant professional body reconsiders the complaint and/or order compensation to be paid.

In 1998 the performance of the Ombudsman's office itself came under scrutiny in a study commissioned by the Ombudsman, and the CCS might perhaps have been forgiven for indulging in a wry smile at the results. Although most members of the public seeking information and advice were happy with the service, and so were most lawyers who had professional contact with the Ombudsman's office, the majority of complainants who had their cases formally investigated were dissatisfied. The complained that they were not kept informed, that the processes of dealing with cases were complex and over-lengthy, and the role of the Ombudsman's service was unclear.

The Ombudsman promised that improvements would be made, and has since produced clearer information leaflets explaining the role of the service, and established new systems to keep complainants informed of the progress of their cases. However, she suggested part of the blame must lie with the professions themselves, in that

Table 8.1 Investigations where the Ombudsman found that complaint handling was satisfactory

	Apr 2004 to Mar 2005	Apr 2003 to Mar 2004	Apr 2002 to Mar 2003	Apr 2001 to Mar 2002
Solicitors/Law Society	62.0%	53.3%	67.2%	57.9%
Barristers/GCB	78.7%	86.8%	88.4%	92.9%
Licenced conveyancers/CLC	33.3%	66.7%	61.5%	60.0%
All cases	**63.8%**	**57.5%**	**69.2%**	**60.9%**

Source: *Annual Report of the Legal Services Ombudsman for England and Wales 2004/2005, p. 15.*

lawyers' failure to resolve complaints more effectively in the first place naturally led to delay and dissatisfaction once complainants reached the Ombudsman's service.

A more recent report commissioned by the Ombudsman in 2002 has now found that the Ombudsman was operating an efficient case load workflow system, consistent with best practice and appropriate for an organization of its size and role.

Due to the Government's dissatisfaction with the solicitors' complaints handling process, it has created a new Legal Services Complaints Commissioner (LSCC). The role of the LSCC is to oversee the operation of the Consumer Complaints Service, partly by setting its targets. He or she will have the power to impose large fines on the Law Society if these targets are not met. Ms Zahida Manzoor, the current Legal Services Ombudsman, has been formally appointed to hold this post as well. Her two roles, however, remain distinct: as Ombudsman she is concerned with individual complaints, as LSCC she supervises the complaints handling process as a whole.

Action for negligence

Solicitors can be sued for negligent work like most other professionals. Following the House of Lords' judgment in **Arthur J S Hall & Co** *v* **Simons** (2000), solicitors no longer enjoy any immunity from liability for work connected to the conduct of a case in court.

▍Promotion to the judiciary

In the past, solicitors were only eligible to become circuit judges, but the Courts and Legal Services Act 1990 has opened the way for them to become judges in the higher courts (see Chapter 7: The judges).

Quick quiz 8.2

1 How many solicitors are there?

2 Following the Access to Justice Act 1999, what rights of audience do solicitors have?

3 What percentage of criminal cases are heard in the magistrates' courts?

4 What does the abbreviation 'CCS' stand for?

Barristers

There are around 9,000 barristers in independent practice, known collectively as the Bar. Their governing body is the Bar Council, which, like the Law Society, acts as a kind of trade union, safeguarding the interests of barristers, and also as a watchdog, regulating barristers' training and activities.

Work

Advocacy is the main function of barristers, and much of their time will be spent in court or preparing for it. Until the changes made under the Courts and Legal Services Act in 1990, barristers were, with a few exceptions, the only people allowed to advocate in the superior courts – the House of Lords, the Court of Appeal, the High Court, the Crown Court and the Employment Appeal Tribunal. We have seen that this has now changed, and they are increasingly having to compete with solicitors for this work. Barristers also do some paperwork, drafting legal documents and giving written opinions on legal problems.

Barristers must be self-employed and, under Bar rules, cannot form partnerships, but they usually share offices, called chambers, with other barristers. All the barristers in a particular chambers share a clerk, who is a type of business manager, arranging meetings with the client and the solicitor and also negotiating the barristers' fees. Around 70 per cent of practising barristers are based in London chambers, though they may travel to courts in the provinces; the rest are based in the other big cities.

Not all qualified barristers work as advocates at the Bar. Like solicitors, some are employed by law centres and other advice agencies, Government departments or private industry, and some teach. Some go into these jobs after practising at the Bar for a time, others never practise at the Bar.

Traditionally a client could not approach a barrister directly, but had to see a solicitor first, who would then refer the case to a barrister. In 2004 the ban on direct access to barristers was abolished. Members of the public can now contact a barrister without using a solicitor as an intermediary. Barristers are today able to provide specialist advice, drafting and advocacy without a solicitor acting as a 'middleman', although the management of litigation will still generally be handled by solicitors. Direct access to the client is permitted where the barrister has been in practice for three years, and has undertaken a short course preparing them for this new mode of operation.

Barristers work under what is called the 'cab rank' rule. Technically, this means that if they are not already committed for the time in question, they must accept any case which falls within their claimed area of specialization and for which a reasonable fee is offered. In practice, barristers' clerks, who take their bookings, may manipulate the rule to ensure that barristers are able to avoid cases they do not want to take. The cab rank rule does not apply where a barrister is approached directly by a potential client, rather than being referred to them by a solicitor. In these circumstances, barristers must follow a principle of non-discrimination, under which they must not refuse work because of the way it is funded or because the client is unpopular.

Qualifications and training

The starting point is normally an upper-second class degree. If this degree is not in law, applicants must do the one-year course leading to the Common Professional Examination (the same course taken by would-be solicitors with degrees in subjects other than law). Mature students may be accepted without a degree, but applications are subject to very stringent consideration, and this is not a likely route to the Bar.

All students then have to join one of the four Inns of Court: Inner Temple; Middle Temple; Gray's Inn; or Lincoln's Inn, all of which are in London. The Inns of Court first emerged in the thirteenth century and their role has evolved over time. Their main functions now cover the provision of professional accommodation for barristers' chambers and residential accommodation for judges, discipline, the provision of law libraries and the promotion of collegiate activities.

Students take the year-long Bar Vocational Course which can now be taken at eight different institutions around the country. The course includes oral exercises, and tuition in interviewing skills and negotiating skills, and as with solicitors' training, more emphasis has been laid on these practical aspects in recent years.

Around 1,600 people take the Bar Vocational Course each year, and each one has to pay approximately £7,000 for the course alone, and then find living expenses on top. Local authority grants are discretionary and only rarely available. Limited financial assistance is available from the Inns of Court.

Students have to dine at their Inn 12 times. This rather old-fashioned and much-criticized custom stems from the idea that students will benefit from the wisdom and

Figure 8.2 One of the dining rooms of the Inns of Court
Source: Photograph by permission of the Masters of the Bench of The Honourable Society of Gray's Inn.

experience of their elders if they sit among them at mealtimes. The dinners are now linked to seminars, lectures and training weekends, in order to provide genuine educational benefit.

After this, the applicant is called to the Bar, and must then find a place in a chambers to serve his or her pupillage. This is a one-year apprenticeship in which pupils assist a qualified barrister, who is known as their pupil master. Competition for pupillage places can be fierce, with only about 600 pupillage vacancies available each year. In the past funding for pupillage has been a problem. But pupils should now normally be paid a minimum of £10,000 a year. Pupils are required to take a further advocacy course before the end of pupillage, as part of the increased emphasis on practical skills.

Pupillage completed, the newly qualified barrister must find a permanent place in a chambers, known as a tenancy. This can be the most difficult part, and some are forced to 'squat' – remaining in their pupillage chambers for as long as they are allowed, without becoming a full member – until they find a permanent place. There are only around 300 tenancies available each year – one to every two pupils.

In 1993, the Royal Commission on Criminal Justice recommended that barristers should have to undertake further training during the course of their careers, after noting that both preparation of cases and advocacy were failing to reach acceptable standards. In response, the Bar Council introduced a continuing education programme. Barristers must now complete a minimum of 42 hours of continuing education in the prescribed subjects by the end of their first three years of practice. There is also a continuing professional development scheme for established practitioners which was introduced in January 2001.

▌ Queen's Counsel

After ten years in practice, a barrister may apply to become a Queen's Counsel, or QC (sometimes called a silk, as they wear gowns made of silk). This usually means they will be offered higher-paid cases, and need do less preliminary paperwork. The average annual earnings of a QC are £270,000, with a small group earning over £1 million a year. Not all barristers attempt or manage to become QCs – those that do not are called juniors, even up to retirement age. Juniors may assist QCs in big cases, as well as working alone. Since 1995, solicitors can also be appointed as QCs, but there are currently only eight QCs who come from the solicitor profession.

The future of the QC system is now in doubt. The Office of Fair Trading in 2001 suggested that the system was merely a means of artificially raising the price of a barrister's services. The Bar Council has counter-argued that, actually, the system is an important quality mark which directs the client to experienced, specialist lawyers where required.

In the past the appointment process for QCs was similar to that for senior judges, including the system of secret soundings, and with civil servants, a Cabinet Minister and the Queen all involved. In 2003 the appointment process was suspended, following criticism of the QC system. Appointments were provisionally recommenced in 2004 but relying on a new appointment process. The Government is no longer involved. Instead, responsibility for appointment has been placed in the hands of the two professional bodies: the Bar Council and the Law Society. They will select candidates on the basis of merit, following an open competition. The secret soundings system has been abolished and replaced by structured references from judges, lawyers and clients who have seen the candidate in action. A wider diversity of people are expected to be appointed, including more solicitor-advocates. The title of QC has been retained for the time being, though the Law Society would like to see it replaced with another name, to mark a clean break from the past, when the system clearly favoured barristers. Commenting on the new appointment procedures, the Law Society president stated:

> Consumers can be assured that holders of the QC designation under the new scheme have been awarded it because of what they know not who they know, and that their superior expertise and experience has been evaluated by an independent panel on an objective basis.

The future of QCs will be reconsidered in 2006. In the mean time, the Lord Chancellor has commissioned a long-term market study into the benefits of the silk system for consumers and solicitors, the results of which are expected to be available in 2006 or 2007. The Government's current view is that the badge of QC is a well-recognized and respected 'kitemark' of quality both at home and abroad. The existence of QCs helps enhance London's status as the centre of international litigation and arbitration.

Task 8.3

In July 2003 the Government issued a Consultation Paper, *The Future of Queen's Counsel*. The Foreword to this Consultation Paper has been written by the Minister for Constitutional Affairs, Lord Falconer. It states:

'There has long been a debate about the relevance and use of the rank of Queen's Counsel. The time has come to bring that debate to a head, and to reach conclusions, after full consultation on the way ahead. Over the last four centuries, the QC system has become a well-established part of our legal structure. But the legal system must meet the needs of the public. The system must be capable of identifying those with the skills and expertise to deal with any particular dispute. In particular, it should be able to recognise the wide variety of skills needed to provide the public with the legal service it needs. This paper therefore explores whether the current QC system is objectively in the public interest and whether it commands public confidence.'

Questions

The Consultation Paper asks for views from the public on a range of questions. Consider how you would to these questions asked by the Government:

1 Do you consider that the rank of QC in its current form benefits the public? What are the reasons for your view?

2 Do you think that the current QC system should be abolished or changed? What are the reasons for your view?

3 If you consider that the QC rank should be abolished, do you consider that it should be replaced by another form of quality mark (whether it be granted by the state, the professions, and independent body or the proposed Judicial Appointments Commission)?

▌Complaints

Until recently barristers enjoyed an immunity from liability for negligent work in court. This immunity had been recognized by the courts in the case of **Rondel _v_ Worsley** (1969). The main justification for the immunity was that clients would seek to use litigation against their barrister to indirectly reopen litigation that had already been lost. This immunity was dramatically abolished by the House of Lords in **Arthur J S Hall & Co _v_ Simons** (2000). The House ruled that there was no longer any good reason to treat barristers any differently from other professionals, so that their negligence could give rise to liability in tort. Despite this judgment, in the most recent House of Lords' case on the point, **Moy _v_ Pettman Smith** (2005), the House proceeded to treat a barrister more leniently than other professionals. A barrister had been sued for negligently failing to settle a case. The House concluded that she had not been negligent, and in reaching this conclusion it repeatedly referred to what could be expected from a barrister of her 'seniority and purported experience'. This is notably different from the way the work of other professionals has been judged in comparable situations. A doctor's work, for example, in a case of alleged negligence is usually judged by the standards of 'reasonably competent practitioners' and the courts ignore their level of seniority.

In the past the only avenue for complaints was the Bar Council but, if upheld, these complaints merely resulted in disciplinary action against the barrister, giving no redress to the client. In 1997 reforms were introduced. The complaints procedure is now overseen by a Complaints Commissioner. The Commissioner is not a lawyer and has complete independence from the Bar Council in the decisions that are made. If the Commissioner considers that the complaint may be justified, it will be referred to the Professional Conduct and Complaints Committee (PCC) for consideration. The PCC is a

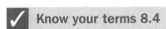

✓ Know your terms 8.4

Define the following terms:

1 Limited liability partnership
2 Bar Council
3 Pupillage
4 Queen's Counsel

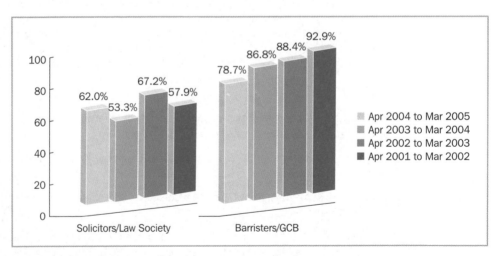

Figure 8.3 Investigations where ombudsman complaint handling was satisfactory

Source: _Annual Report of the Legal Services Ombudsman for England and Wales 2004/2005_, p. 56.

Committee of the Bar Council consisting of barristers and non-lawyers. If the PCC agrees that the complaint may be justified it sends the complaint to a disciplinary panel for a final decision on whether the complaint is justified.

If the complaint is successful, the barrister can be required to apologize, to repay fees or to pay compensation of up to £5,000 to a complainant where that complainant is the barrister's client. The barrister can be subjected to a fine or prevented from practising as a barrister either permanently or temporarily.

The Legal Services Ombudsman oversees the Bar's handling of complaints in the same way as with complaints about solicitors (see p. 128).

Promotion to the judiciary

Suitably experienced barristers are eligible for appointment to all judicial posts, and the majority of current judges have practised at the Bar (for details of appointments, see Chapter 7: The judiciary).

Background of barristers and solicitors

Lawyers have in the past come from a very narrow social background, in terms of sex, race and class; there have also been significant barriers to entrants with disabilities. In recent years the professions have succeeded in opening their doors to a wider range of people, so that they are more representative of the society in which they work.

White, middle-class men dominate in most professions, excluding many people who would be highly suited to such careers. A narrow social profile created particular problems for the legal professions in the past. First, it meant that the legal professions have been seen as unapproachable and elitist, which put off some people from using lawyers and thereby benefiting from their legal rights (this issue is examined in Chapter 11). Secondly, the English judiciary is drawn from the legal professions and, if their background is narrow, that of the judiciary will be too (this issue is examined in Chapter 7). Increasingly, the professions are becoming representative of the society in which they function.

Women

The number of women in the professions has increased dramatically since the 1950s. In 1987 women accounted for less than 20 per cent of all solicitors; now 41 per cent of solicitors are women. Today there are more women qualifying for the solicitor profession than men.

For the barrister profession in 2002 equal numbers of men and women qualified to practise and 32 per cent of barristers are women.

The problem now for women is less about entry into the professions and more about pay, promotion and working conditions. Female solicitors earn less than male solicitors. Despite the fact that there are more women achieving first and upper second class law degrees than men, in 1998 the Law Society's Annual Statistical Survey found that new female entrants were earning on average 4.4 per cent less than new male entrants. Women who become partners in law firms earn on average £6,000 less than men in the same position.

Fewer women are being promoted to become partners in their law firm. Over 50 per cent of male solicitors are partners in their firm, compared to only 23 per cent of female solicitors. This cannot simply be explained by the fact that the average age of women solicitors is younger: 88 per cent of male solicitors in private practice with 10–19 years of experience were partners, compared with 63 per cent of female solicitors with the same experience. There is a similar problem in the barrister profession. In 2003, 112 men were made Queen's Counsel, but only 9 women.

A growing problem exists of women choosing to leave the profession early. This is either because they find it impossible to combine the demands of motherhood with a legal career or because they are frustrated at the 'glass ceiling' which seems to prevent women lawyers from achieving the same success as their male counterparts. Solicitor firms tend not to have provisions in place for flexible or part-time working for solicitors. Those that do, tend to discourage solicitors from taking advantage of them (*Research Study No. 26 of the Law Society Research and Policy Planning Unit* (1997)). The Law Society has recognized that in order to retain women and to ensure that the investment in their training is not lost, the profession must consider more flexible work arrangements (including career breaks) to allow women (and men) to continue to work as well as carrying out caring responsibilities.

The legal profession also needs to tackle the long-hours culture to stem the flow of women lawyers leaving the profession. The macho culture of working long hours forces women, who often have to juggle work and family, out of the legal world.

Ethnic minorities

Again, the picture is improving. The number of solicitors from ethnic minority groups has increased recently. In 2003, 8 per cent of practising solicitors came from an ethnic minority. This compares with 4 per cent in 1995. In 2003, 17 per cent of trainee solicitors were from a minority ethnic group. There are still, however, very few male Afro-Caribbean solicitors.

As regards the Bar, in 1989, 5 per cent of practising barristers came from an ethnic minority, in 2003 they made up 11 per cent of practising barristers and 20 per cent of pupils. This compares favourably with other professions.

Regrettably, there have been some reports in the media of black candidates doing less well in legal examinations than white candidates, particularly at the Bar. It has been suggested that oral examinations may be particularly vulnerable to subjective marking.

The Law Society has recognized that obstacles still exist for ethnic minorities in the solicitor profession. This is because most solicitor firms do not follow proper recruitment procedures, do not have an equal opportunities policy and practice, and the levels of discrimination within society at large are reflected in the perception of solicitors and their clients.

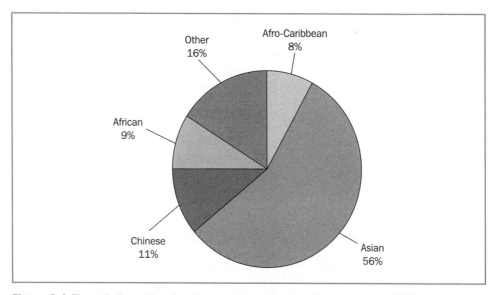

Figure 8.4 The ethnic origin of solicitors from minority ethnic groups, 2002

Source: Law Society website. Fact Sheet 3: Solicitors from minority ethnic groups (www.lawsociety.org.uk). © The Law Society.

Class

The biggest obstacle to a career in law now seems to be class background. Law degree students are predominantly middle class, with fewer than one in five coming from a working-class background. A 1989 Law Society Survey found that over a third of solicitors had come from private schools, despite the fact that only 7 per cent of the population attend such schools. In recent years, more lawyers have been educated in the state sector, but this progress could soon be reversed. This is because the lack of funding for legal training has made it very difficult for students without well-off parents to qualify, especially as barristers.

The chair of the Bar Council has warned that government plans to allow universities to charge top-up fees will stop students from poorer backgrounds pursuing a career in law.

One possible source of change for the future is the number of part time law degrees and Legal Practice Courses now available to mature students, who tend to come from a much broader range of backgrounds than those who attend university straight from school. Students on part-time courses can support themselves by continuing to work while they study in the evenings and at weekends.

Disability

Much attention has been paid to the under-representation of working-class people, ethnic minorities and women in the legal profession, but disabled people are less often discussed. Skill as a lawyer requires brains, not physical strength or dexterity, yet it seems there are still significant barriers to entry for disabled students, particularly to the Bar. Part of the problem is simply practical: a quarter of court buildings are over

100 years old and were never designed to offer disabled access. Most now have rooms adapted for disabled people, but need notice if they are to be used, which is hardly feasible for junior barristers who often get cases at very short notice. The other main barrier is effectively the same as that for ethnic minorities, working-class people and women: with fierce competition for places, 'traditional' applicants have the advantage.

Steps are being taken to address the problems of disabled applicants to the Bar. In 1992, the Bar's Disability Panel was established. This offers help to disabled people who are already within the profession or are hoping to enter it, by matching them to people who have overcome or managed to accommodate similar problems. The Inner Temple also gives grants for reading devices, special furniture and other aids, with the aim of creating a level playing field for disabled and able-bodied people.

Increasing diversity through educational reforms

The Law Society is considering introducing a radical reform to the way people qualify as solicitors. The proposals are contained in a consultation paper *Qualifying as a Solicitor: a framework for the future*. The emphasis would be on work-based training followed by an assessment by the Law Society of their knowledge and skills. Students would be required to have an honours degree in any subject, followed by work-based learning under the supervision of solicitors. They would then have to pass exams set and monitored by the Law Society where they would have to show an understanding and application of core skills. They would also have to prepare a trainee portfolio for external assessment to show that they were ready to practise. Students could choose to attend courses to help prepare them for the external assessment and exams but these courses would not be compulsory and would not be regulated by the Law Society. No minimum period of study and work experience has been laid down in order to qualify under these proposals.

Students would still be able to qualify by taking a law degree, a legal practice course and a two-year training contract, but they would not be required to take this route, and students who did take this route would still have to pass the external examinations and complete the portfolio during the training contract.

It is intended that this new system of training would broaden access to the profession for a more diverse range of students. This is because it would be more flexible, so that students could choose a pathway that suited their circumstances. The current requirement that all students take an LPC is expensive and not attractive to people from a poorer background who are worried about increasing their debts. The Law Society has stated:

> The existing training pathway – a degree in law, one year on a legal practice course and a two-year training contract – has worked well, and will continue to be the route to qualification for many. But it is a system that favours the young school leaver with a traditional academic education who is prepared to take on a five-figure debt. It makes law a difficult career choice for the rest. That is discriminatory – and not good for the profession.

However, the majority of legal education providers are not happy with these proposed reforms and have signed a petition stating that they have not been adequately consulted about them. One such provider has commented that: 'It's a bit like saying, I've had six months' experience in a butcher's shop, so I can be a surgeon.' And that: 'It will take longer to become a Corgi-registered plumber than a lawyer.'

There is concern that without the course structure of the LPC, consistent standards will not be maintained. The Legal Education Training Group has argued that:

> There is no justification for dismantling the existing framework. It works well; it could be improved, and especially made more flexible, but there is no real doubt that it is a functional and well regarded system. The retrograde nature of the . . . recommendations has not been sufficiently justified. We believe that the recommendations constitute a threat to quality standards, and, if implemented, may bring the profession into disrepute. It may also have an impact on current reciprocal arrangements thus affecting the ability of solicitors to qualify in other jurisdictions.

The Law Society of Scotland also considered in 2002 introducing a final external assessment for entry into the Scottish legal profession. It abandoned the project after two pilot tests produced disastrous results.

It is undoubtedly important that the legal profession should be a career option for all able students from a wide range of backgrounds, and that people should not be prevented from entering the profession because their family is not rich. But there are other ways that this can be achieved. The Charter 88 constitutional reform pressure group has argued that students should be funded throughout their legal training. The Law Society and the Bar Council have made representations to the Department of Education, pointing out that training for other professions such as medicine and teaching is paid or involves reduced fees. In her book *Eve was Framed*, Helena Kennedy QC argues that selection for the Bar in particular has always been based too much on 'connections' and financial resources than on ability. She recommends public funding for legal education and that there should be incentives for barristers' chambers to take on less conventional candidates.

Michael Zander (1988) argued that both the academic and the vocation stages of training could be improved, with a consequent rise in professional standards. Law degrees should include at least preliminary training in areas such as drafting documents and developing interviewing skills. Both pupilage and training contracts can be 'infinitely variable' in quality, according to Zander, 'ranging from excellent to deplorable' depending on where they are undertaken. He suggested a more integrated training was needed, like that undertaken by medical students, with better links between academic and vocational stages.

The former Advisory Committee on Legal Education and Conduct (ACLEC) examined the whole issue of legal training. Its 1996 report suggested that the two branches should no longer have completely separate training programmes at the postgraduate stage. Instead, after either a law degree or a degree in another subject plus the CPE, all students would take a Professional Legal Studies course, lasting around 18 weeks. Only then would they decide which branch of the profession to choose, going on to a Legal Practice Course (for solicitors) or Bar Vocational Course (for barristers) which would be only 15–18 weeks long. This, ACLEC suggested, would prevent the problem of students having to specialize too early. It also recommended that funding should be made available for the CPE course and the vocational stage of training.

Performance of the legal professions

Over the past 30 years, the performance of lawyers has come in for a great deal of criticism. Barristers and solicitors involved in criminal work were criticized by the 1993 Royal Commission on Criminal Justice, which found that defence cases were frequently inadequately prepared, often because the work was delegated to unqualified staff and not properly supervised. Advocacy standards were also low, on the part of both barristers and solicitors, and the Commission suggested that inadequate training might be the reason for this; they particularly criticized the practice of allowing pupil barristers to take on cases during their second six months, and the lack of detailed assessment of pupils' experience during this time. They recognized that both branches of the profession were already increasing advocacy training, but suggested that more work might be needed.

In 1995, the Consumers' Association magazine *Which?* caused a stir with a survey of the standards of advice provided by solicitors. Its researchers phoned a number of solicitors, posing as members of the public seeking advice about simple consumer problems, and the advice given was assessed by the Association's own legal team. The verdict was not good, with much of the advice given being assessed as inadequate or simply wrong. Two years later, the magazine repeated the test and, once again, the results were bad: of the 79 solicitors approached by researchers, the majority gave advice which was incomplete, or in some cases incorrect. *Which?* accepted that lawyers cannot be expected to be experts in every area of law, but argued that if asked something outside their area of expertise, they should admit that and either find out the answer or refer the client to someone else.

The number of complaints made about lawyers continues to rise, according to the 2003 annual report from the Legal Services Ombudsman. Figures from the OSS seem to suggest that the problem is not spread throughout its branch of the profession. It claims 80 per cent of complaints made to the OSS concern the same 950 firms, out of the 8,500 in practice.

A survey undertaken for the Law Society in 2001 found that the public perceive lawyers as formal, expensive and predatory. It may be that they are now being accused of being predatory because of the intensive television advertising by companies who pass work on to solicitors.

One of the most common areas for complaint is costs. The Law Society's Written Practice Standard requires solicitors to give clients written information about all aspects of financing their case, including how the fee is calculated, arrangements for payment, and liability for the other side's costs. However, a 1995 report by the National Association of Citizens' Advice Bureaux (NACAB), *Barriers to Justice*, concluded that few clients actually received clear information about costs, and that this was part of the reason why fees were so often the cause of complaints. NACAB recommended that solicitors should have to agree with clients a timetable for

Figure 8.5 Advertisement by the Law Society

Source: By kind permission of The Law Society.

regular updates on costs, confirm the arrangement in writing and provide leaflets giving information about costs.

Research carried out in 2005 for the consumer group *Which?*, showed that three out of ten people did not feel they got value for money from solicitors and one-third did not feel they received a good service.

Barristers' prices have also been the subject of considerable criticism and, in particular, the fees charged by what the press have called 'super silks' – QCs whose annual earnings can top £1 million. As a result of this criticism, the House of Lords looked into the issue, and reported in October 1998 that the fees being charged in some cases were excessive. The report accused barristers' clerks of 'deliberately pitching fees at a very high level' (a conclusion which was not all that surprising since securing the best possible fee for his or her barrister is part of a clerk's job). The report was welcomed by the Legal Action Group, which said that the excessively high fees charged by some QCs were undermining public confidence in the legal system.

The legal profession suffers from a negative public image. A survey of over 1,000 consumers and 100 lawyers carried out in 2005 found that while most lawyers consider themselves forward-thinking and up-to-date, the public think quite the opposite. The consumers said the main attributes they associated with lawyers were that they were good with people but also ruthless and ambitious. The Law Society launched a pilot campaign in 2005 to try to change the public's view of the profession. The adverts portrayed solicitors as heroes to encourage the public to consult solicitors about their legal problems. Interestingly, research on the public's attitude to the campaign found that on average 78 per cent of respondents found the positioning of solicitors as heroes credible.

The future of the profession

A number of Government reports have been published in recent years pushing for changes in the professions. In 2001 the Office of Fair Trading (OFT) issued a report entitled *Competition in the Professions* (2001). This looked primarily at the restrictive practices of barristers and solicitors. These professions were criticized for imposing unjustified restrictions on competition and urged the professions to take prompt action to put an end to these practices.

Professor Zander (2001b) criticized the report, stating:

> What is deplorable about these developments is the simplistic belief that equating the work done by professional people to business will necessarily improve the position of the consumer, when the reality is that sometimes it may rather worsen it. Certainly one wants competition to ensure that professional fees are no higher than they need to be and that the professional rules did not unnecessarily inhibit efficiency. But what one looks for from the professional even more is standards, integrity and concern for the client of a higher order than that offered in the business world. To damage those even more important values in the name of value for the consumer in purely economic terms may be to throw out the baby with the bath water.

The Government accepted that the legal professions should be subject to competition law. It subsequently issued a consultation paper, *In the Public Interests?*, which questioned the competitiveness of legal services given primarily by solicitors working in solicitor firms.

The Bar Council has made some changes in the light of the OFT report, but has rejected many of its key recommendations. Direct access to the Bar has been increased (see p. 155). Employed barristers can now under take litigation work for their employer. To exercise this right they will have to undertake 12 weeks' training with a practising litigator. The Office of Fair Trading considers this latter reform inadequate, and has confirmed it will continue to investigate the ban on independent barristers litigating without the intermediary of a solicitor. The stumbling block is over whether barristers should be allowed to handle clients' money – something the Bar Council is resolutely against.

In July 2003, the Government established an independent review into the regulation of legal services. The review was chaired by Sir David Clementi and considered which regulatory framework 'would best promote competition, innovation and the public and consumer interest in an efficient, effective and independent legal sector'. The Government has accepted most of the recommendations made by Sir David Clementi and is expected to produce a White Paper on the subject shortly. This will be followed by legislation. A range of reforms are likely to be introduced in 2006 in the proposed Regulation of Legal Services Bill, each of which will be considered in turn.

Regulation of the legal professions

Sir David Clementi looked at how improvements in the provision of legal services could be made through changes to the regulation of the professions. At the moment the professions regulate themselves through their professional bodies, the Law Society and the Bar Council. Sir David Clementi considered that the present regulatory arrangements did not prioritize the public's interest. He therefore considered whether the professions should be stripped of their right to regulate themselves and whether instead an independent regulator should be established. The professional bodies would have merely represented their professions and not regulated them. Clementi commented:

> Among the suggested advantages of this approach are the clear independence of the regulator, clarity of purposes for both regulator and representative bodies and consistency of rules and standards across the profession and services. An independent regulator would be well placed to make tough, fair enforcement decisions and to facilitate lay/consumer input into the decision making processes.
>
> Disadvantages might include creating an overly bureaucratic and inefficient organisation, with consequent issues of costs and unwieldy procedure. A further argument is that it fails to recognise the significance of strong roots within the profession and their importance on the international stage. Divorcing the regulatory functions from the profession might lessen the feeling of responsibility professionals have for the high standard of their profession and their willingness to give time freely to support the system.

Ultimately, Clementi concluded that an Independent Legal Services Board should be established but this would just oversee the way the existing professional bodies regulated the professions. The Legal Service Board would have a duty to promote the public and consumer interests, and would be led by a part-time chair and a full-time chief executive, who would both be non-lawyers and the majority of the Board's members would be non-lawyers. All the members of the Board would be selected on merit by the relevant Government Minister. The professional bodies would be required to separate their regulatory and representative functions. They would still take care of the day-to-day regulation of the professions and disciplinary matters, though they could cease to be legally recognized if they failed to carry out their duties satisfactorily.

Sir David Clementi hopes that this reform would achieve consistency and transparency, while keeping costs down and leaving regulation close to those who provide the services. The proposal has been generally well received, though the Bar is unhappy that it is to lose the power to regulate itself. It is anxious that the new Board should take a light touch approach to avoid stifling innovation. It is also concerned that the Board will be clearly independent of government politics, but the planned arrangements for appointment to the Board suggest this may not be the case. The Legal Aid Practitioners Group has commented that Clementi's proposals 'may give the government too much control over the lawyers whose challenges to them are essential in a free and democratic society'.

Regulation of claims management companies

Sir David Clementi failed to address the hot topic of the regulation of claims management companies. These companies advertise heavily for clients seeking legal services. The clients are then passed on to solicitors who pay the company for the referral. There has been concern that some of these companies have behaved unscrupulously. Advertisements on television for personal injury claims have been criticized as encouraging people with no genuine cause of action to bring legal proceedings. In his report Sir David Clementi simply said 'it is for government to decide which types of legal services should be regulated, as these are public policy decisions'. The Government has announced that it intends to introduce legislation on this subject. Claims management companies will be regulated by a Claims Standard Council, which itself will be overseen by the Legal Services Board.

The Law Society relaxed its restrictions on advertising in 1986, but the law firms have been slow to take up this opportunity. Following problems with the claims management companies, solicitor firms are starting to spend more on marketing themselves.

Legal disciplinary practices

Legal disciplinary practices (LDPs) would consist of solicitors, barristers and legal executives being able to work together to provide legal services. Non-lawyers could be involved in the management and ownership of these practices. The OFT report, Sir David Clementi's report and the Government's consultation document *In the Public Interests?*, have all come out in favour of the creation of LDPs. At the moment the regulations of the legal professions stop these being created, because they include rules that, for example, ban employed solicitors from giving advice directly to the public, and require that legal service providers to the public must be owned exclusively by lawyers.

If LDPs are introduced, solicitors could be employed by such organizations as supermarkets, banks, insurance firms and accountants to provide legal services directly to the public. Non-lawyers would simply need to pass a 'fit to own' test set by the Legal Services Board before they could invest in a legal disciplinary practice. Thus, an insurer would not be able to own a personal injury firm to avoid a conflict of interest. The first people who are likely to become part of the management team of the new LDPs are people who are already senior in managing solicitor firms, such as finance directors, human resource managers and IT managers.

In support of this reform, Sir David Clementi has stated:

> The review favours a regulatory framework which permits a high degree of choice: choice both for the consumer, in where he goes for legal services, and for the lawyer, in the type of economic unit he works for.

The proposal has become known as the 'Tesco Law' because big organizations would be able to buy law firms. The Government considers that bigger organizations might provide advice more efficiently. The Law Society sees the reform as an important means of attracting external investment into law firms and therefore business expansion.

However, the Bar Council is unhappy with this reform proposal. It has pointed out that outside commercial involvement does not always mean better and cheaper services. Large, wealthy companies would be allowed to employ a few solicitors and lots of paralegals (individuals with more limited legal qualifications) to offer these services. This could be primarily a telephone service, offered from a centralized location and focused at only the better paid work. Many high street law firms could be forced to close. The Lord Chancellor has admitted that the new proposed business structures could affect the future of small high street solicitor firms.

The Bar Council has stated that the current ban on barristers forming partnerships actually promotes competition between the 10,000 barristers in private practice, and preserves their fundamental independence, which is at the core of the justice system. It is unhappy that non-lawyers could become owners and investors in legal practices. Non-lawyers would not be bound by the ethical codes of standard that apply to legal professionals. The independence of the legal practice would be put at risk. It considers that the current proposed safeguards would be inadequate to prevent improper interference by external investors with the actual business of delivering legal services. The Bar Council would like to see corporate ownership restricted to a 25 per cent stake in a law firm.

Multi-disciplinary partnerships

Multi-disciplinary partnerships would bring together lawyers with other professionals, such as accountants, surveyors and estate agents. These organizations would be able to provide legal and non-legal services, so that they could be described as a 'one-stop shop', providing a range of services to their clients.

Sir David Clementi has not recommended that these should be allowed, he was cautious about them and said the Government should only consider introducing multi-disciplinary partnerships once some experience had been gained from the introduction of Legal Disciplinary Practices. The Government has said that it is considering introducing multi-disciplinary partnerships in the future. The Bar Council is unhappy with this possibility, and has commented:

> The unraveling Enron case should remind us all of the strong public interest that resides in independent professions. Multi-disciplinary partnerships would be dominated by accountancy mega-firms, hungry for corporate consultancy work, and who would regard the independence of the Bar as a matter of secondary importance.

▌Office for Legal Complaints

Sir David Clementi recommended that an Office for Legal Complaints should be created to hear complaints against all legal professions. This reform is discussed on p. 128.

▌Fusion of the professions

The divided legal profession dates from the nineteenth century, when the Bar agreed to give all conveyancing work and all direct access to clients to the solicitors, in return for sole rights of audience in the higher courts and the sole right to become senior judges for barristers. However, since the late 1960s, there have been a series of moves towards breaking down this division. Following the Access to Justice Act 1999, solicitors automatically have rights of audience, though they still have to undertake training in order to exercise these rights. It is likely that an increasing number of solicitors will undertake this training to become solicitor-advocates.

There has been much discussion over recent years as to whether the professions will eventually fuse. When the Courts and Legal Services Act 1990 was passed, it was thought that it might be the first step in Government plans to fuse the two professions by legislation. Until 1985, the two branches had been largely left alone to divide work between themselves, and had made their own arrangements for this; the abolition of the solicitors' monopoly on conveyancing was the first major Government interference in this situation, and the Courts and Legal Services Act was obviously a much bigger step towards regulation by Government rather than the professions themselves. Even if the Government did not force fusion, it has been suggested, it could happen anyway if large numbers of solicitors take up rights of audience.

Alternatively, it has been suggested that the Bar might survive, but in a much reduced form, and there is much debate about which areas would suffer most. Barristers generally fall into two groups: those who specialize in commercial fields, such as company law, tax and patents; and those who have what is called a common law practice, which means that they deal with a fairly wide range of common legal issues, such as crime, housing and family law. Some legal experts believed that commercial lawyers would be most likely to survive, since they have a specialist knowledge that solicitors cannot provide. However, for several years now, solicitors in city firms have been becoming more specialist themselves, and if able to combine specialist knowledge with rights of audience, they would clearly be a threat to the commercial Bar. In addition, such firms offer high incomes, without the insecurity of self-employment at the Bar, and therefore they are able to attract first-rate students who once would have automatically been attracted to the more prestigious Bar. As these entrants work their way up through law firms, the Bar's traditional claim to offer the best expertise in high-level legal analysis will be difficult to sustain.

Others have suggested that common law barristers have a better chance of surviving competition from solicitors. They cater for the needs of ordinary high street solicitors, who generally have a wide-ranging practice, and spend much of their time seeing clients and gathering case information. This leaves little opportunity to swot up on the finer details of every area of law with which clients need help, so where specialist legal analysis is needed, they refer the client to a barrister with experience in the relevant area.

The Inns of Court (discussed on p. 131) set up a Working Party on the future of the Inns of Court which reported in 2000. The aim of the Working Party was to review the impact of the Access to Justice Act 1999, which has made it easier for more solicitors and employed barristers to qualify to appear in the higher courts. It recommended that membership of the Inns should be offered to solicitors entitled to appear in the higher courts, on payment of an entrance fee of £1,000. The report warns that if the Inns cease to be of relevance to the profession they run the risk of decline. The Inns are financially dependent on rents from their properties, which are priced at the very top of the market. If the Bar does decline in numbers – as many predict – they could well find themselves left with property they cannot let at rents no one wants to pay. One of the greatest threats to the future of the Bar is the fact that employed lawyers' rights of audience have increased. Much of the work that the Bar currently gets from the Crown Prosecution Service in particular is likely to disappear as the advocacy will be done 'in-house'.

When Sir David Clementi was appointed in 2003 to review the legal professions, there were fears that this might be the moment when the Government forced the two professions to fuse and abolished the Bar Council and Law Society. In fact these fears proved ill-founded.

Below we look at some of the arguments for and against fusion of the two professions.

Task 8.5

One day a week the quality papers have a section dedicated to looking at legal issues. *The Times* law section comes out every Tuesday. Job advertisements for work in the legal field are placed in this section. Select two job advertisements and consider:

- Is the advertiser looking to recruit a barrister, solicitor or legal executive?
- In what area of law would the person recruited work?
- How much would they be paid?

Task 8.6

Read the following passage and answer the questions below.

Professor Zander (2001) has criticized the report of the Office of Fair Trading on anti-competitive practices in the legal professions. He has written:

> What is deplorable about these developments is the simplistic belief that equating the work done by professional people to business will necessarily improve the position of the consumer, when the reality is that sometimes it may rather worsen it. Certainly one wants competition to ensure that professional fees are no higher than they need to be and that the professional rules do not unnecessarily inhibit efficiency. But what one looks for from the professions even more is standards, integrity and concern for the client of a higher order than that offered in the business world. To damage those even more important values in the name of value for the consumer in purely economic terms may be to throw out the baby with the bath water.

Questions

1 In this context, who is the consumer?

2 What are the benefits identified of allowing competition among legal professionals?

3 What values does Zander argue need protecting by the legal professionals more than by the business world?

4 What is meant by the saying 'to throw out the baby with the bath water'?

Arguments for fusion of the professions

Expense

With the divided profession a client often has to pay both a solicitor and a barrister, sometimes a solicitor and two barristers, and as Michael Zander (1999) puts it, 'To have one taxi meter running is less expensive than to have two or three'. However, the Bar Council prepared a report called *The Economic Case for the Bar. A Comparison of the Costs of Barristers and Solicitors* (2000). This paper claimed that it was generally more economical to employ the services of a barrister, particularly a junior, for work within his or her area of expertise than to use a solicitor. In broad terms it stated that the differences in charge-out rates make it from 25 per cent to 50 per cent cheaper to employ the services of a junior barrister than an assistant solicitor in London. A major factor is that barristers' overheads are approximately half those of solicitors. However, the paper is misleading, as without direct access to clients for barristers it is not an either/or situation. The reality is that a client does not pay for either a solicitor or a barrister, but if the client employs a barrister, the client must pay for both, along with the cost of the solicitor preparing the papers for the barrister.

Inefficiency

A two-tier system means work may be duplicated unnecessarily, and the solicitor prepares the case with little or no input from the barrister who will have to argue it in court. Barristers are often selected and instructed at the last moment – research by

Table 8.2 Moves towards fusion

Year	Moves towards fusion
1969	Following the Royal Commission on Assizes and Quarter Sessions, the Lord Chancellor was given the power to allow solicitors extended rights of audience where there were not enough barristers.
1972	A Practice Direction from the Lord Chancellor's Department stated that solicitors could appear in appeals or committals for sentencing from the magistrates' to the Crown Court, where they had appeared for that client in the magistrates' court.
1979	The Royal Commission on Legal Services unanimously rejected a proposal for the fusion of the professions.
1985	A Practice Direction permitted solicitors to appear in the Supreme Court in formal or unopposed proceedings, and when judgment is given in open court.
1986	The Law Society document, *Lawyers and the Courts: Time for Some Changes*, proposed that all lawyers should undergo the same training, work two or three years in 'general practice', and then choose to go on to train as barristers if they wished. The Bar Council rejected this idea.
1988	The Marre Committee was set up by the Bar Council and the Law Society to look at, among other things, whether any changes were needed in the structure of the profession. It largely advocated maintaining the status quo.
1990	The Courts and Legal Services Act 1990 (CLSA) contained the following provisions: ■ direct access to barristers by certain professional clients; ■ access to the higher levels of the judiciary for solicitors; ■ multi-disciplinary partnerships to be allowed, subject to the agreement of the professions' ruling bodies; ■ rights of audience in all courts should be extended to 'suitably qualified' persons, not necessarily barristers or solicitors. Applications for this right had to be made to the Lord Chancellor's Advisory Committee and then approved by the Lord Chancellor and four judges.
1992	Solicitor advocates were introduced (discussed on p. 125).
1999	Following the Lord Chancellor's report, *Modernising Justice* (1998), the Access to Justice Act 1999 was passed. This replaces the Lord Chancellor's Advisory Committee with the new Legal Services Consultative Panel, which takes over the role of regulating rights of audience. The procedure for approving changes to the rules on rights of audience is simplified and the Lord Chancellor has a new power, subject to parliamentary approval, to change rules which are unduly restrictive. This last power is designed to ensure that the legal professions themselves cannot cling on to restrictive rules and prevent reform. All barristers and solicitors now automatically acquire full rights of audience, though they are only able to exercise them by successfully completing the necessary training.
2001	The Office of Fair Trading issued its report on anti-competitive practices in the professions, which is discussed on p. 142.
2004	The Government established the Clementi Committee to review the regulation of the profession.

Bottoms and McLean in Sheffield revealed that in 96 per cent of cases where the plea was guilty, and 79 per cent where it was not guilty, clients saw their barrister for the first time on the morning of the trial. In this situation important points may be passed over or misunderstood.

Waste of talent

Prospective lawyers must decide very early on which branch of the profession they wish to enter, and if, having chosen to be a solicitor, the lawyer later discovers a talent for advocacy, he or she may be denied the chance to use it to the full.

Other countries

All common law countries have bodies of specialist advocates, and possibly need them, but no other country divides its legal profession in two as England does.

Arguments against fusion

Specialization

Two professions can each do their different jobs better than one profession doing both.

Independence

The Bar has traditionally argued that its cab-rank principle guarantees this, ensuring that no defendant, however heinous the charges, goes undefended; and that no individual should lack representation because of the wealth or power of the opponent. The fact that barristers operate independently, rather than in partnerships, also contributes. However, the Courts and Legal Services Act does provide for solicitors with advocacy certificates to operate on a cab-rank basis, which has somewhat weakened the Bar's argument. In addition, successful barristers do get round the cab-rank rule in practice.

Importance of good advocacy

Our adversarial system means that the presentation of oral evidence is important; judges have no investigative powers and must rely on the lawyers to present the case properly.

The 1979 Royal Commission suggested that fusion would lead to a fall in the quality of the advocacy, arguing that although many solicitors were competent to advocate in the magistrates' and county courts, arguing before a jury required different skills and greater expertise, and if rights were extended it was unlikely that many solicitors would get sufficient practice to develop these.

Access to the Bar

Critics of moves towards fusion argue that it may result in many leading barristers joining the large firms of commercial solicitors, so making their specialist skills less accessible to the average person. Smaller practices might generate insufficient business to justify partnership with a barrister and find it difficult to secure a barrister of equal standing to the opponent's; they would be reluctant to refer a client to a large

Table 8.3 Comparison of barristers and solicitors

	Barrister	Solicitor
Number	9,000	92,000
Professional organization	Bar Council	Law Society
Professional course	Bar Vocational Course (BVC)	Legal Practice Course (LPC)
Apprenticeship	Pupillage	Training contract

firm, for fear of losing them permanently. A major drift towards large firms could worsen the already uneven distribution of solicitors throughout the country.

The judiciary

A reduction in the number of specialist advocates might make it more difficult to make suitable appointments to the Bench; although the potential candidates would increase, they would not be as well known to those carrying out the selection process. On the other hand, this might eventually mean appointments would have to be made on a more open, regulated system, and from a wider social base.

Use of court time

Court cases are not given a fixed time, only a date; depending on the progress of previous cases they may appear at any time during a morning or afternoon session, or be held over until another day – the idea behind this is that the clients and their lawyers should wait for courts, rather than the other way round. It has been suggested that barristers are best organized for this, though there seems no reason why, within a united profession, those lawyers who specialize in court work could not organize themselves accordingly.

Legal executives

Most firms of solicitors employ legal executives, who do much of the same basic work as solicitors. Their professional body is the Institute of Legal Executives. Although technically they are under the supervision of their employers, in practice many experienced executives specialize in particular areas – such as conveyancing – and take almost sole charge of that area. From the firm's point of view, they are a cheaper option than solicitors for getting this work done, and in many cases will be more experienced in their particular area than a solicitor. However, clients are usually unaware that when they pay for a solicitor, they may be receiving the services of a legal executive.

Following the Courts and Legal Services Act 1990 and the Access to Justice Act 1999, the Institute of Legal Executives is now able to grant its members the rights to conduct litigation on the completion of suitable training. The first six legal executives qualified as advocates in the year 2000 and now have extended rights of audience in civil and matrimonial proceedings in the county court and magistrates' courts.

Legal executives are generally less well paid than solicitors. A survey carried out by the Institute of Legal Executives in 2001 found that a third of legal executives earned between £15,000 and £21,000, while 11 per cent earned over £27,000. If Legal Disciplinary Practices are introduced legal executives may be able to own one of these.

Qualifications and training

To qualify as a legal executive, a person works full-time and studies part-time. Studying will either be undertaken at a local college or through distance learning with ILEX Tutorial College. It takes on average six years to fully qualify as a legal executive, though students with a law degree benefit from exemptions from some of the examinations. Only about 600 people qualify each year as legal executives, with many people failing to complete their education. Once qualified as a legal executive, a person can undertake further part-time study to become a solicitor, unless they have unsuccessfully attempted the Legal Practice Course before becoming a legal executive.

Reading on the web

Sir David Clementi's report, *Review of the Regulatory Framework for Legal Services in England and Wales* is available at:

http://www.legal-services-review.org.uk

The consultation paper issued by the Government in 2003 on the future of QCs is available on the Department for Constitutional Affairs' website:

http://www.dca.gov.uk/consult/qcfuture/index.htm

The report of the Office of Fair Trading, *Competition in the Professions* (2001), is available on its website:

http://www.oft.gov.uk/default.htm

The Bar Council's website can be found at:

http://www.barcouncil.org.uk/index.asp

The Law Society's website can be found at:

http://www.lawsociety.org.uk/

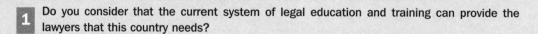

Question and answer guides

1 Do you consider that the current system of legal education and training can provide the lawyers that this country needs?

Answer guide

The first thing to note about this question is that it is not asking what the present system of legal education and training is; it wants to know how well that system performs. You do need to show that you are aware of the system, but a detailed description of it will waste time and gain few marks.

Your introduction should point out what you understand by the term lawyers – we suggest that you concentrate on barristers and solicitors in your answer, even though technically judges are also lawyers. Then you need to state what you think are the qualities this country needs in its lawyers – you might mention legal knowledge and practical skills, efficiency, cost-effectiveness, and an ability to use their skills for the benefit of all the members of society, for example.

You can then go on to outline the system of legal education and training but **keep it brief!** There is no point in writing pages of detailed description, because that is not what the question asks for. You need to point out that training for barristers and solicitors is different, and then just mention the stages for each.

The main part of your essay should be concerned with assessing whether the system provides the qualities you have mentioned in your introduction, and we suggest you consider them in turn. The following are points you might like to make:

- the need for legal knowledge and practical skills. You could mention the various criticisms of lawyers' performance, and point out that both professions are moving towards a more practicalapproach;
- the need for a cost-effective, efficient service. Here you might mention some of the disadvantages of the fact that we train two different types of lawyers to play two different roles – the criticisms of the divided profession in terms of cost and inefficiency are relevant here. You could also put forward the argument that a divided profession is wasteful of talent, especially as it divides so early on;
- the need for lawyers to be accessible to all members of the community. Here you will need to use some of the material on unmet legal need from Chapter 11, pointing out that the middle-class image of solicitors puts many people off using them, especially for problems such as social security and employment. You can then point out that the system of training contributes directly to this problem, because it is so difficult for a student without well-off parents to survive financially during training, and so the profession continues its middle-class base.

You might want to bring in the issue of whether we need professional lawyers at all, mentioning the work done by unqualified legal advisers in agencies such as the Citizens' Advice Bureaux. You could also discuss here the market control theory which suggests that professions exist not to provide the best services, but as a way of controlling competition – so the emphasis on high academic qualifications can be seen as a way of limiting entry to the market.

It would be a good idea to point out that one of the reasons why this question is so important is that legal education and training provides not only lawyers, but eventually the judiciary – point out, for example, that only when the legal profession becomes more mixed in terms of race, class and sex will the judiciary follow suit. You could discuss the reforms that the Law Society is currently considering introducing to the process of qualifying as a solicitor. These reforms aim to increase the diversity of people joining the profession.

Your conclusion should sum up whether you feel legal education does provide the lawyers we need.

2 **Are the current arrangements for complaining about the performance of a lawyer satisfactory?**

Answer guide

Your essay might start by explaining that this is an area of the legal system which has very recently undergone major changes, as a result of enormous criticism of the previous arrangements. You can then go on to explain what the complaints systems are: the Bar's Complaints Commissioner; the Consumer Complaints Service; the Legal Services Ombudsman and the Legal Services Complaints Commissioner. Do not, however, spend too much time simply describing these systems – the main part of your answer should focus on how satisfactory they are. For this part, you need to point out how the new systems are an improvement over the old ones, and then go on to point out that even so, they have themselves been the subject of criticisms. In order to give your essay a coherent structure, deal with each system in turn, discussing its good and bad points before moving on to the next.

Finally, you should look at what might be done to meet some of the criticisms and, in particular, Sir David Clementi's recommendation that a new independent Office for Legal Complaints should be introduced.

Chapter summary

The three main professions in the legal field are:

- solicitors
- barristers, and
- legal executives.

Solicitors

- *Work*: traditionally solicitors focused primarily on paperwork but they are now doing more advocacy.
- *Qualifications and training*: usually a university degree, followed by a conversion course if this was not in law. Then they take the one-year Legal Practice Course and a two-year training contract.
- *Complaints*: can be made to the Consumer Complaints Bureau, the Legal Services Ombudsman and the courts.

Barristers

- *Work*: traditionally advocacy, but they also do some paperwork.
- *Qualifications and training*: usually a university degree, followed by a conversion course if this is not in law. Then the one-year Bar Vocational Course and one-year pupillage.
- *Complaints*: can be made to the Complaints Commissioner, the Legal Services Ombudsman and the courts.

Background of barristers and solicitors

Barristers and solicitors have traditionally come from a very narrow social background, in terms of class, race and sex, and disabled people are under-represented. They now come from a wider range of backgrounds, but there is a problem with promotion and retention of women and people from minority groups.

Increasing diversity through educational reforms

The Law Society is considering introducing a radical reform to the way people qualify as solicitors. The emphasis would be on work-based training along with an assessment by the Law Society of their knowledge and skills.

The future of the profession

A number of Government reports have been published in recent years pushing for changes in the professions. In July 2003, the Government established an independent review into the regulation of legal services, chaired by Sir David Clementi. A range of reforms is likely to be introduced in the near future, each of which will be considered in turn.

Regulation of the legal professions

Sir David Clementi concluded that an Independent Legal Services Board should be established but this would just oversee the way the existing professional bodies regulated the professions.

Regulation of claims management companies

There has been concern that some claims management companies have behaved unscrupulously. The Government has announced that it intends to introduce legislation to improve the regulation of these companies.

Legal disciplinary practices

Legal disciplinary practices (LDPs) would consist of solicitors, barristers and legal executives being able to work together to provide legal services. Non-lawyers could be involved in the management and ownership of these practices. If LDPs are introduced, solicitors could be employed by such organizations as supermarkets, banks, insurance firms and accountants to provide legal services directly to the public. The proposal has become known as the 'Tesco Law' because big organizations would be able to buy law firms.

Multi-disciplinary partnerships

Multi-disciplinary partnerships would bring together lawyers with other professionals, such as accountants, surveyors and estate agents. These organizations would be able to provide legal and non-legal services, so that they could be described as a 'one-stop shop', providing a range of services to their clients. Sir David Clementi has not recommended that these should be allowed for the time being.

Office for Legal Complaints

Sir David Clementi recommended that an Office for Legal Complaints should be created to hear complaints against all legal professions.

Moves towards fusion?

Since the late 1960s there has been a series of moves towards breaking down the division between barristers and solicitors.

Chapter 9

The jury system

Introduction

The jury system was imported to Britain after the Norman conquest. Today the jury is considered a fundamental part of the English legal system though, as we shall see, only a minority of cases are tried by a jury. The main Act that now governs jury trial is the Juries Act 1974.

Today, the jury has attained symbolic importance, so that Lord Devlin wrote in 1956:

> Trial by jury is more than an instrument of justice and more than one wheel of the constitution; it is the lamp that shows that freedom lives.

This statement led to a classic rebuttal by the academic Penny Darbyshire (1991) who wrote an article entitled 'The Lamp that shows that Freedom Lives – Is it worth the Candle?' She argued in that article that

juries are not random, not representative, but anti-democratic, irrational and haphazard legislators, whose erratic and secret decisions run counter to the rule of law.

The function of the jury

The jury has to weigh up the evidence and decide what are the true facts of the case – in other words, what actually happened. The judge directs the jurors as to what is the relevant law, and the jurors then have to apply the law to the facts that they have found and thereby reach a verdict. If it is a criminal case and the jury has given a verdict of guilty, the judge will then decide on the appropriate sentence. In civil cases the jury decides on how much money should be awarded in damages.

When are juries used?

Criminal cases

Though juries are symbolically important in the criminal justice system, they actually only operate in a minority of cases and their role is constantly being reduced to save money. Criminal offences are classified into three groups: summary only offences, which are tried in the magistrates' courts; indictable offences, which are tried in the Crown Court; and either way offences, which, as the name suggests, may be tried in either the magistrates' courts or the Crown Court. The majority of criminal offences are summary only, and because these are, in general, the least serious offences, they are also the ones most commonly committed (most road traffic offences, for example, are summary only). As a result, 95 per cent of criminal cases are heard in the magistrates' courts, where juries have no role (this proportion also includes cases involving either way offences where the defendant chooses to be tried by magistrates). Juries only decide cases heard in the Crown Court. Even among the 5 per cent of cases heard there, in a high proportion of these the defendant will plead guilty, which means there is no need for a jury and, on top of that, there are cases where the judge directs the jury that the law demands that they acquit the defendant, so that the jury effectively makes no decision here either. The result is that juries actually decide only around 1 per cent of criminal cases.

On the other hand, it is important to realize that even this 1 per cent amounts to 30,000 trials, and that these are usually the most serious ones to come before the courts – though here too the picture can be misleading, since some serious offences, such as assaulting a police officer or drink-driving, are dealt with only by magistrates, while even the most trivial theft can be tried in the Crown Court if the defendant wishes.

Despite its historical role in the English legal system, and the almost sacred place it occupies in the public imagination, juries have come under increasing attack in recent years. Successive governments have attempted to reduce their use in criminal cases in order to save money. The Criminal Law Act 1977 removed the right to jury trial in a significant number of offences, by making most driving offences and relatively minor criminal damage cases summary only. Since 1977, more and more offences have been removed from the realm of jury trial by being made summary only. The sentencing powers of magistrates have been increased by the Criminal Justice Act 2003. Prior to that Act, magistrates could only sentence a person to six months' imprisonment for a single offence. Following the passing of the 2003 Act, magistrates can sentence offenders to up to 12 months' imprisonment for a single offence, and this could be increased further to 18 months by delegated legislation. The Government hopes that by increasing the magistrates' sentencing powers, more cases will be tried in the magistrates' court rather than being referred up to the Crown Court to be tried by an expensive jury.

The Criminal Justice Act 2003 also allows trial by judge alone in the Crown Court in two situations:

■ where a serious risk of jury tampering exists; or
■ where the case involves complex or lengthy financial and commercial arrangements.

In this second scenario, trial by judge alone would be possible where the trial would be so burdensome upon a jury that it is necessary in the interests of justice for the case to be heard without a jury. Alternatively, it would be possible where the trial would be likely to place an excessive burden on the life of a typical juror. The

Figure 9.1 The Old Bailey, the Central Criminal Court in London
Source: © EMPICS.

Government agreed with the opposition not to implement this part of the legislation while alternative proposals for specialist juries and judges sitting in panels were investigated. The relevant legislative provisions can only be brought into force by a parliamentary order approving its implementation, which will require debates and a vote in both Houses of Parliament was initiated at the end of 2005 but, following strong opposition, it remains unclear if and when this provision will be brought into force.

Civil cases

In the past most civil cases were tried by juries, but now less than one per cent of civil cases are tried by a jury. Today the Supreme Court Act 1981 gives a qualified right to jury trial of civil cases in four types of case:

■ libel and slander
■ malicious prosecution
■ false imprisonment
■ fraud.

In these cases jury trial is to be granted, unless the court is of the opinion that the trial requires any prolonged examination of documents or accounts, or any scientific or local investigation which cannot conveniently be made with a jury. This right is exercised most frequently in defamation actions, although its use may be more limited now that the Defamation Act 1996 has introduced a new summary procedure for claims of less than £10,000, which can be heard by a judge alone.

In all other cases the right to jury trial is at the discretion of the court.

Qualification for jury service

Before 1972, only those who owned a home which was over a prescribed rateable value were eligible for jury service. The Morris Committee in 1965 estimated that 78 per cent of the names on the electoral register did not qualify for jury service under this criteria, and 95 per cent of women were ineligible. This was either because they lived in rented accommodation or because they were the wife or other relative of the person in whose name the property was held. The Committee recommended that the right to do jury service should correspond with the right to vote. This reform was introduced in 1972. Despite this reform, there continued to be a problem that in practice juries were not truly representative of the society which they served. While it was understandable that some people with criminal convictions were disqualified from jury service, a wide range of other people were either excluded or excused from jury service.

Ineligibility

Five categories of people were ineligible for jury service:

1 The judiciary.
2 Those concerned with the administration of justice, such as barristers, solicitors, prison officers, police officers and even secretaries working for the Crown Prosecution Service.
3 The clergy. The Runciman Commission which reported in 1993 saw no logical reason for the existence of this exception and recommended its abolition.
4 People with mental ill-health.
5 People on bail in criminal proceedings. This disqualification was introduced by s. 40 of the Criminal Justice and Public Order Act 1994 following a recommendation made by the Runciman Commission.

Excusal as of right

People who had duties that were considered more important than jury service could choose whether or not they wished to serve. These included MPs, members of the House of Lords, members of the armed forces and doctors and nurses. People over 65 could also be excused as of right.

Discretionary excusal

Others could be excused at the discretion of the judge if they could show good reason, such as childcare problems, holidays booked which would clash with the jury service, personal involvement with the facts of the case, or conscientious objection. Where appropriate, jury service could be deferred rather than excused completely.

Reform of qualification rules

The basis of the use of juries in serious criminal cases is that the 12 people are randomly selected, and should therefore comprise a representative sample of the population as a whole. This ideal came closer with the abolition of the property qualification and with the use of computers for the random selection process. Despite this, research carried out for the Home Office (*Jury Excusal and Deferral* (2000)) found that each year only two-thirds of the people summoned for jury service made themselves available to do it. About 15 per cent of summoned jurors failed to attend court on the day or had their summonses returned as 'undelivered'. Because enforcement has been poor, it became widely known that a jury summons could be ignored with impunity.

In his *Review of the Criminal Courts* (2001), Sir Robin Auld argued that the many exclusions and excusals from jury service deprived juries of the experience and skills of a wide range of professional and successful people. Their absence created the impression that jury service was only for those not important or clever enough to get out of it. He was keen to make juries more representative of the general population. He wanted jury service to become a compulsory public duty for all, to stop middle-class professionals opting out. He proposed that everyone should be eligible for jury service, save for the mentally ill.

The Government accepted these recommendations. The Criminal Justice Act 2003, s. 321 and Schedule 33 amended the Juries Act 1974. This Act now provides that potential jury members must be:

■ aged 18 to 70;
■ on the electoral register;
■ resident in the UK, Channel Islands or Isle of Man for at least five years since the age of 13;
■ not a mentally disordered person; and not disqualified from jury service.

Most of the grounds for ineligibility and excusal have been removed. Only military personnel can be excused from jury service and only the mentally ill are ineligible for jury service. The rules disqualifying people with certain criminal convictions from jury service remain. As a result, in future juries should become much more representative of society.

Sir Robin Auld also recommended that potential jurors should no longer only be selected from the electoral register. Many people are not registered to vote in elections, even though they are entitled to do so. To reach as many people as possible he therefore proposed that a range of publicly maintained lists and directories should be used. The Government has not adopted this recommendation.

? **Quick quiz 9.1**

1 Does the jury decide the sentence of an offender?

2 For which civil cases is there a qualified right to a trial by jury?

3 What age group can sit on a jury?

4 Which categories of people were disqualified from sitting on a jury before the Criminal Justice Act 2003?

Summoning the jury

Every year almost half a million people are summoned to do jury service. In 2001 a Central Juror Summoning Bureau was established to administer the juror-summoning process for the whole of the country. Computers are used to produce a random list of potential jurors from the electoral register. Summons are sent out (with a form to return confirming that the person does not fall into any of the disqualified or ineligible groups), and from the resulting list the jury panel is produced. This is made public for both sides in forthcoming cases to inspect, though only names and addresses are shown. It is at this stage that jury vetting may take place (see below). Jurors also receive a set of notes which explain a little of the procedure of the jury service and the functions of the juror.

Jury service is compulsory and failure to attend on the specified date, or unfitness for service through drink or drugs, is contempt of court and can result in a fine.

The jury for a particular case is chosen by random ballot in open court – the clerk has each panel member's name on a card, the cards are shuffled and the first 12 names called out. Unless there are any challenges (see p. 162), these 12 people will be sworn in. In a criminal case there are usually 12 jurors and there must never be fewer than nine. In civil cases in the county court there are eight jurors.

Jury vetting

Jury vetting consists of checking that potential jurors do not hold 'extremist' views which some feel would make them unsuitable for hearing a case. It is done by checking police, Special Branch and security service records.

Attorney-General's guidelines exist stating when jurors should be vetted. These state that vetting might be necessary in certain special cases, such as terrorism. Authorization from the Attorney-General is required, who will be acting on the advice of the Director of Public Prosecutions. Checking whether a person has a criminal record is permissible in a much wider range of cases without special permission.

The limits on vetting for previous convictions were, however, stressed again in **R v Obellim and Others** (1996). The case concerned a criminal trial in which the judge had received a written question from the jury, which displayed a lot of knowledge about police powers and led him to suspect that one of the jurors might have such previous convictions as should have disqualified him or her. The judge ordered a security check on the jury, without telling the defence counsel, who only discovered the check had taken place when the jury complained about it after delivering its verdict.

The defendant, who was convicted, appealed on the ground that the check on jury members might have prejudiced them. The Court of Appeal agreed, and quashed the conviction, stating that it was questionable whether the check should have been ordered at all on such a ground, and it certainly should not have been carried out without informing defence counsel.

Vetting for any purpose remains controversial. Supporters claim that it can promote impartiality by excluding those whose views might bias the other members of the jury, and make them put pressure on others, as well as protecting national security and preventing disqualified persons from serving. Opponents say it infringes the individual's right to privacy, and gives the prosecution an unfair advantage, since it is too expensive for most defendants to undertake, and they do not have access to the same sources of information as the prosecution. Only on very rare occasions has the defence been granted legal aid to make its inquiries into the panel.

The whole process is still not sanctioned by legislation and, despite the publication of the Attorney-General's guidelines, it is impossible to know whether they are being followed – 60 potential jurors were vetted by MI5 for the Clive Ponting case (see p. 169), despite the fact that there was no apparent threat to national security.

Challenges

As members of the jury panel are called, and before they are sworn in, they may be challenged in one of two ways:

Challenge for cause. Either side may challenge for cause, on the grounds of privilege of peerage, disqualification, ineligibility or assumed bias. Jurors cannot be questioned before being challenged to ascertain whether there are grounds for a challenge. A successful challenge for cause is therefore only likely to succeed if the juror is personally known, or if jury vetting has been undertaken. If a challenge for cause is made, it is tried by the trial judge.

Stand by. Only the prosecution may ask jurors to stand by for the Crown. Although there are specified grounds for this, in practice no reason need be given, and this is generally how the information supplied by jury vetting is used.

Abolition of the peremptory challenge

Until 1988 there was a third type of challenge, peremptory challenge, available only to the defence. This meant that the defence could challenge up to three jurors without showing cause, which was equivalent to the prosecution's power to 'stand by' a juror. This was abolished, amid much opposition, on the recommendation of the Roskill Committee on fraud trials, on the grounds that it interfered with the random selection process and allowed defence lawyers to 'pack' the jury with those they thought were likely to be sympathetic. This was felt to be a particular problem when there were several defendants as (theoretically) they could combine their rights to peremptory challenge.

This limited process of challenging the jury should be contrasted with the system in the USA where it can take days to empanel a jury, particularly where the case has received a lot of pre-trial media coverage. Potential jury members can be asked a wide range of questions about their attitudes to the issues raised by a case, and a great deal of money may be spent employing special consultants who claim to be able to judge which way people are likely to vote, based on their age, sex, politics, religion and other personal information.

In a high-profile 1998 case, **R** *v* **Andrews**, the defence wanted to use the American approach to establish whether members of the jury panel were likely to be biased against the defendant. She was accused of murdering her boyfriend, and the case had received an enormous amount of publicity since Ms Andrew had initially told police that her boyfriend was killed by an unknown assailant in a 'road rage' incident, sparking off a media hunt for the killer. Her lawyers wanted to issue questionnaires to the jury panel to check whether any of them showed a prejudice against her. The trial judge refused the request and when Ms Andrews was convicted, she appealed, arguing that the failure to allow questioning of the jury meant her conviction was unsafe. The argument was rejected by the Court of Appeal, which stated that questioning of the jury panel, whether orally or by written questionnaire, should be avoided in all but the most exceptional cases, such as where potential jurors might have a direct or indirect connection to the facts of the trial (for example, if they were related to someone involved in the trial, or had lost money as a result of the defendant's actions).

Figure 9.2 **Tracie Andrews, the defendant in** R *v* Andrews **(1998), arrives at the High Court in London to find out if her Court of Appeal bid for freedom has succeeded, after being jailed for life for murdering her fiancé, Lee Harvey, who she had claimed was killed by a mystery motorist in a road rage attack**

Source: © EMPICS.

Discharge of the jury

The judge may discharge any juror, or even the whole jury, to prevent scandal or the perversion of justice. The courts have had to consider whether a jury needs to be discharged where there is a risk of racism. In **Gregory** *v* **United Kingdom** (1997) Gregory was a black defendant accused of robbery. During his trial the jury had handed the judge a note asking that one juror be excused because of racial bias. The judge did not excuse the juror, but instead issued a strong direction to the jury to decide the case on the evidence alone. Gregory was convicted on a majority verdict and brought a case before the European Court of Human Rights, claiming that the judge should have discharged the whole jury, and that failure to do so infringed his right to a fair trial under the European Convention on Human Rights. The European Court of Human Rights, however, held that in the circumstances, issuing a clear and carefully worded warning to the jury was sufficient to ensure a fair trial.

This case was distinguished in **Sander** *v* **United Kingdom** (2000). The applicant was an Asian man, who had been tried in the Crown Court with another Asian man on a charge of conspiracy to defraud. During the trial, a juror passed a note to the judge alleging that certain of his fellow jurors had made racist remarks and jokes. The juror who made the complaint was initially segregated from the rest of the jury while the court considered representations made by the lawyers. The judge then asked the complainant to rejoin the other jurors and instructed them to consider whether they were able to put aside any prejudices which they had and to try the case solely on the evidence. All of the jurors signed a letter to the judge stating:

> We utterly refute the allegation of possible racial bias. We are deeply offended by the allegation. We assure the Court that we intend to reach a verdict solely according to the evidence and without racial bias.

One juror, who believed that the allegations were directed at him, wrote a separate letter to confirm that he was not racially biased. The judge concluded that there was no real risk of bias and allowed the trial to continue with the same jury, and rejected the defence request to discharge the jury. At first instance, the applicant was convicted and his co-accused was acquitted.

The applicant appealed against his conviction up to the European Court of Human Rights. He complained that he had been denied the right to a fair trial before an impartial court, guaranteed by Art. 6(1) of the European Convention on Human Rights. The European Court held that it was not possible to state whether some of the jurors were actually biased as the matter had not been investigated. The fact that at least one juror had made comments that could be construed as jokes about Asians was not evidence of actual bias. But it was also important for the jurors to be viewed as objectively impartial, in other words, that not only were they as a matter of fact impartial, but also they would appear to an observer to be impartial. There was doubt as to the credibility of the letter which denied the allegations because the juror who had made the allegations also signed the letter. The identity of the juror who had made the allegations was revealed by his separation from the other jurors and this must have compromised his position with his fellow jurors, and inhibited him in the further discussion of the case. An admonition by a judge, 'however clear, detailed and forceful would not change racist views overnight'. Even though it was not established that the jurors had such views, the judge's direction could not dispel the reasonable impression and fear of a lack of impartiality based on the original note. The fact that the jury had acquitted one Asian defendant was irrelevant since the case against him was much weaker. The judge should have discharged the jury. Thus, the court concluded that the appellant had not received a fair trial and Art. 6(1) had been breached.

The court distinguished its earlier decision of **Gregory** v **United Kingdom** (1997), mainly on the ground that in that case there was no admission by a juror that he had made racist comments, nor an indication as to which juror had made the complaint and the complaint was vague and imprecise.

Professor Zander (2000) has criticized the decision of **Sander** v **United Kingdom**. He controversially argues that:

> The decision in **Sander** is disturbing since it suggests that the Strasbourg court does not sufficiently understand or value the jury system. The great strength of the system is that generally the verdict of twelve ordinary citizens is felt to be understandable in terms either of the evidence or of the jury's sense of equity. This is despite the fact that most jurors probably have prejudices, which will often include racial prejudice. To pretend otherwise is naïve. But the process of deliberation in the jury room tends to neutralise individual prejudices. The possibility of a majority verdict provides an additional safeguard against the effect of prejudice but in fact in the great majority of cases the verdict is unanimous.

Table 9.1 How jury service was avoided

Disqualification	People who had been sentenced to prison or a young offenders' institute or its equivalent could be disqualified from jury service.
Ineligibility	Five categories of people were ineligible for jury service, including the judiciary and the mentally ill.
Excusal as of right	Certain professionals and those over 65 could choose whether or not to do jury service.
Discretionary excusal	People could be excused from doing jury service if they showed good reason.
Discharge	People could be discharged from jury service if there was doubt over their capacity to do jury service. Jurors could also be discharged to prevent scandal or the perversion of justice.
Challenge for cause	A potential juror could be prevented from sitting on a jury on the grounds of privilege of peerage, disqualification, ineligibility or assumed bias.
Stand by	The prosecution could request that a potential juror was not allowed to sit on the jury without having to give reasons for this.

The secrecy of the jury

Once they retire to consider their verdict, jurors are not allowed to communicate with anyone other than the judge and an assigned court official, until after the verdict is delivered. Afterwards they are forbidden by s. 8 of the Contempt of Court Act 1981 from revealing anything that was said or done during their deliberations. Breach of this section amounts to a criminal offence.

The arguments in favour of secrecy have been stated by McHugh J as:

■ it ensures freedom of discussion in the jury room;
■ it protects jurors from outside influences, and from harassment;
■ if the public knew how juries reached a verdict, they might respect the decision less;
■ without secrecy, citizens would be reluctant to serve as jurors;
■ it ensures the finality of the verdict;
■ it enables jurors to bring in unpopular verdicts;
■ it prevents unreliable disclosures by jurors and misunderstanding of verdicts.

The arguments against secrecy and in favour of disclosure are that this reform would:

■ make juries more accountable;
■ make it easier to enquire into the reliability of convictions and rectify injustices;
■ show where reform is required;
■ educate the public;
■ ensure each juror's freedom of expression.

Research into the work of juries has always been made difficult by the requirement for secrecy. The Runciman Commission (1993) recommended that the 1981 Act should be amended so that valid research can be carried out into the way juries reach their verdicts. The *Review of the Criminal Courts* (2001), however, took the opposite view.

The House of Lords' case of **R** *v* **Mirza** (2004) drew attention to the problem of jury secrecy where, after the trial, a juror writes to the court expressing their concern with how the verdict was reached. There was a suggestion in one of the cases being considered in **R** *v* **Mirza** that some of the jurors were racist. Now that a majority verdict is possible, a letter after verdict is often the only option open to a juror where a verdict has been reached that they did not agree with. The House of Lords took the view that, due to the secrecy of the jury, it could not investigate what had happened in the jury room. However, the trial court could make such an inquiry before a verdict was reached, and if an appeal was launched, the Court of Appeal could ask a judge to provide a report about the trial. A Practice Direction has now been issued stating that trial judges should ensure that the jury is alerted to the need to bring any concerns about fellow jurors to the attention of the judge immediately, and not to wait until the case is concluded. The point should be made that, unless that is done while the case is continuing, it may be impossible to put matters right.

The Government has now issued a consultation paper, *Jury Research and Impropriety* (2005) which looks at when someone should be allowed to break the secrecy of the jury deliberations. It is considering allowing academics to watch jury deliberations for the purpose of carrying out research into how jury's work in practice, with a view to improving the criminal process if this would help juries do their job. Researchers would have to follow a strict set of conditions and follow a code of conduct agreed with the Lord Chief Justice.

In response to this consultation paper, the civil liberties group, Justice, has stated that it is in favour of allowing properly regulated jury research, but would not allow juries to be taped and would not allow researchers access to the jury room. Michael Zander is also opposed to allowing research which involved 'bugging' the jury room as he fears it would undermine the public's confidence in the jury system and therefore could ultimately lead to its abolition.

The verdict

Ideally juries should produce a unanimous verdict, but in 1967 majority verdicts were introduced of ten to two (or nine to one if the jury has been reduced during the trial). This is now provided for in the Juries Act 1974. When the jury withdraws to consider its verdict, it must be told by the judge to reach a unanimous verdict. If, however, the jury has failed to reach a unanimous verdict after what the judge considers a reasonable period of deliberation, given the complexity of the case (not less than two hours), the judge can direct that it may reach a majority verdict. The foreman of the jury must state in open court the numbers of the jurors agreeing and disagreeing with the verdict.

Arguments in favour of the jury system

Public participation

Juries allow the ordinary citizen to take part in the administration of justice, so that verdicts are seen to be those of society rather than of the judicial system, and satisfy the constitutional tradition of judgment by one's peers. Lord Denning described jury service as giving 'ordinary folk their finest lesson in citizenship'.

The Home Office has carried out research into the experience of being a juror: Matthews, Hancock and Briggs, *Jurors' Perceptions, Understanding, Confidence and Satisfaction in the Jury System: a study in six courts* (2004). The research questioned 361 jurors about their jury service. More than half (55 per cent) said they would be happy to do it again, 19 per cent said they would not mind doing jury service again, but 25 per cent said they would never want to be a juror again. About two-thirds felt that their experience had boosted their opinion of the jury system and they were impressed by the professionalism and helpfulness of the court staff and the performance of the judge. A minority were unhappy with the delays in the system, the trivial nature of some cases and the standard of facilities. Thirty-six per cent of jurors felt intimidated or very uncomfortable in the courtroom, primarily because they were worried about meeting defendants or their family members coming out of court or in the street.

Certainty

The jury adds certainty to the law, since it gives a general verdict which cannot give rise to misinterpretation. In a criminal case the jury simply states that the accused is guilty or not guilty, and gives no reasons. Consequently, the decision is not open to dispute.

Ability to judge according to conscience

A major milestone in the history of the jury was in **Bushell's Case** (1670). Before this, judges would try to bully juries into convicting the defendant, particularly where the crime had political overtones, but in **Bushell's Case** it was established that the jury's members were the sole judges of fact, with the right to give a verdict according to their conscience, and could not be penalized for taking a view of the facts opposed to that of the judge. The importance of this power now is that juries may acquit a defendant, even when the law demands a guilty verdict.

Because juries have the ultimate right to find defendants innocent or guilty, they have been seen as a vital protection against oppressive or politically motivated prosecutions, and as a kind of safety valve for those cases where the law demands a guilty verdict, but genuine justice does not. For example, in the early nineteenth century, all felonies (a classification of crimes used at the time, marking out those considered most serious) were in theory punishable by death. Theft of goods or money above the value of a shilling was a felony, but juries were frequently reluctant to allow the death penalty to be imposed in what seemed to them trivial cases, so they would often find that the defendant was guilty, but the property stolen was worth less than a shilling.

There are several well-known recent cases of juries using their right to find according to their consciences, often concerning issues of political and moral controversy, such as **R v Kronlid** (1996). The defendants were three women who broke into a British Aerospace factory and caused damage costing over £1.5 million to a Hawk fighter plane. The women admitted doing this – they had left a video explaining their actions in the plane's cockpit – but claimed that they had a defence under s. 3 of the Criminal Law Act 1967, which provides that it is lawful to commit a crime in order to prevent another (usually more serious) crime being committed, and that this may involve using 'such force as is reasonable in all the circumstances'.

The defendants pointed out that the plane was part of a consignment due to be sold to the Government of Indonesia, which was involved in oppressive measures against the population of East Timor, a region forcibly annexed by Indonesia in 1975. They further explained that Amnesty International had estimated that the Indonesians had killed at least a third of the population of East Timor, and that the jet was likely to be used in a genocidal attack against the survivors. Genocide is a crime and therefore, they argued, their criminal damage was done in order to prevent a crime. However, the prosecution gave evidence that the Indonesian Government had given assurances that the planes would not be used against the East Timorese, and the British Government had accepted this and granted an export licence. Acquitting the women was therefore a criticism of the British Government's position on the issue, as well as the actions of the Indonesian Government, and in the face of the clear evidence that they had caused the damage, they were widely expected to be convicted. The jury found them all not guilty.

Other cases have involved what were seen to be oppressive prosecutions in cases involving the Government, such as **R** *v* **Ponting** (1985), where the defendant, a civil servant, was prosecuted for breaking the Official Secrets Act after passing confidential information to a journalist – even though doing so exposed a matter of public interest, namely the fact that the then Government had lied to Parliament. Ponting was acquitted.

Quick quiz 9.2

1 Explain the case of **Gregory** *v* **United Kingdom** (1997).

2 Give three arguments in favour of the secrecy of the jury and three arguments against.

3 What is the minimum number of jurors who must vote in favour of a conviction or an acquittal in order to reach a verdict?

4 Why is **Bushell's Case** considered to be a major milestone in the history of the jury?

Task 9.3

The Judicial Studies Board has issued a specimen direction which judges can give to a jury to explain their different roles during a jury trial. This specimen direction is as follows:

'Our functions in this trial have been and remain quite different. Throughout this trial the law has been my area of responsibility, and I must now give you directions as to the law which applies in this case. When I do so, you must accept those directions and follow them.

I must also remind you of the prominent features of the evidence. However, it has always been your responsibility to judge the evidence and decide all the relevant facts of this case, and when you come to consider your verdict you, and you alone, must do that.

You do not have to decide every point which has been raised; only such matters as will enable you to say whether the charge laid against the defendant has been proved. You will do that by having regard to the whole of the evidence and forming your own judgement about the witnesses, and which evidence is reliabe and which is not.

The facts of this case are your responsibility. You will wish to take account of the arguments in the speeches you have heard, but you are not bound to accept them. Equally, if in the course of my review of the evidence, I appear to express any views concerning the facts, or emphasise a particular aspect of the evidence, do not adopt those views unless you agree with them; and if I do not mention something which you think is important, you should have regard to it, and give it such weight as you think fit. When it comes to the facts of this case, it is your judgement alone that counts.'

Questions

1 Does the jury have to follow the judge's directions on the law?

2 Does the jury have to follow the judge's view of the facts?

Criticisms of the jury system

Lack of competence

Lord Denning argued in *What Next in the Law?* (1982) that the selection of jurors is too wide, resulting in jurors that are not competent to perform their task. Praising the 'Golden Age' of jury service when only 'responsible heads of household from a select band of the middle classes' were eligible to serve, he claimed that the 1972 changes have led to jurors being summoned who are not sufficiently intelligent or educated to perform their task properly. Denning suggested that jurors should be selected in much the same way as magistrates are, with interviews and references required. This throws up several obvious problems: a more complicated selection process would be more time-consuming and costly; finding sufficient people willing to take part might prove difficult; and a jury that is intelligent and educated can still be biased, and may be more likely to be so if drawn from a narrow social group.

Particular concern has been expressed about the average jury's understanding of complex fraud cases. The Roskill Committee concluded that trial by random jury was not a satisfactory way of achieving justice in such cases, with many jurors 'out of their depth'. However, the Roskill Committee was unable to find accurate evidence of a higher proportion of acquittals in complex fraud cases than in any other kind – many of their conclusions were based on research by Baldwin and McConville (1979), yet none of the questionable acquittals reported there was in a complex fraud case.

The 'perverse verdicts' problem

It is a matter of fact that juries acquit proportionately more defendants than magistrates do; research from the Home Office Planning Unit suggests that an acquittal is approximately twice as likely in a jury trial. Many critics of the jury system argue that this is a major failing on the part of juries, arising either from their inability to perform their role properly, as discussed above, or from their sympathy with defendants, or both.

This is a difficult area to research, as the Contempt of Court Act 1981 prohibits asking jurors about the basis on which they reached their decision. What research there is generally involves comparing actual jury decisions with those reached by legal professionals, or by shadow juries, who sit in on the case and reach their own decision just as the official jurors are asked to do.

A piece of research commissioned by the Roskill Committee on fraud trials concluded that jurors who found difficulty in comprehending the complex issues involved in fraud prosecution were more likely to acquit. They suggested that the jurors characterized their own confusions as a form of 'reasonable doubt' leading them to a decision to acquit.

A study by McCabe and Purves, *The Jury at Work* (1972), looked at 173 acquittals, and concluded that 15 (9 per cent) defied the evidence, the rest being attributable to weakness of the prosecution case or failure of their witnesses, or the credibility of the accused's explanation. McCabe and Purves viewed the proportion of apparently perverse verdicts as quite small and, from their observations of shadow juries, concluded that jurors did work methodically and rationally through the evidence, and tried to put aside their own prejudices.

However, Baldwin and McConville's 1979 study (*Jury Trials*) examined 500 cases, both convictions and acquittals, and found that up to 25 per cent of acquittals were questionable (as well as 5 per cent of convictions), and concluded that, given the serious nature of the cases concerned, this was a problem. They describe trial by jury as 'an arbitrary and unpredictable business'.

Zander (1988) points out that the high rate of acquittals must be seen in the light of the high number of guilty pleas in the Crown Court. It must also be noted that many acquittals are directed or ordered by the judge: according to evidence from the Lord Chancellor's Department to the Runciman Commission, in 1990–1 40 per cent of all acquittals were ordered by the judge because the prosecution offered no evidence at the start of the trial. A further 16 per cent of the acquittals were directed by the judge after the prosecution had made its case as there was insufficient evidence to leave to the jury. Thus the jury was only responsible for 41 per cent of the acquittals, which was merely 7 per cent of all cases in the Crown Court. Bearing in mind the pressures on defendants to plead guilty, it is not surprising that those who resist tend to be those with the strongest cases – and, of course, the standard of proof required is very high. Nor is it beyond the bounds of possibility that part of the difference in conviction rates between magistrates and juries is due to magistrates convicting the innocent rather than juries acquitting the guilty.

In a high-profile case the Court of Appeal overturned a jury decision in civil proceedings on the basis that the jury decision had been perverse. In **Grobbelaar *v* News Group Newspapers Ltd** (2001) a jury had awarded the professional goalkeeper, Bruce Grobbelaar, £85,000 on the basis that he had been defamed in *The Sun* newspaper. *The Sun* had published a story claiming that Grobbelaar had received cash to fix football matches. It had obtained secretly taped videos of Grobbelaar where he apparently admitted receiving money in the past to lose matches, and appeared to accept cash following a proposal to fix matches in the future. A criminal prosecution of Grobbelaar had failed and he sued in the civil courts for defamation. Grobbelaar accepted that he had made the confessions and accepted cash, but claimed that he had done so as a trick in order to bring the other person to justice. The jury accepted his claim and awarded damages. *The Sun*'s appeal was allowed on the basis that the jury's decision had been perverse. The Court of Appeal found Grobbelaar's story 'incredible'. The House of Lords allowed a further appeal. It considered it wrong to overturn the jury's verdict as perverse, as the verdict could have been given an alternative explanation.

▌Bias

Jurors may be biased for or against certain groups – for example, they may favour attractive members of the opposite sex, or be prejudiced against the police.

Bias appears to be a particular problem in libel cases, where juries prejudiced against newspapers award huge damages, apparently using them punitively rather than as compensation for the victim. Examples include the £500,000 awarded to Jeffrey Archer in 1987, and the £300,000 to Koo Stark a year later, as well as **Sutcliffe v Pressdram Ltd** (1990), in which *Private Eye* was ordered to pay £600,000 to the wife of the Yorkshire Ripper. In the latter case Lord Donaldson described the award as irrational, and suggested that judges should give more guidance on the amounts to be awarded – not by referring to previous cases or specific amounts, but by asking juries to think about the real value of money (such as what income the capital would produce, or what could be bought with it). The Courts and Legal Services Act 1990 now allows the Court of Appeal to reduce damages considered excessive.

For a discussion of cases concerned with potentially racist jurors, see p. 164.

Representation of ethnic minorities

Black defendants have no right to have black people sitting on the jury. In **R v Bansal** (1985) the case involved an Anti-National Front demonstration and the trial judge ordered that the jury should be drawn from an area with a large Asian population. However, this approach was rejected as wrong in **R v Ford** (1989). The Court of Appeal held that race could not be taken into account when selecting jurors, and that a judge could not discharge jurors in order to achieve a racially representative jury.

Manipulation by defendants

The Government's consultation paper, *Determining Mode of Trial in Either Way Cases* (1998), suggests that manipulation of the right to jury trial by defendants is a major problem. It claims that many guilty defendants choose jury trial in a bid to make use of the delay such a choice provides. The report puts forward three reasons why guilty defendants want to do this. First, delay may put pressure on the Crown Prosecution Service to reduce the charge in exchange for the defendant pleading guilty and so speed up the process. Secondly, it may make it more likely that prosecution witnesses will fail to attend the eventual trial, or at least weaken their recollections if they do attend, so making an acquittal more likely. Thirdly, if a defendant is being held on remand, he or she is kept at a local prison, and allowed additional visits and other privileges not given to convicted prisoners. Time spent on remand is deducted from any eventual prison sentence, so for a defendant on remand who calculates that he or she is likely to be found guilty and sentenced to imprisonment, putting off the trial for as long as possible will maximize the amount of the sentence that can be spent under the more favourable conditions. Such manipulation is obviously undesirable from the point of view of justice, and it also wastes a great deal of time and money, since many defendants who manipulate the system in this way end up pleading guilty at the last minute (resulting in what is known as a 'cracked trial'), so that the time and money spent preparing the prosecution's case is wasted; in most cases, state funding will also have been spent on the defence case.

However, those who support jury trials argue that this is a declining problem. In 1987, defendants choosing jury trial accounted for 53 per cent of either-way cases sent to the Crown Court, but by 1997, the proportion had fallen to 28 per cent.

Jury nobbling

This problem led to the suspension of jury trials for terrorist offences in Northern Ireland, and has caused problems in some English trials. In 1982 several Old Bailey trials had to be stopped because of attempted 'nobbling', one after seven months, and the problem became so serious that juries had to sit out of sight of the public gallery, brown paper was stuck over the windows in court doors, and jurors were warned to avoid local pubs and cafés and eat only in their own canteen. In 1984, jurors in the Brinks-Mat trial had to have police protection to and from the court, and their telephone calls intercepted.

A new criminal offence was created under the Criminal Justice and Public Order Act 1994 to try to give additional protection to the jury. This provides under s. 51 that it is an offence to intimidate or threaten to harm, either physically or financially, certain people involved in a trial including jurors.

A more radical reform was introduced in the Criminal Procedure and Investigation Act 1996. Section 54 of the Act provides that where a person has been acquitted of an offence and someone is subsequently convicted of interfering with or intimidating jurors or witnesses in the case, then the High Court can quash the acquittal and the person can be retried. This is a wholly exceptional development in the law since traditionally acquittals were considered final, and subsequent retrial a breach of fundamental human rights. Following the Criminal Justice Act 2003, where there is a real risk of jury nobbling a case can be heard by a single judge.

Absence of reasons

When judges sit alone their judgment consists of a detailed and explicit finding of fact. When there is a jury it returns an unexplained verdict which simply finds in favour of one party or another. The former is more easily reviewed by appellate courts because the findings and the inferences of the trial judge can be examined. But when the appellate court is faced with a jury's verdict, it must support that verdict if there is any reasonable view of the evidence which leads to it.

Article 6 of the European Convention on Human Rights requires courts to give reasons for their judgments. In his review of the criminal courts Sir Robin Auld considered this matter in relation to the unreasoned jury verdict. However, he concluded that the European Court of Human Rights would take into account the way the British jury trial works as a whole and not find a violation of Art. 6.

Problems with compulsory jury service

Jury service is often unpopular but a refusal to act as a juror amounts to a contempt of court. Resentful jurors might make unsatisfactory decisions: in particular, jurors keen to get away as soon as possible are likely to simply go along with what the majority say, whether they agree or not.

Excessive damages

In the past, juries in civil cases have awarded very high damages. The Court of Appeal now has the power either to order a new trial on the ground that damages awarded by a jury are excessive or, without the agreement of the parties, to substitute for the sum awarded by the jury such sum as appears to the court to be proper.

Cost and time

A Crown Court trial currently costs the taxpayer around £7,400 per day, as opposed to £1,000 per day for trial by magistrates. The jury process is time-consuming for all involved, with juries spending much of their time waiting around to be summoned into court.

Distress to jury members

Juries trying cases involving serious crimes of violence, particularly rape, murder or child abuse, may have to listen to deeply distressing evidence, and in some cases to inspect graphic photographs of injuries. One juror in a particularly gruesome murder case told a newspaper how he felt on hearing a tape of the last words of the victim as, fatally injured, she struggled to make herself understood on the phone to the emergency services:

> It was your worst nightmare. I've watched American police programmes where you have a murder every 15 seconds, pools of blood, chalk lines where the bodies were . . . that's nothing compared to the sound of this tape. You cannot believe the shock that runs through you, the fear when you know this is what happened. (*The Sunday Times*, 13 April 1997)

At the end of the case, most members of the jury were in tears, and after delivering their verdict, it was over an hour before they could compose themselves sufficiently to leave the jury room. The problem is made worse by the fact that jurors are told not to discuss the case with anyone else.

The potential for distress to jurors was recognized in the recent trials of Rosemary West and the killers of James Bulger, where the jurors were offered counselling afterwards, and since these cases the Lord Chancellor's Department has provided that court-appointed welfare officers should be made available. However, these are provided only in cases judges deem to be exceptional, and only if jurors request their help.

Other criticisms

See also the notes on jury vetting, the non-representative nature of juries, and the termination of peremptory challenges. The material on mode of trial discussed at p. 271 is also relevant.

Quick quiz 9.4

1 On what basis did the Court of Appeal allow the appeal of *The Sun* newspaper in the case of **Grobbelaar** v **News Group Newspapers Ltd** (2001)?

2 When can a retrial be ordered under the Criminal Procedure and Investigation Act 1996, s. 54?

3 Does the failure of the jury to give reasons violate the right to a fair trial contained in Art. 6 of the European Convention on Human Rights?

4 Which is cheaper, a Crown Court trial or a trial in a magistrates' court?

Reform of the jury

A wide range of reform proposals have been put forward for the reform of the jury system.

Serious fraud trials

The Government plans to remove jury trials from most serious fraud cases (see p. 170), a reform that has been heavily criticized. There has been an on-going debate as to whether juries are suitable for such cases. Public attention was drawn to this issue by the collapse of the trial of six men accused of fraud relating to the awarding of contracts for the construction of the Jubilee Line extension on the London Underground system (**R** v **Rayment** (2005)). The trial lasted two years, the longest ever jury trial, before it collapsed having cost the taxpayer £60 million. It had suffered from a range of delays due to illness, scheduled holidays and paternity leave among the jury and lawyers, since it began in February 2000. Legal arguments also involved substantial periods where the jury was not required to hear evidence. In the last seven months before the case was dropped, the jury heard evidence on only 13 days of the 140 available. The prosecution eventually dropped the case after deciding there had been so many interruptions that a fair trial had become impossible.

 Know your terms 9.5

Define the following terms:

1 Jury vetting
2 Stand by
3 Peremptory challenge
4 Summary offence

To try to prevent such a waste of time and money occurring again, the Lord Chief Justice issued a protocol requiring judges to exercise strong case management over cases likely to last more than eight weeks, including strict deadlines. The aim is to reduce the length of such trials to a maximum of three months. Trials would only be allowed to go on longer than six months in 'exceptional circumstances'. In addition, since April 2005 large criminal cases are monitored by a case management panel chaired by the Director of Public Prosecutions.

But the Government has decided not to wait to see whether this new Protocol leads to shorter fraud trials with juries sitting, and instead has decided to remove juries from such cases by bringing into force s. 43 of the Criminal Justice Act 2003. It may not succeed in doing this as it faces strong opposition.

The use of a single judge has the advantages of making trials quicker, reducing the likelihood of 'perverse' verdicts, and defeating the problem of jury nobbling (in Northern Ireland single judges have long been used in some cases because of the problem of jury nobbling). However, the benefits of public participation in the legal system would be lost, and all the problems associated with judicial bias and the restricted social background of judges (described in Chapter 10) would be let loose on cases which involve vital questions for both the individuals concerned and society as a whole. The Bar Council believes that juries should be retained in all cases where the defendant faces serious loss of liberty or reputation. It considers that fraud cases can appear complex, but if they are properly managed juries are capable of deciding the case, which usually comes down to determining whether the defendant has been dishonest.

Using a bench of perhaps three or five judges would give a little more protection against individual bias, but would still not give the benefit of community participation that the jury offers (and would also require massive investment to train the increased number of judges that would be required).

Abolishing juries

It can be argued that since juries have already been abolished in all but a handful of civil cases with no apparent ill effects, and that they decide only 1 per cent of criminal cases anyway, the system really no longer needs them at all and they should be abolished. The pros and cons of this argument naturally depend on what would be put in their place.

Lay participation and increased speed (and lower costs) could be achieved by allowing magistrates to decide all criminal cases, but it is highly unlikely that society would ever wish to trust decisions on the most serious crimes to non-legally qualified judges. Of course, it could be argued that that is exactly what the jury system does, but in that case the number of jurors, and the advantages of random selection in terms of representing society as a whole is thought by supporters to outweigh the amateur status of jurors – and in jury trials, the judge is always there to offer guidance on matters of law, and to decide the sentence in criminal cases.

The Government's 1998 consultation paper on the criminal justice system considered four possible options for serious fraud trials:

- abolishing the use of juries in fraud trials completely and replacing them with a specially trained single judge and two lay people with expertise in commercial affairs;
- replacing juries with a specially trained single judge or panel of judges, possibly with access to advisers on commercial matters;
- retaining jury trial but restricting the jury's role to deciding questions of dishonesty, with the judge deciding other matters; or
- replacing the traditional, randomly selected jury with a special jury, selected on the basis of qualifications or tests, or drawn from those who can demonstrate specialist knowledge of business and finance.

In his review of the criminal justice system in 2001, Sir Robin Auld favoured the first option of a specially trained single judge and two lay people with expertise on the subject. Under his recommendations, a panel of experts would be set up and the trial judge would select the lay members after giving the parties the opportunity to make written representations as to their suitability. The judge would be the sole judge of law, procedure, admissibility of evidence and sentence. All three would be judges of fact and they would therefore decide the verdict together. A majority of any two would suffice for a conviction. The defendant would always have the option of choosing, with the consent of the court, a trial by judge alone.

There are weaknesses in this proposal. The selection process and limited powers of the lay members would risk undermining their stature in the eyes of the public. The power to convict on a majority of two to one could be seen as undermining the usual requirement in criminal law that, in order to convict, a defendant should be found guilty beyond reasonable doubt.

The Government is currently considering allowing trials without a jury for some terrorist cases where sensitive evidence cannot be made public.

Task 9.6

If you were charged with committing a fraud, what type of trial would you prefer?

■ Would you prefer your case to be heard in a magistrates' court or a Crown Court?
■ Would you want your case to be heard by a professional judge, by a jury or by a combination of lay people sitting with a judge and jointly deciding your guilt?

Why would you prefer this type of trial?

▌ Improving the performance of the jury

As well as favouring a reduction in the role of the jury discussed above, Sir Robin Auld made a range of specific recommendations to improve the performance of the jury.

Help the jury to work effectively

The Auld Review recommended that in order to assist a jury in their work, the prosecution and defence advocates should prepare a written summary of the case and the issues that needed to be decided. This 'case and issues' summary would be agreed by the judge and distributed to the jurors at the start of the trial.

The judge would sum up the case at the end of the trial by forming questions which needed to be considered by the jurors. Juries would reach verdicts by answering these questions during their deliberations. Where the judge thought it appropriate he or she would be able to require the jury publicly to answer each of the questions and to declare a verdict in accordance with those answers. Sir Robin Auld argues that this would strengthen the jury as a tribunal of fact, provide a reasoned basis for jury verdicts and reduce the risk of perverse verdicts. While there can only be benefits from presenting the case more clearly to the jury, the use of questions which the jury may be forced to answer publicly seems to be an unnecessary restriction on the jurors' freedom to reach a decision in accordance with their conscience as well as in accordance with the law.

Professor Zander (2001) has criticized these recommendations. He argues persuasively that Sir Robin Auld demonstrates

> an authoritarian attitude that disregards history and reveals a grievously misjudged sense of the proper balance of the criminal justice system. For centuries the role of the jury has included the power to stand between the citizen and unjust law. . . . [G]etting it right does not necessarily mean giving the verdict a judge would have given. . . . To want to inquire whether they reached their decision in the 'right' way, is foolish because it ignores the nature of the institution.

Prevent perverse verdicts

The Auld Review was concerned by the risk of juries reaching perverse verdicts. Rather than seeing these as a potential safeguard of civil liberties, the Review seems to consider these as an insult to the law. It has therefore recommended that legislation should declare that juries have no right to acquit defendants in defiance of the law or in disregard of the evidence. The prosecution would be given a right to appeal against what it considered to be a perverse acquittal by a jury.

Sir Robin Auld recommended that where appropriate, the trial judge and the Court of Appeal should be allowed to investigate any alleged impropriety or failure in the way the jury reached its verdict, even where this is supposed to have happened during the traditionally secret deliberations of the jury. Such an investigation might look at accusations that some jurors ignored or slept through the deliberation or that the jury reached its verdict because of an irrational prejudice or whim, deliberately ignoring the evidence.

These recommendations show insufficient respect for the jurors and have been rejected by the Government.

Reserve jurors

One recommendation of the *Review of the Criminal Courts* (2001) was that where appropriate for long cases judges should be able to swear in extra jurors. These reserve jurors would be able to replace jurors who are unable to continue to hear a case because, for example, of illness.

Black jurors

It has been argued by the Commission for Racial Equality that consideration needs to be given to the racial balance in particular cases. They suggest that where a case has a racial dimension and the defendant reasonably believes that he or she cannot receive a fair trial from an all-white jury, then the judge should have the power to order that three of the jurors come from the same ethnic minority as the defendant or the victim. Both the Runciman Commission (1993) and Sir Robin Auld's *Review of the Criminal Courts* (2001) have given their endorsement to this proposal but it has never been implemented.

The Society of Black Lawyers had, in addition, submitted to the Runciman Commission that there should always be a right to a multiracial trial, that peremptory challenges should be reinstated and that certain cases with a black defendant should be tried by courts in areas with high black populations, and panels of black jurors who would be available at short notice should be set up. These proposals have not been implemented either.

The problems caused by lack of racial representation on juries can be seen in the high-profile Rodney King case in Los Angeles, where a policeman was found not guilty of assaulting a black motorist despite a videotape of the incident showing brutal conduct. The case was tried in an area with a very high white population, while the incident itself had occurred in an area with a high black population. However, the decision in **R** *v* **Ford** (1989), that there is no principle that a jury should be racially balanced, still holds.

Peremptory challenge was abolished because it was said to have interfered with the principle of random selection, especially in multi-defendant trials. However, Vennard and Riley's study (1988) found that the peremptory challenge was used in only 22 per cent of cases, with no evidence of widespread pooling of challenges, and research for the Crown Prosecution Service in 1987 showed that the use of peremptory challenge had no significant effect on the rate of acquittals.

Peremptory challenge could in fact be used to make juries more balanced in terms of race and sex, and it seems rather unjust that while the defence have had their right to a peremptory challenge removed, the prosecution is still allowed to stand by for the Crown.

Reading on the web

The consultation document *Jury Research and Impropriety* (2005), considering when the law should allow the secrecy of jury deliberations to be broken, can be found on the Department for Constitutional Affairs' website at:

   http://www.dca.gov.uk/consult/juryresearch/_cp0405.pdf

Leaflets on jury service are published on the Court Service website at:

   http://www.courtservice.gov.uk/

Question and answer guides

1 Evaluate how important the jury is in the English legal system.

Answer guide

Your introduction should **briefly** outline what the jury is, what it does and when, and how it is selected. You should discuss the fact that in terms of the number of cases juries decide, the importance of the jury has declined over time, and mention that this process is continuing with the current plans to limit defendants' opportunities to choose jury trial. You can then go on to discuss how important the jury is in the areas where it does still operate. Work through the advantages of the jury, pointing out how these make the jury important in the legal system. Follow this with a look at the disadvantages of the system, again linking these points to the issue of the jury's importance. If you have time, run through the alternatives to juries and state whether (and why) you think any of these could provide a partial or complete replacement for juries.

Since the question asks you to evaluate the jury system, you should conclude by saying whether you think the advantages outweigh the disadvantages, and perhaps giving your opinion on whether the jury should be abolished, or still has a valuable role to play. If you feel it should be abolished, you might suggest which of the alternatives should replace it, while if you feel it should be retained, you could point out any reforms that you feel should be made. ('London Qualifications Ltd.', accepts no responsibility whatsoever for the accuracy or method in the answers given.)

2 'We believe that twelve persons selected at random are likely to be a cross-selection of the people as a whole and thus represent the views of the common man' (Lord Denning MR in R v Sheffield Crown Court, ex parte Brownlow (1980)). Do you consider that this statement justifies the use of juries in criminal cases? Is there any other satisfactory justification?

Answer guide

Here you first need to discuss to what extent juries are representative, mentioning the limitations on random selection imposed by the rules on eligibility, disqualification and jury vetting. Having outlined this, you should say whether in your opinion this alone justifies trial by jury in criminal cases, and why, using the material on public participation as an advantage of the jury system (p. 167).

Then move on to the other justifications for jury trials in criminal cases, which are of course the advantages listed on pp. 167–8. You should make it clear whether you feel these are alternative justifications to the principle of representing society, or complementary ones. You can then point out that despite these justifications, there are problems with the jury system, and work through the disadvantages we have listed (remember that this question deals with juries in criminal trials only, and leave out irrelevant material such as the problems with damages for libel). Go through the alternatives to the jury system as well if you have time.

Your conclusion should sum up whether you think that the principle of random selection and representativeness and/or any of the other advantages you have discussed outweigh the disadvantages strongly enough to justify the use of juries in criminal trials. If you conclude that the justifications are not sufficient, you should say what you feel should replace the jury system and why.

3 (a) Explain the role of juries in criminal and civil cases. (15)

(b) To what extent is it true that juries are randomly selected? (30)
(OCR)

Answer guide

(a) The material you need to answer this question is contained at pp. 156–9. You would want to divide your answer clearly between a discussion of criminal cases and a discussion of civil cases. As regards criminal cases, you need to highlight the fact that juries sit in the Crown Court and hear indictable offences and some either-way offences where defendants plead not guilty. They listen to the evidence and decide whether the defendant is guilty or innocent. They usually reach a unanimous verdict, though a majority verdict is possible. Occasionally they will be directed by the judge to find the defendant not guilty if there is inadequate evidence in law for the defendant to be found guilty. Juries are not involved in deciding the appropriate sentence; that is left to the professional judge.

As regards the role of juries in civil cases, they usually sit in the High Court though occasionally they can sit in the county court. They hear only a very small number of cases, but for those cases they normally decide both the issue of liability and the amount of any financial award of damages.

Finally, in explaining the jury's role, you could discuss the fact that they are there to provide a trial by one's peers. They offer an important layman's contribution to the legal system.

(b) The material you need to answer this question can be found at pp. 159–65. You could divide your answer by looking first at factors that support the suggestion that juries are randomly selected, such as the fact that they are selected through the use of a computer from the electoral roll. You could then look at the factors that have in the past undermined this random selection, which were highlighted by Sir Robin Auld and are discussed on p. 160.

Your conclusion might point out that while juries are not a complete cross-section of society, they are more representative than professional judges.

Chapter summary

When are juries used?

Juries only decide about 1 per cent of criminal cases and a very small number of civil cases.

Qualifications for jury service

Potential jury members must be:

■ aged 18 to 70;
■ on the electoral register; and
■ resident in the UK, Channel Islands or Isle of Man for at least five years since the age of 13.

Jury vetting

Jury vetting consists of checking that the potential juror does not hold 'extremist' views which some feel would make them unsuitable for hearing a case. It is done by checking police, Special Branch and security service records.

The secrecy of the jury

Once they retire to consider their verdict, jurors are not allowed to communicate with anyone other than the judge and an assigned court official, until after the verdict is delivered.

Arguments in favour of the jury system

Juries allow ordinary citizens to participate in the administration of justice and decide cases according to their conscience.

Criticisms of the jury system

In practice, juries are not representative of the general population. Some of their judgments are perverse; they can be biased and susceptible to manipulation.

Reform of the jury

Proposals have been put forward for restricting the role of juries or abolishing juries altogether. Significant reform proposals were drawn up by Sir Robin Auld but many of these have been rejected by the Government.

Chapter 10

Magistrates

Introduction

Like juries, lay magistrates have a long history in the English legal system, dating back to the Justices of the Peace Act 1361, which, probably in response to a crime wave, gave judicial powers to appointed lay people. Their main role then, as now, was dealing with criminals, but they also exercised certain administrative functions, and until the nineteenth century the business of local government was largely entrusted to them. A few of these administrative powers remain today.

There are over 28,000 lay magistrates (also called justices of the peace, or JPs), hearing over 1 million criminal cases a year – 95 per cent of all criminal trials, with the remaining being heard in the Crown Court. They are therefore often described as the backbone of the English criminal justice system. Lay magistrates do not receive a salary, but they receive travel, subsistence and financial loss allowances.

There are also 105 professional judges who sit in the magistrates' courts. These are now called 'district judges (magistrates' courts)' following a reform introduced by the Access to Justice Act 1999. They had previously been known as stipendiary magistrates. They receive a salary of over £90,000. On top of the permanent district judges (magistrates' courts) there are also deputy district judges who work part time usually with a view to establishing their competence in order to get a full-time position in the future. These professional judges are appointed by the Queen on the recommendation of the Lord Chancellor, and must have a seven-year general advocacy qualification, meaning that they have had a right of audience in at least the lower courts for a minimum of seven years. Following the Access to Justice Act 1999, they are appointed to a single Bench with national jurisdiction. They act as sole judge in their particular court, mostly in the large cities and London in particular, where 46 are based. They are part of the professional judiciary, and most of the comments about magistrates in this chapter do not apply to them.

Selection and appointment

Lay magistrates are appointed by the Lord Chancellor in the name of the Crown, on the advice of Local Advisory Committees. For historical reasons, magistrates in Lancashire, Greater Manchester and Merseyside are appointed by the Chancellor of the Duchy of Lancaster in the name of the Crown. Candidates are interviewed by the committee, which then makes a recommendation to the Minister who usually follows the recommendation.

Members of the Local Advisory Committees are appointed by the Minister. Two-thirds of them are magistrates, and the Minister is supposed to ensure that they have good local knowledge, and represent a balance of political opinion. Their identity was at one time kept secret, but names are now available to the public.

Candidates are usually put forward to the committee by local political parties, voluntary groups, trade unions and other organizations, though individuals may apply in person. The only qualifications laid down for appointment to the magistracy are that the applicants must be under 65 and live within 15 miles of the commission area in which they will work. These qualifications may be dispensed with if it is considered to be in the public interest to do so. In practice, they must also be able to devote an average of half a day a week to the task, for which usually only expenses and a small loss of earnings allowance are paid. Legal knowledge or experience is not required; nor is any level of academic qualification.

Certain people are excluded from appointment, including police officers, traffic wardens and members of the armed forces; anyone whose work is considered incompatible with the duties of a magistrate; anyone who due to a disability could not carry out all the duties of a magistrate; people with certain criminal convictions; undischarged bankrupts; and those who have a close relative who is already a magistrate on the same Bench.

In 1998 the procedures for appointing lay magistrates were reviewed. The reforms aimed to make the appointment criteria open and clear. Thus a job description for magistrates was introduced which declares that the six key qualities defining the personal suitability of candidates are: having good character, understanding and communication, social awareness, maturity and sound temperament, sound judgement and commitment and reliability. Positions are now advertised widely, including in publications such as *Inside Soaps* to attract a wider range of people.

Following the implementation of the Courts Act 2003, magistrates are appointed nationally rather than locally.

Removal and retirement

Magistrates have to retire at 70. Under the Criminal Justice Act 2003, the Lord Chancellor can remove a lay magistrate from office:

■ on the ground of incapacity or misbehaviour,
■ on the ground of a persistent failure to meet the prescribed standards of competence, and
■ if the Minister is satisfied that the lay justice is declining or neglecting to take a proper part in the exercise of his or her functions as a magistrate.

In addition magistrates are prevented from exercising their functions if they suffer from an incapacity.

Quick quiz 10.1

1 Who appoints lay magistrates?

2 What is the role of the Local Advisory Committees?

3 What qualifications does a person need to become a magistrate?

4 At what age must a magistrate retire?

Background

Class

The 1948 Report of the Royal Commission on Justices of the Peace showed that approximately three-quarters of all magistrates came from professional or middle-class occupations. Little seems to have changed since. Research carried out by Rod Morgan and Neil Russell (2000) found that more than two-thirds of lay magistrates were, or had been until retirement, employed in a professional or managerial position. Their social backgrounds were not representative of the community in which they served. For example, in a deprived metropolitan area, 79 per cent of the Bench members were professionals or managers compared to only 20 per cent of the local population.

Know your terms 10.2

Define the following terms:

1 Stipendiary magistrate
2 Justice of the Peace
3 The Bench
4 Royal Commission

One of the reasons for this may be financial; while employers are required to give an employee who is appointed as a magistrate reasonable time off work, not all employers are able or willing to pay wages during the employee's absence. To meet this difficulty, lay magistrates receive a loss of earnings allowance, but this is not overly generous and will usually be less than the employee would have earned.

A further problem is that employees who take up the appointment against the wishes of their employer may find their promotion prospects jeopardized. This means that only those who are self-employed, or sufficiently far up the career ladder to have some power of their own, can serve as magistrates without risking damage to their own employment prospects. The outcome is that those outside the professional and managerial classes are proportionately under-represented on the Bench, which is still predominantly drawn from the more middle-class occupations. The minimum age for appointment has been raised to 65 in the hope that working-class people, who were prevented from serving during their working lives, will do so in retirement, though so far the change has had little impact.

In the past the Government sought to achieve a social balance on the bench by taking into account a person's political affiliation when making appointments. This stemmed from the time when people tended to vote along class lines, with people from the working class voting predominantly for the Labour Party. Political opinion is no longer a reliable gauge of a person's social background and the Government has therefore replaced the question about 'political associations' on the application form for magistrates. It has been replaced by a question about the applicant's employment. The Department for Constitutional Affairs believes that this will provide a better means of achieving a socially balanced Bench.

Age

There are few young magistrates – most are middle-aged or older. Only 4 per cent are under the age of 40, and almost a third are in their 60s. The problems concerning employment are likely to have an effect on the age as well as the social class of magistrates; people at the beginning of their careers are most dependent on the goodwill of employers for promotion, and least likely to be able to take regular time off without damaging their career prospects. They are also more likely to be busy bringing up families.

While a certain maturity is obviously a necessity for magistrates, younger justices would bring some understanding of the lifestyles of a younger generation.

Politics

Government figures released in 1995 showed that a high proportion of magistrates were Conservative supporters, and few voted Labour. A sample survey of 218 new appointments as magistrates in England and Wales showed that 91 were Conservative voters, 56 Labour, 41 Liberal Democrat, 24 had no political affiliation, and four voted for the Welsh party, Plaid Cymru. A report analysing the figures for 1992 compared the proportion of Conservative voters among magistrates to the proportion in their local area: in two Oldham constituencies, 52 per cent of the local people voted Labour, but only 27 per cent of magistrates, and slightly more magistrates than constituents in general voted Conservative. In Bristol, Labour had won 40 per cent of the votes, slightly more than the Tories; of the magistrates, 142 said they were Tory, and only 85 described themselves as Labour supporters.

Table 10.1 **Ethnicity: lay magistrates and population generally**

	White	Black Caribbean, Black African, Black other	Indian, Pakistani, Bangladeshi, Chinese	Other	Not known	Total
Magistrates England and Wales						
Number	21,950	430	541	186	2,825	25,932
Percentage	85%	2%	2%	1%	11%	100%
General population for England and Wales (1991 census)	94%	2%	3%	1%	–	100%

The data excludes magistrates in the Duchy of Lancaster.

Source: R. Morgan and N. Russell (2000), *The Judiciary in the Magistrates' Courts*, Home Office RDS Occasional Paper No. 66.

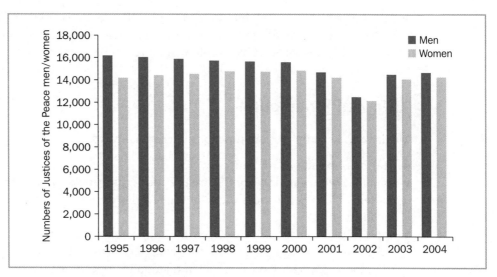

Figure 10.1 Justices of the Peace, 1995–2004[a]

[a] As at 1 January of each year. From 2000 onwards figures compiled on a financial year basis.

Source: K. Dibdin, A. Sealy and S. Aktar, *Judicial Statistics Annual Report 2004*, p. 128.

Race

The Lord Chancellor's Department reported in 1987 that the proportion of black magistrates was only 2 per cent. The figures for 2003 show that lay magistrates increasingly reflect the ethnic diversity of contemporary Britain. Just over 6 per cent of magistrates come from ethnic minority communities, who make up 7.9 per cent of the general population, but there is considerable variation locally and the fit between the local benches and the local communities they serve is, in several instances, very poor.

Sex

The sexes are fairly evenly balanced among lay magistrates with 51 per cent men and 49 per cent women. However, district judges (magistrates' courts) are primarily male, with only 13 women holding this position.

Training

The Magistrates' Commission Committees are responsible for providing training under the supervision of the Judicial Studies Board. Magistrates are not expected to be experts on the law, and the aim of their training is mainly to familiarize them with court procedure, the techniques of chairing and the theory and practice of sentencing. They undergo a short induction course on appointment, and have to undergo basic continuous training comprising 12 hours every three years. Magistrates who sit in juvenile courts or on domestic court panels receive additional training. In order to chair a court hearing a magistrate must, since 1996, take a chairmanship course, the syllabus of which is set by the Judicial Studies Board. Since 1998 the training has included more 'hands on' practical experience, sessions in equality awareness and experienced magistrates act as monitors of more junior members of the Bench.

Criminal jurisdiction

Magistrates have three main functions in criminal cases:

■ hearing applications for bail;

■ trial: magistrates mainly try the least serious criminal cases. They are advised on matters of law by a justices' clerk, but they alone decide the facts, the law and the sentence;

■ appeals: in ordinary appeals from the magistrates' court to the Crown Court, magistrates sit with a judge. But, following a reform by the Access to Justice Act 1999, they no longer have this role in relation to appeals against sentence.

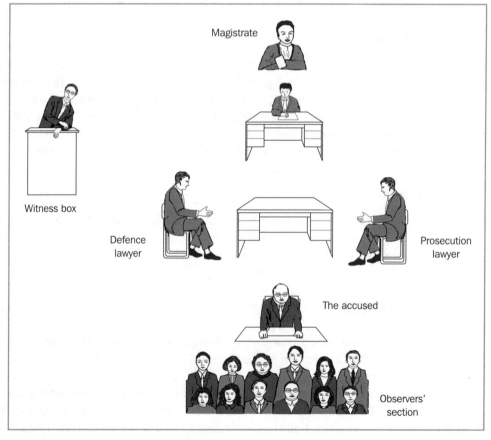

Figure 10.2 Layout of a magistrates' court

Source: F. Mahar and M.J. Duffy, *AQA General Certificate of Education Law Teachers' Guide 2001/2*. © Fareen Mahar.

Magistrates also exercise some control over the investigation of crime, since they deal with applications for bail and requests by the police for arrest and search warrants.

Lay magistrates generally sit in groups of three. However, s. 49 of the Crime and Disorder Act 1998 provides that certain pre-trial judicial powers may be exercised by a single justice of the peace sitting alone. These include decisions to extend or vary the conditions of bail, to remit an offender to another court for sentence and to give directions as to the timetable for proceedings, the attendance of the parties, the service of documents and the manner in which evidence is to be given. These powers of single justices were tested in six pilot studies and, having proved to be successful, were applied nationally in November 1999.

The role of magistrates in the criminal justice system has been effectively increased in recent years. Some offences which were previously triable either way have been made summary only, notably in the Criminal Law Act 1977, where most motoring offences and criminal damage worth less than £2,000 were made summary only (since raised to £5,000 in the Criminal Justice and Public Order Act 1994). The Government proposed at the time that thefts involving small amounts of money should also be made summary offences, but there was great opposition to the idea of removing the right to jury trial for offences which reflected on the accused's honesty. The proposal was dropped, but is still suggested from time to time.

The vast majority of new offences are summary only – there was controversy over the fact that the first offence created to deal with so-called 'joy-riding' was summary, given that the problem appeared to be a serious one, and critics assume that it was made a summary offence in the interests of keeping costs down. Since then, the more serious joy-riding offence, known as aggravated vehicle-taking, which occurs when joy-riding causes serious personal injury or death, has been reduced to a summary offence by the Criminal Justice and Public Order Act 1994. Other serious offences which are summary only include assaulting a police officer, and many of the offences under the Public Order Act 1986.

The Courts Act 2003 has given district judges (magistrates' court) for the first time limited powers to sit in the Crown Court. This is so that they can deal with some preliminary administrative matters.

Civil jurisdiction

Magistrates' courts are responsible for granting licences to pubs and betting shops, and have jurisdiction over domestic matters such as adoption. When hearing such cases they are known as family proceedings courts. The Child Support Agency has taken over most of their work in relation to fixing child maintenance payments.

The courts' domestic functions overlap considerably with the jurisdiction of the county court and the High Court, though some uniformity of approach is encouraged by the fact that appeals arising from these cases are all heard by the Family Division of the High Court.

The fact that for domestic matters different procedures and law are applied in the different courts, and cases are generally assigned to the magistrates' court because

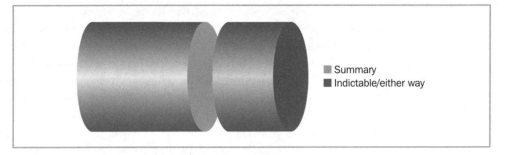

Figure 10.3 **Magistrates' courts: types of cases**
Source: *Crown Prosecution Service Annual Report 2004–2005*, p. 36, Chart 2.

they fall within certain financial limits, has led to the criticism that there is a second-class system of domestic courts for the poor, with the better off using the High Court and county courts where cases are heard by professional and highly qualified judges. Because of this, magistrates sitting in domestic cases must receive special training and the Bench must contain both male and female magistrates.

The justices' clerk and legal advisers

There are about 250 justices' clerks in the country. Most must have a five-year magistrates' court qualification, that is to say, they must be qualified as barristers or solicitors with a right of audience in relation to all proceedings in the magistrates' courts for at least five years, though some hold office by reason of their length of service. In the past there have been problems with recruiting suitably qualified people, partly because the local organization of the courts meant there was no clear career structure. This led many clerks to leave for the Crown Prosecution Service where pay and promotion prospects were better.

The justices' clerks delegate many of their powers in practice to legal advisers (previously known as court clerks). This wide delegation has caused concerns about the qualifications of the people to whom these powers are being delegated. In an effort to raise standards, since 1 January 1999 all newly appointed legal advisers must be qualified solicitors or barristers. Those in post prior to this date who have a specialist diploma in magisterial law have ten years in which to requalify. There is an exemption for legal advisers aged 40 or over on 1 January 1999. Not surprisingly, this reform was angrily received by legal advisers who did not have the requisite qualification.

A Practice Direction was issued by the High Court in 2000 clarifying the powers of the magistrates' clerk – Practice Direction (Justices: Clerk to Court) (2000). This was issued to make it clear that their powers conform to the European Convention on Human Rights following the passing of the Human Rights Act 1998.

The primary function of the justices' clerk and legal adviser is to advise the lay magistrates on law and procedure. They are not supposed to take any part in the actual decision of the Bench; legal and procedural advice should be given in open court, and the justices' clerk and legal adviser should not accompany the magistrates if they retire to consider their decision. Section 49(2) of the Crime and Disorder Act 1998 provides that many of the pre-trial judicial powers that are exercisable by a single justice of the peace can be delegated to a justices' clerk. Their independence is guaranteed by s. 29 of the Courts Act 2003. In the past, the justices' clerk also had considerable administrative functions, but these are increasingly being passed to other staff.

Task 10.3

Visit a magistrates' court. You can find the address of a local magistrates' court by looking in a telephone directory. Write up a report of your visit by answering the following questions:

About the court

1 What was the name and address of the court?

2 What was the court building like? Was it old or modern? Was it clean and in good decorative order? Were the waiting areas comfortable? Was there access to refreshments? Was it easy to find your way around the building, with rooms clearly signposted and labelled?

3 Did you find the court staff helpful? Were there any explanatory leaflets available?

About the proceedings

Take one of the cases that you watched and answer the following questions:

1 Were the proceedings heard by lay magistrates or a professional judge? Were they male or female and what was their approximate age? What did they wear? Were they polite to the parties?

2 Was the case a civil or criminal matter?

3 Were the parties represented by a lawyer?

4 What was the case about?

5 Did any witnesses give evidence?

6 If you heard the whole case, what was its outcome?

7 Did you think that the court came to the right decision?

Lay magistrates versus professional judges

In recent years there has been some discussion as to whether lay magistrates should be replaced by professional judges. There have been suspicions that this may be on the Government's political agenda. These suspicions have been fuelled by the increasing role of justices' clerks and the commission of research in the field by Rod Morgan and Neil Russell. Their report *The Judiciary in the Magistrates' Courts* (2000) has provided some useful up-to-date information to support the debate on the future role of lay magistrates in the criminal justice system. That research concluded:

At no stage during the study was it suggested that . . . the magistrates' courts do not work well or fail to command general confidence. It is our view, therefore, that eliminating or greatly diminishing the role of lay magistrates would not be widely understood or supported.

Advantages of lay magistrates

Cost

It has traditionally been assumed that because lay magistrates are unpaid volunteers, they are necessarily cheaper than their professional colleagues. However, it is not clear that this is the case. The research by Rod Morgan and Neil Russell (2000) found that a simple analysis of the direct costs for the Magistrates' Courts Service of using the two types of magistrates shows that lay magistrates are extraordinarily cheap compared to professional judges. The direct average cost of a lay justice is £495 per annum, that of a district judge £90,000. However, lay magistrates incur more indirect costs than professional judges. They are much slower than professional judges in hearing cases, as one professional judge handles as much work as 30 lay magistrates. Lay magistrates therefore make greater proportionate use of the court buildings. They need the support of legally qualified legal advisers. Administrative support is required for their recruitment, training and rota arrangements. When all the overheads are brought into the equation the cost per appearance for lay and professional magistrates becomes £52.10 and £61.78 respectively. These figures have to be seen in the context that professional judges are currently more likely to send someone to prison which is more expensive than the alternative sentences frequently imposed by lay magistrates. They are almost twice as likely to remand defendants in custody and they are also twice as likely to sentence defendants to immediate custody, a finding that may be partly attributable to their hearing the most serious cases.

Switching to Crown Court trials would be extremely expensive. The Home Office Research and Planning Unit has estimated that the average cost of a contested trial in the Crown Court is around £13,500, with guilty pleas costing about £2,500. By contrast, the costs of trial by lay magistrates are £1,500 and £500 respectively. This is partly a reflection of the more serious nature of cases tried in the Crown Court, but clearly Crown Court trials are a great deal more expensive overall.

Table 10.2 **The cost of appearing before lay and professional magistrates (per appearance)**

	Lay magistrates	Professional magistrates
	£	£
Direct costs (salary, expenses, training)	3.59	20.96
Indirect costs (premises, administration staff, etc.)	48.51	40.82
Direct and indirect costs	52.10	61.78

Source: R. Morgan and N. Russell (2000), *The Judiciary in the Magistrates' Courts*, Home Office RDS Occasional Paper No. 66.

Lay involvement

This is the same point as that cited in favour of the jury (see p. 167). Lay magistrates are an ancient and important tradition of voluntary public service. They can also be seen as an example of participatory democracy. Lay involvement in judicial decision-making ensures that the courts are aware of community concerns. However, given the restricted social background of magistrates, and their alleged bias towards the police, the true value of this may be doubtful. Magistrates do not have the option, as juries do, of delivering a verdict according to their conscience.

Weight of numbers

The simple fact that magistrates must usually sit in threes may make a balanced view more likely.

Local knowledge

Magistrates must live within a reasonable distance of the court in which they sit, and therefore may have a more informed picture of local life than professional judges.

▌ Disadvantages of lay magistrates

Inconsistent

There is considerable inconsistency in the decision-making of different Benches. This is noticeable in the differences in awards of state funding and the types of sentences ordered. To achieve the fundamental goal of a fair trial similar crimes committed in similar circumstances by offenders with similar backgrounds should receive a similar punishment. But in Teeside 20 per cent of convicted burglars are sentenced to immediate custody, compared to 41 per cent in Birmingham.

In 1985, the Home Office noted in *Managing Criminal Justice* (edited by David Moxon) that, though Benches tried to ensure their own decisions were consistent, they did not strive to achieve consistency with other Benches. The researchers Flood-Page and Mackie found in 1998 that district judges (magistrates' courts) sentenced a higher proportion of offenders to custody than lay magistrates after allowing for other factors. There are also marked variations in the granting of bail applications: in 1985, magistrates' courts in Hampshire granted 89 per cent of bail applications, while in Dorset only 63 per cent were allowed.

The Government announced that it intended to put an end to the disparity in sentencing patterns in different areas, a situation which was described as 'postcode sentencing'. In order to do this a Sentencing Guidelines Council was established under the Criminal Justice Act 2003 to ensure greater consistency in sentencing across England and Wales.

Inefficient

Most of the public sampled in the research by Rod Morgan and Neil Russell (2000) were largely unaware that there were two types of magistrate. When enlightened and questioned, a majority considered that magistrates' court work should be divided equally between the two types of magistrate or that the type of magistrate did not matter. However, professional court users have significantly greater levels of confidence in the district judges (magistrates' court). They regard these judges as quicker than lay justices, more efficient and consistent in their decision-making, better able to control unruly defendants and better at questioning CPS and defence lawyers appropriately. In practice, straightforward guilty pleas to minor matters are normally dealt with by panels of lay magistrates, whereas serious contested matters are increasingly dealt with by a single, professional judge who decides questions of both guilt and sentence. Rod Morgan and Neil Russell question whether the work should be distributed in the opposite way.

Bias towards the police

Police officers are frequent witnesses, and become well known to members of the Bench, and it is alleged that this results in an almost automatic tendency to believe police evidence. One magistrate was incautious enough to admit this: in **R** *v* **Bingham J J, ex parte Jowitt** (1974), a speeding case where the only evidence was that of the motorist and a police constable, the chairman of the Bench said: 'Quite the most unpleasant cases that we have to decide are those where the evidence is a direct conflict between a police officer and a member of the public. My principle in such cases has always been to believe the evidence of the police officer, and therefore we find the case proved.' The conviction was quashed on appeal because of this remark.

Magistrates were particularly criticized in this respect during the 1984 miners' strike, for imposing wide bail conditions which prevented attendance on picket lines, and dispensing what appeared to be conveyor-belt justice.

Background

Despite the recommendations of two Royal Commissions (1910 and 1948) and the *Review of the Criminal Courts* (2001) that magistrates should come from varied social backgrounds, magistrates still appear to be predominantly middle class and middle-aged, with a strong Conservative bias.

The selection process has been blamed for the general narrowness of magistrates' backgrounds: Elizabeth Burney's 1979 study into selection methods concluded that the process was almost entirely dominated by existing magistrates who over and over again simply appointed people with similar backgrounds to their own.

The effect of their narrow background on the quality and fairness of magistrates' decisions is unclear. A survey of 160 magistrates by Bond and Lemon (1979) found no real evidence of significant differences in approach between those of different classes, but they did conclude that political affiliation had a noticeable effect on magistrates' attitudes to sentencing, with Conservatives tending to take a harder line. The research did not reveal whether these differences actually influenced the way magistrates carried out their duties in practice, but there is obviously a risk that they would do so.

In 1997, there was a slight controversy when, on winning the General Election, the Labour Lord Chancellor called for more Labour-voting candidates to be recommended for appointment as magistrates by Advisory Committees. His reasoning was that the political make-up of the magistrates needed to reflect that of the general population, which had shifted towards Labour. The Labour Government has now reversed its position, having concluded that it is no longer necessary to seek a political balance among magistrates because people no longer vote along class lines.

Some feel that the background of the Bench is not a particular problem: in *The Machinery of Justice in England* (1989) Jackson points out that 'Benches do tend to be largely middle to upper class, but that is a characteristic of those set in authority over us, whether in the town hall, Whitehall, hospitals and all manner of institutions'.

However, a predominantly old and middle-class Bench is unrepresentative of the general public and may weaken confidence in its decisions, on the part of society in general as well as the defendants before them. Jackson's argument that those 'set in authority over us' always tend to be middle to upper class is not a justification for doing nothing.

Quick quiz 10.4

1 Describe the four main functions of the magistrates in criminal matters.

2 How many lay magistrates normally sit to hear a case?

3 What is the role of the justices' clerk?

4 In what way has the magistrates' decision-making been found to be inconsistent?

Suggested reforms

Professional judges

Professional judges could either replace lay magistrates, or sit together with them. In no other jurisdiction do lay judges alone or in panels deal with offences of the seriousness dealt with in the English and Welsh magistrates' courts by lay magistrates. But putting a professional judge in all magistrates' courts would be very expensive, and is unlikely to happen, though the Royal Commission on Criminal Justice did recommend in 1993 that more use should be made of professional judges. It is understood that the former Home Secretary, Jack Straw, favoured replacing all lay magistrates with professional judges. Rod Morgan and Neil Russell (2000) calculated that if the work of lay magistrates was transferred to professional judges, one professional judge would be needed for every 30 magistrates replaced.

The role of the justices' clerk

The current Government seems to be moving in the direction of allowing justices' clerks to have increased powers to manage cases, while limiting their administrative functions. These reforms could be taken further by appointing them to the Bench, making them legally qualified chairpersons, or giving them formal powers to rule on all points of law, while leaving the determination of the facts to the lay justices. The academic Penny Darbyshire has, however, sounded a note of caution to such developments. In an article in 1999 she argues that case management is not an administrative activity but a judicial one. She considers that such powers should not be delegated to justices' clerks unless they are selected and screened as judges and given the same protection as judges to ensure their independence.

In its submission to the Auld Review of the Criminal Courts (discussed on p. 177), the Association of Magisterial Officers, which represents staff in magistrates' courts, called for a major transfer of powers from lay magistrates to justices' clerks. The union argued that the role of lay magistrates should be restricted to arbiters of fact. Justices' clerks would take on full responsibility for all pre-trial issues apart from the grant or removal of bail. Where lay magistrates were involved, they would act as 'wingers' in three-person tribunals chaired by justices' clerks. The clerks' decision on points of law would be final, but any decision on the facts would be by simple majority. Sir Robin Auld rejected this submission and essentially recommended that the role of justices' clerks should remain unchanged.

The selection process

The *Review of the Criminal Courts* (2001) recommended that steps should be taken to make magistrates reflect more broadly than at present the communities they serve. Increased loss of earnings allowances and crèche facilities at courts (to help young parents) are ways of attracting a more varied range of candidates. Legislation preventing employers from discriminating against magistrates would be difficult to enforce, but might at least make employers more wary about being seen to discriminate, and thus encourage more working class and younger applicants.

The Auld Review (2001) recommended that Local Advisory Committees should be equipped with the information they need to enable them to submit for consideration for appointment candidates that will produce and maintain Benches broadly reflective of the communities they serve. This would include the establishment and maintenance of national and local databases of information on the make-up of the local magistracy. Membership of Local Advisory Committees could be broadened to include members of the ethnic minorities and the working class, perhaps drawn from community organizations and trade unions.

Improvements in consistency

Achieving precise uniformity in sentencing and the granting of bail throughout the country is probably impossible, given the number of cases handled by magistrates' courts; but more detailed guidelines, regularly updated, more training, and some supervision by the higher courts could at least curb the more significant variations.

▌A District Division

The Government commissioned a major review of the criminal courts by Sir Robin Auld. The Review (2001) was primarily focused on the practices and procedures of the criminal courts and a wide range of recommendations were made. The central recommendation of the report was essentially that a new criminal court should be created (though it would for administrative purposes be a division of a court), which would be called the District Division.

Instead of having a separate Crown Court and magistrates' court there would be a single unified criminal court containing three divisions. The three divisions would be the Crown Division (currently the Crown Court), the Magistrates' Division (currently the magistrates' court) and a new intermediate District Division.

Cases before the District Division would be heard by a judge and two lay magistrates. The District Division would deal with a middle range of either-way cases which were unlikely to attract a sentence of more than two years' imprisonment. This would include most burglaries and thefts as well as some assault cases.

Only the judge would be able to determine questions of law, but the judge and lay magistrates would together be judges of fact. The order of proceedings would be broadly the same as in the Crown Division. The judge would rule on matters of law, procedure and inadmissibility of evidence, in the absence of the magistrates where it would be potentially unfair to the defendant to do so in their presence. The judge would not sum up the case to the magistrates, but would retire with them to consider the court's decision. They would reach their verdicts together, each having an equal vote. The judge would give a reasoned judgment and he or she would have sole responsibility for determining the sentence. Defendants would lose their right to insist on a jury trial. Instead, cases would be allocated by magistrates to the relevant Division according to their seriousness.

These recommendations of Sir Robin Auld would have significantly increased the role of magistrates in the criminal justice system, but also represented a major attack on jury trials since they would have significantly reduced the number of cases being heard by a jury. The proposals were heavily criticized by supporters of the jury system. It is questionable whether they would have produced any financial savings. The Law Society expressed its concern that an intermediate court 'would add an unnecessary level of bureaucracy'. After reflection, the Government rejected these recommendations.

▌Community justice centres

The Government is planning to set up some pilot community justice centres which would be modelled on similar centres that have been established in America. These centres aim to bring together the courts and a range of relevant agencies, such as the social services and drug charities, to tackle the underlying problems in a community that lead to crime and anti-social behaviour. As well as bringing offenders to justice, the centres aim to develop crime prevention and to solve community problems. The centres would also offer mediation for minor disputes.

Reading on the web

The research of Rod Morgan and Neil Russell, *The Judiciary in the Magistrates' Courts* (2000), is available on the Home Office website in the section dedicated to the Research Development and Statistics Directorate:

http://www.homeoffice.gov.uk/rds/pdfs/occ-judiciary.pdf

The website of the Magistrates Association, which represents the interests of magistrates, is available at:

http://www.magistrates-association.org.uk

General information about magistrates is available on the Department for Constitutional Affairs website. This site includes information about the appointment process and training:

http://www.dca.gov.uk/magistrates.htm

The BBC's website provides some introductory information on magistrates:

http://www.bbc.co.uk/crime/fighters/magistratescourt.shtml

Question and answer guides

As well as the following examples, the role of magistrates may also be considered as part of a question on lay involvement in the criminal justice system generally, and in questions on the criminal justice system itself.

1 'Magistrates' courts are cheap, but it is wrong that matters of vital concern to the citizen should be decided by amateurs.' In your opinion, how far is this statement true?

Answer guide

You need to address the three points made by this question in turn. First, are magistrates cheap? This is covered in the first point under 'Advantages of lay magistrates' at p. 192. Secondly, can they be fairly described as amateurs? You could mention here that lay magistrates do not have legal qualifications, but do have some training – you might refer to the extra training given to magistrates dealing with family and juvenile cases and to those acting as the chairperson. You should also mention the role of the justices' clerk, who can guide them on the law.

You then need to point out what matters of vital concern they decide – these will mainly be criminal, and you should note that some summary and either-way offences can be serious, and even those which appear minor, such as driving offences, can have serious consequences for individuals. You could also draw attention to the fact that the criminal jurisdiction of the magistrates' court has been increased, with more offences being made summary only. In civil cases, the magistrates' family jurisdiction can be seen as being of vital importance for the citizen.

The main emphasis in your essay should be on the next part: do you think it is right that amateur magistrates should decide such important cases? Do not be tempted simply to list the advantages and disadvantages of magistrates – although that is the information you will use, you must relate it to the idea of magistrates as amateurs. Obvious points to make would be those about inconsistency, and possibly about bias towards the police.

You might then go on to state any advantages of magistrates which could outweigh, or balance out, the problems of being amateurs – their local knowledge, and the fact that they involve the community, for example. You could make a brief comparison between trial by magistrates and trial by jury, drawing attention to the fact that juries too are lay people who have also been accused of providing amateur justice. You could also compare trial by magistrates with the other alternatives – those listed as alternatives to juries (p. 177) are also alternatives to magistrates. You might point out that one of the allegations made against magistrates – that they come from a narrow social background – is even more true of professional judges. If you have time, run through some of the suggested reforms to magistrates, such as better training.

Your conclusion should state your opinion – you might say that magistrates are amateur and should not be given such vital matters to deal with, or that their advantages outweigh their amateur status. You could conclude that if reforms were made, the position would be improved, or even suggest that amateur status is a positive advantage – it all depends what the rest of your answer has argued – but you should give some opinion.

2 **Recent reforms have increased the powers of magistrates in the criminal justice system. Are their powers now too great – or too small?**

Answer guide

You need to start by outlining the criminal powers of magistrates, and particularly those powers which have come about as a result of recent changes – these are described in the section on criminal jurisdiction in this chapter (p. 188). You could point out that there are also areas where magistrates have lost powers – the abolition of committal proceedings, and the decreased use of magistrates' warrants (see Chapter 12). You could point to the recent reforms discussed at p. 189 allowing magistrates to exercise certain case management powers on their own. The main part of your essay should concentrate on whether their powers should be increased or decreased.

You need to go through any reasons why it might be seen as a good idea to increase the powers of magistrates – cost is obviously one, and you might also consider some of the other advantages of magistrates, such as local knowledge or community involvement, which also justify increased powers.

Then consider any reasons why magistrates' powers should not be increased, or should even be decreased. The problems of bias towards the police and inconsistency are clearly relevant here.

If you have time, you could run through any of the relevant reforms mentioned in this chapter, and if you have been arguing that magistrates' powers are too great, say whether you think those powers would be acceptable, or could be increased, if these reforms were carried out.

3 Study the extract below and then answer the questions which follow.

> Over 95 per cent of criminal trials take place in a magistrates' court. A Bench of usually three justices of the peace will hear the evidence, decide whether the accused is innocent or guilty and, if guilty, pass sentence. They also hear committal proceedings. Yet these men and women are not trained lawyers, they are not paid for their work and they sit in court perhaps once a month. Magistrates' courts are regularly criticized for inconsistency. Sentences for the same offence vary widely from one court to another; applications for legal aid and bail are granted far more often in one court than they are in another. Even more seriously, magistrates are accused of being far too willing to accept police evidence and to convict.

(a) How are justices of the peace appointed? *(4 marks)*

(b) Explain what is meant by 'committal proceedings'? *(4 marks)*

(c) What are the advantages of trial in a magistrates' court? *(8 marks)*

(d) What changes would you recommend to improve the working of the magistrates' courts? *(9 marks) (London)*

▶

Answer guide

(a) It was seen at p. 183 that justices of the peace are appointed by the Lord Chancellor on the recommendation of Local Advisory Committees. At pp. 185–7 it was mentioned that there has been criticism of the types of persons who are in practice selected.

(b) Committal proceedings are discussed at p. 273 in the chapter on the criminal trial process. In summary, they assess the evidence for offences triable either way to see whether there is a *prima facie* case to put to a jury in a Crown Court.

(c) Some advantages of trial by magistrates are discussed at p. 192.

(d) Possible reforms are discussed at p. 196. As the question is phrased widely to include 'the workings of the magistrates' courts' you could also look at whether the current trend to increase the workload of the magistrates' courts should be reversed. ('London Qualifications Ltd.', accepts no responsibility whatsoever for the accuracy or method in the answers given.)

Chapter summary

Introduction

There are 30,000 lay magistrates and 105 professional judges who sit in the magistrates' courts.

Selection and appointment

Lay magistrates are appointed by the Lord Chancellor (whose role is currently being carried out by the Minister for Constitutional Affairs) in the name of the Crown, on the advice of Local Advisory Committees.

Background

More than two-thirds of lay magistrates are employed in a professional or managerial position, or were until they retired. Almost a third of magistrates are in their sixties. A high proportion are Conservative voters. Lay magistrates do, however, increasingly reflect the ethnic diversity of contemporary Britain and the sexes are fairly evenly balanced.

Training

The Magistrates' Commission Committees are responsible for providing training under the supervision of the Judicial Studies Board.

Jurisdiction

Magistrates are primarily concerned with criminal matters but they exercise a limited jurisdiction over some civil matters.

The justices' clerk and legal adviser

The primary function of the justices' clerk and legal adviser is to advise the lay magistrates on law and procedure. They are not supposed to take any part in the actual decision of the Bench.

Lay magistrates versus professional judges

In recent years there has been some discussion as to whether lay magistrates should be replaced by professional judges.

PART 3

Dispute resolution

This Part looks at the formal and informal methods available in England and Wales to solve disputes. The formal methods pass through either the criminal justice system or the civil justice system and include a structured appeal process. Less formal methods fall within the concept of alternative methods of dispute resolution and include references to ombudsmen. All of these methods of resolving disputes require funding, and we look first at the different sources of funding available in Chapter 11 Access to justice.

AQA Examination Board

Chapters 11–14 and 17–20 cover AS module 2: Dispute solving

Chapter 15 covers AS module 3: The concept of liability

OCR Examination Board

Chapters 11–17 and 19–20 cover The English legal system module

WJEC Examination Board

Chapters 11–14 and 17–20 cover the Machinery of justice module

---

Chapter 11 Paying for legal services

Since society requires that all its members keep the law, it follows that all members of society should be not only equally bound by, but equally served by, the legal system. Legal rights are after all worthless unless they can be enforced. Yet justice may be open to all, but only in the same way as is the Ritz Hotel. In other words, anyone can go there, but only if they can afford it – and just like the Ritz Hotel, legal advice and help can be very expensive. As a result, many people simply cannot afford to enforce their legal rights and are therefore denied access to justice.

What is more, cost is not the only thing which stops many ordinary people from using the legal system. Other issues such as awareness of legal rights, the elitist image of the legal profession and even its geographical situation, all contribute to the problem which legal writers call 'unmet legal need'. In the following section, we look at what unmet legal need really means, and the causes of it; later in the chapter we consider the various attempts which have been made to resolve the problem, including the provision of state funding, which, as we will see, has been the subject of radical reforms.

Unmet need for legal services

Unmet legal need essentially describes the situation where a person has a problem that could potentially be solved through the law, but the person is unable to get whatever help he or she needs through the legal system.

Research carried out by Pascoe Pleasence and others for the Legal Services Commission in 2004 has found that over a three-and-a-half-year period, more than one in three adults experienced a civil law problem; one in five took no action to solve their problem; and around 1 million problems went unsolved because people did not understand their basic rights or know how to seek help. About 15 per cent of people who sought advice did not succeed in obtaining any. The research revealed that civil law problems are not evenly distributed. Groups vulnerable to social exclusion suffer more problems more often. The survey showed civil justice problems were experienced by:

- four in five people living in temporary accommodation;
- two in three lone parents; and
- more than half of unemployed people.

Many civil justice problems trigger other problems and increase the risk of social exclusion. For example, an accident could lead to personal injury, which could lead to loss of income and then the loss of a person's home.

Research by Richard White in 1973 suggested four situations where someone would fail to get the legal help they needed:

■ the person fails to recognize a problem as having legal implications and so does not seek out legal advice;

■ the problem is recognized as being a legal one, but the person involved does not know of the existence of a legal service that could help, or his/her own eligibility to use it;

■ the person knows the problem is a legal one, and knows of the service that could help with it, but chooses not to make use of it because of some barrier, such as cost, ignorance of state funding, or the unapproachable image of solicitors;

■ the person knows there is a legal problem and wants legal help, but fails to get it because the person cannot find a service to deal with it.

Of these reasons, the barrier of cost has traditionally received most attention, and it is an important one; a 1991 *Which?* report found one in ten people were put off seeking legal advice by cost. Simply obtaining legal advice from a private solicitor is expensive, and taking a case to court much more so – and in English law, losers in civil cases must usually pay the costs of the winner as well as their own costs. This gives the rich three major advantages: they can hire good lawyers and pay for the time needed to do the job properly; they can afford to take the risk of losing litigation; and they can use their wealth to bully a less well-off opponent, by dragging out the case or making it more complex (and therefore more expensive). Bear in mind that 'the rich' does not just mean the millionaire in the Rolls-Royce, but also the employer you might want to sue for unfair dismissal, the company whose products could make you ill, or the builder who left you with a leaky roof, and you can see the problem.

However, as White's research shows, cost is not the only reason why people fail to secure help with their legal problems. This is backed up by the 1973 research of Abel-Smith *et al.*, which compared people's own perception of their need for legal help and the action they took to get it. Almost all the respondents consulted a solicitor when they felt they needed advice on buying a house (though, of course, this only includes those with sufficient means to buy their own home). For employment problems though, only 4 per cent consulted a solicitor; 34 per cent took advice from some other source and 62 per cent took no advice at all. For social security problems, solicitors were consulted by even fewer people: just 3 per cent saw a solicitor, while 16 per cent took other advice and 81 per cent took none at all. Yet in all these cases, the people surveyed realized that they did need some legal advice.

Similarly, Zander (1988) has pointed out that even the poorest members of society consult solicitors about divorce, while the middle classes seem no more likely than working-class people to consult solicitors about employment or consumer problems.

American sociologists Mayhew and Reiss put forward a 'social organization' theory to explain why solicitors are consulted in some cases and not others. This theory suggests that certain types of work are related to social contact – most people know people who have used solicitors for conveyancing and divorce and it becomes an obvious step to take. As Zander points out, lawyers adjust the services they offer to demand and so it becomes a self-fulfilling prophecy.

Research carried out by Professor Hazel Genn in 1998 categorized the different types of people who are confronted by a legal problem. Five per cent were labelled as 'lumpers'. This group had low incomes, low education levels and were frequently unemployed. They were unable to see any way out of their money and employment problems and therefore did absolutely nothing. This could lead to a 'cluster' of problems where the person was increasingly incapable of helping him or herself. The next group was described as 'self-helpers' and had only a 50 per cent chance of resolving their legal problems. They often believed until the last minute that nothing could be done to help them and when they tried to take action they found they had gone, or been sent, to the wrong place; or were confronted by queues, unanswered telephones and restricted opening times. Professor Genn found that social distress could be caused where legal problems were left unresolved. By contrast, if people got good-quality early advice, they could help themselves.

Another problem, identified by the Royal Commission on Legal Services (1979), is the uneven geographical distribution of solicitors throughout the country. The Commission highlighted research showing that while there was one solicitor's office for every 4,700 people in England and Wales, their distribution varied enormously, from one office for every 2,000 people in prosperous owner-occupier areas such as Bournemouth and Guildford, to one for every 66,000 in working-class areas such as Huyton in Liverpool. The Commission concluded that the low rates for state-funded work had much to do with this; most private firms need to subsidize such work with privately funded work, and the poorer areas may not provide enough of this to keep more than a few solicitors in each area in business. Other advice agencies, such as law centres and Citizens' Advice Bureaux, may also be thin on the ground in some, particularly rural, areas. The image of lawyers as predominantly white, male and from privileged backgrounds may also contribute to the problem, making them unapproachable to many people.

In its 1999 report *A Balancing Act; Surviving the Risk Society*, the National Association of Citizens' Advice Bureaux (NACAB) suggested that the problem of unmet legal need may still be growing. It pointed out that changes in society are forcing more and more people to take on responsibility for their own welfare, in areas where the state would once have made provision, while insecurity in work, housing and family relationships is increasing. This means more and more people are placed in situations where they need to assert their legal rights – divorce, homelessness, debt or employment problems, for example – but are unable to do so because there is too little access to free, independent legal advice.

In the following sections, we look at the attempts that successive governments have made to ease the problem of unmet legal need by providing state-funded legal help, and then at a range of other approaches to the problem.

State-funded legal services

The system of state-funded legal help in this country goes back over half a century. After the Second World War, the Labour Government introduced a range of measures designed to address the huge inequalities between rich and poor. These included the National Health Service, the beginnings of today's social security system and, in 1949, the first state-funded legal aid scheme. The legal aid scheme was designed to allow poorer people access to legal advice and representation in court: this would be provided by solicitors in private practice, but the state, rather than the client, would pay all or part of the fees. By the 1980s, the system had developed into six different schemes, covering most kinds of legal case, and administered by the Legal Aid Board. But the growing cost of these schemes was causing concern. In the 1990s the Conservative Government sought to keep the escalating costs down by reducing financial eligibility for the schemes, which in turn led to criticisms that they were also reducing access to justice. As a result of all this, the Labour Government passed the Access to Justice Act 1999 which made major changes to the system.

Before looking at the new system of state funding, it is useful to look at the system that it replaced, in order to consider what problems the changes are designed to address, and how successful they are likely to be.

Legal aid before the Access to Justice Act 1999

The six schemes which made up the legal aid scheme until the 1999 Access to Justice Act was brought into force were:

- the legal advice and assistance scheme (known as the 'green form' scheme because of the paperwork used);
- assistance by way of representation (ABWOR);
- civil legal aid;
- criminal legal aid;
- duty solicitor schemes in police stations;
- duty solicitor schemes for criminal cases in magistrates' courts.

Each scheme had its own rules on eligibility and some included means and/or merits tests. A means test assesses eligibility on the basis of the applicant's disposable income, which is the money left each week after paying for certain essential living expenses; and sometimes disposable capital, which effectively means savings. Only those with disposable incomes below the limit laid down for the type of legal aid required were eligible for help. Merits tests assess whether the applicant's case is likely to succeed, and whether it is sufficiently important to justify state funding. The specific details of the means and merits tests varied according to the type of legal aid, and some imposed neither test.

Legal aid was not always free – for civil and criminal legal aid, clients whose income or savings were above a certain limit were expected to contribute towards their legal costs. And with civil legal aid, it frequently acted more like a loan, since the costs could be deducted from the damages awarded to the successful client.

The Lord Chancellor was the Government Minister responsible for the legal aid scheme, but its day-to-day administration was undertaken by the Legal Aid Board, through area directors and committees.

The six schemes that existed before the Access to Justice Act 1999 came into force will now be considered in more detail.

The green form scheme

This was set up to provide legal advice and assistance in any civil or criminal matter, except conveyancing and drawing up wills. The assistance given included drafting letters and other documents and advising clients who intended to represent themselves in court on what to say, but did not cover representation in court by the solicitor.

Assistance by way of representation (ABWOR)

This was an extension of the green form scheme, which provided representation in a limited number of situations and was subject to a means test.

Civil legal aid

This covered all the work involved in bringing or defending a civil case, including representation in court by a solicitor or barrister.

Criminal legal aid

Like civil legal aid, this covered the whole range of legal advice, assistance and representation, including the cost of a barrister if the case was heard in the Crown Court.

Duty solicitor schemes in police stations

This scheme has been retained following the 1999 reforms. Duty solicitor schemes in the police station were set up in response to the provisions of the Police and Criminal Evidence Act 1984, which provides a right to legal advice for suspects detained by the police. The idea is to ensure that access to a solicitor for advice and assistance is available 24 hours a day to anyone detained by the police. Clients are not, however, obliged to use duty solicitors, and can still consult their own solicitors.

The scheme is free and available to anyone who is being questioned by the police regardless of whether they have been arrested. There are no means or merits tests.

The Legal Services Commission plans to save money by providing some of this advice through a national telephone service. It intends to establish a telephone service, called Criminal Defence Service Direct, which would be available for people detained in police stations for summary offences, such as theft and being drunk and disorderly.

Duty solicitor schemes in magistrates' courts

This scheme has also been retained following the 1999 reforms. Solicitors on a rota basis are present at the courts to advise unrepresented defendants. There is no means or merits test.

Quick quiz 11.1

1 What did Professor Hazel Genn mean when she described some people as 'lumpers'?

2 When was the first state-funded legal aid scheme established?

3 Name the six schemes that existed before the Access to Justice Act 1999 came into force.

4 What was the name of the body responsible for administering the old legal aid scheme?

Problems with the six schemes

Even by the early 1980s, it was clear that there were severe problems with the state-funded schemes. They had become extremely costly – by 1997, state-funded legal aid was costing £1.6 billion, six times higher than in 1979 – yet even the huge amounts being spent were failing to deliver real access to justice for all levels of society. Despite its cost, the legal aid system suffered from a range of problems which will now be considered.

Eligibility

Eligibility levels for the means-tested schemes were drastically lowered after 1992. In 1979, 79 per cent of adults were eligible for civil legal aid, including those who would have had to pay contributions, but by 1993 this had dropped to 48 per cent, which was still the level in 1999.

The result of this was that while the very poor could get legal aid, and the rich, as ever, could afford their own legal costs, the vast majority of people on moderate incomes faced a choice between incurring severe financial burdens, or simply being unable to assert their legal rights.

Even for those who did still qualify for legal aid, eligibility for free help ran out at an extremely low level, and above that, the contributions payable could be very expensive, especially for those at the top end of the eligibility scale.

Funding

Lawyers constantly claimed that the system was underfunded and that lawyers working within it were badly paid. The underfunding risked creating a second-class service, not necessarily because of lack of quality in the lawyers themselves, but because they simply could not afford to spend the same amount of time on a case as a privately-funded lawyer.

Fraud and misuse

In 1997, the Government revealed that over the previous year, more than 25,000 individuals granted legal aid were later discovered not to have been entitled to it. Newspapers estimated that these claims were costing up to £60 million a year.

Patchy coverage

The piecemeal development of the statutory schemes brought about considerable overlap between schemes, while failing to fill important gaps. One of the most significant was that legal aid was not available for cases brought before most tribunals.

Standards of work

A number of problems with criminal legal aid were uncovered by the 1993 Royal Commission on Criminal Justice, which was set up to look at the whole of the criminal justice system after a series of miscarriages of justice were uncovered in the late 1980s and early 1990s. The most serious allegation, made in research by McConville *et al.* (1993), was that the standard of legally aided criminal defence work was very low. Much of it was done by unqualified staff; there was little investigative work, and solicitors pushed clients towards pleading guilty rather than taking time to prepare an effective defence. McConville claimed that the heavy workloads and low pay of legal aid work forced solicitors to see their clients as 'economic units', to be processed as quickly as possible.

Means test for criminal legal aid

In 1997–98 contributions made by defendants to the cost of their criminal legal aid amounted to £6.2 million, but the direct cost of administering means testing and enforcing contributions was around £5 million.

State funding of legal services today

With the passing of the Access to Justice Act 1999 the Labour Government introduced some major reforms to the provision of state-funded legal services. Through these reforms the Government hoped to improve the quality and accessibility of the legal services on offer, while keeping a tighter control on their budget. On 1 April 2000 the Legal Aid Board was replaced by the Legal Services Commission. It currently has a budget of approximately £2 billion a year. The Commission is an executive non-departmental public body reporting to the Minister for Constitutional Affairs. The Minister provides guidance to the Commission on his priorities but is not allowed to give guidance about the handling of any individual case.

In order to develop the standard and accessibility of legal services, the Legal Services Commission has established a quality mark, is building partnerships with the different suppliers of legal services and has set up a website.

Quality mark

The Commission has created a new quality mark to help people make more informed choices about the legal service providers they use. The mark is applied to all kinds of legal services, from providers of information and general advice agencies to specialist solicitors. To be awarded a quality mark, the service providers have to meet set quality standards, so that users of their services know when they see the mark that those standards have been met.

Community Legal Service Partnerships

The Legal Services Commission has a duty to liaise with other funders of legal services (such as local councils, which help to fund local advice centres) in order to develop a network of legal service providers. National, regional and local plans have been developed to match the services available in a particular area to the needs of the people living there. To do this, the Commission has set up Community Legal Service Partnerships (CLSPs) in each local authority area, involving the Commission, the local authority and other significant funders of legal services, to co-ordinate funding and planning. These partnerships provide a forum for sharing expertise, developing and improving services and for monitoring what is happening locally. They should facilitate the creation of effective local referral networks in every area and ensure that funding is appropriately targeted.

As we have seen, gaps in the geographical distribution of legal services increase unmet legal need. The Commission and the CLSPs are encouraging the voluntary sector to use the Internet and mobile services to reach more remote communities.

Website

The Legal Services Commission website can be found at **www.clsdirect.org.uk**. The website provides basic information for members of the public.

The schemes

The Legal Services Commission administers two schemes: the Community Legal Service, which is concerned with civil matters, and the Criminal Defence Service, which is concerned with criminal matters. These two schemes will be considered in turn.

The Community Legal Service

Funding

Whereas previously legal aid in civil cases was available on a demand-led basis (meaning that all cases which met the merits and means tests would be funded), there is now a Community Legal Service Fund, containing a fixed amount of money, set each year as part of the normal round of government spending plans.

The detailed way in which the fund is to be spent is decided by a Funding Code, drawn up by the Legal Services Commission and approved by the Lord Chancellor, which sets out the criteria and procedures to be used when deciding whether a particular case should be funded. The Commission has a duty to obtain the best value for money, which the explanatory notes to the Access to Justice Act 1999 define as taking into account 'a combination of price and quality'. In other words, the Commission is not obliged to choose the cheapest possible service, but it is not obliged to choose the best quality one either; it has to find the best balance between the two.

Levels of funded legal services

Community Legal Service

Figure 11.1 The logo of the Community Legal Service

Source: Legal Services Commission.

Only solicitors or advice agencies holding a contract with the Legal Services Commission are able to provide advice or representation directly funded by the Commission. For specialist areas of law such as family law, immigration, mental health and clinical negligence only specialist firms are funded to do the work. The merits test for civil legal aid has been replaced by the new Funding Code discussed above. This Code lays down the rules as to which cases should receive funding. Direct funding is provided for different categories of legal service, as follows:

Legal Help. Legal Help provides initial advice and assistance with any legal problem. A means test is applied. This level of service covers work previously carried out under the 'green form' scheme.

Legal Representation. Funding is available for a person to be represented in court proceedings. Both a means and a merits test are applied. This scheme replaces civil legal aid.

Help at Court. Help at Court allows somebody (a solicitor or adviser) to speak on another's behalf at certain court hearings, without formally acting for them in the whole proceedings. A means test is applied.

Approved Family Help. Approved Family Help provides help in relation to a family dispute, including assistance in resolving that dispute through negotiation or otherwise. This overlaps with the services covered by Legal Help, but also includes issuing proceedings and representation where necessary to obtain disclosure of information from another party, or to obtain a consent order where the parties have reached an agreement.

Family Mediation. This level of service covers mediation for a family dispute, including finding out whether mediation appears suitable or not.

Coverage

Certain types of case have been removed from the state-funded system altogether. These are:

■ Personal injury cases (with the exception of clinical negligence cases). Instead these are funded by conditional fee agreements which are discussed later in this chapter.
■ Cases of defamation and malicious falsehood. Legal aid was never available for defamation. When the legal aid system was first established in 1949, defamation was excluded because the Attorney-General of the day was concerned that it would produce frivolous and unnecessary claims. While he accepted that the reputation of a poor person is just as deserving of legal protection as that of a wealthy person, he was worried that the legal aid scheme would be seriously overloaded

if every slander uttered across the back garden wall could be pursued at the expense of the state. In some cases, behaviour which would normally be classed as defamation could be categorized as the related tort of malicious falsehood, for which legal aid was available. Now, neither is eligible for state funding. Under the Access to Justice Act 1999, legal aid can exceptionally be made available for such cases, but this has only happened once. Proceedings for defamation and malicious falsehood can, instead, be brought under a conditional fee agreement, discussed at p. 215.

■ Disputes arising in the course of a business. Business traders can insure against the cost of having to bring or defend a legal action, and the Government believes that taxpayers should not be required to meet the legal costs of those who fail to do so.

■ Matters concerning the law relating to companies, partnerships, trusts (trusts are a way of holding property, and as such, tend mainly to affect wealthier people), or boundary disputes (for example, disputes between neighbours as to where each party's garden begins and ends).

The Government considers that none of these types of case are sufficiently important to justify public funding. Approximately 80,000 people are injured each year at work, on the road or during a leisure activity. It has been estimated that personal injury cases accounted for around 60 per cent of cases previously funded by legal aid. However, the Access to Justice Act 1999 provides that a Government Minister can direct the Commission to provide services for excluded categories in exceptional circumstances.

Eligibility

There will continue to be both merits and means tests for some forms of state funding of civil legal services. A single means test applies. State funding is not available if a person earns more than £2,288 per month and if a person has £8,000 in savings.

The old merits test has been replaced by the criteria set out in the Funding Code, and this is intended to be more flexible than the previous test, in that different criteria can be applied to different types of case, depending on their priority. For example, the chances of success might be relevant in many types of case, but would not be in cases about whether a child should be taken into local authority care.

Suppliers

In the past, a person who wanted help with a problem covered by legal aid could go to any lawyer and, provided the client met the relevant means and merits tests, that lawyer would be paid by the Government for the help given in that particular case. This situation was beginning to change even before the 1999 Act was passed. In 1994 the Legal Aid Board began a quality-assurance scheme called franchising. Law firms could apply for a franchise in particular areas of work, and would have to pass quality control tests in order to get one, but would then be able to attract more work in that area. Similar agreements were made, on a pilot basis, with advice agencies, so that they could provide advice and assistance in specific areas. The Act takes this idea further, so that only solicitors and advice agencies holding contracts with the Legal Services Commission are able to get state funding.

The 1999 Act also gives the Commission power to make grants to service providers, such as advice centres, and to employ staff directly to deliver legal services to the public. This latter point means that the Commission could, if it wished, create a system of lawyers employed by the state to provide legal help to the public, though there appear to be no plans to do so with regard to civil cases at the moment.

Future changes

The Act allows for a new way of funding legal help for individuals, which at present the Government has no plans to use. It provides for a scheme in which people could be given state funding, but would be required to agree that, if they win their case, they will pay back the state funding (which they would presumably claim from the losing party), plus a further sum. This would make it possible to fund certain types of case on a self-financing basis, with the extra sums paid by winning litigants funding the costs of those who lose their cases.

Quick quiz 11.2

1 When was the Community Legal Service established?

2 What is the name of the body that administers the Community Legal Service?

3 What does 'CLSP' stand for?

4 What are the five different categories of legal service that get direct funding as part of the Community Legal Service?

The Criminal Defence Service

In April 2001 a Criminal Defence Service was introduced, replacing the old system of criminal legal aid. This Criminal Defence Service is administered by the Legal Services Commission.

Funding

Unlike legal aid in civil cases, state-funded criminal defence will continue to be given on a demand-led basis; there will be no set budget and all cases which fit the merits criteria will be funded.

Levels of funded legal services

As part of this service the Commission directly funds the provision of criminal legal services, employs public defenders and pays for duty solicitor schemes. Thus under the Criminal Defence Service, legal services are provided by both lawyers in private practice and employed lawyers. The Government believes that a mixed system of public and private lawyers will provide the best value for money for the taxpayer. The salaried service is intended to provide a benchmark to assess whether prices charged by private practice lawyers are reasonable, as well as filling in gaps in the system.

Direct funding

Only solicitor firms having a contract with the Legal Services Commission are able to offer state-funded criminal defence work. Unlike the contracts for civil matters, the contracts for criminal defence matters do not limit the number of cases that can be taken on, nor the total value of the payments that may be made. Contracted solicitors will be paid for all work actually undertaken in accordance with the contract. Solicitors with a contract should be able to provide the full range of criminal defence services, from the time of arrest until the end of the case (unlike with the previous system, where defendants could receive assistance relating to the same alleged offence under several different schemes, each resulting in a separate payment for the lawyers involved). In certain cases – such as serious fraud trials – there are panels of firms or individual lawyers who specialize in the relevant type of case, and defendants will be required to choose from that panel. State funding can support three types of service.

Advice and assistance. Funding is available for the provision of advice and assistance from a solicitor, including giving general advice, writing letters, negotiating, getting a barrister's opinion and preparing a written case. A means test is applied but people who are eligible do not have to make any contribution to the legal costs. It does not cover representation in court.

When a person is questioned by the police, he or she has a right to free legal advice from a contracted solicitor and no means test is applied.

Advocacy assistance. Advocacy assistance covers the costs of a solicitor preparing a client's case and initial representation in certain proceedings in both the magistrates' court and the Crown Court and in certain other circumstances. There is no means test but there is a merits test.

Representation. When a person has been charged with a criminal offence, representation covers the cost of a solicitor to prepare the person's defence and to represent him/her in court. It may also be available for a bail application. It will sometimes pay for a barrister, particularly for the Crown Court and for the cost of an appeal.

Decisions to grant representation in individual cases are made by the magistrates' courts. Representation will be granted when it is in the 'interests of justice'. The court may decide that it is in the interests of justice to grant representation where, for example, the case is so serious that on conviction a person is likely to be sent to prison or to lose their job, where there are substantial questions of law to be argued, or where the defendant is unable to follow the proceedings and explain their case because they do not speak English well enough or are suffering from a psychiatric illness.

Previously, criminal legal aid was means tested. Under the new scheme the means test has been abolished. Instead, for cases heard in the Crown Court orders can be issued at the end of a trial to recover the defence costs against wealthy people who have been convicted of an offence. This reform reflected the fact that in most cases the defendants are too poor to pay for their own legal services – in the past only 1 per cent of applicants were refused legal aid. The hope is that by abolishing the means test altogether the criminal process will be speeded up.

Public defenders

Since May 2001 the Legal Services Commission directly employs a number of criminal defence lawyers, known as public defenders. The plans envisage a start-up phase for the salaried service of four years, to run alongside a research programme. The research is looking into a range of issues, including the cost-effectiveness and the quality of the service provided by the pilot projects. There are six regional offices being piloted at the moment. The public defenders can provide the same services as lawyers in private practice and have to compete for work. The Government has promised that clients will not be forced to choose a public defender, but public defenders will be allocated slots on duty solicitor schemes in police stations and magistrates' courts where they will meet potential clients. It is then anticipated that, because there are many repeat offenders, there will be an expanding client base.

 Know your terms 11.3

Define the following terms:

1 Approved Family Help
2 Means test
3 Criminal Defence Service
4 Public defender

There has been strong opposition to the introduction of public defenders. The explanatory notes to the Access to Justice Act state that the idea is to provide flexibility, so that employed lawyers could be used if, for example, there is a shortage of suitable private lawyers in remoter areas. The notes point out that using salaried lawyers will also give the Commission better information about the real costs of providing the services. Public defenders will not necessarily be cheaper than solicitors in private practice, but they will provide an element of competition. They are required to follow a code of conduct guaranteeing certain standards of professional behaviour, including duties to avoid discrimination, to protect the interests of those whom they are defending, to avoid conflicts of interest and to maintain confidentiality.

At the moment, public defenders are only employed in eight public defenders' offices scattered around the county, but the intention is for them to be available nationally in the future. People suspected of crime will therefore have a choice only between these public defenders, and lawyers who have a contract with the Commission, though within that limited range it is intended that there should be some choice in all but the most exceptional circumstances.

Duty solicitor schemes

The duty solicitor schemes have remained unchanged by the reforms. Duty solicitors are available at police stations and magistrates' courts and offer free legal advice.

Coverage

The aim of the Criminal Defence Service, according to the explanatory notes to the Access to Justice Act, is to ensure that individuals involved in criminal investigations or criminal proceedings 'have access to such advice, assistance and representation as the interests of justice require'.

Eligibility

State funding for criminal cases is no longer subject to a means test. Instead, it is automatically granted if the merits test is satisfied. The merits test has remained unchanged under the 1999 Act. Where cases are tried in the Crown Court (which is substantially more costly than the magistrates' courts), at the end of the case the judge has the power to order a defendant to pay some or all of the costs of his or her defence. The Legal Services Commission is able to investigate the financial position of defendants in such cases, in order to help the judge decide whether to make such an order.

Community Legal Service Direct

In 2004, Community Legal Service Direct was established. This is a national telephone and website service providing free legal advice on civil law matters. Members of the public can telephone the helpline on 0845 345 4345 for advice on such matters as housing, social security benefits and debt. Alternatively, they can visit the website at **www.clsdirect.org.uk**. This website is visited over 50,000 times each month. The Community Legal Service Direct is intended to provide an alternative to face-to-face advice, which will be particularly attractive to those with mobility problems, caring responsibilities or accommodation in a remote area. In addition, some people may feel more comfortable talking about their problems with the relative anonymity of a telephone line, rather than in a face-to-face meeting.

Other participants in the Community Legal Service

There are a number of non-profit-making agencies which give legal advice and sometimes representation, and initiatives by the legal profession and other commercial organizations also address the issue of access to justice.

Law centres

Law centres offer a free, non-means-tested service to people who live or work in their area. They aim to be accessible to anyone who needs legal help, and in order to achieve this usually operate from ground floor, high street premises, stay open beyond office hours, employ a high proportion of lay people as well as lawyers and generally encourage a more relaxed atmosphere than that found in most private solicitors' offices. Most law centres are run by a management committee drawn from the local area, so that they have direct links with the community.

The first law centres were established in 1969 today there are around 50 of them. The Law Society allowed them to advertise (before the restriction on advertising was lifted for solicitors in general) in exchange for the centres not undertaking certain areas of work which were the mainstay of the average high street solicitor – small personal injury cases, wills and conveyancing. Their main areas of work are housing, welfare, immigration and employment.

Law centres are largely funded by grants from central and local government, though a few have also managed to secure some financial support from large local private firms. This method of funding means that they do not have to work on a case-by-case basis but can allocate funding according to community priorities.

Because they do not depend on case-by-case funding, law centres have developed innovative ways of solving legal problems. As well as dealing with individual cases, they run campaigns designed to make local people aware of their legal rights, act as a pressure group on local issues such as bad housing, and take action where appropriate on behalf of groups as well as individuals. The reasoning behind this approach is that resources and time are better used tackling problems as a whole, rather than aspects of those problems as they appear case by case. For example, if a council has failed to replace lead piping or asbestos in its council houses, it would seem more efficient to approach the council about all the properties rather than take out individual cases for each tenant as they become aware that they have a problem.

Law centres also provide valuable services in areas not covered by the statutory schemes, such as inquests, and several have set up duty solicitor schemes to deal with housing cases in the county court and help prevent evictions. They may offer a 24-hour general emergency service.

Most law centres face long-term problems with funding; several have closed, and others go through periodic struggles for survival. It is hoped that the Access to Justice Act, with its emphasis on making the most of voluntary advice services, will mean better funding in future. The danger is that local authorities will withdraw funding as funding becomes available from the Legal Services Commission.

Citizens' Advice Bureaux

There are around 700 Citizens' Advice Bureaux across the country, offering free advice and help with a whole range of problems, though the most common areas at the moment are social security and debt. They are largely staffed by trained volunteers, who can become expert in the areas they most frequently deal with. Where professional legal help is required, some bureaux employ solicitors, some have regular help from solicitor volunteers and others refer individuals to local solicitors who undertake state-funded work. The bureaux are overseen by the National Association of Citizens' Advice Bureaux and must conform to its standards and codes of practice.

Task 11.4

Imagine that you are homeless with two children. You want to find out whether you have any rights to accommodation. Go to the Legal Services Commission website at **www.clsdirect.org.uk** and see whether you can find any useful information.

The Citizens' Advice Bureau provides advice on line at **www.adviceguide.org.uk**. Compare the information that is available on this website.

One of their major advantages is a very high level of public awareness – because they are frequently mentioned in the press and have easily recognizable high street offices, most people know where they are and what they do.

Like law centres, they have come under considerable financial pressure in recent years, with the result that many can only open for a very limited number of hours a week. The Access to Justice Act may mean better funding in future.

Other sources of legal help

Some local authorities run money, welfare, consumer and housing advice centres to provide both advice and a mechanism for dealing with complaints, while charities such as Shelter, the Child Poverty Action Group and MIND often offer legal help in their specialist areas. Other organizations, such as trade unions, motoring organizations, such as the AA and RAC, and the Consumers' Association give free or inexpensive legal help to their members. Some university law faculties run 'law clinics', where students, supervised by their tutors, give free help and advice to members of the public.

There are a number of Internet sites giving basic legal advice for free, and some magazines publish legal advice lines, which charge a premium rate for readers to phone and get one-to-one legal advice from qualified solicitors. It is also possible to insure against legal expenses, either as a stand-alone policy, or more usually, as part of household, credit card or motor insurance.

As we saw earlier, cost is not the only cause of unmet legal need; a reluctance among many ordinary people to bring problems to lawyers is also recognized. In recent years the profession has taken steps to address the issue, including the use of advertising and public relations campaigns. Many high street firms now advertise their services locally, while some of the firms currently involved in suing cigarette manufacturers for illnesses caused by smoking attracted potential clients by advertising specifically for people with smoking-related diseases. In 1994, the Law Society set up Accident Line, under which accident victims can get a free initial interview with a solicitor specializing in personal injury.

Task 11.5

In 2003 the Government issued a consultation paper *Delivering Value for Money in the Criminal Defence Service*. The Government wished to consult the public on proposed changes to the Criminal Defence Service. The end of the document contained a list of questions on which it wished to know the public's views before proceeding to introduce any reforms. These questions included the following:

1 Do you consider that access to free police station advice should be reduced? Would this adversely affect the rights of clients?
2 What types of police station advice should still be funded?
3 What impact would restricting the court duty solicitor scheme have upon the rights of the defendants?
4 What impact do you consider restricting the court duty solicitor scheme would have on the administration of the magistrates' courts?
5 What impact do you consider restricting the court duty solicitor scheme would have upon the number of defendants appearing without representation?

Question

If you were preparing a response to the Government, how would you answer these question?

The Access to Justice Act: an assessment

The Access to Justice Act 1999 was the subject of much opposition during the legislative process, and though some of the criticisms were addressed during the passing of the Act, some of this opposition remains. Below we detail the main criticisms, but first we look at some of the advantages claimed for the new system.

Advantages of the Access to Justice Act reforms

Control of costs

As we have seen, the cost of the previous legal aid system was a major problem. The Government claims that the issuing of contracts, the fixed budget for state funding in civil cases and the fact that the Funding Code will set out clear criteria which reflect agreed priorities, will now mean that costs can be kept under control.

A recent report from the National Audit Office (2003) has identified significant improvements that have taken place in the administration of state funding of legal services, with the creation of the Community Legal Service. The new funding arrangements have led to greater control and targeting of resources and better scrutiny of suppliers.

Better allocation of resources

The Funding Code for civil matters will be designed to reflect agreed priorities, so money can be channelled into those areas which the Government considers reflect best the needs of society, whereas the demand-led approach of the past could not do this.

Higher standards of work

By limiting state funding to contracted lawyers and firms who have passed quality control standards, the Government claims that standards of work should be consistently high. The quality assurance mark will be used to spread high standards beyond law firms, to any organization which might offer legal advice to the public. In addition, the Lord Chancellor suggested (*The Times*, 7 September 1999) that the creation of defence lawyers employed by the Commission would create a 'healthy rivalry' with private criminal lawyers and so stimulate them to give a better service.

Disadvantages of the reforms

Access to justice

The reforms were intended to improve access to justice, but they seem to have achieved the opposite. Because many state-funded legal services can only be obtained from lawyers who have a contract with the Legal Services Commission, members of the public are finding it increasingly difficult to find a state-funded lawyer with the relevant expertise close to their home.

Part of the problem is that many law firms have in the past done a small amount of legal aid work alongside their privately funded work. Such firms have not wanted to bid for block contracts because they have not wanted to increase the amount of comparatively poorly paid state-funded work they take on. There are now only 5,000 solicitor firms offering state-funded legal services, compared with 11,000 under the old legal aid system. Between January 2000 and June 2003 the number of civil contracts offered for housing law fell by a third from 743 to 489. In the same period, contracts for debt law fell by more than half, from 462 to 206. One result, many fear, will be the creation of a two-tier legal profession, with one set of firms doing poorly paid state-funded work and another doing exclusively private work.

The National Audit Office (2003) has identified a problem of lawyers opting out of contracting in family work. It also points to a need for more lawyers to undertake work in community care, housing and mental health. A study undertaken by the Citizens' Advice Bureaux (2004) has reinforced this picture of growing gaps in the supply of state-funded legal services, what it calls 'advice deserts'. Their survey found that people were often having to travel up to 50 miles to find a lawyer. Over two-thirds of Citizens' Advice Bureaux said they had difficulty finding a legal aid immigration lawyer for clients, and 60 per cent reported problems finding solicitors to deal with housing and family law problems.

State funding is not available for legal representation at most tribunals.

Community Legal Service Partnerships

A review of the Community Legal Service Partnerships (CLSPs) has been carried out by consultancy firm Matrix and Sheffield University. This found that CLSPs had failed to achieve their goals and were proving ineffective. More than half the advisers working for the CLSPs 'did not believe their CLSPs had been effective in improving access to justice for the public'. A study by the Advice Services Alliance (2004) found that many CLSPs were 'dying on their feet'. It found that the lawyers involved felt they were wasting their time.

Problems with conditional fee agreements

The Access to Justice Act 1999 removed personal injury cases from the state funding system, so that these can only be funded privately or by a conditional fee agreement. Much of the criticism of the current funding arrangements is concerned with the use of these conditional fee agreements which are discussed at pp. 226–7.

Cost-cutting

Critics, including the legal professions and some MPs, have accused the Government of putting cost-cutting before access to justice. The chairperson of the Legal Aid Practitioners Group, Richard Miller, told *The Lawyer* newspaper in December 1998 that he believed the fixed budget for civil matters was designed to make it easy for the Government to cut the amount spent in later years: 'The Legal Services Commission will simply be able to say, this is the budget and if there are any more cases, tough luck.'

There are particular concerns that civil cases will suffer from the priority given to criminal defence work. In order to meet its obligations to guarantee a fair trial under human rights legislation, the Government has had to continue to allow the funding for criminal defence to be demand-led. It has admitted, however, that there is a fixed overall budget for legal services, which means that the budget for civil cases is effectively whatever is left over once criminal defence work is paid for.

Public defenders

The legal profession has fiercely opposed the idea of the Commission employing its own lawyers to do criminal defence work. Both the Bar Council and the Criminal Law Solicitors Association have expressed concern that lawyers who are wholly dependent on the state for their income cannot be sufficiently independent to defend properly people suspected of crime – people who, by definition, are on the opposite side to the state. Interviewed by *The Lawyer* newspaper in December 1998, Bar Council chairperson, Heather Hallett QC, pointed to the example of the United States, where public defenders have been used for some years, arguing that as a result, the justice system there has become geared towards administrative convenience and cost cutting, leading to an emphasis on plea bargaining and uncontested cases.

The experience of foreign jurisdictions such as the United States and Canada shows that any system of public defenders must be properly funded and staffed if it is to retain the confidence of providers, users and the courts. Unfortunately they are frequently under-funded in practice, relying as a result on inexperienced lawyers with excessive caseloads and who are not respected by their clients, opponents or the court.

Research carried out by Cyrus Tata *et al.* (2004) has evaluated the success of the Public Defence Solicitors Office in Scotland in its first three years. The research compared the performance of the public defenders with that of solicitors in private practice receiving state funding. The conclusions of this research were mixed. It found that public defender clients pleaded guilty earlier than clients of solicitors in private practice. But it found no evidence to suggest that public defenders put explicit pressure on clients to plead guilty. Instead, the clients criticized the public defenders for being too neutral and too willing to go along with whatever the client decided. The change in economic incentives involved in receiving a salary rather than a legal aid payment appeared to produce a change in behaviour, because solicitors in private practice earn very little if a client immediately pleads guilty, so ending the case, compared to where there is a late guilty plea. Public defender clients were more likely to be convicted. Representation by a public defender increased the chances of a client being convicted from around 83 per cent to 88 per cent. This was primarily because clients of private solicitors were more likely to plead late, allowing for a greater chance in the meantime for the case against them to be dropped by the prosecution, for example because a witness fails to attend the trial. There was no difference between the sentences handed down.

The levels of trust and satisfaction expressed by public defender clients who had not volunteered to use the service, but been obliged to do so, was consistently lower than those expressed by clients using private practitioners. They were less likely to say that their solicitor had done 'a very good job' in listening to what they had to say; telling them what was happening; being there when they wanted them; or having enough time for them. They were also less likely to agree strongly that the solicitor had told the court their side of the story or treated them as though they mattered. Part of the problem appears to have been that clients resented not being able to choose their solicitor and this choice has now been reinstated. Those who had chosen to use the public defender service were more positive about the service. However, they were still significantly less likely than private clients to agree strongly that their lawyer had told the court their side of the story or had treated them as if they mattered, rather than as 'a job to be done'. Public defenders tended to be seen as more 'business-like' and less personally committed than private solicitors. Public defender clients were less likely to say that they would use the service again compared to clients of private solicitors.

The research concluded:

> From a managerial perspective, the fact that public defenders resolved cases at an earlier stage has advantages. It has the potential to save legal aid costs and also reduce court and prosecution costs, inconveniencing fewer witnesses. Clients were spared the wait and worry of repeated court [hearings] and were less likely to be held in detention pending the resolution of their case.

At the moment, surprisingly, the public defender service is proving more expensive than private solicitors. The average cost of a case handled by the public defender service is over £800 compared to £506 for private practice. The Legal Aid Practitioners Group has suggested that this is because the tax payer has to pay the salary of public defenders even if they have failed to attract clients, while private solicitors are only paid for the work they do.

Small businesses

Research has been carried out at the Institute of Advanced Legal Studies into the impact of the Access to Justice Act funding reforms (*Breaking the Code: the Impact of Legal Aid Reforms on General Civil Litigation* (Goriely and Gupta, 2001)). It highlights problems resulting from the removal of state funding for legal services relating to business disputes. The removal of state funding in this area has attracted little attention, which has led the researchers to comment:

> The problem with any discussion of 'businessmen' is that the phrase is laden with overtones. It conjures up an image of a man in a 'business suit', possibly flying 'business class' to a 'business meeting'.

While this is an accurate picture of some business people, it is far from accurate for many others. The Government justified excluding business disputes from state funding on the basis that such cases did not lead to social exclusion and, according to the Government, 'it is not thought justified to spend public money helping businessmen, who fail to insure against the risk of facing legal costs'.

In fact, the research has found that the withdrawal of state funding for business disputes is leaving low-paid workers, such as self-employed cleaners and taxi drivers, with no means of redress if their businesses run into legal difficulties. The researcher, Ms Goriely, found that 'Business failure is a fast track to social exclusion'. When small businesses fail, the impact on a person's life can be enormous. People often end up losing 'their homes, their savings, their marriages, their health and their self-esteem'. Legal expenses insurance is often too expensive and specifically excludes the kinds of difficulties that failing small businesses face. Many policies have clearly been developed for businesses with million-pound turnovers, not for self-employed builders and taxi drivers.

Lack of independence from Government

State-funded work is likely to become the most important source of income for those firms which hold contracts – in some cases, even the only source of income. There are therefore concerns that the threat of losing their contract if they make themselves unpopular with the Government might lead firms to shy away from taking on cases that challenge Government action, or might in any other way embarrass or annoy the Government.

Poorer standards of work

A survey carried out in 1999 for the Legal Aid Practitioners Group found that 84 per cent of legal aid firms believed the Act's reliance on exclusive contracts would reduce the quality of legal services.

The Consumers' Association undertook research in 2001 into the experiences of people seeking help from the Community Legal Service. The research consisted of in-depth interviews of people who had sought help from the service, particularly those from vulnerable groups in society. It found that community centres and law centres provided the best help and advice, but many people felt that the legal system gave them a second-rate service. The research criticized the apparent lack of commitment and poor communication of some solicitors. There were still not enough solicitors and advisers specializing in areas like social security, housing, disability discrimination, employment and immigration law. People with disabilities complained of poor physical access to buildings.

The Legal Services Commission has paid for some research into the impact of different funding arrangements on the quality of the provision of legal services (*Quality and Cost: Final Report on the Contracting of Civil, Non-family Advice and Assistance Pilot* (2001)). A study was undertaken over two years of 80,000 cases handled by 43 not-for-profit agencies and 100 solicitor firms. The solicitor firms were randomly allocated to one of three payment groups: those who continued to be paid as under the old green form system; those paid a fixed sum and left to determine how many cases it was reasonable for them to do for the money; and those paid a fixed sum and given a specific number of cases which had to be undertaken. The research concluded that where the payment system gave firms an incentive to do work cheaply, the quality of work suffered. Thus firms in the third group performed worst on most indicators, with 20 per cent of the contracted advisers doing poor quality work. Group 2, in general, performed better than Group 1.

In his *Review of the Criminal Courts* (2001), Sir Robin Auld has recommended that changes should be made to the arrangements for the payment of defence lawyers so that they are rewarded for carrying out adequate case preparation.

Quick quiz 11.6

1 Give three advantages of the Access to Justice Act 1999 reforms.

2 Give three disadvantages of the Access to Justice Act 1999 reforms.

3 Research carried out by the Consumers' Association raised concerns about the standards of work carried out by the Community Legal Service. What were these concerns?

4 What has been the impact on small businesses of the reforms of state-funded legal services?

Over-billing

Lawyers may be charging the Government too much for their work. Audits conducted by the Legal Services Commission of case files kept by suppliers suggest that 35 per cent of suppliers were claiming 20 per cent more than they should have been, although some suppliers have complained about the basis of some of these decisions.

The cost of criminal cases

It seems that currently 1 per cent of criminal cases consume 49 per cent of the budget for the Criminal Defence Service. Following the publication of a consultation paper, *Delivering Value for Money in the Criminal Defence Service* (Lord Chancellor's Department, 2003), the Government has tried to reduce the cost of these cases. Lawyers working on cases lasting more than five weeks, or costing more than £150,000 have to negotiate contracts for payment at each stage of the case. In addition, the Government is currently planning to re-introduce means tests for criminal cases in the magistrates' court (apart from the first hearing to avoid court delays), so that those who can afford to pay for their legal services are required to do so. Relevant provisions are contained in the Criminal Defence Service Bill. When means testing was applied before, the administration costs were high compared to the legal fees paid as a result. In addition, there is a substantial risk that means testing could cause delays in the criminal justice system, both because evidence of means will need to be obtained and because the number of unrepresented defendants is likely to increase.

The Government paper *A Fairer Deal for Legal Aid* gives details of plans to reduce the length of high cost criminal cases, by for example, removing juries from serious fraud cases and improving case management by judges. Lawyers will not be paid for time spent when a trial overruns.

The Government is also hoping to reduce the cost of criminal cases by introducing a new form of competitive tendering for some criminal defence work in London. The details of the plans are contained in a consultation paper, *Improving Value for Money for Publicly Funded Criminal Defence Services in London* (2005). The changes would affect criminal defence work carried out in London police stations and Magistrates' Courts. At the moment solicitor firms who have a contract with the Legal Services Commission are paid an hourly rate for carrying out this work. The plan is that solicitor firms would have to bid for a contract to carry out a percentage of the work in a particular area, with the bid stating how much the firm would charge per case. It is expected that smaller firms will not win contracts, so that a reduced number of larger firms will increasingly carry out this work. The Law Society has criticized these proposed reforms, claiming that they will lower the quality of advice and representation available to legally aided clients. A review of this method of purchasing publicly funded legal services is being carried out by Lord Carter who will report on his findings in 2006.

At the moment, the Government allocates a single budget to both civil and criminal state funding of legal services. Within this budget criminal defence work takes priority. So while the cost of criminal legal aid is expanding, this leaves less and less for civil legal aid. In 2004 the national legal aid budget was £2 billion, and 60 per cent of this was spent on criminal legal aid. Spending on civil legal aid has fallen from £564 million in 2000 to £483 million in 2003.

Reliance on private practice

When the legal aid system was first set up the Government had a choice between using the existing private practice structures or setting up a totally separate system of lawyers, who would be paid salaries from public funds (as doctors are in the NHS), rather than being paid on a case-by-case basis. They chose to give legal aid work to lawyers in private practice. This continues to be the case for state funding under the Community Legal Service, with the sole exception of the criminal defenders. Kate Markus, writing in *The Critical Lawyer's Handbook* (1992), argues that this causes five main problems. First, rather than responding to need, state-funded practitioners in private practice are ruled by the requirements of running a business in a highly competitive marketplace. Private practitioners have to make a profit, even where they are paid by the state, and therefore often feel that they must limit the time they spend on state-funded cases. This problem severely limits the services they can offer to the clients. It is also the reason why so many lawyers have refused to do state-funded work, which, given the funding problems, has never been able to compete with privately paid work in terms of the salaries paid.

Secondly, private solicitors' practices are very much geared towards legal problems concerning money and property, which means that as far as general high street solicitors are concerned, their expertise is often not developed in those areas affecting the poorer client.

The third problem, which we have mentioned before, is that solicitors in private practice may be seen as intimidating by the majority of poorer clients. They are then put off bringing their problems to them, especially in areas where they are not sure whether it is appropriate to involve a lawyer.

The fourth issue Markus highlights is that private practice is geared largely to litigation (bringing cases to court), which is not always the best solution to the kind of problems facing the poorer members of society. Let us say, for example, that a local council is failing to fulfil its obligations to tenants, with the result that many of them are living in unacceptable housing. Each affected family could take the council to court, but that would be expensive and time-consuming, and only solve the problem for those families who actually did so. But with access to good legal advice on their rights, the tenants could get together and put pressure on the council themselves, potentially solving a problem affecting lots of people in one action, and much more cheaply. Law centres (see below) often work this way, but the working practices of private practitioners, and the case-by-case way in which legal aid was funded, made it impossible for them to do much, if any, of this kind of work.

Finally, Markus makes the point that any system which seeks to make justice truly accessible has to address the problem of widespread ignorance of legal rights and how to assert them; after all, if a person with a legal problem is unaware that there might be a legal right which could solve it, he or she will not even think of getting legal help in the first place. That means educating people about their rights, and private practice, where every task a lawyer does has to be paid for, is simply not set up to do that kind of work.

Conditional fee agreements

In the USA, a great many cases brought by ordinary individuals are funded by what are called contingency fees, or 'no win, no fee' agreements. Lawyers can agree with clients that no fee will be charged if they lose the case, but if they win, the fee will be an agreed percentage of the damages won. This obviously gives the lawyer a direct personal interest in the level of damages, and there have been suggestions that this is partly responsible for the soaring levels of damages seen in the US courts.

In the English legal system, contingency fees are banned, but in 1990 the Courts and Legal Services Act (CLSA) made provision for the introduction of conditional fee agreements. Under a conditional fee agreement, solicitors can agree to take no fee or a reduced fee if they lose, and raise their fee by an agreed percentage if they win, up to a maximum of double the usual fee. The solicitor calculates the extra fee (usually called the 'uplift' or 'success fee') on the basis of the size of the risk involved – if the client seems very likely to win, the uplift will generally be lower than in a case where the outcome is more difficult to predict. The rule that the losing party must pay the winner's costs remains, so a party using a conditional fee agreement will usually take out insurance to cover this if he or she should lose.

The Access to Justice Act 1999 makes some changes to the arrangements for conditional fee agreements in order to promote their use. Where a person who has made a conditional fee agreement wins his or her case, it will be possible for the court to order the losing party to pay the success fee, as well as the normal legal costs. Thus the success fee is now only ever payable by the losing party, which is a complete reversal of the previous situation. This provision is designed to meet the criticism that damages are

> ✓ **Know your terms 11.7**
>
> Define the following terms:
>
> 1 Duty solicitor
> 2 Pilot scheme
> 3 Law centre
> 4 Conditional fee agreement

calculated to compensate the litigant for the damage done to him or her, so if the 'uplift' has to come out of the client's damages, the amount left will be less than the court calculated as necessary for the purpose of full compensation.

Similarly, where a winning litigant has taken out insurance to provide for payment of the other side's costs if he or she loses, the court can order that the other side also pays the cost of the insurance premium. As a result, people who are bringing actions for remedies other than the payment of money can use a conditional fee arrangement. These changes have caused problems in practice. The cost of after-the-event insurance has increased considerably, and some clients are finding it difficult to obtain such insurance. There has been a lot of litigation over paying these extra costs by the losing party. To try to reduce this problem, new rules of court have been written, which fix the success fee for particular types of litigation, such as road traffic accidents, depending on the circumstances of the case. For example, where litigation involves an accident at work and the employee brings a claim on the basis of a conditional fee agreement; if that action is successful, the employer's insurer will pay the employee's solicitor their normal costs, plus a success fee of 25 per cent of these costs if the case settled before trial, and a 100 per cent success fee for a riskier case that went to trial. It might be better if the sums were simply covered by judges increasing the award of damages to take into account these extra expenses.

The Access to Justice Act 1999 made conditional fee agreements available for all cases apart from medical negligence. The Government is now considering stopping state funding for medical negligence actions, so that these too would fall within the remit of conditional fee agreements. The consultation paper, *A New Focus for Civil Legal Aid: encouraging early resolution; discouraging unnecessary litigation* (2005), suggests that medical negligence cases could be transferred to the conditional fee agreement system after research into the possible impact of this change has been completed. It is questionable whether conditional fees are appropriate for such cases. They are generally very difficult for claimants to win – the success rate is around 17 per cent, compared with 85 per cent for other personal injury claims (often caused by road accidents). While the outcome of litigation arising from a road accident is often reasonably easy to predict, medical negligence cases require detailed reports before anyone can hazard a guess about whether any party is to blame. The evidence is that solicitors will only take on a case under a conditional fee agreement if they estimate there is at least a 70 per cent chance of being successful. It can cost between £2,000 and £5,000 simply to do the initial investigations necessary to assess accurately whether the case is worth pursuing. As a result, solicitors would be very unlikely to want to take on such cases on a conditional fee basis, and even if they did, the uncertainty of outcome means that insurance against losing would be extremely expensive, possibly amounting to thousands of pounds. On the other hand, removing state funding could be an effective way of reducing the National Health Service's legal costs. In 2003 the NHS was facing a record £4.4bn bill in outstanding negligence claims.

The Government is currently considering introducing collective conditional fee agreements. These are designed for bulk users of legal services such as trade unions and insurers.

■ Advantages of conditional fee agreements

Cost to the state

Conditional fee agreements cost the state nothing – the costs are entirely borne by the solicitor or the losing party, depending on the outcome. By removing the huge number of personal injury cases from state funding and promoting conditional fee agreements for them instead, the Government claims it can devote more resources to those cases which still need state funding, such as tenants' claims against landlords, and direct more money towards suppliers of free legal advice, such as Citizens' Advice Bureaux.

Wider access to justice

The Government believes that conditional fee agreements will allow many people to bring or defend cases, who would not have been eligible for state funding and who could not previously have afforded to bring cases at their own expense. As long as they can afford to insure against losing, and can persuade a solicitor that the case is worth the risk, anyone will be able to bring or defend a case for damages. Critics point out that there are a number of problems with this argument (see below).

Performance incentives

Supporters claim conditional fees encourage solicitors to perform better, since they have a financial interest in winning cases funded this way.

Wider coverage

Conditional fee agreements are allowed for defamation actions, and cases brought before tribunals: two major gaps in the provision of state funding.

Public acceptance

The Law Society suggests that clients have readily accepted conditional fee agreements in those areas where they have been permitted in the past. Within two years of the agreements being introduced, almost 30,000 conditional fee agreements had been signed, and by 1999 around 25,000 were in operation.

Fairness to opponents

There are restrictions on the costs state-funded clients can be made to pay to the other side, which can give them an unfair advantage, particularly in cases where both sides are ordinary individuals but only one has qualified for state funding. The requirement for insurance in conditional fee cases solves this problem.

■ Disadvantages of conditional fee agreements

Uncertain cases

Most of those who have criticized the legislation on conditional fee agreements accept that they are a good addition to the state-funded system, but are concerned that they may not be adequate as a substitute. In particular, critics – including the Bar, the Law Society, the Legal Action Group, and the Vice-Chancellor of the Supreme Court, Sir Richard Scott – have expressed strong concerns that certain types of case will lose out under the new rules. They suggest that solicitors will only want to take on cases under conditional fee agreements where there is a very high chance of winning. It was for this reason that medical negligence cases have been kept within the state-funded system.

Unfair trials

Where legal aid is refused, a subsequent trial may prove to be unfair if one party is unrepresented by a lawyer as a result, and the other party benefited from legal representation. This can amount to a breach of Art. 6 of the European Convention which guarantees the right to a fair trial. The problem was highlighted by the case which has come to be known as the McLibel Two. The defendants were two environmental campaigners who had distributed leaflets outside McDonalds' restaurants. These leaflets criticized the nutritional content of the food sold in the restaurants. McDonalds sued the two defendants for defamation. The defendants were refused legal aid because it is not generally available for defamation cases (see p. 211). They therefore represented themselves throughout the proceedings, with only limited help from some sympathetic lawyers who provided a small amount of assistance for free. McDonald's were represented by a team of specialist lawyers. The libel trial lasted for 313 days and was the longest civil action in English legal history. The defendants lost the case and were ordered to pay £60,000 in damages (later reduced to £40,000 on appeal). They challenged the fairness of the UK proceedings in the European Court of Human Rights. That challenge was successful. The European Court held that the McLibel Two had not had a fair trial in breach of Art. 6 of the European Convention on Human Rights and there had been a breach of their right to freedom of expression under Art. 10 of the Convention.

Claimants misled

The Citizens Advice Bureau has issued a report entitled *No Win, No Fee, No Chance* (2005). This expresses concern that consumers are being misled by the term 'no win, no fee'. Often consumers find that the system costs them more than they gain. Consumers are subjected to aggressive and high-pressured sales tactics from unqualified employees of claims management companies. These companies receive a fee from solicitors for passing them a case. Consumers can be subjected to inappropriate marketing tactics, for example, accident victims have been approached in hospital. Consumers are not informed clearly of the financial risks that the legal proceedings will involve, and are misled into believing that the system will genuinely be 'no win, no fee'. In fact, consumers may need to take out an insurance policy to offset any legal expenses incurred if they lose the case and are required to pay the other side's costs. If the claim is, for example, against the council for failure to repair a council flat, a building surveyor may need to be paid as well as the lawyers. These legal expenses can be artificially inflated by unscrupulous claims management companies. The consumer can be encouraged to take out a loan to pay the monthly instalments of the insurance policy. The consumer frequently discovers that these expenses have wiped out any compensation they win. The injured person does not as a result benefit from the compensation they are entitled to. In some cases, the consumer even ends up owing money. In one case handled by the Citizens Advice Bureau a woman was left with just £15 from a £2,150 compensation payout, and in another case a man received compensation of £1,250 for an accident at work, but owed nearly £2,400 for insurance relating to the litigation.

In **Bowen and ten others** *v* **Bridgend County Borough Council** (2004) the litigation had arisen when employees of a claims management company had knocked on council tenants' doors suggesting that claims could be made. An action was brought against the council for failing to carry out housing repairs. The claimants had taken out loans to pay for insurance policies to cover any legal expenses they incurred. The average compensation paid to claimants was £1,631, but the claimants' solicitors sought an average of £8,000 in costs against the local authority. In fact, the court only ordered £250 to be paid, holding that many of the legal fees were unjustified and not payable.

The Government has issued a consultation paper, *Making Simple CFAs a Reality* (2004). This is looking at how conditional fee agreements can be improved. It is also intending to improve the regulation of claims management companies through provisions contained in the Compensation Bill.

Insurance costs

There are concerns that insurance against losing can be expensive. In the area of personal injury, the Law Society provides an affordable insurance scheme, but in other areas the only suppliers are private insurance companies, which charge according to risk, so that clients with cases where the outcome is uncertain may be faced with very high premiums.

Both the Law Society and the Bar have suggested that a better idea would be the establishment of a self-financing contingency fund, which would pay for cases on the understanding that successful litigants would pay a proportion of their damages back to the fund. As we said earlier, this is allowed by the Act, but the Government has said it has no plans to use the power at the moment.

Insurance pressures

There may also be pressure to settle from insurance companies, some of which have been known to threaten to withdraw their cover if a client refuses to accept an offer of settlement that the insurance company considers reasonable. Clearly the insurance company's primary interest will be to avoid having to pay out, so it is not difficult to see that their idea of a reasonable settlement might be very different from the client's – or from what the client could expect to get if the case continued.

Financial involvement of lawyers

The Bar has criticized the idea of allowing lawyers a financial interest in the outcome of a case. In a letter to the Lord Chancellor, the Chair of the Bar Council argued that since clients generally lack the knowledge to assess their chances of winning their case, lawyers will be able to charge whatever they think they can get away with (within the set limits). This seems a rather strange argument for a representative of the legal profession to put forward, and critics have widely suggested that the real reason behind this and the other criticisms made by the legal profession is that lawyers were reluctant to lose the no-risk income that state-funded legal aid allowed them.

The evidence on solicitors' approach to the uplift on fees is currently rather inconclusive. A 1997 report by the Policy Studies Institute on the effects of the changes made under the Courts and Legal Services Act 1990 found that the average uplift was 43 per cent, less than half the 100 per cent maximum allowed – but within that average, one in ten solicitors was charging between 90 per cent and 100 per cent. The author of the study, Stella Yarrow, commented that the number of cases assessed as having a low chance of success was surprisingly large, suggesting that solicitors might be underestimating the chances of winning in order to increase the uplift.

In 1999, the Forum of Insurance Lawyers (Foil) suggested that the chance to make extra money was encouraging solicitors to push clients into conditional fee agreements, even where the clients did not need such an agreement. Around 17 million people in Britain have some form of legal expenses insurance attached to their home, car or credit card insurance, and in many cases this will pay their legal costs for them. However, Foil points out, many people have this insurance without realizing it, and it claims that instead of suggesting that clients check whether they have it, solicitors are persuading them into unnecessary conditional fee agreements.

Abuse in defamation proceedings

There is concern that conditional fee agreements are being used inappropriately in defamation proceedings, and thereby threatening the right to freedom of expression. Following a critical newspaper article, it is easy for a person to bring proceedings for defamation at no expense to themselves, but the newspaper is forced to incur considerable expense to defend such a claim. While it may be clear that a newspaper article damages the reputation of the claimant, the burden of proof will pass to the defendant to show, for example, that the article was true or fair comment. As a result there needs to be strong case management by judges in defamation cases and the capping of costs where appropriate.

Are lawyers always necessary?

As we have seen, many of the non-statutory advice schemes use advisers who are not legally qualified. Some of these lay advisers appear as advocates in tribunals and in some cases have been granted discretionary rights of audience in the county courts, as well as giving legal advice. In particular, advisers for charities such as MIND have shown themselves to be more than a match for most solicitors in their knowledge of the law in their fields. Many solicitor firms also employ non-qualified workers to do legal work.

The skills of a good adviser are not always the same as those of a good lawyer; what the client needs is someone who can interview sympathetically, ascertain the pertinent facts from what may be a long, rambling and in some cases emotional story, analyse the problem and suggest a course of action. The preliminary skills are just as likely to be possessed by a lay person as by a lawyer, even if a lawyer may be needed to advise on the course of action.

Nor are lawyers considered to be the best advocates in every situation. The National Consumer Council advised against allowing them to represent clients in the small claims court, on the grounds that they could make the procedure unnecessarily long-winded and legalistic.

However, critics identify two possible problems in the growing use of lay advisers. First, although most organizations are scrupulous in training their advisers, some may be more casual, and there is no obligatory check on advisers before they are allowed to deal with cases. The general public may not always be in a position to assess the quality of the advice they are given. Secondly, the large number of overlapping agencies means it can be difficult for consumers of legal advice to find the best provider for them and can be wasteful of scarce resources. The Government hopes that the development of Community Legal Service Partnerships will help to tackle this problem.

Proposals for further reform

With the Access to Justice Act 1999 the Government introduced major reforms to the provision of state funding of legal services. The Government has set up the Fundamental Legal Aid Review to look at the long-term future of the Community Legal Service. The study will focus on the use of state funding to meet the needs of society, to prevent social exclusion, and to save money through innovation in the delivery of legal services. This review is expected to be completed in early 2005. The Government has also issued a consultation paper, *The Independent Review of the Community Legal Service*, in 2004, considering ways of improving the Community Legal Service so that it is more effective and transparent. The following are some additional proposals that have been made, addressing not just cost, but many of the other problems associated with unmet legal need.

A national legal service?

Perhaps the most radical reform would be to take the statutory scheme entirely out of the hands of private practice and establish a nationwide network of salaried lawyers on the law centre model. All funding could be given on a block rather than case-by-case basis, for centres to use in whatever ways best meet the needs of their own locality, in consultation with management committees representing the community.

This would deal with some of the criticism of the current schemes made by Kate Markus and discussed above (p. 225). In particular, the advantages of this idea include:

- state-funded work would no longer have to compete with private work for lawyers' time;
- state funding would no longer have to include an element of profit for the lawyer;
- resources could be more flexibly employed, on a combination of individual case-work and litigation, education and campaigning, or any other approach that suited particular problems;
- this more flexible approach to dealing with problems would get away from the over-emphasis on litigation by solicitors in private practice;
- the ability to run educational campaigns would help deal with public ignorance of legal rights;
- law centres appear not to suffer from the unapproachable image of the legal profession in general;
- law centres have been successful in attracting problems not previously brought to lawyers, especially welfare and employment cases;
- a nationwide network of such centres would help overcome the uneven distribution of solicitor firms.

The 1979 Royal Commission on Legal Services did suggest the establishment of a nationwide network of centrally financed Citizens Law Centres, but felt that these should be restricted to individual casework only and not get involved in general work for the community. This idea would fail to take advantage of one of the real strengths of the law centre movement, and the fact that solicitors in private practice would still be allowed to undertake state-funded work would limit the improvements to be made in cost efficiency. The Law Centres Federation rejected the idea.

No-fault compensation

Instead of looking to conditional fee agreements to secure justice for those injured in accidents, such cases could be removed from the litigation arena by the establishment of a system of no-fault compensation for personal injury cases, as was done in New Zealand.

Class actions

Some people would like to see the American approach to class actions introduced to the UK (see, for example, Howard Epstein (2003)). In America, a single claimant can bring an action for damages on behalf of a whole class of claimants, who may be assumed to have suffered the same harm. After an award of damages has been made the lawyer can then locate those who are entitled to share it.

Encouraging ADR

The Government has issued a consultation paper, *A New Focus for Civil Legal Aid: encouraging early resolution; discouraging unnecessary litigation* (2005). This paper suggests that state funding of legal services should be shifted from supporting litigation to supporting pre-trial settlements. This change would be achieved by introducing new pay structures which would provide incentives to settle disputes before going to court.

Reading on the web

The website of Community Legal Service Direct is:

http://www.clsdirect.org.uk

The judgment of the European Court of Human Rights in the McLibel Two case, was application number 6841/01 and can be found on the court's website at:

http://www.echr.coe.int/echr

The report of the National Audit Office (2003), *Community Legal Service: The Introduction of Contracting*, HC 89 2002–03, is available on its website:

http://www.nao.org.uk

The website of the Legal Services Commission is:

http://www.legalservices.gov.uk/

The website of the Community Legal Service is:

http://www.clsdirect.org.uk

Question and answer guides

1 Critically evaluate the Access to Justice Act 1999 with regard to the problem of unmet legal need.

Answer guide

You should begin your answer by explaining what unmet legal need is, and discussing its causes. You should then briefly describe the changes made by the Access to Justice Act and then, in the main part of your answer, talk about how the provisions of the Act are designed to meet the problem of unmet legal need. The material you need for this is mainly to be found in the section on the advantages of the Act, but remember to direct your answer towards the question asked. You could do this either by taking each of the causes of unmet legal need in turn, and explaining which provisions address each problem and how, or by taking the relevant provisions in turn and talking about what aspects of the problem of unmet legal need they address and how (which of these approaches you take is not really important, so long as you do choose one that gives your essay a good, well-organized structure and shows you are using the material you have to really answer the question). You should then talk about the drawbacks of the Access to Justice Act, pointing out how these will compromise its ability to deal with the problem of unmet legal need. Finally, you could set your answer in a broader context (always a good way of showing the examiners that you really know the subject) by pointing out that the Access to Justice Act, although clearly aimed at dealing with the problem of unmet legal need, also had to address other issues, such as cost, and the need to get value for money, and so never intended to solve the problem of unmet legal need at any cost, but to do what it could with limited resources. Your conclusion can then state whether, in view of this broader context, you feel the Act does provide a satisfactory – if not perfect – solution to the problem.

2 **(a)** (i) Explain what is meant by a conditional fee agreement and when it is used; and
(ii) Describe the other ways of funding legal help and representation when bringing a civil claim. [30]

(b) Explain the criticisms that have been made of conditional fees and the other methods of funding. [15] *(OCR)*

Answer Guide

(a) (i) The material you need to answer this question is contained on p. 226–7. In particular, you need to state that a conditional fee agreement is an agreement between a solicitor and a client involved in civil litigation. Under the agreement the client does not have to pay the solicitor. Instead, either the client or the solicitor will pay for insurance cover. If the client wins, the solicitor is paid the normal fee with an uplift to reflect the risk he/she had taken by bringing the case under a conditional fee agreement. The uplift is paid by the losing side along with any award of damages. If the client loses, the solicitor is paid nothing and the other side's costs are paid by the insurance company.

(ii) The other ways of funding legal help and representation are either through the private funds of the client or by state funding. The material you need to answer this question is contained on pp. 209–17.

(b) You could divide your answer to this part of the question into three parts, looking at the criticisms of conditional fees, state funding and private funding separately. For criticisms of conditional fees, see pp. 228–9. For criticism of public funding, see pp. 219–26. The main problem with trying to pay for legal services from private funds is that legal proceedings can be extremely expensive, and there is always the risk that a person will have to pick up the bill for the other side's legal costs if he or she loses the case.

Chapter summary

Unmet need for legal services

Unmet legal need essentially describes the situation where a person has a problem that could potentially be solved through the law, but the person is unable to get whatever help he or she needs to use the legal system.

Legal aid before the Access to Justice Act 1999

The six schemes which made up the legal aid scheme until the 1999 Access to Justice Act was brought into force were:

■ the legal advice and assistance scheme (known as the 'green form' scheme because of the paperwork used);
■ assistance by way of representation (ABWOR);
■ civil legal aid;
■ criminal legal aid;
■ duty solicitor schemes in police stations; and
■ duty solicitor schemes for criminal cases in magistrates' courts.

State funding of legal services today

With the passing of the Access to Justice Act 1999 the Labour Government introduced some major reforms to the provision of state-funded legal services. On 1 April 2000 the Legal Aid Board was replaced by the Legal Services Commission. In order to develop the standard and accessibility of legal services, the Legal Services Commission has established a quality mark, is building partnerships with the different suppliers of legal services and has developed a website.

The Legal Services Commission administers two schemes: the Community Legal Service which is concerned with civil matters and the Criminal Defence Service which is concerned with criminal matters.

The Community Legal Service

Direct funding is provided for different categories of legal service as follows:

■ Legal Help
■ Legal Representation
■ Help at Court
■ Approved Family Help, and
■ Family Mediation.

The Criminal Defence Service

State funding can provide direct funding for three types of service in the criminal field:

■ Advice and assistance
■ Advocacy assistance, and
■ Representation.

In addition, the Legal Services Commission employs public defenders and pays for duty solicitor schemes.

Conditional fee agreements

In 1990 the Courts and Legal Services Act made provision for the introduction of conditional fee agreements. The scope for their use was increased by the Access to Justice Act 1999.

Chapter 12

The police

The criminal justice system is one of the most important tools available to society for the control of anti-social behaviour. It is also the area of the English legal system which has most potential for controversy, given that through the criminal justice system the state has the means to interfere with individual freedom in the strongest way: by sending people to prison.

An effective criminal justice system needs to strike a balance between punishing the guilty and protecting the innocent; our systems of investigating crime need safeguards which prevent the innocent being found guilty, but those safeguards must not make it impossible to convict those who are guilty. This balance has been the subject of much debate in recent years: a large number of miscarriages of justice, where innocent people were sent to prison, suggested the system was weighted too heavily towards proving guilt, yet shortly after these cases had been uncovered, there were claims, particularly from the police, that the balance had tipped too far in the other direction. It may be that the incorporation of the European Convention on Human Rights into British law will lead to a further shift in the balance, as the British courts interpret such rights as the right to a 'fair trial' contained in Art. 6 of the Convention.

The miscarriages of justice

In recent years confidence in the criminal justice system has been seriously dented by the revelation that innocent people had been wrongly convicted and sentenced to long periods in prison. High-profile cases have included the Guildford Four, the Birmingham Six and the Tottenham Three. We will look closely at just one of these cases to see where the system went wrong before examining in detail the rules that govern the criminal justice system.

The Birmingham Six

In November 1974, 21 people died and 162 were injured when IRA bombs exploded in two crowded pubs in the centre of Birmingham. The bombs caused outrage in Britain, and led to a wave of anti-Irish feeling.

Figure 12.1 The Birmingham Six outside the Old Bailey after their convictions were quashed

Source: © EMPICS.

The six Irishmen, who became known as the Birmingham Six, were arrested after police kept a watch on ports immediately after the bombings. The police asked them to undergo forensic tests in order to eliminate them from their enquiries. The men had told the police that they were travelling to Northern Ireland to see relatives; this was partly true, but their main reason for travelling was to attend the funeral of James McDade, an IRA man. Although some of the six may well have had Republican sympathies, none were actually members of the IRA. They were unaware, until McDade was killed, that he was involved in terrorism. Nevertheless, they all knew his family, and intended to go to the funeral as a mark of respect, a normal practice in Northern Ireland which would not necessarily suggest support for the dead person's political views.

Perhaps not surprisingly given the situation at the time, the men did not mention the funeral when the police asked why they were travelling and, equally unsurprisingly, when the police searched their luggage and found evidence of the real reason for their journey, they became extremely suspicious. When the forensic tests, conducted by a Dr Skuse, indicated that the men had been handling explosives, the police were convinced their suspicions were right.

At their trial, the case rested on two main pieces of evidence: the forensic tests and confessions which the men had made to the police. The six claimed that while at the police station, they had been beaten, kicked and threatened with death; they were also told that their families were in danger and would only be protected if the men confessed. There was clear evidence that the six were beaten up; photos taken three days after their admission on remand to Winston Green prison show serious scars. However, the men were also beaten up by prison officers once they were remanded in custody, and the prosecution used this beating to explain the photographic evidence, stating that there had been no physical abuse by the police and that, therefore, the confessions were valid. Yet a close examination of the confessions would have made it obvious that they were made by people who knew nothing about the bombings: they contradicted each other, none of them revealed anything about the way the terrorist attacks were carried out that the police did not know already, and some of the 'revelations' proved to be untrue – for example, three of the men said the bombs were left in carrier bags, when forensic evidence later showed them to have been in holdalls. The men were never put on identity parades, even though at least one person who had been present in one of the bombed pubs felt he could have identified the bombers. Nevertheless, the six were convicted and sentenced to life imprisonment, the judge commenting 'You have been convicted on the clearest and most overwhelming evidence I have ever heard in a case of murder'. On appeal, the judges reprimanded the trial judge for aspects of his summing up and a character attack on a defence witness; they acknowledged the weaknesses in the forensic evidence, yet concluded that this evidence would have played a small part in the jury's decision; and as far as the confession evidence was concerned, a judge mentioned the black eye on one of the defendants, 'the origin of which I have forgotten', but said 'I do not think it matters much anyway'. The appeal was dismissed.

Fourteen prison officers were subsequently tried for assaulting the six men; their victims were not allowed to appear as witnesses, and they were all acquitted. Evidence given suggested that the men had already been injured when they arrived at the prison. The six then brought a civil action for assault against the police force. This claim was struck out. Lord Denning's judgment summed up the legal system's attitude to the case, pointing out that if the six won, and proved they had been assaulted in order to secure their confessions, this would mean the police had lied, used violence and threats, and that the convictions were false; the Home Secretary would have to recommend a pardon or send the case back to the Court of Appeal. The general feeling seemed to be that such serious miscarriages were simply unthinkable, and so the system for a long time turned its back on the growing claims that the unthinkable had actually happened.

In January 1987, the Home Secretary referred the case back to the Court of Appeal. The appeal took a year; the convictions were upheld. The Lord Chief Justice, Lord Lane, ended the court's judgment with remarks which were to become notorious: 'The longer this hearing has gone on, the more convinced this court has become that the verdict of the jury was correct. We have no doubt that these convictions were both safe and satisfactory.'

In the end, it took 16 years for the six to get their convictions quashed. In 1990, another Home Secretary referred the case back to the Court of Appeal. A new technique had been developed, known as electrostatic document analysis (ESDA) which could examine the indentations made on paper by writing on the sheets above. The test suggested that notes of a police interview with one of the six had not been recorded contemporaneously, as West Midlands detectives had claimed in court.

The scientific findings in the Maguire case also meant that the nitroglycerine tests could no longer be relied on. The prosecution decided not to seek to sustain the convictions and the six were finally freed in 1991.

The response to the miscarriages of justice

The miscarriages of justice described above, and others, showed that there was something seriously wrong with the criminal justice system. On 14 March 1991, when the Court of Appeal quashed the convictions of the Birmingham Six, the Home Secretary announced that a Royal Commission on Criminal Justice (RCCJ) would be set up to examine the penal process from start to finish – from the time the police first investigate to the final appeal. The RCCJ (sometimes called the Runciman Commission, after its chairperson) considered these issues for two years, during which they received evidence from over 600 organizations and asked academics to carry out 22 research studies on how the system works in practice. In July 1993 they published their final report. In examining the criminal justice system, we will consider some of the research presented to the RCCJ, its recommendations and some changes that have subsequently been made.

The Human Rights Act 1998

The passing of the Human Rights Act 1998, incorporating the European Convention on Human Rights into domestic law, will have a significant impact on all stages of the criminal justice system. The provisions of the European Convention could potentially provide an important safeguard against abuses and excesses within the system. Of particular relevance in this field are Art. 3 prohibiting torture and inhuman or degrading treatment; Art. 5 protecting the right to liberty including the right not to be arrested or detained by the police without lawful authority; Art. 6 guaranteeing a fair trial; and Art. 8 which recognizes the right to respect of an individual's right to private and family life. The powers of arrest, stop and search and the refusal of bail are all likely to be the subject of legal challenges on the basis that their exercise has breached the Convention. For example, in **Caballero** *v* **United Kingdom** (2000) the UK Government accepted that the law on bail breached Art. 5 of the Convention and the domestic law was reformed as a result.

Quick quiz 12.1

1 Which Act incorporated the European Convention on Human Rights into domestic law?

2 Which article of the European Convention on Human Rights protects the right to a fair trial?

3 Which case triggered the establishment of the Royal Commission on Criminal Justice in 1991?

4 Who chaired the 1991 Royal Commission?

Civilian support staff

The Police Reform Act 2002 allows a range of civilians to exercise police powers. The most significant in practice are likely to be the community support officers. These are civilians who are employed by a police authority. The only qualifications required for the post are that the chief officer is satisfied the person is suitable, capable and has been adequately trained. They are paid two-thirds of a regular police officer's salary. Their powers include the right to issue fixed penalty notices for such anti-social behaviour as dropping litter, cycling on footpaths, dog fouling and drinking alcohol in public. They are able to carry out searches and road checks. Where a suspect fails to provide his name and address, or if the community support officer reasonably suspects the details to be inaccurate, the community support officer may deprive the individual of their liberty (using reasonable force if necessary) for up to 30 minutes until a police officer arrives.

The Police Federation is unhappy that community support officers were given this power to detain suspects, commenting:

> Community Support Officers are supposed to just be the eyes and ears of the police service and therefore should not be placed in potentially confrontational situations, which detaining someone clearly is. They do not have the appropriate experience, the right training or adequate safety equipment to deal with this, which places the wellbeing of the public, police officers and themselves in jeopardy. By giving them more powers, we are effectively

Figure 12.2 Community support officers in uniform
Source: © EMPICS.

taking them away from the communities they serve and creating even greater confusion as to the differences between CSOs and police officers.

The creation of civilian support officers has been highly controversial. The Government's view is that the use of civilians for matters that are essentially administrative and routine will allow more police time for investigative work. In addition, the police role in the establishment of community safety accreditation schemes may lead to a greater degree of police influence over the activities of private security guards and store detectives. But some have criticized this development as a step towards privatizing policing. The Home Affairs Committee (2002) saw a danger of

> civilians with insufficient training, working in poor conditions, for less money while doing jobs that until recently were undertaken by police officers.

The shops and shopping centres which are likely to seek accreditation are, ironically, areas in which there is arguably adequate policing and private security. This reform may result in over-policing of safe areas without increasing the protection in areas in real need of extra reassurance policing.

Police powers

Most people's first contact with the criminal justice system involves the police, and because they have responsibility for investigating crimes, gathering evidence, and deciding whether to charge a suspect, they play an important part in its overall operation. They also have wide powers over suspects, which may be used to help convict the guilty or, as the miscarriages of justice have shown, abused to convict the innocent.

The main piece of legislation regulating police powers is the Police and Criminal Evidence Act 1984 (PACE). This Act was intended to replace a confusing mixture of common law, legislation and local bye-laws on pre-trial procedure with a single coherent statute. The Act provides a comprehensive code of police powers to stop, search, arrest, detain and interrogate members of the public. It also lays down the suspect's rights. The Criminal Justice and Public Order Act 1994 (CJPOA) extended police powers significantly. It introduced some of the recommendations of the RCCJ, and other changes that the RCCJ was opposed to, for example the abolition of the right to silence. Police powers have been further increased by the Serious Organized Crime and Police Act 2005.

As well as the statutory rules on police powers, contained in PACE and the CJPOA, there are codes of practice, drawn up by the Home Office under s. 66 of PACE, which do not form part of the law, but which provide extra detail on the provisions of the legislation. Breach of these codes cannot be the ground for a legal action, but can give rise to disciplinary procedures, and if they are breached in very serious ways, evidence obtained as a result of such a breach may be excluded in a criminal trial. It has been argued that some of the code provisions should be legally enforceable and form part of PACE itself.

Pre-arrest powers

Even without carrying out an arrest, the police enjoy a range of powers to stop and search a member of the public.

Common law powers

Police officers are always free to ask members of the public questions in order to prevent and detect crime, but members of the public are not obliged to answer such questions, nor to go to a police station or be detained at a police station unless they are lawfully arrested. In **Rice v Connolly** (1966), the appellant was spotted by police officers in the early hours of the morning, behaving suspiciously in an area where burglaries had taken place that night. The officers asked where he was going and where he had come from; he refused to answer, or to give his full name and address, though he did give a name and the name of a road, which were not untrue. The officers asked him to go with them to a police box for identification purposes, but he refused, saying, 'If you want me, you will have to arrest me'. He was arrested and eventually convicted of obstructing a police officer in the execution of his duty. His conviction was quashed on appeal on the basis that nobody is obliged to answer police questions.

The line between maintaining the freedom not to answer questions and actually obstructing the police would appear to be a thin one. In **Ricketts v Cox** (1982), two police officers, who were looking for youths responsible for a serious assault, approached the defendant and another man in the early hours of the morning. The defendant was said to have been abusive, unco-operative and hostile to the officers, using obscene language which was designed to provoke and antagonize the officers and eventually trying to walk away from them. The magistrates found that the police acted in a proper manner and were entitled to put questions to the two men; the defendant's behaviour and attitude amounted to an obstruction of the police officers in the execution of their duty. An appeal was dismissed, and the implication appears to be that while merely refusing to answer questions is lawful, rudely refusing to do so may amount to the offence of obstruction.

An even more problematic area is the question of how far the police are allowed to detain a person without arresting them. The courts appear to have concluded that under common law the police cannot actually prevent a person from moving away, though they can touch them to attract their attention (they also have some statutory powers in this area, discussed below). Two schoolboys, in **Kenlin v Gardiner** (1967), were going from house to house to remind members of their rugby team about a game. Two plain-clothed police officers became suspicious and, producing a warrant card, asked what they were doing. The boys did not believe the men were police officers, and one of them appeared to try to run away. A police officer caught hold of his arm, and the boy responded by struggling violently, punching and kicking the officer, at which point the second boy got involved and struck the other officer. Both boys were convicted of assaulting a police constable in the execution of his duty in the magistrates' court, but an appeal was allowed, on the grounds that the police did not have the power to detain the boys prior to arrest, and so the boys were merely acting in self-defence.

Under the Police Reform Act 2002, s. 50, a police officer can require a person behaving in an anti-social manner to give their name and address.

Quick quiz 12.2

1 What does 'PACE' stand for?

2 What does 'CJPOA' stand for?

3 What is the legal status of the codes of practice drawn up by the Home Office under s. 66 of PACE?

4 At common law can the police physically detain a person without carrying out an arrest?

Stop and search under PACE

PACE repealed a variety of often obscure and unsatisfactory statutory provisions on stop and search; the main powers in this area are now contained in s. 1 of PACE. Under s. 1 a constable may search a person or vehicle in public, for stolen or prohibited articles (defined as offensive weapons, articles used for the purpose of burglary or related crimes and professional display fireworks). This power can only be used where the police have 'reasonable grounds for suspecting that they will find stolen or prohibited articles' (s. 1(3)). The Criminal Justice Act 2003 extended the power to stop and search to cover searches for articles intended to cause criminal damage. This reform is aimed at people suspected of causing graffiti and who might be carrying cans of spray paint in their pockets.

The exercise of the power to stop and search is also governed by Code of Practice A. This Code starts by stating:

> 1.1. Powers to stop and search must be used fairly, responsibly, with respect for people being searched and without unlawful discrimination. The Race Relations (Amendment) Act 2000 makes it unlawful for police officers to discriminate on the grounds of race, colour, ethnic origin, nationality or national origins when using their powers.

The requirement of reasonable suspicion is intended to protect individuals from being subject to stop and search on a random basis, or on grounds that the law rightly finds unacceptable, such as age or racial background. Code of Practice A provides guidance on the meaning of 'reasonable grounds for suspecting'. Paragraph 2.2. of Code A states:

> Reasonable suspicion can never be supported on the basis of personal factors alone without reliable supporting intelligence or information or some specific behaviour by the person concerned. For example, a person's race, age, appearance, or the fact that the person is known to have a previous conviction, cannot be used alone or in combination with each other as the reasons for searching that person. Reasonable suspicion cannot be based on generalisations or stereotypical images of certain groups or categories of people as more likely to be involved in criminal activity.

Research by Quinton and others (2000) for the Home Office, found evidence that in practice some stop and search decisions were being based on 'broad generalisations and more superficial criteria'.

Before searching under these powers, police officers must, among other things, identify themselves and the station where they are based, and tell the person to be searched the grounds for the search. If not in uniform, police officers must provide documentary identification (s. 2(3)). Reasonable force may be used (s. 117), but the suspect cannot be required to remove any clothing in public, except for an outer coat, jacket or gloves (s. 2(9)). Police officers must ask anyone stopped to give their name and address and to define their ethnicity.

Any stolen or prohibited articles discovered by the police during the search may be seized (s. 1(6)). A written record of the search must be made at the time of the search, unless there are exceptional circumstances which would make this wholly impracticable. The record should state why the person was stopped and what the outcome was. The person searched must be given a copy of this immediately.

In the past the police could, and frequently did, carry out a search where there was no statutory power to search but with the consent of the member of the public. These searches could then take place without any of the legislative safeguards. In practice some people would 'consent' to a search in that they would offer no resistance to it, because they did not know their legal rights. Since 2003 voluntary searches are no longer allowed.

Other powers to stop and search

Various statutes give specific stop and search powers regarding particular offences. For example, the Misuse of Drugs Act 1971, s. 23, allows the police to stop and search anyone who is suspected on reasonable grounds to be in unlawful possession of a controlled drug.

Following the 11 September attack on the United States, the Anti-Terrorism Crime and Security Act 2001 was passed. Section 44 of that Act allows the Home Secretary to secretly authorize the police to carry out random stop and searches in the fight against terrorism. These powers have been used extensively.

There are clearly potential dangers in granting wide stop and search powers to the police if there is a possibility that the powers will be abused, with harassment of ethnic minority groups being a particular concern.

Powers of arrest

Powers of arrest allow people to be detained against their will. Such detention is only lawful if the arrest is carried out in accordance with the law. An arrest can take place either with or without a warrant.

Arrest with a warrant

Under s. 1 of the Magistrates' Courts Act 1980, criminal proceedings may be initiated either by the issue of a summons requiring the accused to attend court on a particular

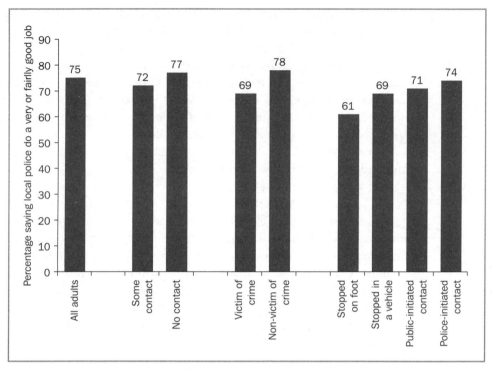

Figure 12.3 Rating of the local police by type of contact

Source: S. Nicholas and A. Walker (2004), *Crime in England and Wales 2002/2003: Supplementary Vol. 2: Crime, disorder and the criminal justice system and public attitudes and perceptions*, p. 11, Figure 2.1.

day or, in more serious cases, by a warrant of arrest issued by the magistrates' court. The police obtain a warrant by applying in writing to a magistrate, and backing up the application with an oral statement made on oath. The warrant issued must specify the name of the person to be arrested and general particulars of the offence. When an arrest warrant has been granted, a constable may enter and search premises to make the arrest, using such reasonable force as is necessary (PACE, s. 117).

Arrest without a warrant

The powers of the police to arrest without a warrant were increased by the Serious Organized Crime and Police Act 2005. The extension of police arrest powers were considered in the consultation paper, *Modernising Police Powers to Meet Community Needs* (2004). The reforms have simplified the police powers of arrest, but at the same time they have given the police more powers than they need, and are open to abuse.

In the past, s. 24 of PACE only allowed a person to be arrested for quite serious offences, known as arrestable offences, unless certain additional requirements were satisfied when an arrest would also be possible for a minor offence. The 2005 Act amended PACE, so that now a police officer can arrest a person for committing any offence if this is necessary. Police officers must reasonably suspect that a person has committed, is committing, or is about to commit an offence and have reasonable grounds for believing that it is necessary to arrest that person. It will be necessary to carry out an arrest if:

■ the person will not give their name and address, or the police officer reasonably suspects that the name or address given is false; or
■ the arrest will prevent the person from causing physical injury to him or herself or another person; suffering physical injury; causing loss or damage to property; committing an offence against public decency; or obstructing the highway;
■ to protect a child or other vulnerable person;
■ to allow the prompt and effective investigation of the offence or of the conduct of the person in question; or
■ to prevent the person disappearing.

These last two reasons are likely to justify an arrest in most cases. Further guidance on the issue is contained in a Code of Practice. In **G** *v* **DPP** (1989) it was held that a belief of the police officer concerned that suspects generally give false names was not sufficient to satisfy the general arrest conditions.

The same rules apply to the concept of reasonable suspicion for arrest as were discussed for stop and search powers. Its meaning in the context of an arrest was considered by the House of Lords in **O'Hara** *v* **Chief Constable of the Royal Ulster Constabulary** (1996). A two-stage test was identified. First, there must be actual suspicion on the part of the arresting officer (the subjective test) ànd, secondly, there must be reasonable grounds for that suspicion (the objective test). This approach was upheld by the European Court of Human Rights in **O'Hara** *v* **United Kingdom** (2002).

Citizen's arrest

A member of the public is entitled to arrest a person in certain circumstances. This power to carry out a citizen's arrest is contained in s. 24A of PACE. The exercise of the citizen's power of arrest is limited to indictable offences where the person has reasonable grounds for believing that arrest is necessary. If the citizen has made a mistake, and an offence has not actually been committed by anyone, the citizen may be liable for damages (**Walters** *v* **WH Smith & Son Ltd** (1914)). For example, if a man hears somebody shout 'Stop thief' and seeing a woman running away with a handbag wrongly assumes she is the thief, he can be sued for damages by that woman if he tries to grab her.

Manner of arrest

PACE requires that at the time of the arrest, or as soon as practicable after the arrest, the person arrested must be informed that they are under arrest, and given the grounds for that arrest, even if it is perfectly obvious that they are being arrested and why (s. 28). This is in line with the pre-existing case law, where in **Christie** *v* **Leachinsky** (1947) Viscount Simon said: 'No one, I think, would approve a situation in which when the person arrested asked for the reason, the policeman replied "that has nothing to do with you: come along with me" . . .'.

There is no set form of words that must be used, and colloquial language such as 'You're nicked for mugging' may be acceptable.

Quick quiz 12.3

1 What is the main statutory provision allowing the police to stop and search a member of the public?

2 Which code of practice provides guidance on the meaning of 'reasonable suspicion'?

3 When do the police have a power to arrest without a warrant under s. 24 of PACE?

4 What is meant by a 'citizen's arrest'?

Search of the person after arrest

The police have the power to search arrested persons on arrival at the police station, and to seize anything which they reasonably believe the suspect might use to injure anyone, or use to make an escape, or that is evidence of an offence or has been obtained as the result of an offence (s. 54).

Intimate searches and fingerprinting

Section 55 of PACE gives police the power to conduct intimate searches of a suspect, which means searches of the body's orifices. Such a search must be authorized by a superintendent, who must have reasonable grounds for believing that a weapon or drug is concealed, and must be carried out by a qualified doctor or nurse.

The safeguards on the use of this power caused problems for the police when confronted with drug dealers. The dealers frequently stored drugs in their mouths, knowing that search of the mouth was regarded as an intimate search that needed to be carried out by a member of the medical profession with special authorization. To address this problem, s. 65 of PACE, as amended by the CJPOA 1994, now provides that a search of the mouth is not an intimate search.

The police are permitted to take fingerprints from a suspect under s. 61 of PACE. Section 62 of PACE states that intimate samples, including blood, saliva or semen, can be taken from a suspect, but in some cases the suspect's written consent is required, though this is becoming increasingly rare following the Criminal Evidence (Amendment) Act 1997. Non-intimate samples, such as hair or nail clippings, can be taken from a suspect without their consent, under s. 63, although this procedure must be authorized by an officer at the level of inspector or above. The authorization must be in writing and recorded on the custody record.

These powers have been extended by the Criminal Justice and Police Act 2001, which allows what the Act calls 'speculative searches', whereby fingerprints, samples or information drawn from them can be checked against other similar data available to the police. These changes broadly reflect the recommendations of the RCCJ. The powers of the police to take and retain DNA samples are also contained in the 2001 Act.

The Criminal Justice and Court Services Act 2000 allows the compulsory drug testing of alleged offenders.

Police detention

Under PACE, suspects can be detained without charge for up to four days, although there are some safeguards designed to prevent abuse of this power. PACE provides that an arrested person must be brought to a police station as soon as practicable after the arrest, though this may be delayed if their presence elsewhere is necessary for an immediate investigation (s. 30). On arrival at the police station, the arrested person should usually be taken to the custody officer, who has to decide whether sufficient evidence exists to charge the person. If, on arrest, there is already sufficient evidence to charge the suspect, he or she must be charged and then released on bail unless there are reasons why this is not appropriate. Such reasons include the fact that the defendant's name and address are not known, there are reasonable grounds for believing that the address given is false or that the suspect may commit an offence while on bail (s. 38(1)). A person who has been charged and is being held in custody must be brought before magistrates as soon as practicable, and in any event not later than the first sitting after being charged with the offence (s. 46).

If there is not sufficient evidence to charge the suspect, then the person can be detained for the purpose of securing or obtaining such evidence – often through questioning (s. 37). Where a person is being detained and has not been charged, a review officer should assess whether there are grounds for continued detention after the first six hours and then at intervals of not more than nine hours (s. 40). These reviews can sometimes be carried out by telephone. As a basic rule, the police can detain a person for up to 36 hours from the time of arrival at the police station (this was increased from 24 hours by the Criminal Justice Act 2003). After this time the suspect should generally be either released or charged (s. 41). However, there are major exceptions to this. Continued detention for a further 12 hours can be authorized by the police themselves, if the detention is necessary to secure or preserve evidence and the offence is an indictable offence (meaning an offence which can be tried in the Crown Court rather than the magistrates' court).

Further periods of continued detention, up to 96 hours, are possible with approval from the magistrates' court. After 96 hours the suspect must be charged or released. In fact prolonged detention is rare, with only 5 per cent of suspects detained for more than 18 hours, and 1 per cent for more than 24 hours.

The custody officer is responsible for keeping the custody record (which records the various stages of detention) and checks that the provisions of PACE in relation to the detention are complied with. These theoretical safeguards for the suspect have proved weak in practice. PACE seems to contemplate that custody officers will be quasi-judicial figures, who can distance themselves from the needs of the investigation and put the rights of the suspect first. In practice, this has never been realistic; custody officers are ordinary members of the station staff, and likely to share their view of the investigation. In addition, they will often be of a more junior rank than the investigating officer. They are therefore highly unlikely to refuse to allow the detention of a suspect, or to prevent breaches of PACE and its codes during the detention.

▌ Police interrogation

The usual reason for detaining suspects is so that the police can question them, in the hope of securing a confession. This has come to be a very important investigative tool, since it is cheap (compared, for example, to scientific evidence) and the end result, a confession, is seen as reliable and convincing evidence by judges and juries alike. Research by Mitchell (1983) suggests that a high proportion of suspects do make either partial or complete confessions.

Unfortunately, as the miscarriages of justice show, relying too much on confession evidence can have severe drawbacks. Instances of police completely falsifying confessions, or threatening or beating suspects so that they confess even when they are innocent, may be rare but the miscarriages show that police have been willing to use these techniques where they think they can get away with it. In addition, there are less dramatic, but probably more widespread problems. The 1993 Royal Commission raised questions about the poor standard of police interviewing; research by John Baldwin (*Video Taping Police Interviews with Suspects: an Evaluation*, 1992) suggested that police officers went into the interview situation not with the aim of finding out whether the person was guilty, but on the assumption of guilt and with the intention of securing a confession to that effect. Interviews were often rambling and repetitious; police officers dismissed suspects' explanations and asked the same questions over and over again until they were given the answer they wanted. In some cases the researchers felt this treatment amounted to bullying or harassment, and in several cases the 'admissions' were one-word answers given in response to leading questions. Suspects were also offered inducements to confess, such as lighter sentences.

Obviously the implication here is that, under this kind of pressure, suspects might confess to crimes they did not commit – as many of the miscarriage of justice victims did. But such false confessions do not only occur where the suspects are physically threatened. A study by psychologist G.H. Gudjonsson (*The Psychology of Interrogations, Confessions and Testimony*, 1992) found that there were four situations in which people were likely to confess to crimes they did not commit. First, a minority may make confessions quite voluntarily, out of a disturbed desire for publicity, to relieve general feelings of guilt or because they cannot distinguish between reality and fantasy – it has been suggested that this was partly the case with Judith Ward. Secondly, they may want to protect someone else, perhaps a friend or relative, from interrogation and prosecution. Thirdly, they may be unable to see further than a desire to put an end to the questioning and get away from the police station, which can, after all, be a frightening place for those who are not accustomed to it. A psychologist giving evidence to the 1993 Royal Commission commented that 'Some children are brought up in such a way that confession always seems to produce forgiveness, in which case a false confession may be one way of bringing an unpleasant situation [the interrogation] to an end'. Among this group there may also be a feeling that, once they get out of the police station, they will be able to make everyone see sense, and realize their innocence. Unfortunately this does not always hapen.

Finally, the pressure of questioning, and the fact that the police seem convinced of their case, may temporarily persuade the suspect that they must have done the act in question. Obviously the young and the mentally ill are likely to be particularly vulnerable to this last situation, but Gudjonsson's research found that its effects were not confined to those who might be considered abnormally suggestible. Their subjects included people of reasonable intelligence who scored highly in tests on suggestibility, showing that they were particularly prepared to go along with what someone in authority was saying. Under hostile interrogation in the psychologically intimidating environment of a police station, even non-vulnerable people are likely to make admissions which are not true, failing to realize that once a statement has been made, it will be extremely difficult to retract.

Safeguards for the suspect

Certain safeguards are contained in PACE to try to protect the suspect in the police station. Some of these – the custody officer, the custody record, and the time limits for detention – have already been mentioned, and we will now look at the rest. It has been claimed that these safeguards would prevent miscarriages of justice in the future, yet the police station where Winston Silcott was questioned was meant to be following the PACE guidelines on a pilot basis. PACE officially came into force in January 1986 and Mark Braithwaite was arrested in February of that year, yet he was denied access to the legal advice guaranteed by the Act.

The caution

Under Code C, a person must normally be cautioned on arrest, and a person whom there are grounds to suspect of an offence must be cautioned before being asked any questions regarding involvement, or suspected involvement, in that offence. Until recently, the caution was: 'You do not have to say anything unless you wish to do so but what you say may be given in evidence.' Since the abolition of the right to silence (see p. 253), the correct wording is: 'You do not have to say anything, but it may harm your defence if you do not mention when questioned anything which you later rely on in court. Anything that you do say may be given in evidence.'

Tape-recording

Section 60 of PACE states that interviews must be tape-recorded. This measure was designed to ensure that oppressive treatment and threats could not be used, nor confessions made up by the police. Sadly, it has proved a weaker safeguard than it might seem. In the first place, research presented to the RCCJ showed that police routinely got round the provision by beginning their questioning outside the interview room – in the car on the way to the police station, for example. In addition, they appeared quite willing to use oppressive questioning methods even once the tape-recorder was running – the RCCJ listened to tapes of interviews with the 'Cardiff Three', victims of another miscarriage of justice whose convictions were quashed in December 1992, and expressed concern at the continuous repetitive questioning that the tapes revealed. The Home Office is carrying out pilot schemes for the use of video recordings in interviews. However, video recording is unlikely to be introduced at a national level in the near future as the cost of establishing such a scheme would be about £100 million.

The right to inform someone of the detention

Section 56 of PACE provides that on arrival at a police station, a suspect is entitled to have someone, such as a relative, informed of their arrest. The person whom the suspect chooses must be told of the arrest, and where the suspect is being held, without delay.

This right may be suspended for up to 36 hours if the detention is in connection with an indictable offence, and the authorizing officer reasonably believes that informing the person chosen by the suspect would lead to interference with, or harm to, evidence connected with a serious arrestable offence; the alerting of other suspects; interference with or injury to others; hindrance in recovering any property gained as a result of a serious arrestable offence, or in drug-trafficking offences; hindrance in recovering the profits of that offence.

The right to consult a legal adviser

Under s. 58 of PACE, a person held in custody is entitled to consult a legal adviser privately and free of charge. The House of Lords ruled in **R v Chief Constable of the Royal Ulster Carstabulary, ex parte Begley** (1997) that there was no equivalent right under common law. The right to see a legal adviser may be suspended for up to 36 hours on the same grounds as the right to have another person informed. The legal adviser will either be a solicitor or, since 1995, an 'accredited representative'. To become an accredited representative a person must register with the Legal Services Commission with a signed undertaking from a solicitor that he or she is 'suitable' for this work. Once registered, representatives can attend police stations on behalf of their solicitor and deal with summary or either-way offences, but not indictable-only offences. Within six months the representative must complete and submit a portfolio of work undertaken. This will include two police station visits where the representative observed his/her instructing solicitor, two visits where the solicitor observed the representative and five visits which the representative completed on his/her own. If representatives pass the portfolio stage, they then have to take a written and an oral examination, at which point they are fully qualified to represent clients in the police station for any criminal matters. The right to see a legal adviser may be suspended for up to 36 hours on the same grounds as the right to have another person informed.

An 'appropriate adult'

PACE and Code C provide that young people and mentally disordered or mentally handicapped adults must have an 'appropriate adult' with them during a police interview, as well as having the usual right to legal advice. This may be a parent, but is often a social worker. Surprisingly, Evans's 1993 research for the RCCJ found that parents were not necessarily a protection for the suspect, since they often took the side of the police and helped them to produce a confession.

Treatment of suspects

PACE codes stipulate that interview rooms must be adequately lit, heated and ventilated, that suspects must be allowed to sit during questioning, and that adequate breaks for meals, refreshments and sleep must be given.

Record of the interview

After the interview is over, the police must make a record of it, which is kept on file. Baldwin's 1992 research checked a sample of such records against the taped recordings, and concluded that even those police forces considered to be more progressive were often failing to produce good quality records of interviews. Half the records were faulty or misleading, and the longer the interview, the more likely the record was to be inaccurate. These findings were backed up by a separate study carried out by Roger Evans (1993). He found that in some summaries the police stated that suspects had confessed during the interview, but, on listening to the tape recordings, the researchers could find no evidence of this, and felt that the suspects were in fact denying the offence.

Exclusion of evidence

One of the most important safeguards in PACE (ss. 76 and 78) is the possibility for the courts to refuse to admit evidence which has been improperly obtained. Given that the reason why police officers bend or break the rules is to secure a conviction, preventing them from using the evidence obtained in this way is likely to constitute an effective deterrent.

Article 8 of the European Convention on Human Rights protects the right to privacy. Article 8(2) adds that interference with that right is permitted if it is in accordance with the law and necessary in a democratic society for the prevention of crime. A careful balance has to be drawn by the law where surveillance techniques are used, for example, by bugging a private home. Breach of Art. 8 can give rise to a right to damages, but there is no guarantee that the evidence will be excluded at trial as the ordinary rules in ss. 76 and 78 of PACE apply.

The right to silence

Until 1994, the law provided a further safeguard for those suspected of criminal conduct, in the form of the traditional 'right to silence'. This essentially meant that suspects were free to say nothing at all in response to police questioning, and the prosecution could not suggest in court that this silence implied guilt (with some very limited exceptions).

Once PACE was introduced, the police argued that its safeguards, especially the right of access to legal advice, had tipped the balance too far in favour of suspects, so that the right to silence was no longer needed. Despite the fact that the Royal Commission on Criminal Justice (1993) opposed this view, the Government agreed with the police, and the right to silence was abolished by the Criminal Justice and Public Order Act 1994. This does not mean that suspects can be forced to speak, but it provides four situations in which, if the suspect chooses not to speak, the court will be entitled to draw such inferences from that silence as appear proper. The four situations are where suspects:

■ when questioned under caution or charge, fail to mention facts which they later rely on as part of their defence and which it is reasonable to expect them to have mentioned (s. 34);
■ are silent during the trial, including choosing not to give evidence or to answer any question without good cause (s. 35);
■ following arrest, fail to account for objects, substances or marks on clothing when requested to do so (s. 36);
■ following arrest, fail to account for their presence at a particular place when requested to do so (s. 37).

No inferences from silence can be drawn where a suspect was at a police station and has been denied access to legal advice (s. 34(2)(A)).

Interviews outside the police station

PACE states that, where practicable, interviews with arrested suspects should always take place at a police station. However, evidence obtained by questioning or voluntary statements outside the police station may still be admissible. Since such interviews are not subject to most of the safeguards explained above, the obvious danger is that police may evade PACE requirements by conducting 'unofficial' interviews – such as the practice known as taking the 'scenic route' to the station, in which suspects are questioned in the police car. The RCCJ found that about 30 per cent of suspects report being questioned prior to arrest.

▌Cautions

In appropriate cases an offender can be issued with a caution rather than being subjected to a full criminal prosecution. This is a formal warning to offenders about what they have done, and their conduct in the future. Home Office guidelines lay down the criteria on which the decision to caution should be made. A caution can only be given where the offender admits guilt, and there would be a realistic prospect of a successful prosecution. In the case of a juvenile, the parents or guardian must consent to a caution being given. If these criteria are met, other factors to be taken into account are the seriousness of the offence and the extent of the damage done; the interests and desires of the victim; the previous conduct of the offender; the family background of the offender; and the offender's conduct after the offence, such as a willingness to make reparation to the victim.

Formal cautions are recorded and if the person is convicted of another offence afterwards can be cited as part of their criminal record. The 1980s saw a substantial increase in the use of cautioning, with the number of cautions given doubling between 1983 and 1993, peaking at 311,300 cautions for that year, primarily to juveniles. There has subsequently been a slight decline in their use, with the figures for 1995 showing a 6 per cent reduction in the use of cautions.

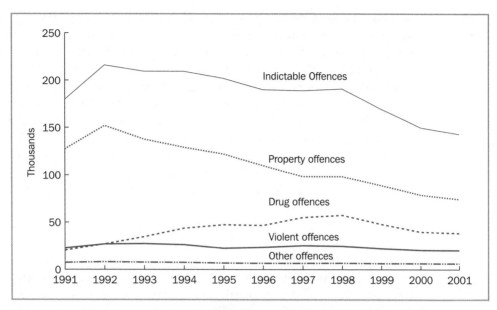

Figure 12.4 Offenders cautioned for indictable offences by offence group, 1991–2001
Source: Home Office (2002), *Criminal Statistics England and Wales 2001*, p. 34, Figure 5.7.

The Criminal Justice Act 2003 introduced conditional cautions. Conditions can seek either to facilitate rehabilitation or to ensure that reparation is made. Failure to comply with the conditions can trigger a criminal trial for the offence. This is a dangerous reform as cautions will take on the form of a punishment administered outside the court system. As such, they might well breach the European Convention on Human Rights.

Bail

A person accused, convicted or under arrest for an offence may be granted bail, which means they are released under a duty to attend court or the police station at a given time. The right to bail has been reduced in recent years amid concern that individuals on bail reoffend and fail to turn up at court for their trial. Fourteen per cent of those bailed to appear at court fail to do so (*Criminal Justice Statistics 2003*) and nearly 25 per cent of defendants commit at least one offence while on bail (Brown (1998) *Offending While on Bail*, Home Office, Report No. 72). The criteria for granting or refusing bail are contained in the Bail Act 1976. There is a general presumption in favour of bail for unconvicted defendants, but there are some important exceptions. Bail need not be granted where there are substantial grounds for believing that, unless kept in custody, the accused would fail to surrender to bail, or would commit an offence, interfere with witnesses or otherwise obstruct the course of justice. In assessing these risks, the court may take account of the nature and seriousness of the offence and the probable sentence, along with the character, antecedents, associations and community ties of the defendant. Following the Criminal Justice and Court Services Act 2000, a court considering the question of bail must take into account any drug misuse by the defendant. The Criminal Justice Act 2003 has created a presumption against bail for a person charged with an imprisonable offence, who tests positive for a specified Class A drug and refuses treatment, unless there are exceptional circumstances. This provision may breach Art. 5 of the European Convention on Human Rights which guarantees the right to freedom of the person.

The courts need not grant bail when the accused should be kept in custody for their own protection, where the accused is already serving a prison sentence or where there has been insufficient time to obtain information as to the criteria for bail. If the court does choose to grant bail in such cases, its reasons for doing so must be included in the bail record. The presumption in favour of bail is reversed where someone is charged with a further indictable offence which appears to have been committed while on bail.

The Criminal Justice and Public Order Act 1994, following concern at offences being committed by accused while on bail, provided that a person charged or convicted of murder, manslaughter, rape, attempted murder or attempted rape could never be granted bail if they had a previous conviction for such an offence. This complete ban breached the European Convention on Human Rights. The law has now been reformed by the Crime and Disorder Act 1998, under which such a person may only be granted bail where there are exceptional circumstances which justify doing so. Thus Sion Jenkins, who was convicted of the murder of his foster-daughter Billy-Jo, was on bail throughout most of the proceedings.

When bail is refused for any of the stated reasons, other than insufficient information, the accused will usually be allowed only one further bail application; the court does not have to hear further applications unless there has been a change in circumstances. Where the remand in custody is on the basis of insufficient information, this is not technically a refusal of bail, so the accused may still make two applications.

Bail can be granted subject to conditions, such as that the accused obtain legal advice before their next court appearance or that the accused or a third party give a security (which is a payment into court that will be forfeited if the accused fails to attend a court hearing). When a defendant fails to attend court any money held by the court is immediately forfeited and it is up to the person who paid that money to show why it should not be forfeited. A defendant refused bail, or who objects to the conditions under which it is offered, must be told the reasons for the decision, and informed of their right to appeal. The prosecution also has increasing rights to appeal against a decision to grant bail.

The Criminal Justice Act 2003 has given the police the power to grant bail at the place of arrest. This is called 'street bail'. It means that the police do not have to take suspects to the police station and undertake lengthy paperwork. A form is completed on the street and later entered in police records. The power is unlikely to be used much until compulsory ID cards have been introduced.

In 1992 the average proportion of unconvicted and unsentenced prisoners was 22 per cent of the average prison population. Many of these remand prisoners, who have not been convicted of any offence, are kept in prison for between six months and a year before being tried, despite the fact that 60 per cent of them go on to be acquitted or given a non-custodial sentence.

Criticism and reform

Criticisms and suggestions for reform have been made throughout this chapter, but the following have been the subject of particular debate.

A graduate profession

The work of a police officer requires a wide range of skills, both intellectual and personal. At the moment the only qualifications that a person needs to join the police force is a handful of GCSEs. Now that increasing numbers of young people are going to university it is time to transform the police force into a graduate profession. Only then would the United Kingdom have an efficient police force with the skills to combat crime effectively. At the moment the police force struggles with the paperwork that their job requires because they have an inadequate education. Without better preparation for their career, the police will continue to be perceived by many in the public as slow, lazy and inefficient. With the creation of community support officers, the higher pay and status of the police can only be justified if they actually have better qualifications and skills.

Racism and the police

Britain is a multicultural and ethnically diverse community. Three per cent of the population aged ten and over is of black ethnic origin, 5 per cent of Asian origin. Successful policing requires that all members of British society must have confidence in the police force. Following the fatal stabbing of Stephen Lawrence, a black teenager who was an A-level student from south London, by a group of racist youths in 1993, defects in several aspects of the English legal system failed to bring his killers to justice. Following concern at the handling of the police investigation into the killing, a judicial inquiry headed by a former High Court judge, Sir William Macpherson, was set up by the Government in 1997 and its report was published in February 1999. It found that the Metropolitan Police suffered from institutional racism. This is defined as existing where there is a

> collective failure of an organisation to provide an appropriate and professional service to people because of their colour, culture and ethnic origin. It can be seen or detected in processes, attitudes and behaviour which amount to discrimination through unwitting prejudice, ignorance, thoughtlessness and racist stereotypical behaviour.

The presence of institutional racism was reflected in the fact that the first senior officer at the scene of the crime assumed that what had occurred had been a fight; it was also expressed in the absence of adequate family liaison and the 'patronising and thoughtless approach' of some officers to Mr and Mrs Lawrence; and it could be seen in the side-lining of Stephen Lawrence's friend, the surviving victim of the attack. There was, furthermore, a refusal to accept, by at least five officers involved in the case, that this was a racist murder. Finally, there was the use of inappropriate and offensive language by police officers, including, on occasion, during their appearance before the Inquiry itself. It found that racism awareness training was 'almost non-existent at every level', and concluded that institutional racism could only be tackled effectively if there was an 'unequivocal acceptance that the problem actually exists'.

The inquiry, however, concluded that institutional racism was not 'universally the cause of the failure of this investigation'. The investigation by the Metropolitan Police was 'marred by a combination of professional incompetence, institutional racism and a failure of leadership by senior officers'.

The Report contained 20 recommendations for reform. In March 1999, the Government issued its Action Plan in response to the Macpherson Report. A steering group, chaired by the Home Secretary, has been established to oversee the programme of reform. In the past the Race Relations Act 1976 did not apply to the police, so that there was no legal remedy if a black person thought they had been stopped by the police because of racial prejudice. Now the Race Relations (Amendment) Act 2000 has been passed. This Act amends the 1976 Act, making it unlawful for a public authority, including the police, to discriminate in carrying out any of their functions. Police forces have reviewed their provision of racism awareness training. Targets have been set for the recruitment and retention of ethnic minority police officers. Currently 2.6 per cent of police officers are from an ethnic minority. The recommendation that the use of racist language in private should be criminalized has been rejected.

While the Macpherson Report is one step towards tackling institutional racism in the police, it is worrying that Lord Scarman's report into the Brixton riots of 1981 had already identified this problem, and though some progress was subsequently made, this has clearly not been sufficient. In 1999/2000 the British Crime Survey suggested that there were 143,000 racially motivated crimes committed and yet only 1,832 defendants were prosecuted for such offences.

A particularly sensitive area of policing is the power to stop and search. A police operation against street robberies in Lambeth (South London) in 1981, codenamed SWAMP 81, involved 943 stops, mostly of young black men, over a period of two weeks. Of these, only 118 led to arrests and 75 to charges, one of which was for robbery. The operation, which had no noticeable effect on the crime figures, shattered relations between the police and the ethnic community, and was one of the triggers of the Brixton riots that occurred soon afterwards. Nevertheless, in his report on the Brixton disorders, Lord Scarman thought such powers necessary to combat street crime, provided that the safeguard of 'reasonable suspicion' was properly and objectively applied. But in 1999 the Macpherson Report concluded that the 'perception and experience of the minority communities that discrimination is a major element in the stop and search problem is correct'.

In accordance with recommendations made by Macpherson, the police are now required to monitor the use of stop and search powers, and 'consider in particular whether there is any evidence that they are being exercised on the basis of stereotyped images or inappropriate generalisations'. Regrettably, these statistics show that an increasing proportion of those stopped and searched by the police are black.

Home Office statistics (*Statistics on Race and the Criminal Justice System 2003*) show that while black people make up only 3 per cent of the population, 14 per cent of stop and searches were carried out on black people, an increase by more than a third on the previous year. The Commission for Racial Equality (2004) has concluded that stop and search has been used disproportionately against black and Asian people. This has:

> led to the perception among some communities that stop and search is being used in a discriminatory way – affecting confidence levels in the police and in some cases reducing the willingness of people to assist with the investigation of crime.

An increasing worry is the number of black murder victims and the failure of the police to bring the offenders to court. Between 2000 and 2003, 10 per cent of homicide victims were black. The police were statistically less likely to identify suspects for homicides involving black and Asian victims than for white victims, though this can partly be explained by the method of killing used.

Police corruption

The police exercise an extremely delicate role in society and, as criminals are able to generate large sums of money from their criminal conduct, the danger of corruption is real. High risk areas include the handling of informers and positions within drug, vice and crime squads where constant vigilance is required. Where corruption is rife, one can no longer fall back on the idea of a few rotten apples and accept that the system itself must be corrupting its members.

Sir Paul Condon made anti-corruption a touchstone of his tenure as Commissioner of the Metropolitan Police. He has estimated that there may be as many as 250 corrupt officers in his force, some of whom are directly involved in very serious criminal activity, and has dedicated resources to their detection. A more proactive approach can be expected at a national level, as New Scotland Yard has established a special squad concentrating on corruption in the police and the Association of Chief Police Officers established in 1998 a Taskforce on Corruption. During the course of that year, 28 police officers were convicted of corruption-related offences, and at the end of the year, 153 police officers were suspended for alleged corruption and similar matters.

'Bobbies on the beat'

Four billion pounds is spent each year on police patrols, but the reality is that at any one time only 5 per cent of police officers are out on patrol. The Audit Commission report, *Streetwise: Effective Police Patrol* (1996), notes that the public are keen to see more 'bobbies on the beat' and that this provides the public with a feeling of security. A review of research in 1998 found that random patrols are ineffective in reducing crime but that targeted patrols on crime hot spots can be effective (Nuttall *et al. Reducing Offending: An Assessment of Research Evidence on Ways of Dealing with Offending Behaviour* (1998)).

Police conduct

During 1997, well over 6,000 complaints of alleged rudeness and incivility by police officers were recorded. Her Majesty's Inspectorate of Constabulary undertook a wideranging exploration of the level of integrity in the police because it was recognized that 'public confidence was becoming seriously affected by the bad behaviour of a small minority of police'. In *Police Integrity: Securing and Maintaining Public Confidence* (1999) Her Majesty's Inspectorate reported that: 'Numerous examples were found in all forces visited of poor behaviour towards members of the public and colleagues alike, including rudeness, arrogance and discriminatory comment.' In the Inspectorate's view, one consequence of tolerating bullying, rudeness and racist or sexist behaviour is that 'corruption and other wrongdoing will flourish'.

The right to silence

The abolition of the right to silence has been one of the most severely criticized changes to the criminal justice system in recent years. As the academic John Fitzpatrick has written, the basis of the right to silence is the presumption of innocence, which places the burden of proof on the prosecution: 'this burden begins to shift, and the presumption of innocence to dwindle, as soon as we are obliged to explain or justify our actions in any way' (*Legal Action*, May 1994).

Those who objected to the right to silence claimed that only the guilty would have anything to hide and that the innocent should therefore have no objection to answering questions. It was suggested that the calculated use of this right by professional criminals was leading to serious cases being dropped for lack of evidence, and that 'ambush' defences (in which defendants remain silent till the last moment and then produce an unexpected defence) were leading to acquittals because the prosecution had no time to prepare for the defence.

These arguments were put to the RCCJ, by a Home Office Working Group among others, but, after commissioning its own research into the subject the RCCJ rejected the idea of abolishing the right to silence. This research, by Leng (1993), and McConville and Hodgson (1993), showed that in fact only 5 per cent of suspects exercised their right to silence, and there was no evidence of an unacceptable acquittal rate for these defendants. Nor was there any serious problem with ambush defences.

As we have seen, the Conservative Government decided to ignore the RCCJ recommendations and abolish the right to silence – a somewhat strange decision considering that it was the same Government which set up the Commission in the first place. The law reform body, Justice, has claimed that this decision will lead to increased pressure on suspects and, in turn, to more miscarriages of justice. It studied the effects of removing the right to silence in Northern Ireland (which took place five years before removal of the right in England and Wales). Apparently, suspects frequently failed to understand the new caution and were put under unfair pressure to speak, while lawyers found it difficult to advise suspects when they did not know the full case against them. Most importantly, Justice claims that while at first trial judges were cautious about drawing inferences of guilt from a suspect's silence, five years on, they were giving such silence considerable weight, and in some cases treating it almost as a presumption of guilt.

Deaths in police custody

Almost 700 people have died in police custody or in contact with the police since 1990. Very few police officers have been prosecuted following a death in custody, and none has been convicted. A report on the subject by Vogt and Wadham (2002), *Deaths in Custody: Redress and Remedies*, for the pressure group Liberty, concluded that these deaths were not being adequately investigated. The police, the Police Complaints Authority (now the Independent Police Complaints Commission) and the coroner could all be involved. These investigations were ineffective, secretive, slow and insufficiently independent.

Reading on the web

The revised Code A for PACE can be found on the Home Office website at:

http://www.homeoffice.gov.uk/news-and-publications/publication/ operational-policing/PACE_Chapter_A.pdf

The report for the pressure group Liberty, *Deaths in Custody: Redress and Remedies*, by Greta Vogt and John Wadham is available on the Liberty website:

http://www.liberty-human-rights.org.uk

Information on the criminal justice system is available at:

http://www.cjsonline.org/index.html

Question and answer guide

1 Tyrone, aged 16, has missed the last bus and has to walk home. It is 2 am and a police officer driving past in a police car sees Tyrone and stops. The police officer tells Tyrone to empty his pockets. Tyrone is tired and becomes annoyed at this. He refuses to do so and keeps on walking. The police officer then grabs Tyrone by the shoulder and pushes him into the police car. Tyrone is taken to the local police station.

(a) Explain what powers the police have to stop and search someone, and when the police have the right to arrest someone. *(30 marks)*

(b) Advise Tyrone on whether the police officer acted lawfully within his powers. *(15 marks)* *(OCR)*

Answer guide

You need to divide your answer into two parts, looking first at the power to stop and search and secondly the power to arrest. The power to stop and search is contained in s. 1 of PACE, ▶

accompanied by the Code of Practice A (discussed at p. 317). The power of the police to arrest without a warrant is contained in s. 24 of PACE (discussed at pp. 246). There is also a power to arrest with a warrant (discussed at p. 245).

Part (b) of the question requires you to apply the law outlined in your answer to part (a) to the facts of the case. Looking first at the power to stop and search, the only apparent reason that the police had for stopping Tyrone was that it was 2 am and Tyrone was young. These are not sufficient grounds to give rise to reasonable suspicion for the purposes of a s. 1 stop and search. The police officer was required to tell Tyrone the reason for the search and as he failed to do so the subsequent search is likely to be considered unlawful.

As regards the power to arrest, again, the police officer does not appear to have grounds for reasonable suspicion that Tyrone has committed, is committing or will commit an offence for the purposes of a s. 24 arrest. Reasons had to be given for the arrest which have not been given. It is not clear whether the amount of force used by the police officer in grabbing Tyrone by the shoulder and pushing him into the car would fall within the legal limit of 'reasonable force'. It is therefore likely that the police officer's actions were unlawful.

Chapter summary

Introduction
The criminal justice system needs to strike a balance between punishing the guilty and protecting the innocent. Recent miscarriages of justice have raised concerns as to whether this balance is being achieved.

The organisation of the police
The organisation of the police is becoming increasingly centralized.

Civilian support staff
The Police Reform Act 2002 allows a range of civilians or exercise police powers.

Pre-arrest powers of the police
Even without carrying out an arrest, the police enjoy a range of powers to stop and search a member of the public, in particular under s. 1 of PACE.

Powers of arrest
An arrest can take place either with or without a warrant. The powers of the police to arrest without a warrant were increased by the Serious Organised Crime and Police Act 2005.

Citizen's arrest
A member of the public is entitled to arrest a person in certain circumstances. This power to carry out a citizen's arrest is contained in s. 24A of PACE.

Police detention
Under PACE the police can detain a suspect for up to four days without charge.

Police interrogation
The usual reason for detaining suspects is so that the police can question them, in the hope of securing a confession. Certain safeguards exist to protect people while they are being

detained and questioned. These include the tape-recording of police interviews in the police station and the right to inform someone of the detention. Since 1994 the right to silence has been effectively abolished.

Bail

A person accused, convicted or under arrest for an offence may be granted bail, which means the person is released under a duty to attend court or the police station at a given time.

Criticism and reform

A range of criticisms and reform proposals have been put forward relating to the police:

A graduate profession

Now that increasing numbers of young people are going to university it is time to transform the police force into a graduate profession. Only then would the UK have an efficient police force with the skills to combat crime effectively.

Racism and the police

Following the unsuccessful police investigation into the murder of the black teenager Stephen Lawrence, Sir William Macpherson found that the Metropolitan police suffered from institutional racism. A particularly sensitive area of policing is the power to stop and search and the targeting of black people can have a detrimental effect on the relationship of the police with black people generally.

Police corruption

The police exercise an extremely delicate role in society and, as criminals are able to generate large sums of money from their criminal conduct, the danger of corruption is real.

The right to silence

The abolition of the right to silence has been one of the most severely criticized changes to the criminal justice system in recent years.

Deaths in police custody

Almost 700 people have died in police custody or in contact with the police since 1990. Very few police officers have been prosecuted following a death in custody, and none have been convicted.

Chapter 13 The criminal trial process

The adversarial process

The English system of criminal justice can be described as adversarial. This means each side is responsible for putting their own case: collecting evidence, interviewing witnesses and retaining experts. In Court they will present their own evidence and attack their opponent's evidence by cross-examining their adversary's witnesses. Both parties only call those witnesses likely to advance their cause and both parties are permitted to attack the credibility and reliability of the witnesses testifying for the other side. The role of the judge is limited to that of a referee ensuring fair play, making sure that the rules on procedure and evidence are followed. It is often compared with a battle with each side fighting their own corner. The adversarial system is typical of common law countries. The alternative is an inquisitorial system, which exists in most of the rest of Europe. Under that system, a judge (known in France as the *juge d'instruction*) plays the dominant role in collecting evidence before the trial. During the course of a lengthy investigation, the judge will interview witnesses and inspect documents, and the final trial is often just to rubber stamp the investigating judge's findings.

In the light of the recent miscarriages of justice, some people suggested that we should introduce an inquisitorial system into England. Arguments were put forward that the inquisitorial system provides a properly organized and regulated pre-trial phase, with an independent figure supervising the whole investigation. The Royal Commission on Criminal Justice ordered research into the French and German criminal justice system (Leigh and Zedner, 1992). The researchers rejected the idea of introducing the inquisitorial system into England. They did not think that the *juge d'instruction* was a real protection against overbearing police practices, except in rare cases where physical brutality was involved. Furthermore, despite the fact that only 10 per cent of cases go before the *juge d'instruction* in France, the system is over-burdened and works slowly. In Germany and Italy the powers of the investigating judge have been transferred to the public prosecutor, to avoid potential conflict between the functions of investigator and judge.

In recent years the English system has shifted slightly towards an inquisitorial system in an effort to achieve greater efficiency. Thus, the role of the judge has been increased, through, for example, an emphasis on judicial case management.

Criminal Procedural Rules

In 2005, the main rules on criminal procedure that apply to the trial and pre-trial process were brought together in new Criminal Procedure Rules. These rules did not introduce any radical changes to the law and practice, but they aim to make the relevant rules more accessible as they are all now brought together in one place. They emphasize that the judges need to take an active role in case management. Rule 3 states that active case management includes:

(a) the early identification of the real issues;

(b) the early identification of the needs of witnesses;

(c) achieving certainty as to what must be done, by whom, and when, in particular by the early setting of a timetable for the progress of the case;

(d) monitoring the progress of the case and compliance with directions;

(e) ensuring that evidence, whether disputed or not, is presented in the shortest and clearest way;

(f) discouraging delay, dealing with as many aspects of the case as possible on the same occasion, and avoiding unnecessary hearings;

(g) encouraging the participants to cooperate in the progression of the case; and

(h) making use of technology.

The emphasis on case management in criminal proceedings is clearly influenced by its relative success in the civil system. It is hoped that through the use of active case management, cases will progress more rapidly through the criminal system and fewer cases will collapse.

Quick quiz 13.1

1 Where should an arrested person normally be taken immediately after arrest?

2 If a person is charged and not released on bail, what do the police have to do?

3 How long can a person be held in a police station without being charged?

4 Is a person obliged to answer questions in a police station?

The Crown Prosecution Service

Until 1986, criminal prosecutions were officially brought by private citizens rather than by the state; in practice most prosecutions were brought by the police (though technically they were prosecuting as private citizens). Although the police obviously employed solicitors to help them in this task, their relationship with those solicitors was a normal client relationship, and so the police were not obliged to act on the solicitors' advice.

In 1970, a report by the law reform pressure group, Justice, criticized the role of the police in the prosecution process (*The Prosecution in England and Wales*, 1970). It argued that it was not in the interests of justice for the same body to be responsible for the two very different functions of investigation and prosecution. This dual role prevented the prosecution from being independent and impartial: the police had become concerned with winning or losing, when the aim of the prosecution should be the discovery of the truth. As a result, there was a danger of the police withholding from the defence information that might make a conviction less likely.

The prosecution process was reviewed by the Royal Commission on Criminal Procedure (RCCP) in 1981. Their report highlighted a range of problems. There was a lack of uniformity, with differing procedures and standards applied across the country on such matters as whether to prosecute or caution, and the system prevented a consistent national prosecution policy. The process was inefficient, with inadequate preparation of cases. The RCCP agreed with Justice that, in principle, investigation and prosecution should be separate processes, conducted by different people. As a result of these findings, the RCCP recommended the establishment of a Crown Prosecution Service, divided into separate local services for each police force area.

The Government followed the main recommendations, though it opposed the establishment of separate local services. The Crown Prosecution Service (CPS) was set up under the Prosecution of Offences Act 1985, as a national prosecution service for England and Wales. The service as a whole is headed by the Director of Public Prosecutions (DPP). The DPP reports on the running of the service to the Attorney-General. The only formal mechanism for accountability of the CPS is the requirement that an annual report must be presented to the Attorney-General, who is obliged to lay it before Parliament. The Attorney-General is responsible in Parliament for general policy, but not for individual cases.

The establishment of the CPS means that the prosecution of offences is now separated from their detection and investigation, which is undertaken by the police.

▌Administration of the CPS

When the CPS first started to operate in 1986, it was organized into 31 areas, each with a Chief Crown Prosecutor. These were subsequently increased to 38, but in 1993, in an effort to improve efficiency, the areas were enlarged into just 13 across the country. The administration was centralized around headquarters in London, with the DPP playing an increased role in the direct administration of the CPS. In the light of continuing concern over the functioning of the CPS, a review was carried out by a body chaired by Sir Ian Glidewell which reported in 1998. The *Review of the Crown Prosecution Service* (also known as the Glidewell Report) heavily criticized the CPS. It concluded that the 1993 reform had been a mistake, as it made the organization too centralized and excessively bureaucratic. It found that there was a problem with judge-ordered acquittals (where the case is too weak to be left to the jury), which constituted over 20 per cent of acquittals in 1996. Not all of these were due to poor case preparation by the CPS, as some involved errors in witness warnings by the police. But many were due to inadequate compilation of case papers between committal and trial by non-qualified staff who lacked supervision; the drafting of inadequate or erroneous indictments; and counsel being briefed too late to put things right.

Glidewell concluded that the CPS 'has the potential to become a lively, successful and esteemed part of the criminal justice system, but . . . sadly none of these adjectives applies to the service as a whole at present'.

The key recommendation of the Report was that there should be a devolution of powers from the centre to the regions, with the London headquarters playing a more limited role. This would involve replacing the 13 CPS areas with 42 areas corresponding to police force areas.

The Glidewell Report proposed that teams of CPS lawyers, police and administrative caseworkers (together known as a Criminal Justice Unit), should be established to prepare and deal with many straightforward cases in their entirety (in other words both the case preparation and the court advocacy); the section which dealt with the most serious cases, called Central Casework, needed more staff, with more training and closer monitoring; there should be at least one full-time CPS lawyer in each Crown Court; CPS lawyers should be allowed to concentrate more on court work rather than paperwork; and the DPP ought to play a lesser role in the administration of the CPS and concentrate largely on the prosecution and legal process.

The Government accepted the main recommendations of the Glidewell Report and the new 42 areas of the CPS came into effect on 22 April 1999.

Charging and prosecuting defendants

The normal practice has been for the police to decide whether to charge a defendant and then after charge send the file to the CPS to proceed with the prosecution. The Criminal Justice Act 2003 (s. 28) has moved the decision to charge from the police to the CPS. The police only retain the right to charge for certain minor offences. Lord Auld recommended this reform in his *Review of the Criminal Courts*. The hope is to improve the relationship between the CPS and the police so that they work efficiently together in the preparation of cases for trial. The police had in the past felt very unhappy about the number of prosecutions that have been discontinued after they have decided to charge a suspect. Six pilot schemes were established around the country where the decision to charge was moved from the police to the CPS, and these proved to be very successful. Convictions rose by 15 per cent. The instances of charges being reduced or dropped fell from 51 per cent to 18 per cent. The Attorney-General concluded that: 'Getting cases right from the start means less abandoned prosecution, less of the frustrating delays and more criminals brought to justice.'

When the CPS receives the file, it reviews whether a prosecution should be brought on the basis of criteria set out in the Code for Crown Prosecutors. This Code is issued by the CPS under s. 10 of the Prosecution of Offences Act 1985. The latest edition of the Code explains that this decision is taken in two stages. First, prosecutors must ask whether there is enough evidence to provide a 'realistic prospect of conviction', that is to say that a court is more likely than not to convict. If the case does not pass this evidential test, the prosecution must not go ahead, no matter how important or serious the case may be. If the case does pass the evidential test, the CPS must then consider whether the public interest requires a prosecution. For example, a prosecution is more likely to be in the public interest if a conviction is likely to result in a significant sentence, if the offence was committed against a person serving the public (such as a police officer) or if the offence is widespread in the area where it was committed. On the other hand, a prosecution is less likely to be in the public interest where the defendant is elderly, or suffering from significant mental or physical ill-health.

At the end of this two-stage test, the CPS may decide to go ahead with the prosecution, send the case back to the police for a caution instead of a prosecution, or take no further action. The decision is theirs, and the police need not be consulted.

The CPS continues to have no involvement in cases where the police decide not to charge, including those where the offender is given a caution.

The clear distinction that was initially drawn between the police and the CPS has been weakened by recent reforms. Following the Glidewell Report and the Narey Report (*Review of Delay in the Criminal Justice System* (1997)), some CPS staff now work alongside police officers in Criminal Justice Units to prepare cases for court.

Private prosecutions

Private prosecutions can still be brought, and although statistically these are few, they can play an important role, particularly in highlighting or encouraging public concern over relevant issues.

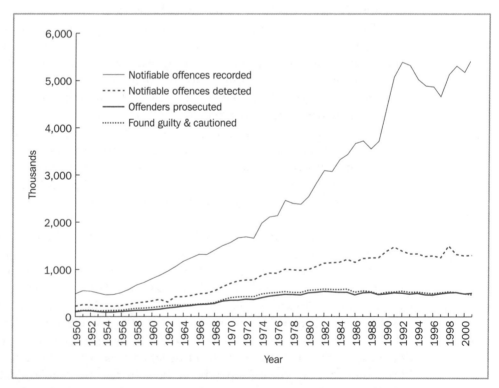

Figure 13.1 Recorded crime, prosecutions and 'known' offenders, 1950–2001

Source: Home Office (2002), *Criminal Statistics England and Wales 2001*, p. 16, Figure 1.2.

The family of Stephen Lawrence, a teenager murdered in south London, took out a private prosecution against three men suspected of the killing, after the CPS dropped the case because it said there was insufficient evidence. Unfortunately, the private prosecution was unsuccessful for lack of evidence. The case primarily relied on the identification evidence of Duwayne Brooks. This was weak because the attack had lasted only for a matter of seconds. He was unable to be specific about the number of attackers, saying that it was a 'group of 4 to 6'. In his initial statement to the police, he said that, 'Of the group of 6 youths, I can only really describe one of them'. At one identification parade, he identified a member of the public. At another he identified no one, although there was a suspect present. He had originally said Stephen had been hit on the head although he was later found to have sustained no head injuries. The judge summed up by saying: 'Where recognition or identification is concerned, [Brooks] simply does not know whether he is on his head or his heels . . . Adding one injustice to another does not cure the first injustice done to the Lawrence family.' The judge withdrew the case from the jury and ordered an acquittal. The decision to bring the private prosecution has been criticized as their acquittal prevented the suspects from being prosecuted for the same offence in the future when stronger evidence might have been available (see p. 406 for a discussion of the double jeopardy rule).

Public defenders

The Access to Justice Act 1999 provides for the appointment of public defenders service. For a discussion of public defenders, see p. 215.

Quick quiz 13.2

1 Which Royal Commission led to the creation of the Crown Prosecution Service?

2 In what year was the Crown Prosecution Service established?

3 Could your neighbour prosecute you for causing criminal damage to his fence?

4 Who is the top person in the Crown Prosecution Service?

Appearance in court

Persons charged with an offence can be called to court by means of a summons, or by a charge following arrest without a warrant. Arrest under a warrant signed by a magistrate under s. 1(1) of the Magistrates' Courts Act 1980 is not common today, and its main use is to arrest those who, having been granted bail, do not turn up for trial.

In order to have a summons served, the prosecutor must give a short account of the alleged offence, usually in writing, to the magistrates or their clerk (a process called laying an information). The information may be substantiated by an oral statement from the police, given on oath before a magistrate; such a statement must be given if the information is to be used as the basis for a warrant for arrest. A summons setting out the offence is then issued and served, either in person or, for minor offences, through recorded delivery or registered post.

The defendant is entitled to plead guilty by post for any summary offence for which the maximum penalty does not exceed three months' imprisonment (s. 12 of the Magistrates' Courts Act 1980). In this situation the defendant does not need to attend court, and the procedure is frequently used for traffic offences. In the past, delays were caused when people failed to respond to the summons in which they were given the opportunity to plead guilty by post: neither pleading guilty by post nor turning up for the court hearing. This led to the case being adjourned while witness statements were prepared or arrangements made for witnesses to attend. To avoid such adjournments in future, the Magistrates' Courts (Procedure) Act 1998 was passed which allows witness statements to be served with the original correspondence, so that if the defendant fails to respond the case can be tried at the first hearing.

Under s. 57 of the Crime and Disorder Act 1998, if an accused is being held in custody, all pre-trial hearings can take place using a live TV link between the court and the prison. The accused will be treated as if he or she is present at the court.

Classification of offences

There are three different categories of criminal offence: summary, indictable and triable either way.

Summary offences

These are the most minor crimes, and are only triable summarily in the magistrates' court. 'Summary' refers to the process of ordering the defendant to attend the court by summons, a written order usually delivered by post, which is the most frequent procedure adopted in the magistrates' courts. There has been some criticism of the fact that more and more offences have been made summary only, reducing the right to trial by jury.

Indictable offences

These are the more serious offences, such as rape and murder. They can only be heard by the Crown Court. The indictment is a formal document containing the alleged offences against the accused, supported by brief facts.

Offences triable either way

These offences may be tried in either the magistrates' court or the Crown Court. Common examples are theft and burglary.

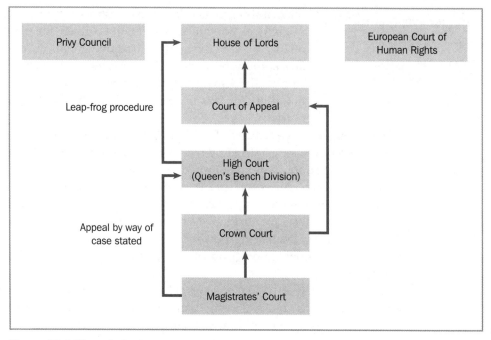

Figure 13.2 The criminal court system

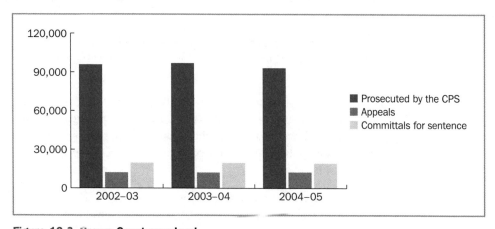

Figure 13.3 Crown Court caseload
Source: *Crown Prosecution Service Annual Report 2004–2005*, p. 38, Chart 5.

Mode of trial

Where a person is charged with an offence triable either way, he or she can insist on a trial by jury, otherwise the decision is for the magistrates. In reaching this decision the magistrates will take into account the seriousness of the case and whether they are likely to have sufficient sentencing powers to deal with it. Since 1996 the

Know your terms 13.3

Define the following terms:

1 Inquisitorial system
2 Custody officer
3 Bail
4 Remand

magistrates are also able to take into account the defendant's plea of guilty or not guilty, which will be given, for triable either-way offences, before the mode of trial decision. If the defendant indicates a guilty plea, the court proceeds to sentence or commits the case to the Crown Court for sentence. If the defendant pleads not guilty, or fails to indicate a plea, the court decides the mode of trial.

The Criminal Justice Act 2003, Schedule 3, has made certain changes to the mode of trial procedures. When deciding whether the case should stay in the magistrates' court, the magistrates will be informed of the defendant's prior convictions. If the magistrates decide summary trial is appropriate, defendants will have the right to ask for an indication of sentence on plea of guilty before deciding which court to choose. Committal for sentence has been abolished for less serious either-way cases. Magistrates' sentencing powers have been increased from 6 to 12 months' custody, in the hope that magistrates will send fewer cases to the Crown Court for sentencing.

Dr Andrew Herbert (2003) has carried out research into the magistrates' decision to send cases to the Crown Court. He has concluded that the reforms in the Criminal Justice Act 2003 are doomed to fail to reduce the number of cases referred to the Crown Court. The main Home Office reason for the recent reform attempts has been to reduce costs and increase efficiency. The chief finding of the research is that the magistrates overwhelmingly reject this reason for changing the court venue:

> There was a virtual consensus among those interviewed that there was no need for any significant change in the division of business between the higher and the lower courts.

Magistrates felt that the existing law produced a fair and realistic choice of court. They resented reforms being made for economic or political reasons. Some of the magistrates interviewed pointed to the importance of their judicial independence, so that Government policy would not persuade them to keep more cases. One of the magistrates said:

> I would never agree to retaining cases on economic grounds. I am fed up with political speak. There should not be pressure put on us. We are trained to do a job and should be left to do it.

The lawyers interviewed thought that lay magistrates were already being asked to handle cases at the extreme of their ability and were not capable of dealing with more serious cases. This is significant in practice because lay magistrates usually follow the agreed recommendation of the CPS and defence lawyers. Lay magistrates reached a decision contrary to the agreed recommendations in only one case out of 123 cases observed.

There are now serious moves to reduce the use of jury trials. These developments are discussed in Chapter 9 at p. 177.

Task 13.4

Complete the following table.

Type of offence	Trial court
Summary	
Triable either way	
Indictable offence	

▌Sending for trial

The 'sending for trial' hearing is a new procedure created by s. 51 of the Crime and Disorder Act 1998, and is intended to be quicker than the old committal procedures which were finally abolished by the Criminal Justice Act 2003. Until this reform was introduced, a case might have given rise to half a dozen hearings in a magistrates' court before being sent up to the Crown Court for trial. Under the new system, every adult charged with an indictable offence has to appear only once in a magistrates' court to determine issues concerning funding from the Legal Services Commission, bail and the use of statements and exhibits. The magistrates' court then provides defendants with a statement of the evidence against them as well as a notice setting out the offence(s) for which they are to be sent for trial and the place where they are to be tried. They are then sent immediately for trial in the Crown Court. The Crown Court has taken over from the magistrates' court all remaining case-management duties.

▌Plea and case management hearings

The plea and case management hearings were introduced by the new Criminal Procedure Rules in 2005 and replace the old plea and direction hearings. They aim to encourage early preparation of cases before trial, with a view to reducing the number of 'cracked' trials. These hearings are normally held in open court with the defendants present, who are required to plead guilty or not guilty to the charges against them. This process is known as the 'arraignment'. If the defendants plead guilty, the judge will proceed to sentence the defendants wherever possible. Where they plead not guilty the prosecution and defence will have to identify the key issues, and provide any additional information required to organize the actual trial, such as which witnesses will have to attend, facts that are admitted by both sides, and issues of law that are likely to arise.

Quick quiz 13.5

1 Name the three different categories of offence.

2 Is the English criminal justice system adversarial or inquisitorial?

3 What is meant by 'case management' in the Criminal Procedural Rules?

4 A jury sits in which court?

Plea bargaining

Plea bargaining is the name given to negotiations between the prosecution and defence lawyers over the outcome of a case; for example, where a defendant is choosing to plead not guilty, the prosecution may offer to reduce the charge to a similar offence with a smaller maximum sentence, in return for the defendant pleading guilty. Although plea bargaining is well known in the US criminal justice system, for many years the official view was that it did not happen here, although those involved in the system knew quite well that in fact it happened all the time. Its existence in the English penal system was confirmed in a 1977 study by McConville and Baldwin, and it is now recognized to be a widespread phenomenon.

Effective plea bargaining requires the active cooperation of the judge, but following the Court of Appeal case of **R** *v* **Turner** (1970) judges were not allowed to get involved in plea bargaining in the UK. That case effectively banned judges from indicating what sentence they would give if a defendant pleaded guilty. The case was not always followed in practice. In the 1993 Crown Court Study carried out by Professor Zander, 86 per cent of prosecution barristers, 88 per cent of defence barristers and 67 per cent of judges thought that **Turner** should be reformed so as to permit realistic discussion of plea, and especially sentence between the defence and prosecution lawyers and the judge. The ban was dramatically removed by the Court of Appeal case of **R** *v* **Goodyear** (2005). Defendants can now request in writing an indication from the judge of their likely sentence if they plead guilty. Following such a request, trial judges are allowed to indicate in public the maximum sentence they would give on the agreed facts of the case. This indication binds the judge, so that a higher sentence cannot subsequently be given. Judges cannot state what sentence they would give if the case went to trial as this risked placing undue pressure on defendants to plead guilty.

Should plea bargaining be allowed?

It can be argued that plea bargaining offers benefits on all sides: for the defendant, there is obviously a shorter sentence; for the courts, the police and ultimately the taxpayers, there are the financial savings made by drastically shortening trials. In fact, without a high proportion of guilty pleas, the courts would be seriously overloaded, causing severe delays which in turn would raise costs still further, especially given the number of prisoners remanded in custody awaiting trial.

Despite this, plea bargaining has been widely criticized as being against the interests of justice. Several studies have shown that the practice may place undue pressure on the accused and persuade innocent people to plead guilty: Zander and Henderson (1993) concluded that each year there were some 1,400 possibly innocent persons whose counsel felt they had pleaded guilty in order to achieve a reduction in the charges faced or in the sentence. Critics also point out that the judge should be, and be seen to be, an impartial referee, acting in accordance with the law rather than the dictates of cost efficiency. In addition, plea bargaining goes against the principle that offenders should be punished for what they have actually done. As well as leading to cases where people are punished more leniently than their conduct would seem to demand, it may lead to quite inappropriate punishments. For example, the high rate of acquittals in rape trials frequently leads to the prosecution reducing the charge to an ordinary offence against the person, in exchange for a guilty plea; this means that offenders who might usefully be given psychiatric help never receive it.

The trial

Apart from the role played by the jury in the Crown Court, the law and procedure in the Crown Court and magistrates' court are essentially the same. The burden of proof is on the prosecution, which means that it must prove, beyond reasonable doubt, that the accused is guilty; the defendant is not required to prove his or her innocence.

Defendants should normally be present at the trial, though the trial can proceed without them if they have chosen to abscond. A lawyer should usually represent them in their absence (**R** *v* **Jones** (2002)).

The trial begins with the prosecution outlining the case against the accused, and then producing evidence to prove its case. The prosecution calls its witnesses, who will give their evidence in response to questions from the prosecution (called examination-in-chief). These witnesses can then be questioned by the defence (called cross-examination), and then if required, re-examined by the prosecution to address any points brought up in cross-examination.

When the prosecution has presented all its evidence, the defence can submit that there is no case to answer, which means that on the prosecution evidence, no reasonable jury (or Bench of magistrates) could convict. If the submission is successful, a verdict of not guilty will be given straight away. If no such submission is made, or if the submission is unsuccessful, the defence then puts forward its case, using the same procedure for examining witnesses as the prosecution did. The accused is the only witness who cannot be forced to give evidence.

Once the defence has presented all its evidence, each side makes a closing speech, outlining their case and seeking to persuade the magistrates or jury of it. In the Crown Court, this is followed by the judge's summing up to the jury. The judge should review the evidence, draw the jury's attention to the important points of the case, and direct the jury on the law if necessary, but must not trespass on the jury's function of deciding the true facts of the case. At the end of the summing up, the judge reminds the jury that the prosecution must prove its case beyond reasonable doubt, and tries to explain in simple terms what this means.

Evidence of bad character and previous convictions

In the past, previous convictions have only exceptionally been available to the court when determining guilt. Following the Criminal Justice Act 2003, this evidence will be more widely available. About 70 per cent of defendants have past convictions so this reform will be important in practice. Critics argue that admitting this evidence undermines the presumption of innocence. It increases the risk of miscarriages of justice, with the courts being distracted by the defendant's past convictions, rather than focusing on the actual evidence about whether the defendant committed the particular offence before the court.

Task 13.6

Look in both a local and a national newspaper and find examples of criminal cases that are being processed through the criminal justice system. Select one article from the national paper and one from the local paper and consider the following questions:

■ What offence has been committed?
■ What stage in the criminal process has the case reached?
■ Was the accused granted bail?
■ Will the case be heard by a magistrates' court or Crown Court? If the case has already gone to court, which court heard the case?
■ What sentence is likely to be imposed/has already been imposed on the accused?

Models of criminal justice systems

In order to judge the effectiveness of a criminal justice system (or anything else for that matter), you need first to know what that system sets out to do. The academic Herbert Packer (1968) has identified two quite different potential aims for criminal justice systems: the 'due process' model; and the 'crime control' model. The former gives priority to fairness of procedure and to protecting the innocent from wrongful conviction, accepting that a high level of protection for suspects makes it more difficult to convict the guilty, and that some guilty people will therefore go free. The latter places most importance on convicting the guilty, taking the risk that occasionally some innocent people will be convicted. Obviously, criminal justice systems tend not to fall completely within one model or the other: most seek to strike a balance between the two. This is not always easy: imagine for a moment that you are put in charge of our criminal justice system, and you have to decide the balance at which it should aim. How many innocent people do you believe it is acceptable to convict? Bear in mind that if you answer 'none', the chances are that protections against this may have to be so strong that very few guilty people will be convicted either. Would it be acceptable for 10 per cent of innocent people to be convicted if that means 50 per cent of the guilty were also convicted? If that 10 per cent seems totally unacceptable, does it become more reasonable if it means that 90 per cent of the guilty are convicted? It is not an easy choice to make.

Looking at the balance which a criminal justice system seeks to strike, and how well that balance is in fact struck, is a useful way to assess the system's effectiveness. As mentioned at the beginning of this chapter, in recent years this balance has been the subject of much debate and disagreement as regards our criminal justice system, with the police, magistrates and the Government claiming that the balance has been tipped too far in favour of suspects' rights, at the expense of convicting the guilty. On the other hand, civil liberties organizations, many academics and the lawyers involved in the well-known miscarriages of justice feel that the system has not learned from those miscarriages, and that the protections for suspects are still inadequate.

Criticism and reform

Criticisms and suggestions for reform have been made throughout this chapter, but the following have been the subject of particular debate:

Racism and the CPS

A report prepared by the Crown Prosecution Inspectorate in 2003 has criticized the CPS for failing to weed out weak cases against ethnic minorities. The report says acquittal rates for black and Asian defendants stand at 42 per cent, compared to 30 per cent for white defendants. The CPS is therefore failing in its duty to eliminate differential treatment. The Inspectorate is of the view that as members of minority groups are more likely to be stopped by the police, the CPS should consider whether the behaviour of the arresting officer 'might have been inappropriate or provocative'. It concludes:

> The CPS would appear to be discriminating against ethnic minority defendants by failing to correct the bias [of police] and allowing a disproportionate number of weak cases against ethnic minority defendants to go to trial.

Racism and the courts

Research was undertaken in 2003 by Roger Hood and others, which was published in a paper called 'Ethnic minorities in the criminal courts: perceptions of fairness and equality of treatment'. The research found that over recent years members of the ethnic minorities were increasingly satisfied that the criminal courts were racially impartial. Several judges said that attitudes had changed a lot and many lawyers also reported that racial bias or inappropriate language was becoming a thing of the past. This improvement was partly due to the fact that judges and magistrates are increasingly receiving training in racial awareness, and partly due to improvements in society as a whole.

While there has been this improvement in the courts, there still remains a significant minority of defendants who consider that they have been treated unfairly because of their race. One in five black defendants in the Crown Court, one in ten in the magistrates' courts and one in eight Asian defendants in both types of court considered they had been treated unfairly because of their race. Most complaints were about sentencing, which were perceived to be higher than for white defendants. Very few perceived racial bias in the conduct or attitude of judges or magistrates – only 3 per cent in the Crown Court and 1 per cent in the magistrates' courts. There were no complaints about racist remarks from the Bench. Of some concern is the fact that black lawyers had a more negative view of proceedings. A third of black lawyers said they had personally witnessed incidents in court that they regarded as 'racist'.

Black defendants and lawyers felt that the authority and legitimacy of the courts would be strengthened if more ethnic minorities were employed in the criminal justice system. Many judges agreed that more could be done to avoid the impression that the courts were 'white dominated institutions'.

■ The Crown Prosecution Service

The CPS ran into problems from the very beginning. Because the Home Office had apparently underestimated the cost of the new service, the salaries offered were low, making it impossible to find sufficient numbers of good lawyers. As a result, the CPS gained a reputation for incompetence and delay. In 1996 a MORI poll found that 70 per cent of CPS lawyers responding to a questionnaire considered that the CPS was either below average or one of the worst places to work. In 1990 the House of Commons Public Accounts Committee noted that the CPS appeared to be costing almost twice as much as the previous prosecution arrangements, and the numbers of staff required was practically double that originally envisaged.

Relations between the police and the CPS have not been good: the police resented the new service and its demands for a higher standard of case preparation from police. While the CPS saw a high rate of discontinued cases as a success story, the police saw this as letting offenders off the hook. Reforms introduced following the Glidewell Report aim to improve relations between the police and the CPS, with police and CPS staff working in integrated teams and the creation of 42 prosecuting authorities which correlate with the 42 police forces. Following the 1997 Narey Report into delay in the criminal justice system, CPS staff now work alongside police officers in police stations to prepare cases for court. However, it may be that these reforms could go to the opposite extreme. The CPS was created to put an end to the close and often cosy relations between police officers and the lawyers who used to prosecute their cases, as this could lead to malpractice.

Some of the teething problems have now been ironed out, but problems still remain. There is doubt as to how far the CPS provides an independent perspective

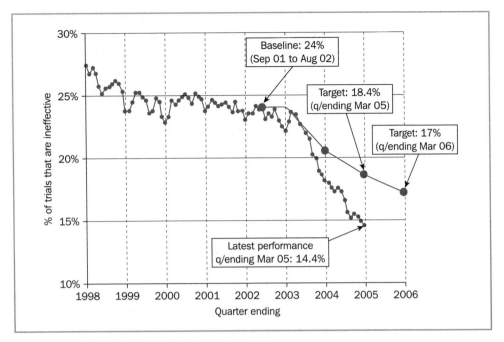

Baseline: 24%
(Sep 01 to Aug 02)

Target: 18.4%
(q/ending Mar 05)

Target: 17%
(q/ending Mar 06)

Latest performance
q/ending Mar 05: 14.4%

Figure 13.4 Ineffective trials in Crown Court cases

Source: Crown Prosecution Service Annual Report 2004–2005, p. 9.

on deciding whether or not to prosecute. Since the police still take the initial decision on whether to pass the file to the CPS, such decisions are taken without the CPS being able to exercise any control, which leads to wide variations in cautioning rates. Where the police do refer a case for prosecution, the CPS makes up its mind on the basis of information with which it is provided – it cannot ask for further enquiries to be made. Given that the police, once satisfied that the suspect is guilty, will tend to look for evidence that supports this conclusion, and see any material that points in another direction as mistaken or irrelevant, the file may paint a very partial picture of the true situation.

The Criminal Justice Act 2003 has moved the power to charge from the police to the Crown Prosecution Service, with the exception of some very minor offences

Decisions by the CPS not to prosecute

In 1990 the Home Affairs Committee expressed concern at the large proportion of discontinued cases which were not dropped until the court hearing, and was surprised that the CPS undertook no systematic analysis of the reasons for discontinuance.

In 1993 the RCCJ found that the CPS did exercise the power to discontinue appropriately, citing one study (Moxon and Crisp, 1994) which suggested that nearly a third of discontinuances were dropped on public interest grounds. Of these, nearly half were discontinued because the offence was trivial and/or the likely penalty was nominal. Only 5 per cent of the cases were discontinued before any court appearance, and where cases were terminated at the court, the decision to discontinue was often taken before the hearing but not communicated to the defendant in time to save a court appearance – either because the decision had been taken too late in the day or because the CPS did not know where the defendant was.

Task 13.7

Look at the diagram and then answer the questions that follow.

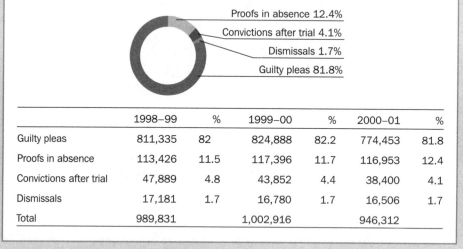

	1998–99	%	1999–00	%	2000–01	%
Guilty pleas	811,335	82	824,888	82.2	774,453	81.8
Proofs in absence	113,426	11.5	117,396	11.7	116,953	12.4
Convictions after trial	47,889	4.8	43,852	4.4	38,400	4.1
Dismissals	17,181	1.7	16,780	1.7	16,506	1.7
Total	989,831		1,002,916		946,312	

Figure 13.5 Magistrates' courts: case results
Source: The Crown Prosecution Service Annual Report 2000–2001.

Questions

1 What percentage of defendants pleaded guilty in the magistrates' courts in 2000–2001?

2 Between 1998 and 2001 what has been the trend in the conviction rates in the magistrates' courts following a trial?

3 Between 1998 and 2001 what has been the trend in cases being dismissed by the magistrates' courts?

In assessing the incidence of weak cases in the Crown Court (which may be cases that should have been discontinued), the numbers of ordered and directed acquittals are relevant. According to the 1996 Judicial Statistics, in one in every five cases a judge ordered an acquittal.

New arrangements are being piloted in which the CPS will offer to meet victims of certain crimes, including racially aggravated crime, to explain its decisions not to prosecute or to substantially alter charges. This is part of a much wider plan to improve victim and witness care across the whole of the criminal justice system.

Cracked and ineffective trials

Know your terms 13.8

Define the following terms:

1 Indictable offences
2 Committal proceedings
3 Plea bargaining
4 Cracked trials

The Government has been concerned by the problem of cracked and ineffective trials. Cracked trials occur when a case is concluded without a trial, usually because the defendant has pleaded guilty at a very late stage. An ineffective trial happens when a hearing is cancelled on the day it was due to go ahead. Over a quarter of Crown Court hearings are cancelled on the day of the trial. Of these, a quarter are due to a witness not attending (*Criminal Justice: Working Together*, National Audit Office, 1999). This is sometimes because they are too frightened to give evidence. It is frequently too late to arrange for another case to slot into the court timetable. Cracked and ineffective trials are a waste of public money and resources and can cause unnecessary stress for victims and witnesses keen for justice to be done without delay. Statistics published by the Office for Criminal Justice Reform suggest that in 2003 as many as 20 per cent of Crown Court trials were ineffective.

Following the introduction of the plea before venue proceedings and the reduction in sentence for early pleas (see p. 310), the number of cracked trials was halved but remains a problem.

To try to deal with the problem of cracked trials, the Courts Act 2003 has given the criminal courts a power to award costs against third parties who cause a case to collapse or be delayed.

Conviction rates

Recent years have seen a large rise in reported crime but falling conviction rates. For example, for sexual offences there were 21,107 cases reported in 1980 and 31,284 by 1993. By contrast, the convictions in those years were 8,000 in 1980 and only 4,300 in 1993. In 2002 the Audit Commission reported that criminals only have a one in 16 chance of being caught and convicted.

Victims and witnesses

Victims and other witnesses play a vital role in getting convictions and thereby achieving justice. In 2003, more than 5 per cent of Crown Court cases did not go ahead on the first day because a witness failed to turn up. Twenty-two per cent of Crown Court cases and more than a quarter of magistrates' court cases that collapsed did so because prosecution witnesses failed to turn up.

There is now a growing awareness that the criminal justice system has paid insufficient attention to the needs of victims and witnesses of crime. For many years victims of crime had virtually no rights. In English legal theory and practice, victims are not parties to the prosecution, but are only witnesses. Traditionally, victims have had no legal right to participation, consultation or even information about their cases. By comparison, suspects and defendants do have rights, even if not all of them are enforceable in practice. Organizations such as Victim Support have campaigned for many years to persuade the Government to recognize that victims are not simply witnesses, and that they should have distinct rights.

The Macpherson Report, which followed the failure to convict the murderers of Stephen Lawrence, suggested that the Government should consider allowing victims or their families to become 'civil parties' to criminal proceedings. This is the approach taken in countries such as France and ensures the provision of all relevant information to victims and their families.

In 2002 the Government planned to introduce a Victims Bill which would have significantly increased the rights of victims, but the Bill was dropped for lack of parliamentary time.

One attempt to redress the balance has been the establishment of a Victim's Charter in 1990. The Criminal Injuries Compensation Scheme provides limited financial compensation to the victims of some forms of crime. Dedicated witness care units have been set up to improve the experience of victims and witnesses of crime. Their needs should be assessed at the start of the criminal process, to identify their specific requirements, such as childcare needs and the risk of intimidation. Witness care officers should then help to guide individuals through the criminal justice system.

The Audit Commission (2003) found that the majority of victims and witnesses felt they had been treated with respect by the police, but were less complimentary about their treatment by the courts. Many witnesses were unaware they could reclaim travel and other expenses incurred, and said their expenses were increased by delays in the court system. Once at court, witnesses reported intimidation, such as name-calling by the defendant's family and friends who were around in the corridors. Non-smoking policies meant people (including the defendant and the victims) gathered around the entrance to the court, causing stress not only to those wanting to smoke, but also to witnesses arriving to enter the building.

The report concludes:

> There is a tension between supporting victims and witnesses through a court case and the adversarial nature of a trial. Many witnesses have no idea what to expect in court, and perceptions are often based on media and dramatic portrayals. Many also perceive that the current culture of the court is not one that responds to witness needs and demands as readily as it does to those of court professionals and the defence.

The Lord Chancellor has promised that by 2008 all Crown Court buildings and 90 per cent of magistrates' courts will have separate facilities for victims and prosecution witnesses.

A victim can now make a Victim Personal Statement which is presented to the trial court. This should be considered by the court prior to passing sentence. The court can take into account the effect of the offence on the victim when passing sentence, but not the victim's opinions on what the sentence should be.

Victims have repeatedly complained of the lack of information they receive from the criminal justice system about the progress of their case. The Witness Satisfaction Survey in 2000 showed that more than half of prosecution witnesses were not kept informed about the progress of the case and over 40 per cent were not told the verdict but had to find out for themselves. Under the Criminal Justice and Court

Services Act 2000 victims of certain types of offence have a right to information about the case and can make representations about the offender's release. The offences giving rise to these rights are sexual and violent offences where the offender has been sentenced to prison for 12 months or more.

Since October 2002 the CPS has a responsibility to inform victims of key casework decisions such as the dropping of charges and, in serious cases, the victim has the opportunity of a face-to-face meeting with a senior prosecutor.

The Youth Justice and Criminal Evidence Act 1999 allows courts to issue special measures directions. These directions seek to reduce the stress and problems experienced by vulnerable and intimidated witnesses giving evidence to courts. The directions can allow the courts to put up a screen between the witness and the defendant, their evidence can be video-recorded in advance and submitted as a video to the court, or it can be given by a live TV link, the public can be asked to leave the court and the lawyers can remove their wigs and gowns.

The Home Office has undertaken research into the use of these special measures by the courts: *Are Special Measures Working? Evidence from surveys of vulnerable and intimidated witnesses* (2004). This found that a large number of witnesses are getting the benefit of these special measures. The vast majority of people who used these special measures to give evidence found them helpful, particularly live link TV and video-recorded evidence. One-third of witnesses using special measures said that they would not have been willing and able to give evidence without them.

The Labour Party's 2005 election manifesto promised that lawyers, known as victim's advocates, will be able to represent victims of rape and murder in court, to ensure victims' rights are taken into account at the trial. The advocate would advise the victims or their families and object to aggressive questions asked in cross-examination.

The role of the media and public opinion

It is noticeable that all the serious miscarriages of justice occurred in cases where a particular crime had outraged public opinion, and led to enormous pressure on the police to find the culprits. In the case of the 'Birmingham Six', feelings ran so high that the trial judge consented to the case being heard away from Birmingham, on the ground that a Birmingham jury might be 'unable to bring to the trial that degree of detachment that is necessary to reach a dispassionate and objective verdict'. Given the graphic media descriptions of the carnage the real bombers had left behind them, it was in fact debatable whether any jury, anywhere, would have found it easy to summon up such detachment. The chances of a fair trial must have decreased even further when, halfway through the trial, the *Daily Mirror* devoted an entire front page to photographs of the six, boasting that they were the 'first pictures' (implying that they were the first pictures of the bombers).

The miscarriages of justice were characterized by a reluctance to refer cases back to appeal. While campaigning by some newspapers and television programmes was eventually to help bring about the successful appeals, other sections of the media, and in particular the tabloid newspapers, were keen to dismiss the idea that miscarriages of justice might have occurred. Nor was there a great amount of public interest in the alleged plight of the Birmingham Six or the other victims – in stark contrast to the petitioning on behalf of Private Lee Clegg during 1995. There was a common feeling of satisfaction that someone had been punished for such terrible crimes, and the public did not want to hear that the system had punished the wrong people.

Even when the miscarriages of justice were finally uncovered, a lingering 'whispering campaign' suggested that the victims of those miscarriages had been let off on some kind of technicality – that there had been police misbehaviour, but that those accused of the bombings and so on were really guilty. Again, tabloid newspapers were only too pleased to contribute to this view. On the day that the report of the Royal Commission on Criminal Justice was published, the *Daily Mail* printed an article entitled 'The true victims of injustice'. In it, victims of the bombings expressed anger that the Guildford Four and the Birmingham Six had been released – as though justice for those wrongly convicted of a crime somehow meant less justice for the victims of that crime – and raised doubts as to their innocence. The newspaper commented that 'the decent majority' were more concerned to see measures designed to convict criminals than to prevent further miscarriages of justice.

On the other hand, in the case of Stephen Lawrence, a young black student murdered at a bus stop in south London in an apparently racially motivated attack, one branch of the media saw itself as a vital tool in fighting for justice. The refusal of five youths, who many suspected to be the murderers, to give evidence at the coroner's court led to the *Daily Mail* labelling them as the killers on its front pages, despite the fact that they had already been acquitted by a criminal court.

The implications of all this for the criminal justice system are important. Clearly, such a system does not operate in a vacuum, and in jury trials in particular public opinion can never really be kept out of the court room. That does not mean that juries should not be used in emotive cases, nor that the media should be gagged. What it does mean is that, in those cases which arouse strong public opinion, the police, the prosecution, judges and defence lawyers must all be extra-vigilant to ensure that the natural desire to find a culprit does not take the place of the need to find the truth – and to make clear to juries that they must do the same. In addition, measures must be taken to prevent 'trial by newspaper' – the Contempt of Court Act 1981 already provides powers in this respect, but in using these powers the courts must be able to take into account the profits to be made from crime 'scoops' by newspapers, and punish breaches of the law accordingly. Rather than impose fines, which can be paid from the increased profits, preventing newspapers from publishing for a day or more might be a greater deterrent.

The law of contempt relating to payments to witnesses in criminal cases and the publication of information before trials are currently being reviewed by the Government. It is considering proposals to legislate against payments and to control trial publicity.

Fears that the media are prejudicing the course of justice have led the Government to issue a consultation document on proposals to ban payments by the media to potential witnesses in criminal trials. The issue was highlighted by breaches of the Press Complaints Commission's Code of Practice during Rosemary West's trial. The

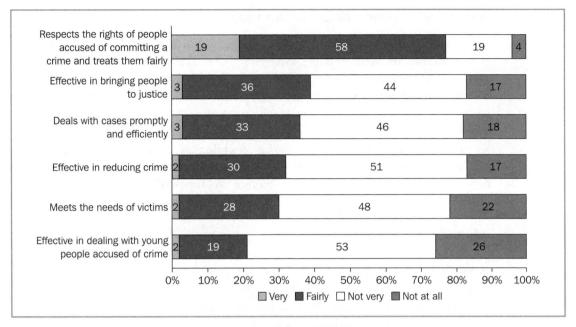

Figure 13.6 Confidence in the criminal justice system, 2002/03

Source: S. Nicholas and A. Walker (2004) *Crime in England and Wales 2002/2003, Supplementary Vol. 2: Crime, disorder and the criminal justice system and public attitudes and perceptions*, p. 2, Figure 1.1.

Code of Practice has been tightened up to ban any payments to potential witnesses. Under the Courts Act 2003, newspapers which publish material that causes trials to collapse can now be punished with a heavy fine.

The Government has published a consultation paper, *Broadcasting Courts* (2004). This paper considers whether television cameras should be allowed into courts so that the public can gain an insight into the workings of the law. The current idea is that cameras would only be permitted into the Court of Appeal. The Lord Chancellor has commented:

> Most people's knowledge and perception of what goes on in court comes from court reporting and from fictionalized accounts of trials. But the medium that gives most access to most people, television, is not allowed in court. Is there a public interest in allowing people, through television, to see what actually happens in our courts in their name?

For the first time ever cameras were allowed into an English court room, when a pilot study was carried out in the Court of Appeal. Criminal and civil cases were filmed and edited for mock news pieces and documentaries. These pictures were not broadcast to the public, but circulated to Ministers, senior judges and representatives from legal professional bodies so that they could consider their impact. In America, cameras are frequently allowed into a court room, but the Lord Chancellor has commented:

> We don't want our courts turned into US-style media circuses. We will not have OJ Simpson-style trials in Britain. Justice should be seen to be done. But our priority must be that justice is done.

Recommendations of Sir Robin Auld

In his *Review of the Criminal Courts* (2001) Sir Robin Auld made a wide range of recommendations, some of which have already been considered at relevant points in this book. Other interesting recommendations included codification, increased use of information technology and the introduction of standard timetables (described below).

Codification

Sir Robin Auld recommended that the law covering offences, court procedures, evidence and sentencing should be codified. This would make the law simpler and more accessible for the legal professions and members of the public to whom these rules can be applied. The Government seems committed to doing this at some point in the future.

Information technology

Sir Robin Auld has emphasized the need for much greater use to be made of information technology in the criminal justice system. In particular, he is particularly keen to see the introduction of single electronic case files, managed by a new Criminal Case Management Agency. The Government is currently investing in information technology for the criminal justice system.

Standard timetables

The Review proposes that there should be a move away from all forms of pre-trial hearings. Instead, standard timetables would be issued and the parties would be required to co-operate with each other in order to comply with these timetables. There would then be a written or electronic 'pre-trial assessment' by the court (discretionary for the magistrates' court) of the parties' readiness for trial. Only if the court or the parties are unable to resolve all matters in this way would there be a pre-trial hearing.

Expert witnesses

The case of Sally Clark has highlighted potential problems with the use of expert witnesses. Sally Clark was a solicitor who was convicted of killing her two young sons. In 2003, the Court of Appeal found her conviction to be unsafe. An expert witness gave potentially misleading evidence about the chances of a woman having two of her children die naturally from unexplained causes. He stated that the chances of a second child dying from natural causes in the same family were one in 73 million. This evidence probably heavily influenced the jury's decision to convict, but the figure was subsequently criticized by statistitians as not having a genuine scientific foundation. In addition, a Home Office pathologist failed to inform the court that one of the dead children had been suffering from an illness that could have accounted for his death. In its annual report for 2004, the Criminal Cases Review Commission has criticized expert witnesses. It considers that high fees are tempting experts to give strong evidence to please their client, to ensure that they will be asked to give expert evidence in the future. Some experts earn more than £1,500 a day and are keen to keep this source of income. They are frequently doctors who are employed by the NHS and earn some extra money by working privately at the same time as expert witnesses. The Criminal Cases Review Commission is concerned that unless expert witnesses are more tightly regulated there will be a risk of more miscarriages of justice.

▌ Community Justice Centres

The Government is considering establishing Community Justice Centres, which have apparently operated successfully in New York. These would seek to tackle low level crime and anti-social behaviour. Court sentences would combine punishment with support to deal with the cause of the offending behaviour, such as alcoholism. A pilot centre has been set up in North Liverpool.

Task 13.9

Read the extract from the introduction of the Auld Report and answer the questions that follow.

The scheme of the Report is to examine the purpose, structure and working of the criminal courts in the criminal justice system and to consider:

■ Re-structuring and improving the composition of the criminal courts, introducing new criteria and procedures for allocating work between them and better matching of courts to cases;

■ Introducing a new structure for direction and better management of the criminal justice system as a whole, with a view to improving the quality of justice, efficiency and effectiveness of the criminal process;

■ Removing work from the criminal process that should not be there, and providing within it alternative forms of disposal for certain types of case;

■ Improving preparation for trial and trial procedures, and reform of the law of criminal evidence; and

■ Simplification of the **appellate structure** and its procedures.

Throughout, I have tried to keep an eye on our **newly acquired domestic law of human rights**, the potential of information technology, not only to improve existing and familiar ways of doing things, but to re-shape our practices and procedures, and to the urgent need to enhance public confidence in the criminal justice system as a whole.

(Extract from Sir Robin Auld, *Review of the Criminal Courts* (2001))

Questions

1 Sir Robin Auld wrote that he had considered removing work from the criminal process that should not be there. What type of cases do you think could be removed from the criminal system?

2 What does 'appellate structure' mean?

3 What is Sir Robin Auld referring to when he states 'our newly acquired domestic law of human rights'?

4 Sir Robin Auld refers to the issue of public confidence. How much confidence do you have in the criminal justice system?

Reading on the web

The revised Code A for PACE can be found on the Home Office website at:

**http://www.homeoffice.gov.uk/news-and-publications/publication/
operational-policing/PACE_Chapter_A.pdf**

The Code for Crown Prosecutors is available on the Crown Prosecution Service's website:

http://www.cps.gov.uk

The report for the pressure group Liberty, *Deaths in custody, redress and remedies*, by Greta Vogt and John Wadham is available on the Liberty website:

http://www.liberty-human-rights.org.uk

The Auld Report is available on:

http://www.criminal-courts-review.org.uk

Criminal Statistics England and Wales 2001 is published at:

http://www.official-documents.co.uk/document/cm56/5696/5696.htm

The Home Office Report, *Crime in England and Wales 2002/2003*, is published at:

http://www.homeoffice.gov.uk/rds/pdfs2/hosb703.pdf

Information on the criminal justice system is available at:

http://www.cjsonline.org

The website of the Crown Prosecution Service is:

http://www.cps.gov.uk

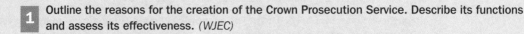

Question and answer guides

1 Outline the reasons for the creation of the Crown Prosecution Service. Describe its functions and assess its effectiveness. *(WJEC)*

Answer guide

You should briefly define what the CPS is, and then divide your answer into the two parts suggested by the question. First, discuss why the CPS was felt to be needed. Then go on to describe what the CPS does and, in assessing its effectiveness, state how you think the creation of the CPS has improved the criminal justice system, if at all, and point out the problems with it, including a discussion of the Glidewell reforms.

2 To what extent can miscarriages of justice be avoided? *(London)*

Answer guide

There is a range of approaches that could be taken to answering this question. You could start by discussing the information contained under the subheading 'Models of criminal justice systems' at p. 276 and the material in the introduction to this chapter. This highlights the fact that the law has to draw a balance between the desire to convict the guilty and the need to prevent innocent people from being wrongly convicted.

You could then move on to mention briefly some of the high-profile miscarriage of justice cases, such as the 'Birmingham Six' and the Stephen Lawrence investigation. You could point to ways these miscarriages could have been avoided by, for example, the introduction of a corroboration rule for confession evidence, stricter controls of the activities of the police in the police station and more money for the defence to challenge forensic evidence. The material contained in the section headed 'Safeguards for the suspect' at p. 251 could be considered; all of these provisions are means of preventing miscarriages of justice.

In your conclusion, you could return to the concept of a balance and discuss the fact that a miscarriage of justice occurs not only when an innocent person is convicted but also when a guilty person is not convicted. It is impossible to create a system where no miscarriages of justice could ever occur, but the aim should be to minimize them. You could question how far such developments as the abolition of the right to silence are likely to achieve this. ('London Qualifications Ltd.', accepts no responsibility whatsoever for the accuracy or method in the answers given.)

3 **Anne has been charged with murder.**

(a) **(i) Describe and comment on the role of her solicitor and barrister in her case both before and during the trial; and**
(ii) Explain the steps the Crown Prosecution Service will take in her case before the trial.
[35]

(b) **Outline the criticisms which have been made of the Crown Prosecution Service. [10]** *(OCR)*

Answer guide

(a) (i) Your answer to this part of the question would draw from both material in this chapter and Chapter 8 on the legal professions. Looking first at the role of the solicitor, the solicitor would be able to give individual advice during and after police questioning. He or she could interview witnesses about the case and put together a file for the defence. This would be used to give instructions to Anne's barrister about the case. The solicitor would be able to represent Anne at a magistrates' court during the preliminary proceedings for the case. He or she would even be able to represent Anne in the Crown Court if he or she has completed the necessary training (see p. 126). Otherwise, the solicitor would sit behind the barrister during the plea and case management hearing and the actual trial.

As regards Anne's barrister, because this is a serious case a QC (discussed on p. 132) is likely to be employed as well as a junior barrister. The QC would do most of the advocacy work and the junior barrister would provide support. The barrister(s) would see Anne after the solicitor had done some initial work on the case. He or she would normally receive a file containing the instructions from the solicitor and then interview Anne prior to the trial. The barrister would, in particular, give Anne some initial advice as to her plea. He or she could represent Anne in the magistrates' court and Crown Court instead of the solicitor. This would include cross-examining witnesses and examining defence witnesses.

At the end of your answer to this part of the question you could take a critical approach to the subject, looking at the advantages and disadvantages of using both a barrister and a solicitor. In particular, you could highlight that the two professionals can provide expertise in their different areas: the barrister can offer independent advice on the case and the solicitor can offer an accessible contact for Anne. The disadvantages of using both professions is that problems can arise if communications are poor between the barrister and solicitor and the barrister is dependent on the solicitor preparing the case properly. While Anne is unlikely to have to pay for her legal representation, use of two professionals will be expensive for the taxpayer.

(ii) The Crown Prosecution Service would receive the file from the police to decide whether to charge and bring a prosecution. It would decide if there was sufficient evidence to give rise to a reasonable chance of conviction and whether it was in the public interest to proceed with the prosecution. An employee of the Crown Prosecution Service (who need not be a lawyer) can present the prosecution case in the magistrates' court. The Crown Prosecution Service will then usually instruct an independent barrister to take the case to the Crown Court, though it does have the right now to use one of its own employees.

(b) The material you need to answer this question is contained at p. 278.

Chapter summary

The adversarial process

The English system of criminal justice can be described as adversarial. This means each side is responsible for putting their own case. The role of the judge is limited to that of a referee ensuring fair play. The adversarial system is typical of common law countries. The alternative is an inquisitorial system, which exists in most of the rest of Europe.

Criminal Procedural Rules

In 2005, the main rules on criminal procedure that apply to the trial and pre-trial process were brought together in new Criminal Procedure Rules.

The Crown Prosecution Service

Most prosecutions are now brought by the Crown Prosecution Service. Significant reforms of this body were introduced following the Glidewell Report which was published in 1998.

Appearance in court

Persons charged with an offence can be called to court by means of a summons, or by a charge following arrest without a warrant.

Classification of offences

There are three different categories of offence: summary offences, indictable offences and offences triable either way.

Mode of trial

Where a person is charged with a triable either way offence, they can insist on a trial by jury, otherwise the decision is for the magistrates.

Disclosure

The issue of disclosure is concerned with the responsibility of the prosecution and defence to reveal information related to the case prior to the trial.

Plea bargaining

Plea bargaining is the name given to negotiations between the prosecution and defence lawyers over the outcome of a case.

The trial

Apart form the role played by the jury in the Crown Court, the law and procedure in the Crown Court and magistrates' court are essentially the same. The burden of proof is on the prosecution.

Models of criminal justice systems

The academic, Herbert Packer (1968), has identified two quite different potential aims for criminal justice systems: the 'due process' model; and the 'crime control' model.

Criticism and reform

The following issues have been the subject of particular debate:

Racism and the CPS
The CPS is failing to weed out weak cases against ethnic minorities.

Racism and the courts
Over recent years members of the ethnic minorities are increasingly satisfied that the criminal courts are racially impartial.

The Crown Prosecution Service
The CPS ran into problems from the very beginning and has continued to be the subject of much controversy.

Cracked and ineffective trials
The Government has been concerned by the problem of 'cracked and ineffective trials'.

Conviction rates
Recent years have seen a large rise in reported crime but falling conviction rates.

Victims and witnesses
There is now a growing awareness that the criminal justice system has paid insufficient attention to the needs of victims and witnesses of crime.

Chapter 14

Young offenders

Introduction

Offenders who are under 18 years old are dealt with differently from adults by the criminal justice system. There have in the past been a number of reasons for this, including a belief that children are less responsible for their actions than adults, a wish to steer children away from any further involvement in crime, and the feeling that sentencing can be used to reform as well as, or instead of, punishing them. However, in recent years the mood towards young offenders has become more severe due to a widespread public perception of mounting youth crime and the killing of the toddler James Bulger by two 10-year-old boys. The Audit Commission found that in some neighbourhoods 26 per cent of known offenders were aged under 18 (*Misspent Youth: Young People and Crime*, 1997). At present one in three young men is found guilty of a criminal offence by the age of 22 and nine out of ten under-17s are reconvicted within two years of release from a custodial sentence. Youth crime costs the public services £1 billion a year. In fact, some of the public's fears are exaggerated. The Home Office British Crime Survey for 1998 found that two-thirds of the people questioned for the survey believed that young people were becoming increasingly involved in crime between 1995 and 1997, while official statistics showed the numbers remaining constant, or declining. Only 17 per cent of known offenders are aged between 10 and 17.

The Government stated in its White Paper, *No More Excuses – A New Approach to Tackling Youth Crime in England and Wales* (1998) that it wanted to reverse the 'excuse culture' that had developed within the youth justice system. A change in approach was signalled by the passing of the Crime and Disorder Act 1998. This piece of legislation was central to the Government's approach to youth crime. The Act sought to reduce offending by young people in two ways: first, by promoting strategies for the prevention of youth crime and, secondly, by creating a range of extended powers available to the police and the courts to deal with young offenders and their parents. Its key provisions are now contained in the Powers of Criminal Courts (Sentencing) Act 2000 (PCC(S)A).

Section 37 of the Act specifies that the aim of the youth justice system is to prevent offending by young people. A Youth Justice Board for England and Wales has been established under s. 41 of the 1998 Act. Its principal functions are to monitor, set

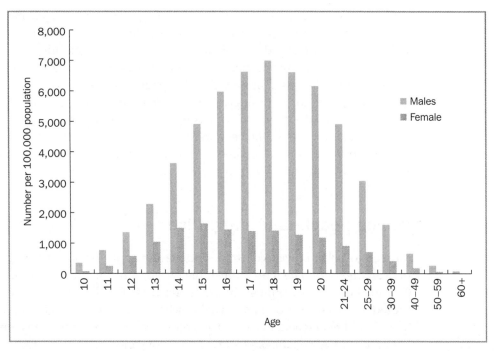

Figure 14.1 Persons found guilty of, or cautioned for, indictable offences per 100,000 population by age group, 2001

Source: Home Office (2002), *Criminal Statistics England and Wales 2001*, p. 29, Figure 5.3.

standards and promote good practice for the youth justice system. Its main focus to date has been to try and speed up the youth justice system, encourage the creation of programmes aimed at preventing youth crime and assist in the implementation of the provisions in the 1998 Act concerning young offenders.

Local authorities must formulate and implement a youth justice plan setting out how youth justice services are to be provided and funded (s. 40). They must, acting in co-operation with police authorities, probation committees and health authorities, establish one or more youth offending teams whose duty it is to co-ordinate the provision of youth justice services and to carry out their functions under the youth justice plan (s. 39).

Some of these reforms appear to have been successful as youth reoffending in 2002 dropped by a quarter.

Criminal liability

Under criminal law children under 10 cannot be liable for a criminal offence at all. In the past there was also a well-established presumption that children between the ages of 10 and 14 were not criminally liable. This presumption could be rebutted by the prosecution successfully adducing evidence that the child knew right from wrong and knew that what he or she was doing was more than just naughty. In 1998 this rebuttable presumption was repealed by the Crime and Disorder Act 1998. In this respect children aged 10 and above are now treated like adults. British children are almost alone in Europe in being regarded as criminals at the age of 10.

The United Nations Committee on the Rights of the Child has condemned the United Kingdom for imposing criminal liability on young children. In a report in 2002, it criticized the 'high and increasing numbers of children being held in custody at earlier ages for lesser offences and for longer custodial sentences'. It has called on the Government to raise the age of criminal responsibility to 14 or above, which would bring it into line with most other European countries.

Young people and the police

Most of the police powers concerning adults also apply to young suspects, but because they are thought to be more vulnerable, some extra rules apply. For example, Code C of the Police and Criminal Evidence Act 1984 (PACE) states that young suspects should not be arrested or interviewed at school and, when brought to a police station, they should not be held in a cell. The police must find out who is responsible for the young person's welfare as quickly as possible and then inform that person of the arrest, stating where and why the suspect is being held. If the person responsible for the young person's welfare chooses not to come to the police station, the police must find another 'appropriate adult', who should be present during the various stages of cautioning, identification, intimate searches and questioning. Where the suspect's parent is not present, the appropriate adult will often be a social worker, though it may be anyone defined as a responsible adult, except someone involved in the offence, a person of low intelligence, someone hostile to the young person, or a solicitor acting in a professional capacity.

The role of the adult is to ensure that the young person is aware of their rights, particularly to legal advice. The adult should be told that their function is not just that of observer, but also of adviser to the young person, ensuring that the interview is conducted properly and facilitating communication between suspect and interviewer. Unfortunately, research by Brown (1993) suggests that some adults are so overawed by the whole process that they are of little use as advisers; they may even side with the interviewer.

Remand and bail

A young person charged with an offence has the right to bail under the Bail Act 1976 (see Chapter 12). Where the police refuse bail, children under 17 are usually remanded to local authority accommodation, which can range from remand fostering schemes to accommodation with high levels of supervision. Secure accommodation can, however, be used if children persistently offend while on bail. Those under 17 should not usually be held in police custody before being brought to court. Instead, they should be held in local authority accommodation.

Reprimands and warnings

People involved in administering the criminal justice system have, in the past, been concerned to try and stop a young offender from a cycle of court appearances, punishments and further offending, often aggravated by contact with other offenders during the process. The police therefore tried to divert the young offenders from the criminal justice system by issuing them with a caution rather than bringing a prosecution. A caution is an official warning about what the young offenders have done, designed to make them see that they have done wrong and deter them from further offending (it is quite separate from the caution administered before questioning, concerning the right to silence).

However, there was growing concern that the caution procedure was being overused in practice, so that young repeat offenders were acting with a sense of impunity. Section 65 of the Crime and Disorder Act 1998 therefore abolished the system of cautions for young offenders aged between 10 and 17, and replaced it with a new system of reprimands and warnings.

Section 65 of the Crime and Disorder Act 1998 provides that a first offence can be met with a reprimand, a final warning or a criminal charge, depending on its seriousness. The usual sequence will be a reprimand for a first offence, followed by a warning for a subsequent offence, followed by a charge on a third occasion (or a warning where the offender has not received a warning for at least two years and the offence is not serious enough for a charge).

Before the police can issue a reprimand or warning, four conditions must be satisfied:

1 there must be sufficient evidence;
2 the young person must admit the crime;
3 the young person must have no previous convictions; and
4 it is not in the public interest to bring a prosecution.

Quick quiz 14.1

1 At what age can a child be criminally liable?

2 If a young person is refused bail, where will he or she be held on remand?

3 What is the usual sequence for the use of reprimands and warnings?

4 What are the four conditions that must be satisfied before the police can issue a reprimand or warning?

Figure 14.2 John Venables and Robert Thompson as children
Source: Mercury Press Agency.

The reprimand or warning will be given in the presence of an 'appropriate' adult. Where a warning has been given, the officer must refer the offender to a youth offending team as soon as practicable. The youth offending team will assess the offender to determine whether a rehabilitation scheme aimed at preventing the person from reoffending is appropriate. Where it is appropriate, a scheme should be established for the offender.

Trial

Young offenders are usually tried in youth courts, which are a branch of the magistrates' court. Other than those involved in the proceedings, the parents and the press, nobody may be present unless authorized by the court. Parents or guardians of children under 16 must attend court at all stages of the proceedings, and the court has the power to order parents of older children to attend.

In limited circumstances young persons can be tried in a Crown Court, for example, if the offence charged is murder, manslaughter or causing death by dangerous driving. They may sometimes be tried in an adult magistrates' court or the Crown

Court if there is a co-defendant in the case who is an adult. Following a Practice Direction discussed below, a separate trial should be ordered unless it is in the interests of justice to do otherwise. If a joint trial is ordered, the ordinary procedures apply 'subject to such modifications (if any) as the court might see fit to order'.

The trial procedures for young offenders have been reformed in the light of a recent ruling of the European Court of Human Rights. This found that John Venables and Robert Thompson, who were convicted by a Crown Court of murdering the 2-year-old James Bulger in 1993, did not have a fair trial in accordance with Art. 6 of the European Convention on Human Rights. It concluded that the criminal procedures adopted in the trial prevented their participation:

> The public trial process in an adult court with attendant publicity was a severely intimidating procedure for 11-year-old children . . . The way in which the trial placed the accused in a raised dock as the focus of intense public attention over a period of three weeks, had impinged on their ability to participate in the proceedings in any meaningful manner.

Following this decision, a Practice Direction was issued by the Lord Chief Justice laying down guidance on how young offenders should be tried when their case is to be heard in the Crown Court. The language used by the Practice Direction follows closely that used in the European decision. It does not lay down fixed rules but states that the individual trial judge must decide what special measures are required by the particular case, taking into account 'the age, maturity and development (intellectual and emotional) of the young defendant on trial'. The trial process should not expose that defendant to avoidable intimidation, humiliation or distress. All possible steps should be taken to assist the defendant to understand and participate in the proceedings. It recommends that young defendants should be brought into the court out of hours in order to become accustomed to its layout. John Venables and Robert Thompson had both benefited from these familiarization visits. The police should make every effort to avoid exposure of the defendant to intimidation, vilification or abuse.

As regards the trial, it is recommended that wigs and gowns should not be worn and public access should be limited. The courtroom should be adapted so that, ordinarily, everyone sits on the same level. In the Bulger trial, the two defendants sat in a specially raised dock. The decision to raise the dock had been done so that the defendants could view the proceedings, but the Court of Human Rights noted that while it did accomplish this, it also made the defendants aware that everyone was looking at them. Placing everyone on the same level should alleviate this problem. In addition, the Practice Direction states that young defendants should sit next to their families or an appropriate adult and near their lawyers.

The Practice Direction suggests that only those with a direct interest in the outcome of the trial should be permitted within the court. Where the press is restricted, provision should be made for the trial to be viewed through a CCTV link to another court area.

It seems that in most other European countries, children aged under 14 who commit offences do not appear before criminal courts, but are dealt with by civil family courts as children in need of compulsory measures of care.

Task 14.2

In 2003 the Youth Justice Board published its annual report *Gaining Ground in the Community*. This report examined the types of crime being committed by young offenders and the experience of young people as victims of crime. The report states:

Types of offence

Both the annual MORI Youth Survey and the data from Young Offending Teams provide information on the types of crimes being committed by young people. The most common offences committed by young people brought into contact with the youth justice system fall into the following categories;

- Motoring offences (23%)
- Theft and handling (17.8%)
- Violence against the person (13%)
- Criminal damage (10.2%)
- Public order offences (6.7%)

Victimisation and fears of young people

There are continuing high levels of fear among young people, according to the MORI Youth Survey, with a third of respondents saying that they felt unsafe in their local area after dark. Over half of young people in school are worried about being physically assaulted or being the victim of theft. A third worry about bullying and racism.

Some 46% of young people in school and 61% of excluded young people say that they have been a victim of crime in the last 12 months. Two-thirds of young people who have been victims of crime say that the perpetrator of the offence is another young person aged under 18.

Questions

1 What type of crime is a young person most likely to commit?

2 Are you frightened to go out in your local area after dark?

3 What percentage of young people have been the victim of a crime in the last 12 months?

4 Have you been the victim of a crime?

▌ Time limits

In 1998 the criminal justice system took, on average, four and a half months to process a young offender from the time of arrest to sentence. The Audit Commission found that in 1997 cases were generally adjourned on four occasions before completion. The Crime and Disorder Act 1998 aimed to reduce this period as there is concern that delays in the system are undermining the impact of the sentence on the offender. In cases involving persons under the age of 18, s. 44 provides that time limits may be applied from arrest to the commencement of proceedings and from conviction to sentence. The Home Secretary commented:

> Young people must be made to recognise and accept responsibility for their crimes – at the time, not many months later. Only when this happens will there be serious pressure on young offenders to change their behaviour rather than settle into a life of crime.

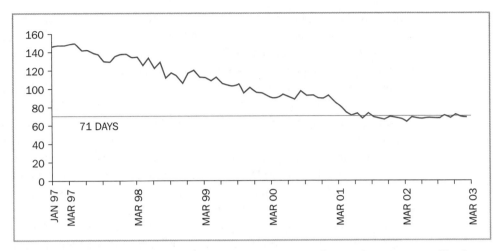

Figure 14.3 Average time between arrest and sentence for persistent young offenders, England and Wales, January 1997 to March 2003

Source: *Crown Prosecution Service Annual Report 2002–2003*, p. 14.

In order to assist practitioners in delivering the current target, the Government has provided guidelines on the length of time each stage of the youth justice process should take in a straightforward case involving a persistent young offender. These are as follows:

Arrest to charge	2 days
Charge to first appearance at court	7 days
First appearance to start of trial	28 days
Verdict to sentence	14 days

By 2004 the Government had succeeded in cutting the time taken to deal with most persistent young offenders in the magistrates' courts from 142 days to 56 days.

 Quick quiz 14.3

1 Which court usually hears trials of young offenders?

2 When can a young person be tried in the Crown Court?

3 Which Article of the European Convention on Human Rights was violated by the mode of trial of Robert Thompson and John Venables?

4 In 2004 what was the average time from arrest to sentence for young offenders?

Zero tolerance

The Labour Party has described its approach to young offenders as being one of 'zero tolerance'. This is a concept that was developed by academics during the 1980s and was adopted by President Ronald Reagan as part of his war against drugs. The principle behind zero tolerance is the 'broken windows theory'. Under this theory, when a neighbourhood shows such signs of decay as graffiti, litter and broken windows, decent people leave, disorder takes over and the area slides into crime. The theory demands that even the most minor offences be pursued with the same vigilance as serious ones, to create a deterrent effect.

Zero tolerance policing was used in New York under the leadership of Mayor Guilliani. The results in New York were impressive, with falls of 50 per cent in overall crime and of nearly two-thirds in the murder rate. But some of the police methods have been criticized as aggressive by the pressure group Human Rights Watch. Critics also suggested that problematic people were simply shifted from rich to poor neighbourhoods – by putting thousands of homeless people on to buses and sending them to remote hostels. There may be other reasons for the drop in crime, such as a reduction in the number of young people in the general population, as this group is statistically more likely to offend. Thus, for example, San Diego saw a significant reduction in crime over a similar period without using zero tolerance policing, but by building partnerships between the police and the public.

 Know your terms 14.4

Define the following terms:

1 Remand
2 Caution-plus
3 Appropriate adult
4 Zero tolerance

A recent use of zero tolerance policy has been by the police in Los Angeles in an attempt to curtail the activities of gang members. Concern had developed that gangs in Los Angeles were disrupting neighbourhoods by dealing in drugs, painting graffiti on walls, urinating on private property, having all-night parties and committing violence and murder. The Los Angeles police, in conjunction with local prosecutors, strictly applied existing law by issuing civil court injunctions against gang members which prevented them from, for example, 'standing, sitting, walking, driving, gathering or appearing any where in public view' in a four-block area where their activities were disruptive. Since the imposition of the zero tolerance policy, some local residents say that the injunctions have returned their neighbourhoods to normal, allowing their children once again to play outside. Opponents of the policy claim that it breaches individuals' rights to freedom of association and speech.

One of the main forms of implementation of the zero tolerance policy by the Labour Government is through the introduction of anti-social behaviour orders, discussed at p. 328. Zero tolerance policing was spearheaded in the UK in Cleveland. Home Office statistics suggest that the policing method was successful in reducing offences targeted by the policy. Between January and December 1997 reported burglary in Cleveland dropped by 26 per cent, robbery by 25 per cent and overall reported crime by 18 per cent. This was the highest reported reduction in England and Wales. At the same time, the area has seen a threefold increase in the incidence of stop and searches. Its clear-up rate had also declined from 27 per cent in 1993 to 25 per cent in 1997, a figure that is 3 per cent below the British average.

Reading on the web

The Youth Justice Board has a website that can be found at:

http://www.youth-justice-board.gov.uk

Question and answer guide

Louise, aged 16, has been seen by a police officer stabbing an old lady and snatching her handbag. He arrests her and takes her to the police station.

(a) Explain the rules concerning the police powers to question Louise about the offence.

(b) If Louise is charged and prosecuted, which court(s) are likely to deal with her case at first instance?

Answer guide

(a) Note that, because of Louise's age, you are talking about a young offender and not an adult. The general rules concerning a suspect in the police station are explained in Chapter 12, but you also need to include the particular rules that apply to Louise because of her age, which are detailed at p. 294.

(b) Special rules apply to the trial of young offenders, which are discussed in this chapter at pp. 296–7. Because of the gravity of this case, you would need to discuss the fact that while most cases involving young offenders are heard by the youth courts, this case might be heard by the Crown Court.

Chapter summary

Introduction

Offenders under 18 are in some respects dealt with differently from adult offenders by the criminal justice system. In 1998 a Youth Justice Board was established to monitor, set standards and promote good practice.

Criminal liability

Children under 10 cannot be liable for a criminal offence.

Young people and the police

An adult responsible for a young person's welfare or an appropriate adult should normally be present in the police station with the young person.

Remand and bail

Young offenders should normally be granted bail, and when bail is refused they should not be held in adult prisons or remand centres.

Reprimands and warnings

In 1998 the system of cautions for young offenders was abolished and replaced by a new system of reprimands and warnings.

Trial

Young offenders are usually tried in youth courts, and only occasionally can they be tried in the Crown Court. The European Court of Human Rights found that John Venables and Robert Thompson, who were convicted by a Crown Court of murdering the two-year-old James Bulger in 1993, did not receive a fair trial in accordance with Art. 6 of the European Convention on Human Rights. As a result, a Practice Direction was issued by the Lord Chief Justice, which lays down guidance on how young offenders should be tried when their case is heard in the Crown Court.

Time limits

The Government has set targets for the handling of cases involving young offenders to try and speed up the youth justice system.

Zero tolerance

The Labour Party has described its approach to young offenders as being one of 'zero tolerance', which means that the law will be strictly enforced in order to reduce crime.

Chapter 15   Sentencing

The Criminal Justice Act 2003

The Home Office undertook a review of sentencing that was carried out by John Halliday and published in 2001. A wide range of recommendations were contained in his report, *Making Punishment Work, Report of the Review of the Sentencing Framework for England and Wales*. Central to the approach of the Halliday Review is that the courts should have a greater role in the implementation of sentences and that offenders should spend more time under supervision after their release from custody. He also wanted to see a greater predictability in sentencing so that the sentencing practice would have a stronger deterrent effect on potential offenders. He was particularly concerned by the approach of the courts to persistent offenders, whom he thought committed a disproportionate amount of crime.

The Government accepted many of the Report's recommendations and introduced significant reforms to the sentencing system in the Criminal Justice Act 2003.

Purposes of sentencing

This chapter is concerned with the sentencing of those convicted of crimes, including the types of punishment available, and how the choice between them is made by the sentencer. But first, we need to consider why people are punished at all – what is the punishment supposed to achieve? Section 142 of the Criminal Justice Act 2003 states that:

> Any court dealing with an [adult] offender in respect of his offence must have regard to the following purposes of sentencing –
>
> (a) the punishment of offenders,
> (b) the reduction of crime (including its reduction by deterrence),
> (c) the reform and rehabilitation of offenders,
> (d) the protection of the public, and
> (e) the making of reparation by offenders to persons affected by their offences.

Each of these purposes of sentencing will be examined in turn.

▌Punishment of offenders

Punishment is concerned with recognizing that the criminal has done something wrong and taking revenge on behalf of both the victim and society as a whole. This can also be described as retribution. Making punishments achieve retribution was a high priority during the last years of the Conservative Government with Michael Howard as the Home Secretary. In the White Paper of 1990, *Crime, Justice and Protecting the Public*, reference was made to the need for sentences to achieve 'just deserts', stating that punishments should match the harm done, and show society's disapproval of that harm. The problem with this is that other factors all too often intervene: for example, those from stable homes, with jobs, are more likely to get non-custodial sentences than those without, who may be sent to prison even though their crime more properly fits a non-custodial sentence.

▌The reduction of crime

Crime is a harm which society wishes to eradicate. One way of reducing crime is through using a sentence as a deterrent. Deterrence is concerned with preventing the commission of future crimes; the idea is that the prospect of an unpleasant punishment will put people who might otherwise commit crime off the idea. Punishments may aim at individual deterrence (dissuading the offender in question from committing crime again), or general deterrence (showing other people what is likely to happen to them if they commit crime).

One problem with the use of punishment as a deterrent is that its effectiveness depends on the chances of detection: a serious punishment for a particular crime will not deter people from committing that offence if there is very little chance of being caught and prosecuted for it. This was shown when Denmark was occupied during the Second World War. All the Danish police were interned, drastically cutting the risk for ordinary criminals of being arrested. Despite increases in punishment, the number of property offences soared.

Linked with this problem is the fact that a deterrent effect requires the offender to stop and think about the consequences of what they are about to do, and, as the previous Government's 1990 White Paper pointed out, this is often unrealistic:

> Deterrence is a principle with much immediate appeal . . . But much crime is committed on impulse, given the opportunity presented by an open window or unlocked door, and it is committed by offenders who live from moment to moment; their crimes are as impulsive as the rest of their feckless, sad or pathetic lives. It is unrealistic to construct sentencing arrangements on the assumption that most offenders will weigh up the possibilities in advance and base their conduct on rational calculation. Often they do not.

The deterrent effect of punishment on individuals becomes weaker each time they are punished. The more deeply a person becomes involved with a criminal way of life, the harder it is to reform and, at the same time, the fear of punishment becomes less because they have been through it all before.

It has been argued that, to deal with this problem, offenders should be given a severe sentence at an early stage – which politicians like to call a 'short, sharp, shock' – rather than having gradually increased sentences which are counterbalanced by the progressive hardening of the offender to the effects of punishment. Successive attempts at the 'short, sharp, shock' treatment have, however, shown it to have no meaningful effect on reconviction rates. The approach was introduced under the Detention Centre Order, created by the Criminal Justice Act 1982; it was abolished in the Criminal Justice Act 1988.

Where a specific crime is thought to be on the increase, the courts will sometimes try to stem this increase by passing what is called an exemplary sentence. This is a sentence higher than that which would normally be imposed to show people that the problem is being treated seriously, and make potential offenders aware that they may be severely punished. There is some debate as to whether exemplary sentences actually work; their effectiveness depends on publicity, yet British newspapers tend to highlight only those sentences which seem too low for an offence which concerns society, or which seem too high for a trivial offence. In addition, even where there is publicity, the results may be negligible – Smith and Hogan (2002) point to an exemplary sentence passed for street robbery at a time when mugging was the subject of great social concern. The sentence was publicized by newspapers and television, yet there was no apparent effect on rates of street robbery even in the area where the case in question took place. We should also question whether exemplary sentences are in the interests of justice, which demands that like cases be treated alike; the person who mugs someone in the street when there has not been a public outcry about that offence is no better than one who mugs when there has.

Reform and rehabilitation

The aim of rehabilitation is to reform offenders, so that they are less likely to commit offences in the future – either because they learn to see the harm they are causing, or because, through education, training and other help, they find other ways to make a living or spend their leisure time. During the 1960s, a great deal of emphasis was placed on the need for rehabilitation, but the results were felt by many to be disappointing. By 1974 the American researcher Robert Martinson was denouncing rehabilitation programmes for prisoners in his paper *What Works*, in which he came to the conclusion that 'nothing works'.

Although rehabilitation sounds like a sensible aim, Bottoms and Preston argue in *The Coming Penal Crisis* (1980) that rehabilitative sentences are fundamentally flawed. First, such sentences assume that all crime is the result of some deficiency or fault in the individual offender; Marxist academics argue that crime is actually a result of the way society is organized. Secondly, they discriminate against the less advantaged in society, who are seen as in need of reform, whereas when an offender comes from a more privileged background, their offence tends to be seen as a one-off, temporary slip. This means that punishment is dictated not by the harm caused, but by the background of the offender. Thirdly, in some cases the pursuit of reform can encourage inexcusable interference with the dignity and privacy of individuals.

This has included, in some countries, implanting electrodes in the brain, and in the UK in the 1970s experiments were carried out involving hormone drug treatment for sex offenders.

In light of the fact that there is a growing prison population, there seems to be a renewed interest in the idea of rehabilitation. Over the past five years, offending behaviour programmes have been developed in many of the prisons of England and Wales. From an initial fragmented range of courses on such matters as anger management, alcohol and drug abuse, domestic violence and victim awareness, the emphasis is now on programmes aimed at changing the way the prisoners think, such as 'Reasoning and Rehabilitation' and 'Enhanced Thinking Skills'. 'Reasoning and Rehabilitation' courses do not look directly at the prisoners' offending; instead, over a 35-session course run by prison probation officers and psychologists, they focus on six key areas – impulse control, flexible thinking (learning from experience), means-end testing (predicting probable outcomes of behaviour), perspective taking (seeing other people's points of view), problem solving and social skills. 'Enhanced Thinking Skills' courses follow a similar pattern, but over 20 sessions. Attendance on the courses is voluntary – but a long-term prisoner is unlikely to be released early without having completed one.

In 1998–99, 3,000 prisoners successfully completed one of these programmes, but this still represents only a very small proportion of the prison population. The number completing a programme is expected to increase significantly over the next few years. Whether a prisoner has the opportunity to undertake a course depends on the establishment in which he or she is being held. Not all prisons run these courses and in most of the ones that do, priority is given to prisoners serving four years or more, in other words, those who have to apply for early release. Yet many persistent offenders are in prison for less than four years. It is common to find people who have had a series of successive two- and three-year sentences, separated by mere weeks and often only days of freedom before they have reoffended and returned to prison. The senior judge, Lord Bingham, would like to see offending behaviour programmes made a legal requirement for all prisoners.

But how far will efforts to change the way a prisoner thinks reduce reoffending? One of the main problems faced by prisoners on release is a lack of work and consequent lack of an honest income or legitimate ways to spend their time. Many prisoners come out with the best of intentions but faced with empty days and even emptier pockets, they soon succumb to their old temptations. There is a danger that prisoners released into their old environment without having acquired any practical or vocational skills to help them on their way will fall back into a life of crime.

A recent report of the Parliamentary Penal Affairs Group, *Changing Offending Behaviour – Some Things Work* (1999) found that 'cognitive behavioural' programmes did work. But in addition, they argued that there is increasing evidence that programmes focused directly on the needs of the offender in relation to the offending behaviour are successful in reducing the risk of reoffending. The types of needs that can be tackled include the need for employment, education, improved social skills and a break from negative peer groups. The need to tackle alcohol and drug problems was also highlighted.

Protection of the public

By placing an offender in custody, you prevent them from committing further offences and the public are thereby protected. While this has its merits where highly dangerous offenders are concerned, it is an extremely expensive way of dealing with crime prevention and, since prison is often the place where criminals pick up new ideas and techniques, may be ultimately counter-productive.

Reparation

The Government has been developing ways in which offenders can provide remedies to their victims or the community at large. This is known sometimes as restorative justice, and has been pioneered for young offenders. So far, it seems to have been surprisingly successful in reducing reoffending and increasing victim satisfaction with the criminal justice system. Offenders can be required, for example, to write letters of apology to their victims, help to repair damage they have caused or take part in other community work.

Sentencing practice

When an offender is convicted in the Crown Court, it is the trial judge alone (without the help of the jury) who determines the appropriate sentence. On conviction in the magistrates' court, the magistrates can determine the sentence themselves or, under s. 3 of the Powers of Criminal Courts (Sentencing) Act 2000 (PCC(S)A), the defendant can be committed to the Crown Court for sentence. If sentenced by the magistrates' court, the maximum sentence that can be imposed for a summary offence has been increased from six months to 12 months by the Criminal Justice Act 2003, s. 154. The minimum is five days (s. 132 of the Magistrates' Courts Act 1980).

Once the defendant has been found guilty, it must be decided first what category of sentence is appropriate and then the amount, duration and form of that sentence.

In recent years there has been a considerable amount of legislation trying to control and regulate the sentencing practices of the judges. The legislature has increasingly sought to reduce the discretion available to the judiciary in selecting the sentence. We will look first at the legislative provisions and then at the common law practice known as the tariff system.

 Quick quiz 15.1

1 What are the five purposes of sentencing identified by the Criminal Justice Act 2003?

2 The White Paper, *Crime, Justice and Protecting the Public* (1990), identified one reason why a sentence might not act as a deterrent in practice. What reason was this?

3 What problems are identified by Bottoms and Preston in the use of rehabilitative sentences?

4 Does the jury, the judge or both together select the offender's sentence in the Crown Court?

▌Legislation

Parliamentary legislation has for a minority of offences fixed the sentence that must be imposed. Since 1997 it has applied minimum sentences to some offenders. Some rules have also been laid down restricting the judiciary's choice of sentence.

Mandatory sentences

Certain offences have a mandatory sentence when committed for the first time. The most notable example of this is murder, which has a mandatory sentence of life imprisonment.

Minimum sentences

There are also now minimum sentences for certain firearms offences under the Criminal Justice Act 2003, s. 287. These minimum sentences were introduced in an attempt to tackle the growing problem of criminals using guns.

General restrictions on sentences

The legislation has divided sentences into four categories: custodial sentences, community sentences, fines and certain miscellaneous sentences. A custodial or community sentence can only be ordered where certain statutory conditions are satisfied. The judges must give reasons for their sentence and explain the effect of the sentence to the offender (Criminal Justice Act 2003, s. 174).

Custodial sentences

A custodial sentence is defined by s. 76 of the PCC(S)A 2000. For a person aged 18 or over it is a sentence of imprisonment or a suspended sentence. For a person under 18 a custodial sentence includes detention in a young offenders' institution or a sentence of custody for life.

A court should not pass a custodial sentence unless it considers that the crime was so serious that only a custodial sentence is justified (s. 152, Criminal Justice Act 2003). Section 153 of the Criminal Justice Act 2003 directs the court to impose the shortest custodial term that is commensurate with the seriousness of the offence(s), subject to certain exceptions. Section 143 of the 2003 Act states that:

> In considering the seriousness of any offence, the court must consider the offender's culpability in committing the offence and any harm which the offence caused, was intended to cause or might foreseeably have caused.

The court also has to take into account previous convictions, failure to respond to previous sentences and the commission of an offence while on bail (s. 143, Criminal Justice Act 2003).

Where a judge intends to impose a custodial sentence (unless the sentence is fixed by law), a pre-sentence report must normally be prepared by the probation service, containing background information about the defendant. This will assist the judge in selecting the appropriate sentence.

Community sentences

Section 148 of the Criminal Justice Act 2003 states that a community sentence can only be imposed if the offence was 'serious enough to warrant such a sentence'. Where a court passes a community sentence, the particular requirements of the sentence must be the most suitable for the offender. The restrictions on liberty imposed by the order must be 'commensurate with the seriousness of the offence, or the combination of the offence and one or more offences associated with it'.

Dangerous offenders

The Criminal Justice Act 2003 has introduced a new scheme for the sentencing of dangerous adults. The scheme applies to offenders who have committed a specified sexual or violent offence and have been assessed as dangerous. Such offenders can receive an extended sentence and their release is at the discretion of the Parole Board. The most dangerous offenders who continue to pose a risk to the public may be kept in prison for an indeterminate period. These measures will allow the state to hold offenders in prison for longer than is required by the gravity of their offence in order to protect the public. Once released, sex offenders may in the future be required to take regular lie detector tests to try and detect if they are committing or planning to commit any further offence, under provisions in the Management of Offenders and Sentencing Bill. This would be a controversial reform, partly because lie detectors are only 90 per cent accurate.

▌The tariff system

The legislation regulates the type of sentence imposed and its focus on the seriousness of the crime clearly has implications for the length of a custodial or community sentence or the amount of a fine. In deciding the latter issues, judges also rely on what has been called the tariff principle, first recognized by Dr David Thomas in his book *Principles of Sentencing* (1970).

The tariff system is based on treating like cases alike: people with similar backgrounds who commit similar offences in similar circumstances should receive similar sentences. That does not mean that judges apply a rigid scale of penalties, but that for most types of criminal offence it is possible to identify a range within which the sentence for different factual situations will fall.

The system works in two stages: calculation of the initial tariff sentence, and then the application of secondary tariff principles. To begin with, the judge will take the tariff sentence that is generally thought appropriate for the offence. This may then be lowered by taking into account secondary tariff principles such as mitigating factors – reasons why the defendant should be punished less severely than the facts of the case might suggest (Criminal Justice Act 2003, s. 166). These include youth or old age; previous good character; the 'jump effect' (a requirement that sentences for repeat offenders should increase steadily rather than by large jumps); provocation; domestic or financial problems; drink, drugs or ill-health; and any special hardship offenders may have to undergo in prison, such as the fact that sex offenders and police informers may have to be held in solitary confinement for their own protection. In some cases, where an offender has already been held on remand, the courts may reduce the tariff sentence on the basis that the shock of being locked up has already constituted a severe punishment. The offender's behaviour after committing the offence may also be a factor, including efforts to help the police and/or compensate the victim. A plea of guilty is usually taken as a sign of remorse and an offender's sentence can now be reduced by up to a third in the light of the stage at which they indicate an intention to plead guilty and the circumstances in which that indication is given (s. 152, Criminal Justice Act 2003 and guidelines issued by the Sentencing Guidelines Council). As far as the offence itself is concerned, the fact that it was committed on impulse and not premeditated may be a mitigating factor. Offenders benefit from a reduced sentence, or even immunity from sentence, if they give evidence against other criminals (Serious Organized Crime and Police Act 2005). This is sometimes called 'Queen's evidence'.

There may also be aggravating factors, as a result of which the court may want to pass an exemplary sentence. The Court of Appeal has stated that the correct way to deal with this is to ignore mitigating factors and not to increase the initial tariff. Under the Criminal Justice Act 2003, a court must treat the fact that an offence was racially or religiously motivated as an aggravating factor that increased the seriousness of the offence. Any previous convictions, which are recent and relevant, should be regarded as an aggravating factor which will increase the severity of the sentence.

Sentencing Guidelines Council and Sentencing Advisory Panel

The Court of Appeal plays a central role in developing the tariff system by providing guidance to the judges of first instance as to the appropriate sentence for certain types of offence and offender. The Crime and Disorder Act 1998 created a Sentencing Advisory Panel to assist in the development of a fair sentencing practice. The Court of Appeal was required to consider the views of this Panel in framing its sentencing guidelines, and it has taken account of a range of guidelines produced by the Sentencing Advisory Panel.

The Criminal Justice Act 2003, ss. 167–73 has established a new Sentencing Guidelines Council. This will produce a set of sentencing guidelines for all criminal courts (and guidelines on allocation of cases between courts). The courts will be obliged to take these guidelines into account when determining what sentence to impose, and will have to give reasons if they depart from a recommended sentence in a guideline. The aim of these guidelines is to help the courts to approach sentencing from a common starting point. They will also enable practitioners and the general public to know the starting point for each offence. The Council will have seven judicial members and five non-judicial members, and will be chaired by the Lord Chief Justice.

The Sentencing Advisory Panel now tenders its advice to the Sentencing Guidelines Council, instead of the Court of Appeal. There is a risk that the Council will simply duplicate the work of the Panel, and it is questionable whether we need both these bodies.

Individualized sentences

In some cases, the courts prefer not to use the tariff system, but to impose a sentence aimed at dealing with the individual needs of the offender. There are four main types of offender for whom individualized sentencing is used: young offenders; intermediate recidivists; inadequate recidivists; and those who need psychiatric treatment. Individualized sentences are often given to young offenders in the hope of steering them away from a life of crime. Intermediate recidivists are offenders in their late twenties or early thirties, with a criminal record dating back to their childhood; rather than simply ordering steadily increasing tariff sentences for them, the courts may give an individualized sentence if there is evidence that a new approach may work. Inadequate recidivists are middle-aged or elderly offenders who have a long history of committing relatively minor crimes, which have resulted in imprisonment and most other types of sentence; individualized sentences may be ordered for them on the simple basis that their record shows increasing tariff sentences to have been ineffective in stopping their offending. Finally, offenders who need psychiatric treatment are given individualized sentences within which such treatment can be undertaken.

Types of sentence

It was mentioned above (pp. 308–9) that there are four main categories of sentence: custodial sentences; community sentences; fines; and other miscellaneous sentences. The death penalty has been abolished. We will now look at the particular forms that the four existing sentences can take.

Fines

A fine may be imposed for almost any offence other than murder. Offences tried in the magistrates' court carry a set maximum, depending on the offence; the highest is £5,000. This will be increased to £15,000 if the Management of Offenders and Sentencing Bill is passed. There is no maximum in the Crown Court. The courts must ensure that the amount of the fine reflects the seriousness of the offence, and also takes account of the offender's means, reducing or increasing it as a result (Criminal Justice Act 2003, s. 167). Magistrates' courts can arrange for the automatic deduction of a fine from the offender's earnings, known as an 'attachment of earnings order', when imposing the fine or following a failure to pay. Under ss. 300 and 301 of the Criminal Justice Act 2003 the court has the power to impose unpaid work or curfew requirements on a fine defaulter or to disqualify them from driving, rather than sending them to prison.

The Courts Act 2003 seeks to improve the information available to magistrates on offenders' means prior to sentence, and to ensure that enforcement action is taken promptly. The Act has introduced a new framework for fine enforcement. Fines officers will manage and collect fines for the court. Discounts of up to 50 per cent will be given to those who pay promptly. If the offender fails to pay promptly the fine can be increased by the fines officer by up to 50 per cent without the case being referred back to the courts. The fines officer may also issue a 'further steps notice'. This could, for example, require payments to be deducted automatically from an offender's pay, for their property to be seized and sold, or their car clamped. Once clamped the car can be removed for sale or other disposal and any proceeds will be used to discharge or reduce the offender's outstanding fine.

The fine is the most common sentence issued by the court, with three-quarters of all offenders sentenced at magistrates' courts in 2000 being issued a fine. The number of fines issued has decreased in recent years and the researchers Flood-Page and Mackie (1998) concluded that 'there seems to have been a general disenchantment with financial penalties'.

Advantages

Evidence suggests that people are less likely to reoffend after being sentenced to a fine than following other sentences, though this can be partly explained by the type of offenders that are given fines in the first place. Fines also bring income into the system, and they do not have the long-term disruptive effects of imprisonment.

Disadvantages

There have been high rates of non-payment, a problem which the Courts Act 2003 is intended to tackle. A third of fines are never paid, so that in 2000–01, according to the National Audit Office, £74 million of fines were written off (mainly because the offender could not be traced). Not only does this make the sentence ineffective, but repeated non-payment of a fine can lead to a custodial sentence, with the result that some inmates of English prisons are there for very minor offences, such as failure to pay for a television licence.

Research carried out for the Home Office, *Enforcing Financial Penalties* (1997), found that the majority of fine defaulters were out of work (only 22 per cent of the men and 11 per cent of the women had any paid employment, even part time). Predominant among reasons for non-payment were changes in circumstances through illness or job loss, and financial difficulties brought on by other debts.

A wide range of enforcement methods are available to the courts, including attachment of earnings orders and the automatic deduction of fines from social security benefits. In practice, these enforcement methods are only rarely used. The 1997 Home Office study highlighted practical difficulties in trying to arrange the deduction of fines from social security benefits. Some magistrates felt that attachment of earnings orders removed the responsibility from the defaulter for ensuring that the fine was paid, which was seen as part of the punishment. The Government is now planning to establish a National Enforcement Service, which should be fully operational in 2007. This will employ 4,000 enforcement officers who will wear a uniform and be responsible for ensuring fines are paid and other court orders obeyed.

Fines can be unfair, since the same fine may be a very severe punishment to a poor defendant, but make little impact on one who is well off. In an attempt to address this problem, the Criminal Justice Act 1991 originally laid down a system of unit fines for the magistrates' courts. A maximum number of units was allocated to each offence, up to a total of 50. Within that maximum, the court had to determine the number of units which was commensurate with the seriousness of the case. The value of the unit depended on the offender's disposable weekly income (their income after having deducted any regular household expenses), with the minimum value of a unit being £4, and the maximum £100. The unit fines system aimed to even out the effects of fines so that, although the sums to be paid were different, the impact on the offender would be similar. The pilot schemes for the unit fines suggested that fines were paid more quickly and there was a drop in debtors ending up in prison, because of the more realistic assessment of the fines.

Unfortunately, the idea aroused huge public opposition after press coverage of what seemed to be high fines for relatively minor offences and very low fines for the unemployed – despite the fact that even if some of these were unfair, they were less unfair than the previous system. There was public uproar when a man received a £1,200 fine for dropping a crisp packet. As a result, unit fines were abolished, and the courts reverted to their previous practice, except that they are now required to take into account ability to pay when setting fines.

The Government is currently planning to reintroduce the unit fine scheme. The relevant legislative provisions are contained in the Management of Offenders and Sentencing Bill which is being considered by Parliament. The maximum income unit for high earners will be £75. The offence of being drunk and disorderly, for example, will carry a penalty of up to 10 units, so that its maximum fine will be £750. At the moment the maximum fine for this offence is only £200. The Home Office hope that the scheme will restore public confidence in the use of fines as an effective and fair punishment. It has commented:

> A fine is meant to have equal impact on the rich and poor. This formalizes the process. The scheme should provide for greater consistency and fairness as the financial penalty should bear equally on offenders of differing means.

The scheme is likely to be in operation in 2006.

Fixed-penalty fines

In order to clamp down on loutish behaviour the police have been given the power to impose fixed-penalty fines by the Criminal Justice and Police Act 2001. These fines can be imposed for such offences as being drunk in a public place and being drunk and disorderly. A police officer may give a person aged 16 and over a penalty notice if there is reason to believe that the person has committed a penalty offence (s. 2). The fine for each offence is fixed by the Home Secretary and can be for up to a quarter of the maximum fine applicable to the offence. Recipients must either pay the fine within 21 days or opt for trial (they will not be marched off to the cash machine by the police officer, as was originally suggested). If they fail to do either, then a sum which is one and a half times the penalty will be registered against them for enforcement as a fine. If the person pays the fixed-penalty fine there is no criminal conviction or admission of guilt associated with the payment of the penalty.

Figure 15.1 Wormwood Scrubs, an example of a Victorian prison
Source: © EMPICS.

The system of fixed-penalty fines is currently being piloted, and if these pilot schemes are successful they will be extended nationwide. The pilots have been criticized by the police. Fifty per cent of the fines have not been paid, and there is a problem with people giving false names and addresses.

Advantages

In the past much minor offending escaped sanction because of the need to focus police and court resources on more important matters. It is hoped that fixed-penalty fines will provide a quick and efficient way of dealing with low-level, but disruptive criminal behaviour.

Disadvantages

Fixed-penalty fines take place outside the protective framework of the court system, and there is therefore a danger of abuse and corruption.

Custodial sentences

For adult defendants, a custodial sentence means prison. Most of those given custodial sentences do not serve the full sentence in custody, but are released early on licence. The Government promised in its 2005 election manifesto that every offender released from custody would be placed under supervision to help their successful reintegration into society.

Task 15.2

Read the following extract and answer the questions that follow.

Tagging is harder than prison because I have to make an effort every day

'I don't like tagging. It's harder than prison because I have to make an effort every day', Mark, 27, who has a long list of drug-related burglaries on his record, says. But it imposed a strict, disciplined framework on his life for the first time in years. This would not, on its own, keep him out of trouble – but it would give Mark and his probation officer the chance to start other longer-term programmes that might.

Tagging's intrusion into family life has produced mixed results. Some women, in particular, found the enforced presence of their partner added to both tension in their relationship and the risk of violence. Others welcomed a period in which the partner learnt to see more of his children.

'He really resented our home being his prison', one wife said, 'and when I went out to work part time and left him to put the children to bed it was – well, he thought it was the end of the world. But after a bit, when he saw how they responded, he was really proud. It won't change everything, but it has done a lot of good.'

Not everyone agrees and research in Scotland revealed that some parents of tagged young adults were resentful about the role of unpaid jailers which they felt had been forced upon them.

Extensive Home Office research has concluded that tagging is 'offence neutral' – that is, it has no real impact on longer-term reoffending rates. But electronic monitoring can be positively used. Politicians have capitalised on its usefulness in terms of crisis management of prison numbers.

In technology terms, electronic tagging schemes are basic – much more sophisticated technology, using satellites to track offenders rather than simply enforcing a curfew, is already in use in the US and could soon be available here.

If all tagging can do is provide a short-term fix, the enormous investment already made will simply have been wasted. Using technology in ways that make a real impact on crime figures and on reoffending rates must be the aim.

(Adapted from an article by Dick Whitfield which was published in *The Times*, 11 March 2003.)

Questions

1 Why did some parents in Scotland resent the tagging of their children?

2 Does tagging currently reduce the longer-term reoffending rates?

3 What does the author consider should be the aim of using technology?

4 Do you think that tagging is a good idea?

Custody plus

John Halliday's report on sentencing (discussed at p. 303) argued that prison sentences of less than 12 months had little meaningful impact on criminal behaviour, because only half of the sentence time was actually served in prison, and the person was then released without conditions. The Prison Service had little opportunity to tackle criminal behaviour as the period served in custody was so short. In addition, such sentences could have long-term adverse effects on family cohesion, employment and training prospects – all of which are key to the rehabilitation of offenders. This was particularly regrettable, as these sentences are used for large numbers of persistent offenders who are likely to reoffend.

Halliday recommended that to tackle this weakness in short prison sentences there should be a new sentence which he described as 'custody plus'. The Government has adopted this reform in the Criminal Justice Act 2003. Under s. 181, all sentences for less than 12 months' custody will be replaced by custody plus (or intermittent custody, discussed below). After spending a maximum of three months in custody, the offender will be released and subjected to at least six months' post-release supervision in the community. The court can attach specific requirements to the sentence, based upon those available under a community sentence. If an offender fails to comply with the terms of the community part of the sentence he or she will be returned to custody.

Sentences for more than 12 months will require the offender to spend half their time in custody (unless they obtain early release on home detention curfew), and the remainder of their sentence under supervision in the community. It is hoped that these reforms will provide a more effective framework within which to address the needs of offenders.

Intermittent custody

Intermittent custody has also been introduced by the Criminal Justice Act 2003, following a recommendation in the Halliday Report. This allows offenders to serve their custodial sentence intermittently, returning to prison at night or at the weekend. It is hoped that this will enable offenders to continue their employment and education and keep their family ties, which should reduce the risk of reoffending. At the moment the prison facilities are not suitable for such arrangements but the Home Secretary wants consideration to be given to this matter. Two pilot schemes have been established. From Monday to Friday purpose-built prison units are occupied by unemployed prisoners who are allowed home at weekends. From Friday to Sunday employed offenders (including those doing community work) and some offenders who are looking for work, stay at these prisons but are allowed out for the rest of the week.

▌ Suspended sentence

Under ss. 189–94 of the Criminal Justice Act 2003 a custodial sentence can be suspended. A court is able to suspend a short custodial sentence for between six months and two years. The offender can be required to undertake certain activities in the community.

If the offender breaches the terms of the suspension the suspended sentence will be activated. The commission of a further offence during the entire length of suspension will also count as breach, and the offender's existing suspended sentence will be dealt with at the time the court sentences him or her for the new offence. Courts have a discretion to review an offender's progress under a suspended sentence.

Suspended sentences were created in 1967 and were intended to be used as an alternative to a custodial sentence. In practice, they have sometimes been used in the past where a community sentence would have been adequate. If the offender then commits another offence the suspended sentence is activated, so that the offender ends up in prison.

Home detention curfew

Home detention curfews were introduced by the Crime and Disorder Act 1998. Prisoners sentenced to between three months' and four years' imprisonment can be released early (usually 60 days early) on a licence that includes a curfew condition. This requires the released prisoners to remain at a certain address at set times, during which period they will be subjected to electronic monitoring. Most curfews are set for 12 hours between 7 pm and 7 am. The person can be recalled to prison if there is a failure to comply with the conditions of the curfew condition or in order to protect the public from serious harm. Private contractors fit the electronic tag to a person's ankle, install monitoring equipment which plugs into the telephone system in their home and connects with a central computer system, and notify breaches of curfew to the Prison Service.

Research has been carried out by Dodgson (2001) and others into the first 16 months' experience of home detention curfew. It found that only 5 per cent were recalled to prison. The main reasons for recall were breach of the curfew conditions (68 per cent) or a change of circumstances (25 per cent). The use of home detention curfew appeared to have eased the transition from prison to the community. Offenders were very positive about the scheme, with only 2 per cent saying that they would have preferred to have spent their time in prison. Prior to release, over a third of prisoners said that the prospect of being granted home detention curfew influenced their behaviour in prison. Other household members were also very positive about the scheme.

Sentences for murder

An area that has caused considerable controversy and litigation in recent years is the question of the release of prisoners sentenced to life imprisonment, and in particular the Home Secretary's involvement in this decision. In the recent past, the final decision as to when murderers should be released on licence lay with a politician, the Home Secretary. This was found to be in breach of the European Convention on Human Rights in the case of **R (Anderson)** *v* **Secretary of State for the Home Department** (2002). The danger was that Home Secretaries might be influenced by issues of political popularity rather than the justice in the particular case. The matter was highlighted in the case of Myra Hindley, who was convicted for life in 1966 for the murder of two children and for her involvement in the killing of a third.

The Home Secretary, however, seems anxious to retain some control in this area. Provisions have been added to the Criminal Justice Act 2003 which aim to promote consistency in the sentencing of murderers. Under these provisions, judges are required to slot offenders into one of three categories according to the severity of their crime. For the first category, actual life will be served by those convicted of the most serious and heinous crimes: multiple murderers, child killers and terrorist murderers. For the second category, there is a starting point of 30 years. This category includes murders of police and prison officers and murders with sexual, racial or religious motives. For the third category, the starting point is 15 years. In addition, there are 14 mitigating and aggravating factors which will affect the sentence imposed. Judges are able to ignore these guidelines, provided they explain why. Once the minimum term has expired, the Parole Board will consider the person's suitability for release, and if appropriate, direct their release.

There are at present 22 people serving whole-life tariffs in England and Wales, none in Europe and 25,000 in America (along with 3,500 people under sentence of death).

Quick quiz 15.3

1 What was the name of the academic who first recognized that judges rely on the tariff principle?

2 What is the automatic sentence for murder?

3 What is the role of the Sentencing Guidelines Council?

4 What is a fixed penalty fine?

Advantages of custodial sentences

The previous Conservative Government claimed that prison 'works', in the sense that offenders cannot commit crime while they are in prison, and so the public is

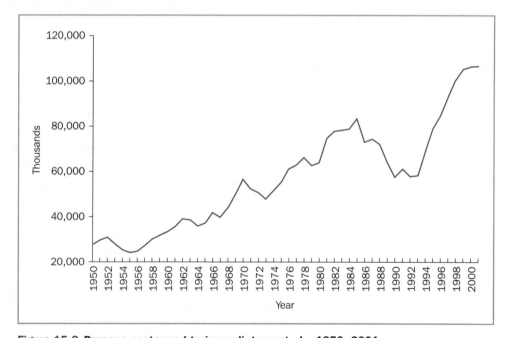

Figure 15.2 Persons sentenced to immediate custody, 1950–2001

Source: Home Office (2002), *Criminal Statistics England and Wales 2001*, p. 18, Figure 1.3.

protected. The current Government claims that prison can be made to work both by protecting the public and by making use of the opportunity for rehabilitation.

Disadvantages of custodial sentences

Fifty-nine per cent of prisoners are reconvicted within two years of being released. In her book, *Bricks of Shame* (1987), Vivienne Stern highlights several reasons why imprisonment lacks any great reformative power, and may even make people more, rather than less, likely to reoffend. Prisoners spend time with other criminals, from whom they frequently acquire new ideas for criminal enterprises; budget cuts have meant there is now little effective training and education in prisons, while the stigma of having been in prison means their opportunities for employment are fewer when they are released; and families often break down, so that the ex-prisoner may become homeless. The result, says Stern, is that 'going straight can present the quite unattractive option of a boring, lonely existence in a hostel or rented room, eking out the Income Support'. All this can also mean that prison punishes the innocent as well as the guilty, with the prisoner's family suffering stigma, financial difficulties, the misery of being parted from the prisoner and often family breakdown in the end.

Stern rejects the idea that prison works because it protects the public. She points out that although it may prevent the individual offending for a while, the percentage of crime that is actually detected and prosecuted is so small that imprisonment has little effect on the crime rate.

Prisons are also extremely expensive – at £36,000 a year per prisoner, three weeks in prison costs as much as a lengthy community sentence. To this must be added the costs associated with the family breakdown and unemployment that imprisonment frequently causes. As well as those who find themselves in prison through non-payment of fines, many of those actually sentenced to prison have committed relatively minor offences and could be dealt with just as effectively, and far more cheaply, in the community.

The conditions within prisons continue to cause concern. While all prisoners are now supposed to have 24-hour access to toilet facilities, with the practice of 'slopping out' ended in 1996, other problems remain. A continuing area of concern that has been highlighted in the Prison Ombudsman's report for 1998 is the failure of the Prison Service's internal complaints system to investigate complaints adequately. Lord Woolf in his inquiry into the prison disturbances that took place in 1990 found that one of the root causes of the riots was that prisoners believed they had no other effective method of airing their grievances.

Where prison conditions are poor, there is an increased risk of suicide. Between 1999 and 2003 a total of 434 people committed suicide in prison. There were over 16,000 incidents of self-harm recorded in 2003. A report of the Joint Committee on deaths in custody in 2004 found that the young, the mentally unstable and women are most at risk.

The number of people in prison has been growing at an alarming rate over recent years. In 2004 the United Kingdom was holding over 75,000 prisoners, an increase of more than 50 per cent in the last ten years. This figure is expected to reach 80,000 by 2009. Seventy per cent of sentenced prisoners are serving 12 months or less. This

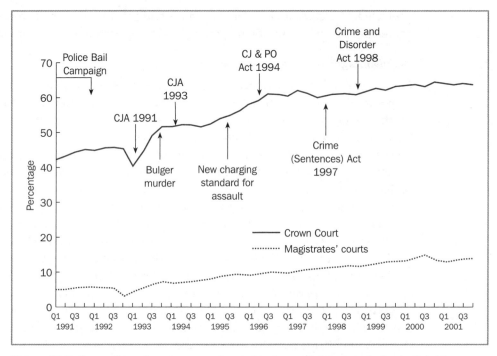

Figure 15.3 Proportion of persons sentenced to immediate custody for indictable offences by type of court, 1991–2001

Source: Home Office (2002), *Criminal Statistics England and Wales 2001*, p. 81, Figure 7.4.

increase in the prison population is not due to an increase in criminal activity, but simply that heavier sentences are being imposed. A Home Office bulletin issued in 2000 showed the courts in England and Wales to be among the toughest in western Europe in terms of numbers imprisoned, while a Council of Europe study revealed that defendants in English courts get longer sentences for assault, robbery or theft than they do elsewhere in Europe. Average prison populations in Europe are approximately one-third lower as a proportion of the population to that of the United Kingdom. A report carried out by the businessman Patrick Carter in 2003 estimated that the increased use of custody had only reduced crime by 5 per cent at the most.

The Chief Inspector of Prisons claimed in an interview for *The Guardian* in 2001 that the prison population could be cut to 40,000 if 'the kids, the elderly, the mentally ill, the asylum seekers, those inside for trivial shoplifting or drug offences' were taken away. The inevitable result of a growing prison population is prison over-crowding. In 1996 matters reached crisis point and this led to a controversial scheme whereby a converted ship was used as a floating prison. In *Prison Sardines* (1996), a Howard League report, it was noted that at the end of February 1996, 46 prisons were overcrowded, with Usk Prison in Gwent being 75 per cent overcrowded.

The Home Office has issued a five year strategic plan (*Cutting Crime – Delivering Justice: strategic plan for criminal justice 2004–08*). This states that the Government wishes to stop the drift towards longer custodial sentences. One way that it is hoped this will be achieved, is by requiring the Sentencing Guidelines Council to consider the capacity of prisons when advising judges and magistrates on sentencing – this requirement is included in clause 37 of the Management of Offenders and Sentencing Bill.

 Quick quiz 15.4

1 Do you think that 'prison works'?

2 How much does it cost to keep a person in prison for a year?

3 In 2004 how many people were in prison in the UK?

4 Do you think intermittent custody will reduce re-offending?

Community sentence

Recent Governments have been anxious to emphasize that community sentences impose substantial restrictions on the offender's freedom and should not be seen as 'soft options'. Home Office statistics show that 56 per cent of offenders given community sentences reoffend within two years.

The Criminal Justice Act 2003 has established a single community order which can be applied to an offender aged 16 or over. This order can contain a range of possible requirements. These are:

- an unpaid work requirement
- an activity requirement
- a programme requirement
- a prohibited activity requirement
- a curfew requirement
- an exclusion requirement
- a residence requirement
- a mental health treatment requirement
- a drug rehabilitation requirement
- an alcohol treatment requirement
- a supervision requirement
- an attendance centre requirement (where the offender is aged under 25).

Each of these requirements will be considered in turn:

Unpaid work requirement

The offender can be required to perform, over a period of 12 months, a specified number of hours of unpaid work for the benefit of the community. The number of hours must be between 40 and 300. The kind of work done includes tasks on conservation projects, archaeological sites and canal clearance. This requirement allows useful community work to be done, and may give offenders a sense of achievement which helps them stay out of trouble afterwards.

Activity requirement

Under an activity requirement offenders must present themselves to a specified person, at a specified place, for a maximum of 60 days, and/or take part in specified activities for a certain number of days. An activity requirement may include such tasks as receiving help with employment, group work on social problems and providing reparation to the victim.

Programme requirement

A programme requirement obliges the offender to participate in an accredited programme on a certain number of days. Programmes are courses which address offending behaviour, such as anger management, sex offending and drug abuse.

Prohibited activity requirement

The court can instruct an offender to refrain from participating in certain activities. For example, it might forbid an offender from contacting a certain person, or from participating in specified activities during a period of time. The court can make a prohibited activity requirement which prohibits a defendant from possessing, using or carrying a firearm.

Curfew requirement

An offender can be ordered to remain in a specified place or places for periods of not less than two hours or more than 12 hours in any one day for up to six months. The court should avoid imposing conditions which would interfere with the offender's work or education, or cause conflict with their religious beliefs. A specified person must be made responsible for monitoring the offender's whereabouts. Courts can require offenders to wear electronic tags, in order to monitor that they are conforming to their curfew order.

Advantages

Tagging costs about £4,000 a year compared with £24,000 for a prison place. Curfew orders have the potential to keep offenders out of trouble and protect the public, without the disruptive effects of imprisonment. In the US city of Atlanta, a night curfew has been imposed on anyone under 16. This was introduced to protect children, but has also had the effect of considerably reducing juvenile crime. While such use of curfew orders on those who have not been convicted of crimes intrudes on the right to freedom of movement, the results show that, as a sentence, it could prove very useful.

At the moment electronic tags are used that set off an alarm if a curfew is breached, but cannot identify where the criminal has then gone. The government is now considering a more technologically advanced system which can track the precise movements of the offender. This could have the advantage, for example, of making sure that a convicted paedophile does not enter a school building.

Disadvantages

The Penal Affairs Consortium have argued that the money spent on electronic tagging would be better spent on constructive options such as supervision requirements, which work to change offenders' long-term attitudes towards offending. Opponents of electronic tagging claim it is degrading to the person concerned, but its supporters – including one or two well-known former prisoners – point out that it is far less degrading than imprisonment. This argument applies only where tagging is used as an alternative to imprisonment: its opponents claim that it is likely to be used in practice to replace other non-custodial measures. Existing research suggests, however, that curfew orders with tagging are being seen as a genuine alternative to custody (Nuttall *et al.* (1998)).

Exclusion requirement

An offender can be required to stay away from a certain place or places at set times. Electronic tags can be used to monitor compliance with this requirement. It is aimed at people, such as stalkers, who present a particular danger or nuisance to a victim. An exclusion requirement is similar in many respects to a curfew requirement. However, whereas under a curfew requirement an offender has to remain at a specified place, an exclusion requirement prohibits an offender from entering a specific place.

Residence requirement

A residence requirement obliges the offender to reside at a place specified in the order for a specified period.

Mental health treatment requirement

A court can direct an offender to undergo mental health treatment for certain period(s) as part of a community sentence or suspended sentence order, under the treatment of a registered medical practitioner or chartered psychologist. Before including a mental health treatment requirement, the court must be satisfied that the mental condition of the offender requires treatment and may be helped by treatment, but is not such that it warrants making a hospital or guardianship order (within the meaning of the Mental Health Act 1983). The offender's consent must be obtained before the requirement is imposed.

Drug rehabilitation requirement

As part of a community sentence or suspended sentence the court may impose a drug rehabilitation requirement, which includes drug treatment and testing. In order to impose such a requirement, the court must be satisfied that the offender is dependent on or has a propensity to misuse any controlled drug and therefore requires and would benefit from treatment. In addition, the court must be satisfied that the necessary arrangements are or can be made for the treatment and that the offender has expressed a willingness to comply with the drug rehabilitation requirement. The treatment provided must be for a minimum of six months.

A court may provide for the review of this requirement, and such reviews must take place if the order is for more than 12 months. Review hearings provide the court with information about the offender's progress, including the results of any drug tests.

Alcohol treatment requirement

A court can require an offender to undergo alcohol treatment to reduce or eliminate the offender's dependency on alcohol. The offender's consent is required. This requirement must last at least six months.

Supervision requirement

The offender can be placed under the supervision of a probation officer for a fixed period of between six months and three years. Home Office research into the probation service (Mair and May, *Offenders on Probation* (1997)) found that 90 per cent of the people supervised thought that their supervision had been useful. The most common reason given for this view was that it offered them someone independent to talk to about their problems. A third mentioned getting practical help or advice with specific problems and about 20 per cent mentioned being helped to keep out of trouble and avoid offending. The research concluded:

> The message contained in this report is a good one for the probation service; it is viewed favourably by most of those it supervises, and seems to work hard at trying to achieve its formal aims and objectives as stated in the National Standards. However, this should not lead to any sense of complacency. It is arguable that any agency which provided similar help to that provided by the probation service to the poor and unemployed would be seen in an equally positive light.

Due to staff shortages, particularly in London, some offenders who are subject to a supervision requirement, are merely being required to turn up and have their names ticked off.

Attendance centre requirement

Attendance centres are discussed at p. 344.

▌Miscellaneous sentences

A range of other sentences are also available to the court. These include:

Compensation orders

Where an offence causes personal injury, loss or damage (unless it arises from a road accident), the courts may order the offender to pay compensation. This may be up to £1,000 in a magistrates' court and is unlimited in the Crown Court. Orders can also be made for the return of stolen property to its owner, or, where stolen property has been disposed of, for compensation to be paid to the victim from any money taken from the offender when arrested.

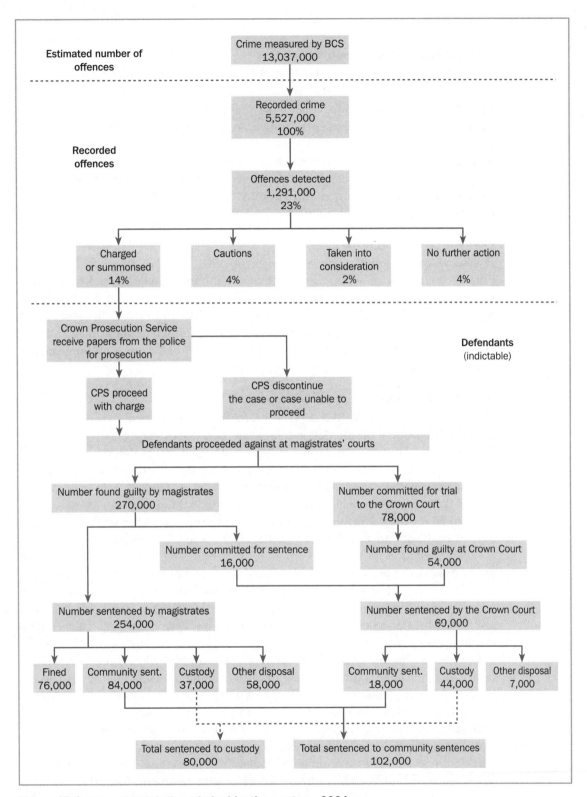

Figure 15.4 Flows through the criminal justice system, 2001

Source: Home Office (2002), *Criminal Statistics England and Wales 2001*, p. 15, Figure 1.1.

Confiscation and civil recovery orders

Under the Proceeds of Crime Act 2002, the powers to confiscate property have been increased. The Act is intended to attack the profits of organized crime. The recovery rates had been disappointing under the previous law. For the first time, the Act permits the use of civil recovery of the proceeds of criminal conduct, even where a person has not been convicted. It puts the burden of proof on the private individual to account for any property for which the source is not clear. The Assets Recovery Agency is established, which has wide powers both to investigate a person's financial affairs, and to bring proceedings to recover property which represents property obtained through unlawful conduct.

Financial reporting order

Following conviction for one of a range of offences suggesting involvement in organized crime, such as drug importation and money laundering and where there is a risk of repeat offending, a court can issue a financial reporting order. Provisions for this order are contained in the Serious Organized Crime and Police Act 2005. It requires offenders to give the authorities regular information about their financial affairs for up to 20 years, to try and prevent the individual from profiting from any criminal enterprise.

Mental health orders

Under the Mental Health Act 1983, the Crown Court can order the detention of offenders in hospital on conviction for an imprisonable offence if they are suffering from a mental disorder, the nature or degree of which makes detention in hospital for medical treatment appropriate; and, if psychopathic disorder or mental impairment is present, the court is satisfied that the treatment is likely to help the condition or stop it getting worse. The order can only be made if the court considers such an order to be the most suitable way of dealing with the case. Alternatively, the court may place the offender under the guardianship of a local authority.

Where detention in hospital is ordered by the Crown Court, and it believes the public needs to be protected from the offender, it can make an order restricting their discharge either for a specified period or without limit. A magistrates' court can make an order for detention in a hospital when an offender has been convicted of an imprisonable offence, or even if the offender has not been convicted, if the court is satisfied as to guilt.

There has been growing concern about offences committed by persons benefiting from care in the community. The case of Michael Stone was particularly distressing. He was accused of killing Lin and Megan Russell in a brutal attack in the countryside. It appears that he suffers from a severe personality disorder but could not be detained under the current legislation because his condition was not treatable. The Home Secretary therefore announced plans in 1999 to introduce new powers to detain individuals. These would allow indefinite detention without trial of dangerous persons with severe and untreatable personality disorders. A court could make a care and treatment order where a person posed a significant risk of serious harm to others as a result of their severe personality disorder.

Binding over to be of good behaviour

This order dates back to the thirteenth century and the relevant legislative provisions can be found in the Justices of the Peace Act 1361 and the Magistrates' Courts Act 1980. A binding over order can be made against any person who is before the court and has 'breached the peace' – not just the defendant, but also any witness. People who are bound over have to put up a sum of money and/or find someone else to do so, which will be forfeited if the undertaking is broken. A person who refuses to be bound over can be imprisoned, despite the fact that they may not have been convicted of any offence. The order usually lasts for a year.

Absolute and conditional discharges

If the court finds an offender guilty of any offence (except one for which the penalty is fixed by law), but believes that in the circumstances it is unnecessary to punish the person and a community rehabilitation order is inappropriate, it may discharge the defendant either absolutely or conditionally.

An absolute discharge effectively means that no action is taken at all, and is generally made where the defendant's conduct is wrong in law, but no reasonable person would blame them for doing what they did. A conditional discharge means that no further action will be taken unless the offender commits another offence within a specified period of up to three years. This order is commonly made where the court accepts that the offender's conduct was wrong as well as illegal but the mitigating circumstances are very strong. If an offender who has received a conditional discharge is convicted of another offence during the specified period, they may, in addition to any other punishment imposed, be sentenced for the original offence. A discharge does not count as a conviction unless it is conditional and the offender reoffends within the specified period.

Deferred sentences

Section 1 of the PCC(S)A 2000 allows the courts to defer passing sentence for a period of up to six months after conviction. The Act contains few guidelines on the use of this power, but does state that it can be exercised only with the consent of the offender, and where deferring sentence is in the interests of justice. The Criminal Justice Act 2003 has added that the power to defer passing sentence is only exercisable if offenders undertake to comply with any requirements as to their conduct that the court considers appropriate. Failure to comply with a requirement will result in the offender being brought back to court early for sentence. If the offender commits another offence during the deferment period the court will deal with both sentences at once.

Deferred sentences are intended for situations where the sentencer has reason to believe that, within the deferral period, the offender's circumstances will materially change, with the result that no punishment will be necessary, or that the punishment imposed should be less than it would have been if imposed at the time of conviction. For example, offenders may make reparation to the victim, settle down to employment or otherwise demonstrate that they have changed for the better.

Disqualification

 Know your terms 15.5

Define the following terms:

1 Retribution
2 Intermediate recidivist
3 Absolute discharge
4 Deferred sentence

This is most common as a punishment for motoring offences, when offenders can be disqualified from driving. Under ss. 146–7 of the PCC(S)A 2000, a court may disqualify a person from driving as a punishment for a non-motoring offence. A conviction for offences concerning cruelty to animals may also lead to disqualification from keeping pets or livestock.

Anti-social behaviour orders

Anti-social behaviour orders are civil orders issued by a court to protect the public from behaviour that causes harassment, alarm and distress. Section 1 of the Crime and Disorder Act 1998 provides that bodies such as local authorities or the police may apply under civil procedures to a court for an anti-social behaviour order (ASBO). An ASBO can also be ordered as part of a criminal sentence. The order will be made against a person aged 10 or over who has acted in an anti-social manner, that is, a manner which is likely to cause harassment, alarm or distress to someone not in the same household as the person described in the order, and who is likely to do so again. Guidance on the legislation provided by the Home Office suggests that typical behaviour which might fall within this provision includes 'serious vandalism or persistent intimidation of elderly people'. The court has power to prohibit that person from doing anything described in the order for a period of not less than two years. For example, a person could be prohibited from entering a certain geographical area. Thus, in 2002, a woman was banned from going near her local police station for three years, as she had been harassing police officers. While the ASBO is obtained using civil procedures, breach of the ASBO can give rise to the criminal sanctions of a fine or five years' imprisonment.

There has been much controversy over the way ASBOs have been used in practice. The pressure groups Liberty, the National Association of Probation Officers (Napo) and the Howard League for Penal Reform have together formed a campaign group, ASBO Concern, calling for a public review of the way anti-social behaviour orders are used. Initially, ASBOs were intended to deal primarily with anti-social behaviour by neighbours and young people, but they are increasingly being used for a wider range of problems. For example, an anti-social behaviour order was issued in 2004 against Sony Music Entertainment (UK) Ltd, to stop flyposting around the country.

A survey published by the probation officers union, NAPO, has revealed that ASBOs are being inappropriately used against the mentally ill (*Anti-Social Behaviour Orders: analysis of the first six years* (2004). As a result people who are unable to control their behaviour due to mental ill-health are being sanctioned, when treatment would actually be more effective and humane. NAPO give an example of a man who had been standing on a windowsill and moaning while pretending to dance with a Christmas tree. An ASBO was issued against him banning him from shouting, swearing and banging windows. He breached the order in August 2004, and was imprisoned for two months for continuing to moan in public. He breached the order again and was imprisoned for four months.

Forty-five per cent of ASBOs have been issued against children. Nearly half of children subject to such an order have breached it, with ten young people each week being placed in custody for breaching an ASBO. Custodial sentences are being handed down for breach of an ASBO where the triggering anti-social conduct was not actually criminal.

The local authorities and police feel that it is necessary for photographs of people sanctioned with an ASBO to be made public in order for the ASBO to be effectively enforced. Photographs have been posted on council websites, leaflets distributed and local newspapers informed. There is concern that such publicity simply stigmatizes families, could lead to a surge in vigilantism and does nothing to tackle the underlying causes of a person's anti-social behaviour. In **R (Stanley, Marshall and Kelly** *v* **Metropolitan Police Commissioner** (2004) the High Court held that the authorities were entitled to 'name and shame' people who have been subjected to an ASBO, and it did not amount to a breach of their right to a private and family life which are guaranteed by Art. 8 of the European Convention.

Appeals against sentence

The defence may appeal against a sentence considered too harsh, while the prosecution can appeal if they feel the sentence was too low. In addition, ss. 35 and 36 of the Criminal Justice Act 1988 give the Attorney-General the power to refer a case to the Court of Appeal where the sentence is believed to have been too lenient.

Task 15.6

Try to visit a Crown Court. This will give you an opportunity both to see a jury at work and to see defendants being sentenced. You can find the address of your local Crown Court by looking in a telephone directory. Alternatively, Crown Court addresses are available on the Court Service's website at: http://www.courtservice.gov.uk/HMCSCourtFinder

You are unlikely to be able to see a whole case from beginning to end as they tend to spread over several days. Near the entrance to the court will be a list of cases that are going to be heard and employees at the reception will also be able to help advise you on suitable cases to watch. Some cases will merely be concerned with sentencing an offender, who has been convicted at an earlier stage. Try to see at least one sentencing hearing as well as trying to see a case where a jury is sitting. Note that the jury are never involved in the sentencing decision. Write up a report of your visit by answering the following questions:

About the court

1 What was the name and address of the court?

2 What was the court building like? Was it old or modern? Was it clean and in good decorative order? Were the waiting areas comfortable? Was there access to refreshments? Was it easy to find your way around the building, with rooms clearly signposted and labelled?

3 Did you find the court staff helpful? Were there any explanatory leaflets available?

About the proceedings involving a jury

Choose one hearing involving a jury and answer the following questions:

1 How many men and how many women were sitting on the jury?

2 Were there any black jurors?

3 How did the jurors behave during the case?

4 Did the jurors take notes?

5 Did the jurors ask any questions?

6 Did the jurors appear to be paying attention?

7 Was the professional judge male or female?

8 What was the ethnic origin of the judge?

9 What did you think of the way the judge behaved during the case?

About the sentencing process

Choose one hearing where the offender was sentenced and answer the following questions:

1 What offence had the offender committed?

2 Was the offender male or female?

3 Approximately how old do you think the offender was?

4 Was the offender represented by a lawyer?

5 Did the court refer to a pre-sentence report?

6 Did the defence lawyer present any arguments in mitigation in favour of a lighter sentence?

7 What sentence did the offender receive?

8 How did the offender react to his or her sentence?

9 Did the judge explain the choice of sentence?

10 Do you think that the court gave the right sentence?

Write up a short oral presentation about your visit to present to the other students with whom you are studying.

Problems with sentencing

The role of the judge

We have seen that the sentence in England is traditionally a decision for the judge, which can lead to inconsistent punishments, especially among magistrates' courts. This situation clearly offends against the principle of justice that requires like cases to be treated alike.

The Government has tried to restrict judicial discretion through legislative guidelines and has also set up a Sentencing Advisory Panel, a Sentencing Guidelines Council and a Judicial Studies Board. Overseen by the Ministry for Constitutional Affairs, the Judicial Studies Board has functions that include running seminars on sentencing, which seek to reduce inconsistencies; courses for newly appointed judges; and refresher courses for more experienced members of the judiciary. The Board also publishes a regular bulletin summarizing recent legislation, sentencing decisions, research findings and developments in other countries, while the Magistrates' Association issues a *Sentencing Guide for Criminal Offences* to its members.

Other jurisdictions generally allow judges less discretion in sentencing. In the USA, for example, many states use 'indeterminate' sentencing by which a conviction automatically means a punishment of, say, one to five years' imprisonment, and the exact length of the sentence is decided by the prison authorities. However, in this country, control of sentencing is seen as an important aspect of judicial independence, and the introduction of more legislative controls has been criticized as interfering with the judiciary's constitutional position.

Racism

Critics of sentencing practice in England have frequently alleged that members of ethnic minorities are treated more harshly than white defendants. For example, in 2001, 21 per cent of the prison population was from an ethnic minority, which is significantly higher than their representation in the general population. This difference becomes much less if only UK nationals are considered, because one in four black people in prison is a foreign national, often imprisoned for illegally importing drugs. Whether these figures actually point to racial discrimination in sentencing is the subject of much debate.

What is clear from recent research is that some members of the ethnic minorities perceive the sentencing process as racist. Research undertaken in 2003 by Roger Hood and others (*Ethnic Minorities in the Criminal Courts: Perceptions of Fairness and Equality of Treatment*) investigated how far black and Asian defendants considered that they had been treated unfairly by the courts because of their race. Most complaints about racial bias concerned sentences perceived to be more severe than those imposed on a similar white defendant.

In addition to any racism in the system, the legal and procedural factors which affect sentencing may account for some of the differences in the punishment of black and white offenders. More black offenders elect for Crown Court trial and plead not guilty, which means that if convicted they would probably receive harsher sentences, because the sentences in the Crown Court are higher than those in the magistrates' court and they would not benefit from a discount for a guilty plea. Research by Flood-Page and Mackie in 1998 found that there was no evidence that black or Asian offenders were more likely than white offenders to receive a custodial sentence when all relevant factors were taken into account.

The experience of black people when in the prison system has also given rise to concern. An internal report commissioned by the Prison Service in 2000 found a blatantly racist regime at Brixton prison, where black staff as well as inmates suffered from bullying and harassment. The head of the Prison Service acknowledged that the service is 'institutionally racist' and that 'pockets of malicious racism exist'. He promised to sack all prison officers found to be members of extreme right-wing groups such as the British National Party. Prison officers' training now includes classes on race relations.

■ Sexism

There is enormous controversy over the treatment of women by sentencers. On the one hand, many claim that women are treated more leniently than men. In 2001, 19 per cent of known offenders were women. In 2003, women made up only 6 per cent of the prison population, but their numbers are growing. A Home Office study carried out by Hedderman and Hough in 1994 reported that, regardless of their previous records, women were far less likely than men to receive a custodial sentence for virtually all indictable offences except those concerning drugs, and that when they do receive prison sentences these tend to be shorter than those imposed on men. Flood-Page and Mackie also found in 1998 that women were less likely to receive a prison sentence or be fined when all relevant factors were taken into account. This has been variously attributed to the fact that women are less likely to be tried in the Crown Court; chivalry on the part of sentencers; assumptions that women are not really bad, but offend only as a result of mental illness or medical problems; and reluctance to harm children by sending their mothers to prison.

On the other hand, some surveys have suggested that women are actually treated less leniently than men. A 1990 study by the National Association for the Care and Resettlement of Offenders found that one-third of sentenced female prisoners had no previous convictions, compared with 11 per cent of men, and most of them were in prison for minor, non-violent offences. Because they are usually on lower incomes than men, women are thought more likely to end up in prison for non-payment of fines.

Several critics have suggested that women who step outside traditional female roles are treated more harshly than both men and other women. Sociologist Pat Carlen (1983) studied the sentencing of a large group of women, and found that judges were more likely to imprison those who were seen as failing in their female role as wife and mother – those who were single or divorced, or had children in care. This was reflected in the comments made by sentencers, including, 'It may not be necessary to send her to prison if she has a husband. He may tell her to stop it', and 'If she's a good mother we don't want to take her away. If she's not, it doesn't really matter.'

Today women represent the fastest-growing sector of the prison population, their numbers nearly trebled in the space of nine years from 1,300 in 1992 to 4,300 in 2002. About one-fifth of the total female prison population have been sentenced as drugs couriers and, of these, some seven out of every ten are foreign nationals (Penny Green, *Drug Couriers: A New Perspective* (1996)). HM Chief Inspector of Prisons, Sir David Ramsbotham, has commented 'There is considerable doubt whether all the women in custody [at Holloway] really needed to be there in order for the public to be protected' (*Report on Holloway Prison* (1997)). Helen Edwards, the Chief Executive of NACRO, has observed that 'the vast majority of women in prison do not commit violent offences and much of their offending relates to addiction and poverty. Prison is not an appropriate, necessary or cost-effective way of dealing with these problems.'

The needs of women prisoners have wrongly been assumed to be the same as those of men. The Chief Inspector of Prisons has emphasized that female prisoners have different social and criminal profiles, as well as different health care, dietary and other needs. The Home Office published a study of women in prison: *Women in Prison: A Thematic Review* (Ramsbotham, 1997). Their survey revealed that the great majority of women in prison come from deprived backgrounds. Over half had spent time in local authority care, had attended a special school or had been in an institution as a child. A third had had a period of being homeless, half had run away from home, half reported having suffered violence at home (from a parent or a partner) and a third had been sexually abused. Forty per cent of sentenced women prisoners had a drug dependency, and alcohol problems were also found to be very common. Almost 20 per cent had spent time in a psychiatric hospital prior to being imprisoned and 40 per cent reported receiving help or treatment for a psychiatric, nervous or emotional problem in the year before coming into prison. Nearly two in five reported having attempted suicide.

The Government has established a three-year plan, called 'The Women's Offending Reduction Programme'. This aims to increase the opportunities for tackling women's offending in the community. Each year about 17,000 children are separated from their mother when she is put into prison.

Privatisation

Criminal justice has, historically, been regarded as a matter for the state. Recently, however, first under the Conservative Government in the early 1990s, and now under Labour, various parts of the system have been privatized, including ten prisons. The Home Secretary said in 1998 that all new prisons would be privately built and run. Such moves have not generally been seen as runaway successes. Privatized prison escort services have come in for severe criticism, with prisoners managing to escape or not being brought to the court on time.

Reading on the web

The guide entitled *Restorative Justice: helping to meet local need* (2004), published by the Office for Criminal Justice Reform, is available on the Home Office website at:

http://www.homeoffice.gov.uk/documents/rj-local-needs-guidance

The report of the National Association of Probation Officers entitled *Anti-Social Behaviour Orders: analysis of the first six years*, is available on their website at:

http://www.napo.org.uk

The report of John Halliday on sentencing is available at:

http://www.homeoffice.gov.uk/documents/halliday-report-sppu

Information about the confiscation powers can be found at:

http://www.assetsrecovery.gov.uk

Question and answer guides

1 Margaret, aged 26, is charged with manslaughter and has appeared before Hattown magistrates.

(i) What are the powers of Hattown magistrates to deal with Margaret?

(ii) How may Margaret obtain funding from the Legal Services Commission?

(iii) If Margaret is convicted what sentences might be passed upon her?

Answer guide

Part (i): the information needed for this part is covered fully in Chapter 10 but essentially the powers of the magistrates concern bail and sending the case to the Crown Court for trial, since manslaughter is a crime triable only on indictment.

Part (ii): these issues are covered in Chapter 11 at pp. 210–11.

Part (iii): as we are given no details about the form of manslaughter or the circumstances, and as Margaret is an adult offender, in theory any of the sentencing options described above could be relevant. You need to outline what these options are and the criteria that would be used to decide which of these is imposed on Margaret.

2 After conviction, how do judges choose the defendant's sentence?

Answer guide

You could start your answer to this question by pointing out the important role that judges have traditionally played in sentencing in our system, highlighting the fact that although there are some mandatory sentences and now greater statutory guidance for judges, they still maintain a wide discretion in sentencing. You could then mention that there are a number of principles which are officially accepted as guiding such judicial decisions but that it is alleged that these decisions may also be affected by certain unadmitted factors, such as racism and sexism.

You can proceed to look first at the official factors that determine how judges choose a sentence. Thus you could discuss the five purposes of sentencing to which a judge must have regard when deciding a sentence under s. 142 of the Criminal Justice Act 2003. You could then move on to look at the process of sentencing, and include a discussion of the statutory guidance, the tariff system and individualized sentences. After this you could examine some of the allegations that racism and sexism also influence judges in arriving at sentencing decisions, mentioning the research studies detailed in the relevant sections in the chapter. ('London Qualifications Ltd.', accepts no responsibility whatsoever for the accuracy or method in the answers given.)

Chapter summary

The Home Office undertook a review of sentencing that was carried out by John Halliday and published in 2001. The Government accepted many of Halliday's recommendations and introduced significant reforms to the sentencing system in the Criminal Justice Act 2003.

Purposes of sentencing

Section 142 of the Criminal Justice Act 2003 states that:

> any court dealing with an [adult] offender in respect of his offence must have regard to the following purposes of sentencing –
>
> (a) the punishment of offenders,
> (b) the reduction of crime (including its reduction by deterrence),
> (c) the reform and rehabilitation of offenders,
> (d) the protection of the public, and
> (e) the making of reparation by offenders to persons affected by their offences.

Sentencing practice

In recent years there has been a considerable amount of legislation trying to control and regulate the sentencing practices of the judges.

Legislation
The legislation applies rules relating to:

- mandatory sentences
- minimum sentences
- general restrictions on sentencing
- dangerous offenders.

The tariff system
In selecting a sentence, judges rely on the tariff system. This system is based on treating like cases alike.

Types of sentence

The judge has the power to impose a wide range of sentences:

Fines
The fine is the most common sentence issued by the court, but there is a major problem with fines not being paid.

Custodial sentences
Adult offenders can be sent to prison. Some offenders will be released early on home detention curfew. The Criminal Justice Act 2003 has introduced custody plus and intermittent custody.

Community sentence
The Criminal Justice Act 2003 has established a single community order that can be applied to an offender aged 16 or over. This order can contain a range of possible requirements. These are:

- an unpaid work requirement
- an activity requirement
- a programme requirement
- a prohibited activity requirement
- a curfew requirement

▶

- an exclusion requirement
- a residence requirement
- a mental health treatment requirement
- a drug rehabilitation requirement
- an alcohol treatment requirement
- a supervision requirement, and
- an attendance centre requirement (where the offender is aged under 25).

Miscellaneous sentences

A range of other sentences is also available to the court. These include:

- compensation orders
- confiscation and civil recovery orders
- mental health orders
- binding over to be of good behaviour
- absolute and conditional discharges
- deferred sentences
- disqualification
- anti-social behaviour orders.

Appeals against sentence

The defence may appeal against a sentence considered too harsh, while the prosecution can appeal if they feel the sentence was too low.

Problems with sentencing

The role of the judge

There has been concern that there is inconsistency in sentencing.

Racism

Critics of sentencing practice in England have frequently alleged that members of ethnic minorities are treated more harshly than white defendants.

Sexism

There is enormous controversy over the treatment of women by sentencers.

Privatisation

Criminal justice has, historically, been regarded as a matter for the state. Recently, however, various parts of the system have been privatized, including ten prisons.

Chapter 16 Sentencing young offenders

Introduction

Sentencing for young offenders has always posed a dilemma: should such offenders be seen as a product of their upbringing and have their problems treated, or are they to be regarded as bad, and have their actions punished? Over the past couple of decades, sentencing policy has swung between these two views. In 1969, the Labour Government took the approach that delinquency was a result of deprivation, which could be 'treated', and one of the aims of the Children and Young Persons Act (CYPA) of that year was to decriminalize the offending of young people. Instead of going through criminal proceedings, they would be handed over to the social services, under either a supervision order or a care order, the latter giving the social services the power to take the young person into some form of custody. The magistracy constantly fought against this approach and, when a Conservative Government was elected in 1970, it declined to bring much of the Act into force and the care order provisions have now been repealed.

The opposite approach introduced by the Conservatives led to the UK having a higher number of young people locked up than any other West European country, but reconviction rates of 75–80 per cent suggested that this was benefiting neither the young offenders themselves, nor the country as a whole.

The philosophy behind the Criminal Justice Act 1982 was that the sentencing of young people should be based on the offence committed and not on the offender's personal or social circumstances, or the consequent chances of reform. This succeeded in lowering the level of detention for young offenders, and the Criminal Justice Act 1991 continued this approach for young persons, and extended it to adults.

Much of the legislation contained in the previous chapter on sentencing is relevant also to young offenders. In this chapter we look at particular areas of law which are specific to sentencing young offenders.

Custodial sentences

Currently, the courts may not pass a sentence of imprisonment on an offender under the age of 18. Such offenders may be detained in other places, such as a young offenders' institution or local authority accommodation, but in order to pass a sentence of this kind, the court must satisfy the same conditions as for adults (discussed in Chapter 14) and in some cases additional criteria as well.

There has been a rapid increase in the number of people under the age of 18 sentenced or remanded to custody. Between June 1993 and 2001 this number had significantly increased from 1,300 to 2,300.

The quality of the custodial accommodation has on occasion given rise to concern. For example, large sums of money have been spent developing the Feltham young offenders' institution near Heathrow Airport. It is now the largest such institution in the United Kingdom with places for 900 young offenders. In 1999 Sir David Ramsbotham was Her Majesty's Chief Inspector of Prisons. He reported that the conditions in Feltham 'were unacceptable in a civilised society'. As the inspector makes clear in a blistering report, the problem was not one of lack of resources, but of staff attitudes and management. This is exemplified by the Inspectorate finding two cases of appalling bedding conditions while there were new and unused mattresses being held in storage. Cell and common areas were dilapidated, dirty and cold. Bedding and linen were unwashed and in a poor state of repair. Despite ample stocks of available clothing in the central stores, the personal clothing provision was pitifully inadequate. All meals had to be taken not in dining rooms but in dirty cells with filthy toilets. Most of the youngsters were locked up for 22 hours a day. A 16-year-old boy who had been on the unit for three months told the inspector: 'I have nothing to do. I get hungry and there's nothing to distract me. If I get depressed, I talk to the chaplain and ask him to pray for me. Most of the time I sleep. My mum's not home during the day and I'm not allowed to phone her in the evening.' The report concluded that 'there were too many examples of distant and disinterested staff throughout the institution who were palpably failing to meet the health and welfare needs of the young people in their charge'. Sir David Ramsbotham has gone as far as describing the conditions in some institutions as 'institutionalised child abuse'.

In response to such criticism the Prison Service is currently seeking to produce a discrete juvenile secure estate within the Prison Service. This approach has already been criticized by the Youth Justice Board in *Creating a Vision for the Secure Juvenile Estate* (1999). It considers that, in order to create a caring, safe and secure environment for young people in custody, institutions should have no more than 150 inmates, while the Prison Service has in mind large facilities with up to 400 places.

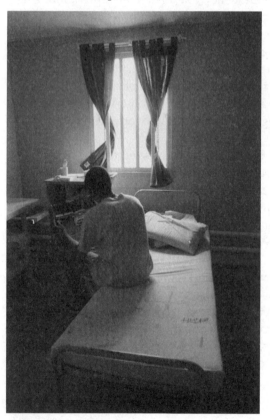

Figure 16.1 Feltham young offenders' institution

Source: © EMPICS.

The Audit Commission (2004) has concluded that placing young offenders in custody is the most expensive and least effective way of tackling crime. Eighty-four per cent of young offenders reconvict within two years after their release from custody.

Task 16.1

Look at the diagram and then answer the questions below.

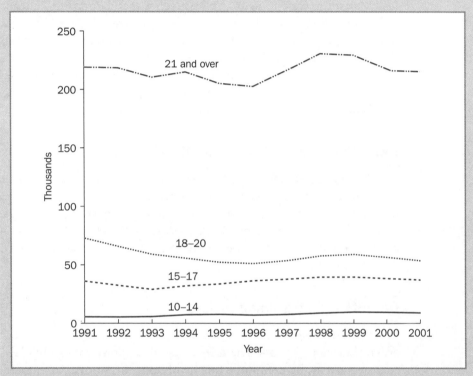

Figure 16.2 Persons sentenced for indictable offences, by age, 1991–2001

Source: Home Office (2002), *Criminal Statistics England and Wales 2001*, p. 78, Figure 7.1.

Questions

1 Which age group is most likely to be given an immediate custodial sentence?

2 Why do you think that people in the above age group are more likely to receive an immediate custodial sentence?

3 Between 1996 and 1998 which age group showed the greatest increase in the use of custodial sentences?

Detention 'during Her Majesty's pleasure'

Under s. 90, PCC(S)A 2000, an offender convicted of murder who was under 18 when the offence was committed must be sentenced to be detained indefinitely, known as 'during Her Majesty's pleasure'.

This form of sentence was considered by the House of Lords in **R** *v* **Secretary of State for the Home Department, ex parte Venables and Thompson** (1997). The two applicants had been convicted of the murder of James Bulger. They were 10 years old at the time of the offence and were given a sentence of detention during Her Majesty's pleasure. The Home Secretary received several petitions signed by thousands of people demanding that the boys serve at least 25 years in custody. In 1994 the Home Secretary, applying the same procedures to children detained at Her Majesty's pleasure as to adults given a mandatory life sentence, decided that the minimum sentence that they should serve was 15 years. The case was taken to the European Court of Human Rights. In **T** *v* **United Kingdom** and **V** *v* **United Kingdom** the court held that it was not compatible with the Convention for the Home Secretary to set tariffs in the case of detention during Her Majesty's pleasure. In response to this finding, the Criminal Justice and Court Services Act 2000 makes provision for the sentencing court to set the tariff in these cases.

Detention under PCC(S)A 2000, s. 91

The PCC(S)A 2000, s. 91, provides that where a person aged 10 or over has been convicted in the Crown Court of an offence with a maximum sentence of 14 years' imprisonment or more, the court may pass a sentence not exceeding that maximum.

Under the Crime (Sentences) Act 1997, s. 28, the Home Secretary must release on licence a life prisoner who was under 18 at the time of the offence when directed to do so by the Parole Board.

Detention and training orders

The only custodial sentence available in the youth court is a detention and training order of up to two years. The use of custody against young children is particularly controversial as, by definition, this involves their removal from their family. Under s. 100 of the PCC(S)A 2000, the courts can make a detention and training order against offenders aged between 12 and 17. Such an order must be for a term of between four and 24 months. Half this period will be spent in detention and the other half under supervision. The detention period can be served in any secure accommodation deemed suitable by the Home Secretary, for example a young offenders' institution, secure training centre, youth treatment centre or local authority secure unit. The order will be available initially for offenders aged at least 12, but the Secretary of State has power to extend it to 10- and 11-year-olds. The sentence of detention in a young offenders' institution will remain available for offenders aged 18 to 20 years.

The privately run Medway Secure Training Centre in Kent was completed in 1998 in order to detain 12- to 14-year-olds. This has places for 40 trainees. As the children detained are very young, it is important that they can maintain links with their families during their detention. Many will be detained far away from home and there will be an assisted visits scheme financed by the Home Office for visits on a weekly basis and arrangements for contact through letters and telephone calls. The

Figure 16.3 European Court of Human Rights in Strasbourg
Source: John Edward Linden/Arcaid.

training and education programmes will include education for 25 hours a week based on the national curriculum, one hour daily for tackling offending behaviour and crime avoidance, regular practical tuition in social skills and domestic training. There will also be the opportunity to acquire and develop interests to occupy leisure time while in custody and after release.

It is debatable whether it is necessary to impose custodial sentences on children by means of a detention and training order. The vast majority of crime committed by this age group is minor property offences, and for more serious cases s. 91 of the PCC(S)A 2000 still applies. Given the problems associated with custodial sentences, putting young persons at risk of custody for more minor offences may not be effective in crime reduction in the long term.

▋ The tariff

Because the maximum custodial sentences for young offenders are usually quite short, the tariff approach described in the chapter on sentencing is of limited application to the sentencing of young offenders, except in the sense that young offenders can usually rely on their youth as strong mitigation.

341

Referral orders

Most young offenders appearing before a youth court for the first time are given a mandatory referral to a youth offender panel if they plead guilty. This order was created by the Youth Justice and Criminal Evidence Act 1999, and the relevant legislative provisions are now contained in s. 16 of the PCC(S)A 2000. Referral orders are automatically made for first-time convictions where the offence is imprisonable, the sentence is not fixed by law and a custodial sentence is not appropriate. The court has a discretion to make a referral order if the defendant has pleaded guilty to a single non-imprisonable offence and this is their first conviction. The youth offender panel agrees a 'programme of behaviour' with the young offender, the primary aims of which are the prevention of reoffending and restorative justice (in other words, that the offender pays back the victim or society in some way). Once agreed, the terms of the programme of behaviour are written in a youth offender contract. This may require the offender, among other things, to compensate financially or otherwise victims or other people whom the panel consider to have been affected by the offence; to attend mediation sessions with victims; to carry out unpaid work in the community or to observe prescribed curfews. The order is administered by the local youth offending team (mentioned on p. 293). Subsequent meetings will be arranged with the panel to review compliance with the contract and a final meeting will determine whether the contract has been satisfactorily completed.

It is hoped that this procedure will prove more effective than the traditional court-sentencing process, which the Home Secretary has criticized in Parliament, saying:

> [T]he young offender is, at best, a spectator in a theatre where other people are the actors. At worst, the young offender is wholly detached and contemptuous of what is going on . . . never asked to engage his brain as to what he has done, or why he hurt the victim.

In many ways the sentence provides the young offender with a second chance. They can admit their guilt knowing what sentence they will receive. Their future employment prospects are not unduly damaged as the offence is deemed spent on the completion of the sentence so that they do not have a criminal record.

Reparation orders

Under s. 73 of the PCC(S)A 2000 a court can hand down a reparation order requiring an offender under the age of 18 to make reparation commensurate with the seriousness of the offence, to the victim or to the community at large. Before making such an order, the court must obtain a report as to what type of work is suitable for the offender and the attitude of the victim or victims to the proposed requirements (s. 74, PCC(S)A 2000). Guidance from the Home Office indicates that the order may require the writing of a letter of apology to the victim, help to be given in repairing damage caused by the offending conduct, the cleaning of graffiti, weeding a garden, collecting litter or doing other work to help the community. The work required must not exceed 24 hours over a period of three months. Most importantly, the order may require a meeting with the victim in an attempt to make the offender understand the emotional and physical damage their actions have caused. For example, a burglar frequently thinks that a burglary will merely require the victim to make an insurance claim. They do not realize the fear and pain it actually causes, partly because traditionally the criminal justice system has been very impersonal. Reparation orders try to personalize the system, by putting offenders face to face with victims, forcing them to see the pain they have caused. The order may be combined with a compensation order if the court considers that financial compensation would also be appropriate. These orders are part of a system of restorative justice, and are becoming increasingly important in the youth justice system.

In the 1998 British Crime Survey, 60 per cent of respondents approved of the concept of reparation orders, though only 40 per cent would be prepared to meet the offender. The orders not only help to rehabilitate criminals, but also help victims and their families come to terms with their feelings of fear and anger caused by the crime and give them positive input into the process of getting the offender to make amends. A small pilot study carried out in Thames Valley found that the young offenders who met the victims in controlled mediation sessions were half as likely to reoffend as those who were given police cautions. In Australia, where restorative justice is practised more widely, there has been a 38 per cent reduction in reoffending after violent criminals met their victims.

Community sentences

A range of youth community orders has been developed to tackle the problem of young offenders.

Supervision orders

These are applied to offenders aged between 10 and 16, and require a probation officer or social services department to supervise the offender for up to three years. The order is basically a junior version of probation, except that a stronger emphasis is placed on assisting the personal development of the young person; it was introduced by the Children and Young Persons Act 1969 to replace community rehabilitation orders for young offenders. The consent of a young person to a basic supervision order is not required.

As with community rehabilitation orders, the supervisor must assist, advise and befriend the offender. Schedule 6 to the PCC(S)A 2000 lays down certain requirements that can be included as part of a supervision order. The young offender can be ordered to live in specified accommodation, attend a particular place, take part in set activities, or any combination of the three, for up to 180 days. The purpose of such requirements is to remove young persons from their home environment and make them take part in challenging activities – these might include rock climbing, pot-holing or even simply attending a local youth club. Youth court magistrates, after consultation with the supervisors, can also specify activities which the offender should not participate in; for this, consent must be obtained from the young person and a parent or guardian. A young offender of compulsory school age can be ordered to comply with arrangements for their education.

If an offender breaches a requirement in a supervision order and the supervisor brings this to the court's attention, the court may change the order, fine the offender up to £100, or make an attendance centre order. If the young offender has reached the age of 17, the court may discharge the order and pass a new sentence for the original offence.

Young offenders over 16 may be made subject to a community rehabilitation order.

▍Attendance centre orders

An offender under 25 convicted of an imprisonable offence may be ordered to go to an attendance centre for a specified number of hours spread over a certain period of time. The number of hours of attendance that may be ordered is not less than 12 (unless the offender is under 14 and 12 hours seems excessive), and not more than 24 in the case of those under 16, and 36 for those aged 16 to 25. Breach of an attendance centre order may result in the offender being sentenced again for the original offence. The centres are normally run by the police, and tend to involve attendance on Saturday afternoons for physical education classes or practical courses. Unless there are special circumstances, such an order should not be made if the offender has previously been sentenced to detention in a young offenders' institute.

▍Curfew orders

A court can impose a curfew order with electronic monitoring of up to six months on an offender under the age of 16 years. Compliance with the curfew order can be monitored through the use of an electronic tag. The use of electronic tagging on young offenders was piloted in two schemes, the results of which were not particularly promising. In Manchester 39 per cent of young offenders breached the curfew order. The majority of the offenders spent their time at home watching more television or sleeping. There is also a danger that some children will wear their tags with pride, seeing them as trophies to be shown off to their peers.

Under the Anti-social Behaviour Act 2003 curfews can be imposed on whole neighbourhoods. The curfew can ban for a specified period children under 16 from being in a public place between 9 pm and 6 am unless they are accompanied by an adult. A police officer who has reasonable cause to believe a child to be in contravention of the ban may inform the local authority of the contravention and take the child home. To date, the police have imposed 150 local curfews, which cover large parts of the country including much of central London. These are the first curfews we have seen in Britain since the Second World War. No other European country imposes curfews on young people. A 14-year-old boy is currently challenging the legality of one such curfew in Richmond as a breach of his human rights.

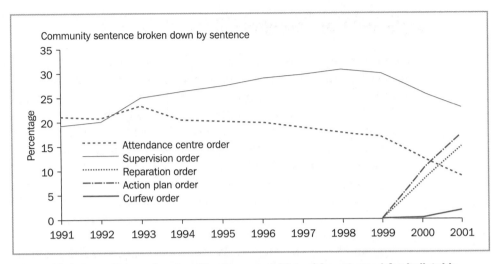

Community sentence broken down by sentence

- - - - - - Attendance centre order
———— Supervision order
·············· Reparation order
—·—·—·— Action plan order
———— Curfew order

Figure 16.4 Percentage of male offenders aged 10 to 14 sentenced for indictable offences who received community sentences, broken down by sentence, 1991–2001
Source: Home Office (2002), *Criminal Statistics England and Wales 2001*, p. 95, Figure 7.10.

Exclusion orders

These are discussed in Chapter 14.

Action plan orders

Action plan orders were introduced in 1998 and are now contained in s. 69 of the PCC(S)A 2000. They are tailored to address the cause of the young person's offending behaviour with the aim of securing the rehabilitation of the offender or the prevention of further offending. Under such an order, a young offender under the age of 18 who is convicted of an offence will be placed under supervision for a maximum of three months and obliged to comply with a series of requirements with respect to his/her actions and whereabouts for a specified period. The Home Office guidance lists examples of requirements to include attendance at anger-management classes, motor-education projects, drug or alcohol misuse programmes, or specified remedial educational classes. The action plan order cannot be combined with a custodial sentence or any other community sentence.

Quick quiz 16.2

1 At what age can a person be sent to prison?

2 What sentence is given to a person under 18 who is convicted of murder?

3 What is a detention and training order?

4 If a young offender, before the court for the first time, pleads guilty, what sentence is he or she likely to receive?

Parents of young offenders

Where a young offender is under 16, a parent or guardian must be required to attend the court hearing, unless the court considers that this would be unreasonable. If the offender is convicted, the court is required to bind over the parents to take proper care and exercise proper control over their child; the courts also have discretion to do this in the case of 16- or 17-year-olds. Although the consent of the parents is required, an unreasonable refusal can attract a fine of up to £1,000. Parents or guardians can also be bound over to ensure that the young offender complies with a community order (s. 150, PCC(S)A 2000).

Where an offender under 16 is sentenced to a fine, the parents are required to pay it. The court may also order parents to pay in the case of 16- and 17-year-old children. The fine will be assessed taking into account the financial situation of the parent, rather than the young offender. Where a local authority has parental responsibility for a young person who is in their care, or has provided accommodation for them, it is to be treated as the young person's parent for these purposes.

In 1997 the Home Office published a study *Women in Prison: A Thematic Review.* It noted that when fines for juvenile offences are imposed on the parent or guardian, this is usually in practice the mother, often alone, and coping in difficult circumstances. If she does not (or cannot) pay the fine, she runs the risk of imprisonment. The report gives the example of Margaret, aged 46 and on income support. She had to pay fines imposed as a result of her son's criminal offences (he was then 16). Magistrates sentenced her to 27 days' imprisonment for a remaining debt of £170.50, despite the fact that she had not personally committed any crime.

Individual support order

Sections 322 and 323 of the Criminal Justice Act 2003 create an individual support order. This order can be made after an anti-social behaviour order (see p. 328) has been issued against a person under 18. The individual support order may require the young person to undertake activities to tackle the underlying causes of their anti-social behaviour.

Child safety orders

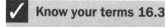

Know your terms 16.3

Define the following terms:

1 Referral order
2 Action plan order
3 Curfew order
4 Child safety order

A local authority can commence civil proceedings for a child safety order to be made by a magistrates' court under ss. 11–13 of the Crime and Disorder Act 1998. It can require children under the age of 10 to be at home at specified times or to avoid certain people or places to limit the risk of their involvement in crime. The order can be made if the child has committed or risks committing an act which would have constituted an offence if the child had been older, he or she has breached a curfew notice or has behaved in an anti-social manner. The aim of this order is to divert children below the age of 10 from behaviour that would bring them into conflict with the criminal law. The child will be placed under the supervision of a social worker or member of a youth offending team for up to three months (and exceptionally 12 months), and the child will be required to comply with the requirements in the order. These requirements are not specified in the Act and are whatever the court considers desirable in the interests of securing that the child receives appropriate care, protection and support and is subject to proper control, and to prevent the repetition of the offending behaviour. It is targeting those children who are 'running wild' but are too young to be the subject of criminal proceedings. Where longer-term intervention is required, care proceedings will be brought by the local authority instead, with a care order continuing until the child becomes an adult. If the child safety order is breached, care proceedings may also be brought.

Parenting orders

Under s. 8 of the Crime and Disorder Act 1998, a court may make a parenting order. The order is designed to help and support parents (or guardians) in addressing their child's anti-social behaviour. It is available in seven situations:

1 A court makes a referral order.
2 A court makes a child safety order.
3 A court makes a sex-offender order against a young person.
4 A court makes an anti-social behaviour order against a young person.
5 A young person has been convicted of an offence.
6 A parent has been convicted for failing to secure their child's attendance at school.
7 A young person has been excluded from school.

The order can be for a maximum of 12 months and consists of two elements. First, the parent will have to attend counselling or guidance sessions for up to three months. Secondly, the parent must comply with certain specific requirements aimed at ensuring that they exercise control over their child. Following the passing of the Anti-social Behaviour Act 2003, this may take the form of a residential course if this is likely to be more effective than a non-residential course and the interference with family life is proportionate. Parents convicted of failing to comply with a parenting order are liable to a fine.

Nearly 3,000 parents participated in 34 parenting programmes across England and Wales between 1999 and 2001. The Youth Justice Board has found that parenting programmes aimed at giving parents support and advice in child rearing reduced reoffending by the children by one-third. They have concluded that while the introduction of these programmes was controversial, they actually provide a powerful way to reach parents who need help and who might otherwise never attend a parenting support service.

Parenting contracts

Under the Anti-social Behaviour Act 2003, s. 25, parenting contracts can be made with youth offending teams or local education authorities. These are designed to

Table 16.1 **New sentences made under the Crime and Disorder Act 1998 between 1998 and 2001**

Type of order	Pilot sites			Live sites	
	1998	1999 (to end May)	2000	2000 (June–Dec)	2001
Action plan order	63	618	274	4,086	8,663
Reparation order	132	907	360	3,673	8,036
Parenting order	5	242	15	352	640
Drug treatment and testing order	5	172	60	262	4,260

Source: Home Office (2002), *Criminal Statistics England and Wales 2001*, p. 96, Table 7F.

provide support for parents when their children are beginning to display anti-social or criminal behaviour, and are intended to prevent the young person from engaging in criminal conduct. This is a voluntary agreement and there is no penalty for its breach.

Reading on the web

Research carried out for the Home Office on referral orders (*Youth Justice: the Introduction of Referral Orders into the Youth Justice System*, 2001 (RDS Occasional Paper No. 70)) is available on the Home Office website:

http://www.homeoffice.gov.uk/rds/pdfs2/hors242.pdf

Question and answer guide

1   **Moira, aged 15, has been seen by a police officer attacking an old man. He arrests her and she is later prosecuted and convicted for the offence of causing grievous bodily harm. What sentence could she receive?**

Answer guide

The material on the general restrictions on sentencing laid down on p. 308 of the previous chapter is relevant here. As to the specific sentences that can be passed, starting with the most serious, custodial sentences, note that Moira cannot be sent to prison; she can only be sentenced to a young offenders' institution. As regards a community sentence, supervision orders and attendance centre orders are specific to young offenders, but the other forms of community sentences discussed in the previous chapter are also relevant here. The sentence actually imposed on an individual young offender is often shorter than for an adult. If a fine were imposed, it would have to be paid by Moira's parents. You might also want to mention the fact that her parents may themselves be subject to sanctions such as being bound over.

Chapter summary

Custodial sentences

The courts may not pass a sentence of imprisonment on an offender under the age of 18. Such offenders may be detained in other places, such as a young offenders' institution or local authority accommodation.

Detention 'during Her Majesty's pleasure'

Under s. 90, PCC(S)A 2000, an offender convicted of murder who was under 18 when the offence was committed must be sentenced to be detained indefinitely, known as 'during Her Majesty's pleasure'.

Detention under s. 91, PCC(S)A 2000

Where a person aged 10 or over has been convicted in the Crown Court of an offence with a maximum sentence of 14 years' imprisonment or more, the court may pass a sentence not exceeding that maximum.

Detention and training orders

Under s. 100, PCC(S)A 2000 the courts can make a detention and training order against offenders aged between 12 and 17. Half the sentence will be spent in detention and the other half under supervision.

Community sentences

Community sentences that have been developed to tackle the problem of young offenders include:

- referral orders
- supervision orders
- attendance centre orders
- curfew orders
- reparation orders, and
- action plan orders.

Parents of young offenders

Certain powers exist to coerce parents to take responsibility for the offending conduct of their children.

Chapter 17

The civil justice system

Introduction

The civil justice system is designed to sort out disputes between individuals or organizations. One party, known as the claimant, sues the other, called the defendant, usually for money they claim is owed or for compensation for a harm to their interests. Typical examples might be the victim of a car accident suing the driver of the car for compensation, or one business suing another for payment due on goods supplied. The burden of proof is usually on the claimant, who must prove his or her case on a balance of probabilities – that it is more likely than not. This is a lower standard of proof than the 'beyond reasonable doubt' test used by the criminal courts and, for this reason, it is possible to be acquitted of a criminal charge yet still be found to have breached the civil law. This happened to the celebrity O.J. Simpson in America who, having been acquitted of murdering his ex-wife and her friend by the criminal courts, was successfully sued in the civil courts for damages by the victim's family.

Major changes have been made to the civil justice system in recent years. After the Civil Justice Review of 1988, reforms were made by the Courts and Legal Services Act 1990. Following continued criticism of the civil justice system, the previous Conservative Government ten years later appointed Lord Woolf to carry out a far-reaching review of the civil justice system. Lord Woolf's inquiry was the sixty-third such review in a hundred years. Lord Woolf made far-reaching recommendations in his report, *Access to Justice*, which was published in 1996. As with the Civil Justice Review, his aim was to reduce the cost, delay and complexity of the system and increase access to justice. Most of his recommendations were implemented in April 1999.

The civil courts

There are two main civil courts which hear civil cases at first instance. These are the county courts and the High Court. There are currently around 300 county courts concerned exclusively with civil work. About 170 of them are designated as divorce county courts and, thereby, have jurisdiction to hear undefended divorces and cases concerning adoption and guardianship.

The High Court is divided into three divisions: the Queen's Bench Division, the Family Division and the Chancery Division. These act in practice as separate courts, with judges usually working within one division only. Lord Woolf recommended that these divisions should remain. The Family Division hears cases concerning marriage, children and the family, such as divorce, adoption and wills. The Chancery Division deals with matters of finance and property, such as tax and bankruptcy. The Queen's Bench Division is the biggest of the three, with the most varied jurisdiction. The major part of its work is handling those contract and tort cases which are unsuitable for the county courts (see below). Sitting as the Divisional Court of the Queen's Bench, its judges also hear certain criminal appeals (originating primarily from the magistrates' courts) and applications for judicial review. High Court judges usually sit alone, but the Divisional Court is so important that two or three judges sit together.

Trials in the High Court are heard either in London or in one of the 26 provincial trial centres. In theory, they are all presided over by High Court judges, but in fact there are not enough High Court judges to cope with the case load. Some cases, therefore, have to be dealt with by circuit judges and others by barristers sitting as part-time, temporary, deputy judges.

Following the Woolf reforms, trial centres have been identified, headed by a Designated Civil Justice. They report to the Head of Civil Justice, a position currently held by Sir Anthony Clarke.

Although most civil cases are dealt with by either the county courts or the High Court, magistrates' courts have a limited civil jurisdiction, and some types of cases are tried by tribunals.

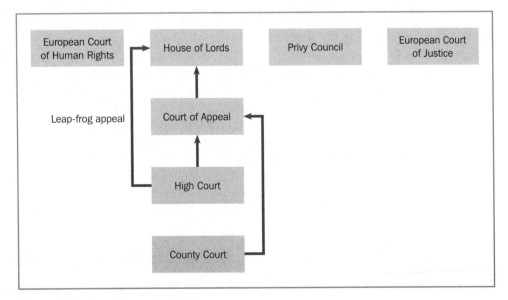

Figure 17.1 The civil court system

Quick quiz 17.1

1 What is the burden of proof in civil cases?

2 What major piece of legislation followed the Civil Justice Review of 1988?

3 What is the name of Lord Woolf's final report on the civil justice system?

4 Name the three divisions of the High Court.

The civil justice system before April 1999

Before the implementation of the Woolf reforms, there were two separate sets of civil procedure rules: the Rules of the Supreme Court in the 'White Book' for the High Court and the Court of Appeal, and the County Court Rules in the 'Green Book' for the county courts. High Court actions were started with a writ, county court ones by a summons, but there were also specialized procedures which required specific documents and formalities to be used. These documents were served on the defendant to a case, and informed the person that an action was being brought against him/her. The rules on serving documents were fairly restrictive and ignored modern modes of communication. Defendants had to acknowledge service. The claimant served a statement of claim if bringing an action in the High Court, or particulars of a claim in the county court. Both were formal pleadings which outlined the facts and legal basis of the action and the remedy sought. The defendant responded with a defence. Either party could request more details from the other, in a document known as 'a request for further and better particulars'. These would then be supplied. Each party provided the other with a list of the documents which they had in relation to the action. The parties could ask to see some or all of this material, a process known as discovery. The trial was conducted along adversarial lines, with each side calling its own witnesses and cross-examining those of the other. As in a criminal hearing, judges relied on the parties to present the evidence, rather than making their own investigations.

The case could be settled out of court at any point in the civil process. The defendant could at any time during the process make a payment into court, which the plaintiff (since 1999 called the claimant) could accept as settlement of the claim. If the plaintiff did not accept it, the process continued as before, but if the case continued to trial and the plaintiff won but was awarded less than the sum paid in, the plaintiff had to pay the defendant's costs from the time of the payment in.

Problems with the civil justice system before April 1999

In his report, *Access to Justice* (1996), Lord Woolf identified a range of problems with the civil justice system.

Too expensive

Research carried out for Lord Woolf's review found that one side's costs exceeded the amount in dispute in over 40 per cent of cases where the claim was for under £12,500. The bill for one claim of just £2,000 came to £69,295. The survey concluded that the simplest cases often incurred the highest costs in proportion to the value of the claim.

Because of the complexity of the process, lawyers were usually needed, making the process expensive. The sheer length of civil proceedings also affected the size of the bill at the end.

Delays

Research carried out for Lord Woolf found the worst delays in personal injury and medical negligence cases, with these actions taking an average time of 54 and 61 months respectively. The average waiting time for a county court claim was 79 weeks. Time limits were laid down for every stage of an action but both lawyers and the courts disregarded them. Often time limits were waived by the lawyers to create an opportunity to negotiate, which was reasonable, but the problem was that there was no effective control of when and why it was done. The High Court's long vacation (the two months during the summer when the judges do not sit) also contributed to delay.

Injustice

Usually an out-of-court settlement is negotiated before the litigants ever reach the trial stage. An out-of-court settlement can have the advantage of providing a quick end to the dispute, and a reduction in costs. But out-of-court settlements can be unfair – see the discussion on this subject at p. 367.

The adversarial process

Many problems resulted from the adversarial process which encouraged tactical manoeuvring rather than cooperation. It would have been far simpler and cheaper for each side to state precisely what it alleged in the pleadings, disclose all the documents it held, and give the other side copies of its witness statements. Attitudes did appear to be slowly changing, with a growing appreciation that the public interest demanded justice be provided as quickly and economically as possible. Some of the procedural rules, for example on expert witnesses, were changed and there was less scope for tactical manoeuvring.

Emphasis on oral evidence

Too much emphasis was placed on oral evidence at trial. This may have been appropriate when juries were commonly used in civil proceedings, but in the twentieth century much of the information the judge needed could be provided on paper and read before the trial. Oral evidence slowed down proceedings, adding to cost and delays.

The civil justice system after April 1999

On 26 April 1999 new Civil Procedure Rules and accompanying Practice Directions came into force. The new rules apply to any proceedings commenced after that date. They constitute the most fundamental reform of the civil justice system in the twentieth century, introducing the main recommendations of Lord Woolf in his final report, *Access to Justice*. He described his proposals as providing 'a new landscape for civil justice for the twenty-first century'.

The Woolf Report was the product of two years' intensive consultation, and was written with the help of expert working parties of experienced practitioners and academics. The recommendations of the Report received universal support from the senior judiciary, the Bar, the Law Society, consumer organizations and the media. In 1996, Sir Richard Scott was appointed as Head of Civil Justice with responsibility for implementing the reforms. The Civil Procedure Act 1997 was passed to implement the first stages of the Woolf Report. Following its election to office, the Labour Government set up its own review of the civil justice system and of Lord Woolf's proposed reforms. It quite reasonably wanted a second opinion before adopting the policies of its predecessors on those issues. The review was chaired by Sir Peter Middleton and took four months to complete. The final report was essentially in favour of implementation of Lord Woolf's proposals. Middleton's report placed an emphasis on the financial implications of the proposals and in particular the opportunities for cost-cutting. In November 1998, an intensive period of training for judges and court staff began, to prepare them for the changes, while the Treasury made available an additional £2 million to implement the reforms.

The reforms aim to eliminate unnecessary cost, delay and complexity in the civil justice system. The general approach of Lord Woolf is reflected in his statement: 'If "time and money are no object" was the right approach in the past, then it certainly is not today. Both lawyers and judges, in making decisions as to the conduct of litigation, must take into account more than they do at present, questions of cost and time and the means of the parties.' Lord Woolf has said that the reforms should lead to a reduction in legal bills by as much as 75 per cent, though it might also mean that some lawyers would lose their livelihoods.

The ultimate goal is to change fundamentally the litigation culture. Thus, the first rule of the new Civil Procedure Rules lays down an overriding objective which is to underpin the whole system. This overriding objective is that the rules should enable the courts to deal with cases 'justly'. This objective prevails over all other rules in case of a conflict. The parties and their legal representatives are expected to assist the judges in achieving this objective. The Woolf Report heavily criticized practitioners, who were accused of manipulating the old system for their own convenience and causing delay and expense to both their clients and the users of the system as a whole. Lord Woolf felt that a change in attitude among the lawyers was vital for the new rules to succeed. According to rule 1.1(2):

Dealing with a case justly includes, so far as is practicable –

a. ensuring that the parties are on an equal footing;

b. saving expense;

c. dealing with the case in ways which are proportionate –

    i. to the amount of money involved;

    ii. to the importance of the case;

    iii. to the complexity of the issues; and

    iv. to the financial position of each party;

d. ensuring that it is dealt with expeditiously and fairly; and

e. allotting to it an appropriate share of the Court's resources, while taking into account the need to allot resources to other cases.

The emphasis of the new rules is on avoiding litigation through pre-trial settlements. Litigation is to be viewed as a last resort, with the court having a continuing obligation to encourage and facilitate settlement. Lord Woolf had observed that it was strange that, although the majority of disputes ended in settlement, the old rules had been mainly directed towards preparation for trial. Thus the new rules put a greater emphasis on preparing cases for settlement rather than a trial.

The new approach to civil procedure will now be examined in more detail.

Quick quiz 17.2

1 Summarize three problems that existed with the civil justice system before April 1999.

2 When did the new Civil Procedure Rules come into force?

3 What is the overriding objective contained in the first rule of the new Civil Procedure Rules?

4 Before 1999 a person bringing an action was called a plaintiff. What is such a person called now?

Civil Procedure Rules

The Lord Chancellor appointed the Civil Procedure Rules Committee to produce and maintain one unified procedural code for both the county court and the High Court. This produced the new Civil Procedure Rules which came into force in April 1999 and replaced the Rules of the Supreme Court and the County Court Rules. The new rules are simpler than their predecessors, providing a broad framework of general application rather than detailed rules covering every contingency. These framework rules are then fleshed out by a number of Practice Directions. There has been an attempt to write the rules in plain English, replacing old-fashioned terminology with more accessible terms. Lord Woolf hoped that the change in language would help to support a change in attitude, away from a legalistic, technical interpretation of words designed to give one party an advantage over their opponent, towards an attitude which was open and fair according to the overriding objective of the new rules.

While the new rules introduce some radical changes to the civil justice system, they also inherit much from the old system. In outline, the procedure is as follows. Before proceedings are commenced, claimants should send a letter to the defendants warning them that they are considering bringing legal proceedings. Almost all proceedings then start with the same document, called a claim form. This replaces the writ for the High Court and the summons for the county court, and other specialist documents. The procedure for starting an action is thus undoubtedly simpler than under the old system. The claim form informs the defendant that an action is being brought against them. When claimants are making a claim for money, they must provide a statement as to the value of the claim in the claim form.

The Practice Direction supplementing Part 7 of the new Civil Procedure Rules (*How to start proceedings – the Claim Form*) specifies in which court proceedings should be started. For non-personal injury actions, a claim may be started in the High Court where the claimant expects to recover more than £15,000 (this limit is expected to be raised to £50,000 in the near future). For personal injury actions, a claim can only be started in the High Court where the claimant expects to recover at least £50,000 for pain, suffering and loss of amenity.

The claim form is served on the defendant to a case. The methods of service have been liberalized to reflect modern modes of communication, including the use of fax and emails. Service will normally be carried out by the court through postage by first class post, unless a party notifies the court that they will serve the documents. Defendants must acknowledge service. The claimant (known before 1999 as the plaintiff) must then serve on the defendant the particulars of claim (previously called the statement of claim in the High Court).

The defendant should respond within 14 days by filing either an acknowledgement of service or a defence with the court. If the defendant fails to do either of these within that period of time, the claimant can enter judgment in default against the defendant (r. 12.3). The mechanics of pleading a defence are now regulated more strictly. Defendants may no longer simply deny an allegation, but must state their reasons for the denial and, if they intend to put forward a different version of events from that given by the claimant, then they must state their own version.

If the defendant files a defence, the court will serve an allocation questionnaire on each party (r. 24.4(1)). This is designed to enable the court to allocate each claim to one of the three tracks discussed at p. 361.

The disclosure procedures (previously known as discovery) are then followed, as discussed below. Either party may seek more details from the other, through a 'request for information'. This procedure merges the old system of interrogatories and requests for further and better particulars. The new rules adopt an amended version of the payment into court procedures discussed at p. 352, which are now called 'Part 36 payments'. If the case is not settled out of court, the case proceeds to trial.

The different formal documents are described as the statement of case, while in the past they were called the pleadings. All statements of case must be verified by a statement of truth. This is a statement signed by the claimant (or his/her legal representative) in the following words: 'I believe that the facts stated in these particulars of claim are true.' The purpose of such a statement is to prevent parties from

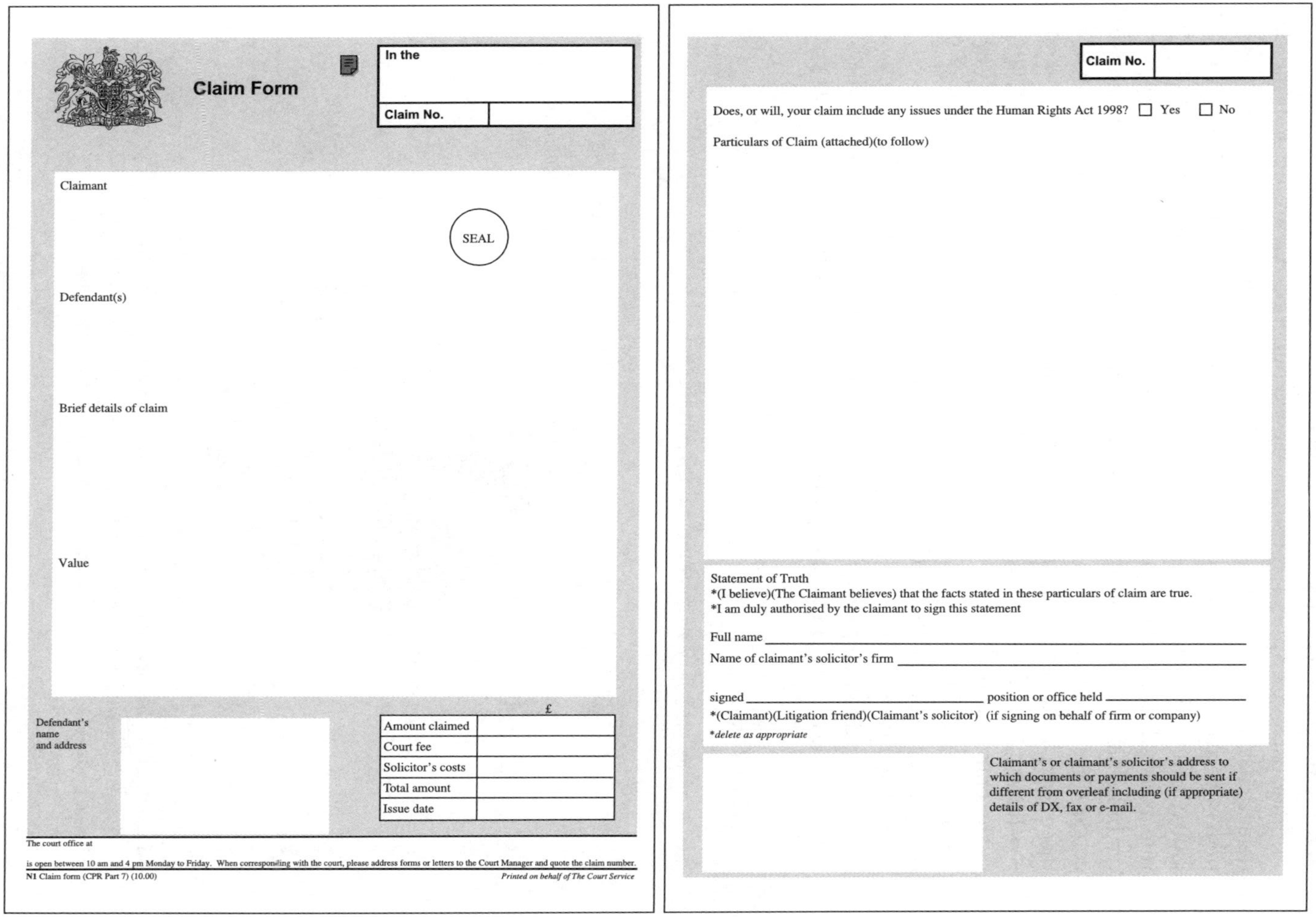

Claim Form

In the

Claim No.

Claimant

Defendant(s)

Brief details of claim

Value

SEAL

Defendant's
name
and address

	£
Amount claimed	
Court fee	
Solicitor's costs	
Total amount	
Issue date	

The court office at

is open between 10 am and 4 pm Monday to Friday. When corresponding with the court, please address forms or letters to the Court Manager and quote the claim number.

N1 Claim form (CPR Part 7) (10.00)

Printed on behalf of The Court Service

Claim No.

Does, or will, your claim include any issues under the Human Rights Act 1998?   ☐ Yes   ☐ No

Particulars of Claim (attached)(to follow)

Statement of Truth
*(I believe)(The Claimant believes) that the facts stated in these particulars of claim are true.
*I am duly authorised by the claimant to sign this statement

Full name

Name of claimant's solicitor's firm

signed _____ position or office held _____

*(Claimant)(Litigation friend)(Claimant's solicitor) (if signing on behalf of firm or company)

*delete as appropriate

Claimant's or claimant's solicitor's address to
which documents or payments should be sent if
different from overleaf including (if appropriate)
details of DX, fax or e-mail.

Figure 17.2 A claim form

Source: Court Service website at www'.mcsi.gov.uk.

putting in facts for purely tactical purposes which they have no intention of relying upon. If a party makes a false statement in a statement of case verified by a statement of truth, the party will be guilty of contempt of court (r. 28.14).

Either party can apply for a summary judgment on the ground that the claim or defence has no real prospect of success. The court can also reach this conclusion on its own initiative. At any stage of the proceedings the parties can enter into 'without prejudice' negotiations to try and settle the dispute out of court. The without prejudice rule makes all negotiations genuinely aimed at settlement, whether oral or in writing, inadmissible in evidence at any subsequent trial. The rule lets litigants make whatever concessions or admissions are necessary to achieve a compromise, without fear of these being held against them if negotiations break down and the case goes to court. It is hoped that this will help and encourage the parties to settle their disputes early.

The emphasis of the new procedural rules is to encourage an early settlement of proceedings. A MORI poll of 100 solicitors carried out in 2000 found that 76 per cent of solicitors believed that the reforms had increased the chances of an early settlement. The majority felt that the reforms had cut the amount of litigation. Between May 1999 and January 2000 there was a 25 per cent reduction in the number of cases issued in the county courts compared with the same period the previous year.

 Task 17.3

Look at the diagram and answer the questions that follow.

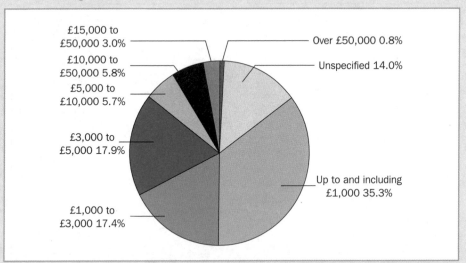

Figure 17.3 County Court claims issued by amount of claim, 2004[1]

1. Figures are based on three months' sample data from selected county courts

Source: K. Dibdin, A. Sealy and S. Aktar, *Judicial Statistics Annual Report 2004*, p. 48.

Questions

1 In 2004, which types of cases were the most likely to be heard by the county court?

2 Which types of cases were least likely to be heard by the county court?

Table 17.1 **Changes in terminology**

Old term	New term
Writ	Claim form
Discovery	Disclosure
Plaintiff	Claimant
Statement of claim	Particulars of claim
Payment into court procedures	Part 36 procedures

Pre-action protocols

The pre-trial procedure is perhaps the most important area of the civil process, since few civil cases actually come to trial. To push the parties into behaving reasonably during the pre-trial stage, Lord Woolf recommended the development of pre-action protocols to lay down a code of conduct for this stage of the proceedings. The pre-action protocols that have been produced to date cover such areas of practice as personal injury, medical negligence and housing cases. They were developed in consultation with most of the key players in the relevant fields, including legal, health and insurance professionals. They are a major innovation and aim to encourage:

- more pre-action contact between the parties;
- an earlier and fuller exchange of information;
- improved pre-action investigation;
- a settlement before proceedings have commenced.

They strive to achieve this through establishing a timetable for the exchange of information, by setting standards for the content of correspondence and by providing schedules of documents that should be disclosed along with a mechanism for agreeing a single joint expert. The pre-action protocols seek to encourage a culture of openness between the parties. This should lead to the parties being better informed as to the merits of their case so that they will be in a position to settle cases fairly, and thereby reduce the need for litigation. If settlement is not reached, the parties should be able to proceed to litigation on a more informed basis. Pre-action protocols should also enable proceedings to run to timetable, and efficiently, if litigation proves to be necessary.

Compliance with a pre-action protocol is not compulsory, but if a party unreasonably refuses to comply, then this can be taken into account when the court makes orders for costs. It may be that these protocols will need 'sharper teeth' in order to be effective.

Alternative dispute resolution

At various stages in a dispute's history, the court will actively promote settlement by alternative dispute resolution (ADR). For a detailed discussion of ADR in the English legal system, see Chapter 19. There is a general statement in the new rules that the court's duty to further the overriding objective by active case management includes both encouraging the parties to use an alternative dispute resolution procedure (if the court considers that appropriate) and facilitating the use of that procedure (r. 1.4(2)(e)). Also, when filling in the allocation questionnaire, the parties can request a one-month stay of proceedings while they try to settle the case by ADR or other means (r. 26.4). The parties will have to show that they genuinely attempted to resolve their dispute through ADR and have not just paid lip-service to the idea, as has been the tendency in the past.

Case management

This is the most significant innovation of the 1999 reforms. Case management means that the court will be the active manager of the litigation. The main aim of this approach is to bring cases to trial quickly and efficiently. Traditionally, it has been left to the parties and their lawyers to manage the cases. The new rules firmly place the management of a case in the hands of the judges, with r. 1.4 emphasizing that the court's duty is to take a proactive role in the management of each case. The judges are given considerable discretion in the exercise of their case management role. Lord Woolf does not feel that this will undermine the adversarial tradition, but he sees the legal professions fulfilling their adversarial functions in a more controlled environment.

Once proceedings have commenced, the court's powers of case management will be triggered by the filing of a defence. When the defence has been filed and case management has started, the parties are on a moving train, trial dates will be fixed and will be difficult to postpone, and litigants will not normally be able to slow down or stop the case unless they settle. The court first needs to allocate the case to one of the three tracks: the small claims track, the fast track or the multi-track (r. 24.6(1)), which will determine the future conduct of the proceedings. To determine which is the appropriate track, the court will serve an allocation questionnaire on each party. The answers to this questionnaire will form the basis for deciding the appropriate track. When considering the allocation questionnaire, the judge will determine whether a case should be subject to summary judgment, or whether a stay of proceedings should be given for ADR; and if neither of these matters applies, whether an allocation hearing should be called or whether the matter can be the subject of a paper determination of the allocation to a particular track.

Quick quiz 17.4

1 What is the name of the document used to commence civil proceedings?

2 If a person wishes to bring an action for £25,000 compensation for a head injury, which court will normally hear the case?

3 What happens if a party does not comply with a pre-action protocol?

4 Under the system of case management, who controls the progress of a case through the civil justice system?

The three tracks

The court allocates the case to the most appropriate track depending primarily on the financial value of the claim, but other factors that can be taken into account include the case's importance and complexity (r. 26.6). Normally:

- small claims track cases deal with actions with a value of less than £5,000;
- fast-track cases deal with actions of a value between £5,000 and £15,000;
- multi-track cases deal with actions with a value higher than £15,000.

The three tracks will now be considered in turn.

The small claims track

The handling of small claims is largely unchanged by the Woolf reforms. In the small claims track, directions will be issued for each case providing a date for the hearing and an estimate of the hearing time, unless the case requires a preliminary hearing appointment to assist the parties in the conduct of the case. This track was previously known as the small claims court, though it was never actually a separate court, but a procedure used by county courts to deal with relatively small claims. It was introduced in response to a report from the Consumers' Association in 1967 which claimed that county courts were being used primarily as a debt-collection agency for businesses: 89.2 per cent of the summonses were taken out by businesses and only 9 per cent by individuals, who were put off by costs and complexity.

Established in 1973, this special procedure aims to provide a cheap, simple mechanism for resolving small-scale consumer disputes. Disclosure is dispensed with and if the litigation continues to trial, it is usually held in private rather than in open court. The hearing is simple and informal, with few rules about the admissibility or presentation of evidence. No experts may be used without leave. It is usually a very quick process, with 60 per cent of hearings taking less than 30 minutes. Costs are limited except where, by consent, a case with a financial value such that it would normally be allocated to the fast track was allocated to the small claims track. The procedure is designed to make it easy for parties to represent themselves without the aid of a lawyer, and state funding for representation is not available. Under the Lay Representatives (Rights of Audience) Order 1992 made under s. 11 of the Courts and Legal Services Act 1990, a party can choose to be represented by a lay person, though the party must also attend.

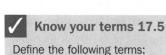

Know your terms 17.5

Define the following terms:

1 Queen's Bench Division
2 The Woolf Report
3 Pre-action protocol
4 Case management

The fast track

Fast-track cases will normally be dealt with by the county court. Upon allocation to the fast track, the court gives directions for the management of the case, and sets a timetable for the disclosure of documents, the exchange of witness statements, the exchange (and number) of expert reports, and the trial date or a period within which the trial will take place, which will be no more than 30 weeks later (compared to an average of 80 weeks before 1999).

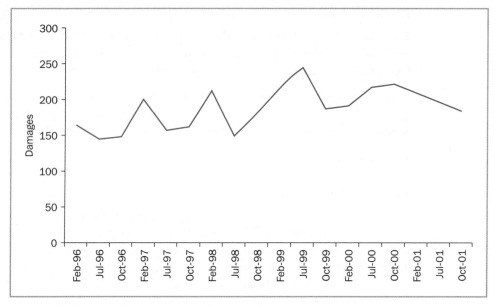

Figure 17.4 Small claims – average time from issue to hearing

Source: Department for Constitutional Affairs (2002), *Civil Justice Reform Evaluation Further Findings*, Figure 12.

A Practice Direction gives an example of a typical timetable that a court may give:

■ disclosure: 4 weeks
■ exchange of witness statements: 10 weeks
■ exchange of experts' reports: 14 weeks
■ hearing: 30 weeks.

Although the parties can vary certain matters by agreement, such as disclosure or the exchange of witness statements, the rules are quite clear that an application must be made to court if a party wishes to vary the date for the trial.

Under this track the maximum length of the trial is normally one day. The relevant Practice Direction states that the judge will normally have read the papers in the trial bundle and may dispense with an opening address. Witness statements will usually stand as evidence in chief. Oral expert evidence will be limited to one expert per party in relation to any expert field and expert evidence will be limited to two expert fields.

In an attempt to keep lawyers' bills down, fixed costs for fast-track trials have been introduced, but the introduction of pre-trial fixed costs has been delayed until additional information is available to inform the development of the revised costs regime. Lord Woolf had recommended that there should be a £2,500 limit on costs for fast-track cases (though clients could enter a written agreement to pay more to their solicitors). Apart from the trial itself, litigants are still committing themselves to open-ended payment by the hour, which Lord Woolf described as being equivalent to handing out a blank cheque. He observed: 'If you and I are having our house repaired, we don't do it on a time and materials basis, because we know it will be a disaster. There is no incentive for the builder to do it in the least time and do it with the most economical materials.'

The multi-track

Upon allocation to the multi-track, the court can give directions for the management of the case and set a timetable for those steps to be taken. Alternatively, for heavier cases, the court may fix a case management conference or a pre-trial review or both. Unlike the fast track, the court does not at this stage automatically set a trial date or a period within which the trial will take place. Instead it will fix this as soon as it is practicable to do so. Thus, this track offers individual case management with tailor-made directions according to the needs of the case. Only the High Court hears multi-track cases.

A proactive approach

Gone are the days when the court waited for the lawyers to bring the case back before it or allowed the lawyers to dictate without question the number of witnesses or the amount of costs incurred. In managing litigation, the court must have regard to the overriding objective, set out in Part 1 of the Woolf Report, which is to deal with cases justly. To fulfil this key objective of the reformed civil justice system, the court is required to:

- identify the issues at an early stage;
- decide promptly which issues require full investigation and dispose summarily of the others;
- encourage the parties to seek alternative dispute resolution where appropriate;
- encourage the parties to cooperate with each other in the conduct of the procedures;
- help the parties to settle the whole or part of the case;
- decide the order in which issues are to be resolved;
- fix timetables or otherwise control the progress of the case;
- consider whether the likely benefits of taking a particular step will justify the cost of taking it;
- deal with a case without the parties' attendance at court if this is possible;
- make appropriate use of modern technology;
- give directions to ensure that the trial of a case proceeds quickly and efficiently.

Disclosure

Before the 1999 reforms, disclosure was known as 'discovery'. The procedure used to involve each party providing the other with a list of all the documents which they had in relation to the action. The parties could then ask to see some or all of this material. The process could be time-consuming and costly. Pre-action disclosure was also available in claims for personal injury and death. Lord Woolf recommended that disclosure should generally be limited to documents which were readily available and which to a 'material extent' adversely affected or supported a party's case, though this could be extended for multi-track cases. This change would have altered significantly the disclosure process and risked going against the philosophy of openness between the parties generally advocated by Lord Woolf. He also favoured extending pre-action disclosure to be available for all proceedings and against people who would not have been parties to the future proceedings. However, the new Civil Procedure Rules are actually very similar to the old rules. These require the disclosure of documents on which they rely or which adversely affect or support a party's case. It is not necessary for this impact to be to a 'material extent'. As under the old rules, additional disclosure will be ordered where it is 'necessary in order to dispose fairly of the claim or to save costs'. The availability of pre-action disclosure was not extended despite the fact that the Civil Procedure Act 1997 provided for its extension. The pre-action protocols are designed to ensure voluntary disclosure is made between likely parties. It seems that the Government wishes to see how the pre-action protocols operate in practice before implementing such changes.

▌Sanctions

Tough rules on sanctions give the courts stringent powers to enforce the new rules on civil procedure to ensure that litigation is pursued diligently. The two main sanctions are an adverse award of costs, and an order for a case or part of a case to be struck out. These sanctions were available under the old rules, but the novelty of the new regime lies in the commitment to enforce strict compliance. There is an increasing willingness of the courts to manage cases with a stick rather than a carrot. The courts can treat the standards set in the pre-action protocols as the normal approach to pre-action conduct and have the power to penalize parties for non-compliance.

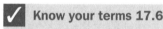 **Know your terms 17.6**

Define the following terms:

1 Adversarial process
2 Multi-track
3 Fast track
4 Disclosure

One of the most significant changes to the civil system made by the Woolf reforms concerned the approach to legal costs. Under the old system there was a basic principle that the loser paid the winner's costs. This principle was only departed from in exceptional circumstances. Although this principle still exists under the new system, it is now treated only as a starting point which the court can readily depart from. Where a party has not complied with court directions, particularly as to time, that party can be penalized by being ordered to pay heavier costs or by losing the right to have some or all of his/her costs paid.

A party who fails to comply with the case timetable or court orders may be struck out. The court has power to strike out a party's statement of case, or part of it where there has been a failure to comply with a rule, practice direction or court order (r. 3.4). This power can be exercised on an application from a party, or on the court's own initiative. Mere delay will be enough in itself to deprive a party of the power to bring or defend an action.

It is up to the defaulting party to apply for relief from sanctions, using the procedure contained in r. 3.9. This is dramatically different from the previous state of affairs where a party in default of a court order was not the subject of any sanction unless the innocent party brought the matter to the court's attention.

Where, during the trial, any representative of a party incurs costs as a result of the representative's own improper, unreasonable or negligent conduct, he or she will not receive payment for those wasted costs. A wasted costs order is essentially a power to 'fine' practitioners who incur the disapproval of the court.

Computerization

The civil courts are in the process of introducing a new computer system. Once it is up and running it is intended that the courts will move from a paper-based system to one where many communications take place electronically. For example, evidence and statements will be exchanged by email.

Money Claim Online

In 2002 Money Claim Online (MCOL) was established. It provides a debt recovery service over the Internet for sums up to £100,000. The debts might be for unpaid goods or services, or rent arrears, for example. Claimants can issue money claims via the Internet at **www.moneyclaim.gov.uk**. Fees are paid electronically by debit or credit card. The defence can use the online service to acknowledge service and file a defence. Most debt claims are undefended and if no defence is filed then the claimant can apply online for a judgment and enforcement. The parties can use the website to check the progress of their case, such as whether a defence has been filed. The service is available 24 hours a day, seven days a week. The new service has proved very popular with creditors, who have issued thousands of claims to date using the new service.

Task 17.7

Read the following extract from Lord Woolf's Report, *Access to Justice*, and answer the questions that follow.

The principles
I have identified a number of principles which the civil justice system should meet in order to ensure access to justice. The system should:
(a) be *just* in the results it delivers;
(b) be *fair* in the way it treats litigants;
(c) offer appropriate procedures at a reasonable cost;
(d) deal with cases with reasonable *speed*;
(e) be *understandable* to those who use it;
(f) be *responsive* to the needs of those who use it;
(g) provide as much *certainty* as the nature of particular cases allows; and
(h) be *effective*, adequately resourced and organised.

The basic reforms
The **interim report** set out a blueprint for reform based on a system where the courts with the assistance of litigants would be responsible for the management of cases. I recommended that the courts should have the final responsibility for determining what procedures were suitable for each case; setting realistic timetables; and ensuring that procedures and timetables were complied with.

The recommendations in my final report, together with the new code of rules, form a comprehensive and coherent package for the reform of civil justice. Each contributes to and underpins the others. Their overall effectiveness could be seriously undermined by piecemeal implementation. My overriding concern is to ensure that we have a civil justice system which will meet the needs of the public in the twenty first century.

(Adapted from Lord Woolf's report, *Access to Justice*)

Questions

1 What is the goal that Lord Woolf hopes his reforms will achieve?

2 One of the principles on which Lord Woolf thinks a civil justice system should be based is that it offers 'appropriate procedures at a reasonable cost'. How far do you think the issue of cost should be taken into account when trying to achieve justice?

3 What is meant by an 'interim report'?

4 Lord Woolf was anxious that his reforms should not be undermined by piecemeal implementation. Has this proved to be a problem?

Criticism of the civil justice system

The transition

The 1999 reforms have generally been very well received, though the immediate transition obviously caused some tensions. There had been fears that the 'big bang' of the implementation would explode into chaos. Sir Richard Scott VC admitted to the Association of Personal Injury Lawyers that the start date had been 'too soon' and had caused something 'approaching panic stations'. Small firms in particular were not able to master the new rules before their implementation as they were only available in December 1999 and amendments continued to be made in the subsequent months. A major irritation for practitioners has been the fact that since the launch of the new Civil Procedure Rules they have been continually amended and extended. A large number of new Practice Directions have been issued and practitioners have found it difficult to keep up with the pace of change. But the explosion never happened; instead there was a rather eerie silence as many lawyers delayed bringing litigation, preferring to wait until others had taken the plunge. There was a huge upsurge of work before 'Woolf day' on 26 April with 360 old-style writs being issued in the High Court on the last Friday of the old system and then a dramatic drop afterwards, with only four claim forms being issued on 26 April. The *Judicial Statistics* published in 2002 show that there has been a significant drop in the number of cases reaching the courts since the Woolf reforms were introduced. The number of claims lodged in the county court in 2002 were down by 7 per cent on the previous year.

Standards

A pilot simulation carried out by civil litigators on behalf of the Lord Chancellor's Department to try and predict the impact of the Woolf reforms on the civil justice system was not encouraging (*Report of the Fast Track Simulation Pilot*, Lord Chancellor's Department Research Secretariat (1998)). Those involved expressed the fear that pressures on practitioners in terms of both time and costs might lead to corner-cutting, devolution of cases to less-experienced fee earners, insufficient time for proper investigation of the claim, and the incurring of irrecoverable costs. They worried too that the openness that Lord Woolf was so keen to encourage as a fundamental principle underlying his reforms might be prejudiced by the 'fear factor'. In other words, solicitors might be secretive during the early stages of the litigation in order to avoid client criticism and potential negligence claims; and be reluctant to tell a client about the weakness of a case.

Enforcement

The enforcement of judgments continues to be a problem. Research carried out by Professor John Baldwin (2003) of Birmingham University has highlighted this weakness in the civil justice system. He concluded that the difficulties with enforcing civil judgments was leaving many claimants disillusioned with the legal system. The danger is that if the system of enforcement is not improved, creditors will look to other methods of securing payment.

Out-of-court settlements

The use of pre-action protocols and claimant offers to encourage pre-trial settlements has diverted cases from being litigated in the courts. As a result only 8 per cent of cases listed for trial settle at the trial, while 70 per cent settle much earlier. The reforms put considerable emphasis on the use of out-of-court settlements which can have the advantage of providing a quick end to the dispute, and a reduction in costs. For the claimant, a settlement means they are sure of getting something, and do not have to risk losing the case altogether and probably having to pay the other side's costs as well as their own. But they must weigh this up against the chances of being awarded a better settlement if the case goes to trial and they win. The defendant risks the possibility that they might have won and therefore had to pay nothing, or that they may be paying more than the judge would have awarded had the claimant won the case, against the chance that the claimant wins and is awarded more than the settlement would have cost.

The high number of out-of-court settlements creates injustice, because the parties usually hold very unequal bargaining positions. In the first place, one party might be in a better financial position than the other, and therefore under less pressure to keep costs down by settling quickly.

Secondly, as Galanter's 1984 study revealed, litigants can often be divided into 'one-shotters' and 'repeat players'. One-shotters are individuals involved in litigation for probably the only time in their life, for whom the procedure is unfamiliar and traumatic; the case is very important to them and tends to occupy most of their thoughts while it continues. Repeat players, on the other hand, include companies and businesses (particularly insurance companies), for whom litigation is routine. They are used to working with the law and lawyers and, while they obviously want to win the case for financial reasons, they do not have the same emotional investment in it as the individual one-shotter. Where a repeat player and a one-shotter are on opposing sides – as is often the case in personal injury litigation, where an individual is fighting an insurance company – the repeat player is likely to have the upper hand in out-of-court bargaining.

A third factor was highlighted by Hazel Genn's 1987 study of negotiated settlements of accident claims. She found that having a non-specialist lawyer could seriously prejudice a client's interests when an out-of-court settlement is made. A non-specialist may be unfamiliar with court procedure and reluctant to fight the case in court. They may, therefore, not encourage their client to hold out against an unsatisfactory settlement. Specialist lawyers on the other side may take advantage of this inexperience, putting on pressure for the acceptance of a low settlement. Repeat players are more likely to have access to their own specialist lawyers, whereas, for the one-shotter, finding a suitable lawyer can be something of a lottery, since they have little information on which to base their choice.

Clearly, these factors affect the fairness of out-of-court settlements. In court, the judge can treat the parties as equals, but for out-of-court negotiations one party often has a very obvious advantage.

The Government's first evaluation of the new Civil Procedure Rules has found that overall the reforms have been beneficial: *Emerging Findings: an early evaluation of the Civil Justice Reforms* (2001). It seems that cases are settling earlier, rather than at the door of the court. Lawyers and clients are now regarding litigation as a last resort, and making more use of alternative methods of dispute resolution. The pre-action protocols have been a success. Their effect has been to concentrate the minds of defendants and make them deal properly with a claim at the early stages rather than months after the issue of proceedings (conditional fee agreements could also be an explanation for this). While generally cases are being heard more quickly after the issue of the claim, small claims are taking longer. But the picture is not quite as straightforward as it looks. Lawyers know that as soon as they issue the claim form they will lose control of the pace of the negotiations and are going to be locked into timetables and procedures which they may find burdensome as well as costly. There is evidence that lawyers are therefore delaying issuing the claim. It is not yet clear whether litigation has become cheaper. The report quotes practitioners who believe the front-end loading of costs caused by the pre-action protocols means that overall costs have actually gone up

In their research paper, *More Civil Justice: the impact of the Woolf reforms on pre-action behaviour* (2002), the Law Society and the Civil Justice Council assessed the success of the new pre-action procedures. Most of the respondents were positive about their introduction. In particular, personal injury practitioners and insurers have welcomed the additional information the protocol requires be disclosed during the early stages of proceedings, as it facilitates early settlement.

▍Court appointed experts

Court appointed experts may tend to increase cost in that the parties will often still employ their own experts.

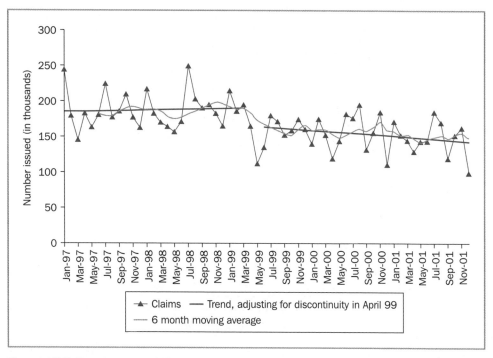

Figure 17.5 County court claims

Source: Department for Constitutional Affairs (2002), *Civil Justice Reform Evaluation Further Findings*, Figure 1.

Small claims track

The small claims procedure is an important part of the civil procedure system, involving around 80,000 actions each year. The procedure is quicker, simpler and cheaper than the full county court process, which is helpful to both litigants and the overworked court system. It gives individuals and small businesses a useful lever against creditors or for consumer complaints. Without it, threats to sue over small amounts would be ignored on the basis that going to court would cost more than the value of the debt or compensation claimed. Public confidence is also increased, by proving that the legal system is not only accessible to the rich and powerful. The academic, John Baldwin, has carried out research into the small claims track, *Lay and Judicial Perspectives on the Expansion of the Small Claims Regime* (2002). It noted that the official statistics show that the recent rises in the small claims limit have not led, as many feared, to the county courts being inundated with new cases. There has been only a slight increase in the number of small claims cases. Most small claims litigants involved in relatively high-value claims are satisfied with the experience. However, there are long-standing concerns about the small claims procedure, which have not been tackled by the 1999 reforms. Small claims are not necessarily simple claims; they may involve complex and unusual points of law. Is the small claimant entitled to be judged by the law of the land or by speedier, more rough-and-ready concepts of fairness?

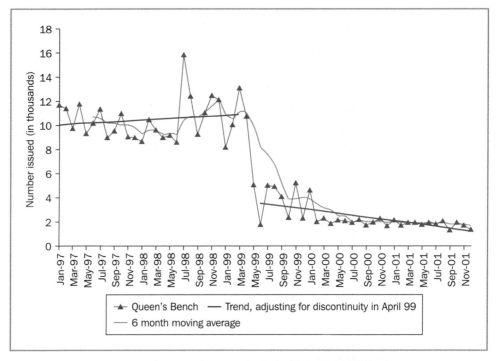

Figure 17.6 Claims in the Queen's Bench Division of the High Court

Source: Department for Constitutional Affairs (2002), *Civil Justice Reform Evaluation Further Findings*, Figure 2.

The Consumers' Association magazine is of the view that the small claims procedure is not simple enough. It reported in 1986 that the process was still 'quite an ordeal', and the level of formality varied widely. The submissions of both the National Consumer Council and the National Association of Citizens' Advice Bureaux to the Civil Justice Review echoed this feeling. The Civil Justice Review recommended that court forms and leaflets should be simplified. The system is still largely used by small businesses chasing debtors, rather than by the individual consumer for whom it was set up. A consultation paper was issued in 1995 suggesting that, in limited cases, the judge might be given the power to award an additional sum of up to £135 to cover the cost of legal advice and assistance in the preparation of the case. If this reform were to be introduced it might assist individual consumers to bring their cases.

There are also problems with enforcement. A survey by the Lord Chancellor's Department in 1986 found that 25 per cent of parties were failing to get the payment owed to them from the defendant following a successful application. A report by the Consumers' Association (November 1997) suggests that many people using the small claims procedure are being denied justice because of slow and inefficient enforcement procedures. The court is not responsible for enforcement, which is left to the winning party to secure. The report found that only a minority of defendants paid up on time and that after six months a substantial minority of people still had not paid their debts. The report's author, Professor John Baldwin, concluded that the enforcement problem was so serious that it threatened to undermine the small claims procedure itself by deterring people from using it.

The Government is currently considering raising the financial level of personal injury cases that can be considered by the small claims procedures from £1,000 to £5,000. The Better Regulation Taskforce (an independent advisory body established in 1997) published a report *Better Routes to Redress* (2004). This suggested that the government should consider raising the limits for personal injury cases to bring them into line with most other civil claims, which can already be considered by the small claims court when they involve claims of up to £5,000. The Taskforce suggested that the reform would 'increase access to justice for many as it will be less expensive, less adversarial and less stressful'. The Government is concerned that procedures and costs should be proportionate to the size of the claim.

At the moment most personal injury cases are heard under the fast track procedure which means costs can be recovered and lawyers can represent clients on a no-win, no-fee basis. If the financial limits were changed about 70 per cent of personal injury cases would be heard by the small claims procedure. On the small claims track, court costs cannot be recovered and lawyers are not able to represent clients on a no-win, no-fee basis. Litigants would therefore frequently be forced to represent themselves. The Association of Personal Injury Lawyers has argued that personal injury cases are complex and people want and need the help of a lawyer to prepare their case. The person being sued is likely to have been insured and will benefit from the specialist help of the insurers lawyers.

Baldwin's research (2002) concluded that the informal small claims procedures inevitably involve a sacrifice in the standards of judicial decision making. He questioned whether this could be justified in claims involving more than the existing fiancial limits.

Compensation culture

There has been some concern that the UK might be developing a compensation culture, which has historically been associated with the USA. A compensation culture implies that people with frivolous and unwarranted claims bring cases to court with a view to making easy money. The phenomenon of a more litigious society can be interpreted in two very different ways. It can be seen as a good thing because more people are asserting their rights and obtaining stronger legal protection. At the same time it can be seen as a bad thing because the law is pushing people into relationships which lack trust and creating confrontational communities.

The Lord Chancellor has concluded that the UK does not have an unhealth compensation culture (accident claims actually fell by 10 per cent in 2004), but the increased number of threats to sue and the resulting fear of being sued is having a negative effect on people's work and behaviour, and this trend needs to be reversed. In 2004 he commented:

> If you have a genuine claim – where someone else is to blame – you should be able to get compensation from those at fault. This is only fair. The victim or taxpayer shouldn't have to pay out where someone else is to blame. But there is not always someone else to blame.

Genuine accidents do happen. People should not be encouraged to always 'have a go' however meritless the claim. The perception that there is easy money just waiting to be had – the so-called 'compensation culture' – creates very real problems. People become scared of being sued; organizations avoid taking risks and stop perfectly sensible activities. It creates burdens for those handling claims and critically it also undermines genuine claims.

The Government is concerned that the problems relating to a compensation culture are being aggravated by the unscrupulous sales tactics of some claims management companies which encourage people who have suffered minor personal injuries to bring litigation. Advertisements are frequently broadcast on television asking the viewers if they have suffered an accident in the last three years. A report on the issue, *Better Routes to Redress* was published in 2004. This recommended that stronger guidelines regarding appropriate advertisements needed to be issued, and the claims management companies needed to be more carefully regulated. However, it did feel that these companies and advertisements should be allowed to continue, as they helped improve access to legal services by spreading information about the services available and the ways that these could be paid for. The Government has decided that claims management companies need to be regulated and relevant provisions are contained in the Compensation Bill currently before Parliament.

The insurers, Norwich Union, have suggested a radical solution to the compensation culture, of abolishing all claims for under £1,000 (*A Modern Compensation System: moving from concept to reality* (2004)). The Law Society has rejected this suggestion, pointing out that denying people their right to seek compensation for claims under

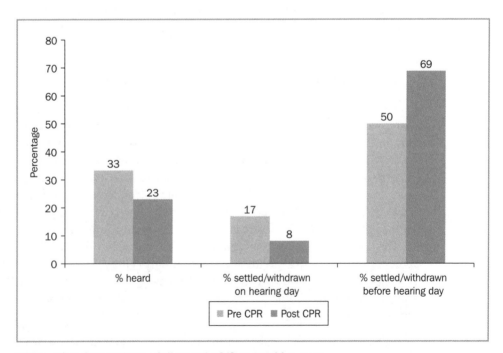

Figure 17.7 Comparison of disposal of 'fast track' cases

Source: Department for Constitutional Affairs (2002), *Civil Justice Reform Evaluation Further Findings*, Figure 6.

£1,000 would prevent the courts from getting to the root cause of injuries and falsely assumes that a loss of £1,000 is a trivial matter.

The Bar Council is concerned that plans to allow private companies to own law firms (see p. 145) would fuel the move towards a compensation culture, as such companies would seek to stimulate demand for legal services to increase profits. The legal sector could as a result become more commercialized with franchising, national brand-building and more television advertising.

Professor Zander's concern

Professor Zander (1998), a leading academic, felt that the reforms were fundamentally flawed, rather than prone to temporary hiccups, and was very vociferous in expressing his opposition to the reforms prior to their implementation. He is reported to have said that they amounted to taking a sledgehammer to crack a nut. Below is an analysis of the main concerns he has expressed.

The causes of delay

Lord Woolf's view was that the chief cause of delay was the way the adversary system was played by the lawyers. Zander has criticized this analysis, pointing out that it is only supported by 'unsubstantiated opinion' rather than real evidence, despite the fact that it forms the basis for most of the subsequent proposals. By contrast, Zander has drawn attention to research carried out for the Lord Chancellor's Department in 1994 into the causes of delay. It identified seven causes: the type of case; the parties; the judiciary; court procedures; court administration; the lawyers

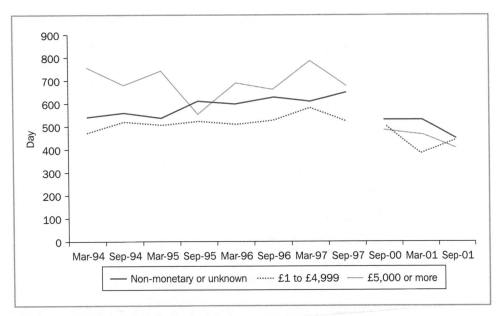

Figure 17.8 Trials – average time from issue to trial by claim value

Source: Department for Constitutional Affairs (2002), *Civil Justice Reform Evaluation Further Findings*, Figure 10.

(mainly due to pressure of work, inexperience or inefficiency); and external factors, such as the difficulty of getting experts' reports including medical reports. Of these seven factors, the last two factors were felt to be the most significant. Not all the reasons for the delay were the fault of the system; for example, in some cases it may be necessary to wait for an accident victim's medical condition to stabilize in order to assess the long-term prognosis. Accident victims in particular often do not seek legal advice until some time after the accident has occurred.

Clearly, if Lord Woolf has wrongly diagnosed the causes of delay, it is unlikely that his reforms will resolve these problems.

The *Judicial Statistics* published by the Court Service in 2002 show that, in the High Court, the time taken between issue and trial has gone up to 173 weeks. The delays have been reduced in the county court, where the average time from issue to trial has fallen from 640 days in 1997 to 500 in 2000–01.

Task 17.8

Visit a county court. You can find the address of a local county court by looking in a telephone directory. Alternatively, you can find the addresses of county courts on the court service website at:

http://www.courtservice.gov.uk/notices/county/ccadd/circuits.htm

Write up a report of your visit by answering the following questions.

About the court

1 What was the name and address of the court?

2 What was the court building like? Was it old or modern? Was it clean and in good decorative order? Were the waiting areas comfortable? Was there access to refreshments? Was it easy to find your way around the building, with rooms clearly signposted and labelled?

3 Did you find the court staff helpful? Were there any explanatory leaflets available?

About the proceedings

Take one of the cases that you watched and answer the following questions.

1 Was the judge male or female and what was their approximate age? What did the judge wear? Was he or she polite to the parties?

2 Were the parties represented by a lawyer?

3 What was the case about?

4 Did any witnesses give evidence?

5 If you heard the whole case, what was its outcome?

6 Did you think that the court came to the right decision?

Use the material you have gathered to prepare an oral presentation for your fellow students about your visit.

Case management

Zander feels that court management is appropriate for only a minority of cases and that the key is to identify these. He has remarked that judges do not have the time, skills or inclination to undertake the task of case management. The court does not know enough about the workings of a solicitor's office to be able to set appropriate timetables. In addition, litigants on the fast track may feel that the brisk way in which a three-hour hearing deals with the dispute is inadequate. Most will not feel that justice has been done by a short, sharp trial with restricted oral evidence and an interventionist judge chivvying the parties to a resolution of their dispute.

A move towards judicial management has already been seen in America, Australia and Canada. A major official study was published by the Institute of Civil Justice at the Rand Corporation in California. This research was not available to Lord Woolf while he was compiling his report. The study was based on a five-year survey of 10,000 cases looking at the effect of the US Civil Justice Reform Act 1990. This Act required certain federal courts to practise case management. Judicial case management has been part of the American system for many years so that, compared with this country, the procedural innovations being studied operated from a different starting point.

The study found that judicial case management did lead to a reduced time to disposition. Its early use yielded a reduction of one and a half or two months to resolution for cases that lasted at least nine months. Also, having a discovery timetable and reducing the time within which discovery took place both significantly reduced time to disposition and significantly reduced the number of hours spent on the case by a lawyer. These benefits were achieved without any significant change in the lawyers' or litigants' satisfaction or views of fairness.

On the other hand, case management led to an approximate 20-hour increase in lawyers' work hours overall. Their work increased with the need to respond to the court's management directions. In addition, once judicial case management had begun, a disclosure cut-off date had usually been established and lawyers felt an obligation to begin disclosure on a case which might be settled.

Thus, the Rand Report found that case management, by generating more work for lawyers, tended to increase rather than reduce costs. If the fixed costs did not reflect the extra cost, then this would be unjust to the lawyers and their clients. The danger is that case management will front-load costs on to cases which would have been settled anyway before reaching court, and which therefore did not need judicial management.

The Rand Report noted that the effectiveness of implementation depended on judicial attitudes. Some judges viewed these procedural innovations as an attack on judicial independence and felt that they emphasized speed and efficiency at the possible expense of justice. The Report concluded, among other things, that judicial management should wait a month after the defence has been entered in case the action settles.

In the research carried out for the Law Society, *The Woolf Network Questionnaire* (2002), 84 per cent of solicitors questioned said they thought the new procedures were quicker and 70 per cent said they were more efficient than the old ones. Greater use of telephone case management conferences was cited as leading to greater efficiency.

Sanctions

Procedural timetables for the fast track are, according to Professor Zander, doomed to failure because a huge proportion of solicitors, for a range of reasons, will fail to keep to the prescribed timetables. This will necessitate enforcement procedures and sanctions on a vast scale which, in turn, will lead to innumerable appeals. Sanctions will be imposed that are disproportionate and therefore unjust, and will cause injustice to clients for the failings of the lawyers. Furthermore, if the judges did impose severe sanctions when lawyers failed to comply with timetable deadlines, it would usually be the litigants rather than the lawyers who would be penalized.

Professor Zander has pointed to the courts' experience of Order 17 under the old County Court Rules as evidence that lawyers are not good at time limits, and sanctions were unlikely to change that. Under that order an action would be automatically struck out if the claimant failed to take certain steps within the time limits set by the rule. From its introduction in 1990 until 1998, roughly 20,000 cases had been struck out on this basis leaving 20,000 people either to sue their lawyers for negligence or to start all over again. In relation to Order 17, the Court of Appeal stated in **Bannister *v* SGB plc** (1997):

> This rule has given rise to great difficulties and has generated an immense amount of litigation devoted to the question whether a particular action has been struck out and if so, whether it should be reinstated. In short, the rule has in a large number of cases achieved the opposite of its object, which was to speed up the litigation process in the county courts.

There is the danger that, if a court does not exercise its power temperately and judiciously, then in its eagerness to dispose of litigation it will actually generate more litigation. This danger is particularly acute where a court exercises powers on its own initiative. If, for example, a court moves to strike out a statement of case on its own initiative, the likely result is that the party affected will apply to have its case reinstated; and if, in fact, it was not a suitable case for striking out, unnecessary cost and delay will be the result.

There is a risk that unrealistic trial dates and timetables will be set, particularly in heavy litigation, at an early stage, and of the judges insisting on their being adhered to thereafter, regardless of the consequences.

In research carried out for the Law Society, *The Woolf Network Questionnaire* (2002), some solicitors said they were reluctant to apply for sanctions against those who did not stick to the pre-action protocols. This was because they felt that the courts were unwilling to impose sanctions for non-compliance in all but the most serious cases, judges were inconsistent in their approach to sanctions and an application for sanctions was likely to cause more delays and additional costs.

Costs

Litigation can be very costly and state funding is often not available (see Chapter 11). Research carried out for the Law Society, *The Woolf Network Questionnaire* (2002), suggests that the cost of engaging in civil litigation has not been reduced by the civil justice reforms. In many cases, especially those involving personal injury, the defendant's costs, and sometimes those of the claimant, will be paid by an insurance company – for example, the parties in a car accident are likely to have been insured and professionals such as doctors are insured against negligence claims. As Hazel Genn's 1987 study showed, where only one party is insured, this can place great pressure on the other, unless the other has been granted state funding. The insured side may try to drag out the proceedings for as long as possible, in the hope of exhausting the other party's financial reserves and forcing a low settlement.

Professor Zander has argued that in many civil cases the claimant wins and the defendant is an insurance company which currently pays the claimant's costs. If, in future, the court can only order the loser to pay fixed and fairly low costs, then the claimant's lawyers will not be able to claim back everything that it was in fact necessary to spend on the case in order to win. He predicts that, as a result, either the work will not be done or the client will have to pay for it out of their damages. Either way, justice will not have been served.

Quick quiz 17.9

1 Name the three tracks for the purposes of case management.

2 If you wish to bring an action for compensation following a disastrous package holiday, claiming £4,000 compensation, to which track would your case be allocated?

3 What is meant by a 'compensation culture'?

4 Did the Rand Report into case management find that it tended to increase or reduce costs?

Reform

Clearly the civil justice system underwent significant reforms in 1999, but further reforms could be made.

Integration

A proposal to integrate the High Court and the county court to produce a simpler system was considered by the Gorell Committee on county court procedure, but rejected, mainly on the ground that hearing big cases in the county courts would prejudice the handling of smaller ones.

The proposal was also considered by the Civil Justice Review (1988), which pointed out that the two-court system was inflexible, making it difficult to make rational allocations of judges' and administrators' time between the different courts. Consequently, some courts have much longer delays than others. In a unified court, all cases would start in the same way and be allocated to different sorts of judges on the basis of their complexity. Judges could be sent where they were needed most, and some higher-level judges could be based outside London.

The recommendation was supported by solicitors, advice centres and consumer organizations but strongly opposed by barristers and judges, for rather unattractive reasons. Barristers feared that solicitors would have greater rights of audience in the unified court and that the London Bar would lose business to provincial solicitors; High Court judges thought that the proposals would reduce their standing and destroy their special way of life, especially if they were expected to be based for long periods of time in the provinces.

In the end the Review rejected the idea of a unified court, on the grounds that there was no general support for it, the financial implications were uncertain, a unified court would require major legislation and a lengthy implementation period and it might have adverse effects on the standing of the High Court judiciary. But the former Head of Civil Justice, Sir Richard Scott VC, has predicted that ultimately the High Court and county courts will merge.

The Department for Constitutional Affairs is looking again at this issue. In a consultation paper, *A Single Civil Court?* (2005) it considers abolishing the county courts, while giving the High Court a wider jurisdiction to hear all civil cases at first instance. The Government is concerned that it is inefficient and costly for the Courts Service to administer two separate civil court systems.

■ An inquisitorial system

In theory, the civil justice system could become an inquisitorial system, in which the judge would take a more investigative role and the two parties would be required to cooperate by revealing all their evidence to each other. Tactics would become less important, and since delay is often a part of these tactics, the whole process could be speeded up. Some would suggest that this system might also be fairer, since being able to afford the best lawyer would be less important.

In fact, a full change from the adversarial system seems extremely unlikely, but there have been proposals for such movement in certain areas: the Civil Justice Review suggested that a paper adjudication scheme might be considered for handling certain claims, which would move to an oral hearing only if the adjudicator felt there were difficulties which made one necessary. The procedure would be compulsory for road accidents and claims under £5,000 and could also be used in other cases where the parties agreed. This idea has been opposed by both the National Consumer Council and the National Association of Citizens' Advice Bureaux, on the basis that those who could afford a skilled lawyer to draft their papers would have too much of an advantage. Some of the Woolf reforms have caused a move towards an inquisitorial approach and a less aggressive form of litigation.

Progress towards full pre-trial disclosure of evidence, and the fact that small claims track arbitrators now take a more interventionist approach, can be seen as moves towards a more inquisitorial system.

Reform of compensation for personal injury

Tort law dictates that the victims of an accident (other than industrial accidents, which are covered by a compensation scheme) can get compensation only if they can prove that the harm caused to them was somebody else's fault. The result of this is that individuals with identical injuries may receive hundreds of thousands of pounds in compensation, or nothing more than state benefits, depending not on their needs but on whether they can prove fault – often very difficult to do conclusively. In many cases, the state has to spend money on state-funded legal representation, but if the case is lost, the only person to benefit from that expenditure is the lawyer. Because of this, it is often suggested that the tort action for personal injury should be abolished and the financial savings should be used to provide improved welfare benefits for all those injured by accidents. New Zealand has adopted such an approach and established a no-fault system of compensation.

Modernization

The Government issued a consultation paper, *Modernising the Civil Courts* (2001). This looked at the possibility of applying the same developments in technology to the Court Service that have been applied to the private sector, such as retail banking. Unfortunately, insufficient money has been invested in developing the IT system that a modern court system requires and so the current IT resources are inadequate. The senior judiciary are concerned that lack of investment in the civil courts is putting at risk London's status as an international centre for commercial litigation. The Master of the Rolls has stated: 'Our civil justice system must keep abreast of technological developments that are happening elsewhere.'

Reading on the web

The research *Emerging Findings: An Early Evaluation of the Civil Justice Reforms* (2001) is available on the Lord Chancellor's website at:

http://www.dca.gov.uk/civil/emerge/emerge.htm

Lord Woolf's final report, *Access to Justice*, is available on the website of the Lord Chancellor's Department at:

http://www.dca.gov.uk/civil/final/index.htm

The website for Money Claim Online can be found at:

www.moneyclaim.gov.uk

A useful source of information about court matters is the Court Service Annual Report:

www.courtservice.gov.uk

Question and answer guides

1 Study the extract below and then answer the questions which follow.

> One of the major divisions in law is between criminal and civil. In reality, the distinction is not always so clear cut. Consider a person attacked and injured by another. Is this a civil matter or criminal? The answer is that it may be either or both. It all depends on what action the victim decides to take. The victim may complain to the police who may bring criminal charges against the assailant. If the police or the Crown Prosecution Service are unwilling to prosecute, then the aggrieved victim may take out a private action against the assailant. The victim would do this by contacting a solicitor and then sue the assailant. It is therefore possible for the same conduct to be prosecuted and also to be followed through the civil courts. This frequently happens in cases of road traffic accidents.

(a) What are the aims of sentencing in a criminal case? *(4 marks)*

(b) What is the burden of proof:
   (i) in a criminal trial
   (ii) in a civil trial? *(4 marks)*

(c) Explain how a criminal trial will differ from a civil action. *(8 marks)*

(d) In what circumstances might a victim prefer to pursue a civil case as an alternative to a criminal prosecution? *(9 marks) (London)*

Answer guide

This question mixes issues from this chapter and from Chapters 12 and 14.

(a) At p. 303 it was mentioned that the five main aims of sentencing are punishment, the reduction of crime, reform and rehabilitation, public protection and reparation.

(b) (i) At p. 275 it was stated that the burden of proof is on the prosecution to prove guilt beyond all reasonable doubt.
   (ii) At p. 350 it was noted that in civil cases the claimant has to prove their case on the balance of probabilities.

(c) Criminal trials are brought by the state unless it is a private prosecution, while civil cases are brought by individuals. The focus of a criminal trial is whether the defendant committed a crime while civil trials are concerned with civil wrongs. Criminal trials have a higher burden of proof and take place in the Crown Court or the magistrates' court. Civil trials normally take place in the High Court or the county court, though some civil procedures are heard by magistrates. A criminal case will be decided either by a lay jury sitting with a professional judge or magistrates. Civil cases are normally decided by professional judges, though rare cases can be heard by a jury or magistrates. A successful criminal prosecution will result in a sentence for punishment, including potentially a custodial sentence. The main remedy in civil cases is damages for compensation.

You could also point to the different procedures; for example, a defendant is either arrested or summoned to attend a criminal court while civil proceedings commence with the issue of a claim form.

(d) Victims have more control in civil cases, the burden of proof is lower and it is therefore easier to win the case. You could illustrate this with the example of O.J. Simpson that was mentioned at p. 350. The victims will usually be awarded damages after a successful civil case, while it is rare for the criminal courts to make reparation or compensation orders. You could look at the problems that arose from the unsuccessful private prosecution brought by Stephen Lawrence's family which is discussed at p. 269. ('London Qualifications Ltd.', accepts no responsibility whatsoever for the accuracy or method in the answers given.)

2 Quickfix Ltd has separate contracts with two companies, Roughs Ltd and Stokes Ltd, to purchase goods. Roughs has failed to deliver some of the goods and it has cost Quickfix £10,000 extra to replace these items, and it wishes to claim the £10,000 from Roughs. Stokes Ltd has delivered faulty goods and Quickfix wishes to claim £80,000 from Stokes.

(a) Explain and comment on the main reforms made to the civil justice system after the Woolf Report. [30]

(b) Advise Quickfix on the type of court and procedure likely to be used for each of its claims [15]. *(OCR)*

Answer guide

(a) You could start by briefly outlining why the civil justice system needed reforming, which is discussed at p. 352. You could then look at the reforms that were introduced following the Woolf Report, which are discussed at p. 354. You could conclude by considering how far these reforms have been successful, an issue considered at p. 366.

(b) You need to divide your answer to this part of the question into two parts, looking first at the proceedings against Roughs for £10,000 and then at the proceedings against Stokes for £80,000. The proceedings against Roughs would fall within the fast-track limits. As the case is worth less than £15,000, the case would have to be started in the county court. The case should be heard within 30 weeks and the trial should normally take only one day.

The litigation against Stokes would fall within the multi-track limits. It could be commenced in either the county court or the High Court. The case would be assigned to a judge, who would decide an appropriate timetable. Note that the parties would be encouraged to try alternative methods of dispute resolution before the cases are heard by the courts.

Chapter summary

Civil courts
There are two main civil courts which hear civil cases at first instance. These are the county courts and the High Court.

The civil justice system before April 1999
Before the implementation of the Woolf reforms, there were two separate sets of civil procedure rules for the county courts and the High Court and Court of Appeal. The system was heavily criticized for being too expensive and slow.

The civil justice system after April 1999

In April 1999 new Civil Procedure Rules and accompanying Practice Directions came into force. The new rules introduce the main recommendations of Lord Woolf in his final report, *Access to Justice*. The reforms aim to eliminate unnecessary cost, delay and complexity in the civil justice system. The ultimate goal is to change fundamentally the litigation culture. Thus, the first rule of the new Civil Procedure Rules lays down an overriding objective which is to underpin the whole system. This overriding objective is that the rules should enable the courts to deal with cases justly. The emphasis of the new rules is on avoiding litigation through pre-trial settlements.

Civil Procedure Rules

For non-personal injury actions, a claim may be started in the High Court where the claimant expects to recover more than £15,000. For personal injury actions a claim can only be started in the High Court where the claimant expects to recover at least £50,000.

Pre-action protocols

To push the parties into behaving reasonably during the pre-trial stage pre-action protocols have been developed. These lay down a code of conduct for this stage of proceedings.

Alternative dispute resolution

At various stages in a dispute's history, the court will actively promote settlement by alternative dispute resolution (ADR).

Case management

Case management has been introduced, whereby the court plays an active role in managing the litigation. To determine the level and form of case management cases have been divided into three types:

■ small claims track
■ fast track, and
■ multi-track.

Sanctions

The courts now have tough powers to enforce the new rules on civil procedure to ensure that litigation is pursued diligently.

Criticism of the 1999 reforms

The 1999 reforms were generally well received, though Professor Zander has been a vociferous critic of the changes, suggesting that they would not succeed in reducing delays and expense.

Chapter 18 | Tribunals

Introduction

Many claims and disputes are settled not by the courts, but by tribunals, each specializing in a particular area. Tribunals decide almost half a million cases every year. Employment tribunals (formally called industrial tribunals) are probably the best known example, but there are many others, dealing with subjects ranging from social security and tax to forestry and patents. Not all are actually called tribunals – the category includes, for example, the Education Appeal Committee, which hears appeals concerning the allocation of school places, and the Criminal Injuries Compensation Board, which assesses applications for compensation for victims of violent crime. The majority deal with disputes between the citizen and the state, though the employment tribunal is an obvious exception.

Tribunals are generally distinguished from the other courts by less formal procedures, and by the fact that they specialize. However, they are all expected to conduct themselves according to the same principles of natural justice used by the courts: a fair hearing for both sides and open and impartial decision-making.

Individual tribunals may differ quite markedly from each other in terms of procedure, workload and membership. For example, employment tribunals operate on an adversarial model, whereas the procedure in the social security tribunals is much more inquisitorial.

History

Tribunals were in existence as long ago as 1799, but the present system has really grown up since the Second World War. The main reason for this was the growth of legislation in areas which were previously considered private, and therefore rarely addressed by the state, such as social security benefits, housing, town and country planning, education and employment.

This legislation gave people rights – to a school place, to unemployment benefit, or not to be unfairly sacked, for example – but its rules also placed limits on these rights. Naturally, this leads to disputes: employer and employee disagree on whether the latter's dismissal was unfair under the terms of the legislation; a social security

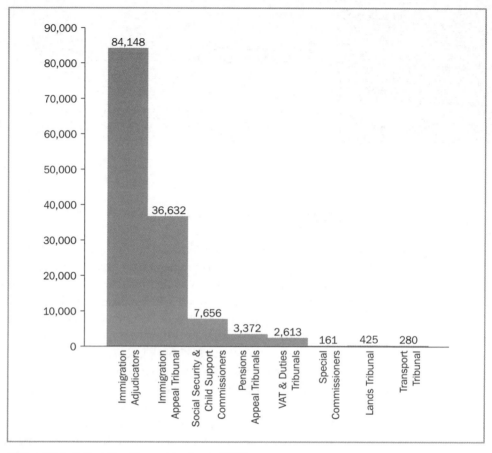

Figure 18.1 Tribunals: Cases received, 2002

Source: K. Dibdin, A. Sealy and S. Aktar, *Judicial Statistics Annual Report 2002*, p. 77.

claimant believes she has been wrongly denied benefit; a landowner disputes the right of the Local Authority to purchase her field compulsorily.

Given the potentially vast number of disputes likely to arise, and the detailed nature of the legislation concerning them, it was felt that the ordinary court system would neither have been able to cope with the workload, nor be the best forum for sorting out such problems, hence the growth of tribunals.

As well as the administrative tribunals dealing with this kind of dispute, there are domestic tribunals, which deal with disputes and matters of discipline within particular professions – trade unions and the medical and legal professions all have tribunals like this, the Solicitors' Complaints Tribunal being an example. The decisions of these tribunals are based on the particular rules of the organization concerned, but they are still required to subscribe to the same standards of justice as the ordinary courts and in the case of those set up by statute, their decisions can be appealed to the ordinary courts – as can those of most administrative tribunals.

The Franks Report

In 1957, the Franks Committee investigated the workings of tribunals. It reported that the tribunal system was likely to become an increasingly important part of the legal system, and recommended that tribunal procedures should be marked by 'openness, fairness and impartiality'. Openness required, where possible, hearings in public and explanations of the reasoning behind decisions. Fairness entailed the adoption of clear procedures, which allowed parties to know their rights, present their case fully, and be aware of the case against them. Impartiality meant that tribunals should be free of undue influence from any government departments concerned with their subject area. The Committee was particularly concerned that tribunals were often on Ministry premises, with Ministry staff.

Following recommendations of the Committee, a Council on Tribunals was established. Its functions are only advisory – it has little real power, and cannot reverse or even direct further consideration of individual tribunal decisions. In 1980, it put forward a report asking for further powers, but they were not granted.

Tribunals today

Composition

Most tribunals consist of a legally trained chairperson, and two lay people who have some particular expertise in the relevant subject area – doctors in the medical appeal tribunal, for example, and representatives of both employees' and employers' organizations in the employment tribunal. The lay members take an active part in decision-making.

Tribunals composed entirely of lay people are considered to have been less effective than those with a legally qualified chairperson.

Status

Tribunals are regarded as inferior to the ordinary courts, even though they are largely independent from them in their own jurisdictions. This was confirmed in the case of **Peach Grey & Co.** *v* **Sommers** (1995), which concerned a claim of wrongful dismissal against a firm of solicitors, heard by an industrial tribunal. The person dismissed had tried to influence a witness due to appear before the tribunal, and his former employers claimed that this was contempt of court. The Divisional Court agreed, and in accepting that it had jurisdiction to punish this contempt, it confirmed that the tribunal is an inferior court.

Workload

The tribunals system handles over a million cases each year. Although they have often been seen as an unimportant part of the legal system, this case load clearly shows that they are now playing a major role.

Employment tribunals

Employment tribunals provide one example of a powerful tribunal playing a central role in today's society. The role of employment tribunals has altered radically since they were first established in 1964. The number of applications has risen dramatically so that in 2001 there were 130,408 applications. The procedure is quicker than that in the civil courts, with 75 per cent of cases being heard within 26 weeks of receipt. A MORI users' survey in 2002 found that both applicants and respondents were satisfied that cases were dealt with impartially and professionally. But the cases have become more legalistic and no longer satisfy the original idea that they should be quick, informal hearings. Only 4 per cent of cases are appealed.

The huge increase in the number of cases has put a strain on the system. The Employment Tribunal System's Taskforce was established to provide a vision of the employment tribunal system for the twenty-first century. It reported in 2002 and the Government hopes to introduce its main recommendations over the next three years.

Appeals from tribunals

There is no uniform appeals procedure from tribunals, though most do allow some right of appeal. The 1992 Tribunals and Inquiries Act provides for appeals to the High Court on points of law from some of the most important tribunals. These appeals are heard by the Queen's Bench Division.

In addition to appeal rights, decisions of tribunals are always subject to judicial review by the High Court on the grounds that they have not been made in accordance with the rules of natural justice or were not within the powers of the tribunal to make (see p. 60).

Controls over tribunals

Aside from the judicial review procedure, which supervises the actual decisions of tribunals, the workings of tribunals are overseen by the Council on Tribunals. This consists of ten to 15 members appointed by the Lord Chancellor. It reviews and reports on the constitution and workings of certain specified tribunals, and is consulted before any changes to their procedural rules are made; it also considers and reports on matters referred to it concerning any tribunal. However, it has no firm say in any of these matters, and cannot overrule any decisions.

Advantages of tribunals

Speed

Tribunal cases come to court fairly quickly, and many are dealt with within a day. Many tribunals are able to specify the exact date and time at which a case will be heard, so minimizing time-wasting for the parties.

Cost

Tribunals usually do not charge fees, and each party usually pays their own costs, rather than the loser having to pay all. The simpler procedures of tribunals should mean that legal representation is unnecessary, so reducing cost, but that is not always the case (see below).

Informality

This varies between different tribunals, but as a general rule, wigs are not worn, the strict rules of evidence do not apply, and attempts are made to create an unintimidating atmosphere. This is obviously a help where individuals are representing themselves.

Flexibility

Although they obviously aim to apply fairly consistent principles, tribunals do not operate strict rules of precedent, so are able to respond more flexibly than courts.

Specialization

Tribunal members already have expertise in the relevant subject area, and through sitting on tribunals are able to build up a depth of knowledge of that area that judges in ordinary courts could not hope to match.

Relief of congestion in the ordinary courts

If the volume of cases heard by tribunals was transferred to the ordinary courts, the system would be completely overloaded.

Awareness of policy

The expertise of tribunal members means they are likely to understand the policy behind legislation in their area, and they often have wide discretionary powers which allow them to put this into practice.

Privacy

Tribunals may, in some circumstances, meet in private, so that the individual is not obliged to have their circumstances broadcast to the general public (but see the first disadvantage below).

Disadvantages of tribunals

Lack of openness

The fact that some tribunals are held in private can lead to suspicion about the fairness of their decisions.

Unavailability of funding from the Legal Services Commission

Full funding from the Legal Services Commission is available for only a small number of minor tribunals. Tribunals are, of course, designed to do away with the need for representation, but the fact is that in many of them ordinary individuals will be facing an opponent with access to the very best representation – an employer, for example, or a Government department – and this clearly places them at a serious disadvantage. Even though the procedures are generally informal compared to those in ordinary courts, the average person is likely to be very much out of his or her depth, and research by Genn and Genn in 1989 found that much of the law with which tribunals was concerned was complex, and their adjudicative process sometimes highly technical; individuals who were represented had a much better chance of winning their case.

There is, however, some dispute as to the desirability of such representation necessarily involving lawyers; although in some cases this will be the more appropriate form of representation, there are fears that introducing lawyers could detract from the aims of speed and informality. If money for tribunal representation were available, it might be better spent on developing lay representation, such as that offered by specialist agencies, including the United Kingdom Immigration Advisory Service and the Child Poverty Action Group, which can develop real expertise in specific areas, as well as general agencies such as the Citizens' Advice Bureaux.

Lack of coherence

Each tribunal has evolved as a solution to a particular problem, adapted to one particular area of law. As a result, most tribunals are entirely self-contained, and operate separately from one another, using different practices and procedures. The result is a system that lacks coherence and which is not providing a uniformly high standard of service.

Not user-friendly

The tribunals were originally intended to be user-friendly, providing easy access to justice. Over time many have become increasingly like courts and it is difficult as a result for claimants without professional legal help to take their case to a tribunal.

Dependent

At the moment, the relevant ministry frequently provides the administrative support for the tribunal, selects the tribunal members, pays their fees and expenses, and lays down the tribunal procedures. This means that tribunals neither appear to be, nor are in fact, independent. Responsibility for tribunals and their administration should not lie with those whose policies or decisions it is the tribunals' duty to consider. Otherwise, for users every case is an 'away game'. The current arrangements in this respect could be the subject of a successful challenge under Art. 6 of the European Convention on Human Rights, which guarantees the right to a fair trial.

Reasons for decisions not always given

Although the majority of tribunals are obliged to explain their reasoning if requested, a few are not.

Lack of accessibility

The Franks Committee recommendation that tribunals should be 'open' requires more than just a rule that hearings should usually be held in public; it also demands that citizens be aware of tribunals and their right to use them. In cases where the dispute is between a citizen and the Government, the citizen will usually be notified of procedures to deal with disputes, but in other cases more thought needs to be given to publicizing citizens' rights.

Problems with controls over tribunals

Diversity

Although they are often considered together, tribunals vary widely in procedure and the subjects with which they deal, and they make thousands of decisions every year in very different types of case. This great diversity makes it difficult to establish mechanisms of supervision that are appropriate to them all.

The Council on Tribunals

The Council is a watchdog with no teeth. It can advise the Government of problems, but has no real power to ensure they are dealt with.

Rights of appeal

There is no absolute right of appeal from a tribunal: such rights exist only where they are laid down in statute with regard to a particular tribunal. Consequently, there is no uniform appeals system, and some tribunals offer no appeal rights at all. An example is the vaccine damage tribunal, set up under the Vaccine Damage Payments Act 1971 to assess claimants' rights to damages for disabilities caused by vaccination. Some tribunal appeals can only be made to the relevant Minister, who can hardly be seen as a disinterested party. Others have appeal rights to the High Court, which is expensive, complex and time-consuming, and therefore seems inconsistent with the basic aims of tribunals.

Judicial review

As always, the controlling effect of the potential for judicial review is limited by the fact that it cannot consider the merits of decisions, and that where wide discretionary powers are given to a Minister, Government department or local authority, the court will find it difficult to prove that many decisions are outside those powers (see p. 60).

Quick quiz 18.1

1 In what year was the Franks Report published?

2 Which advisory body was established following the Franks Report?

3 What is the normal composition of a tribunal?

4 Is funding from the Legal Services Commission available for legal proceedings before tribunals?

Reform

A major review of the tribunals was undertaken by Sir Andrew Legatt. Following this review, the Government has now issued a White Paper containing significant plans to reform the tribunal system.

The Legatt Review of Tribunals

In 2000/2001 the tribunals were the subject of a major review undertaken at the request of the Lord Chancellor by Sir Andrew Leggatt, a retired Lord Justice of Appeal. This is the first systematic examination of tribunals since the Franks Report in 1957. The Review was asked to look at the funding and management of tribunals, their structure and standards and whether they complied with the Human Rights Act 1998.

The Review issued a consultation document in which it agreed with the Franks Committee that the main characteristics required of tribunals are fairness, openness and impartiality, though it saw openness and impartiality as components of the overarching requirement of fairness. The Review proposed certain benchmarks against which the achievement of fairness could be tested. These benchmarks included the following:

- independence from sponsoring departments;
- an accessible and supportive system;
- tribunals exercising a jurisdiction suitable for the area that each is intended to cover;
- simple procedures;
- effective decision-making;
- ensuring that the decision-taking process is suitable for the type of dispute;
- providing proportionate remedies;
- speed in reaching finality;
- authority and expertise appropriate for their task; and
- cost-effectiveness.

The report of the Review, *Tribunals for Users: One System, One Service*, was published in 2001. Of the 70 different administrative tribunals in England and Wales, it found that their quality varied 'from excellent to inadequate'. It identified some significant weaknesses in the current system. In particular, it was concerned by the lack of coherence in the existing tribunal system, the fact that they were not always user-friendly and the absence of independence of the tribunals from the Ministries whose decisions were the subject of the tribunal work. These criticisms have been discussed at pp. 387–8.

Proposals

The Review concluded that the tribunals had to be rationalized and modernized, and that a radical approach was both necessary and justified. Its proposals have four main aims:

- to make the 70 tribunals into one *tribunal system*;
- to render the tribunals independent of their sponsoring departments by having them administered by one Tribunal Service;
- to improve the training of chairpersons and members in the interpersonal skills particularly required by tribunals;
- to enable unrepresented users to participate effectively and without apprehension in tribunal proceedings.

The precise proposals of the Review were as follows:

Tribunal Service

The main proposal of the Review was that a single Tribunal Service should be established which would be responsible for the administration of all the tribunals. According to the Review, this would achieve efficiency, coherence and independence.

Any citizen who wished to apply to a tribunal would simply have to submit their case to the Tribunal Service and the case would be allocated to the appropriate tribunal. This would be a considerable advance in clarity and simplicity for users and their advisers. The single system would enable a coherent, user-focused approach to the provision of information which would enable tribunals to meet the claim that they operate in ways which enable citizens to participate directly in preparing and presenting their own cases.

It is hoped that a Tribunal Service would raise the status of tribunals, while preserving their distinctness from the courts. In the medium term it would yield considerable economies of scale, particularly in relation to the provision of premises for all tribunals, common basic training and the use of information technology. It would provide a single point of contact for users, improved geographical distribution of tribunal centres, common standards, an enhanced corporate image and a greater prospect of job satisfaction for employees on account of the size and coherence of the Tribunal Service.

The Tribunal Service should be an executive agency of the Lord Chancellor's Department (now the Ministry for Constitutional Affairs). The Review considers that the independence of tribunals would best be safeguarded by having their administrative support provided by this department with its extensive experience of managing courts.

In the light of this recommendation the Government intends to introduce a unified Tribunal Service for ten tribunals.

Structure of the tribunal system

The Review proposes that the tribunals should be organized into divisions grouping together coherent areas of work. The first-tier tribunals would be grouped into eight divisions:

- education
- financial
- health and social services
- immigration
- land and valuation
- social security and pensions
- transport
- regulatory and employment.

Tribunal procedure

At the moment all the tribunals have their own rules of procedure. The Review proposes the establishment of a unified set of procedural rules. Its proposals are heavily influenced by the reforms introduced to the rules of civil procedure following the Woolf Report. It considers that at the moment cases take too long and are often ill-prepared. To deal with this problem it favours the increased use of case management, with the imposition of rigorous time constraints supported by sanctions. Each division would have at least one registrar to assist the tribunal members with case management duties. Registrars would have the power to order the production of documents and attendance of witnesses and to issue directions. They would seek to minimize the length of oral hearings by ordering the exchange of documentary evidence before the hearing, and by directing that written arguments from the department whose decision is challenged be sent before the hearing to the tribunal and to the other party. The registrar would consider during pre-hearing procedures (with advice, as needed from the tribunal chairperson) whether the case was suitable for some alternative method of dispute resolution. Where a department fails without reasonable excuse to comply with an order or direction, the tribunal would have the power to allow the application against the department. Tribunals would not have the power to award costs against a party.

The same overarching principle would apply to tribunals as is now enshrined in the Civil Procedure Rules. The tribunals would be under a duty to ensure, so far as practical, that procedures were as speedy, proportionate and cheap as the nature of each case allowed.

Suitable information technology would be provided for work flow management and tracking.

A user-friendly system

 Know your terms 18.2

Define the following terms:

1 The Franks Report
2 Council on Tribunals
3 Queen's Bench Division
4 Overriding objective

The Review considered that tribunal users should be able to prepare and present their cases themselves. The tribunals should give the parties confidence in their ability to participate regardless of their skills or knowledge. Working where possible with user groups, tribunals should do all they can to render themselves understandable, unthreatening, and useful to users. Information about venues, timetables and sources of professional advice should be easily accessible. All judgments should contain reasons written in plain English.

Appeals

The current arrangements for appeals against tribunal decisions have developed haphazardly so that there is a confusing and illogical variety of routes of appeal from tribunal decisions. The Review proposes that the existing appeal system should be replaced by a simple, clear structure which would be capable of developing the law consistently. There would be a single route of appeal for all tribunals. Each new division would have a corresponding appellate tribunal. There would be a right of appeal on a point of law, by permission, on the ground that the decision of the tribunal was unlawful. The appeal route would be from first-tier tribunal to second-tier tribunal and from second-tier tribunal to the Court of Appeal. The appellate body would have the power to quash the decision, to remit it for reconsideration, to grant declaratory relief or (if there was no substantial prejudice) to give no relief. There would be specific provision for certain appeals direct to the Court of Appeal.

The Council on Tribunals

The Review recommends that the Council on Tribunals should continue to exist, with extended powers. It would monitor progress in the implementation of the tribunal system. It would also check that the practices and procedures of the government departments were compliant with the European Convention on Human Rights.

Government reform proposals

The Department for Constitutional Affairs has issued a White Paper, *Transforming Public Services: complaints, redress and tribunals* (2004), proposing wide changes to the tribunal system. In the light of Sir Andrew Legatt's recommendations, the Government is progressively unifying the administration of the tribunal service. It is hoped that the new arrangements will help to improve the standard of Government decision-making, so that its decisions are clearer and more accurate, reduce waiting times, and make tribunal hearings less intimidating. The notion of 'proportionate dispute resolution' will be introduced, which is intended to encourage the resolution of disputes more quickly, using alternative methods of dispute resolution instead of formal tribunal hearings.

The Council of Tribunals will be replaced by an Administrative Justice Council which will examine the whole system of redress following disputes between citizens and the Government.

Quick quiz 18.3

1 Who presided over the 2000/2001 Review of the Tribunals?

2 What was the name of the report produced by the Review of the Tribunals in 2001?

3 What were the four main aims of the Review's proposals?

4 What changes did the Review propose should be made to the appeal process?

Task 18.4

When the Lord Chancellor established the Review of Tribunals by Sir Andrew Leggatt, he set its terms of reference. These terms of reference laid down the work that the Review had to carry out. Read the terms of reference of the Review and then answer the questions below:

Terms of Reference

To review the delivery of justice through tribunals other than ordinary courts of law, constituted under an Act of Parliament by a Minister of the Crown or for the purposes of ministers' functions; in resolving disputes, whether between citizen and the state, or between other parties, to ensure that:

There are fair, timely, proportionate and effective arrangements for handling those disputes, within an effective framework for decision-making which encourages the systematic development of the area of law concerned, and which forms a coherent structure, together with the *superior courts*, for the delivery of administrative justice;

The administrative and practical arrangements for supporting those decision-making procedures meet the requirements of the European Convention on Human Rights for independence and impartiality;

There are adequate arrangements for improving people's knowledge and understanding of their rights and responsibilities in relation to such disputes, and that tribunals and other bodies function in a way which makes those rights and responsibilities a reality;

The arrangements for the funding and management of tribunals and other bodies by Government departments are efficient, effective and economical; and pay due regard both to judicial independence, and to ministerial responsibility for the administration of public funds;

Performance standards for tribunals are coherent, consistent, and public; and effective measures for monitoring and enforcing those standards are established; and tribunals overall constitute a coherent structure for the delivery of administrative justice.

The review may examine, insofar as it considers it necessary, administrative and regulatory bodies which also make judicial decisions as part of their functions.

Questions

1 Why was the Government particularly concerned that the tribunals' procedures met the requirements of the European Convention on Human Rights?

2 In this context, what is meant by the 'superior courts'?

3 The Review was required to consider whether there were 'adequate arrangements for improving people's knowledge and understanding of their rights and responsibilities' in relation to disputes between citizens and the state. If you had been refused a place in the school of your choice, would you have known where to take your dispute?

4 The Review was asked to consider whether 'tribunals overall constitute a coherent structure for the delivery of administrative justice'. What did the Review conclude on this matter?

Reading on the web

The Report of the Review of tribunals by Sir Andrew Leggatt is available on:

http://www.tribunals-review.org.uk/

The website of the Council on Tribunals is:

http://www.council-on-tribunals.gov.uk/

Question and answer guides

1 Evaluate the role of tribunals in the English legal system

Answer guide

You can begin by considering what the role of tribunals is. You should point out that their roles do vary widely, but broadly their job in the legal system can be said to include providing justice in a quick, inexpensive and accessible way, making independent decisions in disputes between the citizen and the state, putting into effect the policy behind legislation, and taking pressure off the courts. You then need to assess how well tribunals do these jobs.

The following are points you might mention:

- *Speed* – they are quicker than courts, but since the Franks Committee they have adopted more court-like procedures, which may slow things down.
- *Cost* – some charge no fees, and costs are not usually awarded against a losing party as they would be in a court. However, the need for representation, and the fact that state funding is not available, may eradicate these advantages for some.
- *Accessibility* – procedures are usually simpler than in courts, but again, the fact that representation is allowed means that powerful litigants will have it, so less powerful ones are disadvantaged by representing themselves.

▶

- *Independence* – though this has improved, there are still criticisms (see pp. 387–8).
- *Helping the citizen to assert rights against the state* – this may be compromised by lack of independence, and also the problems with state funding, putting the individual at a disadvantage.
- *Effecting policy* – tribunals do often have wider discretionary powers than courts.
- *Taking pressure off the courts* – you could point out the vast numbers of cases which arise in the kinds of matters dealt with by tribunals. ('London Qualifications Ltd.', accepts no responsibility whatsoever for the accuracy or method in the answers given.)

2   **Analyse the role played by tribunals in the administration of justice. How far are the methods of supervising and reviewing their judgments adequate?**

Answer guide

The role of tribunals is described above – if you have time, it is worth mentioning some of the assessment points, since you are being asked what role is actually played, rather than just what role tribunals aim to play.

For the second part of the question, you need to outline what methods of supervising tribunals and reviewing their decisions are available. The problems with these methods are outlined above, and you should also refer to the section on judicial review in general (p. 60).

Chapter summary

Introduction

Tribunals are generally different from ordinary courts because of their less formal procedures and the fact that they are very specialist.

History

Tribunals were in existence as long ago as 1799, but the present system has really grown up since the Second World War.

The Franks Report

In 1957 the Franks Committee investigated the workings of tribunals. It recommended that tribunal procedures should be marked by 'openness, fairness and impartiality'. Following its report, the Council on Tribunals was established.

Tribunals today

Composition
Most tribunals consist of a legally trained chairperson, and two lay people who have some particular expertise in the relevant subject area.

Status
Tribunals are generally regarded as inferior to the ordinary courts.

Appeals from tribunals

There is no uniform appeals procedure from tribunals, though most do allow some right of appeal.

Advantages of tribunals

The advantages of tribunals include:

- speed
- cost
- informality
- flexibility
- specialization, and
- privacy.

Disadvantages of tribunals

The disadvantages of tribunals include:

- lack of openness
- unavailability of funding from the Legal Services Commission
- lack of coherence between the different tribunals
- not being user-friendly
- lack of independence
- lack of accessibility, and
- problems with controls.

Reform

In 2000/2001 the tribunals were the subject of a major Review undertaken by Sir Andrew Leggatt. It proposed:

- to make the 70 tribunals into one tribunal system;
- to render the tribunals independent of their sponsoring departments by having them administered by one Tribunal Service;
- to improve the training of chairpersons and members in the interpersonal skills particularly required by tribunals; and
- to enable unrepresented users to participate effectively and without apprehension in tribunal proceedings.

The Government is progressively unifying the administration of the tribunal service.

Chapter 19 Appeals

The appeals system provides a way of overseeing the lower courts, and has two basic functions:

- Putting right any unjust or incorrect decisions, whether caused by errors of fact, law or procedure. An error of fact might be that a victim was stabbed with a knife rather than a broken bottle; an error of law might be that the judge has wrongly defined an offence when explaining to the jury what needs to be proved; and an error of procedure means that the trial has not been conducted as it should have been.
- Promoting a consistent development of the law.

Judicial review is not technically an appeal, though it is a way of reviewing the decisions of courts and tribunals as well as the decisions of the executive. It will be considered after the appeals system.

Appeals in civil law cases

Civil appeals may be made by either party to a dispute. The Government has been concerned at the increasing number of appeals being brought in civil proceedings. In 1990 there were 954 appeals heard and 573 applications outstanding. By 1996, 1,825 appeals were heard and 1,288 applications were outstanding. There has also been a slight increase in the number of appeals following the passing of the Human Rights Act 1998. A review of the Civil Division of the Court of Appeal was undertaken by a committee chaired by Sir Jeffrey Bowman. It produced a report in the spring of 1998. A number of problems were identified as besetting the Court of Appeal. In particular, the court was being asked to consider numerous appeals which were not of sufficient weight or complexity for two or three of the country's most senior judges, and which had sometimes already been through one or more levels of appeal. Additionally, existing provisions concerning the constitution of the court were too inflexible to deal appropriately with its workload. Recommendations were made that were designed to reduce the delays in the hearing of civil appeals, and the Government accepted many of its proposals. The Access to Justice Act 1999 introduced some significant reforms to the civil appeal process.

In the past, permission was required for most cases going to the Civil Division of the Court of Appeal, but not elsewhere. Following the Access to Justice Act 1999, court rule 52 requires permission to appeal to be obtained for almost all appeals. This permission can be obtained either from the court of first instance or from the appellate court itself. Permission will be given where the appeal has a realistic prospect of success or where there is some other compelling reason why the appeal should be heard. More stringent conditions are applied for the granting of permission to appeal case management decisions. The main situation where permission to appeal is not required is where the liberty of the subject is at stake, for example following the rejection of a *habeas corpus* application. The general rule is that appeal lies to the next level of judge in the court hierarchy.

The Access to Justice Act 1999 provides that in normal circumstances there will be only one level of appeal to the courts. Where the county court or High Court has already reached a decision in a case brought on appeal, there will be no further possibility for the case to be considered by the Court of Appeal, unless it considers that the appeal would raise an important point of principle or practice, or there is some other compelling reason for the Court of Appeal to hear it. Thus, in future, second appeals will become a rarity. Only the Court of Appeal can grant permission for this second appeal.

In the Court of Appeal cases are normally heard by three judges but, following the Access to Justice Act 1999, some smaller cases can be heard by a single judge.

Civil appeals will normally simply be a review of the decision of the lower court, rather than a full rehearing, unless the appeal court considers that it is in the interests of justice to hold a rehearing. The appeal will only be allowed where the decision of the lower court was wrong, or where it was unjust because of a serious procedural or other irregularity in the proceedings of the lower court.

From the county court

Appeals from the county court based on alleged errors of law or fact are made to the Civil Division of the Court of Appeal. Appeals from a district judge's decision normally have to go first to a circuit judge and then to the High Court (though exceptionally they will go to the Court of Appeal instead of the High Court).

The Court of Appeal does not hear all the evidence again, calling witnesses and so forth, but considers the appeal on the basis of the notes made by the trial judge, and/or other documentary evidence of the proceedings. Written skeleton arguments should normally be provided to the court so that oral submissions can be kept brief to save time and costs.

The Court of Appeal may affirm, vary (for example, by altering the amount of damages) or reverse the judgment of the county court. It is generally reluctant to overturn the trial judge's finding of fact because it does not hold a complete rehearing. As the trial judge will have had the advantage of observing the demeanour of witnesses giving their evidence, the Court of Appeal will hardly ever question his or her findings about their veracity and reliability as witnesses. From the Court of

Appeal, there may be a further appeal to the House of Lords, for which leave must be granted.

Judicial review by the High Court is also possible.

From the High Court

Cases started in the High Court may be appealed to the Civil Division of the Court of Appeal. The case is examined through transcripts rather than being reheard, as above. From there, a further appeal on questions of law or fact may be made, with leave, to the House of Lords.

The exception to this process is the 'leap-frog' procedure, provided for in the Administration of Justice Act 1969. Under this procedure, an appeal can go directly from the High Court to the House of Lords, missing out the Court of Appeal. The underlying rationale is that the Court of Appeal may be bound by a decision of the House of Lords, so that money and time would be wasted by going to the Court of Appeal when the only court that could look at the issue afresh is the House of Lords. In order to use this procedure, all the parties must consent to it and the High Court judge who heard the original trial must certify that the appeal is on a point of law that either:

(a) relates wholly or mainly to the construction of an enactment or of a statutory instrument, and has been fully argued in the proceedings and fully considered in the judgment of the judge in the proceedings; or

(b) is one in respect of which the judge is bound by a decision of the Court of Appeal or of the House of Lords in previous proceedings, and was fully considered in the judgments given by the Court of Appeal or the House of Lords (as the case may be) in those previous proceedings (s. 12(3)).

The trial judge has a discretion whether or not to grant this certificate, and there is no right of appeal against this decision. Even if a certificate is granted, leave will still need to be obtained from the House of Lords.

From the civil jurisdiction of the magistrates' court

Appeals concerning family proceedings go to the Family Division of the High Court. From there, appeal with leave lies to the Court of Appeal and the House of Lords. Appeals on licensing matters are heard by the Crown Court.

It is also possible for the magistrates to state a case (see p. 402) and for judicial review to be applied.

From tribunals

Tribunals may have their own appeal system – the Employment Appeal Tribunal, for example, hears cases from employment tribunals. Otherwise, appeals from tribunals tend to be limited to points of law, which are usually referred to the High Court. They are also subject to judicial review.

Quick quiz 19.1

1 What are the two basic functions of an appeal system?

2 Which court(s) can give permission to appeal for civil cases?

3 How many judges normally sit in the Court of Appeal?

4 Which court hears civil appeals from the High Court?

Appeals in criminal law cases

Significant reforms have been introduced to the criminal appeal system in the light of heavy criticism following the high-profile miscarriages of justice. The appeal process is supposed to spot cases where there have been wrongful convictions at an early stage so that the injustice can be promptly remedied. A wrongful conviction could arise because of police or prosecution malpractice, a misdirection by a judge, judicial bias, or because expert evidence, such as forensic evidence, was misleading. Sadly, the Court of Appeal in particular failed in the past to detect such problems and this led to demands for reform. The Criminal Appeal Act 1995 was therefore passed to make major amendments to the criminal appeal procedure.

From the magistrates' court (criminal jurisdiction)

There are four routes of appeal:

Rectification

The magistrates can rectify an error they have made under s. 142 of the Magistrates' Courts Act 1980, as amended by the Criminal Appeal Act 1995. The case is retried before a different bench where it would be in the interests of justice to do so and the sentence can be varied.

Right to appeal to the Crown Court

A defendant who has pleaded not guilty may appeal as of right to the Crown Court on the grounds of being wrongly convicted or too harshly sentenced. Only appeals against sentence are allowed if the defendant pleaded guilty. The appeal has to be made within 28 days of the conviction. These appeals are normally heard by a circuit judge sitting with between two and four magistrates (not those who heard the original trial). Each person's vote has the same weight except where the court is equally divided; in such a case the circuit judge has the casting vote.

The court will rehear the facts of the case and either confirm the verdict and/or sentence of the original magistrates, or substitute its own decision for that of the lower court. It can impose any sentence that the magistrates might have imposed – which can occasionally result in the accused's sentence being increased. In 1994 there were 22,600 appeals heard by the Crown Court, of which 43 per cent were successful.

Appeals by way of case stated

Alternatively, either the prosecution or the accused may appeal on the grounds that the magistrates have made an error of law, or acted outside their jurisdiction. The magistrates (or the Crown Court when hearing an appeal from the magistrates) are asked to 'state the case' for their decision to be considered by the High Court. This is, therefore, known as an appeal by way of case stated.

Appeals by way of case stated are heard by up to three judges of the Queen's Bench Division and the sitting is known as a Divisional Court. The court can confirm, reverse or vary the decision; give the magistrates its opinion on the relevant point of law; or make such other order as it sees fit, which may include ordering a rehearing before a different Bench.

Referral by the Criminal Cases Review Commission

The Criminal Cases Review Commission can refer appeals from the magistrates' court to the Crown Court. This body is discussed in more detail from p. 414 onwards. In fact, only 5 per cent of new cases received by the Commission since 1997 have been against convictions by the magistrates.

If an appeal has been made to the Crown Court, either side may then appeal against the Crown Court's decision by way of case stated. If a party has already appealed to the High Court by way of case stated, the party may not afterwards appeal to the Crown Court.

From the Divisional Court there may be a further appeal, by either party, to the House of Lords, but only if the Divisional Court certifies that the question of law is one of public importance and the House of Lords or the Divisional Court gives permission for the appeal to be heard.

Criminal cases tried by magistrates are also subject to judicial review.

In practice, appeals from the decisions of magistrates are taken in only 1 per cent of cases. This may be because most accused plead guilty, and since the offences are relatively minor and the punishment usually a fine, many of those who pleaded not guilty may prefer just to pay up and put the case behind them, avoiding the expense, publicity and embarrassment involved in an appeal.

■ From the Crown Court

There are three types of appeal for cases tried in the Crown Court:

To the Court of Appeal with judicial permission

An appeal on grounds that involve the facts, the law or the length of the sentence can be made to the Court of Appeal. The accused must get permission to appeal from the trial judge or the Court of Appeal. A sentence cannot be imposed that is more severe than that ordered by the Crown Court. An appeal against sentence will only be successful where the sentence is wrong in principle or manifestly severe; the court will not interfere merely because it might have passed a different sanction.

Task 19.2

Look at the diagram and answer the questions that follow.

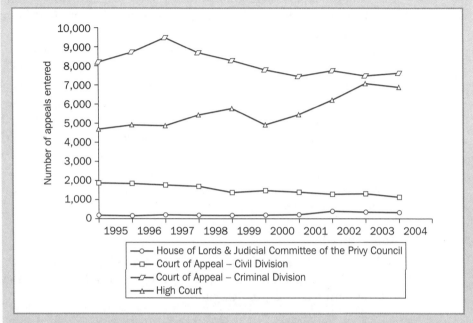

Figure 19.1 Appellate Courts: Appeals entered, 1995–2004

Source: K. Dibdin, A. Sealy and S. Aktar, *Judicial Statistics Annual Report 2004*, p. 6.

Questions

1 Which appellate court hears the fewest cases?

2 Which division of the Court of Appeal is the busiest?

3 Did the High Court's workload increase or decrease in 2003–04?

4 What is the trend in the workload of the House of Lords?

While only the accused can appeal to the Court of Appeal, from there either the accused or the prosecution may appeal on a point of law to the House of Lords, provided that either the Court of Appeal or the House of Lords grants permission for the appeal and that the Court of Appeal certifies that the case involves a matter of law of general public importance.

Referral by the Criminal Cases Review Commission

The Criminal Appeal Act 1995 established the Criminal Cases Review Commission (CCRC), following a proposal made by the Royal Commission on Criminal Justice 1993 (RCCJ). This body is not a court that decides appeals; rather it is responsible for bringing cases, where there may have been a miscarriage of justice, to the attention of the Court of Appeal if the case was originally heard by the Crown Court (or the

Crown Court if the case was originally heard by a magistrates' court). Either a person can apply to the Commission to consider his/her case or the Commission can consider it on its own initiative if an ordinary appeal is time barred. The Commission can carry out an investigation into the case, which may involve asking the police to reinvestigate a crime. Before making a reference, the Commission is able to seek the Court of Appeal's opinion on any matter.

The decision as to whether or not to refer a case will be taken by a committee consisting of at least three members of the Commission. It can make such a reference in relation to a conviction where it appears to them that any argument or evidence, which was not raised in any relevant court proceedings, gives rise to a real possibility that the conviction would not be upheld were the reference to be made. A reference in relation to a sentence will be possible if 'any argument on a point of law, or any information' was not so raised and, again, there is a real possibility that the conviction might not be upheld. Where the Commission refers a conviction or sentence to the Court of Appeal, it is treated as a fresh appeal and the Commission has no further involvement in the case.

Case stated

Following the Access to Justice Act 1999, appeals by way of case stated have been introduced from the Crown Court to the High Court. Previously, these were available only from the magistrates' court.

Second appeal to the Court of Appeal

In exceptional circumstances the Court of Appeal will be prepared to hear an appeal twice, in other words an appeal from its own earlier decision in the same case. This was decided in the landmark case of **Taylor** *v* **Lawrence** (2002). The Court of Appeal had dismissed the first appeal which had been based on the fact that the judge at first instance had been a client of the claimants. After that first appeal, the appellant then discovered that the judge had not been asked to pay for work carried out the night before the case went to court. When this came to light the Court of Appeal ruled that it would hear a second appeal. The Court of Appeal laid down guidelines for future cases on when it would be prepared to hear a second appeal in the same case. It must be clearly established that a significant injustice has probably been done, the circumstances are exceptional and there is no alternative effective remedy. There is no effective remedy if leave would not be available for an appeal to the House of Lords. Leave to appeal would not have been given by the House of Lords in **Taylor** *v* **Lawrence** because the case was not of sufficient general importance and merit.

The approach taken by the Court in **Taylor** *v* **Lawrence** is now contained in Civil Procedure Rule 52.17.

Procedure before the Court of Appeal

Whichever appeal route is taken to reach the Court of Appeal, once the case is before the court, it is dealt with under the same procedure, which will now be considered.

Admission of fresh evidence

The Court of Appeal in criminal cases does not rehear the whole case with all its evidence. Instead, it aims merely to review the lower court's decision. This is at least partly because the Court of Appeal is reluctant to overturn the verdict of a jury, apparently fearing that to do so might undermine the public's respect for juries in general.

The Court of Appeal can admit fresh evidence 'if they think it necessary or expedient in the interests of justice' (Criminal Appeal Act 1968, s. 23(1)). In deciding whether to admit fresh evidence the court must consider whether:

- the evidence is capable of belief;
- the evidence could afford a ground for allowing the appeal;
- the evidence would have been admissible at the trial; and
- there is a reasonable explanation why it was not so adduced.

In addition, under the 1995 Act, the Court of Appeal can direct the Criminal Cases Review Commission to investigate and report on any matter relevant to the determination of a case being considered by the court.

In **Stafford** *v* **DPP** (1974) the Court of Appeal said that if it was satisfied that there was no reasonable doubt about the guilt of the accused, the conviction should not be quashed, even though the jury might have come to a different view. The case of **Stafford** *v* **DPP** was reconsidered in **R** *v* **Pendleton** (2002). **Stafford** *v* **DPP** was not overruled but its interpretation needs to be reconsidered in the light of the later case. In 1986 Donald Pendleton was convicted of murdering a newspaper seller 15 years earlier. In 1999 the Criminal Cases Review Commission referred Mr Pendleton's conviction back to the Court of Appeal. Fresh evidence was available from an expert forensic psychologist to the effect that the appellant had psychological vulnerabilities, which raised serious doubts about the reliability of his statements to the police. The Court of Appeal both received this evidence and accepted the opinion of the expert. However, the appeal was dismissed on the grounds that the conviction was safe because the fresh evidence did not put a 'flavour of falsity' on the content of the interviews. His further appeal to the House of Lords was allowed.

While **Stafford** was not overruled, the House stated that the Court of Appeal had to remember that it was a court of review and that the jury were the judges of fact. The Court of Appeal therefore had to bear in mind:

> that the question for its consideration is whether the conviction is safe and not whether the accused is guilty. . . . It will usually be wise for the Court of Appeal, in a case of any difficulty, to test their own provisional view by asking whether the evidence if given at the trial, might reasonably have affected the decision of the trial jury to convict. If it might, the conviction must be thought to be unsafe.

The case of Hanratty was referred to the Court of Appeal in 2002 by the Criminal Cases Review Commission (**R** *v* **Hanratty** (2002)). Hanratty had been convicted of murder and was later executed. A campaign was subsequently launched to establish his innocence. The Court of Appeal ordered that the body of the defendant be exhumed and samples of his DNA obtained. The prosecution made an application under the Criminal Appeal Act 1968, s. 23, to be allowed to submit fresh evidence consisting of the DNA analysis of evidence collected at the time of the murder. The defence argued against this application primarily on the basis that there was a risk that the evidence had been contaminated after the defendant's arrest. The prosecution's application was successful. The defendant's DNA was found on some of the evidence collected at the time of the murder and Hanratty's appeal was rejected.

Outcome of the appeal

The appellate court can allow the appeal, dismiss it or order a new trial. Under s. 2 of the Criminal Appeal Act 1968 (as amended by the 1995 Act) an appeal should be allowed if the court thinks that the conviction 'is unsafe'. There is conflicting case law as to whether, if a person is found to have had an unfair trial under Art. 6 of the European Convention on Human Rights, this will automatically mean that the conviction is unsafe and should be quashed. Some English judges prefer the view that if the defendant is clearly guilty their conviction should be upheld as safe even if the trial was unfair. This seems to conflict with the view of the European Court of Human Rights, which suggested in **Condron** *v* **United Kingdom** (1999) that the conviction should always be quashed if there has been an unfair trial. The Court of Appeal may order a retrial where it feels this is required in the interests of justice. It will only do so if it accepts that the additional evidence is true but is not convinced that it is conclusive – in other words, that it would have led to a different verdict.

■ Powers of the prosecution following acquittal

In the past there was a general rule that once a person had been tried and acquitted they could not be retried for the same offence, under the principle of double jeopardy. The rule aimed to prevent the oppressive use of the criminal justice system by public authorities. Following the unsuccessful private prosecution of three men suspected of killing Stephen Lawrence, the judicial inquiry into the affair recommended that the principle of double jeopardy should be abolished. It proposed that the Court of Appeal should have the power to permit prosecution after acquittal 'where fresh and viable evidence is presented'.

The Criminal Justice Act 2003, s. 75 has now abolished the double jeopardy rule. The Act introduces an interlocutory prosecution right of appeal against a ruling by a Crown Court judge that there is no case to answer or any other ruling made before or during the trial that has the effect of terminating the trial. A retrial is permitted in cases of serious offences where there has been an acquittal in court, but compelling new evidence subsequently comes to light against the acquitted person. Twenty-nine serious offences are listed in Sched. 5 to the Act, and are most of the offences which carry a maximum sentence of life imprisonment. This is wider than the recommendations of the Law Commission and Sir Robin Auld. The consent of the Director of Public Prosecutions is required to reopen investigations and to apply to the Court of Appeal.

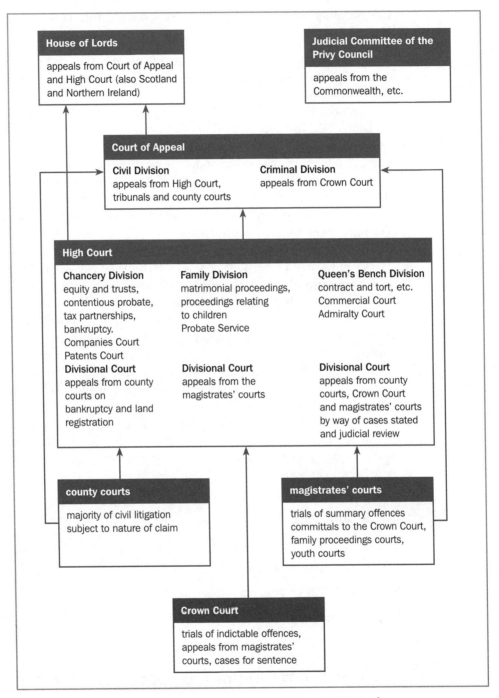

Figure 19.2 An outline of the court structure in England and Wales[1]

1. This diagram is, of necessity, much simplified and should not be taken as a comprehensive statement on the jurisdiction of any specific court.

Source: K. Dibdin, A. Sealy and S. Aktar, *Judicial Statistics Annual Report 2004*, p. 3.

Certain other exceptions to the double jeopardy rule also existed prior to the 2003 Act:

- The prosecution can state a case for consideration of the High Court following the acquittal of a defendant by the magistrates' court. This is restricted to a point of law or a dispute on jurisdiction.
- The prosecution can also, with leave, appeal to the House of Lords against a decision of the Court of Appeal.
- The Criminal Justice Act 1972 gives the Attorney-General powers to refer any point of law which has arisen in a case for the opinion of the Court of Appeal, even where the defendant was acquitted. Defendants are not identified (though they may be represented) and their acquittal remains unaffected even if the point of law goes against them – so this procedure is not, strictly speaking, an appeal. The purpose of this power is to enable the Court of Appeal to review a potentially incorrect legal ruling before it gains too wide a circulation in the trial courts.
- The Criminal Justice Act 1988 enables the Attorney-General to refer to the Court of Appeal cases of apparently too lenient sentencing for certain offences, including cases where it appears the judge has erred in law as to their powers of sentencing. Leave from the Court of Appeal is required. The Court of Appeal may quash the sentence and pass a more appropriate one. This is the first time that the prosecution is involved in the sentencing process. The provision was enacted in response to the Government's view that public confidence in the criminal justice system was being undermined by unduly lenient sentences, which had been given much publicity by the tabloid press.
- The Criminal Procedure and Investigation Act 1996 created a power to order a retrial where a person has been convicted of an offence involving interference with, or intimidation of, a juror, witness or potential witness, in any proceedings which led to an acquittal.

Quick quiz 19.3

1 Which court hears appeals by way of case stated from the magistrates' court?

2 Which court hears appeals from the Divisional Court?

3 What percentage of magistrates' cases are the subject of an appeal?

4 When can the Court of Appeal admit new evidence that was not heard in the original trial?

Criticism and reform of the appeal system

A Supreme Court

Rather unexpectedly, the Government announced in June 2003 that it was going to abolish the House of Lords and replace it with a Supreme Court. It subsequently issued a consultation paper, *Constitutional Reform: a Supreme Court for the United*

Kingdom (2004), which considered the shape that this reform should take. The Constitutional Reform Act 2005 has now been passed, which contains provisions for the creation of the new court. It is expected to start hearing cases in 2008.

The Government was undoubtedly wrong to announce a decision, then consult afterwards merely on the detail, but the decision itself was probably right. There is a natural inclination towards the saying, 'If it isn't broke, don't mend it'. But, with the highest court in the land, one cannot afford to wait until it is broken before one starts to mend. It is now important that the new Supreme Court gets some quality accommodation that matches its status. The judges need space, computer support, research facilities and research assistants. The new court will have to work hard in its early years to establish its reputation nationally and internationally. It must be given all the resources necessary in order to be able to achieve this.

Reasons for abolishing the House of Lords

The consultation paper stated that this reform was necessary to enhance the independence of the judiciary from both the legislature and the executive. It pointed to the growth of judicial review cases and the passing of the Human Rights Act 1998 as two key reasons why this reform was becoming urgent. Article 6 of the European Convention on Human Rights requires not only that the judges should be independent, but also that they should be seen to be independent. The fact that the Law Lords are currently a Committee of the House of Lords can raise issues about the appearance of independence from the legislature.

The Government is, however, anxious to point out that the reform does not imply any dissatisfaction with the performance of the House of Lords as the country's highest court of law:

> On the contrary its judges have conducted themselves with the utmost integrity and independence. They are widely and rightly admired, nationally and internationally. The Government believes, however, that the time has come to establish a new court regulated by statute as a body separate from Parliament.

Six of the current Law Lords are opposed to the reform, considering the change unnecessary and harmful.

Separation from Parliament

The new Supreme Court will be completely separate from Parliament. Its judges will have no rights to sit and vote in the upper House. Only the current Law Lords will have the right to sit and vote in the House of Lords after their retirement from the judiciary.

One advantage of this change will be that the court will no longer sit in the Palace of Westminster, where there is a shortage of space, and could be given more spacious accommodation elsewhere. It is likely to be based in a refurbished gothic building opposite Parliament in Parliament Square.

Jurisdiction

The proposed Court will be the Supreme Court for the whole of the UK. Its jurisdiction will remain the same as that of the House of Lords, but with the addition of jurisdiction in relation to devolution cases. At the moment the Privy Council has the jurisdiction to hear cases concerning the devolution of Scotland, Wales and Northern Ireland. This jurisdiction will be transferred to the new Supreme Court. The reason for the transfer is to remove any perceived conflict of interest in which the UK Parliament, with an obvious interest in a dispute about devolution, appears to be sitting in judgment over the case.

There is no proposal to create a Supreme Court on the US model with the power to overturn legislation. Nor is there any proposal to create a specific constitutional court. The new court will not have the power to give preliminary rulings on difficult points of law. It has been pointed out that English courts do not traditionally consider issues in the abstract, so giving such a power to the Supreme Court would sit very uneasily with our judicial traditions. This is despite the fact that we have become accustomed to this procedure for the European Court of Justice.

The Government recognizes that there are already various entities in the UK which are known as 'supreme courts'. In particular the Court of Appeal, the High Court and the Crown Court are together known as the Supreme Court to allocate jurisdiction to judges and to route work between the courts. But this title is not in common usage and in future the title of Supreme Court will be reserved for the new court to be created in 2008.

Membership

The existing 12 full-time Law Lords will form the initial members of the new court. The Government wants to keep the same number of full-time judges, but to continue to allow the court to call on the help of other judges on a part-time basis. The Lord Chancellor was a member of the Appellate Committee of the House of Lords, but does not have a right to sit in the Supreme Court. A President of the Court will be appointed.

The judges will no longer automatically become Lords. Members of the Supreme Court will be called 'Justices of the Supreme Court'.

Qualifications for membership will remain the same. The Government has rejected the idea that changes should be made to make it easier for distinguished academics to be appointed in order to enhance the diversity of the court. This is disappointing, as the Government itself acknowledges that the current pool of candidates for the post is very narrow, and the Government's statistics themselves show that the current senior judiciary are not representative of society.

Candidates will not be subjected to confirmation hearings before Parliament as these would risk politicizing the appointment process.

Privy Council

The Privy Council will continue to exist and to undertake its work for various Commonwealth and overseas territories. The judges of the Supreme Court will become the judges of the Privy Council and its other members will stay the same. The administrative and support arrangements for the Judicial Committee will remain unchanged. This seems an odd conclusion to reach. If the UK needs a modern, independent court, then it seems likely that the Commonwealth and overseas territories also need this. Failing to make this reform at the same time is failing to respect their needs and interests.

Do we need a second appeal court?

Do we need two courts with purely appellate jurisdiction? Could the House of Lords (or Supreme Court) be abolished altogether, leaving the Court of Appeal as the final appellate court? Efforts to abolish the appellate jurisdiction of the House of Lords date back over a hundred years – in fact the Judicature Act of 1873 contained a section which did just that, but was never brought into force. The following are some of the arguments on both sides.

For abolition

- The Court of Appeal should be sufficient; a third tier is unnecessary and illogical. A.P. Herbert points out that giving appellants the chance to have their case decided by two appellate courts is like having your appendix taken out by a distinguished surgeon and then being referred to another who might confirm the first surgeon's decision, but might just as easily recommend the appendix be replaced! Reversing legal decisions might not pose the same practical problems as reversing medical ones but, nevertheless, it may seem odd that the decisions of the eminent judges in the Court of Appeal can be completely overturned by the House of Lords.
- It allows a litigant with the support of a minority of judges to win. Take the example of a litigant losing a civil case, appealing to the Court of Appeal and losing, but finally winning in the House of Lords. Counting all the judges involved together, the litigant may have had six against them (the original trial judge, the three judges hearing the case in the Court of Appeal, and two out of five in the House of Lords). Yet, if three judges in the House of Lords are in their favour they win the case overall, even though twice as many judges supported their opponent.
- It adds cost and delay to achieving a decision. Usually, QCs are instructed in appeals to the House of Lords, substantially increasing costs, and extra time is taken up. This can add to emotional stress and financial hardship for one or both litigants.
- It has failed to make any adequate contribution to development of the criminal law. This point is made by the eminent criminal law specialists J.C. Smith and Glanville Williams. Unlike the Court of Appeal, the House of Lords has no specialist divisions, and criticisms of the quality of their decisions in criminal appeals may stem from this. Glanville Williams points out that 'It is particularly inapt that a Chancery judge should have the casting vote in the House of Lords in a criminal case, as Lord Cross did in **Hyam**' (see **Hyam** *v* **DPP** (1975)). He also suggests that the age of judges in the House of Lords is a problem, since old men are 'often fixed in their opinions' and 'tend to ignore the opinions of others'; this may be true, but the judges of the Court of Appeal are hardly in the first flush of youth either.

Part of the problem may be due to the strict conditions for appealing to the House of Lords, which mean that few criminal cases get there, and the Law Lords actually have very little chance to make notable contributions to this area of the law.

■ It tends to side with the establishment, and usually the Government. This is the argument advanced by Griffith (see p. 46), but there is little evidence to suggest that the Court of Appeal would be very different in this respect if it became the highest court.

■ The House of Lords offers nothing beyond finality, and that could be more efficiently achieved without it. Jackson, an academic in the field, examined the 15 appeals made to the House of Lords in 1972, and found that eight involved Government departments or national authorities and five were disputes between commercial concerns. He deduced that, in the case of both Government departments and commercial concerns, the reason for taking the case to the House of Lords was nothing more than the fact that it is the final court.

In the case of Government departments, where judicial decisions appear to obstruct them, their object is to remove that obstruction; appeal to the House of Lords may achieve this, but if not, the matter can be put right by legislation. However, they must have the final decision of the judiciary before this can happen, and must therefore go to the House of Lords – not because of any innate quality of its decision-making, but simply because it is the final court. Jackson felt that the commercial cases were also likely to be based on the pursuit of finality. If this is correct, abolishing the House of Lords would enable finality to be achieved more quickly and cheaply.

Against abolition

■ Its small membership allows the House of Lords to give a consistent leadership that the Court of Appeal, with its much greater number of judges, could not, and therefore to guide the harmonious development of the law. Louis Blom-Cooper QC (1972) has argued that, especially since the Practice Direction of 1966 allowing the House of Lords to overrule its own decisions, the Law Lords are in a unique position to be able to reform the law from the top. The much larger size of the Court of Appeal, and its division into different courts, means there would always be a danger of different courts within it applying different views of the law.

■ The combination of the two appellate courts allows the majority of appeals to be dealt with more quickly than the House of Lords could hope to deal with them, while still retaining the smaller court for those matters which require further consideration, and for promoting consistent development of the law.

■ The House of Lords plays a valuable role in correcting decisions by the Court of Appeal – in 1988 it reversed nearly 40 per cent of civil and 33 per cent of criminal appeals that were referred to it.

■ It has made some important contributions to the development of our law, including making marital rape a crime – in **R** *v* **R** (1991) – and confirming the restricted scope of parental rights in a modern society in **Gillick** *v* **West Norfolk and Wisbech Area Health Authority** (1985).

Lord Woolf on appeals

With regard to civil appeals, Lord Woolf (1996) has recommended the introduction of a system where cases could be referred to the Court of Appeal or House of Lords in order to ensure proper development of the law. This would be appropriate where the lower court has reached an unsatisfactory decision but where no appeal has been brought or is possible.

Sir Robin Auld on appeals

In his *Review of the Criminal Courts* (2001), Sir Robin Auld wanted to see a simplification of the appeal process. He recommended that all appeals should apply the same test, and favoured the adoption of the Court of Appeal test. He thought that there should be a single line of appeal from the magistrates' courts to the Court of Appeal. He would therefore abolish appeals from magistrates' courts to the Crown Court by way of rehearing. He would also abolish appeals from the magistrates' court and the Crown Court to the High Court by way of case stated and judicial review.

He thought that the Court of Appeal should be variously constituted according to the nature, legal importance and complexity of its work. In straightforward appeals only two judges would sit. In cases of exceptional legal importance and complexity, a distinguished academic could either be appointed to act as a judge in the case or be invited to submit a written brief to the court on the points in issue.

He thought the Court of Appeal needed to slow down so that appeal hearings were less rushed. More time needed to be allocated for the judges to prepare for cases and to write their judgments.

On points of law of general public importance, where there are conflicting decisions of the Court of Appeal or where the law is in such an unsatisfactory state that only the House of Lords can resolve it, he favoured the introduction of a 'leap-frog' appeal from the Crown Court to the House of Lords, similar to that which exists for civil appeals.

He also favoured giving the prosecution a new right to appeal what it considers to be a perverse acquittal by a jury, a reform which has been criticized by the Bar Council as containing 'grave dangers'.

The Privy Council

The Judicial Committee of the Privy Council hears appeals from Commonwealth countries, such as the Bahamas, Barbados, Bermuda, the Channel Islands, the Falkland Islands, Gibraltar, Jamaica, New Zealand and Trinidad and Tobago. Certain independent Commonwealth countries, including Australia, India, Malaysia, Nigeria, Pakistan and Singapore, have chosen to stop sending their final appeals to London. The Privy Council also hears appeals from, for example, disciplinary proceedings by professional bodies and the courts of the Church of England.

In recent years there has been much debate about the future of appeals to the Judicial Committee of the Privy Council from independent Caribbean countries. All of these countries have retained the mandatory death penalty by hanging for the crime of murder. The Privy Council is seen locally as an obstacle in the desire to execute those on death row. One proposal is to abolish the criminal jurisdiction of the Privy Council.

The Criminal Cases Review Commission (CCRC)

The CCRC was established to replace the old s. 17 procedure contained in the Criminal Appeal Act 1968 and repealed in 1995. Under the old procedure, the Home Secretary could refer a case that had been previously heard in the Crown Court to the Court of Appeal, despite the fact that the normal time limit for appeals had expired or an unsuccessful appeal had already been heard. The Home Secretary had considerable discretion whether or not to make this referral: the statute simply required a reference to be made 'if he thinks fit'.

There were serious difficulties with the s. 17 procedure. The Home Secretary only usually referred cases where new evidence had come to light, and which were continuing to attract media comment and public concern long after the trial had taken place. Each year there were about 730 applications to the Home Office and its equivalent in Northern Ireland, but only ten to 12 of those cases were actually referred to the Court of Appeal.

Problems with the process were highlighted by such cases as the Birmingham Six and the Tottenham Three, where references were only ordered after years of persuasion and publicity. The original appeal of the Birmingham Six was rejected in 1976. It was not until 1987 that the Home Secretary referred their case back to the Court of Appeal though that appeal was rejected. Three years later, he again referred the case to the Court of Appeal and this time the Director of Public Prosecutions did not resist the application so that the court had little choice but to allow the appeal and quash the convictions.

The Court of Appeal showed a general reluctance to allow s. 17 appeals in cases where it had already dismissed an appeal, and in fact appeared to dislike s. 17 referrals generally: in the first (unsuccessful) s. 17 appeal from the Birmingham Six, the court stated that: 'As has happened before in references by the Home Secretary to this court, the longer the hearing has gone on the more convinced this court has become that the verdict of the jury was correct.' As the book by the MP Chris Mullins (1990) on the Birmingham Six points out, this seemed to be a thinly veiled message to the Home Secretary that referring such cases was a waste of time.

Figure 19.3 The Criminal Cases Review Commission's offices in Alpha Tower, Birmingham

Source: The Criminal Cases Review Commission.

A further problem was that, once the reference was made, the appeal was governed by the Criminal Appeal Act 1968, and the expense and responsibility of preparing the appeal lay with the defendant, who would probably be in prison and have been there for quite some time. Legal aid might be available but investigation in these circumstances would be difficult.

It has been hoped that the CCRC will mark a considerable improvement on the old s. 17 procedure, but concerns have already been expressed about the new arrangements. One problem with the Commission is that, while it is predicted that more cases will reach the Court of Appeal than under the s. 17 procedure, one of the weaknesses with that procedure was that even when the case was referred to the Court of Appeal the convictions were often upheld, even though later it was acknowledged that there had been a miscarriage of justice. Thus, cases such as the Birmingham Six had to be repeatedly referred back to the Court of Appeal before the court would eventually overturn the original conviction. In that case the appeal was allowed on the basis that there was 'fresh' evidence as to the police interrogation techniques and the forensic evidence. In reality this evidence had, in essence, been before the Court of Appeal in 1987; the difference was that the court was forced to accept that the evidence raised a lurking doubt in 1991. Only if the other provisions are adequate to improve the Court of Appeal process will the same problems be avoided. An alternative solution would have been to give the Commission the power to decide appeals themselves.

The pressure group, Justice, has criticized the fact that the CCRC has no power to assign in-house staff as investigating officers. It has argued that without this power the Commission could not guarantee the independence of an inquiry. The CCRC has no independent powers to carry out searches of premises, to check criminal records, to use police computers or to make an arrest. To do this it would have to appoint someone who had these powers, usually a police officer. The fact that investigations carried out on behalf of the CCRC will be by the police has caused concern. Many allegations of a miscarriage of justice involve accusations of malpractice by the police. Experience of police investigations into the high-profile miscarriages of justice suggests that these are not always effective, and there is a tendency for the police to close ranks and try to protect each other. Justice has also questioned the independence of the organization as its members are government appointees.

The CCRC issued its third annual report in June 2000. This states that it received a total of 13,193 applications in its first three years. Eighty of these were referred to the courts; all were appeals following conviction in the Crown Court apart from one which was an appeal from the magistrates' court. Twenty-seven of these referrals have resulted in convictions being quashed or sentences modified. One of the first referrals made by the CCRC concerned Derek Bentley. He had been involved with a friend in an unsuccessful burglary. This had resulted in a police chase when his friend had pointed a gun at a police officer and Derek Bentley had said 'let him have it', at which point the friend shot and killed the officer. Derek Bentley was convicted as an accomplice to the murder. He appealed but his appeal was rejected and he was hanged in January 1953.

The circumstances of his conviction gave rise to a long campaign by his family and numerous representations were made to the Home Office. He was given a royal pardon in 1993 but this was in respect of the sentence only. The family continued its campaign for the conviction itself to be quashed and in 1998 the CCRC referred the case to the Court of Appeal which quashed the conviction, stating that the conviction was unsafe because of a defective summing-up by the trial judge to the jury, which had included such prejudicial comments about the defence case that Bentley had been denied a fair trial. This was a notable high-profile success for the CCRC, but it remains to be seen whether the Commission will have success with lower-profile referrals.

The CCRC has found the main reasons for it to refer cases back to the courts are:

- prosecution failings (such as breach of identification and interview procedures or the use of questionable witnesses);
- scientific evidence (such as DNA and fingerprint evidence);
- non-disclosure of evidence;
- new evidence (such as alibis, eye-witnesses or confessions).

The biggest problem facing the CCRC since it was set up is a substantial backlog of cases waiting to be considered. This issue was considered by a Home Affairs Select Committee Report in 1999. It considered that the Commission could reduce the amount of detailed work done on each case without reducing its effectiveness, as its approach was currently 'meticulous to a fault'. It also suggested that the Commission should refer more cases to the Court of Appeal, rather than trying to second-guess the Court of Appeal and only referring cases that are highly likely to be overturned. In its annual report for 1999/2000 the Commission responded:

> Some external commentators have advocated that the Commission should review cases faster by being less thorough, and should refer them more readily to the appropriate courts of appeal. Not referring cases that should be referred, for lack of thoroughness, would perpetuate the very miscarriages of justice that the Commission was set up to review, and would be likely to result in resubmission of cases and judicial review. Referring unmeritorious cases would impose a costly burden on the courts of appeal. Such behaviour would rapidly diminish public confidence in the competence of the Commission, and in the wider criminal justice system.

The CCRC has improved its procedures and been given increased resources to try and deal more speedily with its workload.

There is also a problem of funding submissions to the Commission. At the moment, the Legal Services Commission only pays for two hours of a solicitor's time, which is insufficient for the preparation of such an application. As a result, more than 90 per cent of applicants are not represented by a solicitor.

 Task 19.4

The Chairman of the Criminal Cases Review Commission has written in its third annual report an open letter to the Home Secretary, David Blunkett. This states:

'Although early stakeholder concerns regarding the Commission's likely independence, and ability to investigate miscarriages of justice thoroughly, are now only rarely repeated, there has been persistent, well-founded criticism of the Commission's accumulation of cases awaiting review. That accumulation derives directly from the fact that the Commission's initial funding and corresponding scale of operations were inadequate to cope with the case intake that materialised. The Commission can satisfy the legitimate expectations of Parliament and its other stakeholders only if the resources allocated to it are sufficient for it to minimise its case accumulation.

Projections made in February 1998 suggested that some 50 Case Review Managers (CRMs) would be needed for a few years to enable expeditious progress to be made towards that minimisation. Subsequent funding increases allowed that complement of CRMs to be reached just before 31 March 2002. . . .

There has been an unexpected 12% increase in applications to the Commission, combined with fast CRM turnover and slower recruitment than expected. These factors have retarded progress towards minimisation of the case accumulation.'

Questions

1 What is meant by 'stakeholders'?

2 What is meant by the term 'case accumulation'.

3 What problems have the CCRC encountered in reducing the backlog of cases?

■ Reluctance to overturn jury verdicts

Know your terms 19.5

Define the following terms:

1 The 'leap-frog' procedure
2 Divisional Court
3 Double jeopardy
4 Criminal Cases Review Commission

The Court of Appeal seems to feel that overturning jury verdicts weakens public confidence in the jury system, and it is therefore very reluctant to do it. This view was spelt out during the final, successful appeal of the Birmingham Six, in 1991, in which the Court of Appeal stated:

Nothing in s. 2 of the Act, or anywhere else obliges or entitles us to say whether we think that the appellant is innocent. This is a point of great constitutional importance. The task of deciding whether a man is innocent or guilty falls on the jury. We are concerned solely with the question whether the verdict of the jury can stand.

Rightly or wrongly (we think rightly) trial by jury is the foundation of our criminal justice system . . . The primacy of the jury in the criminal justice system is well illustrated by the difference between the Criminal and Civil Divisions of the Court of Appeal . . . A civil

The Criminal Cases Review Commission states that its values are:

■ Independence
■ Integrity
■ Impartiality
■ Professionalism
■ Accountability
■ Transparency

Figure 19.4 The value of Criminal Cases Review Commission

Source: *Criminal Cases Review Commission Annual Report and Accounts 2004–5.*

> appeal is by way of rehearing of the whole of the case. So the court is concerned with fact as well as law . . . It follows that in a civil case the Court of Appeal may take a different view of the facts from the court below. In a criminal case this is not possible . . . the Criminal Division is perhaps more accurately described as a court of review.

The major problem with the Court of Appeal's approach is that, in many cases, the fault lies not with the decision-making powers of the jury, but in the evidence presented to it. Where a jury has not seen all the evidence, or where the evidence it has heard has been falsified by the police (as was alleged in some of the well-known miscarriages of justice), or where the jury has in any other way failed to have the case properly presented to it, overturning the verdict should not automatically be viewed as a criticism of its ability to make correct decisions. A better way to demonstrate confidence in the jury system might be to order a retrial with a new jury.

The Royal Commission on Criminal Justice 1993 (RCCJ – the Runciman Commission) concluded that the Court of Appeal should show greater willingness to substitute its judgment for that of the jury. The Commission pointed out that in gauging the evidence juries could make errors, particularly where it was a high-profile case in which emotions ran high. We will have to wait and see whether the Criminal Appeal Act 1995 might instigate a change of philosophy in this regard, particularly in the light of the changes to the rules on the admissibility of fresh evidence.

Up to 1995 the Court of Appeal was able to conclude that even if there was found to have been a material irregularity in the trial, it could still uphold the conviction if it thought that no miscarriage of justice had occurred. This was known as 'applying the proviso', but the relevant statutory provision has now been repealed – which may lead to a greater willingness to overturn a jury verdict.

▌Admission of fresh evidence

Until 1995, s. 23 of the 1968 Act, as well as giving the court a discretion to admit new evidence, imposed a duty on the court to receive fresh evidence where it was 'likely to be credible'. In practice, the Court of Appeal was very reluctant to admit fresh evidence, despite the apparently broad drafting of the legislation. One of the reasons for the court's approach was that it was unwilling to turn what was supposed to be a process of review into a full rehearing. But, in effect, defendants could be punished and denied the right to a fair hearing for omissions caused by their lawyers' incompetence, the underfunding of the legal aid system or the prosecution's obstructiveness. The RCCJ concluded that the statutory powers to admit fresh evidence were sufficient; the problem was that in practice they were being given too narrow an interpretation. Thus, they encouraged the Court of Appeal to take a more flexible approach.

Now the appeal court merely has a discretion to receive fresh evidence where 'it is capable of belief'. At the time of the amendment, it was suggested that this provided a wider discretion for the court in the interests of justice. Unfortunately, this does not seem to be reflected in the Court of Appeal's interpretation of the provision. In **R v Jones (Steven Martin)** (1996) the appellant had been convicted of his wife's murder and, on appeal, he applied for the court to receive fresh expert evidence from three forensic pathologists. While on the facts of the case the evidence was allowed, the court stated that in general only new factual evidence as opposed to expert evidence would normally be admitted, noting that the test for admissibility was more appropriate to such evidence as one could rarely consider expert evidence as 'incapable of belief'. This case shows that the legislative amendment to s. 23 may have actually accentuated the problems of the Court of Appeal refusing to admit fresh evidence.

Lord Devlin, in his book *The Judge* (1979), criticized the Court of Appeal's decision in **Stafford** *v* **DPP** (1974) to follow its own view of whether new evidence makes a conviction unsafe (or unsatisfactory), rather than assessing the effect such evidence might have had on the trial jury. He felt that this involves judges in findings of fact, a function that properly belongs to the jury. The jury ends up playing a subordinate part in the verdict, since it has not heard all the evidence. He believes the change from assessing the possible effect of new evidence on the trial jury has not been sanctioned by Parliament and is an attack on the jury system.

▌ Reluctance to order retrials

Many have argued that the Court of Appeal should use its power to order retrials more often. The number of such retrials has been growing, from three in 1990 to 23 in 1992, though they remain rare.

Lord Devlin has argued, as stated above, that a retrial should be ordered wherever fresh evidence could have made a difference to the verdict – the original verdict being clearly unsatisfactory since it was given without the jury hearing all the evidence.

Opponents argue that it may be unfair to the accused to reopen a decided case, and that a second trial cannot be a fair one, especially if some time has passed and/or the case has received a lot of publicity. But, as Lord Devlin argues, this does not stop retrials being ordered where the jury has failed to agree a verdict, nor are prosecutions necessarily stifled because witnesses have to speak of events many years before. In fact, at the same time as the Birmingham Six were told that a retrial 13 years after the original one was inappropriate, the Government was debating the prosecution of war criminals, some 44 years after the end of the Second World War. Shortly after the Six's unsuccessful appeal, an IRA man was brought to trial on charges dating back 13 years.

As far as publicity is concerned, the second jury may well know of the defendant's record and have noted other adverse publicity, as well as knowing that the defendant has already been convicted on a previous occasion for the crime. On the other hand, in all the high-profile miscarriages of justice, no further publicity could have affected the attitudes of potential jurors more than that surrounding the original offences and trials – in fact prejudicial media reporting was one reason given for finding the convictions of the Taylor sisters unsafe and unsatisfactory in 1995.

Many wrongful convictions result from mistaken identity, and it is difficult for the Court of Appeal, which does not usually re-examine witnesses, to assess the strength of such evidence. Retrials might be the best way of dealing with this problem. A general power to order a retrial could also be a way of convicting offenders who escape on a technicality first time round, and might be a more obviously just solution than applying the old proviso, or letting such defendants go free, which has a negative effect on the public, the jury and the victim. However, it could also subject genuinely innocent defendants to a second ordeal.

It has been suggested that wider use of retrials would 'open the floodgates' to a deluge of appeals, yet this does not appear to be a problem in other countries with wider powers of retrial, including Scotland. In any case, Lord Atkin has pointed out, 'Finality is a good thing but justice is better.'

The Runciman Commission considered the issue and concluded that the Court of Appeal should use the power to order a retrial more extensively.

The single test for quashing convictions

Before the 1995 Act, there used to be three grounds on which the Criminal Division of the Court of Appeal could allow an appeal. These were where the court thought that:

■ the jury's verdict was unsafe and unsatisfactory; or
■ there was an error of law; or
■ there was a material irregularity in the course of the trial.

The old law was criticized by the Runciman Commission on the basis that it was unnecessarily complex and that the different grounds for quashing a conviction overlapped. For example, it felt that there was no real difference between the words 'unsafe' and 'unsatisfactory'. In the light of this criticism the law has been reduced by the Criminal Appeal Act 1995 to a single test that the court thinks the conviction is unsafe. This is narrower than that recommended by the Runciman Commission as it had favoured a retrial where the conviction 'may' be unsafe. The Law Society, the Bar, Liberty and Justice all unsuccessfully called on the Government to follow the RCCJ's proposal. The Government's expressed view was that any such doubt implied by the concept of 'may be unsafe' was already implicit in the idea of a conviction being 'unsafe'.

Government ministers insisted that the effect of the new law was simply to restate or consolidate the existing practice of the Court of Appeal. However, the leading criminal law academic, Professor J.C. Smith, and the Director of the pressure group Justice, Anne Owens (1995), have both criticized the new single test on the basis that there is a danger it will be interpreted more narrowly than the previous tests.

Michael Zander (one of the Commissioners and a leading academic on the English legal system), along with one other Commissioner, disagreed with the final proposal. They took the view that where there had been serious police malpractice then the conviction should always be quashed to discourage such conduct, and to prevent the police believing that they could benefit in terms of getting convictions by such behaviour. This is a situation where, under the old law, the Court of Appeal might have stated that the conviction was safe but it would be quashed because it was unsatisfactory. This route is no longer open to the court.

Judicial review

The system of judicial review by the High Court oversees the decisions of public bodies and officials, such as inferior courts and tribunals, local councils and members of the executive including police officers and Government Ministers. Cases are heard by the Queen's Bench Division. Certain public bodies are exempt from judicial review. For example, in **R v Parliamentary Commissioner for Standards, ex parte Al Fayed** (1998) the Court of Appeal ruled that the Parliamentary Commissioner for Standards could not be subjected to judicial review. One of the functions of the Commissioner is to receive and, where appropriate, investigate complaints from the public in relation to the conduct of Members of Parliament. Mohammed Al Fayed, the owner of Harrods, had made such a complaint that Michael Howard, while Home Secretary, had received a corrupt payment. The complaint had been investigated and then rejected and Al Fayed had sought judicial review of this decision. The Court of Appeal ruled that the Parliamentary Commissioner for Standards operated as part of the proceedings of Parliament and its activities were non-justiciable. This is because of the principles of the separation of powers discussed at p. 103.

Unlike the appeal process, judicial review does not examine the merits of the decision. It can only quash a decision if the public body had no power to make it, known as *ultra vires* (*ultra* is Latin for 'beyond' and *vires* is Latin for 'powers'). There are two forms of *ultra vires*: procedural *ultra vires* and substantive *ultra vires*.

Quick quiz 19.6

1 When was the Criminal Appeals Review Commission created?

2 What is the single test that the Court of Appeal applies in deciding whether to allow a criminal appeal?

3 Explain the case involving Derek Bentley.

4 Which court hears cases involving judicial review?

Reading on the web

Any developments in the establishment of a Supreme Court are likely to be signalled on the Department for Constitutional Affairs' website:

http://www.dca.gov.uk/

The annual report of the Criminal Cases Review Commission is published on the Commission's website at:

http://www.ccrc.gov.uk/publications/publications_get.asp

Question and answer guides

1 **Assess the impact of the Criminal Cases Review Commission on the appeal process.**

Answer guide

This is a very topical area, and therefore one which you would be wise to study carefully. You could start your essay by stating what the Commission is, and looking at the reasons for its creation – what were the problems with criminal appeals? You could mention the role that these problems played in the well-known miscarriages of justice – these are highlighted in the section on criticisms in this chapter, while the stories of some of the miscarriages of justice are told in more detail in Chapter 12.

Then move on to look in detail at the Commission itself; its membership, function and powers. One of the points you might want to make is that it is not an appeal court as such, but can merely refer cases for appeal, and that it replaces the old s. 17 procedure under which the Home Secretary referred cases back to appeal. You are asked to assess its impact; this essentially means considering how far it is solving the problems it was set up to address. In answering this, you should highlight ways in which it is an improvement on the previous situation – the problems with the s. 17 procedure are relevant here, for example – and also any criticisms which can be made of it. You could point to the successful appeal in Derek Bentley's case (see p. 415), but that there is now a serious backlog of cases that is rapidly growing.

2 **Gavin is due to be tried at Amcaster Crown Court for robbery of £7,000 from a bank.**

(a) If he is found guilty, what appeal routes are open to him? *(10 marks)*

(b) What appeal rights are available to the prosecution? *(15 marks)*

(c) Is this system of appeals satisfactory? *(25 marks) (Oxford)*

Answer guide

(a) The appeal route is first to the Court of Appeal. The information required for this part of the answer is contained under the heading 'From the Crown Court' at p. 402. Note that reaching the Court of Appeal via the Criminal Cases Review Commission is an exceptional procedure. There is then a further appeal possible to the House of Lords. Following the Access to Justice Act 1999, he could also make an appeal by way of case stated to the High Court.

(b) Here you should discuss the material contained under the sub-heading 'Powers of the prosecution following acquittal' on p. 406.

(c) The material contained in the section 'Criticism and reform of the appeal system' is relevant to this part of the answer. In particular, you would want to discuss how far the Criminal Cases Review Commission is more satisfactory than the old s. 17 procedure, the new rules on the admission of fresh evidence and the whole debate surrounding the House of Lords.

3 **An Act of Parliament gave power to local councils to pass laws for purposes of (among other things) 'ensuring the safety and well-being of all pedestrians and other authorized users of pedestrianized areas', but required the local authority to consult with representatives of all interested parties before any laws were made. The local authority passed a law requiring all**

street entertainers to be in possession of a licence and to perform only in the area designated in the licence. Before doing so, officials of the local authority sought the views of town centre traders, the pedestrian society and a small number of street musicians. In the six months after the law was passed, no licences were granted to any jugglers or fire-eaters. When H, a juggler who had always previously given performances in the area, enquired why he had been refused a licence, he was told that juggling and fire-eating were too dangerous. After his appeal against the refusal to grant a licence had been turned down by a committee established by the local authority to hear complaints, H discovered that the chairman of the committee was the brother of a street entertainer who had been granted a licence and whose earnings were reputed to have risen dramatically since the introduction of the licensing system.

Explain whether there is any way in which H may challenge the actions and decisions by which he has been deprived of his chance to earn money by juggling in the street. *(London)*

Answer guide

The Act of Parliament was a parent Act which gave the local authority the power to make delegated legislation. H can challenge the actions and decisions by which he has been deprived of his chance to earn money through the system of judicial review.

H can found his challenge on two grounds: that the delegated legislation was made in breach of the law and that the decision of the committee had breached the law. Looking first at the delegated legislation, the relevant material on this issue can be found at p. 59. The delegated legislation could be challenged as invalid on the basis of procedural *ultra vires*. It would be claimed that the proper procedures were not followed in its creation. The parent Act required that the local authority consult representatives of all interested parties before making the delegated legislation. H could argue that though representatives of traders and pedestrians were consulted, the consultation of street musicians was not representative of all the street entertainers. You could have referred to the case of **Agricultural, Horticultural and Forestry Training Board** v **Aylesbury Mushrooms Ltd** (1972).

Looking secondly at the decision of the committee, H could argue that there was substantive *ultra vires*. In particular, he could argue that it had been made for an improper purpose as there is a suggestion that the decision may have been taken to favour certain kinds of entertainers, perhaps from personal motives.

He could also point to procedural *ultra vires* on the basis that the rules of natural justice had been violated. There is a strong possibility of bias in the decision-making process, as the chairman of the committee either has a personal financial interest (through his brother) or is likely to favour the local authority decision because of his concern for his brother's livelihood.

Finally, you could point to the different remedies available under these procedures, especially *certiorari* (to quash the decision), *mandamus* (to compel further decision-making that is free of the illegality) and damages. ('London Qualifications Ltd.', accepts no responsibility whatsoever for the accuracy or method in the answers given.)

4 **(a)** Describe the main appeal routes for defendants from the magistrates' court and the Crown Court. [25]

(b) Explain and comment on the role of the Criminal Cases Review Commission. [20]
(OCR June 2001 Machinery of Justice 2568, Question 1)

Answer guide

(a) The material you need to answer this part of the question is contained at pp. 401–3. You need to divide your answer into two parts, looking first at appeals from the magistrates' court and ▶

then at appeals from the Crown Court. As regards appeals from the magistrates' court, the appeal options are discussed on pp. 401–2.

An appeal from the Crown Court is made to the Court of Appeal (Criminal Division) with a further possibility of appeal to the House of Lords. Permission is always required to make these appeals.

You could mention that in practice there are very few appeals from the decisions of the magistrates' courts and very few appeals are made to the House of Lords.

(b) Useful material on the role of the Criminal Cases Review Commission can be found on pp. 403 and 414.

Chapter summary

Appeals in civil law cases

Following the report of Sir Jeffrey Bowman into the Civil Division of the Court of Appeal in 1998, the Access to Justice Act 1999 introduced some significant reforms to the civil appeal process. The Access to Justice Act provides that in normal circumstances there will be only one level of appeal.

From the county court

Appeals based on alleged errors of law or fact are made to the Civil Division of the Court of Appeal. Appeals from a district judge's decision normally have to go first to a circuit judge and then to the High Court.

From the High Court

Cases started in the High Court may be appealed to the Civil Division of the Court of Appeal.

Appeals in criminal cases

From the magistrates' court (criminal jurisdiction)

There are four routes of appeal:

■ the magistrates can rectify an error they have made;
■ a defendant who has pleaded not guilty may appeal as of right to the Crown Court on the grounds of being wrongly convicted or too harshly sentenced;
■ either the prosecution or the accused may appeal to the High Court on the grounds that the magistrates have made an error of law or acted outside their jurisdiction; and
■ the Criminal Cases Review Commission can refer appeals from the magistrates' court to the Crown Court.

From the Crown Court

There are three types of appeal from the Crown Court:

■ an appeal to the Court of Appeal;
■ an application to the Criminal Cases Review Commission; and
■ an appeal by way of case stated from the Crown Court to the High Court.

Powers of the prosecution following acquittal

The general rule is that once a person has been tried and acquitted, he or she cannot be retried for the same offence, under the principle of double jeopardy. Major exceptions have now been developed.

Criticism and reform of the appeal system

The appeal system has been the subject of considerable criticism. There has been concern over the working of the Criminal Cases Review Commission. The Court of Appeal has been criticized for being reluctant to overturn jury verdicts, admit fresh evidence and order retrials. The Government intends to abolish the House of Lords and replace it with a new, independent Supreme Court.

Judicial review

The system of judicial review by the High Court oversees the decisions of public bodies and officials.

Chapter 20

Alternative methods of dispute resolution

Introduction

Court hearings are not always the best methods of resolving a dispute, and their disadvantages mean that, for some types of problem, alternative mechanisms may be more suitable. The main uses of these at present are in family, consumer, commercial, construction and employment cases, but, following Lord Woolf's reforms of the civil justice system, these alternative mechanisms should play a more important role in solving all types of civil disputes.

The Civil Procedure Rule 1.4 requires the court to undertake case management which is stated to include:

> (2)(e) encouraging the parties to use an ADR procedure if the Court considers that appropriate and facilitating the use of such procedure
> (f) helping the parties to settle the whole or part of the case.

In addition, Civil Procedure Rule 26.4 allows the court to grant a stay for settlement by ADR or other means either when one or all of the parties request this, or when the court considers this would be appropriate. If a party fails to use ADR where the court thinks this would have been appropriate, then it can be penalized through a costs order (Civil Procedure Rule 44.5).

In **Halsey** *v* **Milton Keynes General NHS Trust** (2004) the Court of Appeal held that the courts do not, however, have the power to force parties to try ADR, as this might amount to a breach of a person's right to a fair trial under Art. 6 of the European Convention on Human Rights.

> It is one thing to encourage the parties to agree to mediation, even to encourage them in the strongest terms. It is another to order them to do so. It seems to us that to oblige truly unwilling parties to refer their disputes to mediation would be to impose an unacceptable obstruction on their right of access to the Court.

By contrast, in many other countries, such as the United States and Australia, the courts are prepared to force the parties to try ADR.

Problems with court hearings

Alternative methods of dispute resolution have become increasingly popular because of the difficulties of trying to resolve disputes through court hearings. Below are some of the specific problems posed by court hearings.

The adversarial process

A trial necessarily involves a winner and a loser, and the adversarial procedure combined with the often aggressive atmosphere of court proceedings divides the parties, making them end up enemies even where they did not start out that way. This can be a disadvantage where there is some reason for the parties to sustain a relationship after the problem under discussion is sorted out – child custody cases are the obvious example, but in business, too, there may be advantages in resolving a dispute in a way which does not make enemies of the parties. The court system is often said to be best suited to areas where the parties are strangers and happy to remain so – it is interesting to note that in small-scale societies with close kinship links, court-type procedures are rarely used, and disputes are usually settled by negotiation processes that aim to satisfy both parties, and thus maintain the harmony of the group.

Technical cases

Some types of dispute rest on detailed technical points, such as the way in which a machine should be made, or the details of a medical problem, rather than on points of law. The significance of such technical details may not be readily understandable by an ordinary judge. Expert witnesses or advisers may be brought in to advise on these points, but this takes time, and so raises costs. Where detailed technical evidence is at issue, alternative methods of dispute resolution can employ experts in a particular field to take the place of a judge.

Inflexible

In a court hearing, the rules of procedure lay down a fixed framework for the way in which problems are addressed. This may be inappropriate in areas which are of largely private concern to the parties involved. Alternative methods can allow the parties themselves to take more control of the process.

Imposed solutions

Court hearings impose a solution on the parties, which, since it does not involve their consent, may need to be enforced. If the parties are able to negotiate a settlement between them, to which they both agree, this should be less of a problem.

Publicity

The majority of court hearings are public. This may be undesirable in some business disputes, where one or both of the parties may prefer not to make public the details of their financial situation or business practices because of competition.

Alternative dispute resolution mechanisms

Where, for one or more of the reasons explained above, court action is not the best way of solving a dispute, a wide range of alternative methods of dispute resolution (often known as ADR) may be used. Three main forms of ADR can be identified: arbitration, mediation and conciliation:

Arbitration is a procedure whereby both sides to a dispute agree to let a third party, the arbitrator, decide. The arbitrator may be a lawyer, or may be an expert in the field of the dispute. He or she will make a decision according to the law and the decision is legally binding.

Mediation involves the appointment of a mediator to help the parties to a dispute reach an agreement which each considers acceptable. Mediation can be 'evaluative', where the mediator gives an assessment of the legal strength of a case, or 'facilitative', where the mediator concentrates on assisting the parties to define the issues. When a mediation is successful and an agreement is reached, it is written down and forms a legally binding contract unless the parties state otherwise.

Conciliation is similar to mediation but the conciliator takes a more interventionist role than the mediator in bringing the two parties together and in suggesting possible solutions to help achieve an agreed settlement. The term conciliation is gradually falling into disuse and the process is regarded as a form of mediation.

One of the simplest forms of ADR is, of course, informal negotiation between the parties themselves, with or without the help of lawyers – the high numbers of civil cases settled out of court are examples of this. Formal schemes include the Advisory, Conciliation and Arbitration Service (ACAS), which mediates in many industrial disputes and unfair dismissal cases; the role of ombudsmen in dealing with disputes in the fields of insurance and banking, and in complaints against central and local government and public services; the work done by trade organizations such as the Association of British Travel Agents (ABTA) in settling consumer complaints; inquiries into such areas as objections concerning compulsory purchase or town and country planning; the conciliation schemes offered by courts and voluntary organizations to divorcing couples; and the arbitration schemes run by the Institute of Arbitrators for business disputes. We will look at some of these in more detail below. Though procedural details vary widely, what they all have in common is that they are attempting to provide a method

Figure 20.1 The ABTA logo
Source: Association of British Travel Agents.

of settling disagreements that avoids some or all of the disadvantages of the court system listed above.

The Government is keen to promote ADR. It has set up a working party to draw up plans to increase awareness of the availability of ADR and intends to launch a wide-ranging awareness campaign. As part of the Government's commitment to promote alternative dispute resolution, Government legal disputes will be settled by mediation or arbitration whenever possible. Government departments will only go to court as a last resort.

Pressure to use ADR

Following the Woolf reforms of the civil justice system (see p. 354), the Civil Procedure Rules positively encourage the use of ADR. The pre-action protocols direct the parties to consider ADR. When filling out the allocation questionnaire, the parties are invited to apply for a one-month stay of proceedings in order to explore settlement through ADR. Active case management under the Civil Procedure Rule 1.4 involves 'encouraging the parties to use an alternative dispute resolution procedure if the court considers that to be appropriate and facilitating the use of such procedure'. The courts will order a stay of the proceedings for ADR if the parties request it.

The Court of Appeal is now prepared to punish parties who refuse to use ADR by depriving them of costs, even if they are successful in the action: **Dunnett** *v* **Railtrack plc** (2002). A party may turn down an opponent's offer to mediate with impunity if it can satisfy the court that it has compelling reasons for doing so. Thus, in **Hurst** *v* **Leeming** (2002) the court held that when mediation can have no real prospect of success a party may, with impunity, refuse to proceed to mediation.

Examples of ADR

Below are some examples of ADR being used in practice.

Conciliation in unfair dismissal cases

A statutory conciliation scheme administered by ACAS operates before cases of unfair dismissal can be taken to an employment tribunal. ACAS conciliation officers talk to both sides with the aim of settling the dispute without a tribunal hearing; they are supposed to procure reinstatement of the employee where possible, but in practice most settlements are only for damages.

A conciliation officer contacts each party or their representatives to discuss the case and advise each side on the strength or weakness of their position. They may tell each side what the other has said, but if the case does eventually go to a tribunal, none of this information is admissible without the consent of the party who gave it.

Evaluation

 Know your terms 20.1

Define the following terms:

1 Adversarial process
2 Arbitrator
3 ADR
4 ACAS

The success of the scheme is sometimes measured by the fact that two-thirds of cases are either withdrawn or settled by the conciliation process. However, this ignores the imbalance in power between the employer and the employee, especially where the employee has no legal representation – the fact that there has been a settlement does not necessarily mean it is a fair one, when one party is under far more pressure to agree than the other. Dickens's 1985 study of unfair dismissal cases found that awards after a hearing were generally higher than those achieved by conciliation, implying that employees may feel under pressure to agree to any settlement. The study suggested that the scheme would be more effective in promoting fair settlements – rather than settlement at any price – if conciliation officers had a less neutral stance and instead tried to help enforce the worker's rights.

Mediation in divorce cases

In many ways, the court system is an undesirable forum for divorce and its attendant disputes over property and children, since the adversarial nature of the system can aggravate the differences between the parties. This makes the whole process more traumatic for those involved, and clearly is especially harmful where there are children. Consequently, conciliation has for some time been made available to divorcing couples, not necessarily to get them back together (though this can happen), but to try to ensure that any arrangements between them can be made as amicably as possible, reducing the strain on the parties themselves as well as their children.

The Family Law Act 1996 makes changes to the divorce laws and places a greater emphasis on mediation. The Act requires those seeking public funding for representation in family proceedings to attend a meeting with a mediator to consider whether mediation might be suitable in their case.

Evaluation

In divorce cases generally, success depends on the parties themselves and their willingness to cooperate. The parties may find that meeting in a neutral environment, with the help of an experienced, impartial professional helps them communicate calmly, and can make the process of divorce less painful for the couple and their children, by avoiding the need for a court battle in which each feels obliged to accuse the other of being unfit to look after their children – a battle which can be as expensive as it is unpleasant, at a time when one or both parties may be under considerable financial strain.

A three-year study undertaken as a pilot scheme for the new reforms found that eight out of ten couples reached agreement on some issues through mediation, and four in ten reached a complete settlement. However, the Solicitors' Family Law Association (SFLA) points out that because men are usually the main earners in a family, and women's earning abilities may be limited by the demands of childcare, women may need lawyers to get a fair deal financially; in fact the SFLA says the reforms may well turn out to be 'a rogue's charter for unscrupulous husbands'.

Trade association arbitration schemes

The Fair Trading Act 1973 provides that the Director-General of Fair Trading has a duty to promote codes of practice for trade associations, which include arrangements for handling complaints. So far, more than 20 codes have received approval from the Office of Fair Trading (OFT), and there are many other voluntary schemes not yet approved. Many include provisions for an initial conciliation procedure between consumers and retailers or suppliers in case of complaints, often followed by independent arbitration if conciliation fails.

One of the best-known examples is that set up by the Association of British Travel Agents (ABTA), which, in the case of disputes between tour operators and consumers, offers impartial conciliation. If this fails, disputes may be referred to a special arbitration scheme – about half of all claims referred to it succeed, though not always winning the amount originally claimed.

Evaluation

The best of the schemes offer quick, simple dispute resolution procedures, but standards do vary – the National Consumer Council has reported that some are very slow, and there is some concern about the impartiality of arbitrators. These problems could be addressed relatively easily, but the main drawback is the diversity of the codes, and widespread ignorance of their existence, not only among consumers but even among some of the retailers covered by them! Tighter controls by the OFT and better publicity could make them much more useful mechanisms.

Commercial arbitration

Many commercial contracts contain an arbitration agreement, requiring any dispute to be referred to arbitration before court proceedings are undertaken – the aim being to do away with the need for going to court. Arbitrators usually have some expertise in the relevant field, and lists of suitable individuals are kept by the Institute of Arbitration. The parties themselves choose their arbitrator, ensuring that the person has the necessary expertise in their area and is not connected to either of them. Once appointed, the arbitrator is required to act in an impartial, judicial manner just as a judge would, but the difference is that they will not usually need to have technical points explained to them, so there is less need for expert witnesses.

Disputes may involve disagreement over the quality of goods supplied, interpretation of a trade clause or point of law, or a mixture of the two. Where points of law are involved the arbitrator may be a lawyer.

The Arbitration Act 1996 aims to promote commercial arbitration, by providing a clear framework for its use. It sets out the powers of the parties to shape the process according to their needs, and provides that they must each do everything necessary to allow the arbitration to proceed properly and without delay. It also spells out the powers of arbitrators, which include limiting the costs to be recoverable by either party and making orders which are equivalent to High Court injunctions if the parties agree. Arbitrators are also authorized to play an inquisitorial role, investigating the facts of the case – many of them are, after all, experts in the relevant fields.

Arbitration hearings must be conducted in a judicial manner, in accordance with the rules of natural justice, but proceedings are informal and held in private, with the time and place decided by the parties. The arbitrator's decision, known as the award, is often delivered immediately, and is as binding on the parties as a High Court judgment would be, and if necessary can be enforced as one.

The award is usually to be considered as final, but appeal may be made to the High Court on a question of law, with the consent of all the parties, or with the permission of court. Permission will only be given if the case could substantially affect the rights of one of the parties, and provided (with some exceptions) that they had not initially agreed to restrict rights of appeal. The High Court may confirm, vary or reverse the award, or send it back to the arbitrator for reconsideration.

Evaluation

Arbitration fees can be high, but for companies this may be outweighed by the money they save through being able to get the problem solved as soon as it arises, rather than having to wait months for a court hearing. The arbitration hearing itself tends to be quicker than a court case, because of the expertise of the arbitrator – in a court hearing time and therefore money can be wasted in explanation of technical points to the judge.

The ability of the parties to choose their arbitrator promotes mutual trust in and respect for the decision, and arbitration is conducted with a view to compromise rather than combat, which avoids destroying the business relationship between the parties. Privacy ensures that business secrets are not made known to competitors. Around 10,000 commercial cases a year go to arbitration, which tends to suggest that business people are fairly happy with the system and the more detailed framework set out by the 1996 Act is thought likely to increase use even further.

Commercial Court ADR scheme

The Commercial Court has taken a robust approach to the use of ADR. Since 1993, it issues ADR orders for commercial disputes regarded as suitable for ADR. It requires each party to inform the court by letter what steps were taken to resolve the case by ADR and why those efforts failed. This has been the subject of research by the academic, Hazel Genn, which was published in 2002 – *Court-based ADR Initiatives for Non-Family Civil Disputes: The Commercial Court and the Court of Appeal*. ADR was undertaken in a little over half of the cases in which an ADR order had been issued, though the research found that the take-up was increasing in recent years.

Of the cases in which ADR was attempted, 52 per cent settled through ADR, 5 per cent proceeded to trial following unsuccessful ADR, 20 per cent settled some time after the conclusion of the ADR procedure, and the case was still live or the outcome unknown in 23 per cent of cases. Among cases in which ADR was not attempted following an ADR order, about 63 per cent eventually settled. About one-fifth of these said that the settlement had been as a result of the ADR order being made. However the rate of trials among the group of cases not attempting ADR following an ADR order was 15 per cent, compared with only 5 per cent of cases proceeding to trial following unsuccessful ADR.

ADR orders were generally thought to have had a positive or neutral impact on settlement. Orders can have a positive effect in opening up communication between the parties, and may avoid the fear of one side showing weakness by being the first to suggest settlement.

The Court of Appeal mediation scheme

In 1996 the Court of Appeal established a voluntary mediation scheme. Cases are not individually selected, but, with the exception of certain categories of case, a standard letter of invitation is sent to parties involved in appeals. Since 1999, parties refusing to mediate have been asked to give their reasons for refusal. If both parties agree to mediate, the Court of Appeal arranges mediations and mediators provide their services without charge. This scheme was also the subject of Hazel Genn's research that was published in 2002.

Between November 1997 and April 2000, 38 appeal cases were mediated following agreement by both sides. When the scheme had the benefit of a full-time manager, there was a significant increase in the proportion of cases in which both sides agreed to mediate.

About half of the mediated appeal cases settled either at the mediation appointment or shortly afterwards. Among those cases in which the mediation did not achieve a settlement, a high proportion (62 per cent) went on to trial. This suggests that there are special characteristics of appeal cases that need to be considered in selecting cases for mediation. Blanket invitations to mediate, particularly with an implicit threat of penalties for refusal, may not be the most effective approach for encouraging ADR at appellate level. There was some concern that clients felt they were being pushed into mediation and sometimes being pressured to settle. Although solicitors generally approved of the Court of Appeal taking the initiative in encouraging the use of ADR in appropriate cases, it was felt that there was a need for the adoption of a more selective approach, such as that being used in the Commercial Court.

Quick quiz 20.2

1 Which body administers the statutory conciliation scheme in cases of unfair dismissal?

2 Which Act introduced a greater emphasis on mediation in divorce proceedings?

3 If you had a disastrous holiday in Spain which you think is the fault of your travel agent, which body will arrange conciliation and arbitration of any subsequent dispute?

4 What is the name of the Act which lays down the main laws governing the use of arbitration procedures?

Advantages of ADR

Cost

Many procedures try to work without any need for legal representation, and even those that do involve lawyers may be quicker and therefore cheaper than going to court.

In 1998, Professor Genn carried out research into a mediation scheme at Central London County Court. The scheme's objective was to offer virtually cost-free court-annexed mediation to disputing parties at an early stage in litigation. This involved a three-hour session with a trained mediator assisting parties to reach a settlement, with or without legal representation. The scheme's purpose was to promote swift dispute settlement and a reduction in legal costs through an informal process that parties might prefer to court proceedings. Hazel Genn's research did not find clear evidence that mediation saved costs. The overall cost of cases which were settled through mediation was significantly less than those which were litigated; but where mediation was used and the parties failed to reach an agreement, and then went on to litigate, it was possible for costs to be increased.

Accessibility

Alternative methods tend to be more informal than court procedures, without complicated rules of evidence. The process can therefore be less intimidating and less stressful than court proceedings.

Speed

The delays in the civil court system are well known, and waiting for a case to come to court may, especially in commercial cases, add considerably to the overall cost, and adversely affect business.

The research carried out by Professor Genn (1998) found that mediation was able to promote and speed up settlement. The majority (62 per cent) of mediated cases were settled at the mediation appointment.

Expertise

Those who run alternative dispute resolution schemes often have specialist knowledge of the relevant areas, which can promote a fairer as well as a quicker settlement.

Conciliation of the parties

Most alternative methods of dispute resolution aim to avoid irrevocably dividing the parties, so enabling business or family relationships to be maintained.

Customer satisfaction

The research by Hazel Genn (2002) found that ADR generally results in a high level of customer satisfaction.

Problems with ADR

Imbalances of power

As the unfair dismissal conciliation scheme shows, the benefits of voluntarily negotiating agreement may be undermined where there is a serious imbalance of power between the parties – in effect, one party is acting less voluntarily than the other.

Lack of legal expertise

Where a dispute hinges on difficult points of law, an arbitrator may not have the required legal expertise to judge.

No system of precedent

There is no doctrine of precedent, and each case is judged on its merits, providing no real guidelines for future cases.

Enforcement

Decisions not made by courts may be difficult to enforce.

Low take-up rate

There is a low take-up rate for ADR, and the numbers have not increased as much as expected following the introduction of the Woolf reforms. Research carried out for the Lord Chancellor's Department, *Further Findings: a continuing evaluation of the civil justice reforms*, has found that after a substantial rise in the first year following the introduction of the Civil Procedure Rules 1998, there has been a levelling off in the number of cases in which alternative dispute resolution is used.

Hazel Genn's research (2002) found that outside commercial practice, 'the profession remains very cautious about the use of ADR. Positive experience of ADR does not appear to be producing armies of converts'. She looked at the reasons why parties choose not to use ADR. For the Commercial Court ADR scheme, the most common reasons given for refusal to mediate were:

- a judgment was required for policy reasons;
- the appeal turned on a point of law;
- the past history or behaviour of the opponent.

The most common reasons given for not trying ADR following an ADR order in the Court of Appeal were:

- the case was not appropriate for ADR;
- the parties did not want to try ADR;
- the timing of the order was wrong (too early or too late); or
- there was no faith in ADR as a process in general.

In addition, Professor Hazel Genn has suggested that following the Woolf reforms the increased number of pre-trial settlements might mean that fewer people feel the need for ADR in 'run of the mill' cases. The research concluded that an individualized approach to the directing of cases towards ADR is likely to be more effective than general invitations at an early stage in the litigation process. This would require the development of clearly articulated selection principles. The timing of invitations or directions to mediate is crucial. The early stages of proceedings may not be the best time, and should not be the only opportunity to consider using ADR.

The future for ADR

Although ADR appears to meet many of the principles for effective civil justice, the proportion of people with legal problems who choose to use ADR has remained very low, even when there are convenient and free schemes available. It is not altogether clear why this is so. Hazel Genn's research (1998) found that in only 5 per cent of cases did the parties agree to try mediation, despite vigorous attempts to stimulate demand. It was least likely to be used where both parties had legal representation.

At present, many of those contemplating litigation will go first to a solicitor and Professor Genn's research shows widespread misunderstanding about mediation processes amongst solicitors. Many did not know what was involved and were therefore not able to advise clients on whether their case was suitable for any form of ADR, or the benefits that might flow from seeking to use it. Solicitors were apprehensive about showing weakness through accepting mediation in the context of traditional adversarial litigation. Litigants were also hostile to the idea of compromise, particularly in the early stages of litigation.

It is likely that in the future ADR will play an increasingly important role in the resolution of disputes. It is already widely used in the USA, where the law frequently requires parties to try mediation before their case can be set down for trial. It is generally accepted that the UK will see a similar expansion in the use of ADR, as both the courts and the legal profession begin to take ADR more seriously than they once did. Following Lord Woolf's reforms of the civil justice system, the new rules of procedure in the civil courts impose on the judges a duty to encourage parties in appropriate cases to use ADR and to facilitate its use. Parties can request that court proceedings be postponed while they try ADR and the court can also order a postponement for this reason. Backing up this position is the fact that the Government has said, in the explanatory notes to the Access to Justice Act 1999, that in time it hopes to extend public funding to increasingly cover the use of ADR.

Reading on the web

The research carried out by Professor Genn in 1998 on the mediation scheme at Central London County Court is available on the Department of Constitutional Affairs website:

http://www.dca.gov.uk/research/1998/598esfr.htm

Question and answer guides

1 Do you think that the courts offer the best means of solving disputes?

Answer guide

Your introduction might mention the fact that although courts are accepted as a means of resolving disputes, there are some types of dispute where they are not helpful, and so other methods of dispute resolution have developed. You can then examine the disadvantages of courts as means of dispute resolution, and then relate these disadvantages to the types of dispute where courts have not been found to offer the best solution.

You could then go through the four types of alternative dispute resolution we have examined, pointing out why they have advantages over the court system for those types of dispute. In this essay you could also look at tribunals (see Chapter 18), and examine how and why they provide a useful alternative to courts.

You might then discuss some of the disadvantages of alternative methods of dispute resolution, pointing out the kinds of case for which these disadvantages might make them unsuitable. Your conclusion might simply point out that courts may provide the best way of solving some disputes, but be unhelpful in others.

2 How can people resolve their disputes without using the courts or tribunals? How satisfactory are these alternative methods of dispute resolution?

Answer guide

This question uses much the same material as the previous one, but you are required to evaluate the alternative methods of dispute resolution. Also note that you could not bring tribunals into this answer. ('London Qualifications Ltd.', accepts no responsibility whatsoever for the accuracy or method in the answers given.)

▶

3 Read the following extract carefully before answering the questions based on it.

> This idea [of ADR] is not new of course: conciliation, arbitration, mediation have always been important elements of the means of dispute settlement. However, this is a new *element* in that modern societies have developed *new reasons* to prefer such alternatives. It is important to stress the fact that such new reasons include the very essence of the access movement, that is the fact that the judicial process now is, or should be, open to larger and larger segments of the population, indeed in theory at least to the entire population. This is, of course, the cost of access to justice, which is the cost of democracy itself; a cost that advanced societies must be ready and happy to bear.
>
> Alternative dispute process is an area in which the Ford Foundation developed a pioneer programme as early as 1978, which launched a broad search for what was called 'new approaches to conflict resolution', dealing particularly with 'complex public policy disputes', 'regulatory disputes', 'disputes arising out of social welfare programmes', all of which were intended to 'find ways to resolve disputes outside the formal system' . . .
>
> *Source*: Capalletti, 'Alternative Dispute Resolution Processes within the framework of the World-Wide Access to Justice Movement' (1993) Vol. 56 *Modern Law Review* 282 at p. 283.

(a) State the functions of ADR with reference to the above extract. [5]

(b) Identify and describe the different forms of ADR. [10]

(c) Explain the advantages and disadvantages of ADR. [10] *(WJEC)*

Answer guide

(a) The main function of ADR is to promote the resolution of disputes in a less formal manner than court litigation. The use of ADR should assist the goal of opening access to justice to the general population, without increasing the costs to society to excessive levels.

(b) Different forms of ADR are discussed at p. 428, including arbitration and mediation.

(c) The problems with the formal court system are discussed at p. 435. It is hoped that ADR will avoid these problems, and its key advantages are discussed on p. 434.

Chapter summary

Introduction

Following Lord Woolf's reforms of the civil justice system, ADR should play a more important role in solving all types of civil disputes. ADR has become increasingly popular because of problems resolving disputes through court hearings.

Alternative dispute resolution mechanisms

Three main forms of ADR can be identified:

- arbitration
- mediation, and
- conciliation.

Conciliation in unfair dismissal cases

A statutory conciliation scheme administered by the Advisory, Conciliation and Arbitration Service (ACAS) operates before cases of unfair dismissal can be taken to an employment tribunal.

Mediation in divorce cases

The Family Law Act 1996 has made changes to the divorce laws and places a greater emphasis on mediation.

Trade association arbitration schemes

The Fair Trading Act 1973 provides that the Director-General of Fair Trading has a duty to promote codes of practice for trade associations. Many include provisions for an initial conciliation procedure, often followed by independent arbitration if conciliation fails.

Commercial contracts

Many commercial contracts contain an arbitration agreement, requiring any dispute to be referred to arbitration before court proceedings are undertaken.

Commercial Court ADR scheme

Since 1993 the Commercial Court has issued ADR orders for disputes regarded as suitable for ADR.

The Court of Appeal mediation scheme

The Court of Appeal has a voluntary mediation scheme, under which a standard letter is sent to the parties inviting them to enter mediation.

Advantages of ADR

The advantages of ADR include:

■ cost
■ accessibility
■ speed
■ expertise
■ conciliation of the parties, and
■ customer satisfaction.

Problems with ADR

The problems with ADR are that:

■ there may be a serious imbalance of power between the parties
■ an arbitrator may lack legal expertise
■ there is no system of precedent
■ enforcement may be difficult, and
■ low take-up rate.

The future of ADR

It is likely that in the future ADR will play an increasingly important role in the resolution of disputes.

PART 4

The concept of liability

This Part explores the whole concept of liability in English law, looking specifically at liability in criminal and tort law. Criminal liability is imposed on conduct felt to be against the general interests of society. The crime is punished by the state (called the Crown for these purposes) and the primary aim is to punish the wrongdoer. Tort law is concerned with the imposition of civil liability. Civil liability is imposed either for the commission of a tort or for breach of a contract and this Part concentrates on the former. A tort involves breach of a duty which is fixed by the law. It can give rise to litigation between the wrongdoer and the victim and the aim is to compensate the victim for the harm done.

There are some areas in which the distinction between criminal and tortious liability is blurred: in some tort cases, damages may be set at a high rate in order to punish the wrongdoer, while in criminal cases, the criminal can be ordered to compensate the victim financially, though this is still not the primary aim of criminal proceedings, and the awards are usually a great deal lower than would be ordered in a tort action. There are cases in which the same incident may give rise to both criminal and tortious proceedings. An example would be a car accident, in which the driver might be prosecuted by the state for dangerous driving, and sued by the victim for the injuries caused.

Part 4 starts with the criminal law and explores the basic requirements of *actus reus* and *mens rea* in order for criminal liability to be imposed and introduces the exception of strict liability offences. It then applies these concepts of *actus reus* and *mens rea* to the non-fatal offences against the person. In civil law the grounds for imposing liability for negligence are analysed and the remedy of damages in tort law examined.

> **AQA Examination Board**
>
> Chapters 21–25 cover AS module 3: The concept of liability

Chapter 21

Elements of a crime

A person cannot usually be found guilty of a criminal offence unless two elements are present: an *actus reus*, Latin for 'guilty act'; and *mens rea*, Latin for 'guilty mind'. Both these terms actually refer to more than just moral guilt, and each has a very specific meaning, which varies according to the crime, but the important thing to remember is that to be guilty of an offence, an accused not only must have behaved in a particular way, but also must usually have had a particular mental attitude to that behaviour. The exception to this rule is a small group of offences known as crimes of strict liability, which are discussed in the next chapter.

The definition of a particular crime, either in statute or under common law, will contain the required *actus reus* and *mens rea* for the offence. The prosecution has to prove both of these elements so that the magistrates or judge and jury are satisfied beyond all reasonable doubt of their existence. If this is not done, the person will be acquitted, as in English law all persons are presumed innocent until proven guilty – **Woolmington** *v* **DPP** (1935).

Actus reus

An *actus reus* can consist of more than just an act, it comprises all the elements of the offence other than the state of mind of the defendant. Depending on the offence, this may include the circumstances in which it was committed, and/or the consequences of what was done. For example, the crime of rape requires unlawful sexual intercourse by a man with a person without their consent. The lack of consent is a surrounding circumstance which exists independently of the accused's act.

Similarly, the same act may be part of the *actus reus* of different crimes, depending on its consequences. Stabbing someone, for example, may form the *actus reus* of murder if the victim dies, or of causing grievous bodily harm (GBH) if the victim survives; the accused's behaviour is the same in both cases, but the consequences of it dictate whether the *actus reus* of murder or GBH has been committed.

Conduct must be voluntary

If the accused is to be found guilty of a crime, his or her behaviour in committing the *actus reus* must have been voluntary. Behaviour will usually only be considered involuntary where the accused was not in control of his or her own body (when the defence of insanity or automatism may be available) or where there is extremely strong pressure from someone else, such as a threat that the accused will be killed if he or she does not commit a particular offence (when the defence of duress may be available).

In the much criticized decision of **R** *v* **Larsonneur** (1933), a Frenchwoman was arrested as an illegal immigrant by the authorities in Ireland, and brought back to the UK in custody where she was charged with being an alien illegally in the UK and convicted. This is not what most of us would describe as acting voluntarily, but it apparently fitted the courts' definition at the time. It is probably stricter than a decision would be today, but it is important to realize that the courts do define 'involuntary' quite narrowly on occasion.

Types of *actus reus*

Crimes can be divided into three types, depending on the nature of their *actus reus*.

Action crimes. The *actus reus* here is simply an act, the consequences of that act being immaterial. For example, perjury is committed whenever someone makes a statement which he/she does not believe to be true, while on oath. Whether or not that statement makes a difference to the trial is not important to whether the offence of perjury has been committed.

State of affairs crimes. Here the *actus reus* consists of circumstances, and sometimes consequences, but no acts – they are 'being' rather than 'doing' offences. The offence committed in **R** *v* **Larsonneur** is an example of this, where the *actus reus* consisted of being a foreigner who had not been given permission to come to Britain and was found in the country.

Result crimes. The *actus reus* of these is distinguished by the fact that the accused's behaviour must produce a particular result – the most obvious being murder, where the accused's act must cause the death of a human being.

Result crimes raise the issue of causation: the result must be proved to have been caused by the defendant's act. If the result is caused by an intervening act or event, which was completely unconnected with the defendant's act and which could not have been foreseen, the defendant will not be liable. Where the result is caused by a combination of the defendant's act and the intervening act, and the defendant's act remains a substantial cause, then he or she will still be liable.

Causation

With result crimes, the prosecution must prove that the defendant caused the result of the offence. In many cases this will be obvious: for example, where the defendant shoots or stabs someone, and the victim dies immediately of the wounds. Difficulties may arise where there is more than one cause of the result. This might be the act or omission of a third party which occurs after the defendant's act, and before the result constituting the offence, or some characteristic of the victim which means that the victim suffers a result which a fitter person would not have suffered.

Much of the case law in this field has been concerned with the offence of murder, where it must be shown that the offender caused the death of the victim, but the cases are equally relevant to any other result offence, including non-fatal offences against the person.

Defendants can only be held responsible for results where their acts are both a 'factual' and a 'legal' cause of the result constituting the offence.

Factual causation

In order to establish factual causation, the prosecution must prove two things:

■ That *but for* the conduct of the accused, the result of the offence would not have occurred as and when it did. Thus, a defendant will not be liable for a death if the victim would have died at the same time regardless of the defendant's act (or omission). In **R v White** (1910), the defendant gave his mother poison but, before it had a chance to take effect, she died of a heart attack which was not caused by the poison. He was not liable for her death.

■ That the original injury arising from the defendant's conduct was *more than a minimal cause* of the result constituting the offence. This is known as the *de minimis* rule. So pricking the thumb of a woman bleeding to death would hasten her death, for example, but not enough to be the real cause of it.

Legal causation

Even if factual causation is established, the judge must direct the jury as to whether the defendant's acts are sufficient to amount in law to a cause of the result of the offence. Legal causation can be proved in any one of the following three ways or by a combination of them:

1. The original injury was an operative and significant cause of the result

Under this criterion the prosecution must show that at the time of the result of the offence occurring, the original harm caused by the defendant was still an 'operative and substantial' cause of the result. In **R v Smith** (1959), a soldier was stabbed in a barrack-room brawl. He was dropped twice as he was being taken to the medical officer, and then there was a long delay before he was seen by a doctor, as the doctor mistakenly thought that his case was not urgent. When he did eventually receive treatment, it was inappropriate for the injuries he was suffering from and harmful. Nonetheless, the court took the view that these intervening factors had not broken the chain of causation so that the original wound was still an operative cause and the accused was liable for murder.

The same principle was followed in **R v Malcherek and Steel** (1981). The victims of two separate attacks had been kept on life-support machines; these were switched off when tests showed that they were brain-dead. The two defendants argued that when the hospital switched off the machines the chain of causation was broken, thereby relieving the defendants of liability for murder. The court rejected this argument on the ground that the original injuries were still an operative cause of their victim's death.

In **R** *v* **Cheshire** (1991), a dispute developed in a fish and chip shop, ending with the defendant shooting his victim in the leg and stomach, and seriously wounding him. The victim was taken to hospital, where his injuries were operated on, and he was placed in intensive care. As a result of negligent treatment by the medical staff, he developed complications affecting his breathing, and eventually died. His leg and stomach wounds were no longer life-threatening at the time of his death. The court stated that the critical question for the jury to answer was 'Has the Crown proved death?' Negligent medical treatment could only break the chain of causation if it was so independent of the accused's acts, and such a powerful cause of death in itself, that the contribution made by the defendant's conduct was insignificant. This means that medical treatment can only break the chain of causation in the most extraordinary cases; incompetent or even grossly abnormal treatment will not suffice if the original injury is still an operative cause of death.

An example of such an extraordinary case might be **R** *v* **Jordan** (1956). The defendant was convicted of murder after stabbing the victim, but the conviction was quashed by the Court of Appeal when it heard new evidence that, at the time of the death, the original wound had almost healed, and the victim's death was brought on by the hospital giving him a drug to which he was known to be allergic – treatment that was described as 'palpably wrong'. It was held that the wound was no longer an operative cause of death. **Jordan** was described in the later case of **R** *v* **Smith** as a very particular case dependent upon its exact facts, and in **Malcherek** as an exceptional case, and is therefore unlikely to be used as a precedent. It seems that the law still requires very extraordinary circumstances for medical treatment to break the chain of causation.

It was pointed out in **R** *v* **Mellor** (1996) that the burden of proof is on the prosecution, so the defence do not have to prove that there was, for example, medical negligence in order to avoid liability. In that case the accused attacked a 71-year-old man breaking his ribs and facial bones. The victim died two weeks later of bronchopneumonia, which would probably not have been fatal if, on the day of his death, he had been given oxygen. This failure may have constituted medical negligence. Certain passages in the judge's summing-up implied that there was a burden on the defence to prove medical negligence. He cited with approval the vital question on causation laid down in **Cheshire**, and it was accepted that the jury had been misdirected. Nevertheless the conviction was upheld as the evidence against the appellant was overwhelming so that a correctly directed jury would have convicted.

2. The intervening act was reasonably foreseeable

An intervening act which is reasonably foreseeable will not break the chain of legal causation. For example, if the defendant knocks the victim unconscious, and leaves him or her lying on a beach, it is reasonably foreseeable that when the tide comes in, the victim will drown, and the defendant will have caused that death. However, the defendant would not be liable for homicide if the victim was left unconscious on the seashore and run over by a car careering out of control off a nearby road as this could not have been foreseen. In **R** *v* **Pagett** (1983), the defendant was attempting to escape being captured by armed police, and used his girlfriend as a human shield. He shot at the police, and his girlfriend was killed by shots fired at him in self-defence by the policemen. The defendant was found liable for the girl's death as it was reasonably foreseeable that the police would shoot back and hit her in response to his shots. This is despite the fact that the police appear to have been negligent, as the mother of the girl subsequently succeeded in a claim for negligence in respect of the police operation in which her daughter was killed.

In cases involving medical treatment, only grossly abnormal treatment will be treated as not reasonably foreseeable, according to **Cheshire**. Treatment falling within the 'normal' band of incompetence will be regarded as foreseeable.

A defendant will avoid liability if a victim responds to their conduct in a way that is so daft that it could not have been foreseen. This issue arose in **R** *v* **Corbett** (1996) when a mentally disabled man had been drinking heavily all day with the defendant. An argument ensued and the defendant started to hit and head-butt the victim who ran way. The victim fell into a gutter and was struck and killed by a car. At Corbett's trial for manslaughter the judge directed that he was the cause of the victim's death if the victim's conduct of running away was within the range of foreseeable responses to the defendant's behaviour. An appeal against this direction was rejected.

In **R** *v* **Dear** (1996) the Court of Appeal suggested that if the defendant's conduct was still an operative and significant cause of the death, the defendant would in law be the cause of that death, regardless of whether or not any intervening factors were foreseeable. The accused's daughter told him that she had been sexually assaulted. On hearing this allegation the accused stabbed the alleged abuser repeatedly with a knife. The victim died two days later. On appeal against his conviction for murder the appellant argued that he was not the cause of the death. He contended that the deceased had committed suicide either by reopening his wounds or, the wounds having reopened themselves, by failing to seek medical attention and the suicide broke the chain of causation. The appeal was dismissed as the injuries inflicted on the deceased were an operative and significant cause of the death. In such a case as this it was not necessary to consider the degree of fault in the victim or to consider how foreseeable the victim's conduct was. This approach has been criticized on the basis that it ignores previous authorities which state that the chain of causation is broken if the victim's conduct was so daft that it could not have been foreseen. It may be that this case will be distinguished from those authorities on the basis that the operative and substantive test had been satisfied on the facts of the case, and not in the earlier authorities; or it may be that **R** *v* **Dear** will not be followed.

3. The 'thin skull' test

Where the intervening cause is some existing weakness of the victim, the defendant must take the victim as he or she finds him. Known as the 'thin skull' rule, this means that if, for example, a defendant hits a person over the head with the kind of blow which would not usually kill, but the victim has an unusually thin skull which makes the blow fatal, the defendant will be liable for the subsequent death. The principle

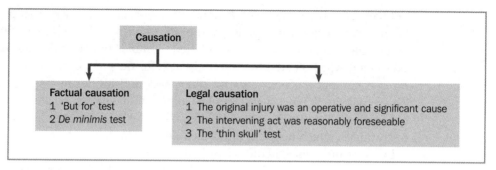

Figure 21.1 Factual and legal causation compared

has been extended to mental conditions and beliefs, as well as physical characteristics. In **R** *v* **Blaue** (1975), the victim of a stabbing was a Jehovah's Witness, a church
which, among other things, forbids its members to have blood transfusions. As a
result of her refusal to accept a transfusion, the victim died of her wounds. The Court
of Appeal rejected the defendant's argument that her refusal broke the chain of
causation, on the ground that the accused had to take his victim as he found her.

Omissions

Criminal liability is rarely imposed for true omissions at common law, though there
are situations where a non-lawyer would consider that there had been an omission
but in law it will be treated as an act and liability will be imposed. There are also
situations where the accused has a duty to act, and in these cases there may be
liability for a true omission.

Act or omission?

It must first be decided whether in law you are dealing with an act or an omission.
There are three situations where this question arises: continuing acts, supervening
faults and euthanasia.

Continuing acts

The concept of a continuing act was used in **Fagan** *v* **Metropolitan Police
Commissioner** (1969) to allow what seemed to be an omission to be treated as an act.
The defendant was told by a police officer to park his car close to the kerb; he obeyed
the order, but in doing so he accidentally drove his car on to the constable's foot. The
constable shouted, 'Get off, you are on my foot'. The defendant replied, 'Fuck you,
you can wait', and turned off the ignition. Convicted of assaulting the constable in
the execution of his duty, the defendant appealed on the grounds that at the time he
committed the act of driving on to the officer's foot, he lacked *mens rea*, and though
he had *mens rea* when he refused to remove the car, this was an omission, and the
actus reus required an act. The appeal was dismissed, on the basis that driving on to
the officer's foot and staying there was one single continuous act, rather than an act

followed by an omission. So long as the defendant had the *mens rea* at some point during that continuing act, he was liable.

The same principle was held to apply in **Kaitamaki v R** (1985). The accused was charged with rape, and his defence was that at the time when he penetrated the woman, he had thought she was consenting. However, he did not withdraw when he realized that she was not consenting. The court held that the *actus reus* of rape was a continuing act, and so when Kaitamaki realized that his victim did not consent (and therefore formed the necessary *mens rea*) the *actus reus* was still in progress.

Supervening fault

A person who is aware that he or she has done something which has endangered another's life or property, and does nothing to prevent the relevant harm occurring, may be criminally liable, with the original act being treated as the *actus reus* of the crime. In particular, this principle can impose liability on defendants who do not have *mens rea* when they commit the original act, but do have it at the point when they fail to act to prevent the harm they have caused.

This was the case in **R v Miller** (1982). The defendant was squatting in a building. He lay on a mattress, lit a cigarette and fell asleep. Some time later, he woke up to find the mattress on fire. Making no attempt to put the fire out, he simply moved into the next room and went back to sleep. The house caught fire, leading to £800-worth of damage. Miller was convicted of arson. As the fire was his fault, the court was prepared to treat the *actus reus* of the offence as being his original act of dropping the cigarette.

A rare example of the principle in **Miller** being applied by the courts is the case of **Director of Public Prosecutions v Santra-Bermudez** (2003). A police officer had decided to undertake a search of the defendant, as she suspected that he was a ticket tout. Initially she had asked him to empty his pockets and in doing so he revealed that he was in possession of some syringes without needles attached to them. The police officer asked the defendant if he was in possession of any needles or sharp objects. He replied that he was not. The police officer proceeded to put her hand into the defendant's pocket to continue the search when her finger was pricked by a hypodermic needle. When challenged that he had said he was not in possession of any other sharp items, the defendant shrugged his shoulders and smirked at the police officer. The defendant was subsequently found guilty of an assault occasioning actual bodily harm (discussed on p. 00). This offence is defined as requiring the commission of an act, as opposed to an omission, but the appeal court applied the principles laid down in **Miller**. By informing the police officer that he was not in possession of any sharp items or needles, the defendant had created a dangerous situation, he was then under a duty to prevent the harm occurring. He had failed to carry out his duty by telling the police officer the truth.

Euthanasia

Euthanasia is the name given to the practice of helping severely ill people to die, either at their request, or by taking the decision that life support should be withdrawn when the person is no longer capable of making that decision. In some countries euthanasia is legal but, in this country, intentionally causing someone's death can constitute murder, even if carried out for the most compassionate reasons. However, in the light of the case of **Airedale National Health Service Trust *v* Bland** (1993), liability will only be imposed in such cases for a positive act, and the courts will sometimes say there was a mere omission when strictly speaking there would appear to have been an act, in order to avoid imposing criminal liability. The case concerned Anthony Bland, who had been seriously injured in the Hillsborough football stadium disaster when only 17 years old. As a result, he suffered irreversible brain damage, leaving him in a persistent vegetative state, with no hope of recovery or improvement, though he was not actually brain-dead. His family and the health trust responsible for his medical treatment wanted to turn off his life-support machine, but in order to ensure that this did not make them liable for murder, they went to the High Court to seek a declaration that if they did this they would not be committing any criminal offence or civil wrong.

The declaration was granted by the High Court and upheld by the House of Lords. Since the House was acting in its civil capacity, strictly speaking the case will not be binding on the criminal courts, but it will be highly persuasive. Part of the decision stated that turning off the life-support system should be viewed as an omission, rather than an act. Lord Goff said:

> I agree that the doctor's conduct in discontinuing life support can properly be categorized as an omission. It is true that it may be difficult to describe what the doctor actually does as an omission, for example where he takes some positive step to bring the life support to an end. But discontinuation of life support is, for present purposes, no different from not initiating life support in the first place. In each case, the doctor is simply allowing his patient to die in the sense that he is desisting from taking a step which might, in certain circumstances, prevent his patient from dying as a result of his pre-existing condition: and as a matter of general principle an omission such as this will not be unlawful unless it constitutes a breach of duty to the patient.

In this case, it was pointed out that there was no breach of duty, because it was no longer in Anthony Bland's interests to continue treatment as there was no hope of recovery.

The decision of **Bland** was found to conform with the European Convention on Human Rights by the High Court in **NHS Trust A *v* M** and **NHS Trust B *v* H** (2000). In particular, there was no violation of the right to life protected by Art. 2 of the Convention. The High Court stated that the scope of Art. 2 was restricted to positive acts, and did not apply to mere omissions.

Offences capable of being committed by omission

Where the conduct in question is genuinely an omission, and not one of the categories just discussed, the next question is whether the particular offence can, in law, be committed by omission. The rules here are contained in both statute and common law with regard to the particular offences – for example, murder and manslaughter can be committed by omission, but assault cannot (**Fagan *v* Metropolitan Police Commissioner**, above).

An example of the offence of murder being committed by an omission is **R *v* Gibbins and Proctor** (1918). In that case, a man and a woman were living together with the man's daughter. They failed to give the child food and she died. The judge directed that they were guilty of murder if they withheld food with intent to cause her grievous bodily harm, as a result of which she died. Their conviction was upheld by the Court of Appeal.

A duty to act

Where the offence is capable in law of being committed by an omission, it can only be committed by a person who was under a duty to act (in other words, a duty not to commit that omission). This is because English law places no general duty on people to help each other or save each other from harm. Thus if a man sees a boy drowning in a lake, it is arguable that under English criminal law the man is under no duty to save him, and can walk past without incurring criminal liability for the child's subsequent death.

A duty to act will only be imposed where there is some kind of relationship between the two people, and the closer the relationship the more likely it is that a duty to act will exist. So far, the courts have recognized a range of relationships as giving rise to a duty to act, and other relationships may in the future be recognized as so doing.

Special relationship

Special relationships tend to be implied between members of the same family. An obvious example of a special relationship giving rise to a duty to act is that of parents to their children. In **R *v* Lowe** (1973), a father failed to call a doctor when his nine-week-old baby became ill. He had a duty to act, though on the facts he lacked the *mens rea* of an offence partly because he was of low intelligence.

Voluntary acceptance of responsibility for another

People may choose to take on responsibility for another. They will then have a duty to act to protect that person if the person falls into difficulty. In **Gibbins and Proctor** a woman lived with a man who had a daughter from an earlier relationship. He paid the woman money to buy food for the family. Sadly, they did not feed the child, and the child died of starvation. The woman was found to have voluntarily accepted responsibility for the child and was liable, along with the child's father, for murder.

In **R *v* Stone and Dobinson** (1977), Stone's sister, Fanny, lived with him and his girlfriend, Dobinson. Fanny was mentally ill, and became very anxious about putting on weight. She stopped eating properly and became bedbound. Realizing that she was ill, the defendants had made half-hearted and unsuccessful attempts to get medical help and after several weeks she died. The couple's efforts were found to have been inadequate. The Court of Appeal said that they had accepted responsibility for Fanny as her carers, and that once she became bedbound the appellants were, in the circumstances, obliged either to summon help or else to care for her themselves. As they had done neither, they were both found to be liable for manslaughter.

Table 21.1 Duty to act

Existence of a duty to act	Case authority
Special relationship	**R v Lowe**
Voluntary acceptance of responsibility for another	**R v Stone and Dobinson**
Contract	**R v Pittwood**
Statute	
Defendant created a dangerous situation	**R v Miller**

Contract

A contract may give rise to a duty to act. This duty can extend not just for the benefit of the parties to the contract, but also to those who are not party to the contract, but are likely to be injured by failure to perform it. In **R v Pittwood** (1902), a gatekeeper of a railway crossing opened the gate to let a car through, and then forgot to shut it when he went off to lunch. As a result, a haycart crossed the line while a train was approaching, and was hit, causing the driver's death. The gatekeeper was convicted of manslaughter.

Statute

Some pieces of legislation impose duties to act on individuals. For example s. 1 of the Children and Young Persons Act 1933 imposes a duty to provide for a child in one's care. Failure to do so constitutes an offence.

Defendant created a dangerous situation

Where a defendant has created a dangerous situation they are under a duty to act to remedy this. This duty is illustrated by the case of **R v Miller** (1982) which is discussed on p. 449.

Termination of the duty

The duty to act will terminate when the special relationship ends, so a parent, for example, probably stops having a duty to act once the child is grown up.

Criticism

It will depend on the facts of each case whether the court is prepared to conclude that the relationship is sufficiently close to justify criminal liability for a failure to act to protect a victim. This approach has been heavily criticized by some academics, who argue that the moral basis of the law is undermined by a situation which allows people to ignore a drowning child whom they could have easily saved, and incur no criminal liability so long as they are strangers. In some countries, legislation has created special offences which impose liability on those who fail to take steps which could be taken without any personal risk to themselves in order to save another from death or serious personal injury. The offence created is not necessarily a homicide offence, but it is an acknowledgement by the criminal law that the individual should have taken action in these circumstances. Photographers involved in the death of Princess Diana were prosecuted for such an offence in France.

Quick quiz 21.1

1 Explain the 'but for' test.

2 What is meant by the 'thin skull' test?

3 What was the *ratio decidendi* of **R** v **Miller** (1982)?

4 Does a stranger owe a duty to act to save a baby drowning in a puddle?

Mens rea

Mens rea is Latin for 'guilty mind' and traditionally refers to the state of mind of the person committing the crime. The required *mens rea* varies depending on the offence. We will consider the two most important forms of *mens rea*: intention and subjective recklessness.

When discussing *mens rea*, we often refer to the difference between subjective and objective tests. Put simply, a subjective test involves looking at what the particular defendant was thinking (or in practice, what the magistrates or jury believe the defendant was thinking), whereas an objective test considers what a reasonable person would have thought in the defendant's position.

Intention

Intention is a subjective concept: a court is concerned purely with what the particular defendant was intending at the time of the offence, and not what a reasonable person would have intended in the same circumstances.

The case law in this field has developed in the context of the law of murder, where the *mens rea* required is that of an intention either to kill or to cause grievous bodily harm. But the law laid down in these cases applies more widely to any offence where intention can satisfy the *mens rea* element.

To help comprehension of the legal meaning of intention, the concept can be divided into two: direct intention and indirect intention.

Direct intention

Direct intention corresponds with the everyday definition of intention, and applies where the accused actually wants the result that occurs. An example of direct intention to kill is where Ann shoots at Ben because Ann wants to kill Ben.

Indirect intention

Indirect intention is less straightforward. It exists where the accused did not desire a particular result but, in acting as he or she did, realized to the point of virtual certainty that it might occur. For example, a mother wishes to frighten her children and so starts a fire in the house. She does not want to kill her children, but she realizes that there is a virtually certain risk that they may die as a result of the fire. The courts are now quite clear that oblique intention can be sufficient for the imposition of criminal liability: people can intend a result that they do not necessarily want. But in a line of important cases, they have tried to specify the necessary degree of foresight required in order to provide evidence of intention.

In **R** *v* **Moloney** (1985), the defendant was a soldier who was on leave at the time of the incident that gave rise to his prosecution. He was staying with his mother and stepfather, with whom he was apparently on very good terms. The family held a dinner party, during which the appellant and his stepfather drank rather a lot of alcohol. They stayed up after everyone else had left or gone to bed; shortly after 4.00 am a shot was fired and the appellant was heard to say, 'I have shot my father'.

The court was told that Moloney and his stepfather had had a contest to see who could load his gun and be ready to fire first. Moloney had been quicker, and stood pointing the gun at his stepfather, who teased him that he would not dare to fire a live bullet; at that point Moloney, by his own admission, pulled the trigger. In evidence he said, 'I never conceived that what I was doing might cause injury to anybody. It was just a lark.' Clearly he did not want to kill his stepfather, but could he be said to have intended to do so? Lord Bridge pointed out that it was quite possible to intend a result which you do not actually want. He gave the example of a man who, in an attempt to escape pursuit, boards a plane to Manchester. Even though he may have no desire to go to Manchester – he may even hate the place for some reason – that is clearly where he intends to go.

Foresight is merely evidence of intent

Moloney established that a person can have intention where he or she did not want the result but merely foresaw it, yet the courts are not saying that foresight is intention. Foresight is merely evidence from which intention can be found.

Before **Moloney**, in the case of **Hyam** *v* **DPP** (1975), it had looked as though foresight was actually intention, though the judgment in that case was not very clear. The defendant, Pearl Hyam, put blazing newspaper through the letterbox of the house of a Mrs Booth, who was going on holiday with Pearl Hyam's boyfriend; Mrs Booth's two children were killed in the fire. On the facts it appeared that Pearl Hyam did not want to kill the two children; she wanted to set fire to the house and to frighten Mrs Booth. The court held that she must have foreseen that death or grievous bodily harm were highly likely to result from her conduct, and that this was sufficient *mens rea* for murder. In **Moloney** the House of Lords held that **Hyam** had been wrongly decided, and that nothing less than intention to kill or cause grievous bodily harm would constitute the *mens rea* of murder:

merely foreseeing the victim's death as probable was not intent, though it could be evidence of it.

Lord Bridge suggested that juries might be asked to consider the questions: was death or really serious injury a 'natural consequence' of the defendant's act, and did the defendant foresee that one or the other was a natural consequence of his/her act? If the answer was 'yes', the jury might infer from this evidence that the death was intended.

This guidance for juries in turn proved to be problematic. In **R** *v* **Hancock and Shankland** (1986) the defendants were striking miners who knew that a taxi, carrying men breaking the strike to work, would pass along a particular road. They waited on a bridge above it, and dropped a concrete block which hit the taxi as it passed underneath, killing the driver. At their trial the judge had given the direction suggested by Lord Bridge in **Moloney** and they were convicted of murder. On appeal, the House of Lords held that this had been incorrect, and a verdict of manslaughter was substituted. Their Lordships agreed with Lord Bridge that conviction for murder could result only from proof of intention, and that foresight of consequences was not in itself intention, but they were concerned that the question of whether the death was a 'natural consequence' of the defendants' act might suggest to juries that they need not consider the degree of probability. The fact that there might be a ten-million-to-one chance that death would result form the defendants' act might still mean that death was a natural consequence of it, in the sense that it had happened without any interference, but, with this degree of likelihood, there would seem to be little evidence of intention.

Lord Scarman suggested that the jury should be directed that: 'the greater the probability of a consequence, the more likely it is that the consequence was foreseen and that if that consequence was foreseen the greater the probability is that that consequence was also intended . . . But juries also need to be reminded that the decision is theirs to be reached upon a consideration of all the evidence.'

Thus, if a person stabs another in the chest, it is highly likely this will lead to death or grievous bodily harm, and since most people would be well aware of that, it is likely that they would foresee death or serious injury when they acted. If they did foresee this, then that is evidence of intent, from which a jury might conclude that that death was intended. But if you cut someone's finger, that person could die as a result – from blood poisoning, for example – but since this is highly unlikely, the chances are that you would not have foreseen that the person might die when you cut the finger, and your lack of foresight would be evidence that you did not intend the death.

The concept was further clarified in **R** *v* **Nedrick** (1986). The defendant had a grudge against a woman, and poured paraffin through the letterbox of her house and set it alight. The woman's child died in the fire. Lord Lane CJ said:

> Where the charge is murder and in the rare cases where the simple direction is not enough, the jury should be directed that they are not entitled to infer the necessary intention unless they feel sure that death or serious bodily harm was a virtual certainty (barring some unforeseen intervention) as a result of the defendant's action and that the defendant appreciated that such was the case.

> Where a man realizes that it is for all practical purposes inevitable that his actions will result in death or serious harm, the inference may be irresistible that he intended that result, however little he may have desired or wished it to happen . . . The decision is one for the jury to be reached on a consideration of all the evidence.

In other words, Lord Lane considered that even if death or grievous bodily harm is not the defendant's aim or wish, the jury may infer intent if they decide that death or grievous bodily harm was virtually certain to result from what the defendant did, and the defendant foresaw that that was the case. Such foresight was still only evidence from which they might infer intent, and not intent itself, although it would be difficult not to infer intent where the defendant foresaw that death or grievous bodily harm was practically inevitable as a result of his or her acts.

The virtual certainty test in **Nedrick** became the key test on indirect intention. Then confusion was thrown into this area of the law by the Court of Appeal judgment in **R** *v* **Woollin** in 1996. Having given various explanations for his three-month-old son's injuries in the ambulance and in the first two police interviews, Woollin eventually admitted that he had 'lost his cool' when his son had choked on his food. He had picked him up, shaken him and thrown him across the room with considerable force towards a pram standing next to a wall about five feet away. He stated that he had not intended or thought that he would kill the child and had not wanted the child to die. The judge directed the jury that it was open to them to convict Woollin of murder if satisfied that he was aware there was a 'substantial risk' that he would cause serious injury. On appeal, the defence argued that the judge had misdirected the jury by using the term 'a substantial risk', which was the test for recklessness, and failing to use the phrase 'virtual certainty' derived from **Nedrick** for oblique intention. The appeal was rejected by the Court of Appeal, which held that in directing a jury a judge was obliged to use the phrase 'virtual certainty' if the only evidence of intent was the actions of the accused constituting the *actus reus* of the offence and their consequences on the victim. Where other evidence was available, the judge was not obliged to use that phrase, or a phrase that meant the same thing. The Court of Appeal felt that otherwise the jury function as laid down in s. 8 of the Criminal Justice Act 1967 would be undermined. This section states:

A court or jury in determining whether a person had committed an offence,
(a) shall not be found in law to infer that he intended or foresaw a result of his actions by reason only of its being a natural and probable consequence of those actions; but
(b) shall decide whether he did intend or foresee that result by reference to all the evidence, drawing such inferences from the evidence as appear proper in the circumstances.

Thus, Parliament had recognized in that provision that a court or jury could infer that a defendant intended a result of their actions by reason of its being a natural and probable result of those actions. In deciding whether the defendant intended the natural and probable result of his/her actions, s. 8 stated that the court or jury was to take into account all the evidence drawing such inferences as appeared proper. Section 8 contained no restrictive provision about the result being a 'virtual certainty'. The facts of **Woollin** fell within the category of cases where there was more evidence of intention than purely the conduct of the defendant constituting the *actus reus* of the offence

Table 21.2 Chronology of cases on indirect intention

Case	Legal principle
Hyam v **DPP** (1975)	May have wrongly decided that foresight was intention.
R v **Moloney** (1985)	Overturned **Hyam** v **DPP**, as foresight is not intention, it is merely evidence of intent.
R v **Hancock and Shankland** (1986)	Lord Scarman suggested that the jury should be directed that: 'the greater the probability of a consequence, the more likely it is that the consequence was foreseen and that if that consequence was foreseen the greater the probability is that the consequence was also intended . . . But juries also need to be reminded that the decision is theirs to be reached upon a consideration of all the evidence.'
R v **Nedrick** (1986)	Indirect intention can exist where the defendant foresaw a result as a virtual certainty.
R v **Woollin** (1998)	The **Nedrick** test of virtual certainty was confirmed.

and the result of the conduct, for in addition there was the conduct of the defendant in the first two interviews and his description of events to the ambulance controller.

A further appeal was made to the House of Lords. This ruled that the Court of Appeal and the trial judge had been mistaken. It said that the **Nedrick** direction was always required in the context of indirect intention. Otherwise, there would be no clear distinction between intention and recklessness as both would be concerned simply with the foresight of a risk. The **Nedrick** direction distinguishes the two concepts by stating that intention will only exist when the risk is foreseen as a virtual certainty. Accordingly, a conviction for manslaughter was substituted.

Thus the **Nedrick** 'virtual certainty' direction was approved, though two amendments were made to it. First, the original **Nedrick** direction told the jury that 'they are not entitled to *infer* the necessary intention, unless they feel sure that death or serious bodily harm was a virtual certainty'. The House of Lords substituted the word 'find' for the word 'infer'. This change was to deal with the criticism that juries were told in the past that they could 'infer' intention from the existence of the foresight and this suggested that intention was something different from the foresight itself, but did not specify what it was. But the difficulties are not completely resolved by the change from 'infer' to 'find' as a jury is still only 'entitled' to make this finding, and it is still a question of evidence for the jury – it is not clear when this finding should be made. It might be more logical to oblige a jury to conclude that there is intention where a person foresaw a result as virtual certainty.

The second amendment was that the majority of the House of Lords felt that the first sentence of the second paragraph of Lord Lane's statement in **Nedrick**, quoted above ('Where a man realizes . . .'), did not form part of the model direction. So the jury will not normally be pressurized into finding intention by being told that a finding of intention 'may be irresistible'. Thus the model direction now reads as follows:

> Where the charge is murder and in the rare cases where the simple direction is not enough, the jury should be directed that they are not entitled to find the necessary intention

unless they feel sure that death or serious bodily harm was a virtual certainty (barring some unforeseen intervention) as a result of the defendant's actions and that the defendant appreciated that such was the case. The decision is one for the jury to be reached on a consideration of all the evidence.

It is slightly puzzling that in the high-profile case of **Re A (Children) (Conjoined Twins: Medical Treatment)** (2000), concerning the legality of an operation to separate conjoined twins, the Court of Appeal included, as part of the direction on intention that should be given to the jury, the statement from **Nedrick** which the majority of the House of Lords had said no longer formed part of the model direction. The decision of the Court of Appeal had to be given under significant time constraints due to the urgent need to carry out the operation and, with due respect, it is suggested that this part of the Court of Appeal judgment is wrong.

In **R v Matthews** and **Alleyne** (2003) the Court of Appeal stated 'there is very little to choose between a rule of evidence and one of substantive law' and those on the facts of the case a finding of intention was 'irresistible'.

Doctors and euthanasia

Technically in England the act of euthanasia can give rise to liability for murder if the doctor is found to have committed an act that caused the death of a human being with the intention of causing death. This can place doctors in a delicate position when treating terminally ill patients. In relation to the *mens rea* of murder, the law has in this context developed a concept of 'double effect'. This seeks to distinguish between the primary and secondary consequences of an action or course of treatment. An act which causes a death will not be treated as criminal if the action is good in itself. The doctors are merely viewed as having intended the good effect where there is sufficient reason to permit the bad effect. The doctrine of double effect was first formulated by Devlin J in 1957 in the case of Dr John Adams. This doctor had been tried for the murder of an 84-year-old woman whom he had injected with a fatal dose of narcotics when she was terminally ill. In his summing-up, Devlin J stated:

> If the first purpose of medicine, the restoration of health, can no longer be achieved there is still much for a doctor to do, and he is entitled to do all that is proper and necessary to relieve pain and suffering, even if the measures he takes may incidentally shorten human life.

After 42 minutes of deliberation, the jury returned a 'not guilty' verdict. Thus liability for murder can be avoided if beneficial medication is given, despite the certain knowledge that death will occur as a side-effect.

Davies in his *Textbook on Medical Law* (1998) has argued that, although one can sympathize with judicial reluctance to see competent and highly regarded medical practitioners convicted of murder, the doctrine of double effect is both illogical and inconsistent with English criminal law. If a doctor injects a severely ill patient with a powerful painkiller in the certain knowledge that the drug will cause death within a matter of minutes, under the ordinary principles of criminal law (laid down in the cases of **Woollin** and **Nedrick**) this doctor intended to kill. English law has traditionally excluded any considerations of motive in determining criminal responsibility.

The doctrine of 'double effect' was considered in the recent high-profile case concerned with the separation of conjoined twins. In **Re A (Children)** (2000), Jodie and Mary were conjoined twins. They each had their own vital organs, arms and legs. The weaker twin, Mary, had a poorly developed brain, an abnormal heart and virtually no lung tissue. She had only survived birth because a common artery enabled her sister to circulate oxygenated blood for both of them. An operation to separate the twins would require the cutting of that common artery. Mary would die within minutes because her lungs and heart were not sufficient to pump blood through her body. The doctors believed that Jodie had between a 94 and 99 per cent chance of surviving the separation. She would have only limited disabilities and would be able to lead a relatively normal life. If the doctors waited until Mary died naturally and then carried out an emergency separation operation, Jodie would have only a 36 per cent chance of survival. If no operation was performed, they were both likely to die within three to six months because Jodie's heart would eventually fail.

The question to be determined by the Court of Appeal was whether the operation would constitute a criminal offence, and in particular, murder of Mary who would be killed by the operation. Looking at whether the doctors carrying out the operation would have the *mens rea* of murder, submissions were made to the Court of Appeal that the doctrine of double effect should relieve the surgeons of criminal responsibility. It was argued before the Court of Appeal that the surgeons' 'primary purpose' in this case would be to save Jodie, and the fact that Mary's death would be accelerated was a secondary effect which would not justify a conviction for murder. But the majority of the Court of Appeal felt the doctrine of double effect could not apply to these facts, where the side-effect to the good cure for Jodie was another patient's death for whom the act in question provided no benefit. They therefore found that the doctors would have 'murderous intent' if they carried out the operation, though they would avoid liability due to the defence of necessity.

Subjective recklessness

In everyday language, recklessness means taking an unjustified risk. However, its legal definition is not quite the same as its ordinary English meaning and careful direction as to its meaning in law has to be given to the jury.

Its legal definition has radically changed in recent years. It is now clear that it is a subjective form of *mens rea*, so the focus is on what the defendant was thinking. In 1981 in the case of **Metropolitan Police Commissioner** *v* **Caldwell**, Lord Diplock created an objective form of recklessness, but this was abolished in 2003 by the case of **R** *v* **G**. Following the House of Lords' judgment of **R** *v* **G** recklessness will always be interpreted as requiring a subjective test. In that case, the House favoured the definition of recklessness provided by the Law Commission's draft Criminal Code Bill in 1989:

> A person acts recklessly . . . with respect to –
> (i) a circumstance when he is aware of a risk that it exists or will exist;
> (ii) a result when he is aware of a risk that it will occur;
> and it is, in the circumstances known to him, unreasonable to take the risk.

Defendants must always be aware of the risk in order to satisfy this test of recklessness. In addition their conduct must have been unreasonable. It would appear that any level of awareness of a risk will be sufficient, provided the court finds the risk taking unreasonable.

Until the case of **R v G**, the leading case on subjective recklessness was **R v Cunningham** (1957). In **R v Cunningham** the defendant broke a gas meter to steal the money in it, and the gas seeped out into the house next door. Cunningham's prospective mother-in-law was sleeping there, and became so ill that her life was endangered. Cunningham was charged under s. 23 of the Offences Against the Person Act 1861 with 'maliciously administering a noxious thing so as to endanger life'.

The Court of Appeal said that 'maliciously' meant intentionally or recklessly. They defined recklessness as where:

> the accused has foreseen that the particular kind of harm might be done and yet has gone on to take the risk of it.

This is called a subjective test: the accused must actually have had the required foresight. Cunningham would therefore have been reckless if he realized there was a risk of the gas escaping and endangering someone, and went ahead anyway. His conviction was in fact quashed because of a misdirection at the trial.

In order to define recklessness, the House of Lords in **R v G** preferred to use the words of the Law Commission's draft Criminal Code Bill (the draft Code), rather than the court's earlier words in **Cunningham**. It is likely therefore in future that the draft Code's definition will become the single definition of recklessness, and the phrasing in **Cunningham** will no longer be used.

There are three main differences between the definition of subjective recklessness in the draft Code, and the definition in **Cunningham**. First, the **Cunningham** test refers only to taking risks as to a result and makes no mention of taking risks as to a circumstance. The Law Commission, in preparing its draft Code, felt that this was a gap in the law. It therefore expressly applies the test of recklessness to the taking of risks in relation to a circumstance. Secondly, the draft Code adds an additional restriction to a finding of recklessness: the defendant's risk-taking must have been 'unreasonable'. To determine whether the risk-taking was unreasonable the courts will balance such factors as the seriousness of the risk and the social value of the defendant's conduct. William Wilson (2003) observes that:

> Jumping a traffic light is likely to be deemed reckless if actuated by a desire to get home quickly for tea but not if the desire was to get a seriously ill person to hospital.

Thirdly, the **Cunningham** test for recklessness only requires foresight of the type of harm that actually occurred. It is arguable that the Law Commission's Draft Code requires awareness of the risk that the actual damage caused might occur (see Davies (2004) listed in the bibliography).

Transferred malice

If Ann shoots at Ben, intending to kill him, but happens to miss, and shoots and kills Chris instead, Ann will be liable for the murder of Chris. This is because of the principle known as transferred malice. Under this principle, if Ann has the *mens rea* of a particular crime and does the *actus reus* of the crime, Ann is guilty of the crime even though the *actus reus* may differ in some way from that intended. The *mens rea* is simply transferred to the new *actus reus*. Either intention or recklessness can be so transferred.

As a result, the defendant will be liable for the same crime even if the victim is not the intended victim. In **R** *v* **Latimer** (1886), the defendant aimed a blow at someone with his belt. The belt recoiled off that person and hit the victim, who was severely injured. The court held that Latimer was liable for maliciously wounding the un-expected victim. His intention to wound the person he aimed at was transferred to the person actually injured.

Where the accused would have had a defence if the crime committed had been completed against the intended victim, that defence is also transferred. So if Ann shot at Ben in self-defence and hit and killed Chris instead, Ann would be able to rely on the defence if charged with Chris's murder.

In **Attorney-General's Reference (No. 3 of 1994)** the defendant stabbed his girlfriend, who was to his knowledge between 22 and 24 weeks pregnant with their child. The girlfriend underwent an operation on a cut in the wall of her uterus but it was not realized at the time that the stabbing had damaged the foetus's abdomen. She subsequently gave birth prematurely to a baby girl who later died from the complications of a premature birth. Before the child's death the defendant was charged with the offence of wounding his girlfriend with intent to cause her grievous bodily harm to which he pleaded guilty. After the child died, he was in addition charged with murdering the child. At the close of the prosecution's case the judge upheld a defence submission that the facts could not give rise to a conviction for murder or manslaughter and accordingly directed the jury to acquit. The Attorney-General referred the case to the Court of Appeal for a ruling to clarify the law in the field. The Court of Appeal considered the foetus to be an integral part of the mother until its birth. Thus any intention to injure the foetus prior to its birth was treated as an intention to injure the mother. If on birth the baby subsequently died, an intention to injure the baby could be found by applying the doctrine of transferred malice. This approach was rejected by the House of Lords. It held that the foetus was not an integral part of the mother, but a unique organism. The principle of transferred malice could not therefore be applied, and the direction was criticized as being of 'no sound intellectual basis'.

> ✓ **Know your terms 21.2**
>
> Define the following terms:
>
> 1 *Actus reus*
> 2 *Mens rea*
> 3 **Cunningham** recklessness
> 4 Transferred malice

Mens rea and motive

It is essential to realize that *mens rea* has nothing to do with motive. To illustrate this, take the example of a man who suffocates his wife with a pillow, intending to kill her because she is afflicted with a terminal disease which causes her terrible and constant pain. Many people would say that this man's motive is not a bad one – in fact many people would reject the label 'murder' for what he has done. But there is no doubt that he has the necessary *mens rea* for murder, because he intends to kill his wife, even if he does not want to do so. He may not have a guilty mind in the everyday sense, but he does have *mens rea*. Motive may be relevant when the decision is made on whether or not to prosecute, or later for sentencing, but it makes no difference with regard to legal liability.

Proof of *mens rea*

Under s. 8 of the Criminal Justice Act 1967, where the definition of an offence requires the prosecution to prove that the accused intended or foresaw something, the question of whether that is proved is one for the court or jury to decide on the basis of all the evidence. The fact that a consequence is proved to be the natural and probable result of the accused's actions does not mean that it is proved that he or she intended or foresaw such a result; the jury or the court must decide.

Mens rea and morality

Problems arise because in practice the courts stretch the law in order to convict those whose conduct they see as blameworthy, while acquitting those whose behaviour they feel does not deserve the strongest censure. For example, the offence of murder requires a finding of intention to kill or to cause serious injury. The courts want to convict terrorists of murder when they kill, yet do they have the requisite *mens rea*? If you plant a bomb but give a warning, do you intend to kill or to cause serious injury? Assuming a fair warning, could death or serious injury be seen as a virtually certain consequence of your acts? What if a terrorist bomber gives a warning that would normally allow sufficient time to evacuate the relevant premises, but owing to the negligence of the police, the evacuation fails to take place quickly enough and people are killed? The courts are likely to be reluctant to allow this to reduce the terrorist's liability, yet it is hard to see how this terrorist could be said to intend deaths or serious injury to occur – in fact the giving of a warning might suggest the opposite. The courts are equally reluctant to impose liability for murder where it is difficult to find real moral guilt, even though technically this should be irrelevant. The problem is linked to the fact that murder carries a mandatory life sentence, which prevents the judge from taking degrees of moral guilt into account in sentencing.

The academic Alan Norrie has written an exciting article on this subject called 'After Woollin' (1999). He argues that the attempt of the law to separate the question of *mens rea* from broader issues of motive and morality is artificial and not possible in practice. He points to the fact that the jury are merely 'entitled to find' indirect intention and that for some offences only direct intention will suffice. In his view through this flexibility the courts want to allow themselves the freedom to acquit in morally appropriate cases. Such moral judgements on the basis of the defendant's motive are traditionally excluded from decisions on *mens rea*.

George Fletcher (*Rethinking Criminal Law*, 2000) has noted how historically there has been a development of the law from terms with a moral content such as 'malice' to the identification of 'specific mental states of intending and knowing'. Fletcher observes that:

Descriptive theorists seek to minimise the normative content of the criminal law in order to render it, in their view, precise and free from the passions of subjective moral judgement . . . [Such a concern] may impel courts and theorists towards value free rules and concepts; the reality of judgement, blame and punishment generates the contrary pressure and insures that the quest for a value free science of law cannot succeed.

Making a judgement on someone that he is a 'murderer' and that he should have a life sentence are both moral judgements. Judges are constantly making judgements on right and wrong and what should happen to wrongdoers. But they have to render these judgements in specialist legal terms using concepts such as 'intention' and 'foresight'. These terms are different from everyday terms of moral judgement, but they are used to address moral issues. Norrie argues:

as a result of this, lawyers end up investing 'nominally descriptive terms with moral force'. Thus terms like 'intent', 'state of mind' and 'mental state' which appear to be descriptive are used to refer to issues that require normative judgement.

In Norrie's view the desire to exclude 'subjective moral judgement' really results from the desire in the past to safeguard a criminal code based on the protection of a particular social order. He considers that:

if one examines the historical development of the criminal law, one finds that a legal code designed to establish an order based on private property and individual right was legitimated by reference to the dangers of subjective anarchy. This argument was the ideological window-dressing justifying the profound institutional changes taking place.

Thus, he considers that the apparently impartial language used to describe *mens rea* is actually very partial and unfair to many. The law is based upon the supposed characteristics of the average person, stressing the free will of the individual. It ignores the 'substantive moral differences that exist between individuals as they are located across different social classes and according to other relevant divisions such as culture and gender'.

One way to avoid this tension between the legal rules and the moral reality is to develop the defences that are available. Defences such as duress explicitly allow moral issues to enter into the legal debate through questions of proportionality.

Coincidence of *actus reus* and *mens rea*

The *mens rea* of an offence must be present at the time the *actus reus* is committed. So if, for example, Ann intends to kill Ben on Friday night, but for some reason fails to do so, then quite accidentally runs Ben over on Saturday morning, Ann will not be liable for Ben's murder. However, there are two ways in which the courts have introduced flexibility into this area: continuing acts, which are described above at p. 434, and the interpretation of a continuous series of acts as a single transaction. An example of the latter occurred in **Thabo Meli** *v* **R** (1954). The defendants had attempted to kill their victim by beating him over the head, then threw what they assumed was a dead body over a cliff. The victim did die, but from the fall and exposure, and not from the beating. Thus there was an argument that at the time of the *actus reus* the defendants no longer had the *mens rea*. The Privy Council held that throwing him over the cliff was part of one series of acts following through a pre-conceived plan of action and therefore the incident could not be seen as consisting of separate acts at all, but as amounting to a single transaction. The defendants had the required *mens rea* when that transaction began, and therefore *mens rea* and *actus reus* had coincided.

Quick quiz 21.3

1 What is the difference between direct and indirect intention?

2 What level of foresight is required for a finding of **Cunningham** recklessness and what level of foresight is required for a finding of indirect intention?

3 Name the most recent House of Lords' judgment on intention.

4 Is a person's motive relevant in determining whether he or she had *mens rea*?

Reading on the web

The full judgment of **R** *v* **Woollin** is available on the House of Lords' judicial business website at:

http://www.parliament.the-stationery-office.co.uk/pa/ld/ldjudgmt.htm#1998

Question and answer guide

1 Critically analyse the situations where a person can be liable in criminal law for an omission to act.

Answer guide

This is not a difficult question – the circumstances in which criminal liability will be imposed for true omissions are clearly explained above. You should also include the situations in which liability is imposed for conduct which would in everyday language be described as an omission, but which in law is an act, and vice versa. Remember that you are asked to analyze the law critically, so it is not good enough simply to provide a description; you should also evaluate the law by pointing out its strengths and weaknesses. For example, you could look at the issue of the drowning child and whether the law is adequate in this situation and you could also consider the approach taken by the courts to **Bland**'s case.

Chapter summary

A person cannot usually be found guilty of a criminal offence unless two elements are present: an *actus reus* and a *mens rea*.

Actus reus

The *actus reus* comprises all the elements of the offence other than the state of mind of the defendant. The defendant's acts must have been voluntary.

Causation

With result crimes, the prosecution must prove that the defendant caused the result of the offence. Defendants can only be held responsible for results where their acts are both a 'factual' and a 'legal' cause of the result constituting the offence.

Factual causation

In order to establish factual causation, the prosecution must prove two things:

■ that but for the conduct of the accused, the result of the offence would not have occurred as and when it did; and
■ that the original injury arising from the defendant's conduct was more than a minimal cause of the result constituting the offence.

Legal causation

Legal causation can be proved in any one of the following three ways or by a combination of them:

■ the original injury was an operative and significant cause of the result;
■ the intervening act was reasonably foreseeable; and
■ the 'thin skull' test.

Omissions

Criminal liability is rarely imposed for true omissions at common law, though there are situations where the accused has a duty to act, and in these cases there may be liability for a true omission.

Mens rea

Mens rea traditionally refers to the state of the mind of the person committing the crime.

Intention

Intention is a subjective concept.

■ *Direct intention*. Direct intention exists where the accused actually wants the result that occurs.
■ *Indirect intention*. Indirect intention exists where the accused did not desire a particular result but, in acting as he or she did, realized to the point of virtual certainty that it might occur. The 'virtual certainty' test was laid down by the Court of Appeal in **Nedrick** and approved by the House of Lords in **Woollin**.

▶

Subjective recklessness

Defendants are reckless where they are aware of a risk and take that risk where it was unreasonable to do so.

Transferred malice

Under the principle of transferred malice, if the defendant has the *mens rea* of a particular crime and does the *actus reus* of the crime, the defendant is guilty of the crime even though the *actus reus* may differ in some way from that intended. The *mens rea* is simply transferred to the new *actus reus*.

Coincidence of *actus reus* and *mens rea*

The *mens rea* of an offence must be present at the time the *actus reus* is committed.

Chapter 22 — Strict liability in criminal law

There are a small number of crimes which can be committed without any *mens rea*, or without *mens rea* regarding at least one aspect of the *actus reus*. These offences are known as strict liability crimes, and most of them have been created by statute, though public nuisance and blasphemous libel are examples of common law strict liability offences.

Which crimes are crimes of strict liability?

Unfortunately, statutes are not always so obliging as to state 'this is a strict liability offence'. Occasionally the wording of an Act does make this clear, but otherwise the courts are left to decide for themselves. The principles on which this decision is made were considered in **Gammon (Hong Kong) Ltd** *v* **Attorney-General of Hong Kong** (1985). The defendants were involved in building works in Hong Kong. Part of a building they were constructing fell down, and it was found that the collapse had occurred because the builders had failed to follow the original plans exactly. The Hong Kong building regulations prohibited deviating in any substantial way from such plans, and the defendants were charged with breaching the regulations, an offence punishable with a fine of up to $250,000 or three years' imprisonment. On appeal they argued that they were not liable because they had not known that the changes they made were substantial ones. However, the Privy Council held that the relevant regulations created offences of strict liability, and the convictions were upheld.

Explaining the principles on which they had based the decision, Lord Scarman confirmed that there is always a presumption of law that *mens rea* is required before a person can be held guilty of a criminal offence. The existence of this presumption was reaffirmed in very strong terms by the House of Lords in **B (A Minor)** *v* **Director of Public Prosecutions** (2000). A 15-year-old boy had sat next to a 13-year-old girl and asked her to give him a 'shiner'. The trial judge observed that '[t]his, in the language of today's gilded youth, apparently means, not a black eye, but an act of oral sex'. The boy was charged with committing an act of gross indecency on a child under the age of 14. Both the trial judge and the Court of Appeal ruled that this was a strict liability offence and that there was therefore no defence available that the boy believed the girl to be over 14. The House of Lords confirmed that there was a presumption that *mens rea* was required, and ruled that the relevant offence was

467

not actually one of strict liability. The House stated that in order to rebut the presumption that an offence required *mens rea*, there needed to be a 'compellingly clear implication' that Parliament intended the offence to be one of strict liability. As the offence had a very broad *actus reus*, carried a serious social stigma and a heavy sentence, it decided that Parliament did not have this intention.

The case has thrown doubt on the old case of **R** *v* **Prince** (1874) which was also concerned with an offence against the person that could only be committed on a girl under a certain age. That offence had been treated as one of strict liability and the reasonable but mistaken belief of the defendant as to her age was therefore found to be irrelevant. The House of Lords described that case as 'unsound' and a 'relic from an age dead and gone'.

There are certain factors which can, on their own or combined, displace the presumption that *mens rea* is required. These can be grouped into four categories which will be considered in turn.

▌ The crime is a regulatory offence

A regulatory offence is one in which no real moral issue is involved, and usually (though not always) one for which the maximum penalty is small – the mass of rules surrounding the sale of food are examples. In **Gammon** it was stated that the presumption against strict liability was less strong for regulatory offences than for truly criminal offences.

This distinction between true crimes and regulatory offences had previously been made in the case of **Sweet** *v* **Parsley** (1970). Ms Sweet, a teacher, took a sublease of a farmhouse outside Oxford. She rented the house to tenants, and rarely spent any time there. Unknown to her, the tenants were smoking cannabis on the premises. When they were caught, she was found guilty of being concerned in the management of premises which were being used for the purpose of smoking cannabis, contrary to the Dangerous Drugs Act 1965 (now replaced by the Misuse of Drugs Act 1971).

Ms Sweet appealed, on the grounds that she knew nothing about what the tenants were doing, and could not reasonably have been expected to have known. Lord Reid acknowledged that strict liability was appropriate for regulatory offences, or 'quasi-crimes' – offences which are not criminal 'in any real sense', and are merely acts prohibited in the public interest. But, he said, the kind of crime to which a real social stigma is attached should usually require proof of *mens rea*; in the case of such offences it was not in the public interest that an innocent person should be prevented from proving that innocence in the interests of making it easier for guilty people to be convicted.

Since their Lordships regarded the offence under consideration as being a 'true crime' – the stigma had, for example, caused Ms Sweet to lose her job – they held that it was not a strict liability offence, and since Ms Sweet did not have the necessary *mens rea*, her conviction was overturned.

Unfortunately, the courts have never laid down a list of those offences which they will consider to be regulatory offences rather than 'true crimes'. Those generally considered to be regulatory offences are the kind created by the rules on hygiene and measurement standards within the food and drink industry, and regulations designed to stop industry from polluting the environment, but there are clearly some types of offences which will be more difficult to categorize.

The statute deals with an issue of social concern

According to **Gammon**, where a statute is concerned with an issue of social concern (such as public safety), and the creation of strict liability will promote the purpose of the statute by encouraging potential offenders to take extra precautions against committing the prohibited act, the presumption against strict liability can be rebutted. This category is obviously subject to the distinctions drawn by Lord Reid in **Sweet** v **Parsley** – the laws against murder and rape are to protect the public, but this type of true crime would not attract strict liability.

The types of offences that do fall into this category cover behaviour which could involve danger to the public, but which would not usually carry the same kind of stigma as a crime such as murder or even theft. The breach of the building regulations committed in **Gammon** is an example, as are offences relating to serious pollution of the environment. In **R** v **Blake** (1996), the defendant was accused of making broadcasts on a pirate radio station and was convicted of using wireless telegraphy equipment without a licence, contrary to s. 1(1) of the Wireless Telegraphy Act 1949. His conviction was upheld by the Court of Appeal which stated that this offence was one of strict liability. This conclusion was reached as the offence had been created in the interest of public safety, given the interference with the operation of the emergency services that could result from unauthorized broadcasting.

In **Harrow London Borough Council** v **Shah** (1999), the offence of selling National Lottery tickets to a person under the age of 16 was found to be an offence of strict liability. The Divisional Court justified this by stating that the legislation dealt with an issue of social concern.

These crimes overlap with regulatory offences in subject area, but unlike regulatory offences, may carry severe maximum penalties. Despite such higher penalties, strict liability is seen to be a necessary provision given the need to promote very high standards of care in areas of possible danger.

The wording of the Act

Gammon states that the presumption that *mens rea* is required for a criminal offence can be rebutted if the words of a statute suggest that strict liability is intended. The House of Lords said in **Sweet** v **Parsley**: 'the fact that other sections of the Act expressly required *mens rea*, for example, because they contain the word "knowingly", is not in itself sufficient to justify a decision that a section which is silent as to *mens rea* creates a [strict liability] offence'. At present it is not always clear whether a particular form of words will be interpreted as creating an offence of strict liability. However, some words have been interpreted fairly consistently, including the following.

'Cause'

In **Alphacell v Woodward** (1972), the defendant was a company accused of causing polluted matter to enter a river. It was using equipment designed to prevent any overflow into the river, but when the mechanism became clogged by leaves, the pollution was able to escape. There was no evidence that the defendant company had been negligent or even knew that the pollution was leaking out. The House of Lords stated that where statutes create an offence of causing something to happen, the courts should adopt a common-sense approach – if reasonable people would say that the defendant has caused something to happen, regardless of whether he or she knew he or she was doing so, then no *mens rea* is required. Their Lordships held that in the normal meaning of the word, the company had 'caused' the pollution to enter the water, and the company's conviction was upheld.

'Possession'

There are many offences which are defined as 'being in possession of a prohibited item', the obvious example being drugs. They are frequently treated as strict liability offences.

'Knowingly'

Clearly, use of this word tells the courts that *mens rea* is required, and it tends to be used where Parliament wants to underline the fact that the presumption should be applied.

The smallness of the penalty

Strict liability is most often imposed for offences which carry a relatively small maximum penalty, and it appears that the higher the maximum penalty, the less likely it is that the courts will impose strict liability. However, the existence of severe penalties for an offence does not guarantee that strict liability will not be imposed. In **Gammon** Lord Scarman held that where regulations were put in place to protect public safety, it was quite appropriate to impose strict liability, despite potentially severe penalties.

Relevance of the four factors

Obviously these four factors overlap to a certain extent – regulatory offences usually do have small penalties, for example. And in **Alphacell v Woodward**, the House of Lords gave its decision the dual justification of applying the common-sense meaning of the term 'cause', and recognizing that pollution was an issue of social concern.

It is important to note that all these categories are guidelines rather than clear rules. The courts are not always consistent in their application of strict liability, and social policy plays an important part in the decisions. During the 1960s, there was intense social concern about what appeared to be a widespread drug problem, and the courts imposed strict liability for many drug offences. Ten years later, pollution of the environment had become one of the main topics of concern, hence the justification for the decision in **Alphacell v Woodward**.

Today, there appears to be a general move away from strict liability, and some newer statutes imposing apparent strict liability contain a limited form of defence, by which an accused can escape conviction by proving that he or she took all reasonable precautions to prevent the offence being committed. However, the courts could begin to move back towards strict liability if it seems that an area of social concern might require it.

Crimes of negligence

Following the decision of **Attorney-General's Reference (No. 2 of 1999)**, it is arguable that crimes of negligence, such as gross negligence manslaughter, are actually crimes of strict liability. This is because in that case the Court of Appeal stated that gross negligence was not a form of *mens rea* and that a person could be found to have been grossly negligent without looking at their state of mind but simply by looking at the gross carelessness of their conduct.

The effect of mistake

Where strict liability applies, an accused cannot use the defence of mistake, even if the mistake was reasonable. The House of Lords' judgment of **B (A Minor) v Director of Public Prosecutions** is slightly misleading on this issue as it seems to blur the distinction between mistakes made in relation to strict liability offences and mistakes made in relation to offences requiring *mens rea*. This distinction is, however, fundamental. As the case was concerned with an offence that required *mens rea*, anything it stated in relation to strict liability offences was merely *obiter dicta* and therefore not binding on future courts.

The European Convention on Human Rights

In **R v Mithun Muhamad** (2002) the Court of Appeal stated that strict liability offences did not automatically breach the European Convention on Human Rights. In **Salabiaku v France** (1988) the European Court of Human Rights stated:

> the Contracting States may, under certain conditions, penalise a simple or objective fact as such, irrespective of whether it results from criminal intent or from negligence.

Quick quiz 22.1

1 What is meant by a strict liability offence?

2 In law is there a presumption that *mens rea* is required or is there a presumption that *mens rea* is not required?

3 Give three examples of words that can rebut the presumption that *mens rea* is required.

4 If a person makes a mistake, what impact can this have on his or her liability for a strict liability offence?

Arguments in favour of strict liability

Promotion of care

By promoting high standards of care, strict liability, it is argued, protects the public from dangerous practices. Social scientist Barbara Wootton (1981) has defended strict liability on this basis, suggesting that if the objective of criminal law is to prevent socially damaging activities, it would be absurd to turn a blind eye to those who cause the harm due to carelessness, negligence or even an accident.

Deterrent value

Strict liability is said to provide a strong deterrent, which is considered especially important given the way in which regulatory offences tend to be dealt with. Many of them are handled not by the police and the Crown Prosecution Service (CPS), but by special government bodies, such as the Health and Safety Inspectorate, which checks that safety rules are observed in workplaces. These bodies tend to work by putting pressure on offenders to put right any breaches, with prosecution, or even threats of it, very much a last resort. It is suggested that strict liability allows enforcement agencies to strengthen their bargaining position, since potential offenders know that if a prosecution is brought, there is a very good chance of conviction.

Easier enforcement

Strict liability makes enforcing offences easier; in **Gammon** the Privy Council suggested that if the prosecution had to prove *mens rea* in even the smallest regulatory offence, the administration of justice might very quickly come to a complete standstill.

Difficulty of proving *mens rea*

In many strict liability offences, *mens rea* would be very difficult to prove, and without strict liability, guilty people might escape conviction. Obvious examples are those involving large corporations, where it may be difficult to prove that someone knew what was happening.

No threat to liberty

In many strict liability cases, the defendant is a business and the penalty is a fine, so individual liberty is not generally under threat. Even the fines are often small.

Profit from risk

Where an offence is concerned with business, those who commit it may well be saving themselves money, and thereby making extra profit by doing so – by, for example, saving the time that would be spent on observing safety regulations. If a person creates a risk and makes a profit by doing so, he or she ought to be liable if that risk causes or could cause harm, even if that was not the intention.

Arguments against strict liability

Injustice

Strict liability is criticized as unjust on a variety of different grounds. First, that it is not in the interests of justice that someone who has taken reasonable care, and could not possibly have avoided committing an offence, should be punished by the criminal law. This goes against the principle that the criminal law punishes fault.

Secondly, the argument that strict liability should be enforced because *mens rea* would be too difficult to prove is morally doubtful. The prosecution often find it difficult to prove *mens rea* on a rape charge, for example, but is that a reason for making rape a crime of strict liability? Although many strict liability offences are clearly far lesser crimes than these, some do impose severe penalties, as **Gammon** illustrates, and it may not be in the interests of justice if strict liability is imposed in these areas just because *mens rea* would make things too difficult for the prosecution. It is inconsistent with justice to convict someone who is not guilty, in the normal sense of the word, just because the penalty imposed will be small.

Even where penalties are small, in many cases conviction is a punishment in itself. Sentencing may be tailored to take account of mitigating factors, but that is little comfort to the reputable butcher who unknowingly sells bad meat, when the case is reported in local papers and customers go elsewhere. However slight the punishment, in practice there is some stigma attached to a criminal conviction (even though it may be less than that for a 'true crime') which should not be attached to a person who has taken all reasonable care.

In addition, as Smith and Hogan (2002) point out in their criminal law textbook, in the case of a jury trial, strict liability takes crucial questions of fact away from juries, and allows them to be considered solely by the judge for the purposes of sentencing. In a magistrates' court, it removes those questions from the requirement of proof beyond reasonable doubt, and allows them to be decided according to the less strict principles which guide decisions on sentencing.

Strict liability also delegates a good deal of power to the discretion of the enforcement agency. Where strict liability makes it almost certain that a prosecution will lead to a conviction, the decision on whether or not to prosecute becomes critical, and there are few controls over those who make this decision.

Ineffective

It is debatable whether strict liability actually works. For a start, the deterrent value of strict liability may be overestimated. For the kinds of offences to which strict liability is usually applied, the important deterrent factor may not be the chances of being convicted, but the chances of being caught and charged. In the food and drinks business particularly, just being charged with an offence brings unwelcome publicity, and even if the company is not convicted, it is likely to see a fall in sales as customers apply the 'no smoke without fire' principle. The problem is that in many cases the chances of being caught and prosecuted are not high. In the first place, enforcement agencies frequently lack the resources to monitor the huge number of potential offenders – the Factory Inspectorate in 1980 had 900 inspectors who were responsible for reporting on at least 600,000 different workplaces. Even where offenders are caught, it appears that the usual response of enforcement agencies is a warning letter. The most serious or persistent offenders may be threatened with prosecution if they do not put matters right, but only a minority are actually prosecuted. Providing more resources for the enforcement agencies and bringing more prosecutions might have a stronger deterrent effect than imposing strict liability on the minority who are prosecuted.

In other areas too, it is the chance of getting caught which may be the strongest deterrent – if people think they are unlikely to get caught speeding, for example, the fact that strict liability will be imposed if they do is not much of a deterrent.

In fact in some areas, rather than ensuring a higher standard of care, strict liability may have quite the opposite effect: knowing that it is possible to be convicted of an offence regardless of having taken every reasonable precaution may reduce the incentive to take such precautions, rather than increase it.

As Professor Hall points out, the fact that strict liability is usually imposed only where the possible penalty is small means that unscrupulous companies can simply regard the criminal law as 'a nominal tax on illegal enterprise'. In areas of industry where the need to maintain a good reputation is not so strong as it is in food or drugs, for example, it may be cheaper to keep paying the fines than to change bad working practices, and therefore very little deterrent value can be seen. In these areas it might be more efficient, as Professor Hall says, 'to put real teeth in the law' by developing offences with more severe penalties, even if that means losing the expediency of strict liability.

Justifying strict liability in the interests of protecting the public can be seen as taking a sledgehammer to crack a nut. It is certainly true, for example, that bad meat causes food poisoning just the same whether or not the butcher knew it was bad, and that the public needs protection from butchers who sell bad meat. But while we might want to make sure of punishment for butchers who knowingly sell bad meat, and probably those who take no, or not enough, care to check the condition of their meat, how is the public protected by punishing a butcher who took all possible care (by using a normally reputable supplier, for example) and could not possibly have avoided committing the offence?

Task 22.2

The Health and Safety Executive is responsible for the enforcement of a wide range of strict liability offences. Its website can be found at **http://www.hse.gov.uk/**

Visit its website and find information on its work in this field.

The fact that it is not always possible to recognize crimes of strict liability before the courts have made a decision clearly further weakens any deterrent effect.

Little administrative advantage

It is also open to debate whether strict liability really does contribute much to administrative expediency. Cases still have to be detected and brought to court, and in some cases selected elements of the *mens rea* still have to be proved. And although strict liability may make conviction easier, it leaves the problem of sentencing. This cannot be done fairly without taking the degree of negligence into account, so evidence of the accused's state of mind must be available. Given all this, it is difficult to see how much time and manpower is actually saved.

Inconsistent application

The fact that whether or not strict liability will be imposed rests on the imprecise science of statutory interpretation means that there are discrepancies in both the offences to which it is applied, and what it actually means. The changes in the types of cases to which strict liability is applied over the years reflect social policy – the courts come down harder on areas which are causing social concern at a particular time. While this may be justified in the interests of society, it does little for certainty and the principle that like cases should be treated alike.

The courts are also inconsistent in their justifications for imposing or not imposing strict liability. In **Lim Chin Aik *v* R** (1963) the defendant was charged with remaining in Singapore, despite a prohibition order against him. Lord Evershed stated that the subject matter of a statute was not sufficient grounds for inferring that strict liability was intended; it was also important to consider whether imposing strict liability would help to enforce the regulations, and it could only do this if there were some precautions the potential offender could take to prevent him from committing the offence. 'Unless this is so, there is no reason in penalizing him and it cannot be inferred that the legislature imposed strict liability merely in order to find a luckless victim.'

In the case of **Lim Chin Aik**, the precaution to be taken would have been finding out whether there was a prohibition order against him, but Lord Evershed further explained that people could only be expected to take 'sensible' and 'practicable' precautions: Lim Chin Aik was not expected to 'make continuous enquiry to see whether an order had been made against him'.

Presumably then, our hypothetical butcher should only be expected to take reasonable and practicable precautions against selling bad meat, and not, for example, have to employ scientific analysts to test every pork chop. Yet just such extreme precautions appear to have been expected in **Smedleys *v* Breed** (1974). The defendants were convicted under the Food and Drugs Act 1955, after a very small caterpillar was found in one of three million tins of peas. Despite the fact that even individual inspection of each pea would probably not have prevented the offence being committed, Lord Hailsham defended the imposition of strict liability on the grounds that 'To construe the Food and Drugs Act 1955 in a sense less strict than that which I have adopted would make a serious inroad on the legislation for consumer protection'. Clearly the subject areas of these cases are very different, but the contrast between them does give some indication of the shaky ground on which strict liability can rest – if the House of Lords had followed the reasoning of **Lim Chin Aik**, Smedleys would not have been liable, since they had taken all reasonable and practical precautions.

Better alternatives are available

There are alternatives to strict liability which would be less unjust and more effective in preventing harm, such as better inspection of business premises and the imposition of liability for negligence (see below).

Reform

The Law Commission's draft Bill

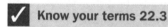
Know your terms 22.3

Define the following terms:

1 Regulatory offence
2 Stigma
3 Draft Bill
4 Law Commission

The Law Commission's draft Criminal Liability (Mental Element) Bill of 1978 requires that Parliament specifically state if it is creating an offence of strict liability. Where this is not done, the courts should assume *mens rea* is required. The practice of allowing the courts to decide when strict liability should be applied, under cover of the fiction that they are interpreting parliamentary intention, is not helpful, leading to a mass of litigation with many of the cases irreconcilable with each other – as with **Lim Chin Aik** and **Smedleys v Breed**, above. If legislators knew that the courts would always assume *mens rea* unless specifically told not to, they would be more likely to adopt the habit of stating whether the offence was strict or not.

Restriction to public danger offences

Strict liability could perhaps be more easily justified if the tighter liability were balanced by real danger to the public in the offence – the case of **Gammon** can be justified on this ground.

Liability for negligence

Smith and Hogan in their criminal law textbook (2002) suggest that strict liability should be replaced by liability for negligence. This would catch defendants who were simply thoughtless or inefficient, as well as those who deliberately broke the law, but would not punish people who were genuinely blameless.

Defence of all due care

In Australia a defence of all due care is available. Where a crime would otherwise impose strict liability, the defendant can avoid conviction by proving that he or she took all due care to avoid committing the offence.

Extending strict liability

Baroness Wootton (1981) advocates imposing strict liability for all crimes, so that *mens rea* would only be relevant for sentencing purposes.

Reading on the web

The website of the Health and Safety Executive can be found at:

> http://www.hse.gov.uk/

The decision of **B (A Minor)** v **Director of Public Prosecutions** (2000) is available on the House of Lords' website at:

> http://www.publications.parliament.uk/pa/ld/ldjudgmt.htm#2000

Question and answer guides

The criminal law question on the AQA examination paper "The Concept of Liability" is unlikely to be solely about strict liability. Instead, if the issue of strict liability arises, it will probably only form one part of the question.

1 Peter, aged 15, was very naughty. He used a catapult to throw stones at children playing in a river. Unfortunately, one of the stones hit a child on the head and he developed a large bruise and suffered shock. The child tried to run away and knocked over Louise who was standing near by. She landed awkwardly and broke her leg.

(a) In a criminal trial, the prosecution usually has to prove *mens rea* unless the crime is one of **strict liability**. Explain the meaning of these terms. *(10 marks)*

(b) With regard to the child's injuries, describe the *actus reus* and *mens rea* of a relevant offence. *(10 marks)*

(c) If Peter was prosecuted for the injuries to Louise, the issue of **causation** would have to be satisfied. Explain the law on causation and apply this law to the facts in this case. *(10 marks)*

Answer guide

(a) The meaning of *mens rea* is discussed in the previous chapter at p. 453, and the meaning of strict liability is discussed in the first part of this chapter. You could have looked at the case of **Gammon (Hong Kong) Ltd** v **A-G** (1985) as an illustration of a strict liability offence. ▶

(b) The offences of either battery or actual bodily harm could have been discussed which are discussed in the next chapter.

(c) Causation is discussed at p. 444.

 Is the imposition of strict liability ever justifiable in criminal law? *(Oxford)*

Answer guide

Avoid the natural temptation of using this question simply as a trigger for writing everything you know on the subject without applying that material to the specific question asked. Obviously, you will want to learn a lot of material before the exam, and it will probably help to follow the structure of this book when you do this, so that for this chapter, for example, you might learn the lists of arguments for and against strict liability. That material will provide the basis for answering many differently worded questions on strict liability, but in the exam, you must angle that material to the actual question being asked. In this question, the key words are 'imposition' and 'justifiable' and these and their synonyms should be used at several points in the essay to show that you are answering the particular question asked. You could start by stating where strict liability is currently imposed, before discussing whether such impositions are justified – in this part you can describe the kind of offences to which strict liability applies, giving examples from case law. You should, however, devote the bulk of your essay to discussing when the imposition of strict liability is justified, if ever in your opinion, and when not, using the arguments for and against it to back up your points.

Chapter summary

Strict liability crimes are crimes which can be committed without any *mens rea*, or without *mens rea* regarding at least one aspect of the *actus reus*.

Which crimes are crimes of strict liability?

The wording of an Act will sometimes make it clear that an offence is one of strict liability; otherwise the courts must decide. There is always a presumption of law that *mens rea* is required before a person can be held guilty of a criminal offence. There are certain factors which can, on their own or combined, displace the presumption that *mens rea* is required. These can be grouped into the four following categories:

■ the crime is a regulatory offence;
■ the statute deals with an issue of social concern;
■ the wording of the Act suggests that *mens rea* is not required; and
■ the smallness of the penalty suggests *mens rea* is not required.

Crimes of negligence

Following the decision of **Attorney-General's Reference (No. 2 of 1999)**, it is arguable that crimes of negligence are actually crimes of strict liability.

The effect of mistake

Where strict liability applies, an accused cannot use the defence of mistake, even if the mistake is reasonable.

The European Convention on Human Rights

Strict liability offences do not automatically breach the European Convention.

Arguments in favour of strict liability

Arguments have been put forward in favour of strict liability including:

■ promotion of care
■ deterrent value
■ easier enforcement, and
■ difficulty in proving *mens rea*.

Arguments against strict liability

Arguments against strict liability include that such offences:

■ cause injustice
■ are ineffective
■ have little administrative advantage
■ are applied inconsistently; and
■ should be replaced by better alternatives.

Chapter 23

Non-fatal offences against the person

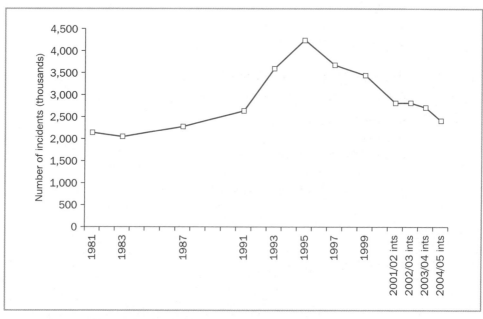

Figure 23.1 Trends in violent crime, 1981 to 2004/05

Source: Crime in England and Wales 2004/2005, p. 73, Figure 5.1.

There are five main non-fatal offences against the person:

- assault
- battery
- actual bodily harm
- inflicting grievous bodily harm or wounding
- causing grievous bodily harm or wounding.

Each of these offences will be considered in turn, starting with the least serious and progressing to the most serious where a life sentence can be imposed.

Assault

The Criminal Justice Act 1988, s. 39 provides that assault is a summary offence with a maximum sentence on conviction of six months' imprisonment or a fine. The Act does not provide a definition of the offence; the relevant rules are found in common law.

Actus reus

This consists of any act which makes the victim fear that unlawful force is about to be used against him or her. No force need actually be applied; creating the fear of it is sufficient, so assault can be committed by raising a fist at the victim, or pointing a gun. Nor does it matter that it may have been impossible for the defendant actually to inflict any force, for example if the gun was unloaded, so long as the victim is unaware of the impossibility of the threat being carried out.

Words alone can constitute an assault

Until the Court of Appeal decision in **R *v* Constanza** (1997), there was some uncertainty as to whether words alone could amount to an assault. **R *v* Constanza**, a case involving stalking, confirmed that they could. The House of Lords took this approach in **R *v* Ireland and Burstow** (1997) so that silent phone calls could amount to an assault. The offence would, for example, be committed if a man shouted to a stranger 'I'm going to kill you' – there is no need for an accompanying act, such as raising a fist, or pointing a gun. The old case of **Meade and Belt** (1823), which had suggested the contrary, must now be viewed as bad law. Some people had gathered around another's house singing menacing songs with violent language and the judge had said 'no words or singing are equivalent to an assault'.

Words can also prevent a potential assault occurring – so, if a person shakes a fist at someone, but at the same time states that they will not harm that person, there will be no liability for this offence. This was the situation in **Tuberville *v* Savage** (1669). The defendant, annoyed by the comments someone had made to him, put his hand on his sword, which by itself could have been enough to constitute an assault, but also said, 'If it were not assize time I would not take such language', meaning that since judges were hearing criminal cases in the town at the time, he had no intention of using violence. His statement was held to negative the threat implied by putting his hand on his sword.

Fearing the immediate infliction of force

It has traditionally been said that the victim must fear the immediate infliction of force: fear that force might be applied at some time in the future would not be sufficient. The courts had often given a fairly generous interpretation of the concept of immediacy in this context. In **Smith *v* Chief Superintendent, Woking Police Station** (1983) the victim was at home in her ground-floor bedsit dressed only in her nightdress. She was terrified when she suddenly saw the defendant standing in her garden, staring at her through the window. He was found liable for assault, on the ground that the victim feared the immediate infliction of force, even though she was safely locked inside. The Court of Appeal said:

> It was clearly a situation where the basis of the fear which was instilled in her was that she did not know what the defendant was going to do next, but that, whatever he might be going to do next, and sufficiently immediately for the purposes of the offence, was something of a violent nature. In effect, as it seems to me, it was wholly open to the justices to infer that her state of mind was not only that of terror, which they did find, but terror of some immediate violence.

However, the requirement that the victim must fear the immediate infliction of force was undermined by the House of Lords in **R *v* Ireland and Burstow** (1997). One of the defendants, Ireland had made a large number of unwanted telephone calls to three different women, remaining silent when they answered the phone. All three victims suffered significant adverse symptoms such as palpitations, cold sweats, anxiety, inability to sleep, dizziness and stress as a result of the repeated calls. He was convicted under s. 47 of the Offences Against the Person Act 1861. This offence is discussed below but what is important here is that for Ireland to have been liable there must have been an assault. Ireland appealed against his conviction on the basis that there was no assault since the requirement of immediacy had not been satisfied. His appeal was dismissed by the Court of Appeal. The court stated that the requirement of immediacy was in fact satisfied as, by using the telephone, the appellant had put himself in immediate contact with the victims, and when the victims lifted the telephone they were placed in immediate fear and suffered psychological damage. It was not necessary for there to be physical proximity between the defendant and the victim. A further appeal was taken to the House of Lords in 1997 and, while the initial conviction was upheld, the House of Lords refused to enter into a discussion of the requirement for immediacy. They said that this was not necessary on the facts of the case as the appellant had pleaded guilty and that, in any case, the existence of immediacy would depend upon the circumstances in each case. It is not sufficient that the victim is immediately put in fear, the fear must be of immediate violence.

In **R *v* Constanza** (1997), a stalking case where the victim had been stalked over a prolonged period of time, the Court of Appeal stated that in order to incur liability

Table 23.1 Location of violent incidents (percentages)

	All violence	Domestic	Mugging	Stranger	Acquaintance
Around the home	27	75	22	5	16
Around work	8	3	1	8	16
Street	24	6	49	25	25
Pub or club	21	3	8	38	23
Transport	4	–	8	7	2
Other location	15	13	12	16	17

Source: Adapted from C. Flood-Page and J. Taylor (eds) (2003) *Crime in England and Wales 2001/2002: Supplementary Volume*, p. 57, Table 3g. Notes not included. Home Office, © Crown Copyright 2003.

for assault, it is enough for the prosecution to prove a fear of violence at some time not excluding the immediate future. If the Court of Appeal in **Constanza** is followed, then there would be no need to fear the immediate infliction of force in the sense of a battery; the offence would include fearing some other type of injury, notably psychological damage. The concept of immediacy would also be considerably weakened.

Causation

Note that, as for all these offences against the person, the issue of causation may be relevant if there is any question that the defendant was not the cause of the relevant result – in the case of assault, if the victim was put in fear of immediate and unlawful force, but the defendant did not cause that fear.

Mens rea

The *mens rea* of assault is either intention or subjective recklessness. The defendant must have either intended to cause the victim to fear the infliction of immediate and unlawful force, or been aware of the risk that such fear would be created and unreasonably taken that risk. The meaning of intention is discussed at p. 453, and recklessness is discussed at p. 459.

Battery

By s. 39 of the Criminal Justice Act 1988, battery is a summary offence punishable with up to six months' imprisonment or a fine, but as with assault, it is left to the common law to define the offence.

Actus reus

The *actus reus* of battery consists of the application of unlawful force on another. Any unlawful physical contact can amount to a battery; there is no need to prove harm or pain, and a mere touch can be sufficient. Often the force will be directly applied by one person to another, for example if one person slaps another across the face, but the force can also be applied indirectly. This was the case in **Fagan v Metropolitan Police Commissioner** (discussed at p. 448), where the force was applied by running over the police officer's foot in the car.

A battery was also, therefore, committed in **Haystead v Director of Public Prosecutions** (2000). The defendant had punched a woman twice in the face while she was holding her three-month-old baby, causing her to drop her child. The baby hit his head on the floor. The defendant was convicted of the offence of battery against the child. He appealed the conviction, arguing that battery required a direct application of force, but this argument was rejected.

The force does not have to be applied to the victim's body; touching his or her clothes may be enough, even if the victim feels nothing at all as a result. In **R v**

Thomas (1985) it was stated *obiter* that touching the bottom of a woman's skirt was equivalent to touching the woman herself.

Mens rea

Again either intention or recklessness is sufficient, but here it is intention or recklessness as to the application of unlawful force.

Offences Against the Person Act 1861, s. 47

According to s. 47:

> Whosoever shall be convicted upon an indictment of any assault occasioning actual bodily harm shall be liable . . . [to imprisonment for five years].

Section 47 of the Offences Against the Person Act 1861 (OAPA) provides that it is an offence to commit 'any assault occasioning actual bodily harm'. This offence is commonly known as ABH. The crime is triable either way and if found guilty the defendant is liable to a maximum sentence of five years.

Actus reus

Despite the fact that the Act uses the term 'assault' for this offence, s. 47 has been interpreted as being committed with either assault or battery. The first requirement is, therefore, to prove the *actus reus* of assault or battery, as defined above. In addition, the prosecution must show that the assault or battery caused ABH. Both **Ireland** and **Constanza**, discussed in the context of assault, were concerned with this offence as the issue of assault arose in the context of the *actus reus* of a s. 47 crime.

Actual bodily harm has been given a wide interpretation. In **R** *v* **Miller** (1954) the court stated: 'Actual bodily harm includes hurt or injury calculated to interfere with health or comfort.' Thus ABH can occur simply where discomfort to the person is caused. However, this was qualified slightly in **R** *v* **Chan-Fook** (1994), where Hobhouse LJ said in the Court of Appeal: 'The word "actual" indicates that the injury (although there is no need for it to be permanent) should not be so trivial as to be wholly insignificant.'

In **R** *v* **Donovan** (1934) the court stated that the injury had to be 'more than merely transient and trifling'. The defendant in **R** *v* **DPP** (2003) relied on this case to argue that he had not caused actual bodily harm because the victim had only momentarily lost consciousness following a kick to the head. He argued that this was only a transient harm and was not therefore sufficient. This argument was rejected by the court. **Donovan** merely required that the injury must not be both 'transient and trifling', on these facts the injury was transient but it was not trifling.

In **Miller**, it was also accepted that ABH included not just physical harm, but also psychological injury, such as shock. In later cases, the courts have made it clear that psychological injury will only count as ABH if it is a clinically recognizable condition.

The defendant in **R** *v* **Chan-Fook** aggressively questioned a man he suspected of stealing his fiancée's jewellery. He then dragged him upstairs and locked him in a room. The victim, frightened of what the defendant would do on his return, tried to escape through the window, but injured himself when he fell to the ground. Charged with an offence under s. 47, the defendant denied striking the victim. The trial judge said, for liability to be incurred, it was sufficient if the victim suffered a hysterical or nervous condition at the time and the defendant was convicted at first instance. His appeal was allowed and Hobhouse LJ said: 'The phrase "actual bodily harm" is capable of including psychiatric injury. But it does not include mere emotions such as fear or distress or panic, nor does it include, as such, states of mind that are not themselves evidence of some identifiable clinical condition.'

The offence of causing actual bodily harm has been applied in the context of stalking, but where the stalking consists of a course of conduct over a period of time, it can be difficult to identify the actual assault that caused the actual bodily harm. In **R** *v* **Cox** (1998) the Court of Appeal did not consider this problem insurmountable. The defendant's relationship with his girlfriend had ended. He started to make repeated telephone calls, some of which were silent, he prowled outside her flat, put through her letterbox a torn piece of a brochure showing details of a holiday she had booked, and, shortly before she was due to depart, he telephoned her to say that she was going to her death and he could smell burning. The complainant began to suffer from severe headaches and stress. The appellant was convicted of assault occasioning actual bodily harm and his conviction was upheld by the Court of Appeal even though it was difficult to identify an act that constituted the assault.

▋ *Mens rea*

The *mens rea* of assault occasioning ABH is the same as for assault or battery. No additional *mens rea* is required in relation to the actual bodily harm, as the case of **R** *v* **Roberts** (1978) shows. Late at night, the defendant gave a lift in his car to a girl. During the journey he made unwanted sexual advances, touching the girl's clothes. Frightened that he was going to rape her, she jumped out of the moving car, injuring herself. It was held that the defendant had committed the *actus reus* of a s. 47 offence by touching the girl's clothes – sufficient for the *actus reus* of battery – and this act had caused her to suffer actual bodily harm. The defendant argued that he lacked the *mens rea* of the offence, because he had neither intended to cause her actual bodily harm, nor seen any risk of her suffering actual bodily harm as a result of his advances. This argument was rejected: the court held that the *mens rea* for battery was sufficient in itself, and there was no need for any extra *mens rea* regarding the actual bodily harm.

The point was confirmed in **R** *v* **Savage** (1991). The defendant went into a local pub, where she spotted her husband's new girlfriend having a drink with some friends. She went up to the table where the group was sitting, intending to throw a pint of beer over the woman. On reaching the table, she said 'Nice to meet you darling' and threw the beer but, as she did so, she accidentally let go of the glass, which broke and cut the woman's wrist. The defendant argued that she lacked sufficient *mens rea* to be liable for a s. 47 offence, because her intention had only been to throw the beer, and she had not seen the risk that the glass might injure the girlfriend. This was rejected because she intended to apply unlawful force (the *mens rea* of battery) and there was no need to prove that she intended or was reckless as to causing actual bodily harm. The conflicting case of **R** *v* **Spratt** (1990) was overruled on this point.

Offences Against the Person Act 1861, s. 20

This section states:

> Whosoever shall unlawfully and maliciously wound or inflict any grievous bodily harm upon any other person either with or without any weapon or instrument shall be guilty of an offence triable either way, and being convicted thereof shall be liable to imprisonment for five years.

Actus reus

The prosecution has to prove that the defendant either inflicted grievous bodily harm or wounded the victim.

Inflicting grievous bodily harm

In **DPP** *v* **Smith** (1961) the House of Lords emphasized that grievous bodily harm (GBH) is a phrase that should be given its ordinary and natural meaning, which was simply 'really serious harm'. This was confirmed in **R** *v* **Saunders** (1985) where the Court of Appeal said that there was no real difference between the terms 'serious' and 'really serious'. The point was again made in **R** *v* **Brown and Stratton** (1998), where the Court of Appeal stated that trial judges should not attempt to give a definition of the concept to the jury. The victim was a transsexual who had undergone gender reassignment treatment, and changed her name to Julie. Stratton was the victim's son and he had felt humiliated when his father had come to the supermarket where he worked, dressed as a woman. With his cousin, Stratton had gone round to Julie's flat and attacked her with fists and part of a chair, resulting in a broken nose, three missing teeth, bruising, a laceration over one eye and concussion. These injuries were found by the Court of Appeal to amount to grievous bodily harm and the defendants were liable under s. 20. **R** *v* **Ireland and Burstow** (1997) recognizes that a really serious psychiatric injury can amount to grievous bodily harm.

In determining whether grievous bodily harm has been inflicted, the courts can take into account the particular characteristics of the victim, such as their age and health. In deciding the severity of the injuries, an assessment had to be made of the effect of the harm on the particular victim. Thus, in **R** *v* **Bollom** (2003) the victim was a 17-month-old child who had bruises over her body. In determining whether these bruises amounted to grievous bodily harm, the court could take into account the frailty of the child.

The difference between actual bodily harm under s. 47 and grievous bodily harm in this section is one of degree – grievous bodily harm is clearly the more serious injury.

The meaning of the word 'inflict' in this section has caused considerable difficulty. For many years it was held that 'inflict' implied the commission of an actual assault. Thus, in **R** v **Clarence** (1888) the Queen's Bench Division decided that a husband could not be said to have inflicted GBH on his wife by knowingly exposing her to the risk of contracting gonorrhoea through intercourse; the wife had not feared the infliction of lawful force at the time of the sexual intercourse. In **R** v **Wilson** (1984) the House of Lords stated that an assault is not necessary, the word 'inflict' simply required 'force being violently applied to the body of the victim, so that he suffers grievous bodily harm'. Thus it was thought that under s. 20 grievous bodily harm had to be caused by the direct application of force. This meant, for example, that it would cover hitting, kicking or stabbing a victim, but not digging a hole for the victim to fall into. In practice, the courts often gave a wide interpretation as to when force was direct. In **R** v **Martin** (1881), while a play was being performed at a theatre, the defendant placed an iron bar across the exit, turned off the staircase lights and shouted 'Fire! Fire!' The audience panicked and, in the rush to escape, people were seriously injured. The defendant was found liable under s. 20, even though strictly speaking it is difficult to view the application of force as truly direct on these facts.

A similarly wide interpretation was given in **R** v **Halliday** (1889). In that case, the defendant's behaviour frightened his wife so much that she jumped out of their bedroom window to get away from him. The injuries that she suffered as a result of the fall were found to have been directly applied, so that he could be liable under s. 20.

However, following the decisions in **R** v **Ireland and Burstow** (1997), the word inflict no longer implies the direct application of force. Burstow had become obsessed with a female acquaintance. He started to stalk her, following her, damaging her car and breaking into her house. He was convicted for this conduct but after his release from prison he continued to stalk her, following her and subjecting her to further harassment, including silent telephone calls, sending hate mail, stealing clothes from her washing line and scattering condoms over her garden. His behaviour caused his victim to suffer severe depression, insomnia and panic attacks. For this subsequent behaviour he was charged with inflicting grievous bodily harm under s. 20 of the Offences Against the Person Act 1861. The trial court convicted, stating that there was no reason for 'inflict' to be given a restrictive meaning. On appeal against his conviction the appellant argued that the requirements of the term 'inflict' had not been satisfied. The appeal was dismissed by both the Court of Appeal and the House of Lords. The House stated that s. 20 could be committed where no physical force had been applied (directly or indirectly) on the body of the victim.

The offence can be committed when somebody infects another with HIV. A prosecution was brought under s. 20 in **R** v **Dica** (2004). The defendant knew that he was HIV positive and had unprotected sexual intercourse with two women. He was prosecuted under s. 20 of the Offences Against the Person Act 1861. His initial conviction was quashed on appeal and a retrial ordered because of a misdirection on the issue of consent, but the Court of Appeal accepted that a person could be liable under s. 20 for recklessly infecting another with HIV.

Wounding

Wounding requires a breaking of the skin, so there will normally be bleeding, though a graze will be sufficient. In **C (A Minor)** *v* **Eisenhower** (1984), the defendant fired an air pistol, hitting the victim in the eye with a pellet. This ruptured a blood vessel in the eye, causing internal bleeding, but the injury was not sufficient to constitute a wounding, as the skin had not been broken. This may seem odd given that for this serious offence the *actus reus* can be satisfied simply by pricking somebody's thumb with a pin.

▌ Mens rea

The *mens rea* for this offence is defined by the word 'maliciously'. In **R** *v* **Cunningham** (1957) it was stated that for the purpose of the 1861 Act maliciously meant 'intentionally or recklessly'.

The case of **R** *v* **Mowatt** (1967) established that there is no need to intend or be reckless as to causing GBH or wounding. The defendant need only intend or be reckless that his or her acts could have caused some physical harm. As Lord Diplock said: 'It is quite unnecessary that the accused should have foreseen that his unlawful act might cause physical harm of the gravity described in the section, i.e. a wound or serious physical injury. It is enough that he should have foreseen that some physical harm to some person, albeit of a minor character, might result.' The leading case on the point is now the House of Lords' judgment in **R** *v* **Savage**; **DPP** *v* **Parmenter** (1992).

In **R** *v* **Grimshaw** (1984) the defendant was in a pub when she heard someone insult her boyfriend. She pushed the glass he was holding into his face. She was found guilty of an offence under s. 20: she had inflicted grievous bodily harm and she had the *mens rea* because she had at least foreseen that he might suffer some harm.

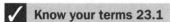

✔ Know your terms 23.1

Define the following terms:

1 Assault
2 Battery
3 Actual bodily harm
4 Maliciously

The Divisional Court decision of **Director of Public Prosecutions** *v* **A** (2000) highlighted the fact that the defendant is only required to have foreseen that some harm *might* occur, not that it *would* occur. In that case the defendant was a 13-year-old boy who had been playing with two air pistols with his friend. He shot his friend in the eye, causing him to lose his sight in that eye. The defendant was charged with committing an offence under s. 20 of the Offences Against the Person Act 1861. He argued that he lacked the requisite *mens rea*. On the issue of *mens rea*, the magistrates were referred by the court clerk to a passage in *Stone's Justices' Manual*, a book frequently used in the magistrates' courts. This passage stated: 'In order to establish an offence under s. 20 the prosecution must prove either that the defendant intended or that he foresaw that his act would cause some physical harm to some person, albeit of a minor nature.' The prosecution appealed against the defendant's acquittal and the appeal was allowed. The passage in *Stone's Justices' Manual* was wrong as it required too high a level of *mens rea*. It was only necessary for the prosecution to show that the defendant had foreseen that some harm *might* occur, not that it *would* occur. In fact, if the defendant had foreseen that the harm would occur, the court could have found an intention to commit that harm under the **Nedrick** test for indirect intention, which exists where the harm is foreseen as a virtual certainty.

Where the offence is concerned with the infection of HIV, the defendant need not have known that he was actually infected, provided he was aware that there was a high risk that he was infected. In the Crown Court case of **R** *v* **Adaye** (2004), Mr Adaye had been informed by his wife that she was HIV positive. Shortly afterwards he started a new sexual relationship with another woman and failed to use condoms. His new partner contracted HIV and he was prosecuted for the s. 20 offence. Mr Adaye had not taken a HIV antibody test and did not conclusively know of his HIV status at the time of transmission. However, the Crown Court held that knowledge of a higher level of risk of HIV infection was sufficient to hold that the defendant had acted recklessly.

Offences Against the Person Act 1861, s. 18

Section 18 provides:

> Whosoever shall unlawfully and maliciously by any means whatsoever wound or cause any grievous bodily harm to any person, with intent to do some grievous bodily harm to any person, or with intent to resist or prevent the lawful apprehension or detainer of any person, shall be guilty of an offence triable only on indictment, and being convicted thereof shall be liable to imprisonment for life.

This is similar to the offence of s. 20, and, like that offence, requires proof of either grievous bodily harm or wounding. The crucial difference is in the *mens rea*: while recklessness can be sufficient for s. 20, intention is always required for s. 18. It is for this reason that s. 18 is punishable with a life sentence, while the maximum sentence for s. 20 is only five years – a person acting with intent is considered to have greater moral fault than a person merely acting recklessly.

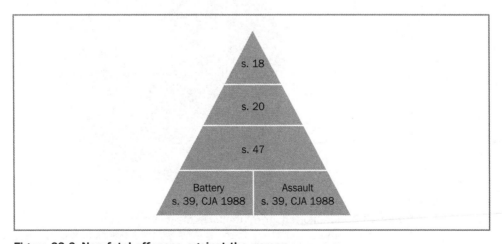

Figure 23.2 Non-fatal offences against the person

▌ *Actus reus*

Wounding and grievous bodily harm are given the same interpretation as for s. 20. In **R** *v* **Ireland and Burstow** (1997) Lord Steyn said that the word 'cause' in s. 18 and 'inflict' in s. 20 were not synonymous, but it is difficult to see how they differ in practice. Both refer to the need for causation.

▌ *Mens rea*

As noted above, the prosecution must prove intention. The intent must be either to cause grievous bodily harm (by contrast with s. 20, where an intention to cause some harm is sufficient), or to avoid arrest.

In addition, the section states that the defendant must have acted 'maliciously'. This bears the same meaning as discussed for s. 20, so if the prosecution has already proved that the defendant intended to cause grievous bodily harm, 'maliciously' imposes no further requirement: a defendant who intends to cause grievous bodily harm obviously intends to cause some harm. If the prosecution has proved the other form of intent, the intent to avoid arrest, then the requirement that the defendant acts maliciously does impose a further requirement: an intent to avoid arrest does not necessarily imply intention, or recklessness as to whether you cause some harm. Therefore, where the prosecution proves intent to avoid arrest, it must also show that the defendant intended to cause some harm, or was reckless as to whether harm was caused.

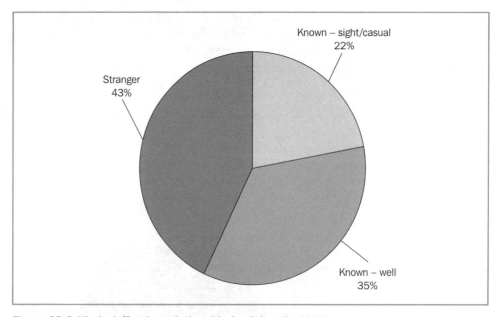

Figure 23.3 Victim/offender relationship in violent incidents

Source: C. Flood-Page and J. Taylor (eds) (2003), *Crime in England and Wales 2001/2002: Supplementary Volume*, p. 57, Figure 3.8. Home Office, © Crown Copyright 2003.

Quick quiz 23.2

1 If a person shouts at you 'I'm going to beat you up', has that person committed an assault?

2 What is the *mens rea* of an assault?

3 What is the *mens rea* of a s. 47 actual bodily harm offence?

4 What is the difference between the s. 20 and s. 18 offences in the Offences Against the Person Act 1861?

Problems with offences against the person

Domestic violence

Domestic violence accounts for 16 per cent of all violent crime (*Crime in England and Wales 2003/2004*, Home Office). This form of violence is defined by the Home Office as: 'Any violence between current and former partners in an intimate relationship, wherever and whenever the violence occurs. The violence may include physical, sexual, emotional and financial abuse.' One in four women and one in six men will be the victims of domestic violence at some point in their lives (Mirlees-Black (1999)). Every minute the police receive a 999 emergency telephone call reporting an incident of domestic violence (Stanko, 2000). Between a quarter and a third of victims of homicide are killed by a partner or former partner (Criminal Statistics (2000)). In 90 per cent of incidents where the couple have children, a child is present or in the next room. Domestic abuse occurs throughout the whole of our society, regardless of social class.

While the law itself does not distinguish between these victims and the person who gets attacked in the streets by a stranger, in practice the victims of domestic assaults rarely receive the law's protection. The first reason for this is simply that very few domestic assaults – research suggests around 2 per cent – are reported to the police. On average, a woman will be assaulted 35 times before she contacts the police (Yearnshire (1997)). If the offences are not reported, obviously they cannot be prosecuted, and the violent partner escapes punishment.

Research among battered wives suggests a variety of reasons for this under-reporting. Women are embarrassed by what the violence says about their relationship, and often blame themselves – a feeling frequently supported by a violent partner's claims that he has been provoked into violence by the woman's behaviour. In the early stages, a woman may make excuses for a man's behaviour, and tell herself that it will not happen again; by the time the violence has been repeated over a long period, she may feel powerless and unable to escape or take any steps towards reporting the offence. This situation can lead to a recognized psychological state, often called battered woman's syndrome, in which the victim loses the ability to see beyond the situation or any means of changing it.

Equally important is the fact that victims may fear that reporting the offence will simply lead to further beatings, given that even if charges are brought, the partner will usually be granted bail, and is highly likely to arrive home and attack her again in revenge for her making the complaint.

These problems are intensified by the traditional police approach to domestic violence which is to avoid involvement, leaving the partners to sort things out themselves. This is prompted partly by the emphasis on the privacy of the home and the family which has been a traditional part of British culture where 'an Englishman's home is his castle'. The expression 'rule of thumb' comes from a rule that a man was allowed to hit his wife with a stick if it was no thicker than this thumb. In addition, there were concerns that the intervention of the legal system might lead to increased marriage breakdown. The assumption was that a couple might divorce if a prosecution were brought, but left alone, they would patch up their differences. The police also claimed that, where prosecutions were brought, by the time the case came to court wives and girlfriends were refusing to give evidence leading to cases collapsing.

In recent years some changes have been made in an attempt to address these problems. A spouse can now be compelled to give evidence against their partner in court proceedings, following the passing of s. 80 of the Police and Criminal Evidence Act 1984, and orders can be made prohibiting violence against a partner and even ousting the violent person from the home, though the effect of such an order in practice may be minimal where the violent partner is really determined to get at the victim.

The Crown Prosecution Service has issued policy guidance on prosecuting cases of domestic violence. This encourages prosecutors to not just rely on the victim's evidence, but to also collect such evidence as medical reports and tape recordings of 999 calls. The prosecution can then proceed even where the victim no longer wishes to pursue the complaint. Special measures can be used during the trial to help the victim give evidence, such as allowing the victim to give evidence behind a screen. Bail conditions can be applied which order the defendant to keep away from the family home and the children's school.

In June 2003 the Government published a consultation paper, *Safety and Justice: the Government's proposals on domestic violence*. This focuses on improving the legal protection available to the victims of domestic violence, using both the civil and criminal systems. This consultation process was followed by the Domestic Violence, Crime and Victims Act 2004, which introduces a range of practical reforms to try and improve the protection afforded to people who are the victim of domestic violence.

The Government promised in its 2005 election manifesto to promote the use of 'advocates' in domestic violence, murder and rape cases. These advocates would be volunteers providing support to the victims during the criminal justice process. It also promised to develop specialist courts to deal with domestic violence.

The law and legal procedure alone cannot deal with this problem; a cultural change is required that would make domestic violence as unacceptable as any other kind of violent behaviour. Society tends to ignore domestic abuse or even consider it acceptable. One boy in five believes it is alright to hit a woman. One girl in ten agrees with this view.

Task 23.3

Read the following newspaper article and then answer the questions below.

Grim facts of domestic violence

The figures make depressing reading. One in four women and one in six men experience domestic violence in their lifetimes. An average of two women a week in England and Wales are killed by current or former partners. Domestic violence incidents make up nearly a quarter of all violent crimes and yet surveys say that only between 11 and 35 per cent of such events are reported to the police. This crime degrades both victim and perpetrator. And it is no respecter of age, race, sex or nationality. There are no significant differences in numbers between ethnic groups and it is the under-25s in all sections of society who are most likely to be affected. A study among Asian, Afro-Caribbean and Arab women found that half of those who had experienced domestic violence waited five years before they sought help.

Perhaps most depressing of all, a survey of 1,300 schoolchildren found that one in three boys thought violence against women was acceptable.

Academic research estimated the cost of dealing with domestic violence in the Hackney area alone in 1996 was £90 per household, equivalent to £278 million a year for Greater London alone. Multiply that nationally and the financial costs are huge.

So what are we to do to improve this state of affairs? The Government is committed to tackling domestic violence on every front. There are initiatives by the Department for Constitutional Affairs, the Home Office, the Crown Prosecution Service and the police. Type the words 'domestic violence' into an internet search engine and it will throw up the contact details of dozens of aid groups covering every race, religious, ethnic, sexual, geographic and national grouping.

Education is the only solution. If we are serious about reducing the rate of domestic violence, we need to tackle the issue in the classroom, not the police interview room.

(Article written by Marilyn Stowe and published in *The Times* on 1 July 2003.)

Questions

1 What is meant by 'domestic violence'?

2 Can men be victims of domestic violence?

3 Which age group is more likely to be the victim of domestic violence?

4 Research suggested that one in three schoolboys thought violence against women is acceptable. Do you think violence against women is acceptable?

5 What do you think is the best way of reducing domestic violence?

Definitions of the offences

Criticism is also often made of the way the offences themselves are defined. There is still no clear statutory definition of assault and battery, while the definitions of the more serious offences are contained in an Act passed back in 1861, with much of the vocabulary antiquated and even misleading, such as 'assault' in s. 47 and 'maliciously' in s. 18.

The requirement that the threat must be of immediate force in order to fall within an assault means that there is a gap in the law. Currently, if a person shouts that he or she is going to kill you, that may be an assault; but if the threat is to kill you

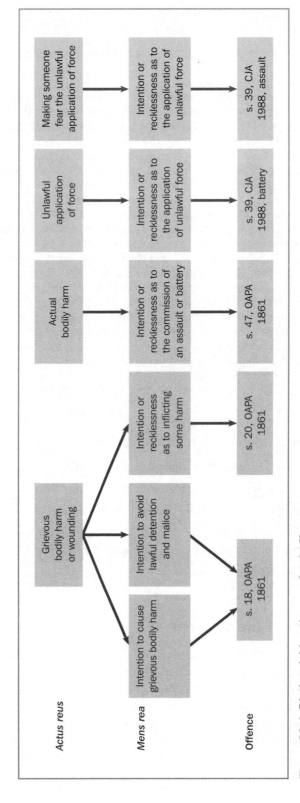

Figure 23.4 Distinguishing the non-fatal offences

Table 23.2 Trial and sentence of the non-fatal offences

Offence	Type of offence	Maximum sentence
Assault	Summary	Six months
Battery	Summary	Six months
s. 47, OAPA 1861	Summary	Five years
s. 20, OAPA 1861	Triable either way	Five years
s. 18, OAPA 1861	Indictable only	Life

tomorrow, it is not. The Law Commission has produced a draft Criminal Law Bill in the belief that prompt reform of this area is necessary, and which creates an offence that would cover this example.

Structure of the offences

The 1861 Act was merely a consolidating Act which gathered together a whole host of unrelated provisions from existing statutes. No attempt was made to rationalize the provisions. As a result the offences lack a clear structured hierarchy. First, while assault and battery can only be punished with a maximum of six months' imprisonment, and a s. 47 offence can be punished by five years, the only real difference between them is that ABH is caused – yet ABH can mean as little as causing discomfort to the person. Secondly, the s. 20 offence is defined as a much more serious offence than one covered by s. 47, and yet they share the same maximum sentence of five years.

A third problem is that the only significant difference between s. 20 and s. 18 offences is arguably a slightly more serious *mens rea*, and yet the maximum sentence leaps from five years to life. This can perhaps be justified by the fact that a defendant who intends to cause GBH within s. 18 has the *mens rea* of murder, and it is merely chance which dictates whether the victim survives, leading to a charge under s. 18, or dies, leading to a charge of murder and a mandatory life sentence if convicted.

Reform

Modernising the legislation

In 1980 the Criminal Law Revision Committee recommended that this area of the law should be reformed. Its proposals were incorporated into the draft code of the criminal law prepared by the Law Commission. The Law Commission again considered the matter at the beginning of the 1990s, producing a report and draft Criminal Law Bill on the issue in 1993. In February 1998, the Home Office produced a consultation document in furtherance of its commitment to modernise and improve the law. This presents a draft Offences Against the Person Bill modelled largely, but not entirely, on the Law Commission's 1993 draft Criminal Law Bill. There now looks as if there is a real possibility that legislation may follow. The draft Bill updates the language used for these offences by talking about serious injury rather than grievous bodily harm, and avoiding the words 'maliciously' and 'wounding' altogether. Under the draft Bill s. 18 is replaced by 'intentionally causing serious injury', with a maximum sentence of life (clause 1); s. 20 by 'recklessly causing serious injury', with a maximum sentence of seven years (clause 2); and s. 47 by 'intentionally or recklessly causing injury' with a maximum sentence of five years (clause 3). Thus the offence replacing s. 47 would remove the requirement of an 'assault', which would be tidier and avoid the problem of finding an assault where there is a course of conduct (see **R** *v* **Cox** on p. 485). The draft Bill still proceeds to use the term 'assault' for conduct which would better be described as two separate offences of assault and battery (clause 4).

Task 23.4

The Home Office consultation document, *Violence: Reforming the Offences Against the Person Act 1861*, includes an annexe with a draft Offences Against the Person Bill. You can find this draft Bill on the Home Office website at **http://www.old.homeoffice.gov.uk/docs/vroapa.htm**

Look at the Bill and find out how 'intention' is defined for the purposes of this Bill.

Statutory definitions are given for the mental elements of the offences which would continue to give recklessness a subjective meaning. Difficulties could arise as the statutory definitions differ from the common law definitions and if, for example, a jury was also faced with an accusation of murder, they would have to understand

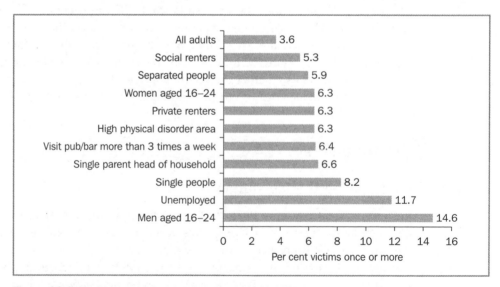

Figure 23.5 Adults most at risk of violence, 2004/05

Source: S. Nicholas, D. Povey, A. Walker and C. Kershaw, 'Adults most at risk of violence, 2004/05', British Crime Survey Interviews, *Crime in England and Wales 2004/2005*, p. 84, Figure 5.7.

and apply two different tests for intention. The most serious offence in clause 1 could be committed by an omission but not the lesser offences. Injury is defined (clause 15) to include physical and mental injury, but 'anything caused by disease' is not an injury of either kind, except for the purpose of clause 1. So it would be an offence under clause 1 to intentionally infect another with AIDS but no offence to recklessly do so under clause 2.

Liability for infecting another with a disease

In the case of **R** *v* **Dica** the Court of Appeal accepted that in principle a defendant could be liable under s. 20 of the Offences Against the Person Act 1861 for recklessly infecting another with AIDS. There is, however, much debate on whether criminal liability should be imposed for infecting another with a disease, particularly sexually transmitted diseases, such as AIDS. The World Health Report lists AIDS as the fourth biggest world killer, with an estimated 5,000 new infections every day, and the number of HIV patients in Britain is increasing. Clearly it is in everybody's interests to stop the spread of AIDS, but there is much controversy over whether the criminal law can help to achieve this. The United Nations has put forward a range of reasons why the criminal law should get involved in preventing the transmission of AIDS in a document entitled *Criminal Law, Public Health and HIV Transmission: a policy options paper*. However, there are concerns that criminalizing this type of activity risks discriminating against the ill. Where the relevant disease is AIDS, many of those infected belong to some of the more vulnerable groups in society. Prior to the **Dica** case, the Home Office had rejected criminalizing the reckless transmission of disease because:

> the government is particularly concerned that the law should not seem to discriminate against those who are HIV positive, have AIDS or viral hepatitis or who carry any kind of disease.

A counter-argument to this is that the criminal law will only step in if an ill person behaves in a reprehensible manner, not simply because they are ill.

Another concern is that criminalizing such conduct could prove to be counter-productive in terms of protecting public health. The involvement of the criminal law in the field, may encourage secrecy and constitute an obstacle to educating the public about AIDS. If the reckless transmission of a disease is criminalized, people might avoid having health checks, so that they can claim that they were not reckless in having unprotected sexual intercourse, because they did not know that they were carrying an infection. It could also encourage those who know they are infected, to engage in casual sexual intercourse after which they cannot be traced, rather than being in a long-term sexual relationship. Following a criminal conviction for HIV transmission in Scotland, two academics, Bird and Brown (2001), carried out research into the impact of the case on HIV transmission in Scotland. They suggested that following the conviction there was evidence of a 25 per cent reduction in HIV testing. They also found that even a modest fall in the uptake of HIV testing as a result of the judgment could produce a third increase in sexually transmitted HIV infections.

It may be appropriate to impose criminal liability where a person has intentionally infected another, but it will frequently be difficult to prove this intention in this type of case, and it is much more controversial to impose liability for reckless infection. In 1993 the Law Commission proposed the creation of an offence of recklessly causing serious injury, which would have covered the reckless transmission of disease (*Legislating the Criminal Code: Offences Against the Person and General Principles*, Law Com. No. 218.) Five years later, however, the Home Office rejected this proposal (*Violence: Reforming the Offences Against the Person Act 1861*). It would have restricted liability for the transmission of a disease to where there was intention to cause serious injury. An intention to cause a lesser harm would not be sufficient and recklessness would not be sufficient. The Government considered that 'it would be wrong to criminalize the reckless transmission of normally minor illnesses such as measles or mumps'.

In the context of AIDS, its transmission can be prevented by the use of a condom, and it is not unreasonable to expect people to use a condom when they know that failure to do so risks giving their partners a disease that will ultimately kill them.

Task 23.5

The following extract is the introduction to the Home Office consultation paper, *Violence: Reforming the Offences Against the Person Act 1861*. Read the passage and answer the questions that follow. (The underlined words are the subjects of questions.)

1.1 This paper sets out proposals for the reform of the criminal offences used to prosecute violence against individual people. The vocabulary of offences of violence against the person is part of the common currency of everyday life. Court reports and drama have made the very words grievous bodily harm and actual bodily harm deeply familiar. However, familiarity does not mean that such time-hallowed offences are readily understood or that they provide an effective means for the courts to deal with violent behaviour. Criminal law that applies to violence against the person derives from both common and statute law, but the unrepealed parts of the Offences Against the Person Act 1861 provide the bulk of the statutory offences. That Act was itself not a coherent restatement of the law, but a consolidation of much older law. It is therefore not surprising that the law has been widely criticised as archaic and unclear and that it is now in urgent need of reform.

1.2 Reforming the law on violence against the person is not just an academic exercise – criminal cases involving non-fatal offences against the person make up a large part of the work of the courts and cost a great deal of taxpayers' money. In 1996 83,000 cases came before the courts. It is therefore particularly important that the law governing such behaviour should be robust, clear and well understood. Unclear or uncertain criminal law risks creating injustice and unfairness to individuals as well as making the work of the police and courts far more difficult and time-consuming. The Government's aim is that the proposed new offences should enable violence to be dealt with effectively by the courts and that the law should be set out in clear terms and in plain, modern language. That is what the draft Bill contained in this consultation paper does. It is intended to help not only practitioners of the law but anyone who finds themselves involved in court cases, whether as a defendant, victim or witness.

1.3 The proposals in this paper are based on the work of the Law Commission as set out in its report No. 218: *Offences Against the Person and General Principles*. That report examined the current state of the law in great detail and proposed a new set of offences ranging from intentional serious injury to assault, as well as rationalising and codifying other offences. The Government is deeply grateful to the Law Commission for the careful and painstaking work that they have done on this subject, and for the principled way they have approached it.

1.4 The purpose of this consultation paper is to set out both the rationale and the detail of the Government's proposals, how they relate to those of the Law Commission, and to invite comments on them. The Government recognises that reforming the law in this area can raise important questions of policy, principle and practice and wishes to ensure that the implications of its proposals are fully appreciated and that all those affected have an opportunity to contribute their views.

Questions

1 What is meant by 'court reports and drama'?

2 What does 'unrepealed' mean?

3 What is meant by 'consolidation' of the law?

4 What type of law does the Government want to introduce?

Stalking

The problems of stalking have attracted considerable media attention. 'Stalking', like 'shoplifting' and 'football hooliganism', is not a technical legal concept but one used in everyday language. It describes a campaign of harassment, usually with sexual undertones. Such conduct raises two important questions which concerned Western legal systems in the late twentieth century: what are the boundaries of acceptable sexual behaviour and how far should psychiatric damage be recognized by the law? So any legal developments in this area are very sensitive.

In response to public concern, the Protection from Harassment Act 1997 was passed. As well as enacting certain civil wrongs, it creates several new criminal offences. Section 1 prohibits a person from pursuing a course of conduct which they know or ought to know amounts to harassment of another. This is punishable by a maximum of six months' imprisonment. Section 4 contains the offence of aggravated harassment where, in addition, the defendant knows or ought to know that they placed the victim in fear of violence on at least two occasions. This is punishable with up to five years' imprisonment.

It is questionable whether this piece of legislation was necessary. The Act follows a pattern witnessed in other areas (for example, joyriding and dangerous dogs) of addressing a narrowly conceived social harm, backed by a single issue pressure group campaign, with a widely drawn provision which overlaps with existing offences. The new offences in the 1997 Act are broadly defined and there is a danger that they could impinge upon other activities hitherto regarded as legitimate, such as investigative journalism and door-to-door selling. Cases such as **R v Ireland and Burstow** and **R v Constanza** show that the courts were prepared to adapt existing criminal law offences to include this type of harmful conduct. On the other hand, some people feel that these cases artificially distorted the existing law, ignoring accepted authorities, and that a fresh legislative approach was required with this specific problem in mind. In practice, the value of the 1997 Act may be that it includes a power to make restraining orders forbidding the defendant from pursuing any conduct which amounts to harassment and a power of arrest to enforce these orders.

Reading on the web

The Home Office consultation paper *Violence: Reforming the Offences Against the Person Act 1861* (1998) is available on the Home Office website at:

  http://www.old.homeoffice.gov.uk/docs/vroapa.htm

The decision of **R** v **Ireland and Burstow** can be found on the House of Lords' website at:

  http://www.publications.parliament.uk/pa/ld/ldjudgmt.htm#1997

Question and answer guides

1 J who is 17 and K who is 16 years old decide to plan an initiation ceremony for a new student, L, at their college. They agree to blindfold the newcomer and paint his hands and face red. Unfortunately, L is allergic to a chemical in the paint and, when painted, suffers a severe asthma attack. He becomes very unwell, being unable to breathe properly, and nearly faints. J and K become frightened and run off. After 20 minutes L is found and taken to hospital, where he recovers after a few days' rest. Should J and K be charged with any offence? How might the courts deal with them on a finding of guilt? *(London)*

Answer guide

In many cases where there are two possible defendants their liability will need to be discussed separately, but here the defendants have done exactly the same thing so they can be dealt with together – the only difference is their age but as they are both over 14 this does not affect their criminal liability. Note that you are not being asked what offences they may have committed, but specifically with what they should be charged. This means that there are two separate elements to this part of the question: for what offences they might be liable, and whether they should be charged with those offences.

Looking first at the offences for which they may be liable, it is often easiest when answering problem questions to start with the most serious relevant offence and then work your way down to the least serious. Bear in mind that there is no death, so you are only concerned with non-fatal offences. The most serious possible offence would be s. 18 of the Offences Against the Person Act 1861. There is no wounding, so you will need to establish that there is GBH; whether the injuries are sufficient for this will be a question of fact for the jury to decide, but it seems unlikely. There must also be *mens rea* of intention to cause GBH, which again seems unlikely on the facts.

The next offence down is s. 20, for which GBH would again need to be proved. *Mens rea* would be easier to prove as you only need to show intention or recklessness as to causing some harm, but on these facts it would still be possible to find that J and K did not intend to cause any harm at all and neither did they see the risk (remember the recklessness must be subjective). The most likely offence is s. 47, with its wider *actus reus* and *mens rea*.

The question of whether or not they should be charged and the issue of sentencing young offenders are discussed in Chapters 12 and 15. ('London Qualifications Ltd.', accepts no responsibility whatsoever for the accuracy or method in the answers given.)

2 Has the time come to repeal the Offences Against the Person Act 1861 and replace it with a modern piece of legislation?

Answer guide

The question requires a discussion of ss. 18, 20 and 47 of the Offences Against the Person Act 1861. The offences of assault and battery are not defined in the 1861 Act, but are relevant to the definition of s. 47.

Over the years there has been considerable criticism of the 1861 Act. There have been difficulties in interpreting the scope of these offences, as is reflected in cases such as **R** v **Ireland and Burstow** and **R** v **Roberts**. Specific criticisms are discussed at pp. 491–2. The language is becoming dated and there have been proposals put forward for repealing this Act and replacing it with a more modern piece of legislation. These reform proposals are discussed at p. 495.

Chapter summary

There are five main non-fatal offences against the person:

- assault
- battery
- actual bodily harm
- inflicting grievous bodily harm or wounding, and
- causing grievous bodily harm or wounding.

Assault

Actus reus
This consists of any act which makes the victim fear that unlawful force is about to be used against them.

Mens rea
The *mens rea* of assault is either intention or subjective recklessness. The defendant must have either intended to cause the victim to fear the infliction of immediate and unlawful force, or seen the risk that such fear would be created.

Battery

Actus reus
The *actus reus* of battery consists of the application of unlawful force on another.

▶

Mens rea

Again, either intention or subjective recklessness is sufficient, but here it is intention or recklessness as to the application of unlawful force.

Offences Against the Person Act 1861, s. 47

Actus reus

The first requirement is to prove the *actus reus* of assault or battery. In addition, the prosecution must show that the assault or battery caused actual bodily harm.

Mens rea

The *mens rea* is the same as for assault or battery. No additional *mens rea* is required in relation to the actual bodily harm.

Offences Against the Person Act 1861, s. 20

Actus reus

The prosecution has to prove that the defendant either inflicted grievous bodily harm or wounded the victim.

Mens rea

The *mens rea* for this offence is defined by the word 'maliciously'. In **R** v **Cunningham** it was stated that for the purposes of the 1861 Act maliciously meant 'intentionally or recklessly' and the test for recklessness is subjective.

Offences Against the Person Act 1861, s. 18

Actus reus

The defendant must have caused grievous bodily harm or wounded the victim.

Mens rea

The defendant must have intended to cause grievous bodily harm or to avoid arrest. If the defendant intended to avoid arrest, there is an additional requirement that he or she acted maliciously.

Chapter 24 Negligence

Negligence is the most important tort in modern law. It was first recognized in the 1932 case of **Donoghue** *v* **Stevenson**, and concerns breach of a legal duty to take care, with the result that damage is caused to the claimant. The tort of negligence comprises three elements: a duty of care, breach of that duty and damage resulting from the breach.

The duty of care

Negligence is essentially concerned with compensating people who have suffered damage as a result of the carelessness of others, but the law does not provide a remedy for everyone who suffers in this way. One of the main ways in which access to compensation is restricted is through the doctrine of a duty of care. Essentially, this is a legal concept which dictates the circumstances in which one party will be liable to another in negligence: if the law says you do not have a duty of care towards the person (or organization) you have caused damage to, you will not be liable to that party in negligence.

It is interesting to note that in the vast majority of ordinary tort cases which pass through the court system, it will usually be clear that the defendant does owe the claimant a duty of care, and what the courts will be looking at is whether the claimant can prove that the defendant breached that duty – for example, in the huge numbers of road-accident cases that courts hear every year, it is established that road users owe a duty to other road users, and the issues for the court will generally revolve around what the defendant actually did, and what damage was caused. Yet flick through the pages of this or any other law book, and you soon see that duty of care occupies an amount of space which seems disproportionate to its importance in real-life tort cases. This is because when it comes to the kinds of cases which reach the higher courts and therefore the pages of law books, duty of care arises frequently, and that in turn is because of its power to affect the whole shape of negligence law. Every time a new duty of care is recognized (or declined), that has implications for the numbers of tort cases being brought in the future, the types of situations it can play a part in, and therefore the role which the tort system plays in society.

As a result, the law in this field has caused the courts considerable problems and we can analyze its development in three main stages: the original neighbour principle as established in **Donoghue** v **Stevenson**; a two-stage test set down in **Anns** v **Merton London Borough** (1978), which greatly widened the potential for liability in negligence; and a retreat from this widening following the case of **Murphy** v **Brentwood District Council** (1990).

Development of the duty of care

The neighbour principle

The facts of **Donoghue** v **Stevenson** began when Mrs Donoghue and a friend went into a café for a drink. Mrs Donoghue asked for a ginger beer, which her friend bought. It was supplied, as was usual at the time, in an opaque bottle. Mrs Donoghue poured out and drank some of the ginger beer, and then poured out the rest. At that point, the remains of a decomposing snail fell out of the bottle. Mrs Donoghue became ill, and sued the manufacturer.

Up until this time, the usual remedy for damage caused by a defective product would be an action in contract, but this was unavailable to Mrs Donoghue because the contract for the sale of the drink was between her friend and the café. Mrs Donoghue sued the manufacturer, and the House of Lords agreed that manufacturers owed a duty of care to the end-consumer of their products. The ginger beer manufacturer had breached that duty, causing harm to Mrs Donoghue, and she was entitled to claim damages.

For the benefit of future cases, their Lordships attempted to lay down general rules for when a duty of care would exist. Lord Atkin stated that the principle was that: 'You must take reasonable care to avoid acts or omissions which you can reasonably foresee would be likely to injure your neighbour.' By 'neighbour', Lord Atkin did not mean the person who lives next door, but 'persons who are so closely and directly affected by my act that I ought to have them in contemplation as being so affected when I am directing my mind to the acts or omissions which are called in question'. This is sometimes known as the neighbour principle.

The test of foreseeability is objective; the court does not ask what the defendant foresaw, but what a reasonable person could have been expected to foresee.

Later cases established that the duty had to be owed to the actual claimant; the fact that it was owed to others would not suffice. In an American case, **Palsgraf** v **Long Island Railroad Co.** (1928), two of the defendant's employees helped a passenger board a train. In doing so, they negligently knocked a parcel the passenger was carrying. It contained fireworks, and exploded as it dropped. The explosion shook some scales about 25 feet away, which fell and in turn hit and injured the claimant. The New York Court of Appeals held that she was not entitled to damages, explaining that a duty of care was owed to the holder of the package but not to the claimant who had been standing far away, as there was no reason to foresee that she was in any danger from the contents of the package.

Claimants do not have to be individually identifiable for the defendant to be expected to foresee the risk of harming them. In many cases, it will be sufficient if the claimant falls within a category of people to whom a risk of harm was foreseeable – for example, the end-user of a product, as in **Donoghue** *v* **Stevenson**. The ginger beer manufacturer did not have to know that Mrs Donoghue would drink its product, only that someone would.

In **Haley** *v* **London Electricity Board** (1965) the defendants dug a trench in the street. Their precautions for the protection of passers-by were not sufficient to protect the claimant, because he was blind. He was injured as a result, and the court held that the number of blind people who walk about on their own made it foreseeable that such a person could be injured, and therefore gave rise to a duty of care to take suitable precautions to prevent such injury.

Task 24.1

A headnote is a summary of a case that appears at the beginning of a law report. Below is a headnote from the *All England Law Reports* of the judgment of **Donoghue** *v* **Stevenson**. The section in italics is a list of the key issues that are considered in the case. A lawyer can look at this list to decide whether the case contains any law relevant to the area they are researching. Read the headnote and answer the questions that follow (the words that are the subject of the questions have been underlined).

DONOGHUE (or McALISTER) v STEVENSON

[House of Lords (Lord Buckmaster, Lord Atkin, Lord Tomlin, Lord Thankerton and Lord Macmillan), December 12, 1931, May 26, 1932]

[Reported [1932] AC 562; 101 LJPC 119; 147 LT 281; 48 TLR 494; 76 Sol Jo 396; 37 Com Cas 350]

Negligence – Duty of manufacturer to consumer – No contractual relation – No possibility of examination of product before use – Knowledge that absence of reasonable care in preparation of production will result in injury to consumer – Bottle of ginger-beer purchased from retailer – Dead snail in bottle – Purchaser poisoned by drinking contents – Liability of manufacturer.

A manufacturer of products which he sells in such a form as to show that he intends them to reach the ultimate consumer in the form in which they left him, with no reasonable possibility of intermediate examination, and with the knowledge that the absence of reasonable care in the preparation or putting up of the products will result in injury to the consumer, owes a duty to the consumer to take reasonable care, although the manufacturer does not know the product to be dangerous and no contractual relations exist between him and the consumer.

Per LORD ATKIN: The rule that you are to love your neighbour becomes in law: You must not injure your neighbour; and the lawyer's question: Who is my neighbour? receives a restricted reply. You must take reasonable care to avoid acts or omissions which you can reasonably foresee would be likely to injure your neighbour. Who, then, in law is my neighbour? The answer seems to be persons who are so closely and directly affected by my act that I ought reasonably to have them in contemplation as being so affected when I am directing my mind to the acts or omissions which are called in question.

Per LORD MACMILLAN: A person who for gain engages in the business of manufacturing articles of food and drink intended for consumption by members of the public in the form in which he issues them is under a duty to take care in the manufacture of those articles. That duty he owes to those whom he intends to consume his products. He manufactures his commodities for human consumption; he intends and contemplates that they shall be consumed. By reason of that very fact he places himself in a relationship with all potential consumers of his commodities, and that relationship which he assumes and desires for his own ends, imposes on him a duty to take care to avoid injuring them. He owes them a duty not to convert by his own carelessness an article which he issues to them as wholesome and innocent into an article which is dangerous to life and health.

The appellant and a friend visited a café where the friend ordered for her a bottle of ginger-beer. The proprietor of the café opened the ginger-beer bottle, which was of opaque glass so that it was impossible to see the contents, and poured some of the ginger-beer into a tumbler. The appellant drank some of the ginger-beer. Then her friend poured the remaining contents of the bottle into the tumbler and with it a decomposed snail came from the bottle. As a result of her having drunk part of the impure ginger-beer the appellant suffered from shock and gastric illness. In an action by her for negligence against the manufacturer of the ginger-beer.

Held by LORD ATKIN, LORD THANKERTON, and LORD MACMILLAN (LORD BUCKMASTER and LORD TOMLIN dissenting), on proof of these facts <u>the appellant would be entitled to recover</u>.

Questions

1 In which court was this case heard?

2 What is meant by 'Reported [1932] AC 562'.

3 How many judges heard the case, and what were their names?

4 What is meant by the phrase 'Per LORD ATKIN'?

5 Which judges disagreed with the majority decision?

6 The headnote provides summaries of Lord Atkin's judgment and Lord Macmillan's judgment. In the light of the discussion of the case in this textbook at p. 504, which judgment has been the most influential in the development of the law?

7 Lord Atkin refers to the 'rule that you must love your neighbour'. Where is this rule laid down?

8 What is meant by the phrase 'the appellant would be entitled to recover'?

A two-stage test

The issue of reasonable foresight was never the only criterion for deciding whether a duty of care is owed. As time went on, and a variety of factual situations were established in which a duty of care arose, the courts began to seek precedents in which a similar factual situation had given rise to the existence of a duty of care. For example, it was soon well established that motorists owe a duty of care to other road users, and employers owe a duty to their employees, but where a factual situation seemed completely new, a duty of care would only be deemed to arise if there were policy reasons for doing so. 'Policy reasons' simply mean that the courts take into account not just the legal framework, but also whether society would benefit from the existence of a duty. The apparent need to find such reasons was said to be holding back development of the law.

However, in **Anns** v **Merton London Borough** (1978) Lord Wilberforce proposed a significant extension of the situations where a duty of care would exist, arguing that it was no longer necessary to find a precedent with similar facts. Instead, he suggested that whether a duty of care arose in a particular factual situation was a matter of general principle.

In order to decide whether this principle was satisfied in a particular case, the courts should use a two-stage test. First, they should establish whether the parties satisfied the requirements of the neighbour test – in other words, whether the claimant was someone to whom the defendant could reasonably be expected to foresee a risk of harm. If the answer was yes, a *prima facie* duty of care arose. The second stage would involve asking whether there were any policy considerations which dictated that no duty should exist.

This two-stage test changed the way in which the neighbour test was applied. Previously, the courts had used it to justify new areas of liability, where there were policy reasons for creating them. After **Anns** v **Merton London Borough**, the test would apply unless there were policy reasons for excluding it. This led to an expansion of the situations in which a duty of care could arise, and therefore in the scope of negligence. This expansion reached its peak in **Junior Books** v **Veitchi** (1983) where the House of Lords seemed to go one step further. The House appeared to suggest that what were previously good policy reasons for limiting liability should now not prevent an extension where the neighbour principle justified recovery. It therefore allowed recovery for purely economic loss (meaning financial loss that did not result from injury or damage to property) when previously this kind of claim had not been permitted. This illustrates a problem with the **Anns** test; that it could be applied with little regard for previous case law.

The first stage being relatively easy to pass, there was also a risk that the bounds of liability would be extended beyond what was reasonable, particularly given the judiciary's notorious reluctance to discuss issues of policy – a discussion that was necessary if the second stage was to offer any serious hurdle. For example, in **McLoughlin** v **O'Brian** (1983) Lord Scarman, refusing to impose any limit other than that of mere foreseeability for 'psychiatric injury', said, 'the policy issue as to where to draw the line is not justiciable. The problem is one of social, economic and financial policy. The considerations relevant to a decision are not such as to be capable of being handled within the limits of the forensic process.'

The law today

The growth in liability for negligence set all sorts of alarm bells ringing. The problems of insuring against the new types of liability, and the way in which tort seemed to be encroaching on areas traditionally governed by contractual liability led to a rapid judicial retreat.

In 1990, the case of **Murphy** v **Brentwood District Council** came before a seven-member House of Lords. Their Lordships invoked the 1966 Practice Statement (which allows them to depart from their own previous decisions) to overrule **Anns**. They quoted the High Court of Australia in **Sutherland Shire Council** v **Heyman** (1985), a case in which the High Court of Australia had itself decided not to follow **Anns**:

It is preferable, in my view, that the law should develop novel categories of negligence incrementally and by analogy with established categories, rather than by a massive extension of a prima facie duty of care, restrained only by indefinable 'considerations which ought to negative, or to reduce or limit the scope of the duty or the class of person to whom it is owed'.

The broad general principle with its two-part test envisaged in **Anns** was thereby swept aside, leaving the courts to impose duties of care only when they could find precedent in comparable factual situations.

Rejection of the **Anns** test does not mean that the categories of negligence are now closed, but the creation of new duties of care is likely to involve a much more gradual process, building step-by-step by analogy with previous cases involving similar factual situations. Issues of policy will still arise, as such consideration of policy is an inescapable result of the importance of the judge's position. Some would argue that the judges would do better to face up to this fact honestly, as **Anns** was forcing them to do, rather than often hiding this consideration behind reliance on precedents.

In **Caparo Industries plc *v* Dickman** (1990) it was stated that there are now three questions to be asked in deciding whether a duty of care was owed by the defendant to the claimant. Was the damage to the claimant reasonably foreseeable? Was the relationship between the claimant and the defendant sufficiently proximate? Is it just and reasonable to impose a duty of care? However, although this test does provide a broad framework for the establishment of a duty of care, in practice the detailed rules have come to differ according to the type of damage sustained (the three main categories being personal injury and/or damage to property, pure economic loss, and psychiatric injury); whether the damage was caused by an act or an omission; whether by the claimant or a third party; and whether the defendant(s) fall(s) within a range of groups which have become subject to special rules.

Before we move on to look at the rules surrounding where and when a duty of care will be found, one important procedural point to note is that where a case raises an issue of law, as opposed to purely issues of fact, the defendant can make what is called a striking-out application, which effectively argues that even if the facts of what the claimant says happened are true, this does not give them a legal claim against the defendant. Cases where it is not clear whether there is a duty of care are often the subject of striking-out applications, where essentially the defendant is saying that even if he or she has caused the harm alleged by the claimant, there was no duty of care between them and so there can be no successful claim for negligence. Where a striking-out application is made, the court conducts a preliminary examination of the case, in which it assumes that the facts alleged by the claimant are true, and from there, decides whether they give rise to an arguable case in law – so in a case involving a duty of care, it would be deciding whether, on the facts before it, the defendant owes a duty of care to the claimant. If not, the case can be dismissed without a full trial. If the court finds that there is an arguable case, the striking-out application will be dismissed, and the case can then proceed to a full trial (unless settled out of court). The claimant will still have to prove that the facts are true, and that the complete case is made out, so a case which is not struck out can still be lost at trial.

Quick quiz 24.2

1 Which case established the tort of negligence?

2 What three elements need to be proved for a finding of negligence?

3 What is the 'neighbour principle'?

4 In determining whether a duty of care is owed, are the courts likely to follow **Anns** v **Merton London Borough** or **Murphy** v **Brentwood District Council**?

Physical injury and damage to property

The most straightforward kind of tort case as far as the existence of a duty of care is concerned (and in practice the most common) is one where the defendant has done something which physically injures the claimant, or damages his or her property. In these cases a duty of care will exist where the damage was reasonably foreseeable – essentially, the original neighbour test – and there are no policy reasons against imposing liability (though it is important to remember, in all negligence cases, that establishing the existence of a duty is only a step towards liability; the claimant still needs to prove that the duty was breached and that the breach caused damage). Thus, for example, a motorist automatically owes a duty of care not to cause physical injury to other road users, even though they are likely to be strangers to him or her. The operation of the test can be seen in **Langley** v **Dray** (1998), where the claimant was a policeman who was injured in a car crash when he was chasing the defendant, who was driving a stolen car. The Court of Appeal held that the defendant knew, or ought to have known, that he was being pursued by the claimant, and therefore in increasing his speed he knew or should have known that the claimant would also drive faster and so risk injury. The defendant had a duty not to create such risks and he was in breach of that duty.

Omissions

As a general rule, the duties imposed by the law of negligence are duties not to cause injury or damage to others; they are not duties actively to help others. And if there is no duty, there is no liability. If, for example, you see someone drowning, you generally have no legal duty to save that person, no matter how easy it might be to do so (unless there are special reasons why the law would impose such a duty on you in particular, such as under an employment contract as a lifeguard). This means tort law generally holds people liable for acts (the things people do), not omissions (the things they fail to do).

However, there are two main situations where there may be a duty of care with regard to omissions. The first is where an omission is actually just part of a chain of negligent acts – for example, a driver failing to stop when a pedestrian steps out. These kinds of omissions are often more logically seen as acts done carelessly: the car hits the pedestrian because the driver is driving carelessly, and the omission to stop is merely a sign of that.

The second situation is where there exists what is called a relationship of proximity. This may be between the defendant and the claimant, in which case it imposes a duty on the defendant to protect the claimant from a particular type of harm; or between the defendant and a third person who injures the claimant, which imposes a duty on the defendant to prevent the third person from causing injury or damage. Two cases which illustrate the idea of proximity are **Watson** *v* **British Boxing Board of Control** (2001) and **Sutradhar** *v* **Natural Environment Research Council** (2004). In **Watson**, the claimant was the famous professional boxer Michael Watson, who suffered severe brain damage after being injured during a match. He sued the Boxing Board, on the basis that they were in charge of safety arrangements at professional boxing matches, and evidence showed that if they had made immediate medical attention available at the ringside, his injuries would have been less severe. The Court of Appeal held that there was sufficient proximity between Mr Watson and the Board to give rise to a duty of care, because they were the only body in the United Kingdom which could license professional boxing matches, and therefore had complete control of and responsibility for a situation which could clearly result in harm to Mr Watson if the board did not exercise reasonable care. They therefore had a duty to protect him from that harm.

In **Sutradhar**, the claimant was a resident of Bangladesh, who had been made ill by drinking water contaminated with the poison arsenic. The water came from wells near his home, and his reason for suing the defendants was that, some years earlier, they had carried out a survey of the local water system, and had neither tested for, nor revealed the presence of arsenic. The claimant argued that the defendants should have tested for arsenic, or made public the fact that they had not done so, in order not to lull local people into a false sense of security. The Court of Appeal, however, held that the defendants had no duty of care to users of the water system, because there was insufficient proximity. The defendants were not responsible for providing the claimants with pure water (that was the job of the local water authorities), they had no way of directly warning those who might drink the water that it was not drinkable, and no control over who saw the report and what use they made of it. They therefore had no duty to protect the local people from being harmed by the water.

Breach of a duty of care

At the very beginning of this chapter, we explained that negligence has three elements: a duty of care, breach of that duty and damage caused by the breach. Now that we have looked at the various tests for establishing whether a duty exists between the claimant and the defendant, we can move on to consider what, assuming a duty has been found in any particular circumstances, will constitute a breach of that duty.

Breach of a duty of care essentially means that the defendant has fallen below the standard of behaviour expected in someone undertaking the activity concerned; so, for example, driving carelessly is a breach of the duty owed to other road users, while bad medical treatment may be a breach of the duty owed by doctors to patients. In each case, the standard of care is an objective one: the defendant's conduct is tested against the standard of care which could be expected from a reasonable person. This means that it is irrelevant that the defendant's conduct seemed fine to him or her; it must meet a general standard of reasonableness.

This principle was established in **Vaughan** *v* **Menlove** (1837). The defendant built a haystack on land adjoining the claimant's cottages, and because the haystack was poorly ventilated, it caught alight, causing damage to the cottages. The state of the haystack, and the almost inevitable result of leaving it like that, had been pointed out to the defendant, but he refused to do anything about it, and simply answered that he would 'chance it', apparently because the haystack was insured, so he stood to lose nothing if it caught fire. The defendant argued that he had genuinely acted honestly and in accordance with his own best judgement of the risk, but it was held that this was not enough; in such a situation, a reasonable person would have taken precautions.

As the test is objective, the particular defendant's own characteristics are usually ignored. A striking example of this is that the standard of care required of a driver is that of a reasonable driver with no account taken of whether the driver has been driving for 20 years or 20 minutes, or is even a learner driver. In **Nettleship** *v* **Weston** (1971) the claimant was a driving instructor, and the defendant his pupil. On her third lesson, she drove into a lamp post and the claimant was injured. The court held that she was required to come up to the standard of the average competent driver, and anything less amounted to negligence: 'The learner driver may be doing his best, but his incompetent best is not good enough. He must drive in as good a manner as a driver of skill, experience and care.' However, there are a limited number of situations in which special characteristics of the defendant will be taken into account.

The standard of reasonableness

It is important to realize that the standard of care in negligence never amounts to an absolute duty to prevent harm to others. Instead, it sets a standard of reasonableness: if a duty of care exists between two parties, the duty is to do whatever a reasonable person would do to prevent harm occurring, not to do absolutely anything and everything possible to prevent harm. We can see this principle in operation in **Etheridge** *v* **East Sussex County Council** (1999). The claimant here was a teacher, who was injured in an accident at school: she had been coming up the stairs, when a pupil threw a heavy basketball down them, hitting her on the head. She sued the County Council, which ran the school, alleging that it was negligent in allowing such an accident to happen. However, the court found that the council had taken all reasonable steps to prevent accidents: the school was well run, with no evidence of behavioural problems, and there were rules in place designed to help prevent accidents, and systems for enforcing them. The school was not required to guarantee the safety of every person in the school against every possible way that an accident could happen; its duty was to make the premises reasonably safe and it had done that, so there was no negligence.

A similar approach was taken in **Simonds** v **Isle of Wight Council** (2003). The claimant here was a 5-year-old boy, who was injured while playing, unsupervised, on swings during a school sports day. The boy had had a picnic lunch with his mother near to where the sports day was taking place and, afterwards, his mother sent him back to rejoin the supervised activities. Unknown to her, the little boy instead headed for some nearby swings. While playing there alone, he fell off and broke his arm. The court rejected the mother's claim that the school had a duty of care to prevent accidents happening on the swings. The sports day had been well supervised, and the school had in place measures to prevent children playing on the swings; it was not possible to make a playing field completely free of hazards, only to take reasonable precautions, which the school had done.

In deciding what behaviour would be expected of the reasonable person in the circumstances of a case, the courts consider a number of factors, balancing them against each other. These include special characteristics of the defendant; special characteristics of the claimant; the magnitude of the risk; how far it was practicable to prevent the risk; common practice; and any benefits that might be gained from taking the risk. None of the factors is conclusive by itself; they interact with each other. For example, if a type of damage is not very serious, the precautions required may be quite slight, but the requirements would be stricter if the damage, though not serious, was very likely to occur. Equally, a risk of very serious damage will require relatively careful precautions even if it is not very likely to occur.

Special characteristics of the defendant

Children

Where the defendant is a child, the standard of care is that of an ordinarily careful and reasonable child of the same age. In **Mullin** v **Richards** (1998), the defendant and claimant were 15-year-old schoolgirls. They were fencing with plastic rulers during a lesson, when one of the rulers snapped and a piece of plastic flew into the claimant's eye, causing her to lose all useful sight in it. The Court of Appeal held that the correct test was whether an ordinarily careful and reasonable 15-year-old would have foreseen that the game carried a risk of injury. On the facts, the practice was common and was not banned in the school, and the girls had never been warned that it could be dangerous, so the injury was not foreseeable.

Illness

A difficult issue is what standard should be applied when a defendant's conduct is affected by some kind of infirmity beyond his or her control. In **Roberts** v **Ramsbottom** (1980) the defendant had suffered a stroke while driving and, as a result, lost control of the car and hit the claimant. The court held that he should nevertheless be judged according to the standards of a reasonably competent driver. This may seem extremely unjust, but remember that motorists are covered by insurance; the question in the case was not whether the driver himself would have to compensate the claimant, but whether his insurance company could avoid doing so by establishing that he had not been negligent. This is also one explanation for the apparently impossible standard imposed in **Nettleship** (see p. 511).

Even so, in a more recent case, **Mansfield** *v* **Weetabix Ltd** (1997), the Court of Appeal took a different approach. Here the driver of a lorry was suffering from a disease which on the day in question caused a hypoglycaemic state (a condition in which the blood sugar falls so low that the brain's efficiency becomes temporarily impaired). This affected his driving, with the result that he crashed into the defendant's shop. The driver did not know that his ability to drive was impaired, and there was evidence that he would not have continued to drive if he had known. The Court of Appeal said that the standard by which he should be measured was that of a reasonably competent driver who was unaware that he suffered from a condition which impaired his ability to drive.

Professionals and special skills

The courts also take account of the fact that a particular defendant has a professional skill, where the case involves the exercise of that skill. In such a case, the law will expect the defendant to show the degree of competence usually to be expected of an ordinary skilled member of that profession, when doing his or her duties properly. A defendant who falls short of that level of competence, with the result that damage is done, is likely to be held negligent. It would be ridiculous to demand of a surgeon, for example, no more than the skill of the untrained person in the street when carrying out an operation.

In **Vowles** *v* **Evans** (2003), a rugby player was injured as a result of a decision made by the referee. The Court of Appeal said that the degree of care a referee was legally expected to exercise would depend on his grade, and that of the match he was refereeing; less skill would be expected of an amateur stepping in to help out, than of a professional referee. This means that the same accident might amount to a breach of duty if the referee was a trained professional, but not if he was an amateur. The referee in the case was a professional and was found liable. Similarly, in **Gates** *v* **McKenna** (1998) the court said a stage hypnotist was expected to take the precautions that a 'reasonably careful exponent of stage hypnotism' would take to prevent psychiatric injury to members of his audience.

In assessing the standard of care to be expected in areas where the defendant is exercising special skill or knowledge, the courts have accepted that within a profession or trade there may be differences of opinion as to the best techniques and procedures in any situation. This issue was addressed in **Bolam** *v* **Friern Barnet Hospital Management Committee** (1957), a case brought by a patient who had had electric shock treatment for psychiatric problems, and had suffered broken bones as a result of the relaxant drugs given before the treatment. These drugs were not always given to patients undergoing electric shock treatment; some doctors felt they should not be given because of the risk of fractures; others, including the defendant, believed their use was desirable. How was the court then to decide whether, in using them, the defendant had fallen below the standard of a reasonable doctor?

Its answer was a formula which has been taken as allowing the medical profession (and to a certain extent other professions, as the test has also been adopted in other types of case) to fix its own standards. According to McNair J:

> A doctor is not guilty of negligence if he has acted in accordance with a practice accepted as proper by a responsible body of medical men skilled in that particular art.

Provided that this was the case, the fact that other doctors might disagree could not make the conduct negligent. The practical effect of this decision (which was only given in a High Court case, but was adopted in several later House of Lords cases) was that so long as a doctor could find a medical expert prepared to state that the actions complained of were in keeping with a responsible body of medical opinion, it would be impossible to find him or her negligent.

The House of Lords, however, modified this much-criticized decision in the more recent case of **Bolitho** *v* **City and Hackney Health Authority** (1997). The case involved a 2-year-old boy, who was admitted to hospital suffering breathing difficulties. He was not seen by a doctor. Shortly after his second attack of breathing problems, his breathing failed completely, he suffered a heart attack and died. His mother sued the health authority on his behalf, arguing that he should have been seen by a doctor, who should have intubated him (inserted a tube into his throat to help him breathe), and that it was the failure to do this which caused his death. The doctor maintained that even if she had seen the boy, she would not have intubated him, which meant that the court had to decide whether she would have been negligent in not doing so. The doctor was able to produce an expert witness to say that intubation would not have been the correct treatment, and the claimant was able to produce one who said it would.

In this situation, the **Bolam** principle had always been taken as suggesting that the doctor was therefore not negligent – other medical opinion might disagree with what she did, but she could produce evidence that it was a practice accepted by a responsible body of medical opinion. Lord Browne-Wilkinson, delivering the leading judgment with which the others agreed, thought differently. While agreeing that the **Bolam** test was still the correct one to apply, he said that the court was not obliged to hold that a doctor was not liable for negligence simply because some medical experts had testified that the doctor's actions were in line with accepted practice. The court had to satisfy itself that the medical experts' opinion was reasonable, in that they had weighed up the risks and benefits, and had a logical basis for their conclusion. However, he then went on to water down this statement by suggesting that in most cases the fact that medical experts held a particular view would in itself demonstrate its reasonableness, and that it would only be in very rare cases that a court would reject such a view as unreasonable. The case before the House of Lords, he concluded, was not one of those rare situations, and so the claimant's claim was rejected.

Bolitho was applied in **Marriott** *v* **West Midlands Regional Health Authority** (1999). The claimant suffered a head injury following a fall at home; he spent the night in hospital but was discharged the next day after tests. After continuing to feel ill for a week, he called his GP, who could find nothing wrong but told Mrs Marriott to call him again if her husband's condition got any worse. Four days later, he became partially paralyzed, and this was later discovered to be a result of the original injury. He claimed that the GP had been negligent in not referring him back to the hospital, given that the GP did not have the resources to test for the condition which he was eventually found to have. At trial, Mr Marriott's expert witness claimed that, given the symptoms Mr Marriott had shown, the GP should have sent him back to the hospital for more tests; however, the GP brought expert evidence to suggest that although this would have been a reasonable course of action, keeping a patient at home for review was equally reasonable in the circumstances.

The old **Bolam** approach would have required the judge to find for the GP, given that she could prove that a reasonable body of medical opinion supported her actions, but, following **Bolitho**, the trial judge looked at the reasonableness of this opinion, given the risk to Mr Marriott, and concluded that, in the circumstances, deciding to review his case at home, without asking for further tests, was not a reasonable use of a GP's discretion. She therefore found the GP negligent. The Court of Appeal upheld her approach: a trial judge was entitled to carry out their own assessment of the risk in the circumstances, and was not bound to follow the opinion of a body of experts.

This new approach can also be seen in a case which attracted a lot of media attention in 2004: **A B and others** v **Leeds Teaching Hospital NHS Trust** (2004). The case was brought after it was revealed that some hospitals had been routinely retaining the organs of children who had died in their care, for research purposes. The parents had not been told that this was happening, and many were devastated when they found out. The case was brought by some of the parents who had suffered psychiatric injury as a result of the shock of finding out what had happened.

The hospital stated that the practices they had followed were considered by the medical profession to be in the best interests of bereaved parents, who might be upset to hear about the unpleasant details of a post-mortem examination. The judge accepted that they had acted in good faith, and genuinely believed they were doing what was best for the parents but, he said, they were wrong; they had a duty to give the parents full information and allow them to make an informed decision on whether they wanted their children's organs to be retained.

The use of the **Bolam** test has been extended to cover not just other professionals, but also defendants who do not have the skills of a particular profession, but have made a decision or taken an action which professionals in the relevant area might disagree about. In **Adams** v **Rhymney Valley District Council** (2000) the claimants were a family whose children had died when fire broke out in the house they rented from the defendant council. The house had double-glazed windows which could only be opened with a key, and the claimants had been unable to smash the glass quickly enough to save the children. They argued that the council had been negligent in providing this type of window, and the issue arose of whether it was correct to decide this by applying the **Bolam** test, given that the council was not a window designer. The court held that it was negligent. The court pointed out that, in deciding on the window design, the council had to balance the risk of fire against the risk of children falling out of a more easily opened window, and professional opinions on how this balance should be struck. If a reasonable body of experts in the field would consider that the council's window design struck this balance in an acceptable way, and the court accepted this view as reasonable, there was no negligence, even though other experts might disagree, and even though the council had neither consulted experts, nor gone through the same processes when choosing the design as an expert would have done.

It was also established in **Bolam** (and **Bolitho** does not affect this point) that where a defendant is exercising a particular skill, he or she is expected to do so to the standard of a reasonable person at the same level within that profession or trade. No account is taken of the defendant's actual experience, so that a junior doctor is not expected to have the same level of skill as a consultant, but is expected to be as competent as an average junior doctor, whether he or she has been one for a year or a week. This principle was upheld in **Djemal** v **Bexley Health Authority** (1995), where the standard required was held to be that of a reasonably senior houseman acting as a casualty officer (which was the defendant's position at the time), regardless of how long the defendant had actually been doing that job at that level.

The standard of care imposed is only that of a reasonably skilled member of the profession; the defendant is not required to be a genius, or possess skills way beyond those normally to be expected. In **Wells** v **Cooper** (1958) the defendant, a carpenter, fixed a door handle on to a door. Later the handle came away in the claimant's hand, causing him injury. It was held that the carpenter had done the work as well as any ordinary carpenter would, and therefore had exercised such care as was required of him; he was not liable for the claimant's injury.

In **Balamoan** v **Holden & Co.** (1999) the defendant was a solicitor who ran a country town practice in which he was the only qualified lawyer. The claimant consulted him over a claim for nuisance. During the following two years, he had two 30-minute interviews with non-qualified members of the solicitor's staff, but no contact with the defendant himself. At the end of that time, he was advised that his claim was worth no more than £3,000, and when he refused to accept that advice, his legal aid certificate was discharged and he stopped using the firm. He went on to conduct the nuisance case himself and won a settlement of £25,000. He then sued the solicitor, arguing that but for the solicitor's negligence, in, for example, failing to gather all the available evidence at the time, he could have won £1 million in damages. The Court of Appeal held that the solicitor was only to be judged by the standard to be expected of a solicitor in a small country town (rather than, for example, a specialist firm which might have expert knowledge of big claims). However, if the solicitor delegated the conduct of claims to unqualified staff who could not come up to that standard, he could be held negligent.

A couple of recent cases have established that professionals have a duty not just to take reasonable steps to ensure that their advice is right, but to explain the thinking behind that advice, and any risks involved in taking it, to the person receiving it. In **Chester** v **Afshar** (2002) the claimant had been operated on by the defendant surgeon to treat a back problem. When recommending the surgery, the surgeon had made no mention of any risk of things going wrong. After the operation, the claimant suffered severe nerve damage, which caused paralysis in one leg. She later discovered that this was a known, if unusual, risk of the surgery. She sued the doctor.

The Court of Appeal found that the doctor had not been negligent in the way he carried out the operation; the paralysis was something that could happen even when the surgery was carried out properly, as it had been here. But they stated that the surgeon had been negligent in not warning the claimant of the risk, however slight it might be. The patient had a right to choose what was or was not done to her, and she could only exercise this right if given full information. Providing such information was therefore part of the doctor's duty of care.

A similar approach was taken in the context of advice from lawyers, in **Griffin** *v* **Kingsmill** (2001) and in **Queen Elizabeth's Grammar School Blackburn Ltd** *v* **Banks Wilson (a firm)** (2001). In **Griffin**, the claimant was a young girl who had been seriously injured in a road accident. She brought a case against the person she considered to be responsible for the accident, but there was considerable conflict of evidence whether that person was actually at fault. Her solicitor took advice from a barrister on whether to settle out of court or press on with the case; the barrister said that she had very little chance of success, so the case was settled for £50,000. Had the case gone to court and the claimant won, she could have expected damages of around £500,000.

The girl sued her lawyers, claiming that they had been negligent in advising that her prospects of winning were so poor. The Court of Appeal agreed that they had been negligent in taking this view of the case, but it also went further. With regard to the barrister, they said, his duty was not just to take reasonable steps to give the right advice, but also to give a reasoned explanation of why he considered his advice to be right, with reference to the evidence before him. This had not happened in the case.

In **Queen Elizabeth's Grammar School**, the claimant was a school, and the defendants their solicitors. The defendants had acted for the school in the purchase of some land from a neighbour of the school. The land was the subject of a restrictive covenant (a legal condition which stops certain things being done with or on the land) which limited the height of any building erected on it. When the school revealed its plans for a new building on the land, the owner of the neighbouring land complained that it was too high, and breached the covenant. The wording of the covenant was slightly unclear, but the defendant solicitors advised the school that it allowed a building up to the height of the chimney pots of an existing building. The planned design fitted in with this. At this stage the solicitors did not to refer to the possibility of the covenant's wording carrying any other meaning, when in fact it was possible that the wording meant that any new building could only be as high as the ridge line of an existing one (which means the top of the roof itself).

Once the building work had started, the neighbour again complained, and the school checked again with their solicitors. They repeated their original advice, but would not guarantee that it was right, or that a court would not take a different view. The school decided to have the roof line of the building altered, to make sure they did not infringe the covenant. At such a late stage, this was quite expensive, and they sued the solicitors for their costs.

The Court of Appeal held that there was scope for dispute over the meaning of the covenant, and as the defendants had known that from the start, they should have explained as much to the school, who could then have made sure from the start that there was no risk of breaching the covenant. The implication was that even if the solicitors' advice had turned out to be right (which is unknown as it never became necessary to test the covenant in court) they could still be negligent for not mentioning the possibility that they might be wrong.

In areas such as medicine and technology, the state of knowledge about a particular subject may change rapidly, so that procedures and techniques which are approved as safe and effective may very quickly become outdated, and even be discovered to be dangerous. The case of **Roe** *v* **Minister of Health** (1954) established that, where this happens, a defendant is entitled to be judged according to the standards that were accepted at the time when he or she acted.

The claimant in the case was left paralysed after surgery, because a disinfectant, in which ampoules of anaesthetic were kept, leaked into the ampoules through microscopic cracks in the glass, invisible to the naked eye. Medical witnesses in the case said that until the man's accident occurred, keeping the ampoules in disinfectant was a standard procedure, and there was no way of knowing that it was dangerous; it was only the injuries to the claimant that had revealed the risk. Therefore, the defendant was held not to be liable.

However, once a risk is suspected, the position may change. In **N** *v* **United Kingdom Medical Research Council** (1996), the Queen's Bench Division looked at this issue. In 1959, the Medical Research Council (MRC) started a medical trial of a human growth hormone, which involved giving the hormone to children with growth problems. The children were each given the hormone by one of four different methods. In 1976, the MRC was warned that the hormone could cause Creutzfeld Jakob Disease (CJD, which is the human form of the fatal brain disease generally known as Mad Cow Disease). A year later, the MRC was told that two of the four methods of giving the hormone carried a particular risk of transmitting CJD. Ultimately, several of the children who received the hormone died from CJD, and their parents alleged that the MRC had been negligent in not investigating the risk when it was first suggested in 1976, and suspending the programme until it was proved safe.

The court held that the failure to look into the risk was negligent, and if the MRC had looked into it then, failure to suspend the trial programme would also have been negligent.

Special characteristics of the claimant

A reasonable person would have due regard to the fact that a claimant has some characteristic or incapacity which increases the risk of harm. In **Paris** *v* **Stepney Borough Council** (1951), the claimant was employed by the defendant in a garage. As a result of a previous injury at work, he could only see with one eye. His job included welding, and while he was doing this one day, a piece of metal flew into his good eye and damaged it. No goggles had been provided by the defendant. Although the House of Lords accepted that failing to provide goggles would not have made the defendant liable to a worker with no previous sight problems, in this case it held that the defendant was liable. The risk of injury was small, but the potential consequences to this particular employee if such injury did occur were extremely serious, as he could easily end up completely blind; moreover, the provision of goggles was neither difficult nor expensive.

In a number of recent cases the courts have looked at the issue of claimants who are drunk, and whether this amounts to a characteristic which in some way increases a defendant's duty towards them. In **Barrett** v **Ministry of Defence** (1995), the Court of Appeal took the view that there is no duty to stop someone else from getting drunk, but once the claimant was drunk, it accepted that the defendant had assumed some responsibility for protecting him from the consequences of his intoxication, by virtue of the relationship between them and the fact that the defendant had ordered the claimant to be taken to lie down.

However, without such a relationship, it seems there is no general duty to give extra protection to a drunken claimant. In **Griffiths** v **Brown** (1998), the claimant had got drunk and asked a taxi driver to take him to a particular cashpoint mach-ine. The driver dropped him off on the opposite side of the road from the machine, and he was injured while crossing. He argued that the driver, knowing he was drunk, had a duty not to expose him to the danger of crossing a road. The court rejected this argument: the duty of a taxi driver was to carry passengers safely during the journey, and then stop at a place where they can get out of the car safely; that duty should not be increased by the fact that the claimant was drunk. However, he accepted that the duty might be extended if, for example, a passenger who intended to spend the evening drinking, arranged for a taxi driver to collect him and see him home safely; this clearly accords with the **Barrett** approach that there may be a duty to protect a claimant from the effects of drunkenness where the defendant has actually done something which amounts to assuming responsibility for doing so.

The courts are likely to be more severe on defendants who have actively encour-aged the claimant to get drunk, rather than merely failing to stop him or her. The claimant in **Brannan** v **Airtours plc** (1999) had been on an Airtours holiday, and joined in an evening excursion organized by Airtours, which offered dinner, danc-ing and unlimited free wine. Above the table where he was sitting was a revolving electric fan seven feet from the floor; the party guests had been warned not to climb on to the tables because of the danger from these fans if they did. The claimant did climb on the table, in order to get out of his seat without people nearby having to move, and he was injured. The Court of Appeal held that the fact that the holiday company had actively created an atmosphere where people would drink too much, lose their inhibitions and have less than usual regard for their personal safety was relevant to assessing whether the company had been negligent.

Magnitude of the risk

The greater the risk of harm, the more likely that a court will find that the duty of care has been breached. In considering the scale of the risk, the courts will take into account both the chances of damage occurring, and the seriousness of that damage. In **Bolton** v **Stone** (1951) the claimant was standing outside her house in a quiet street when she was hit by a cricket ball from a nearby ground. It was clear that the cricketers could have foreseen that a ball would be hit out of the ground, and this had happened before, but only six times in the previous 30 years. Taking into con-sideration the presence of a 17-foot fence, the distance from the pitch to the edge of the ground, and the fact that the ground sloped upwards in the direction in which the ball was struck, the House of Lords considered that the chances of injury to someone standing where the claimant was were so slight that the cricket club was not negligent in allowing cricket to be played without having taken any other precautions against such an event. The only way to ensure that such an injury could not occur would be to erect an extremely high fence, or possibly even a dome over the whole ground, and the trouble and expense in such precautions were completely out of proportion to the degree of risk.

A case in which the potential seriousness of an injury was decisive is **Paris** *v* **Stepney Borough Council** (see p. 518).

Practicality of protection

The magnitude of the risk must be balanced against the cost and trouble to the defendant of taking the measures necessary to eliminate it. The more serious the risk (in terms of both foreseeability and degree of potential harm), the more the defendant is expected to do to protect against it. Conversely, as **Bolton** *v* **Stone** shows, defendants are not expected to take extreme precaution against very slight risks. This was also the case in **Latimer** *v* **AEC Ltd** (1952). Flooding had occurred in a factory owned by the defendants following an unusually heavy spell of rain. This had left patches of the floor very slippery. The defendants had covered some of the wet areas with sawdust, but had not had enough to cover all of them. The claimant, a factory employee, was injured after slipping on an uncovered area, and sued, alleging that the defendants had not taken sufficient precautions; in view of the danger, they should have closed the factory. The House of Lords agreed that the only way to eradicate the danger was to close the factory, but held that given the level of risk, particularly bearing in mind that the slippery patches were clearly visible, such an onerous precaution would be out of proportion. The defendants were held not liable.

Where defendants are reacting to an emergency, they are then judged according to what a reasonable person could be expected to do in such a position and with the time available to decide on an action, and this will clearly allow for a lesser standard of conduct than that expected where the situation allows time for careful thought.

Common practice

In deciding whether the precautions taken by the defendant (if any) are reasonable, the courts may look at the general practice in the relevant field. In **Wilson** *v* **Governors of Sacred Heart Roman Catholic Primary School, Carlton** (1997), the claimant, a 9-year-old boy, was hit in the eye with a coat by a fellow pupil as he crossed the playground to go home at the end of the day. The trial judge had looked at the fact that attendants were provided to supervise the children during the lunch break, and inferred from this that such supervision should also have been provided at the end of the school day. The Court of Appeal, however, noted that most primary schools did not supervise children at this time; they also pointed out that the incident could just as easily have happened outside the school gates anyway. Consequently, the school had not fallen below the standard of care required.

In **Thompson _v_ Smiths Shiprepairers (North Shields)** (1984), it was made clear that companies whose industrial practices showed serious disregard for workers' health and safety would not evade liability simply by showing that their approach was common practice in the relevant industry. The case involved a claimant who suffered deafness as a result of working in the defendant's shipyard, and the defendant argued that the conditions in which he worked were common across the industry and therefore did not fall below the required standard of care. Mustill J disagreed, stating that they could not evade liability just by proving that all the other employers were just as bad. He observed that their whole industry seemed to be characterized by indifference to the problem, and held that there were some circumstances in which an employer had a duty to take the initiative to look at the risks and seek out precautions which could be taken to protect workers. He pointed out, however, that this approach must still be balanced against the practicalities; employers were not expected to have standards way above the rest of their industry, though they were expected to keep their knowledge and practices in the field of safety up to date.

Another area where common practice is taken into account is in accidents which take place during sports. In **Caldwell _v_ Maguire and Fitzgerald** (2001), the claimant, Caldwell, was a professional jockey, as were the two defendants. All three were in a race with a fourth jockey, Byrne. At the point where the incident which gave rise to the case happened, Maguire, Fitzgerald and Byrne were neck and neck, with Caldwell close behind. As they approached a bend, Maguire and Fitzgerald pulled ahead in such a way as to leave no room for Byrne. Seeing its path ahead closed off, Byrne's horse veered across Caldwell's path, causing him to fall. The defendants were found to have committed the offence of careless riding under the rules of the Jockey Club, which regulates racing practice; this was the least serious of five possible offences concerning interfering with other riders.

Caldwell sued Maguire and Fitzgerald for causing his injuries, but the Court of Appeal found their conduct did not amount to negligence. They confirmed that a player of sports owes a duty to all the other players, and approved the test of negligence in sports used in the earlier case of **Condon _v_ Basi** (1985), which stated that the duty on a player of sports is to exercise such care as is appropriate in the circumstances. The court went on to explain that this would depend on the game or sport being played, the degree of risk associated with it, its conventions and customs, and the standard of skill and judgement reasonably to be expected of players. As a result, the standard of care would be such that a momentary lapse of judgement or skill would be unlikely to result in liability, and in practice, it might be difficult to prove a breach unless the player's conduct amounted to a reckless disregard for others' safety. Therefore, in this case, the defendants were not negligent, as within the circumstances of the horseracing world, careless riding was accepted as part of the sport, even if not approved of.

Players of sport also have a duty to spectators, but the court stated that as, in the normal course of events, spectators would be at little or no risk from players, a player would have to have behaved with a considerable degree of negligence before he or she could be said to have failed to exercise such care as was reasonable in the circumstances.

Potential benefits of the risk

Some risks have potential benefits for society, and these must be weighed against the possible damage if the risk is taken.

This principle was applied in **Watt** *v* **Hertfordshire County Council** (1954). The claimant was a firefighter. He was among others called to the scene of an accident where a woman was trapped under a car; a heavy jack was needed to rescue her. The vehicle in which the fire officers travelled to the scene was not designed to carry the jack, and the claimant was injured when it slipped. He sued his employers, but the court held that the risk taken in transporting the jack was outweighed by the need to get there quickly in order to save the woman's life. However, the court stated that if the same accident had occurred in a commercial situation, where the risk was taken in order to get a job done for profit, the claimant would have been able to recover.

Quick quiz 24.3

1 When is a duty of care breached?

2 List three factors that the courts will take into account when deciding what behaviour would be expected of the reasonable person in the circumstances of a case.

3 In determining whether a defendant has breached a duty of care, will the courts take into account the age of the defendant?

4 What standard of care is expected of a doctor when treating a patient?

Damage

The negligence must cause damage; if no damage is caused, there is no claim in negligence, no matter how careless the defendant's conduct. In the vast majority of cases this is not an issue: there will be obvious personal injury, damage to property or economic loss. However, there are cases where the claimant perceives that the defendant's negligence has caused damage, yet the law does not recognize the results of that negligence as damage. The cases discussed in this section give an insight into how the law decides what is damage and what is not.

The issue of damage to property was the subject of **Hunter** *v* **Canary Wharf Ltd and London Docklands Development Corporation** (1997). The case arose from the construction of the big tower block known as Canary Wharf in east London. An action concerning the effects of the construction work was brought by local residents, and one of the issues that arose from the case was whether excessive dust could be sufficient to constitute damage to property for the purposes of negligence. The Court of Appeal concluded that the mere deposit of dust was not in itself sufficient because dust was an inevitable incident of urban life. In order to bring an action for negligence, there had to be damage in the sense of a physical change in property, which rendered the property less useful or less valuable. Examples given by the court included excessive dust being trodden into the fabric of a carpet by householders in such a way as to lessen the value of the fabric, or excessive dust causing damage to electrical equipment.

A very different issue was examined in a line of cases beginning with **R v Croydon Health Authority** (1997): can the birth of a child be considered damage? In **R v Croydon** an employee of the defendant had routinely examined the claimant, a woman of childbearing age, and found that she was suffering from a life-threatening heart condition, which could be made worse by pregnancy. The claimant was not told this, and went on to become pregnant and have a child. Although she did want a child, the claimant claimed she would not have become pregnant if she had known of the danger to herself in doing so. In addition to claiming for the fact that her heart condition was made worse by the pregnancy, she claimed for the expenses of pregnancy and the cost of bringing up the child, and was successful at first instance. The defendant appealed against the award of damages for the costs of pregnancy and bringing up the child. The Court of Appeal supported its view: where a mother wanted a healthy child and a healthy child was what she got, there was no loss. The court emphasized that a key factor in this case was that the claimant had wanted a child; the decision might be different, it was suggested, when a child was not wanted.

However, when this issue was addressed in **McFarlane v Tayside Health Board** (1999), the House of Lords found it impossible to view as damage the birth of a healthy child, even to parents who had expressly decided that they did not want more children (the case is a Scottish one, but has been accepted as representing English law too). The claimants were a couple who had four children, and decided that they did not want any more, so Mr McFarlane had a vasectomy. After he was wrongly advised that the operation was successful, Mrs McFarlane became pregnant again, and gave birth to a healthy daughter. The couple sought to sue the health authority, with Mrs McFarlane claiming damages for the pain and discomfort of pregnancy and birth, and both claimants claiming for the costs of bringing up the child.

The House of Lords allowed the claim for pain and discomfort, pointing out that tort law regularly compensated for pain arising from personal injury, and there was no reason to treat pregnancy as involving a less serious form of pain. But their Lordships refused to allow the claim for the costs of bringing up the child, stating that the birth of a normal, healthy baby was universally regarded as a blessing, not a detriment, and therefore could not be viewed as damage. Lord Millett pointed out that although there were disadvantages involved in parenthood (cost being one), they were inextricably linked with the advantages, and so parents could not justifiably seek to transfer the disadvantages to others while themselves having the benefit of the advantages.

Both cases focused on the fact that the baby was healthy, and in **McFarlane** the House of Lords specifically declined to consider what the position is when a baby is born disabled, who would not have been born at all if it were not for a defendant's negligence. The implication seemed to be that they might be prepared to allow that the birth of a disabled child could be considered damage in a way that having a healthy child was not, which said little for their approach to disabled people.

Not long afterwards, this exact issue arose before the Court of Appeal, in **Parkinson** *v* **St James and Seacroft University Hospital NHS Trust** (2001). The claimant, Mrs Parkinson, and her husband had four children, and had decided they neither wanted nor could afford any more, so Mrs Parkinson was sterilized. Due to the hospital's admitted negligence, the operation did not work, and Mrs Parkinson became pregnant again. The child was born with severe disabilities, and Mrs Parkinson claimed for the costs of bringing him up. At first instance the court refused to allow her to claim the basic costs of his maintenance (the amount it would have cost to bring him up if he had not been disabled), following **McFarlane**. However, the judge said she could claim the extra costs which arose from her son's disability. The hospital appealed.

The Court of Appeal allowed Mrs Parkinson's claim for these extra costs, and in her judgment, Hale LJ addressed the idea of whether the birth of a disabled child could be considered damage, if that of a healthy one could not, and in doing so, looked again at the reasoning in **McFarlane**. She argued that one of the most important rights protected by the law of tort was that of bodily integrity – the right to choose what happens to one's own body, and not to be subjected to bodily injury by others. The processes of pregnancy and childbirth, if unwanted, were a serious violation of this right, denying the mother the chance to decide what happened to her own body, and causing discomfort and pain. In addition, she pointed out that child-bearing impacts on a woman's personal autonomy, saying that 'One's life is no longer just one's own, but also someone else's'. Mothers-to-be are expected to alter what they eat, drink and do to safeguard the baby, while after the birth there is a legal responsibility to look after the child, which includes a financial burden. As a result, she said, it was clear that where an unwanted pregnancy happened as a result of negligence, its consequences were capable of giving rise to damages. However, she went on, it was also necessary to take into account the fact that children bring benefits to their parents, and since it was impossible to calculate these, the fairest assumption was that they were sufficient to cancel out the costs. This was what the House of Lords had assumed in **McFarlane**.

Applying this reasoning to the birth of a disabled child, she said that allowing a claim for the extra costs associated with disability made sense. It was acknowledged that a disabled child brought as much benefit to his or her family as any other child, but that as he or she would cost more to bring up, the costs were not cancelled out. Therefore the extra expense should be recoverable.

The same issue took a slightly different shape in **Rees** *v* **Darlington Memorial Hospital NHS Trust** (2002). Here the claimant was a disabled woman, who was almost blind as a result of a hereditary condition. Because of her disability, she did not want to have children, and so chose to be sterilized. The operation was performed negligently, and the claimant had a son, who was not disabled. She was a single parent, and claimed, not for the basic costs of bringing up her son, but for the extra costs of doing so that were caused by her disability. The House of Lords rejected her claim. As in **McFarlane**, they allowed Ms Rees compensation for the pain and stress of pregnancy and birth, but they refused to give compensation for any of the costs of bringing up a child. By a majority, they confirmed the reasoning in

McFarlane, that a child should not be seen in terms of an economic liability, and that the benefits of having a child could not be quantified. They said that the idea of giving someone compensation for the birth of a healthy child would offend most people, especially as that money would come from the hard-pressed resources of the NHS.

However, they said that it was clear that where a defendant's negligence had brought about a pregnancy and birth which the mother did not want and had asked them to prevent, a legal wrong had been done that went beyond the pain and suffering of birth and pregnancy. As examples of the harm this could cause, Lord Bingham cited the situation of a single mother who might already be struggling to make ends meet and would now not only have another child to feed, but would face a longer period before she could work longer hours and earn more money, or the situation of a woman who had been longing to start or resume a much-wanted career, and was now prevented from doing so. The House of Lords held that there should be a financial recognition of this loss, and awarded Ms Rees £15,000 in addition to the compensation for pain and suffering.

The House also took the opportunity to consider whether **Parkinson** had been correctly decided, and said that it was; where a child born as the result of a defendant's negligence was disabled, the parents could claim for the extra costs associated with his or her disability.

Causation

In order to establish negligence, it must be proved that the defendant's breach of duty actually caused the damage suffered by the claimant, and that the damage caused was not too remote from the breach (a legal test which is covered at p. 533 below).

The 'but for' test

Causation is established by proving that the defendant's breach of duty was, as a matter of fact, a cause of the damage. To decide this issue the first question to be asked is whether the damage would not have occurred but for the breach of duty; this is known as the 'but for' test.

The operation of the test can be seen in **Barnett v Chelsea and Kensington Hospital Management Committee** (1968). A night-watchman arrived early in the morning at the defendant's hospital, suffering from nausea after having a cup of tea at work. The nurse on duty telephoned the casualty doctor, who refused to examine the man, and simply advised that he go home and consult his GP if he still felt unwell in the morning. The man died five hours later of arsenic poisoning: he had been murdered. In this case the hospital was being sued for negligence, but the action failed. The court accepted that the defendant owed the deceased a duty of care, and that they had breached that duty by failing to examine him. However, the breach did not cause his death. There was evidence that even if he had been examined, it was too late for any treatment to save him, and therefore it could not be said that but for the hospital's negligence, he would not have died.

A similar result was reached in **Brooks** *v* **Home Office** (1999). The claimant was a woman in prison, who was pregnant with twins. Her pregnancy had been classified as high risk, so she needed regular ultrasound scans. One of these scans showed that one of the twins was not developing properly, but the prison doctor, who had little experience in this area of medicine, waited five days before seeking specialist advice. It was then discovered that the affected twin had died two days after the scan. Ms Brooks sued the Home Office (which is responsible for the prison service), arguing that she was entitled to receive the same standard of health care as a woman outside prison, and that the prison doctor's five-day delay in seeking expert advice fell below this standard. The court agreed with these two points, but it was found that a wait of two days before getting expert advice would have been reasonable, and as the baby had actually died within this time, the doctor's negligence could not be said to have caused its death.

Of course, it is not always clear what would have happened but for the defendant's negligence. This was the situation in **Chester** *v* **Afshar** (2002), the case described on p. 516, concerning the surgeon who failed to warn a patient of the possible risks of an operation. On the point of causation, it was necessary to decide what the patient would have done had she been adequately warned. The hospital argued that causation could only be proved if the claimant could show that, had she been warned of the risk, she would have decided against having the operation at all. In that case, it could be said that but for the surgeon's failure to warn, her injuries would not have happened. But the claimant could not show that: she said that had she been warned, she would have sought further advice on what to do. As it was not possible to say what that advice would have been or how she would have responded to it, the defendants argued that causation was not proved. The surgeon's failure to warn that the operation could go wrong did not in any way increase the risk associated with the operation; that risk was there anyway, and it was a risk the claimant would have taken had she chosen to have the operation later, which she may well have done.

The House of Lords disagreed. They pointed out that the scope of the surgeon's duty of care to his patient included a duty to warn of any risks. Therefore, there had to be a remedy where a doctor failed to fulfil that part of the duty, and a patient was injured as a result of the risk, otherwise that aspect of the duty was meaningless. The House of Lords accepted that it was very difficult to prove causation on conventional principles, and said that this was a case where legal policy required a judge to decide whether justice required the normal approach to causation to be modified. In this case it did. To find otherwise would mean that only those claimants who could categorically say that they would not have had the surgery would benefit from the existence of the duty of care, whereas those who needed time to think or more advice would not. This would leave the duty of care useless where it was needed most. On policy grounds therefore, the test of causation was satisfied and the claimant won her case.

▌ Multiple causes

In some cases, damage may have more than one possible cause. As an example, take the facts of **McGhee** *v* **National Coal Board** (1972). The claimant's job brought him into contact with brick dust, which caused him to develop a skin condition called dermatitis. It was known that contact with brick dust could cause dermatitis, but it was not suggested that merely exposing workers to the dust was negligent, as that was an unavoidable risk of the job he did. However, it was accepted that the risk of developing dermatitis could be reduced if workers could shower before leaving work, as this would lessen the amount of time the dust was in contact with their skin. The defendants had not installed any showers, and the claimant argued that they had been negligent in not doing so. To succeed in his claim, he had to prove that this negligence had caused his dermatitis – but because showers would only have lessened the risk, not removed it, the 'but for' test did not work. It was impossible to say that the damage would not have happened 'but for' the defendant's negligence, but equally impossible to say that it would definitely still have happened without the negligence.

As a result, in cases where there is more than one possible cause of damage, the courts have modified the 'but for' test, in an attempt to find a fair way to decide whether liability should be imposed. Unfortunately, they have come up with not one test, but several. In many cases, the result will differ according to which test is applied, yet it remains difficult to predict which approach a court will take in a particular case.

The simplest approach is that which was actually taken by the House of Lords in **McGhee**. They said that in cases where there was more than one possible cause, causation could be proved if the claimant could show that the defendant's negligence had materially increased the risk of the injury occurring; it was not necessary to show that it was the sole cause. In that case, the lack of showers was held to substantially increase the risk to Mr McGhee, and he won his case.

A similar test was used in **Page** v **Smith (No. 2)** (1996), where the claimant was in a car accident, and claimed that the resulting shock reactivated a previous physical illness, ME. The defendant claimed that the claimant had not proved that the accident had caused the recurrence of his illness. The Court of Appeal held that the question to be answered was, as in **McGhee**, 'did the accident, on the balance of probabilities, cause or materially contribute to or materially increase the risk of' the claimant developing the symptoms of which he complained.

The same test was applied in **Athey** v **Leonati** (1999). The claimant had been injured in two separate car crashes, and afterwards developed severe back pain, which was diagnosed as a condition called a disc herniation. However, he had had a history of minor back problems before the accidents, and medical evidence could not show whether the disc herniation was caused by these pre-existing problems, by the accidents, or by a combination. The Court of Appeal confirmed that in cases where the 'but for' test was unworkable, causation could be established if the claimant could show that the defendant had materially contributed to the risk of the injury developing.

As we can see, the **McGhee** test has been used in cases over the past 30 years (and continues to be good law). During the same period, however, the courts have also used a completely different test, which in many cases would give the opposite result to the **McGhee** rule. This test was used in **Wilsher** v **Essex Area Health**

Authority (1988), a tragic case concerning a claimant who was born prematurely, with a number of health problems associated with being born too early. He was put on an oxygen supply, and as a result of a doctor's admitted negligence, was twice given too much oxygen. He eventually suffered permanent blindness, and the hospital was sued. However, medical evidence suggested that although the overdoses of oxygen could have caused the blindness, it could also have been caused by any one of five separate medical conditions from which the baby suffered. The House of Lords held that the claimant had to prove, on a balance of probabilities, that the defendant's breach of duty was a material cause of the injury; it was not enough to prove that the defendant had increased the risk that the damage might occur, or had added another possible cause of it. On the facts of the case, the defendant's negligence was only one of the possible causes of the damage, and this was not sufficient to prove causation.

Loss of a chance cases

A third approach is taken to causation in cases which involve what is called 'loss of a chance'. Often these are medical negligence cases, and a typical example might involve a claimant being diagnosed with cancer, who has a certain percentage chance of being cured, but has that chance reduced by their doctor's delay in diagnosing or treating the illness. The court then has to decide whether the delay can be said to have caused the patient not to have been cured, or whether that would have been the situation even if the doctor had not acted negligently. Loss of a chance can also involve financial losses, where a claimant misses out on the chance of a money-making deal, or a well-paid job, because of the defendant's negligence.

A key case on loss of chance with respect to injury or illness is **Hotson** *v* **East Berkshire Health Authority** (1987). Here the claimant, a young boy, had gone to hospital after falling from a rope and injuring his knee. An X-ray showed no apparent injury, so he was sent home. Five days later, the boy was still in pain, and when he was taken back to the hospital, a hip injury was diagnosed and treated. He went on to develop a condition known as avascular necrosis, which is caused when the blood supply to the site of an injury is restricted, and eventually results in pain and deformity. This condition could have arisen as a result of the injury anyway, but medical evidence showed that there was a 25 per cent chance that if he had been diagnosed and treated properly on his first visit to the hospital, the injury would have healed and the avascular necrosis would not have developed. The Court of Appeal treated this evidence as relevant to the issue of damages, holding that it meant his action could succeed but he should receive only 25 per cent of the damages he would have got if the condition was wholly due to the defendant's negligence.

The House of Lords, however, ruled that this was the wrong approach; what was really in issue was whether the claimant had proved that the defendant's negligence caused his condition. The House held that he had not: the law required that he should prove causation on a balance of probabilities, which means proving that it was more likely that the defendant had caused his condition than not. What the medical evidence showed was that there was a 75 per cent chance of his developing the condition even if the negligence had not occurred. Proving causation on a balance of probabilities required at least a 51 per cent chance that the negligence caused the damage, so he could not prove his case.

This approach was challenged in **Gregg v Scott** (2005). The claimant had visited his GP, complaining of a lump under his left arm, but the doctor said it was nothing to worry about. Nine months later, the lump was still there, so the claimant consulted another GP, who referred him to a surgeon. The lump was diagnosed as cancer, and it was shown to have grown during the time between visiting the first and second GPs. The claimant was treated, and the cancer went into remission, but it was not known whether he was actually cured.

The claimant sued the doctor on the basis that the delay had made is less likely that he would be cured, but it was not possible to say with certainty whether this was the case. Statistics showed that out of every 100 people who developed the same kind of tumour, 17 would be cured if they had prompt treatment, but not if their treatment was delayed by a year; 25 would be cured even if their treatment was delayed by a year; and 58 would be incurable regardless of how much treatment they had and when. The claimant said that, on the basis of these figures, he had originally had a 42 per cent chance of being cured (adding together the figures for those who would be cured even if treatment was delayed, and those who would only be cured if they received prompt treatment). By delaying his treatment, the doctor had reduced his chances to 25 per cent.

The House of Lords rejected this argument, and confirmed that personal injury cases could not be won on the basic of 'loss of a chance'. The rule remained that the claimant could succeed only if he could prove that the defendant's negligence made it more likely than not that he would not be cured. Since it was impossible to know whether, at the time of seeing his GP, Mr Gregg fell into the incurable 58 per cent or the potentially curable 42 per cent, it was impossible to prove the effect of the negligence on a balance of probabilities.

Damages for loss of a chance have, however, been allowed in cases where the loss is purely financial. In **Stovold v Barlows** (1995), the claimant claimed that the defendant's negligence had caused him to lose the sale of his house. The Court of Appeal decided there was a 50 per cent chance that the sale would have gone ahead had the defendant not been negligent, and on this basis they upheld the claimant's claim, but awarded him 50 per cent of the damages that he would normally have won (thus following the approach it had taken in **Hotson**, and not that taken by the House of Lords in that case).

In **Allied Maples Group v Simmons & Simmons** (1995) the defendants hoped to make a particular business deal, but were prevented from doing so by the claimant's negligence; it was possible that the deal might not have gone ahead for other reasons even if the negligence had not happened. The Court of Appeal held that where the damage alleged depends on the possible action of a third party (in this case the other party to the deal), the claimant must prove that the chance was a substantial one, as opposed to pure speculation on what might have happened. If so, the action can succeed on causation, and the evaluation of the chance will be taken into account when calculating damages.

Multiple tortfeasors

In the cases discussed above, the question has been whether damage was caused by the defendant, or by one or more non-negligent acts or situations, such as accident or illness. What happens when the damage was definitely caused by negligence, but there is more than one party which could have been responsible? This often arises in cases concerning work-related illnesses which take many years to develop, so that it is not always clear at which point during the claimant's working life the damage was done. In **Holtby v Brigham & Cowan** (2000) the claimant suffered asbestosis as a result of breathing asbestos dust at work over a long period; he had been employed by the defendants for approximately half that time, and by other firms doing similar work for the rest; for reasons which are not important here, he was only suing the defendants. The Court of Appeal stated that the defendants were liable if it was proved that their negligence had made a material contribution to the claimant's disability; their negligence did not have to be the sole cause of it. However, if the injury had also been partially caused by the negligence of others, the defendants would only be liable for the proportion they had caused. In deciding how big this proportion was, the judge followed the practice of insurance companies and related it to the amount of time the claimant had been exposed to the defendants' negligence and, erring on the side of the claimant, set the proportion of liability at 75 per cent.

This approach can, however, work harshly against claimants, and this was revealed – and eventually to some extent corrected – in **Fairchild v Glenhaven Funeral Services Ltd** (2002). This case also concerned employees who had worked with asbestos, but here the disease caused was mesothelioma, an invariably fatal cancer that is almost always caused by asbestos. It is not entirely clear how mesothelioma is caused, but it is believed to be triggered by a single fibre of asbestos penetrating a cell in the lining of the lung, which then becomes malignant and eventually grows into a tumour. This makes it different from asbestosis, which generally gets worse the more asbestos the person is or has been exposed to; with mesothelioma, the single event of the fibre entering the lung causes the disease. It may take up to 30 years to do so, but essentially the person's fate is sealed when the fibre enters the lung, and the amount of previous or subsequent exposure is irrelevant. This was what caused problems for the claimants in **Fairchild**.

The claimants (or their husbands, as some of the men had already died, and their widows sued) had been exposed to asbestos over long periods during their working lives, as a result of negligence by a series of different employers. By the time they sued, many of the companies were no longer worth claiming against, so they sued only those that were. Previously, in mesothelioma cases, the courts had taken the approach that all significant exposure to asbestos up to around ten years before the symptoms developed could be said to have contributed to the causation of the disease. But in **Fairchild**, the High Court held that it was necessary for the claimant to prove which fibre had caused the disease, and only the employer at that time would be liable. Since it was impossible to know, let alone prove, which fibre had caused the disease, this ruling had the potential to mean that mesothelioma sufferers would never be able to sue those who had caused their disease.

As there are over 1,300 cases of the disease each year, and the figure is expected to more than double over the next 20 years, the decision caused considerable anxiety. But to many people's surprise, the Court of Appeal upheld the High Court's approach, and confirmed that where a claimant with mesothelioma has been exposed to asbestos by different employers at different times, and it cannot be proved, on a balance of probabilities, which period of exposure caused the illness, he or she could not recover damages from any of the employers.

On a strict definition of causation, this at first sight looks plausible, if callous, but a closer look shows a number of problems. First, although the disease is caused by one inhalation of fibres and not cumulative exposure, you do not have to be a mathematical genius to work out that the more times you are exposed to asbestos, the higher the chance that on one of those occasions you will breathe some in. On this basis, it would not seem difficult to argue that each of the employers had increased the claimants' risk of getting the disease, just as the employer in **McGhee** had.

Secondly, the focus on the one 'guilty fibre' somehow suggests that only the employer for whom the claimant was working at the time the fibre was inhaled did anything wrong – whereas in fact all of them had negligently exposed their employees to a substance which had the potential to kill them, prematurely and painfully. Ignoring this fact does not sit well with tort's claim to act as a deterrent to careless and dangerous behaviour.

Thirdly, the parties who would actually be paying any damages would be insurance companies, which had been taking premiums for decades during which the risks of asbestos were well known, and now wanted to escape liability. In fact while the case was awaiting its House of Lords hearing, the insurance companies concerned offered the claimants a full settlement, which, if accepted, would have meant the cases would not be heard. As a result, although the **Fairchild** claimants would have been compensated, thousands of other victims would have remained at the mercy of the Court of Appeal judgment. The president of the Association of Personal Injury Lawyers, Frances McCarthy, called the offer 'a cynical and underhanded attempt to prevent the cases being heard'.

In the event, the House of Lords did hear the case, and came to a different view. They said that where an employee had been negligently exposed by different defendants, during different periods of employment, to inhalation of asbestos, a modified approach to proof of causation was justified. In such a case, proof that each defendant's wrongdoing had materially increased the risk of contracting the disease was sufficient to satisfy the causal requirements for his or her liability. Applying that approach, the claimants could prove causation on a balance of probabilities, and the defendants were liable.

Other issues in causation

An interesting development in the area of causation can be seen in **Bolitho** *v* **City and Hackney Health Authority** (1997), the case discussed earlier concerning the little boy brought to hospital with breathing difficulties (see p. 514). The doctor in the case had argued that even if she had attended the little boy, she would not have intubated him, so that her failure to attend could not therefore be a cause of his death. Had this argument been allowed to succeed, it would mean that a patient who could prove that a doctor was negligent in not attending could lose the action on the basis that even if the doctor had attended he or she would have behaved negligently. The House of Lords rightly refused to accept this, and stated that causation could be established if the claimant proved either that the doctor would have intubated if she had attended; or that she *should* have intubated if she had attended, because it would be a breach of duty not to have done so.

The case of **Pickford** *v* **Imperial Chemical Industries plc** (1998) stresses that the onus is always on the claimant to prove causation. In that case the claimant was a secretary who had suffered severe pains in her hands after her employers greatly increased the amount of typing she had to do, a condition usually known as repetitive strain injury (RSI). Evidence was presented that the condition could be caused by physical or psychological factors or a combination of the two, and the defendants suggested that the cause in this case was psychological. The Court of Appeal held that the claimant had to prove that her condition was caused by the typing and not merely associated with it, and she had not done that. The defendants were not required to prove that the cause was psychological.

Intervening events

In some cases, an intervening event may occur after the breach of duty, and contribute to the claimant's damage. Where such an event is said to break the chain of causation, the defendant will only be liable for such damage as occurred up to the intervening event. In such cases the intervening event is called a *novus actus interveniens*.

Where there is an intervening event but the original tort is still a cause of the damage, the defendant remains liable. In **Baker** *v* **Willoughby** (1969) the claimant injured his left leg as a result of the defendant's negligence. After the accident he was shot in the left leg by an armed robber, and ended up having his leg amputated. The robber was not caught and so could not be sued for the incident.

The defendant argued that his liability only extended to the point at which the armed robbery occurred, when the effects of his negligence were overtaken by the robber's shooting. However, in this context the 'but for' test is not strictly applied: it would be inaccurate to suggest that the damage would not have occurred but for the breach of duty, for the claimant's leg would have been damaged later anyway, as a result of the robbery. However, the House of Lords took the approach that tort law compensates as much for the inability to lead a full life as for the specific injury itself. This inability continues even where the original injury had been superseded by a later one.

However, **Baker** *v* **Willoughby** was not followed in the decision of **Jobling** *v* **Associated Dairies** (1982). As a result of the defendant's breach of duty, the claimant hurt his back at work in 1973, which rendered him disabled and reduced his earning capacity by 50 per cent. In 1976, the claimant was diagnosed as suffering from a back condition, known as myelopathy, which had no connection with the accident. By the end of that year he was unable to work. The defendants argued that they should only be liable for the effects of the back injury up to the point at which the myelopathy occurred, to which the claimant responded that the case of **Baker** *v* **Willoughby** should apply. The House of Lords found unanimously in favour of the defendants' argument, applying the 'but for' test strictly. The risk of unrelated medical conditions occurring was habitually taken into account when calculating damages for future loss of earnings. It could therefore not be ignored when it had already developed.

Interestingly, both **Baker** and **Jobling** were followed in **Murrell** *v* **Healy** (2001), though with reference to different aspects of the case. Murrell was injured in a car accident in May 1995. It was obviously not his year, as he was involved in another car accident in November, causing new injuries. He settled out of court with the driver in the first accident, and was paid compensation of £58,500. One of the questions at issue was how far the damages payable by the second driver should be reduced because of the payment Murrell had received from the first. The Court of Appeal held that the second driver was liable to compensate Murrell for the additional damage that the accident caused to an already injured victim. So if, for example, Murrell had originally been capable of heavy work, and after the first accident, was only capable of light work, the second driver had no liability for that loss. But if the second accident had meant that he was then not even capable of light work, the second driver was liable to compensate him for that. This was held to be the other side of the rule in **Baker**; if the first tortfeasor's liability is not reduced by the second tort, then the second tortfeasor cannot be liable for losses caused by the first tortfeasor.

A second problem in the case was that Murrell's inability to work was also caused by a knee and hip problem, which had not been proved to be caused by either of the accidents. Here the court followed **Jobling**, holding that where a claimant has been injured by a tort but is also suffering from an unrelated condition that makes them unable to work, that condition reduces the damages payable by the tortfeasor. The correct approach was to try to assess what the claimant's life would have been like had the tort not happened, so problems which would have existed then could not be ignored.

Remoteness of damage

As well as proving that the defendant's breach of duty factually caused the damage suffered by the claimant, the claimant must prove that the damage was not too remote from the defendant's breach. Like the issue of duty of care, the remoteness test is a legal test (rather than a factual one) which forms one of the ways in which the law draws the line between damage which can be compensated in law, and that which cannot. This means that there are some circumstances where the defendant will undoubtedly have caused damage in fact, but in law it is considered that he or she should not have to compensate the claimant for it.

The test of remoteness

The traditional test of whether damage was too remote was laid down in **Re Polemis** (1921), and essentially imposed liability for all direct physical consequences of a defendant's negligence; it became known as the direct consequence test. The case concerned the renting of a ship, an arrangement known as a charter. The people renting the ship, called the charterers, had loaded it with tins of petrol, and during the voyage these leaked, releasing large amounts of petrol vapour into the hold. The ship docked at Casablanca, and was unloaded. The workers unloading it had positioned some heavy planks as a platform over the hold, and as a result of their negligence, one of the planks fell into the hold. It caused a spark, which ignited the petrol vapour, and ultimately the ship was completely burnt, causing the owners a loss of almost £200,000. They sued the charterers.

The trial judge had found as a fact that the charterers could not reasonably have foreseen that the fire was likely to occur as a result of the plank falling into the hold, though they might reasonably have foreseen that some damage to the ship might result from that incident. However, the Court of Appeal held that this was irrelevant; the charterers were liable for any consequence that was a direct result of their breach of duty, even if such consequences might be different from and much more serious than those which they might reasonably have foreseen. A consequence would only be too remote if it was 'due to the operation of independent causes having no connection with the negligent act, except that they could not avoid its results'.

As time went on and the tort of negligence grew, the direct consequence test came to be seen as rather hard on defendants. As a result, a new test was laid down in **Overseas Tankship (UK) Ltd** *v* **Morts Dock & Engineering Co. (The Wagon Mound)** (1961), which is usually referred to as **Wagon Mound No. 1** (a second case, **Wagon Mound No. 2**, arose from the same incident, but raised different issues; it is discussed later (see p. 537)). The incident which gave rise to the litigation was an accident which occurred in Sydney Harbour, Australia. In **Wagon Mound No. 1** the defendants were the owners of a ship which was loading oil there, and owing to the negligence of their employees, some of it leaked into the water and spread, forming a thin film on the surface. Within hours, the oil had spread to a neighbouring wharf, owned by the claimants, where another ship was being repaired by welders. It caused some damage to the slipway, but then a couple of days later, further and much more serious damage was caused when the oil was ignited by sparks from the welding operations.

The trial judge found that the damage to the slipway was reasonably foreseeable, but given that the evidence showed that the oil needed to be raised to a very high temperature before it would catch fire, the fire damage was not reasonably foreseeable. Nevertheless, as the Australian courts were also following **Re Polemis**, he found the defendants liable for both types of damage.

The Privy Council, however, took a different view, stating that **Re Polemis** was no longer good law. The new test of remoteness was the foresight of the reasonable person: was the kind of damage suffered by the claimant reasonably foreseeable at the time of the breach of duty? Under this test, the defendants in **Wagon Mound No. 1** were only liable for the damage to the slipway, and not for the fire damage. The reasonable foreseeability test as set down in **Wagon Mound No. 1** is now the standard test for remoteness of damage in negligence.

▌ Type of damage

Under the remoteness of damage test, a defendant will only be liable if it was reasonable to foresee the type of damage that in fact happened – in **Wagon Mound No. 1** it was clear that this covered the damage to the slipway, but not the fire damage. However, this has led to some difficult distinctions in other cases, as the contrasting decisions in **Doughty** v **Turner Manufacturing Co.** (1964) and **Hughes** v **Lord Advocate** (1963) show.

In **Doughty** the claimant was an employee who was injured when an asbestos cover was knocked into a vat of hot liquid. A chemical reaction between the asbestos and the liquid caused the liquid to bubble up and erupt over the edge of the vat, burning the claimant. The chemical reaction was not foreseeable, but the claimant argued that it was foreseeable that the lid falling in would cause some liquid to splash out, and the result of this was likely to be burning, the same injury as resulted from the liquid erupting. The court disagreed, holding that an eruption was different in kind to a splash.

In **Hughes**, Post Office employees had opened a manhole in the street, and left it open when they finished work for the day, covering it with a canvas shelter and surrounding it with paraffin lamps. The claimant, an 8-year-old boy, picked up one of the lamps and took it into the shelter. While playing there, he knocked the lamp into the manhole, and paraffin vapour from the lamp ignited, causing an explosion in which the claimant fell into the hole and was badly burnt. The defendants claimed that although they could have foreseen a risk that someone might be burnt, they could not have foreseen injuries caused by an explosion, and so the damage was too remote. The House of Lords rejected this view: if it was reasonably foreseeable that the damage would be burning, it did not matter that the burns were produced in an unforeseeable way.

Recent cases seem to suggest that the less narrow approach is gaining favour. In **Page** v **Smith (No. 2)** (1996) (see p. 527), it was argued that where some form of personal injury was foreseeable, the fact that the damage suffered was psychiatric rather than physical did not make it too remote; they were both types of personal injury and that was foreseeable. Similarly, in **Margereson** v **JW Roberts Ltd** (1996) the Court of Appeal considered the case of claimants who had contracted the lung disease mesothelioma as a result of playing near the defendant's asbestos factory as children. The court held that it was not necessary for mesothelioma to be a reasonably foreseeable result of exposure to the asbestos dust, it was sufficient that some form of lung damage was reasonably foreseeable.

However, the case of **Brown** v **Lewisham and North Southwark Health Authority** (1999) makes it clear that the courts can still manipulate the foreseeability concept as a potential restriction on liability. The case involved a complicated medical negligence claim. The claimant had had heart surgery at Guy's, a London hospital, after which he was given a blood-thinning drug called Heparin and discharged to travel by train and taxi to his local hospital in Blackpool; at the time of his discharge, he was suffering from a chest infection. A few days later he was diagnosed as having a deep vein thrombosis (a potentially fatal blood clot) in his leg, and was given

Heparin again. In rare cases, patients can develop a reaction, called HITT, to a first dose of Heparin, which results in later doses causing or worsening a thrombosis rather than treating it; this happened to Mr Brown. The hospital failed to recognize it, and gave him another course of Heparin, and eventually the worsening thrombosis meant that he had to have his leg amputated. The claimant sued the health authority which ran Guy's Hospital, on the basis that if he had stayed there, the HITT would have been diagnosed, and he would not have had to undertake the journey to Blackpool and the later courses of Heparin, both of which, it was claimed, had materially contributed to the thrombosis and loss of his leg. However, it was acknowledged that if he had not had the chest infection, it would not have been negligent for the hospital to discharge him when it did, and the chest infection had had nothing to do with his subsequent problems. The Court of Appeal held that causation had not been proved, but Beldam LJ also considered the issue of the type of damage suffered by the claimant. He argued that it was not fair to hold a doctor liable for failing to diagnose the HITT, simply because that doctor was at fault in his treatment of the chest infection:

> . . . it must be shown that the injury suffered by the patient is within the risk from which it was the doctor's duty to protect him. If it is not, the breach is not a relevant breach of duty.

This view would seem to go against the **Page** principle that where some kind of personal injury is foreseeable, any kind of personal injury is sufficient. It is worth noting that although a series of apparently conflicting cases like these can seem confusing, as a student you are not expected to know which path a court would take when faced with this issue; what you have to do is show that you are aware that the cases illustrate different approaches. You can do this by stating that there are conflicting cases, and describing how the decision on the facts before you might go if the courts took, for example, the **Page** approach, and how this might differ if the view expressed in **Brown** was preferred. It is also important to point out any differences in the authority of apparently clashing cases, such as whether one was a House of Lords case and the other from the Court of Appeal, or whether, as in **Brown**, the issue was not decisive because other factors played a part in the judgment.

■ Extent of damage

So long as the type of damage sustained is reasonably foreseeable, it does not matter that it is in fact more serious than could reasonably have been foreseen. The extreme application of this principle is the gruesome-sounding 'thin-skull' rule, which essentially establishes that defendants will be liable even if the reason for the damage being more serious than could be expected is due to some weakness or infirmity in the claimant. In **Smith** v **Leech Brain & Co.** (1962), the claimant was burnt on the lip as a result of the defendant's negligence. He had a pre-cancerous condition, which became cancerous as a result of the burn, and the defendant was held liable for the full result of the negligence.

Quick quiz 24.4

1 What is the 'but for' test?

2 Which case lays down the current test on remoteness?

3 What is the current test for remoteness?

4 If it was reasonably foreseeable that about £10,000 worth of damage would be caused by a fire started by the defendant, will the defendant be liable to pay £1 million in compensation when this amount of damage was actually caused by the fire?

Risk of damage

The case of **Overseas Tankship (UK)** *v* **Miller Steamship Co. (The Wagon Mound No. 2)** (1967) establishes that so long as a type of damage is foreseeable, it will not be too remote, even if the chances of it happening were slim. The case arose from the accident in Sydney Harbour discussed at p. 534 when we looked at **Wagon Mound No. 1**; the defendants were the same but in this case the claimants were the owners of some ships that were also damaged in the fire. When this case was heard, different evidence was brought which led the trial judge to conclude that it was foreseeable that the oil on the water would ignite, and when the case was appealed to the Privy Council, it held that on the evidence before that judge, he was entitled to reach this conclusion. The risk was small but it clearly existed, and therefore the damage was not too remote.

Intervening events

An intervening event will only make damage too remote if the event itself was unforeseeable. The old case of **Scott** *v* **Shepherd** (1773) is still one of the best illustrations of this. The defendant threw a lighted firework into a market hall while a fair was being held there. It landed on a stall, and the stall owner picked it up and tossed it away from his stall; it landed on another, whose owner did the same, and after the firework had seen most of the market, it eventually exploded in the claimant's face, blinding him in one eye. The court held that the defendant was liable; the actions of the stallholders were a foreseeable result of throwing the firework.

In **Humber Oil Terminal Trustee Ltd** *v* **Owners of the Ship Sivand** (1998) the defendants' ship had damaged the claimants' wharf as a result of negligent navigation. The claimants engaged contractors to repair the wharf, and their agreement with the contractors included a clause that obliged the claimants to pay any extra repair costs which might be necessary if the repairers encountered physical conditions which could not have been foreseen. This in fact happened, as the seabed proved unable to take the weight of the jack-up barge the repairers used, and so the barge sank. The claimants were claiming against the defendants for damage caused to the wharf by their negligence, and they sought to add this increased cost to their claim. The defendants argued that the loss of the barge was not foreseeable, and was an intervening act which broke the chain of causation. The Court of Appeal disagreed: although the precise circumstances were not reasonably foreseeable, it was the kind of circumstance envisaged by the contract, and the loss of the barge was not caused by an intervening event, but an existing state of affairs, namely the condition of the seabed, and it did not break the chain of causation.

Proving negligence

The claimant normally has the burden of proof in relation to proving negligence, which can be a considerable obstacle for a claimant. However, there are two exceptions to this rule: where the defendant has a criminal conviction related to the incident in question, and where the principle of *res ipsa loquitur* (Latin for 'the facts speak for themselves') applies.

Criminal convictions

Under s. 11 of the Civil Evidence Act 1968, a defendant's criminal conviction is admissible evidence in a subsequent civil case based on the same facts. This means that if a defendant whose conduct is alleged to have been negligent has already been convicted of a crime for that conduct, that is evidence of negligence, and it is for the defendant to disprove it if he or she can. A common example is where a defendant in a motor accident case has already been convicted of dangerous driving as a result of the accident.

Res ipsa loquitur

There are circumstances in which the facts of the case are such that the injury complained of could not have happened unless there had been negligence, and in such cases, the maxim *res ipsa loquitur* may apply. One example is the case of **Scott** *v* **London and St Katherine's Docks** (1865), where the claimant was injured by some bags of sugar which fell from the open door of the defendant's warehouse above. There was no actual evidence of negligence, but the Court of Appeal held that negligence could be inferred from what had happened, since the bags of sugar could not have fallen out of the door all by themselves. Similarly, in **Mahon** *v* **Osborne** (1939) it was held that a swab left inside the claimant after a stomach operation could not have got there unless someone had been negligent. In such circumstances, the courts may treat the facts themselves as evidence of negligence (but only evidence, which may be rebutted), provided that two other conditions are satisfied: the events are under the control of the defendant or the defendant's employees, and there is no direct evidence of negligence.

Under the control of the defendant

This point is illustrated by two contrasting cases. In **Gee** *v* **Metropolitan Railway Co.** (1873) the claimant fell out of a train just after it left a station, when the door he was leaning against flew open. The railway staff clearly had a duty to ensure that the door was properly shut, and since the train had so recently left the station, it could be inferred from the fact of what happened that they had not shut it properly. However, in a similar case, **Easson** *v* **London and North Eastern Railway** (1944), the train was seven miles past the last station when the door flew open. It was held that the fact that the door had opened in this way did not necessarily mean that railway staff had been negligent, because the situation was not under their exclusive control; any passenger could have interfered with the door during the time since the train had left the station. The staff might have been negligent, but the facts alone were not enough to act as reasonable evidence to that effect.

No direct evidence of negligence

If there is direct evidence of what caused the damage, the courts will examine that, rather than inferring it from the facts alone. In **Barkway** *v* **South Wales Transport Co. Ltd** (1950) the claimant was injured when the bus he was travelling in burst a tyre and crashed. The tyre burst because of a defect that could not have been discovered beforehand, but there was evidence that the bus company should have told drivers to report any blows to their tyres, which could weaken them, and they had not done so. The court held that it should examine this evidence rather than rely on *res ipsa loquitur*.

Using *res ipsa loquitur*

The operation of *res ipsa loquitur* was explained by the Court of Appeal in **Ratcliffe** *v* **Plymouth & Torbay Health Authority** (1998). Here the claimant had gone into hospital for an ankle operation, and had ended up with a serious neurological condition which it was agreed had been triggered by the injection of a spinal anaesthetic. He argued that this was a case of *res ipsa loquitur*; the injection must have been given negligently, or it could not have caused the problem. The health authority produced expert evidence which stated that the condition might be due to the claimant already having a susceptibility to spinal cord damage, and the injection triggering such damage even though it was not given negligently. The Court of Appeal, referring back to **Scott**, stated that where there was no direct evidence of negligence, but a situation was under the management of the defendant and/or the defendant's employees, and the damaging event was such that in the ordinary course of things would not happen if proper care was taken, that in itself could be taken as evidence of negligence, and in the absence of any other explanation, a judge would be entitled to infer that negligence had taken place. However, the defendant could prevent the judge from inferring negligence by either showing that he or she took reasonable care, or supplying another explanation for the events. The court stressed that nothing in the application of *res ipsa loquitur* changed the rule that the burden of proof was on the claimant. The defendant's alternative explanation would have to be plausible, and not merely theoretically possible, but the defendant is not required to prove that it was more likely to be correct than any other. In this case the defendant had provided a plausible explanation and it was up to the claimant to prove that negligence, rather than the claimant's explanation, had caused his injury, which he could not do.

By contrast, a claimant's case succeeded on the basis of *res ipsa loquitur* in **Widdowson v Newgate Meat Corporation** (1997). Here the claimant, who suffered from a serious mental disorder, was knocked down by the defendant's van while he was walking along the side of a dual carriageway at night. Because of his disorder, the claimant was not considered a reliable witness and was not called at the trial; the defendant pleaded that there was no case to answer and offered no evidence. The trial judge declined to apply *res ipsa loquitur* on the ground of a lack of evidence regarding the events leading up to the trial. The Court of Appeal disagreed with this approach: case law had established that where it was impossible to pinpoint an exact act or omission that was negligent, but the circumstances were such that it was more likely than not that the damage was caused by the defendant's negligence, it was up to the defendant to rebut this inference. In this case, the road was deserted and the defendant would have had a clear view of the claimant, so it was more likely than not that his negligence caused the action. The defendant driver had failed to rebut the inference by providing a credible explanation of what happened.

Rebutting the inference of negligence

An inference of negligence under the doctrine of *res ipsa loquitur* can be rebutted by the defendant. In **Ng Chun Piu v Lee Chuen Tat** (1988), a coach driver swerved while travelling along a dual carriageway, and crossed the central reservation, hitting a bus that was moving in the opposite direction. A passenger on the bus was killed, and his personal representatives sued the driver and owner of the coach. The Privy Council ruled that on the facts negligence could be inferred, but the coach driver was able to rebut this inference by explaining that he had had to swerve to avoid a car which had cut in front of him. Therefore the burden of proving negligence remained with the claimant.

In **Ward v Tesco Stores Ltd** (1976), the claimant slipped on some yogurt which had been spilt on the floor of the defendant's supermarket. She put forward evidence that three weeks later, another spill, this time of orange juice, was left on the supermarket's floor for 15 minutes, though she had no evidence of the circumstances leading up to her own accident. The defendant gave evidence that the floor was swept five or six times a day, and that staff were instructed that if they saw a spillage, they should stay by it, and call someone to clean it up. Nevertheless, the Court of Appeal relied on the doctrine of *res ipsa loquitur* to find that negligence could be inferred, and this inference was not rebutted by the defendant's evidence.

▌ The Highway Code

Following the Road Traffic Act 1988, s. 38(7), where a road user fails to comply with any provision of the Highway Code, that fact may be submitted as evidence of negligence.

The defence of contributory negligence

Common law traditionally provided that anyone who was partly responsible for the harm done to them could not recover in tort. Not surprisingly, this caused considerable injustice in some cases, and the Law Reform (Contributory Negligence) Act 1945 now provides that in such cases, the claim need not fail, but the defence of contributory negligence may apply. Where this defence applies, damages can be reduced to take account of the fact that the fault was not entirely the defendant's.

An example of the application of this defence can be seen in **Baker** *v* **Willoughby** (1969). Here the claimant was a pedestrian who had been knocked down by the defendant's car. The defendant had been driving carelessly, but on the other hand, the claimant had had a clear view of the road for the last 200 yards travelled by the car, but had taken no evasive action. The Court of Appeal found that the claimant was 50 per cent contributorily negligent – in other words, that both parties were equally to blame. The practical result of that finding was that the claimant received 50 per cent of the damages he would have got had there been no contributory negligence.

It is important to realize that a finding of contributory negligence cannot be made unless it is first clear that the defendant was negligent. Although obviously the defendant must have a duty of care towards the claimant before this can happen, the claimant does not need to have a duty of care towards the defendant; all that is necessary is that he or she failed to take reasonable care for his or her own safety, and by that lack of care, contributed to the harm suffered.

In many cases, the claimant's negligent behaviour will contribute to causing the accident which results in damage. An obvious example would be a pedestrian who walks out into the path of a car without looking. However, contributory negligence can also apply where the claimant's behaviour does not cause the accident itself, but contributes to the amount of damage done. For this reason, damages to drivers or passengers in road accidents are always reduced if seatbelts have not been worn, since this negligence would usually increase the injuries suffered.

This principle can be seen clearly in economic loss cases, such as **Cavendish Funding Ltd** *v* **Henry Spencer & Sons Ltd** (1998). Here the claimants had lent money for the purchase of a property which had been negligently valued by the defendants. The defendants had valued the building at over £1.5 million, and the claimants had also had a valuation from another company, at around £1 million. The property was actually worth around a quarter of a million. The claimants based their loan on the defendants' valuation and lost money as a result; they sued the defendants for the loss. The Court of Appeal held that the claimants had been contributorily negligent: the discrepancy between the two valuations should have made it clear that something might be wrong, and they should have checked; had they done so, the valuation would have been reduced and they would not have lost so much. The court deducted 25 per cent from their damages for contributory negligence.

The damage to which the claimant's negligence has contributed must fall within the general scope of the risk he or she was taking, but the courts have been willing to give this a fairly wide interpretation. In **Jones** *v* **Livox Quarries** (1952), the claimant was riding on the back of a vehicle called a 'traxcavator' at the quarry where he worked. The vehicle was not designed to carry passengers in this way. The claimant was injured when another vehicle drove into the back of the traxcavator. He argued that his negligence amounted only to taking the risk that he might fall off the back of the traxcavator, but the court held that being hit from behind by another vehicle was also within the range of possible risks arising from riding on the traxcavator, and the claimant's negligence in doing so had contributed to his injury.

The standard of care

The standard of care which the claimant must show for his or her own safety in order to avoid being found contributorily negligent is essentially the same as the standard of care required of a defendant in negligence: that of the reasonable person involved in the relevant activity. Like the standard of care in negligence, it is usually objective, but allowance is made for children, and probably for people with some type of disability which makes it impossible for them to reach the required standard.

A claimant will not be contributorily negligent where he or she has only fallen below the standard of care as a result of an error of judgement: the courts have pointed out that reasonable people do make errors of judgement from time to time, and especially in emergency situations. In **Jones** *v* **Boyce** (1816), the claimant was riding on top of the defendant's coach when one of the horses' reins broke, and it looked as though the coach might topple over. The claimant jumped from the coach, breaking his leg. As it turned out, the coach was kept on the road, so if the claimant had kept his seat, he would not have been injured. Clearly he had contributed to his own injury, but the court held that this did not amount to contributory negligence; he had acted reasonably in the face of what appeared to be a dangerous situation.

In **Griffin** *v* **Mersey Regional Ambulance Service** (1998), the claimant was a motorist who collided with an ambulance being driven on an emergency call. He had failed to see the ambulance because his vision was obscured by another vehicle, which had stopped to let the ambulance through. He was held to be negligent in that he had failed to notice the ambulance's siren and flashing light, or to realize that the other vehicle had stopped to let it through; however, the ambulance driver was negligent because he was driving too fast, and because he should have waited to make sure that there was no traffic in his path before turning.

In **Brannan** *v* **Airtours plc** (1999) the Court of Appeal dealt with a case where the defendant's conduct had made the claimant's error of judgement more likely. In this case the claimant, a holidaymaker, took an evening excursion organised by the defendants, which offered dinner, dancing and unlimited free wine. Above the table here the claimant was sitting, there was a ceiling fan; he climbed onto the table and was injured by the fan. The defendant's employees had warned people not to get up on the tables, but there was evidence that they had also actively created an atmosphere in which people would drink a lot and lose their inhibitions. The holiday company was found to be negligent, but the court reduced the damages by 75 per cent on the basis that the claimant had been contributorily negligent in ignoring warnings given to holidaymakers about the risk of injury if they climbed on tables.

However, the Court of Appeal thought differently; it agreed that there had been some contributory negligence, but stated that the trial judge should have considered the fact that the holiday company had actively created an atmosphere where people would drink a lot and so lose their inhibitions and be less cautious. It reduced the assessment of contributory negligence to 50 per cent. This part of the judgment is an interesting contrast to the views expressed in **Barrett** *v* **Ministry of Defence** (1995), to the effect that adults should take responsibility for their own alcohol consumption and not expect others to prevent them getting drunk (see p. 519).

In **Revill** *v* **Newberry** (1996), the claimant had entered the defendant's land intending to steal from his shed, but was shot by the defendant, who had taken to sleeping in his shed because he was concerned, rightly as it turned out, about the risk of theft and vandalism. He was sued for negligence by the would-be burglar, and successfully raised the defence of contributory negligence.

The case of **Reeves** *v* **Metropolitan Commissioner** (1999) makes it clear that intentionally harming yourself can be contributory negligence. The case concerned the suicide of a suspect in police custody; his widow sued the police, arguing that they were negligent in failing to prevent her husband's death. The court found that the death was caused equally by two factors: police negligence in allowing him to take his own life, and his action in doing so. Therefore he was 50 per cent contributorily negligent.

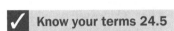

✓ Know your terms 24.5

Define the following terms:

1 *Novus actus interveniens*
2 *Res ipsa loquitur*
3 An objective test
4 Contributory negligence

Children

Where the claimant is a child, the standard of care is that which could reasonably be expected, taking into account the child's age and development. In **Gough** *v* **Thorne** (1966), a 13-year-old girl was injured crossing the road. A lorry driver had stopped to let her cross, and signalled to her that she should cross, so the girl did so, without checking to see whether there was any other vehicle coming up from behind to overtake the lorry. In fact there was a lorry approaching, and it hit and killed her. The court held that taking into account her age, she had not fallen below the expected standard of care and so was not contributorily negligent.

In **Yachuk** *v* **Oliver Blais Co.** (1949), a 9-year-old boy bought some gasoline, a highly inflammable fuel, from the defendant company, saying his mother needed it for her car. He took it away and played with it, and ended up being seriously burnt. The company was found to be negligent in supplying the gasoline to a child of that age, but the boy was not found contributorily negligent on the ground that at his age he could not be expected to know the dangers of gasoline.

Very young children are unlikely ever to be found contributorily negligent, since they cannot be expected to have enough awareness and experience to guard their own safety at all.

■ Reduction of damages

Where contributory negligence is proved, the claimant's damages will be reduced 'to such extent as the court thinks just and equitable having regard to the claimant's share in the responsibility for the damage' (Law Reform (Contributory Negligence) Act 1945, s. 1(1)).

The exact calculations are at the discretion of the court and will vary according to the facts. However, in one of the most common examples of contributory negligence, failure to wear a seatbelt in road accident cases, the courts have laid down a standard set of reductions. In **Froom** v **Butcher** (1976) it was stated that in cases where using a seatbelt would have prevented the claimant's injuries from happening at all, damages should be reduced by 25 per cent. Where the injuries would have happened anyway, but wearing a seatbelt would have made them less serious, damages should be reduced by 15 per cent.

Criticisms of negligence law

In order to highlight the general problems with the law of negligence, we need to look first at what the aims of this area of the law are, in order to provide a gauge by which its success can be measured. The law of negligence has several aims, not all of which are necessarily consistent with each other: to compensate victims of harm caused by others; to mark the fault of those who cause harm; to deter carelessness; to spread the financial costs of harm caused by carelessness; and to do all these things quickly and fairly. To judge how well it achieves these aims, we need to look at both the law itself, and the context in which it operates.

■ Compensating victims of harm

Considering that compensation is generally seen to be its most important function, the law of negligence is remarkably inefficient in this area and, in practice, only a small proportion of victims of harm get compensation through it.

The first reason for this is that, if we take a wide view of harm, many people are caused harm by circumstances in which nobody can be blamed, for example those with genetic illnesses or those who suffer damage of any kind in accidents which are genuinely nobody's fault. You might well ask why they should be compensated, but the wider picture is that, as we shall see, society as a whole spends a lot of money on negligence cases, yet the result is that a few people get large amounts of money in damages, while many other people whose needs are the same, but result from different causes, do not. The question is therefore whether the system we currently have gives good value for our money.

Even among those who have suffered damage in circumstances where someone else might be liable, only a small proportion take legal action. This might come as a surprise given that most of the media seem to be convinced that suing is the most popular hobby in Britain. Certainly, the figures are rising: the 1984 study *Compensation and Support for Injury and Illness* by Harris *et al.* found that just over one in ten seriously injured accident victims made a claim whereas a 1999 study by the right-wing think tank, the Centre for Policy Studies, found that one in seven of people who were sufficiently badly injured to need medical treatment sought legal advice. But even leaving aside the fact that not all of these will have gone on to make a claim, the other side of this figure is that six out of seven people were not seeking compensation for what in many cases will have been serious injury. There are several reasons for this: people are often unaware of the possibility of legal action, or are put off by the inaccessible image of the legal world, and the cost of legal action is extremely high. In recent years, no-win, no-fee actions, and more accessible legal advice (from, for example, accident management companies, who advertise widely and lack the sometimes forbidding image of solicitors) have probably eased these problems to some extent, but a survey by MORI in 2000 suggests that for many people, substantial barriers to taking legal action still exist. The survey found that almost 72 per cent of people would consider making a claim if they were injured through someone else's negligence – but the likelihood of this translating into a similar proportion of actual claims seems slim, given that over 60 per cent thought they would probably not be able to afford legal action, and almost 70 per cent said they knew little or nothing about how to go about making a claim.

Among those who do bring cases, the chances of success are sometimes slim. This is particularly the case in medical negligence, where the **Bolam** ruling (see p. 513) has essentially meant that if doctors stick together, it is extremely difficult to prove them negligent. How far this will change in the light of **Bolitho** (see p. 514) remains to be seen; certainly the judgment in **Bolitho** leaves plenty of room to keep the old standard in all but exceptional cases. Yet there seems no compelling reason why medical negligence should be treated so differently from other areas of negligence, and English law is alone among the major common law jurisdictions in giving doctors this privileged status.

In practice, the vast majority of negligence cases are settled without going to court – sometimes early on, but often almost literally at the door of the court. This saves whichever side would have lost a lot of money, since a trial can drastically raise the costs, and the loser must pay those of the winner as well as their own. From the point of view of adequately compensating those injured though, settlements can be problematic. Hazel Genn's 1987 study, *Hard Bargaining*, showed that in cases where the defendant is an insurance company (which is the case in the vast majority of accident and professional negligence claims) and the claimant an ordinary member of the public, the insurance companies, with their considerable experience of these cases, are able to manipulate the pre-trial process in order to achieve not a fair settlement but the lowest offer they can get away with. What seems to happen is that small claims are overcompensated because it is not cost-effective for insurance companies to fight them, while very big claims (such as, for example, those brought by parents of children damaged by negligence at birth, who will need care throughout their lives) are often undercompensated because the claimants need compensation quickly, and so can be forced to accept a lower settlement than they might get if they went to court.

Because the law on negligence is complicated, cases can be long and involved. Specialist legal representation is usually required, and the expert witnesses often needed to prove fault add to the cost. The result in practice is that only a fraction of the money spent on negligence cases actually goes to the victims of harm.

Marking fault

The original basis of the law of negligence was claimed to be essentially moral: those who carelessly cause harm to others should bear the responsibility for that harm. In fact this was always debatable; for example, the direct consequence test for remoteness of damage, laid down in **Re Polemis** (1921), created cases where the damage the defendant was required to compensate could be wildly out of proportion to his or her fault, and even though this test has been superseded, the 'eggshell-skull' rule can have a similar effect.

Deterring carelessness

The argument here seems obvious: the tort system means that people and organizations know they are liable to be sued if their carelessness causes damage, and therefore its existence should mean that they are more likely to take care to avoid causing harm. In practice, however, the deterrence issue is not so straightforward. First, the possibility of being sued for negligence can only really act as a deterrent if it is clear that everybody who suffers damage through negligence will sue, and as we have seen, that is not the case. Secondly, the presence of insurance means that even if you are sued, your carelessness is quite likely not to cost you anything, giving you little incentive to be careful.

Thirdly, the market system on which our society is run actually makes it much more difficult for businesses to take sufficient care, where such care costs (and it usually does). This is because in a market system, companies have to keep their costs in line with those of other competing companies. Any company which went out on a limb and spent a lot of money on, for example, safety precautions when, as we have seen, there is relatively little chance of being sued for negligence, would soon be put out of business (a fact which was implicitly acknowledged by the courts in **Thompson** *v* **Smith Shiprepairers (North Shields)**, see p. 521).

The objective approach can mean that it is actually impossible for the tortfeasor to reach the required standard; in **Nettleship** *v* **Weston** (1971) (see p. 511) the defendant was judged by standards that in reality she could not have been expected to attain. The decision may have been right, given that the defendant would have been protected by insurance, but as far as deterrence is concerned, it was meaningless.

Another practical problem is that in many cases the standard of care imposed is too vague to be of much use in deterring careless behaviour. In reality, most tortfeasors do not sit and balance the magnitude of the risk against its seriousness, while taking into account their own special characteristics and those of the defendant, and contemplating the possible benefits to society of what they are about to do. In an ideal world perhaps they should, but in practice they do not. What the law of negligence really does is not so much deter carelessness, as attempt to mop up the mess that carelessness leaves behind.

Spreading risk

This is one area where the law of negligence can be seen to work very well at times; rather than leaving loss to lie where it falls, it can pass it on to those most able to bear it financially. The fine judgements needed to do this are not always easy, but there are many cases where the courts have shown obvious good sense in this area.

Having said that, it is worth bearing in mind that, as we have explained, when loss is shifted to insurers, in practice it is actually shifted from them to all of us. This is not necessarily a bad thing, since it spreads the costs of harm thinly – but if this is what society wants to do, it might be more efficiently done by compensating all victims of harm, however caused, through welfare systems based on need and paid for by taxes. In this way much more of the money spent would go to victims of harm, because there would be no need to take out the element of profit for insurance companies, nor the costs of legal actions.

Individualism and negligence

Supporters of the school of thought known as critical legal theory criticize negligence law for the way it focuses almost exclusively on individual fault, when in fact there may be wider issues involved. For example, many of the activities which crop up in negligence cases – transport, industry and medicine, for example – are activities which benefit society as a whole, but also necessarily carry risks. As the judge in **Daborn v Bath Tramways Motor Co. Ltd** (1946) put it:

> If all the trains in this country were restricted to a speed of five miles per hour, there would be fewer accidents, but our national life would be intolerably slowed down.

Thus it can be argued that those people who are injured as a result of such risks bear the brunt of the convenience and other benefits which the relevant activities provide for all members of society. It might therefore be appropriate for society to compensate such victims automatically, rather than making them jump through the hoops of negligence law.

This argument becomes even stronger when the harm suffered by the claimant directly results in a benefit to society, through better knowledge of possible risks. For example, in **Roe v Minister of Health** (1954) (see p. 518) it was only the injury caused to the claimant that revealed the danger of keeping ampoules of anaesthetic in disinfectant. Because the hospital could not have known of the risk beforehand, it was not liable. As a direct result of what happened, the hospital changed its procedures so that it could not happen to any future patients, but the patient whose suffering had caused this progress went uncompensated.

Critical theorists argue that since society benefits in all these cases, society should pay; this would require an acceptance that we have social, as well as individual responsibilities.

An economic solution?

It has been suggested that negligence should be assessed on the basis of an economic formula: if the likelihood of the injury, multiplied by its seriousness, exceeds the cost to the defendant of taking adequate precautions, the defendant would be liable. The rationale behind this approach is that finding negligence effectively transfers the loss from the claimant to the defendant, and for economic reasons, this should only happen where the cost of avoiding the accident is less than paying compensation for it.

While this approach may have practical attractions, it lacks any concept of disapproving the wrongdoer's conduct, and could also raise difficulties when it came to calculating (or guessing) the cost of preventing an accident.

Reading on the web

The House of Lords' judgment in **Bolitho** v **City and Hackney Health Authority** can be found on the House of Lords' judicial business website at:

http://www.publications.parliament.uk/pa/ld/ldjudgmt.htm#1997

Question and answer guides

1 'One of the purposes of the law of torts is said to be to encourage people to take care in what they do and to discourage activities that are dangerous to others.'

Do the rules that courts apply in determining the standard of care in negligence achieve this aim? *(Oxford)*

Answer guide

The first thing to notice here is that you are specifically asked to talk about the rules concerning the standard of care, so even though there is a lot of material on duty of care and the operation of negligence law in practice that is relevant to the issue of whether the law encourages care for the safety of others, in this essay you must stick to discussing the rules on the standard of care.

A good way to start would be to outline the basis of these rules: the standard of reasonableness; the objective approach; and the factors which the courts will weigh against each other to assess reasonableness. You can then go on to discuss each of these areas in more detail, stating how they operate to discourage dangerous behaviour, and highlighting any ways in which they fail to do this. As regards the objective standard, you could point to the fact that it can be vague, and in some cases unachievable. The case of **Nettleship** v **Weston** is relevant here, and in discussing it, you should talk about the implications of insurance in negligence cases: the standard of driving imposed in **Nettleship** may not discourage unsafe driving, since learner drivers are unlikely to be able to reach that standard, however hard they try, but what it does is to ensure that the financial risk is borne by the party who is insured and therefore able to pay. Similar comments apply to the rules on defendants whose conduct is affected by an infirmity over which they have no control, as in **Roberts** v **Ramsbottom**. You could contrast this with **Mansfield** v **Weetabix**, where the standard imposed seems more in keeping with the aim of promoting care, and yet its practical effect was to leave the injured claimant uncompensated, even though the defendant was insured.

In discussing the rules on special characteristics of the defendant, you should talk about the special rules for professionals, and in particular doctors. Discuss the criticisms made of **Bolam** v **Friern Barnet Hospital Management Committee**, and the idea that doctors are in effect allowed to set their own standard of care; how far can such rules effectively discourage medical negligence? Consider whether **Bolitho** v **City and Hackney Hospital Authority** is likely to make a significant difference.

You should also point out that the rules on practicality of protection mean that defendants are not required to eliminate risk, only to take reasonable precautions. The cases of **Latimer** v **AEC** and **Bolton** v **Stone** are relevant here.

To extend the coverage of your essay, you could discuss the fact that, in some cases, the law's emphasis on promoting care in individuals ignores the wider picture and can result in injustice to claimants. On the issue of risks unknown at the time when the defendant acted, you can point out that there is no liability for damage caused as a result of such risks, and this can be justified by the argument that defendants cannot be expected to take care to avoid risks which are not known by anyone to exist. You can then go on to explain that this approach can be unfair to the claimant, whose injury will often result in some advance in knowledge that benefits others (as in **Roe** v **Minister of Health**) yet remains uncompensated because of the law's focus on individual fault.

2 To what extent do the rules relating to causation and remoteness of damage achieve the aim of compensating the claimant for loss and injury? *(Oxford)*

Answer guide

A good way to begin this essay would be to explain that in tort not every injury or loss that is factually caused by someone else will result in that person being required to pay compensation. The law aims to strike a balance between ensuring fair compensation for claimants, and not imposing too harsh a burden on defendants, and the rules on causation and remoteness of damage are part of the legal framework which helps the courts to strike this balance.

The clearest structure then is to take the rules on causation first, moving on to remoteness of damage when you have finished causation. Explain that the basic rule is that claimants must satisfy the 'but for' test, and then go on to talk about the difficulties that cases involving multiple causes have created for the courts, and the variety of approaches taken to them. In discussing these approaches, you need to highlight which of them best fulfil the aim of compensating the claimant, and which have weaknesses in this area.

Go on to discuss the rules on intervening events, again looking at the different approaches, and which seem to serve the claimant's need for compensation best.

You can then turn to remoteness of damage. Talk about the original direct consequence test from **Re Polemis**, describing how this was thought to cause injustice to defendants, but was obviously useful to claimants, and then explain the current reasonable foreseeability test from **Wagon Mound (No. 1)**. You can consider how far the current test achieves the aim of compensating claimants. You might highlight the strange distinctions made using this test, comparing cases such as **Doughty** v **Turner** and **Hughes** v **Lord Advocate**; does the unpredictability such cases cause help claimants seeking compensation? You should also talk about the 'eggshell-skull' rule in personal injury and the apparently similar approach in economic loss cases, and the rule arising from **Wagon Mound (No. 2)**; how far do these rules promote the aim of compensation for the claimant?

3 Mr King and his son Augustus are both injured when their car is involved in a collision with a bus. The collision is caused by the bus driver's negligence. Augustus's hip is badly jarred. Mr King suffers severe spinal injuries. Both are rushed to St Crisp's Hospital where Mr King is left unattended for many hours. The staff X-ray Augustus's head but fail to examine his hip. As a result, Augustus is in much pain for several days, before his hip is finally X-rayed and a fracture identified. Subsequently, Augustus develops a weakness in his hip. The medical ▶

evidence indicates that such a weakness would occur in 80 per cent of patients injured in this way, but that the delay in treatment for the fracture made it virtually certain that the weakness would develop. As a result of the accident, Mr King is paralyzed from the waist down. The medical evidence indicates that this would have occurred even if he had been treated immediately for the injuries which he had sustained.

Advise Mr King and Augustus as to any potential claims they may have. *(Oxford, adapted)*

Answer guide

In problem questions concerning negligence, you should always remember the three elements of the tort: there must be a duty of care between claimant and defendant; breach of that duty of care; and damage to the claimant, which is caused by the defendant and within the rules on remoteness. Although questions rarely require you to look in detail at all these elements, keeping them in mind will help you structure your thoughts and make sure you leave nothing out.

Take the claim of each claimant in turn, dealing completely with each one's claim or claims before starting on the next. Starting with Mr King, there are two possible claims: against the bus driver and against the hospital staff (you should point out that in practice the parties sued would probably be the bus company and the hospital, since they are likely to have vicarious liability for their staff).

As regards the claim against the bus company, we know that drivers owe a duty of care to other road users, and we are told that his driving was negligent, so we know he has fallen below the standard of care; therefore, the issue here seems to be causation and remoteness of damage. Which aspects of the damage caused to Mr King will the bus company be liable for? Clearly personal injury is a foreseeable result of such a crash, so the company will be liable for Mr King's spinal injury. Is it also liable for the paralysis? Here you have to consider whether the failure to treat him immediately is an intervening act, breaking the chain of causation: the medical evidence that the paralysis would have happened anyway shows that the chain of causation was not broken, and so the bus company will be liable for the paralysis too.

As regards the hospital's liability to Mr King, we know that hospital staff have a duty of care towards patients, but we do not know whether the time taken to treat his injuries would fall below the standard of care. Where you are not given enough information to judge a particular issue, it is perfectly reasonable to say so, and you can earn yourself marks if you say what information would help you come to a decision: in this case, you can point to the rule in **Bolam** (and the modification in **Bolitho**) and say that Mr King would have to show that what happened was not in line with the practice followed by a responsible body of doctors. However, you should point out that in fact we do not need this information, since the claim would clearly fail on causation: it cannot be said that but for the hospital's failure to treat him quickly the paralysis would not have happened, so they will have no liability towards him.

Augustus's situation is more complicated, and again, the best way to treat it is by taking each possible claim in turn. Starting with the bus company, we have already dealt with duty of care and breach of duty; once again, the issue is causation and remoteness of damage. Clearly the bus company is liable for Augustus's fractured hip, because personal injury was reasonably foreseeable; is it also liable for the weakness he later develops, or was this caused by the delay in treatment? You should point out that the courts have taken a variety of approaches to this issue; where this is the case, it is a good idea to explore each of the possible approaches and say how each would apply to the facts of the problem. If we take the approach in **Hotson** v **East Berkshire Health Authority**, the question to be asked is whether there was at least a 51 per cent chance of developing the weakness as a result of the accident, and we are told that there was an 80 per cent chance. Under the **Hotson** principle, therefore, the bus company would be liable to Augustus for all his injuries. If we look at the test laid down in **McGhee** v **National Coal Board**, the result is the same: clearly the accident did make a substantial contribution to the injury, even though the hospital's failure to give the right treatment increased it. The situation also satisfies the test in **Wilsher** v **Essex Area Health Authority**, so it seems fairly clear that the bus company is liable for both the hip fracture and the weakness. (You might wonder at this stage why we are looking at the cases on multiple causes, rather than treating the hospital's lack of care as an intervening event. The distinction can be difficult, but where, as here, the hospital has increased the risk, its conduct merely increases the risk of the same injury which the original accident caused; an intervening event usually introduces a new risk or injury. If, for example, Augustus had been given the wrong drugs in hospital and suffered a heart attack, the correct cases to consider would be those on intervening events.)

We know then that Augustus has a claim against the bus company for all his injuries, but it is still worth considering whether the hospital has any liability towards him. It is possible for two or more parties to be liable for the same injury or damage, and in that case, the claimant can sue either of them, though he or she cannot get damages twice for the same injury (this would probably not be necessary here, but might be useful if, for example, the accident had been caused by a hit-and-run driver, who could not be found and sued). The hospital is clearly not liable for the hip fracture, but does it have any liability for the hip weakness? Clearly we cannot say that but for the hospital's lack of care the weakness would not have happened, so we have to look at the cases on multiple causes again. Here Augustus's best argument would be **McGhee**, because he could argue that increasing the risk from 80 per cent to virtually certain amounts to making a substantial contribution to the injury; without the hospital's negligence, he had a 20 per cent chance of not developing hip weakness, but after its negligence, he had almost no chance. By contrast, **Wilsher** offers little hope for Augustus, because it says that the fact that a defendant's negligence has increased the risk of damage is not sufficient. Nor is **Hotson** helpful to Augustus, because we know there is a less than 51 per cent chance that the hospital's negligence caused the damage. In cases like this, where different authorities suggest different answers to the problem, it is worth mentioning any aspects of the problem that lead you to think a court would prefer one approach over another, but you are not required to *know* which view they would take; all you have to do is show you know what cases they could follow, and how the principles in those cases apply to the facts before you.

4 Alan is a professional lorry driver. He was driving on the motorway just after dawn one summer morning when he fell asleep. As a result, his lorry crashed into a taxi that had broken down and was parked on the hard shoulder. Fortunately the taxi driver, Bella, was not injured as she was calling for help from an emergency telephone some distance away. However, her taxi was completely destroyed. Alan was very fortunate not to be injured.

Carol lives in a house near the motorway. She heard the sound of the crash involving Alan and set off, with her binoculars, towards the crash scene so she could get a better look. On the way to the motorway, she fell into a ditch and broke her arm.

(a) Bella and Carol are considering suing Alan for negligence and their solicitors have mentioned to them the requirements of duty, breach and damage.

(i) Taking these into account, discuss Alan's liability to Bella for negligence. *(20 marks)*

(ii) Briefly discuss whether or not Alan owes Carol a duty of care. You may refer to the relevant part(s) of your answer to Question 2(a)(i). *(5 marks)*

(b) Assuming Alan is found liable in negligence to Bella, explain how the court would calculate the damages to be awarded to her. *(10 marks)*

▶

Answer guide

(a) (i) Here you should explain the three elements which will be required if Alan is to be found liable for negligence: a duty of care, breach of that duty, and damaged caused by the breach. The test for a duty of care depends on the kind of damage caused, so you should explain that the damage Bella has suffered would be classified as damage to property. This means that the test for whether Alan owes her a duty of care is the neighbour test as defined in **Caparo** v **Dickman**. Explain the test, point out how it applies to the facts. Then look at whether Alan has breached his duty, referring to the objective standard of care as explained in **Nettleship**. You should point out that as Alan is a professional lorry driver, he will be expected to meet the standards of a competent person in the same job, as explained in cases such as **Vowles v Evans** and **Gates v McKenna**. The issues of damage and causation of that damage are clear, so you need only refer to them in passing.

(ii) The damage here is personal injury, so you can refer back to the test for duty of care in cases of damage to property that you explained in the previous section, as it is the same for personal injury. You should then use cases to explain whether or not you think this test is met in the case of Carol. The issues of foreseeability and proximity are important here.

(b) The law required to answer this part of the question is examined in the next chapter. Note that Bella did not suffer any personal injury. You needed to discuss the distinction between general and special damages. Damages might be available for loss of amenity, loss of earnings and for general expenses incurred, including the cost of replacing the car. You should consider the fact that Bella has an obligation to mitigate her loss.

Chapter summary

Negligence was first recognized in the 1932 case of **Donoghue** v **Stevenson**, and concerns breach of a legal duty to take care, with the result that damage is caused to the claimant. The tort of negligence comprises three elements: a duty of care, breach of that duty and damage resulting from the breach.

The duty of care

The duty of care is a legal concept which dictates the circumstances in which one party will be liable to another in negligence. A person is only liable in negligence if he or she owes a duty of care.

The neighbour principle

Lord Atkin stated in **Donoghue** v **Stevenson** that 'You must take reasonable care to avoid acts or omissions which you can reasonably foresee would be likely to injure your neighbour.' For these purposes my neighbours are 'persons who are so closely and directly affected by my act that I ought to have them in contemplation as being so affected when I am directing my mind to the acts or omissions which are called in question'.

Breach of a duty of care

Breach of a duty of care essentially means that the defendant has fallen below the standards of behaviour expected in someone undertaking the activity concerned. As the test is objective, the particular defendant's own characteristics are usually ignored.

The standard of reasonableness

The standard of care in negligence never amounts to an absolute duty to prevent harm to others. Instead, it sets a standard of reasonableness: if a duty of care exists between two parties, the duty is to do whatever a reasonable person would do to prevent harm from occurring, not to do absolutely anything and everything possible to prevent harm.

Special characteristics of the defendant

The law will take into account certain special characteristics of the defendant. For example, where the defendant is a child, the standard of care is that of an ordinarily careful and reasonable child of the same age.

Special characteristics of the claimant

A reasonable person would have due regard to the fact that a claimant has some characteristic or incapacity which increases the risk of harm.

Magnitude of the risk

The greater the risk of harm the more likely that a court will find that the duty of care has been breached.

Practicality of protection

The magnitude of the risk must be balanced against the cost and trouble to the defendant of taking the measures necessary to eliminate it.

Common practice

In deciding whether the precautions taken by the defendant (if any) are reasonable, the courts may look at the general practice in the relevant field.

Potential benefits of the risk

Some risks have potential benefits for society, and these must be weighed against the possible damage if the risk is taken.

Damage

The negligence must cause damage. If no damage is caused, there is no claim in negligence, no matter how careless the defendant's conduct.

Causation

In order to establish negligence, it must be proved that the defendant's breach of duty actually caused the damage suffered by the claimant, and that the damage caused was not too remote from the breach.

The 'but for' test

Causation is established by proving that the defendant's breach of duty was, as a matter of fact, a cause of the damage. To decide this issue the first question to be asked is whether ▶

the damage would not have occurred but for the breach of duty: this is known as the 'but for' test.

Remoteness of damage

The claimant must prove that the damage was not too remote from the defendant's breach. The test of remoteness currently applied is whether the kind of damage suffered by the claimant was reasonably foreseeable at the time of the breach of duty. This test was laid down in the **Wagon Mound (No. 1)** case.

Type of damage

Under the remoteness of damage test, a defendant will only be liable if it was reasonable to foresee the type of damage that in fact occurred.

Extent of damage

So long as the type of damage sustained is reasonably foreseeable, it does not matter that it is in fact more serious than could reasonably have been foreseen. Under the 'eggshell-skull' rule defendants will be liable even if the reason for the damage being more serious than could be expected is due to some weakness or infirmity in the claimant.

Risk of damage

So long as the type of damage is foreseeable, it will not be too remote, even if the chances of it happening were slim. This principle was laid down in **Wagon Mound (No. 2)**.

Intervening events

An intervening event will only make damage too remote if the event itself was unforeseeable.

Proving negligence

The claimant normally has the burden of proof in relation to proving negligence, which can be a considerable obstacle for a claimant. However, there are two exceptions to this rule: where the defendant has a criminal conviction related to the incident in question, and where the principle of *res ipsa loquitur* applies.

The defence of contributory negligence

The Law Reform (Contributory Negligence) Act 1945 provides that where a person is partly responsible for the harm done to him or her, the defence of contributory negligence may apply. Where this defence applies, damages can be reduced to take account of the fact that the fault was not entirely the defendant's.

Chapter 25

Remedies for torts

A person who is the victim of a tort may seek a remedy from the courts. The principal remedy awarded by a court for a tortious wrong is damages. Damages aim to compensate the claimant financially for the tort they have suffered.

Damages

In the vast majority of cases where damages are claimed they are what is known as compensatory (there are some types of non-compensatory damages, which are discussed at p. 571). The principle behind compensatory damages is that they should put the claimant in the position they would have been in if the tort had never been committed. An award of compensatory damages may be composed of either general or special damages, or both. General damages are designed to compensate for the kinds of damages which the law presumes to be a result of the tort, such as pain and suffering from a personal injury, and loss of future earnings where the claimant's injuries mean that he or she cannot return to a previous employment or cannot work at all. Obviously, the amount of such damages cannot be calculated precisely, but the courts use the awards given for similar injuries in the past as a guideline.

Special damages are those which do not arise naturally from the wrong complained of, and must be specifically listed in pleadings, and proved in court. They generally cover the claimant's financial loss up until the date of trial, and any expenses incurred up to that point, and are therefore susceptible of more exact calculation.

Calculating compensatory damages

The principle of restoring the claimant to the position they would have held if the tort had not been committed is called *restitutio in integrum*. There are essentially two different sorts of losses: pecuniary, which simply means financial, and non-pecuniary, which means losses other than those of money. Examples of pecuniary losses would be loss of earnings as a result of an injury, or a house being worth less than you paid for it because your surveyor negligently failed to spot defects in it. Non-pecuniary losses include pain and suffering after an injury, and what is called loss of amenity (see p. 548). They are usually seen in connection with personal injury cases, and rarely arise in cases concerning money or property, but in **Farley** *v* **Skinner** (2001), damages were given for non-pecuniary losses. The claimant had asked the defendant, a surveyor, to prepare a report on a home he was thinking of buying. Because of where the house was, the claimant was worried that it might be affected by aircraft noise, and he specifically asked the surveyor to check this out. The surveyor negligently reported that it was very unlikely that aircraft noise would be a problem. The claimant bought the house, spent a lot of money on doing it up, then moved in – and discovered that in fact there was a very severe problem with aircraft noise. He decided not to move, but claimed damages from the surveyor.

The House of Lords held that the whole purpose of the claimant in choosing the house had been to buy a place where he could enjoy peace and quiet, and if the surveyor had reported correctly, he would not have bought it. That being the case, the claimant was awarded £10,000 damages.

Pecuniary damages are clearly easier to calculate than non-pecuniary ones, since the claimant's loss can be measured in money. Even so, there are cases where the loss is purely financial, but the issue of what will amount to *restitutio in integrum* is not straightforward. In **Gardner** *v* **Marsh & Parsons** (1997), the claimants had bought a leasehold flat after having it surveyed by the defendants. The surveyors were negligent, failing to discover a serious structural defect, which did not come to light for three years. The lease contained a clause making the freeholder responsible for structural repairs, and the freeholder eventually repaired the defect, but not until two years later. The claimants sued the surveyors for negligence, claiming the difference between the price they paid, and the lower market value of the flat with the defect, but the surveyors claimed that no damages were required since the defect had been repaired, albeit not by them, and there was no loss.

The Court of Appeal disagreed, stating that loss could not be avoided by a claimant's own actions, unless those actions flowed from the original transaction between the parties and were really part of a continuous course of dealing arising from it. In this case the claimants were only able to put right the problem because they had a contract with the freeholder, and even then they had had to go to the trouble of hassling the freeholder to do the repairs; they had also waited a long time for them to be done, during which time they could not sell the flat. The means by which they solved the problem were too remote to be taken into account when deciding the defendants' liability.

In **South Australia Asset Management Corporation** *v* **York Montague Ltd** (1996), the House of Lords heard three appeals, each arising from similar facts: the defendants had each negligently valued a property, and the claimants lent money for the purchase of the property on the strength of those valuations. Soon afterwards, property prices dropped, and the borrowers in each case defaulted on the loan, leaving the lenders with a property worth less than the money they were owed on it. Each of the lenders gave evidence that they would not have granted the loans if they had known the true value of the property, and claimed that their damages should therefore include the loss that they had made through the general drop in property prices, since if they had not made the loan, they would not have made that loss either. For our purposes, the details of one of the cases is sufficient: here the lenders lent £1.75 million on a property that was valued at £2.5 million, but was actually worth £1.8 million. By the time the property market had dropped, it was worth only £950,000.

The Court of Appeal analyzed the cases on the basis of whether the loans would have been granted if the true valuations had been known, and said that where the lenders would not have gone ahead with the loans had it not been for the negligent valuation, the lenders were entitled to recover the difference between the sum lent and the sum recovered when the property was sold, together with a reasonable rate of interest, so that they would be compensated for the drop in market prices. Where a lender would still have gone ahead with the loan even if the correct valuation had been given, but lent a smaller sum, the lender would only be able to recover the difference between what it actually lost and what it would have lost had it lent a lesser amount; any fall in the market could not be compensated.

The House of Lords rejected this argument. Their Lordships said that in order to calculate damages for breach of a duty of care, it was first necessary to determine exactly what the duty consisted of; a defendant would only be liable for consequences arising from negligent performance of that duty. In this case, the defendants did not have a duty to advise the claimants whether or not to make the loan; their duty was to inform the claimants of the value of the property offered as security, and so their liability was limited to the consequences of that advice being wrong, and not to the entire consequences of the loan being made. The consequence of the advice being wrong was that the claimants had less security for the debt than they thought, and that loss should be compensated; in the case detailed above, the correct figure would be £700,000. This would give the claimants the amount of security they thought they had at the time the loan was made, but would not compensate for the drop in property prices, since this was not a consequence of the negligent valuation but would have happened anyway. If the defendants had had a duty to advise the claimants whether or not to make the loan, they would have been liable for all losses arising from the fact that the loan was made, including the drop in property prices, but here their duty did not extend that far so their liability could not either.

In a case with similar facts, **Platform Home Loans Ltd** v **Oyston Shipways Ltd** (1999), the House of Lords held that where part of the loss was due to the claimants' own negligence in making the loan in the first place without adequately assessing the borrower's ability to repay it, the damages could be reduced for contributory negligence.

The main difficulty with applying the principle established in **South Australia** is how the courts identify the duty that was owed. Sometimes this will be obvious, but the case of **Aneco Reinsurance Underwriting Ltd** v **Johnson and Higgins Ltd** (2002) illustrates how complex this question can be. The case concerned a practice common in the insurance industry, called reinsurance. Where an insurer gives cover for a particular risk, they will often seek to protect themselves by reinsuring the same risk, or part of it, with another insurer, so that if the worst happens and the client claims on the insurance, the insurer will get some of their money back by claiming on their reinsurance. The claimants, Aneco, had been asked to provide insurance for a company we will call B. They were happy to do so, but wanted to reinsure part of the risk, and asked the defendants to arrange this for them. Believing this to have been done, they went ahead and issued the policy to B. B later claimed £35 million on the policy, and Aneco then sought to recover some of this under their reinsurance: the policy they believed had been arranged would have given them £11 million. In fact there was no reinsurance cover, due to the defendants' negligence.

The question then arose of how much they could claim in damages. The defendants claimed that, under the principle established in **South Australia**, their duty to Aneco was to ensure that, if B claimed on their insurance policy, Aneco could reduce their own losses by £11 million, by claiming on the reinsurance. They therefore maintained that the damages owed would be £11 million. Aneco, however, sought to claim the whole £35 million. Their reasoning was that when a company seeks reinsurance, they are looking not just for actual cover, but for an impression of how the insurance industry sees the risk in question; if it proves impossible to get reinsurance for a certain risk, it is very probably unwise to offer insurance for it yourself. They argued that, had Johnson and Higgins taken reasonable steps to arrange the reinsurance cover, they would have discovered that no one was willing to provide it, and had they told Aneco that it was proving impossible to reinsure the risk, Aneco themselves would not have gone ahead with the insurance policy, and would never have had to pay out £35 million.

The House of Lords agreed with Aneco, stating that in agreeing to arrange reinsurance, the defendants owed Aneco a duty to advise on the availability of such cover, and in failing to do so they had breached that duty, and were liable to pay the full £35 million. Unfortunately, the House of Lords did not give any guidance as to quite how the extent or content of a duty is to be decided, which makes it very difficult to predict how the principle will be applied in future cases.

Preventing overcompensation

The fact that compensatory damages are designed to put the claimant in the position they would have enjoyed had the tort not happened does not just mean they should not end up worse off as a result of the tort; it also means that they should not end up better off than they would otherwise have been. In **Southampton Container Terminals Ltd** *v* **Schiffarts-Gesellschaft Hansa Australia MBH & Co.** (2001), the defendants' ship collided with the quayside in Southampton, and destroyed the claimants' crane. The defendants admitted liability and the judge awarded the claimants the amount which the crane would have been worth if the claimants had sold it. The claimants appealed, arguing that the principle of *restitutio in integrum* meant they were entitled to the much higher cost of replacing the crane, including transport and installation costs. However, the Court of Appeal found that there was no evidence that the claimants had actually intended to replace the crane, and that its loss had caused inconvenience, but no serious financial loss. The court said that the overriding principle had to be that damages should be reasonable between the parties, and in this case allowing the appeal would result in compensation that was out of all proportion to the loss.

Similarly, although the courts will order compensation for special expenses which the claimant has reasonably incurred as a result of the tort, they will not compensate for expenses which he or she would have faced anyway.

In **Patel** *v* **Hooper & Jackson** (1998), the Court of Appeal allowed the buyer of a residential property who was unable to live in it as a result of a negligent survey to claim the cost of alternative accommodation up until such time as the house could reasonably be expected to have been sold, as well as the difference between the true value of the house and the price paid as a result of the negligent survey. The court held that in the circumstances the cost of alternative accommodation was part of the reasonable cost of the buyer extricating himself from the purchase.

Where loss is non-pecuniary (such as pain and suffering), *restitutio in integrum* is even more difficult, and the general aim is to provide fair and reasonable compensation for the damage done, taking into account all the circumstances. In each case, the exact calculation of damages is a question of fact, and the judge has discretion over whether to allow counsel to refer to decisions in previous similar cases. In practice, such references are frequent.

An (admittedly extreme) example of the difficult questions that can be faced in deciding just how to compensate for a non-pecuniary loss can be seen in **Briody** *v* **St Helen's and Knowsley Area Health Authority** (2001). Medical negligence by the defendant's employee had left the claimant unable to get pregnant naturally. Awards to cover infertility treatment such as *in vitro* fertilization (IVF) had been made in previous cases, but the claimant's condition was such that she could not be helped by such treatments, so she sought damages to cover the cost of a surrogacy procedure, in which an embryo created from the claimant's egg and her partner's sperm would be implanted into a surrogate mother. The agreement arranging this procedure was illegal in England, and was to be carried out in America, though there was evidence that the chances of it working were very small. An alternative option was a procedure that was legal in England, but involved using donor eggs from another woman, rather than the claimant's own; this was said to have a slightly higher chance of success.

The Court of Appeal ruled that damages could not be awarded to cover either option. They agreed that for a woman who wanted children, being deprived of the chance to have them was a very serious loss of amenity, which entitled the claimant to damages for that loss, over and above the pain and suffering arising from her injuries. However, they said that because there was such a slim chance of the first procedure working, it was very different from a claim for IVF treatment, which would usually offer a reasonable chance of success. It was not reasonable to expect the defendant to pay the costs of a treatment which was in fact very unlikely to compensate the claimant's loss. As for the second procedure, since this would not, even if it worked, produce a child that was biologically the claimant's own, the court said that it would not represent *restitutio in integrum*, and would in fact be little different from adoption. This seems rather odd reasoning, given that the claimant herself clearly viewed a baby from a donor egg as some compensation for the inability to have her own child.

▌Mitigation

A person who falls victim to a tort is expected to take reasonable steps to mitigate any loss; the defendant will not be liable for compensatory damages in respect of any losses that could have been prevented by such steps. However, since the situation is the fault of the defendant, not the claimant, the standard of reasonableness is not particularly high, and the claimant is certainly not required to make huge efforts to avoid a loss that is the defendant's fault.

In **Emeh** *v* **Kensington Area Health Authority** (1982), the claimant underwent a sterilization operation carried out by the defendants' employees, but afterwards became pregnant. The defendants rather bizarrely argued that she could have mitigated her financial loss by having an abortion, thereby saving the cost of bringing up the child. Rejecting this argument, the court accepted that in the circumstances it was reasonable to refuse to have an abortion.

Compensation for personal injury

Damages for personal injury (which covers physical or psychiatric harm, disease and illness) raise problems not encountered with other types of loss. In the case of damage to property, for example, financial compensation is both easy to calculate, and an adequate way of making good the loss, by allowing the claimant to buy a replacement or pay for repairs. It is not so easy to calculate the value of a lost limb or permanent loss of general good health, and even if it were, money can never really compensate for such losses. In addition, the court may be required to estimate the amount of future earnings which will be lost, and the future development of the injury; even though personal injury cases may take years to come to trial, the degree of recovery to be expected may still be unclear, and new symptoms may not appear until years later.

Damages for personal injury are divided into pecuniary and non-pecuniary losses. Pecuniary damages are those which can be calculated in financial terms, such as loss of earnings, and medical and other expenses, while non-pecuniary damages cover damages that are less easy to calculate, such as loss of physical amenity, pain, shock and suffering. Within these two broad categories, the courts have defined the following 'heads of damage'.

Pecuniary losses

Pre-trial expenses

The claimant is entitled to recover all expenses actually and reasonably incurred as a result of the accident up to the date of the trial. This includes, for example, loss of, or damage to, clothing and any medical expenses.

Expenses incurred by another

In some cases the claimant will have had to be looked after by a friend or relative. Such carers cannot bring an action themselves directly against the defendant to seek compensation. But in **Donnelly** v **Joyce** (1972) the Court of Appeal recognized that the claimant could normally claim for this loss as part of his or her own claim. In that case the claimant was a child and his mother had to give up work to look after him when he was seriously injured by the defendant's negligence. The claimant succeeded in claiming for the financial loss that his mother had suffered as a result of caring for him.

This principle was extended to cover a slightly more complicated situation in **Lowe** *v* **Guise** (2002). Here, the claimant had been acting as a carer to his disabled brother, for around 77 hours a week. After being injured as a result of the defendant's negligence, he was only able to help his brother for around half that time, and their mother had to take over for the remainder of the time. There was no financial loss as a result of this arrangement, but Mr Lowe nevertheless claimed the value of the services provided to his brother by his mother as part of the amount required to compensate him for his injuries. The court agreed, holding that the help he had been giving his brother was not just a favour, it was a serious responsibility owed by him to his family. Loss of part of it was therefore the loss of something of real value to himself and to his family's welfare, and should be compensated.

The House of Lords decided in **Hunt** *v* **Severs** (1994) that any damages received under this head are awarded to the claimant to compensate the carer and not the claimant. When the claimant received this award he or she should hand the money over to the carer and until he or she did so the money was held under an obligation to do so, known as being held on trust. On this point the House of Lords reversed **Donnelly** *v* **Joyce**, which had viewed such an award as being to compensate the claimant's loss and therefore placing him or her under no legal obligation to hand it over to the carer.

In **Hunt** *v* **Severs** the claimant was the defendant's girlfriend. She was riding on the back of his motorbike when they had an accident and she was seriously injured. On leaving the hospital she started to live with the defendant and they married three years later. At the trial the defendant admitted liability. The claimant claimed £77,000 as the value of the care that the defendant had given her and would give her in future. The trial judge had awarded this amount but the appeal was allowed by the House of Lords, because once it was accepted that the award was made to compensate the carer, it made no sense to make such an award if the carer was also the defendant, for he would be merely making a payment to himself. The fact that in reality it is not the defendant's money but the insurance company's money is traditionally ignored by the court.

This conclusion runs counter to the approach preferred by the Pearson Commission (see p. 574), which argued that damages should be the absolute property of the claimant. The Commission pointed out that any duty to hand some of it over to someone else, such as a carer, would be extremely difficult to supervise. It might also constitute an incentive for members of a family not to help each other but to employ people from outside the family to care for their relations.

Where a spouse provides services in a business context, the courts have decided that there must be an actual loss before the claimant can claim for the cost of the services. In **Hardwick** *v* **Hudson** (1999), the claimant was injured in a car accident. He was a partner in a garage business, and while he was recovering, his wife took over his role at work, without being paid. The claimant argued that this was comparable to carer services supplied free by a relative, but the Court of Appeal disagreed. The claimant's wife was supplying services which the business would otherwise have had to pay for, and in doing that, she could be seen as providing a benefit to the business and actually preventing the claimant from suffering the loss he would have done if he had paid someone to do the work. In fact the couple would have been better off if the wife had been properly employed and paid by the business, under an express or implied contract, as then there would have been a loss and, the court said, the claimant could have sought to recover this from the defendant.

The same principle applies to other benefits provided by third parties. In **Dimond v Lovell** (1999), the claimant was involved in an accident for which the defendant was responsible, and as a result, she had to hire a car. Due to irregularities with the hire contract, it was held to be unenforceable and she ended up not having to pay the hire charges, but she attempted to claim them from the defendant anyway, on the basis that she had had to hire the car because of his negligence. The court compared the situation to that in cases where care was provided free by, for example, a partner, as in **Hunt v Severs**, and held that the same rule applied. Where claimants have received services from a third party at no cost to themselves, the court can award damages to be held in trust for that third party – but where it is not possible to impose a trust for the third party, the damages cannot be awarded to claimants instead. In this case, imposing a trust for the benefit of the car-hire company would have amounted to enforcing an unenforceable contract, and the court could not impose a trust for this purpose.

Pre-trial loss of earnings

The claimant can receive damages for the loss of the earnings or profits which would otherwise have been earned up to the date of the judgment. The amount awarded will be that which the claimant would actually have taken home, after tax and National Insurance contributions have been deducted. Both pre-trial expenses and pre-trial loss of earnings are considered to be special damages.

Future loss of earnings

Claims for future pecuniary loss almost always comprise loss of future earnings, and are regarded as general damages. Obviously they are difficult to calculate, since there is no real way of knowing what the future would have held for the claimant if the accident had not happened.

Damages are usually awarded as a lump sum, but obviously the purpose of damages for loss of future earnings due to personal injury is usually to give the claimant an income to replace the one he or she would have had if the injury had not happened. The courts therefore calculate a figure which, given as a lump sum, would be sufficient to buy an investment called an annuity that would give the claimant the right level of income for life, or however long the effects of the injury were expected to last (an annuity is an arrangement under which a lump sum is invested so as to produce an income).

The starting point for calculating future loss of earnings is the difference between income before the accident and afterwards, which is called the net annual loss. Obviously in some cases the claimant may be so badly injured that no income can be earned, but the principle also covers those who can work, but at less highly paid employment than before. Predicting future earnings can be a matter of guesswork, as the case of **Doyle** *v* **Wallace** (1998) shows. In this case the claimant was badly injured in a road accident and was unable to work. She had been planning to train as a drama teacher if she could get the necessary qualifications, and if not, she planned to get a clerical job. Her income would have been substantially higher as a teacher than as a clerk, but at the time of the accident, it was too early to know whether she would have obtained the necessary qualifications. The trial judge found that she had a 50 per cent chance of qualifying as a drama teacher, and calculated the damages for loss of future earnings on the basis of an income that was halfway between that of a drama teacher and that of a clerical worker. The Court of Appeal upheld this approach.

Another example of the kind of complications courts can face in 'loss of a chance' cases can be seen in **Langford** *v* **Hebran** (2001). Here, the claimant, then 27, had just started training to be a bricklayer, but was also a competitive kickboxer, and had recently won his first (and only) professional fight. After being injured in a car accident caused by the defendant's negligence, he was no longer able to do his job, or his sport, to the same standard. He claimed that, had he not been injured, he would have gone on to become a champion kickboxer, which meant that the court had to assess just how far the claimant was likely to go in his sport. The Court of Appeal, with the help of expert evidence, found that there were four possible levels of success which the claimant could have reached, ranging from holding one national title, to becoming world champion. They then had to assess the chances of him reaching each stage, and decide what that would have been worth to him financially.

The loss of a chance approach is generally used in cases where there is a fairly high degree of uncertainty as to whether the claimant's financial prospects would have improved if the accident had not happened; where it is fairly obvious that they would have improved, there is no need for loss of a chance calculations. In **Herring** *v* **Ministry of Defence** (2004), a part-time soldier was badly injured during a parachute jump. He had intended to apply to join the police force, and therefore claimed damages for loss of future earnings on the basis of the typical police officer's salary. The defendants argued that, as it was not clear whether he would have been accepted into the police force, the claim should be assessed on the basis of loss of a chance, but the Court of Appeal disagreed. On the evidence, it was clear that, even if the claimant had not got into the police force, he would have got a job with similar earning power. His damages could therefore be calculated on the basis of a police officer's salary, with a small reduction for what are called the 'vicissitudes of life' (see below).

Once the court has the net annual loss figure, it adjusts that sum to take into account factors which might have altered the claimant's original earnings, such as promotion prospects, and the figure that they reach as a result of doing so is called the multiplicand. The court then takes the number of years that the disability is likely to continue, and reduces this number by taking into account what are called the 'contingencies (or vicissitudes) of life' – basically, the fact that even if the accident had not happened, the claimant might not have lived or worked until retirement age.

At this stage, a court has before it the annual amount that will compensate the claimant, and the number of years for which this amount should be payable.

However, simply to multiply the first figure by the second would actually overcompensate the claimant. If we take, for example, an annual loss of £10,000, to be payable over 20 years, simple multiplication of these figures gives us £200,000. But a claimant does not actually need a lump sum of £200,000 to produce an annual income of £10,000 over 20 years, because the assumption is that the lump sum is invested, and so makes more money during the 20 years, with the result that the claimant would end up overcompensated. To avoid this, the court assumes that the investment will earn a particular rate of return (called the discount rate), and reduces the lump sum to one which, on the basis of the assumed rate of return, will provide the right rate of compensation, nothing more and nothing less. The sum arrived at is called the multiplier, and the multiplicand multiplied by the multiplier gives the sum necessary to compensate the claimant for loss of future earnings.

Within these calculations, the rate of return on investments that the court assumes is very important – the higher the assumed rate of return, the smaller the lump sum, and if for some reason the claimant is unable in practice to achieve this rate of return on his or her investments, the claimant will be undercompensated.

Until recently, the courts generally assumed a rate of interest of 4–5 per cent per year. This practice was criticized by, among others, the Law Commission in its 1995 report *Structured Settlements and Interim and Provisional Damages* (Law Com. No. 224). It said that the assumed rate of interest was an arbitrary figure; it was possible to achieve this rate of interest, but only with a relatively sophisticated understanding of investments which few claimants would possess, and so many claimants were likely to end up undercompensated. The Commission recommended that the courts should use as their guideline the return given to investors on a type of investment called an Index Linked Government Security (ILGS), which would give a more accurate picture of the kind of returns claimants could hope to get on their lump sums. The practical effect of this would be that multipliers would go up and so, as a result, would damages.

The Damages Act 1996 responded to this recommendation by providing that the Lord Chancellor can prescribe a rate of interest for the purposes of calculating multipliers, and in June 2001, the rate was set at 2.5 per cent. To appreciate how important the precise figure is, it might help to know that if you take a 20-year-old man who is awarded a multiplicand of £70,000, the difference in damages paid between a discount rate of 2 per cent and one of 2.5 per cent would be £225,400.

The Damages Act provides, in s. 1(2), that a court may use a different discount rate 'if any party to the proceedings shows that it is more appropriate to the question'. An attempt to make use of this provision was made in **Warriner** *v* **Warriner** (2002). The claimant had suffered serious brain damage in a road accident and was claiming damages of over £2 million. He wanted to put forward expert evidence to show that a different discount rate should be used, because the amount claimed was large and the claimant's life expectancy was long; it was claimed that the effect of a 2.5 per cent discount rate in this situation would be to undercompensate the claimant. The Court of Appeal refused to hear the evidence, stating that this was not the kind of circumstance intended to be covered by s. 1(2).

They held that the Lord Chancellor had given very careful consideration to setting the discount rate, and that the certainty offered by a set rate was extremely important.

This being the case, the court said that a case could only activate the discretion allowed in s. 1(2) if there was material that supported changing the rate of return, and the Lord Chancellor had not considered that material when setting the rate. That was not the case here: the Lord Chancellor had considered the problems raised by large sums intended to cover long periods and allowed for them when setting the rate; the set rate assumed a relatively low level of investment performance, and in practice, claimants could do better, with prudent investing, and so even out the problem of undercompensation.

In **Cooke *v* United Bristol Healthcare NHS Trust; Sheppard *v* Stibbe; Page *v* Lee** (2003), the Court of Appeal heard three similar cases in which the claimants had all been very severely injured and were likely to need care for the rest of their lives. They argued that, in their circumstances, using the conventional method of assessing damages with the discount rate would leave them substantially undercompensated, because although the discount rate took into account the effects of inflation, the costs of care were increasing at a much faster rate than that of inflation. The Court of Appeal held that it was not possible to take evidence of this into account; Parliament had authorized the Lord Chancellor to set the rate, he had done so, taking inflation into account, and the courts had to respect that.

Non-pecuniary losses

These are losses which are not financial, although the courts can only compensate for them in a financial way. They do this by reference to guidelines produced by the Judicial Studies Board, based on awards in previous cases. The Law Commission's 1995 Report No. 225, *How Much is Enough?*, argued that compensation paid for these losses had fallen behind inflation and should be substantially increased. The Commission suggested that there was no real problem with the very smallest awards, those currently under £2,000, but that above that, claimants were being undercompensated.

In **Heil *v* Rankin** (2000), the House of Lords took the opportunity to look into this claim and agreed with the Law Commission that there was a problem. However, it was held that only those awards currently worth £10,000 or more needed adjustment, with the biggest problem being at the very top end of the scale, with the compensation for what the House of Lords called 'catastrophic injuries'. Where previously £150,000 had been regarded as the top level, this should be raised to £200,000; below that, there should be a tapering scale of increases down to awards of £10,000 or less, which would stay at current levels.

Non-pecuniary losses fall into the following heads of damage.

The primary injury

Damages for the actual injury are usually calculated with reference to a tariff, so that recognized values are placed on similar injuries. For example, minor or temporary eye injuries are 'worth' £1,000–£2,500, a broken leg £4,000–£7,000, lung disease £1,000–£65,000, and quadriplegia £160,000–£200,000. For most sorts of injuries there is a broad range within which damages can fall, allowing courts to take into account factors such as the seriousness of the injury, and how long the effects are likely to last.

Pain and suffering

Damages will be awarded for any pain and suffering which results from the injury itself, or from medical treatment of that injury. The claim may cover pain which the claimant can expect to suffer in the future, and mental suffering arising from the knowledge that life expectancy has been shortened or that the ability to enjoy life has been reduced by disability resulting from the injury.

Where the injury has caused a period of unconsciousness, that period will be excluded from any claim for pain and suffering, as it is assumed that an unconscious person is unaware of pain.

Loss of amenity

Loss of amenity describes the situation where an injury results in the claimant being unable to enjoy life to the same extent as before. It may include an inability to enjoy sport or any other pastime the claimant enjoyed before the injury, impairment of sight, hearing, touch, taste or smell, reduction in the chance of finding a marriage partner, and impairment of sexual activity or enjoyment. Calculation of these damages is based on a tariff laid down by the Court of Appeal, though the tariff figure can be adjusted to take into account the claimant's individual circumstances.

Damages for loss of amenity are not affected by whether the claimant is actually aware of the loss, so unconscious claimants may claim damages as if they had not been unconscious. This was the case in **H West & Son *v* Shephard** (1964). The claimant was a married woman, who was 41 when she was injured. Serious head injuries left her at least partially unconscious, and paralysed in all four limbs. There was no hope of recovery, and her life expectancy was only five years. She was unable to speak, but there was evidence to suggest that she had some awareness of her circumstances. An award of £17,500 for loss of amenity was upheld by a majority in the House of Lords.

Quick quiz 25.1

1 What are the two principal remedies that a court can order for a tortious wrong?

2 How are compensatory damages calculated?

3 Give two examples of the types of things that can be compensated by pecuniary damages following personal injury caused by negligence.

4 If damages are awarded for 'loss of amenity', what are they compensating?

▌Interim awards and provisional damages

Unless there is a statutory provision to the contrary, damages are usually awarded as a once-only lump sum. This can cause problems in personal injury cases, where long after the case is tried, the injury may turn out to have consequences which could not have been foreseen. In order to deal with this situation, the Supreme Court Act 1981 gives the courts power to award provisional damages. Where there is a possibility that the injured person will, as a result of the tort, develop a serious disease or serious physical or mental deterioration in the future, the court can award initial damages based on the claimant's condition at the time of trial, but retain the power to award further damages if the possible future deterioration does in fact happen. The award can only be adjusted once.

A further problem with damages for personal injury is that delays in coming to trial often mean the claimant has no financial help when it is actually needed most. The Supreme Court Act 1981 also provides some mitigation of this situation, by allowing the courts to award interim damages before trial, where the defendant admits liability, and is only contesting the amount of damages claimed. The defendant must also be insured, or be a public body, or have the resources to make an interim payment. Because there is often a long delay between being injured and receiving damages, the Supreme Court Act 1981 makes it mandatory for courts to award interest where damages are more than £200, unless there are special reasons not to do so.

Know your terms 25.2

Define the following terms:

1 *Restitutio in integrum*
2 Pecuniary loss
3 Loss of amenity
4 Interim damages

In **Wadey** *v* **Surrey County Council (No. 2)** (1999) it was decided that courts should disregard any social security benefits received by the claimant when they calculate the interest due on the damages.

Structured settlements

Some compensation payments for personal injury are made in the form of structured settlements. Instead of one lump sum, the claimant receives an initial payment, covering losses up to the date of settlement, and the rest of the damages are paid as a pension, providing a regular income which will usually last for the rest of the claimant's life, and designed to cover future loss of income, medical expense and future non-pecuniary losses such as pain and suffering. Around 100 cases a year result in this kind of payment, usually those involving very serious injuries which leave the victims unable to work or care for themselves.

Currently, courts cannot order damages to be paid in this way, so it is a matter for the parties to agree between themselves the appropriate terms of such a settlement. However, in March 2002, the Government produced proposals to allow courts to order structured settlements where they believe it is appropriate. The department's report suggests that such settlements are the most appropriate means for paying compensation in cases where the claimant has a large loss of future earnings.

Set-offs

As we have said, tort damages are generally calculated to put the claimant in the position he or she would have enjoyed if the tort had never been committed. They are not designed to put the claimant in a better position than if the tort had never been committed, and so the courts will generally take steps to ensure that any other money paid as a result of the injury will be deducted from the damages: this is known as a set-off. The following principles are followed.

Tax

Where a claimant is awarded damages for loss of earnings, the amount payable will be what the claimant would have earned after paying tax – **British Transport Commission** v **Gourley** (1956).

Payments by an employer

Sick pay from an employer is taken into account in assessing damages, and damages are reduced accordingly. In **Hussain** v **New Taplow Paper Mills Ltd** (1988) the House of Lords stated that long-term sick pay from the employer according to the terms of the employment contract could be deducted, as such payments were the equivalent of receiving a salary.

Social security benefits

When the social security system was first set up, the Law Reform (Personal Injuries) Act 1948 provided that the value of certain social security benefits received by claimants should be deducted from the compensation payable to them, and as time went on, the courts extended this approach, so that all benefits were covered by the rule. This prevented claimants from being double-compensated, but it meant that the social security system (and therefore the taxpayer) was, in effect, subsidizing defendants. From the late 1980s, new legislation was enacted, which deducted the value of social security benefits from the compensation received, but gave it to the state, rather than back to the defendant. The situation is now covered by the Social Security (Recovery of Benefits) Act 1997. This provides that the value of social security benefits received by the claimant during the five years immediately following the accident or until the making of the compensation payment (whichever is the earlier) should be deducted from the compensation ordered by the court, and paid to the Secretary of State. The Act treats compensation as having three elements – loss of earnings, cost of care and loss of mobility – and the value of benefits received can only be set off against the corresponding element in the damages award. This means, for example, that if a claimant who has received £7,000 in income support and £3,000 in attendance allowance is awarded £10,000 for loss of earnings and £2,000 for cost of care, he or she will end up with £3,000, because the scheme will not take the outstanding £1,000 in attendance allowance from the sum awarded for loss of earnings. In addition, no part of the value of social security benefits can be deducted from damages awarded for pain and suffering. The previous legislation did not apply to awards of up to £2,500, but the 1997 Act brings such payments within the scheme.

Exceptions

Apparent exceptions to the rule that tort damages should not make claimants better off than they would have been had the tort not been committed are made in the case of disability pensions paid by a claimant's employer, insurance pay-outs and payments made on a charitable basis. This was established in **Parry** *v* **Cleaver** (1970), where Lord Read explained the decision on the basis that set-offs of these kinds of payments would discourage charity and sensible investment in insurance, and might allow tortfeasors to benefit.

The rule has been criticized by the Law Commission in its 1997 consultation paper *Damages for Personal Injury: Collateral Benefits*. The Commission argued that it over-compensates victims, which is both contrary to the aims of tort law, and a waste of resources. It doubted that anyone would be put off buying insurance by the prospect of set-offs, since people buy insurance against income loss generally, not just loss as a result of a tort, so they would still want the cover.

However, in **Longden** *v* **British Coal Corporation** (1998) the House of Lords ignored such criticisms. The claimant in the case had suffered an injury at work, which meant he had to retire at the age of 36. Under a scheme run by his employers, he became entitled to receive a disability pension from that point, instead of the ordinary pension he would have started receiving at the age of 60. The defendants accepted that they could not set off the disability pension against the damages for loss of earnings, following **Parry** *v* **Cleaver**, but argued that the disability pension could be set off against the claimant's claim for loss of the pension he would have started receiving at the age of 60. The House of Lords held that the amounts he would receive from the disability pension after he reached 60 could be set off against the claim for loss of the normal pension, but the payments he received before he was 60 could not.

In **Gaca** *v* **Pirelli General plc** (2004), the Court of Appeal said that the rule could not apply to payouts from insurance policies which had been paid for by the injured person's employer. Mr Gaca had been injured at work, and had received £122,000 from a group insurance scheme paid for by his employers, which covered employees who were disabled at work. Employees were not required to pay for the insurance cover. When Mr Gaca successfully sued his employers for causing his injuries, they sought to deduct the insurance payout from his damages. The Court of Appeal held that they could do so. The situation did not fall within the 'benevolence exception' because allowing the deduction did not discourage benevolence; in fact failing to allow it might well discourage companies from making such payments to injured employees.

Benefits provided by the tortfeasor

In **Hunt** *v* **Severs** (1994), the claimant was very seriously injured in a car accident caused by her fiancé, whom she went on to marry. She sued him (which may seem odd, but bear in mind it would actually be his insurance company that stood to pay damages), and the issue arose of whether she could claim the cost of care that had been provided by him, and would continue to be given by him in the future. There is usually no problem with compensating the cost of care, even if that care is provided by a relative and so not actually paid for, but in this case the House of Lords held that such compensation could not be awarded, because it would amount to double compensation, just as if the defendant had, for example, given the claimant a wheelchair and then been asked to pay compensation for the cost of it.

Quick quiz 25.3

1 When are provisional damages awarded?

2 When are interim damages awarded?

3 Can the courts order compensation to be paid as a structured settlement?

4 Give two examples of money that will be deducted from a person's award of damages.

Fatal accidents

When a claimant dies as a result of a tort, the claim he or she would have had against the tortfeasor passes to that person's estate, meaning that it becomes part of what is inherited as a result of the death. Whoever inherits the estate can recover the losses that the claimant would have claimed for the period between the injury and the death, provided that it is not too brief – Law Reform (Miscellaneous Provisions) Act 1934, s. 1. So if, for example, someone is injured in an accident and dies six months later, the estate can claim damages for pecuniary and non-pecuniary losses, based on the usual principles, for that six-month period.

In addition, the Fatal Accidents Act 1976 establishes two further claims: a claim by dependants of the deceased for financial losses and a claim for the bereavement suffered. As well as the spouse and children of the deceased, dependants can include other relatives, so long as they can prove financial dependence on him or her. A partner who lived as husband or wife with the deceased for at least two years is also classed as a dependant. Dependants will only have a claim if the deceased would have had one, and any defence which could have been used by the defendant can be used against them.

Dependants can claim for financial losses to themselves caused by the death, including earnings spent on the dependants, savings made for their future use, nonessential items such as holidays, and the value of services rendered. So, for example, a man who loses his wife can claim the value of any domestic services she provided for the family. In **Martin** *v* **Grey** (1998), a 12-year-old girl was awarded a record amount of damages for loss of the services provided by her mother, who had been killed. The court held that in calculating the award it was necessary to look at the cost of providing the services a mother would normally provide, whether or not these services had actually been replaced; this might include, for example, the cost of employing a housekeeper or the loss of earnings of the father if he gave up work.

Assessing the loss can be a difficult task, and in **Davies** *v* **Powell Duffryn Associated Collieries Ltd** (1942) Lord Wright laid down some guidance. The court must start with the earnings of the deceased; from this it deducts an amount estimated to cover the deceased's personal and living expenses. The sum left will be the multiplicand. This is then multiplied by the multiplier, which is calculated using the rules described at p. 564, except that the multiplier runs from the date of the death. Benefits received by the dependants, such as social security or insurance payments, are not deducted.

The second claim allowed by the Fatal Accidents Act 1976 is for a fixed award of £10,000 damages for bereavement, which is designed to provide some compensation for the non-pecuniary losses associated with bereavement. It is only available to the husband or wife of the deceased, or, if the deceased was unmarried and a minor, to the parents. It does not give children a claim for the death of a parent.

Non-compensatory damages

As we have seen, compensatory damages are carefully calculated to put claimants in the position they would have enjoyed if the tort had never been committed. In some cases, however, damages may be awarded for different reasons, and these may be less, or much more, than is required to compensate the loss directly. There are four types of non-compensatory damages: contemptuous, nominal, aggravated and exemplary.

Contemptuous damages

Where a court recognizes that the claimant's legal rights have technically been infringed, but disapproves of his or her conduct, and considers that the action should never have been brought, it may order contemptuous damages. These will amount to no more than the value of the least valuable coin of the realm (currently one penny). A claimant awarded contemptuous damages is also unlikely to recover costs. Contemptuous damages are not commonly awarded; their main use is in defamation actions.

Nominal damages

An award of nominal damages is normally made where there has technically been an infringement of a person's legal rights but no actual damage has been done. It comprises a small sum of money, normally £20, and tends to arise in relation to torts which are actionable *per se* (that is, without the proof of damage), such as trespass and libel. Its purpose is to acknowledge that the defendant has violated the claimant's rights, rather than to compensate for loss.

An example of nominal damages being awarded is **Constantine *v* Imperial London Hotels** (1944), where the claimant, a famous West Indian cricketer, was only awarded damages of five guineas, after the defendants wrongfully refused to allow him into one of their hotels, though they allowed him to rent a room in another of their hotels.

A claimant who secures nominal damages will not necessarily be awarded costs as well.

Aggravated damages

Where a defendant has behaved in such a way that the claimant has suffered more than would normally be expected in such a case, a court can show its disapproval by awarding damages which are higher than would normally be appropriate. These are called aggravated damages. A recent example of the kind of case where such aggravated damages are considered appropriate is **Khodaparast** *v* **Shad** (1999). The claimant, an Iranian woman, had sued her ex-boyfriend for libel, after he created photo-montages that appeared to show her advertising pornographic telephone lines, and distributed the images throughout the local Iranian community. As a result, the claimant lost her teaching job at an Iranian school, and had little or no prospect of finding further work within the Iranian community; as her English was poor, this had been her main source of employment. In his pre-trial statements, and later in court, the defendant persisted in denying that he had created the montages, and insisted that they were real pictures of the claimant and quite likely to have come from pornographic magazines; in support of this allegation, he made a number of other untrue claims, including that she 'slept around', associated with prostitutes, and had had 'an improper relationship' with her solicitor. As a result of this behaviour, the trial judge awarded aggravated damages, and his decision was upheld by the Court of Appeal.

Quick quiz 25.4

1 If a person dies as a result of another's negligence, does the death put an end to any possible actions in negligence?

2 List the four types of non-compensatory damages.

3 When are contemptuous damages awarded?

4 When will aggravated damages be awarded?

Exemplary damages

Exemplary damages also involve paying the claimant more than would normally be appropriate, but they differ from aggravated damages in that their purpose is actually to offer a serious punishment to the defendant, and to deter others from behaving in the same way.

The punitive nature of exemplary damages means that they stray into an area which is generally thought to be more appropriate to criminal law, where, of course, there is a higher standard of proof. As a result, their use is very carefully controlled. In a case called **Rookes** *v* **Barnard** (1964), the facts of which are not important here, the House of Lords said that exemplary damages should only be used in cases which fitted into one of the three following categories: statutory authorisation; conduct calculated to make a profit; and oppressive conduct by Government servants.

Statutory authorization

There are a few cases in which exemplary damages are expressly allowed by statute.

Conduct calculated to make a profit

There are clearly some cases, usually involving defamation, where a defendant may calculate that it is worth committing a tort, even at the risk of being sued, because the profit to be made will exceed the cost of compensating the claimant if he or she does sue. For example, an unscrupulous newspaper may calculate that the revenue from increased sales may make it worthwhile to print libellous stories.

It is not necessary for the defendant precisely to calculate the potential profit and compensation, so long as he or she deliberately risks causing damage in order to make a profit. This was the case in **Cassell & Co. Ltd** *v* **Broome** (1972). The claimant was a retired naval officer, and the defendants published a book about a wartime convoy with which the claimant was involved. The claimant successfully sued for libel and was awarded £25,000 exemplary damages. This was upheld by the House of Lords, taking into account the profit which the defendants would have made.

Oppressive conduct by Government servants

Exemplary damages may also be awarded where there has been oppressive, arbitrary or unconstitutional action by Government servants, which includes people exercising governmental functions, such as police officers. The purpose here is to mark the fact that Government servants are also supposed to serve the community, and must use their power accordingly.

An example of such a case is **Huckle** *v* **Money** (1763). The claimant was detained under a search warrant. The detention was for six hours, and involved no ill-treatment; in fact food and drink were provided. Even so, the court upheld an award of £300 damages, stating that entering a person's home with a search warrant that did not have his name on it was a serious breach of civil liberties, and 'worse than the Spanish Inquisition'.

Modern cases have involved local authorities which have practised sexual or racial discrimination in recruiting employees, such as **Bradford City Metropolitan Council** *v* **Arora** (1991).

In addition to falling within one of these categories, it must be clear that the case is one where compensatory damages would be insufficient, and if there is a jury, the members must be fully and carefully directed. Later cases have shed more light on the nature of the direction to be given to juries in particular types of case. In **John** *v* **Mirror Group Newspapers** (1995) the Court of Appeal stated that in defamation cases the jury should be told that an award of exemplary damages could only be made if the publisher had no genuine belief that the published information was true, and in **Thompson** *v* **Commissioner of Police of the Metropolis** (1997) the Court of Appeal stated that in cases of unlawful conduct by the police juries should be told that they can award damages at a level designed to punish the defendant. Such damages were unlikely to be less than £5,000, and might be up to £50,000 where officers of at least the rank of superintendent were directly involved.

Until recently, there was a further restriction on the use of exemplary damages, established in **AB** *v* **South West Water Services Ltd** (1993). In that case it was held that even where a case fell within one of the **Rookes** *v* **Barnard** categories as listed above, exemplary damages could only be awarded if the tort committed was one for which such damages had been awarded in at least one case before **Rookes** *v* **Barnard**. The decision was much criticized as being irrational, since whether exemplary damages were available would depend entirely on which cases had happened to come up before. The House of Lords accepted this criticism and in **Kuddus** *v* **Chief Constable of Leicestershire Constabulary** (2001), they overruled **AB** *v* **South West Water**. However, this decision did not entirely clarify the issue. Their Lordships made it clear that they did not intend that exemplary damages should now be available for any tort, since there were some for which such damages had never been available (namely, negligence, nuisance and the strict liability tort order **Rylands** *v* **Fletcher**) and they did not want to make them available in these areas. They also criticized the basis for the **Rookes** *v* **Barnard** categories, stating that they were no longer in step with modern law; yet they were reluctant to take the radical step of abolishing exemplary damages completely. This has left nobody very much the wiser, so it is probably a good thing that in real life, as opposed to textbooks, exemplary damages play a very small role.

Problems with damages

Lump sums

The fact that damages are paid in a lump sum has disadvantages for the claimant, particularly where the effects of injury worsen after the award is made. The introduction of provisional damages has gone some way towards dealing with this problem, but still does not cover cases where at the time of trial there is no reason to believe that further deterioration will occur.

As well as the future prospects of the claimant's health, the lump sum system requires the court to predict what the claimant's employment prospects are likely to be; in reality this can never be known, so the compensation may well turn out to represent much more or less than the claimant should have had. Perhaps more importantly, there is no way to predict the result of inflation on the award, so that when inflation is high, the award's value can soon be eroded.

A further problem is that there is no way to ensure that the claimant uses the lump sum in such a way as to make sure it provides a lifelong income, where necessary. If the money is used unwisely, the claimant may end up having to live on state benefits, which partly defeats the object of making the tortfeasor compensate for the damage caused.

These issues were considered by the Pearson Commission (1978), which recommended that in cases of death or serious, long-term injury, claimants should be able to receive damages in the form of periodic payments. Assuming that the defendant was insured, the insurer would be responsible for administering the payments, which would be revalued annually to reflect average earnings. In addition, the Commission recommended that the courts should be able to vary awards where changes in the claimant's medical condition affected the level of pecuniary loss. These recommendations were not taken up by the Government.

Degrees of fault

Because the aim of tort damages is to compensate the claimant, rather than punish the defendant, compensation does not take into account the degree of fault involved in the defendant's action. As a result, a defendant who makes a momentary slip may end up paying the same damages as one who shows gross carelessness. The system as it stands seems unable to provide justice for the claimant without injustice to some defendants.

West & Son v Shephard and loss of amenity

The case of **West & Son** *v* **Shephard** (1964), and the principle that a person who is unaware of his or her loss of amenity can still be compensated for it, have been strongly criticized. The main criticism is that the compensation cannot actually be used by the unconscious person, and in most cases will simply end up forming part of his or her estate when that person dies. This being the case, it seems inequitable that relatives in this situation may end up with considerably more than the relatives of someone killed immediately as the result of a tort. But if no such award was made, the court would be treating the claimant like a dead person.

The Law Commission has recommended that this aspect of the law be kept, but the Pearson Commission suggested that awards for non-pecuniary loss should no longer be made to unconscious claimants. The Pearson Commission's recommendation has not been implemented.

Damages for bereavement

The standard payment for bereavement (see p. 571) was raised from £7,500 to £10,000 in 2002, but the Association of Personal Injury Lawyers (APIL) has criticized this as inadequate and unfair. The Association had been pushing for a complete review of bereavement damages, arguing that such damages should be at least equal to those for the most serious injuries; at £10,000, bereavement compensation is a fraction of the £35,000 typically awarded for loss of one eye, for example, or the £200,000 for paralysis. The current situation means that it is cheaper for defendants to kill than to injure.

APIL has also criticized the fact that parents are denied damages for children over 18, which means that unless the child has another next of kin – such as a spouse – defendants do not have to pay anybody bereavement compensation.

▌ The role of exemplary damages

Despite the restrictions imposed by **Rookes** *v* **Barnard** (see p. 572), exemplary damages continue to cause concern, notably in high-profile cases such as the libel actions involving the ex-MP Lord Archer, and Sonia Sutcliffe, the wife of the murderer known as the Yorkshire Ripper. These were seen as examples of juries 'punishing' newspapers beyond what was deserved by the particular libels, and instead using the cases to show their disapproval of newspapers generally.

Critics of the idea of exemplary damages argue that they go beyond the purpose of tort law, and that they introduce the potential for punishment without the safeguards built into the criminal legal system (such as the standard of proof beyond reasonable doubt). Some steps have been taken to meet these criticisms, in the case of **John** *v* **Mirror Group Newspapers** (see p. 573), but there is still a strong body of opinion that would like to see the problem avoided by taking the calculation of damages away from juries, so that in cases where juries are used (in practice, this is usually defamation cases), the jury would deliver only a verdict, with the job of deciding damages left to the judge (as sentencing is in the criminal system).

Reading on the web

A report of the Law Commission entitled *Damages for Personal Injury: Non-pecuniary Loss* (1999) is available on the Law Commission's website at:

http://www.lawcom.gov.uk/lc_reports.htm

The House of Lords' judgment in **Farley** *v* **Skinner** (1998) is available on the House of Lords' judicial business website at:

http://www.publications.parliament.uk/pa/ld/ldjudgmt.htm#2001

Question and answer guide

1 Damages in tort are intended to put the claimant in the position they would have enjoyed if the tort had never been committed. How far does the law do this?

Answer guide

A good way to start this essay would be to briefly summarize the principle of *restitutio in integrum*; if you have studied contract law you could briefly mention how tort damages differ from the principle of damages in contract – one seeks to make good a loss, and the other to protect an expected gain.

You should then go on to discuss the rules on how tort damages are calculated and awarded. As you work through the rules, highlight the cases which reveal the problems associated with these calculations, including the disputed loss cases such as **Gardner** *v* **Marsh** and **South Australia Asset Management** *v* **York Montague Ltd**, the 'loss of a chance' cases such as

Doyle *v* **Wallace** and **Langford** *v* **Hebran**, and the controversy over the discount rate, as high-lighted in **Warriner** *v* **Warriner**. You should also cover the issues of possible overcompensation examined in **Parry** *v* **Cleaver** and **Longden** *v* **British Coal**, with the criticisms made by the Law Commission; the problems with the principle in **West & Son** *v* **Shephard**; and the problems associated with giving damages as lump sums.

In order to look further at the issue of how far *restitutio in integrum* is achieved, you could talk about the areas of tort law where damages simply cannot undo the harm done: the non-pecuniary damages associated with personal injury, and the damage to reputation done by defamation, for example. You should point out problems which arise from these – for the problem of juries awarding excessive damages for defamation may in part be caused by the fact that there is no way to put a price on damage to reputation.

Your conclusion should sum up how far you feel the law achieves the aim of *restitutio in integrum*, but you might also choose to say how far you feel this should be its aim in tort cases – you might mention, for example, the fact that in choosing this aim, the sum of damages cannot take into account degrees of fault.

Chapter summary

The principal remedy awarded by a court for a tortious wrong is damages.

Damages

In the vast majority of cases where damages are claimed they are what is known as compensatory, aiming to put claimants in the position they would have been in if the tort had never been committed. Where the loss suffered is non-pecuniary, it is very difficult to calculate how much compensation is appropriate, but the general aim is to provide fair and reasonable compensation for the damage done, taking into account all the circumstances.

Compensation for personal injury

Damages for personal injury are divided into pecuniary and non-pecuniary losses. Pecuniary losses are those which can be calculated in financial terms, while non-pecuniary losses are not financial and cover damages that are less easy to calculate, such as loss of physical amenity, pain, shock and suffering. Pecuniary losses are divided into the following categories:

■ pre-trial expenses
■ expenses incurred by another
■ pre-trial loss of earnings, and
■ future loss of earnings.

Non-pecuniary losses are grouped into the following categories:

■ the primary injury
■ pain and suffering, and
■ loss of amenity.

The following sources of money will be deducted from an award of damages to prevent a person from being better off as a result of the injury (known as a set-off):

▶

- tax
- payments by an employer, and
- social security benefits.

Non-compensatory damages
There are four types of non-compensatory damages:

- contemptuous damages
- nominal damages
- aggravated damages, and
- exemplary damages.

Appendix 1
Answering examination questions

At the end of each chapter in this book, you will find detailed guidelines for answering exam questions on the topics covered. Many of the questions are taken from actual A-level past papers, but they are equally relevant for candidates of all law examinations, as these questions are typical of the type of questions that examiners ask in this field.

In this section, we aim to give some general guidelines for answering questions on the English legal system.

Citation of authorities

One of the most important requirements for answering questions on the law is that you must be able to back the points you make with authority, usually either a case or a statute. It is not good enough to state that the law is such and such, without stating the case or statute which says that that is the law. Some examiners are starting to suggest that the case name is not essential as long as you can remember and understand the general principle that the case laid down. However, such examiners remain in the minority and the reality is that even they are likely to give higher marks where the candidate has cited authorities; quite simply, it helps give the impression that you know your material thoroughly, rather than half-remembering something you heard once in class.

This means that you must be prepared to learn fairly long lists of cases by heart, which can be a daunting prospect. What you need to memorize is the name of the case, a brief description of the facts, and the legal principle which the case established. Once you have revised a topic well, you should find that a surprisingly high number of cases on that topic begin to stick in your mind anyway, but there will probably be some that you have trouble recalling. A good way to memorize these is to try to create a picture in your mind which links the facts, the name and the legal principle. For example, if you wanted to remember the contract law case of **Redgrave *v* Hurd**, you might picture the actress Vanessa Redgrave and the politician Douglas Hurd, in the situation described in the facts of the case, and imagine one of them telling the other the principle established in the case.

Knowing the names of cases makes you look more knowledgeable, and saves writing time in the exam, but if you do forget a name, referring briefly to the facts will identify it. It is not necessary to learn the dates of cases though it is useful if you know whether it is a recent or an old case. Dates are usually required for statutes. Unless you are making a detailed comparison of the facts of a case and the facts of a problem question, in order to argue that the case should or could be distinguished, you should generally make only brief reference to facts, if at all – long descriptions of facts waste time and earn few marks.

When reading the AS exam questions' 'Question and answer guides' sections at the end of each chapter in this book, bear in mind that for reasons of space, we have not highlighted every case which you should cite. The skeleton arguments outlined in those sections **must** be backed up with authority from cases and statute law.

When discussing the English legal system, as well as citing relevant cases and statutes it is particularly important to cite relevant research and reports in the field being discussed. If there are important statistics in an area, being able to quote some of them will give your answers authority.

There is no right answer

In law exams, there is not usually a right or a wrong answer. What matters is that you show you know what type of issues you are being asked about. Essay questions are likely to ask you to 'discuss', 'criticize' or 'evaluate', and you simply need to produce a good range of factual and critical material in order to do this. The answer you produce might look completely different from your friend's but both answers could be worth 'A' grades.

Breadth and depth of content

Where a question seems to raise a number of different issues – as most do – you will achieve better marks by addressing all or most of these issues than by writing at great length on just one or two. By all means spend more time on issues which you know well, but be sure to at least mention other issues which you can see are relevant, even if you can only produce a paragraph or so about them.

Civil or criminal

In some cases, a question on the English legal system will require you to confine your answer to either the civil or criminal system. This may be stated in the question – for example, 'Discuss the system of civil appeals'. Alternatively, it may be something you are required to work out for yourself, as is often the case with problem questions. For example, a question might state:

> Jane has been charged with criminal damage.
> (a) How may she obtain legal aid and advice? and
> (b) If convicted, to which courts may she appeal?

This question only requires you to discuss the legal aid and advice available in criminal cases, and the criminal appeals system; giving details of civil legal aid and the civil appeals system will waste time and gain you no marks, as would bringing the criminal appeals system into the previous question. Equally, where a question does not limit itself to either civil or criminal legal systems, you will lose marks if you only discuss one.

Because of this danger, it is a good idea to make a point of asking yourself before you answer any legal system question whether it covers just the civil legal system, just the criminal, or both.

The structure of the question

If a question is specifically divided into parts, for example (a), (b) and (c), then stick to those divisions and do not merge your answer into one long piece of writing.

Law examinations tend to contain a mixture of essay questions and what are known as 'problem questions'. Tackling each of these questions involves slightly different skills, so we consider each in turn.

Essay questions

Answer the question asked

Over and over again, examiners complain that candidates do not answer the question they are asked – so if you can develop this skill, you will stand out from the crowd. You will get very few marks for simply writing all you know about a topic, with no attempt to address the issues raised in the question, but if you can adapt the material that you have learnt on the subject to take into account the particular emphasis given to it by the question, you will do well.

Even if you have memorized an essay which does raise the issues in the question (perhaps because those issues tend to be raised year after year), you must fit your material to the words of the question you are actually being asked. For example, suppose during your course you wrote an essay on the advantages and disadvantages of the jury system, and then in the exam you find yourself faced with the question 'Should juries be abolished?' The material in your coursework essay is ideally suited for the exam question, but if you begin the main part of your answer with the words 'The advantages of juries include . . .' or something similar, this is a dead giveaway to the examiner that you are merely writing down an essay you have memorized. It takes very little effort to change the words to 'Abolition of the jury system would ignore certain advantages that the current system has . . .', but it will create a much better impression, especially if you finish with a conclusion which, based on points you have made, states that abolition is a good or bad idea, the choice depending on the arguments you have made during your answer.

During your essay, you should keep referring to the words used in the question – if this seems to become repetitive, use synonyms for those words. This makes it clear to the examiner that you are keeping the question in mind as you work.

Plan your answer

Under pressure of time, it is tempting to start writing immediately, but five minutes spent planning each essay question is well worth spending – it may mean that you write less overall, but the quality of your answer will almost certainly be better. The plan need not be elaborate: just jot down everything you feel is relevant to the answer, including case names, and then organize the material into a logical order appropriate to the question asked. To put it in order, rather than wasting time copying it all out again, simply put a number next to each point according to which ones you intend to make first, second and so forth.

Provide analysis and fact

Very few essay questions require merely factual descriptions of what the law is; you will almost always be required to analyse the factual content in some way, usually highlighting any problems or gaps in the law, and suggesting possible reforms. If a question asks you to analyse whether lay magistrates should be replaced by professional judges you should not write everything you know about magistrates and judges and finish with one sentence saying that magistrates should/should not be kept. Instead, you should select your relevant material and your whole answer should be targeted at answering whether or not magistrates should be kept.

Where a question uses the word 'critically', as in 'critically describe' or 'critically evaluate', the examiners are merely drawing your attention to the fact that your approach should be analytical and not merely descriptive; you are not obliged to criticize every provision you describe. Having said that, even if you do not agree with particular criticisms which you have read, you should still discuss them and say why you do not think they are valid; there is very little mileage in an essay that simply describes the law and says it is perfectly satisfactory.

Structure

However good your material, you will only gain really good marks if you structure it well. Making a plan for each answer will help in this, and you should also try to learn your material in a logical order – this will make it easier to remember as well. The exact construction of your essay will obviously depend on the question, but you should aim to have an introduction, then the main discussion, and a conclusion. Where a question is divided into two or more parts, you should reflect that structure in your answer.

A word about conclusions: it is not good enough just to repeat the question, turning it into a statement, for the conclusion. So, for example, if the question is 'Is the criminal justice system satisfactory?', a conclusion which simply states that the system is or is not satisfactory will gain you very little credit. Your conclusion will often summarize the arguments that you have developed during the course of your essay.

Problem questions

In problem questions, the exam paper will describe an imaginary situation, and then ask what the legal implications of the facts are – for example, 'Jane had suffered physical violence at the hands of her husband for many years. One day she lashes out and kills him. She is arrested by the police and later charged with murder. In which court will Jane be tried? If she is convicted, to what court may she appeal?'

Read the question thoroughly

The first priority is to read the question thoroughly, at least a couple of times. Never start writing until you have done this, as you may well get halfway through and discover that what is said at the end makes half of what you have written irrelevant – or at worst, that the question raises issues you have no knowledge of at all.

Answer the question asked

This means paying close attention to the words printed immediately after the situation is described. In the example given above you are asked to advise about the courts and appeal procedure, so do not start discussing sentencing powers as this is not relevant to the particular question asked. Similarly, if a question asks you to advise one or other of the parties, make sure that you advise the right one – the realization as you discuss the exam with your friends afterwards that you have advised the wrong party and thus rendered most of your answer irrelevant is not an experience you will enjoy.

Spot the issues

In answering a problem question in an examination you will often be short of time. One of the skills of doing well is spotting which issues are particularly relevant to the facts of the problem and spending most time on those, while skimming over more quickly those matters which are not really an issue on the facts, but which you clearly need to mention.

Apply the law to the facts

What a problem question requires you to do is to spot the issues raised by the situation, and to consider the law as it applies to those facts. It is not enough simply to describe the law without applying it to the facts. So in the example given above it is not enough to write about the appeal procedure in general for civil and criminal cases; you must apply the rules of criminal appeal to the particular case of Jane. She has committed an indictable offence that would have been tried by the Crown Court, so you are primarily concerned with appeals from the Crown Court to the Court of Appeal. Nor should you start your answer by copying out all the facts. This is a complete waste of time, and will gain you no marks.

Unlike essay questions, problem questions are not usually seeking a critical analysis of the law. If you have time, it may be worth making the point that a particular area of the law you are discussing is problematic, and briefly stating why, but if you are addressing all the issues raised in the problem you are unlikely to have much time for this. What the examiner is looking for is essentially an understanding of the law and an ability to apply it to the particular facts given.

Use authority

As always, you must back up your points with authority from case or statute law.

Structure

The introduction and conclusion are much less important for problem questions than for essay questions. Your introduction can be limited to pointing out the issues raised by the question, or, where you are asked to 'advise' a person mentioned in the problem, what outcome that person will be looking for. You can also say in what order you intend to deal with the issues. Your conclusion might simply summarize the conclusions reached during the main part of the answer, for example that Jane will be tried in the Crown Court and her main route of appeal will be to the Court of Appeal.

There is no set order in which the main part of the answer must be discussed. Sometimes it will be appropriate to deal with the problem chronologically, in which case it will usually be a matter of looking at the question line by line, while in other cases it may be appropriate to group particular issues together. Problem questions on the English legal system are often broken down into clear parts – a, b, c and so on – so the answer can be broken down into the same parts. Thus with the example about Jane the question was clearly broken into two parts, and so your question should deal with first the trial court and then with the issue of appeal.

Whichever order you choose, try to deal with one issue at a time – for example, finish talking about the trial court before looking at the issue of appeal. Jumping backwards and forwards gives the impression that you have not thought about your answer. If you work through your material in a structured way, you are also less likely to leave anything out.

Appendix 2
A guide to law reports and case references

We have seen that much of the law is contained in cases decided before the courts. It is therefore important that a written record is kept of the decisions of the courts. Lawyers and students of law need to be able to find these written records.

The Law Reports

Over 2,000 cases are published in law reports each year. The most respected series of law reports is called *The Law Reports*, because before publication the report of each case included in the series is checked for accuracy by the judge who tried it. It is this series that should be cited before a court in preference to any other. The series is divided into several sub-series depending on the court which heard the case, as follows:

Appeal Cases (decisions of the Court of Appeal, the House of Lords and the Privy Council).

Chancery Division (decisions of the Chancery Division of the High Court and their appeals to the Court of Appeal).

Family Division (decisions of the Family Division of the High Court and their appeals to the Court of Appeal).

Queen's Bench (decisions of the Queen's Bench Division of the High Court and their appeals to the Court of Appeal).

Neutral citation

In 2001 a form of neutral citation was introduced in the Court of Appeal and Administrative Court. This form of citation was introduced to facilitate reference to cases reported on the internet and in CD-ROMs. Unlike reports in books, these reports do not have fixed page numbers and volumes. A unique number is now given to each approved judgment and the paragraphs in each judgment are numbered. The three forms of the neutral citation are as follows:

Civil Division of the Court of Appeal: [2000] EWCA Civ 1, 2, 3, etc.
Criminal Division of the Court of Appeal: [2000] EWCA Crim 1, 2, 3, etc.
Administrative Court: [2000] EWHC Admin 1, 2, 3, etc.

The letters 'EW' stand for England and Wales. For example, if **Brown** *v* **Smith** is the fifth numbered judgment of 2002 in the Civil Division of the Court of Appeal, it would be cited: **Brown** *v* **Smith** [2002] EWCA Civ 5. If you wished to refer to the fourth paragraph of the judgment, the correct citation is: [2002] EWCA Civ 5 at [4].

Case reference

Each case is given a reference(s) to explain exactly where it can be found in a law report(s). Such a reference can be used to go and find and read the case in a law library which stocks the relevant law report. This is important as a textbook can only provide a summary of the case and has no legal status in itself; it is the actual case which contains the law.

The reference consists of a series of letters and numbers that follow the case name. The pattern of this reference varies depending on the law report being referred to. The usual format is to follow the name of the case by:

A year Where the date reference tells you the year in which the case was decided, the date is normally enclosed in round brackets. If the date is the year in which the case is reported, it is given in square brackets. The most common law reports tend to use square brackets.

A volume number Not all law reports have a volume number, sometimes they simply identify their volumes by year.

The law report abbreviation Each series of law reports has an abbreviation for their title so that the whole name does not need to be written out in full.

The main law reports and their abbreviations are as follows:

All England Law Reports	All ER
Appeal Cases	AC
Chancery Division	Ch D
Criminal Appeal Reports	Cr App R
Family Division	Fam
King's Bench	KB
Queen's Bench Division	QB
Weekly Law Reports	WLR

A page number This is the page at which the report of the case commences.

Neutral citation Where a case has been decided after 2001 the neutral citation for decisions of the Court of Appeal and Administrative Court will appear in front of the law report citation.

Examples of case references

Cozens *v* **Brutus** [1973] AC 854
The case was reported in the Appeal Cases law report in 1973 at p. 854.

DPP *v* **Hawkins** [1988] 1 WLR 1166
The case was reported in the first volume of the Weekly Law Report of 1988 at p. 1166.

R *v* **Angel** (1968) 52 Cr App R 280
The case was reported in the fifty-second volume of the Criminal Appeal Reports at p. 280.

Brown *v* **Smith** [2002] EWCA Civ 5, [2002] QB 432, [2002] 3 All ER 21
The case was the fifth decision to be decided in 2002 by the Civil Division of the Court of Appeal. It was reported in the Queen's Bench law report in 2002 at p. 432 and in the third volume of the All England Law Report in 2002 at p. 21.

Select bibliography

Abel, R. (1988) *The Legal Profession in England and Wales*, Oxford: Basil Blackwell.

Abel-Smith, B., Zander, M. and Brooke, R. (1973) *Legal Problems and the Citizen: a Study in Three London Boroughs*, London: Heinemann Educational.

Alternative Dispute Resolution – A Discussion Paper (1999) London: Lord Chancellor's Department.

Anti-Social Behaviour Orders – Analysis of the first six years (2004), London: National Association of Probation Officers.

Aquinas, St T. (1942) *Summa Theologica*, London: Burns Oates & Washbourne.

Atiyah, P.S. (1979) *The Rise and Fall of Freedom of Contract*, Oxford: Clarendon Press.

Audit Commission (1996) *Streetwise: effective police patrol*, London: HMSO.

Audit Commission (1997) *Misspent Youth: Young People and Crime*, London: Audit Commission Publications.

Audit Commission (2003) *Victims and Witnesses*, London: Audit Commission Publications.

Audit Commission (2004) *Youth Justice*, London: Audit Commission Publications.

Auld, Sir R. (2001) *Review of the Criminal Courts*, London: HMSO.

Austin, J. (1954) *The Province of Jurisprudence Determined*, London: Weidenfeld & Nicolson.

Bailey, S. and Gunn, M. (2002) *Smith, Bailey and Gunn on the Modern English Legal System* (4th edn), London: Sweet & Maxwell.

Baldwin, J. (1992) *The Role of Legal Representatives at the Police Station* (Royal Commission on Criminal Justice Research Study No. 2), London: HMSO.

Baldwin, J. (1992) *Preparing Records of Taped Interviews* (Royal Commission on Criminal Justice Research Study No. 3), London: HMSO.

Baldwin, J. (1992) *Video Taping Police Interviews with Suspects: an Evaluation*, London: Home Office.

Baldwin, J. (1997) Small Claims in County Courts in England and Wales: the bargain basement of civil justice? Oxford: Clarendon Press.

Baldwin, J. (2002) *Lay and Judicial Perspectives on the Expansion of the Small Claims Regime*, London: Lord Chancellor's Department, Research Secretariat.

Baldwin, J. (2003) *Evaluating the Effectiveness of Enforcement Procedures in Undefended Claims in the Civil Courts*, London: Lord Chancellor's Department.

Baldwin, J. and McConville, M. (1979) *Jury Trials*, Oxford: Clarendon Press.

Baldwin, J. and Moloney, T. (1992) *Supervision of Police Investigations in Serious Criminal Cases* (Royal Commission of Criminal Justice Research Study No. 4), London: HMSO.

Bell, J. and Engle, Sir G. (eds) (1995) *Statutory Interpretation*, London: Butterworths.

Bennion, F.A.R. (1990) *Statutory Interpretation*, London: Butterworths.

Bird, S.M. and Brown, A.J. (2001) 'Criminalisation of HIV transmission: implications for public health in Scotland', *British Medical Journal*, 323, pp. 1174–7.

Blackstone, W. (1758) *An Analysis of the Laws of England*, Oxford: Clarendon Press.

Block, B.P., Corbett, C. and Peay, J. (1993) *Ordered and Directed Acquittals in the Crown Court*, London: HMSO.

Blom-Cooper, L. (1972) *Final Appeal: a study of the House of Lords in its judicial capacity*, Oxford: Clarendon Press.

Bond, R.A. and Lemon, N.F. (1979) 'Changes in Magistrates' Attitudes during the First Year on the Bench' in Farrington, D.P. *et al.* (eds) (1979) *Psychology, Law and Legal Processes*, London: Macmillan.

Bottoms, A.E. and Preston, R.H. (eds) (1980) *The Coming Penal Crisis: A Criminological and Theoretical Exploration*, Edinburgh: Scottish Academic Press.

Bowman, Sir J. (1997) *Review of the Court of Appeal (Civil Division)*, London: Lord Chancellor's Department.

Brazier, R. (1998) *Constitutional Reform*, Oxford: Oxford University Press.

Bridges, L. and Choongh, S. (1998) *Improving Police Station Legal Advice: the impact of the accreditation scheme for police station legal advisers*, London: Law Society's Research and Planning Unit: Legal Aid Board.

Brown, D. (1998) *Offending While on Bail*, London: Home Office.

Brown, D. and Neal, D. (1988) 'Show Trials: The Media and the Gang of Twelve' in Findlay, M. and Duff, P. (eds) (1988) *The Jury under Attack*, London: Butterworths.

Brown, D., Ellis, T. and Larcombe, K. (1993) *Changing the Code: Police Detention under the Revised PACE Codes of Practice* (Home Office Research Study No. 129), London: HMSO.

Brownlee, I. (2004) 'The statutory charging scheme in England and Wales: towards a unified prosecution system' [2004], Criminal Law Review 896.

Burney, E. (1979) *Magistrates, Court and Community*, London: Hutchinson.

Campbell, S. (2002) *A Review of Anti-social Behaviour Orders* (Home Office Research Study No. 236), London: Home Office.

Carlen, P. (1983) *Women's Imprisonment: A Study in Social Control*, London: Routledge.

Carter, P. (2003) *Managing Offenders, Reducing Crime*, London: Strategy Unit, Home Office.

Citizens' Advice Bureau (2004) *Geography of Advice*, London: Citizens' Advice Bureau.

Citizens' Advice Bureau (2005) *No win, no fee, no chance*, London: Citizens' Advice Bureau.

Consumer Council (1970) *Justice Out of Reach: A Case for Small Claims Courts: A Consumer Council Study*, London: HMSO.

Cotton, J. and Povey, D. (2004) *Police Complaints and Discipline, April 2002–March 2003*, London: Home Office.

Cretney, S. (1998) *Law, Law Reform and the Family*, Oxford: Clarendon Press.

Criminal Justice: the Way Ahead (2001) Cm 5074, London: Home Office.

Cross, Sir R. (1995) *Statutory Interpretation*, London: Butterworths.

Cutting Crime – Delivering Justice: Strategic Plan for Criminal Justice 2004–08 (2004) Cmnd 6288, London: Home Office.

Darbyshire, P. (1991) 'The Lamp that shows that freedom lives – is it worth the candle?' [1991], *Criminal Law Review* 740.

Darbyshire, P. (1999) 'A comment on the powers of magistrates' clerks' [1999], *Criminal Law Review* 377.

Davies, A. (1998) *Textbook on Medical Law*, London: Blackstone Press.

Davies, M. (2004) 'Tales from the (Thames) River Bank: R *v* G and Another (2004)', *Journal of Criminal Law*.

Denning, A. (1982) *What Next in the Law?*, London: Butterworths.

Department for Constitutional Affairs (2004) *Transforming Public Services: complaints, redress and tribunals*, London: Stationery Office.

Department for Trade and Industry (2004) 'Fairness for all: a new Commission for Equality and Human Rights', Command Paper 6185, London: TSO.

Devlin, P. (1965) *The Enforcement of Morals*, Oxford: Oxford University Press.

Devlin, P. (1979) *The Judge*, Oxford: Oxford University Press.

Dibdin, K., Sealy, A. and Aktar, S. (eds) (2002) *Judicial Statistics Annual Report 2002*, London: Court Service.

Dicey, A. (1982) *Introduction to the Study of the Law of the Constitution*, Indianapolis: Liberty Classics.

Dickens, L. (1985) *Dismissed: A Study of Unfair Dismissal and the Industrial System*, Oxford: Blackwell.

Dodgson, K. and others (2001) *Electronic Monitoring of Released Prisoners: An Evaluation of the Home Detention Curfew Scheme* (Home Office Research Study No. 222), London: Home Office.

Duster, T. (1970) *The Legislation of Morality*, New York: Free Press.

Dworkin, R. (1977) *Taking Rights Seriously*, London: Duckworth.

Dworkin, R. (1986) *Law's Empire*, London: Fontana Press.

Ellis, T. and Hedderman, C. (1996) *Enforcing Community Sentences: Supervisors' Perspectives on Ensuring Compliance and Dealing with Breach*, London: Home Office.

Enright, S. (1993) 'Cost Effective Criminal Justice', *New Law Journal* vol. 143, p. 1023.

Epstein, H. (2003) 'The liberalisation of claim financing', *New Law Journal*, vol. 153, p. 153.

Evans, R. (1993) *The Conduct of Police Interviews with Juveniles*, London: HMSO.

Fletcher, G. (2000) *Rethinking Criminal Law*, Oxford: Oxford University Press.

Flood-Page, C. and Mackie, A. (1998) *Sentencing During the Nineties*, London: Home Office Research and Statistics Directorate.

Freeman, M.D.A. (1981) 'The Jury on Trial', 34 *Criminal Law Review* 65.

Fuller, L. (1969) *The Morality of Law*, London: Yale University Press.

Galanter, M. (1984) *The Emergence of the Judge as a Mediator in Civil Cases*, Madison: University of Wisconsin.

Genn, H. (1982) *Meeting Legal Needs?: An Evaluation of a Scheme for Personal Injury Victims*, Oxford: SSRC Centre for Socio-Legal Studies.

Genn, H. (1987) *Hard Bargaining: Out of Court Settlement in Personal Injury Actions*, Oxford: Clarendon Press.

Genn, H. (1998) *The Central London County Court Pilot Mediation Scheme: Evaluation Report*, London: Lord Chancellor's Department.

Genn, H. (2002) *Court-based ADR Initiatives for Non-Family Civil Disputes: The Commercial Court and the Court of Appeal*, London: Lord Chancellor's Department, Research Secretariat.

Genn, H. and Genn, Y. (1989) *The Effect of Representation at Tribunals*, London: Lord Chancellor's Department.

Goriely, T. and Gupta, P. (2001) *Breaking the Code: the impact of legal aid reforms on general civil litigation*, London: Institute of Advanced Legal Studies.

Green, P. (ed.) (1996) *Drug Couriers: A New Perspective*, London: Quartet.

Griffith, J.A.G. (1997) *Politics of the Judiciary*, London: Fontana Press.

Gudjonsson, G.H. (1992) *The Psychology of Interrogations, Confessions and Testimony*, Chichester: Wiley.

Hale, Sir M. (1979) *The History of the Common Law of England*, Chicago: University of Chicago Press.

Hall, J. (1960) *General Principles of Criminal Law*, Indianapolis: Bobbs-Merrill.

Hall, J. (1963) 'Negligent Behaviour should be Excluded from Criminal Liability', 63 *Criminal Law Review* 632.

Halliday, J. (2001) *Making Punishment Work, Report of the Review of the Sentencing Framework for England and Wales*, London: Home Office.

Harris, P. *et al.* (1984) *Compensation and Support for Illness and Injury*, Oxford: Clarendon Press.

Hart, H.L.A. (1963) *Law, Liberty and Morality*, Oxford: Oxford University Press.

Hart, H.L.A. (1994) *The Concept of Law*, Oxford: Clarendon Press.

Hayek, F. (1982) *Law Legislation and Liberty: A New Statement of the Liberal Principles of Justice and Political Economy*, London: Routledge.

Hedderman, C. and Hough, M. (1994) *Does the Criminal Justice System Treat Men and Women Differently?*, London: Home Office.

Hedderman, C. and Moxon, D. (1992) *Magistrates' Court or Crown Court? Mode of Trial Decisions and Sentencing*, London: HMSO.

Herbert A. (2003) 'Mode of trial and magistrates' sentencing powers: will increased powers inevitably lead to a reduction in the committal rate', *Criminal Law Review* 314.

HM Chief Inspector of Prisons (1997) *Women in Prison: A Thematic Review*, London: Home Office.

HM Inspectorate (1999) *Police Integrity: Securing and Maintaining Public Confidence*, London: Home Office Communication Directorate.

Hohfeld, W.N. and Cook, W.W. (1919) *Fundamental Legal Concepts as Applied in Judicial Reasoning*, London: Greenwood Press.

Home Office (2002) *Statistics on Women and the Criminal Justice System*, London: Home Office.

Home Office (2004) *Are Special Measures Working? Evidence from surveys of vulnerable and intimidated witnesses*, Home Office Research Study 283, London: Home Office.

Home Office (2004) *One Step Ahead: A 21ˢᵗ century strategy to defeat organised crime*, London: Stationery Office.

Home Office Research Development and Statistics Directorate (2000) *Jury Excusal and Deferral* (Research Findings No. 102), London: HMSO.

Hood, R. and others (2003) *Ethnic Minorities in the Criminal Courts: Perceptions of Fairness and Equality of Treatment*, London: Home Office.

Hucklesby, A. (2004) 'Not necessarily a trip to the police station: the introduction of street bail' [2004] *Criminal Law Review* 803.

Idriss, M. (2004) 'Police perceptions of race relations in the West Midlands' [2004] *Criminal Law Review* 814.

Ingman, T. (1987) *English Legal Process*, London: Blackstone Press.

Jackson, R.M. (1989) *The Machinery of Justice in England*, Cambridge: Cambridge University Press.

Johnson, N. (2005) 'The training framework review – what's all the fuss about?' *New Law Journal* 155, 357.

Joseph, M. (1981) *The Conveyancing Fraud*, London: Woolwich.

Joseph, M. (1985) *Lawyers Can Seriously Damage Your Health*, London: Michael Joseph.

Kairys, D. (1998) *The Politics of Law: a Progressive Critique*, New York: Basic Books.

Kelsen, H. (1945) *General Theory of Law and State*, Cambridge, MA: Harvard University Press.

Kennedy, H. (1992) *Eve Was Framed: Women and British Justice*, London: Chatto.

King, M. and May, C. (1985) *Black Magistrates: A Study of Selection and Appointment*, London: Cobden Trust.

Law Commission (1976) *Criminal Law: Report on Conspiracy and Criminal Law Forum*, London: HMSO.

Law Commission (1982) *Offences Against Public Order*, London: HMSO.

Law Commission (1999) *Bail and the Human Rights Act 1998* (Report No. 157), London: HMSO.

Laws, J. (1998) 'The limitations of human rights', *Public Law* [1998] 254.

Lee, S. (1986) *Law and Morals*, Oxford: Oxford University Press.

Leigh, L. and Zedner, L. (1992) *A Report on the Administration of Criminal Justice in the Pretrial Phase in London, France and Germany*, London: HMSO.

Leng, R. (1993) *The Right to Silence in Police Interrogation* (Royal Commission on Criminal Justice Research Study No. 10), London: HMSO.

Levi, M. (1988) 'The Role of the Jury in Complex Cases' in Findlay, M. and Duff, P. (eds) (1988) *The Jury under Attack*, London: Butterworths.

Levi, M. (1992) *The Investigation, Prosecution and Trial of Serious Fraud*, London: HMSO.

Lidstone, K. (1984) *Magisterial Review of the Pre-Trial Criminal Process: A Research Report*, Sheffield: University of Sheffield Centre for Criminological and Socio-Legal Studies.

Llewelyn, K. (1962) *Jurisprudence: realism in theory and practice*, Chicago, IL: University of Chicago Press.

Locke, J. (1967) *Two Treatises of Government*, London: Cambridge University Press.

The Macpherson Report (1999) Cm 4262-I, London: HMSO.

Lord Chancellor's Department (2002) *Further Findings: A Continuing Evaluation of the Civil Justice Report*, London: Lord Chancellor's Department.

Lord Chancellor's Department (2003) *Delivering Value for Money in the Criminal Defence Service*, Consultation Paper, London: Lord Chancellor's Department.

Maine, Sir H. (1917) *Ancient Law*, London: Dent.

Mair, G. and May, C. (1997) *Offenders on Probation* (Home Office Research Study No. 167), London: HMSO.

Making Simple CFAs a Reality (2004), London: Department of Constitutional Affairs.

Malleson, K. (1993) *A Review of the Appeal Process* (Royal Commission on Criminal Justice Research Series No. 17), London: HMSO.

Mansfield, M. (1993) *Presumed Guilty: The British Legal System Exposed*, London: Heinemann.

Markus, K. (1992) 'The Politics of Legal Aid' in *The Critical Lawyer's Handbook*, London: Pluto Press.

Marsh, N. (1971) 'Law reform in the United Kingdom: A new institutional approach', *William and Mary Law Review*, 13, 263.

Marx, K. (1933) *Capital*, London: J.M. Dent.

Matthews, R., Hancock, L. and Briggs, D. (2004) *Jurors' Perceptions, Understanding Confidence and Satisfaction in the Jury Systems: A Study in Six Courts*, London: Home Office.

McCabe, S. and Purves, R. (1972) *The Jury at Work: A Study of a Series of Jury Trials in which the Defendants was Acquitted*, Oxford: Blackwell.

McConville, M. (1992) 'Videotaping Interrogations: Police Behaviour On and Off Camera', *Criminal Law Review*, 907.

McConville, M. and Baldwin, J. (1977) *Negotiated Justice: Pressures to Plead Guilty*, Oxford: Martin Robertson.

McConville, M. and Baldwin, J. (1981) *Courts, Prosecution and Conviction*, Oxford: Oxford University Press.

McConville, M. and Hodgson, J. (1993) *Custodial Legal Advice and the Right to Silence* (Royal Commission on Criminal Justice Research Study No. 16), London: HMSO.

McConville, M., Sanders, A. and Leng, P. (1993) *The Case for the Prosecution: Police Suspects and the Construction of Criminality*, London: Routledge.

Mendelle, P. (2005) 'No detention please, we're British?' *New Law Journal* 155, 77.

Mill, J.S. (1859) *On Liberty*, London: J.W. Parker.

Millar, J., Bland, N. and Quinton, P. (2000) *The Impact of Stop and Search on Crime and the Community*, Police Research Series Paper 127, London: Home Office.

Millar, J., Bland, N. and Quinton, P. (2000) *Upping the PACE? An Evaluation of the Recommendations of the Stephan Lawrence Inquiry on Stop and Search*, Police Research Series Paper 128, London: Home Office.

Mirlees-Black, C. (1999) *Domestic Violence: Findings from the British Crime Survey Self-completion Question*, London: Home Office.

Mitchell, B. (1983) 'Confessions and Police Interrogation of Suspects', *Criminal Law Review*.

Modernising Justice (1997) Cm 4155, London: Home Office.

Montesquieu, C. (1989) *The Spirit of the Laws*, Cambridge: Cambridge University Press.

Mooney, J. (1999) *The North London Domestic Violence Survey: Final Report*, London: Centre for Criminology, Middlesex University.

Moore, R. 'The methods for enforcing financial penalties: the need for a multi-dimensional approach' [2004] *Criminal Law Review* 728.

Morgan, R. and Russell, N. (2000) *The Judiciary in the Magistrates' Courts* (Home Office RDS Occasional Paper No. 66), London: Home Office.

Moxon, D. (1985) *Managing Criminal Justice: A Collection of Papers*, London: HMSO.

Moxon, D. and Crisp, D. (1994) *Case Screening by the Crown Prosecution Service: How and Why Cases are Terminated*, London: HMSO.

Mullins, C. (1990) *Error of Judgement: The Truth about the Birmingham Bombings*, Dublin: Poolbeg Press.

Narey, M. (1997) *Review of Delay in the Criminal Justice System*, London: Home Office.

National Audit Office (1999) *Criminal Justice Working Together*, London: Stationery Office.

No More Excuses – A New Approach to Tackling Youth Crime in England and Wales (1998), London: Home Office.

Nobles, R. (2005) 'The Criminal Cases Review Commission: establishing a workable relationship with the Court of Appeal' [2005], *Criminal Law Review* 173.

Norrie, A. (1999) 'After Woollin', *Criminal Law Review* 532.

Nozick, R. (1975) *Anarchy, State and Utopia*, Oxford: Blackwell.

Nuttall, C., Goldblatt, P. and Lewis, C. (1998) *Reducing Offending: An Assessment of Research Evidence on Ways of Dealing with Offending Behaviour* (Home Office Research Study No. 187), London: Home Office.

Olivercrona, K. (1971) *Law as Fact*, London: Stevens.

Owers, A. (1995) 'Not Completely Appealing', *New Law Journal* vol. 145, 353.

Packer, H. (1968) *The Limits of the Criminal Sanction*, Stanford, CA: Stanford University Press.

Pannick, D. (1987) *Judges*, Oxford: Oxford University Press.

Paterson, A. (1982) *The Law Lords*, London: Macmillan.

Peach, Sir L. (1999) *Appointment Processes of Judges and Queen's Counsel in England and Wales*, London: HMSO.

Pickles, J. (1988) *Straight from the Bench*, London: Coronet.

Pleasence, P. (2004) *Causes of Action: civil law and social justice*, London: HMSO.

Plotnikoff, J. and Wilson, R. (1993) *Information and Advice for Prisoners about Grounds for Appeal and the Appeal Process* (Royal Commission on Criminal Justice Research Study No. 18), London: HMSO.

Pound, R. (1968) *Social Control Through Law*, Hamden: Archon Books.

Quinton, P., Bland, N. and Miller, J. (2000) *Police Stops, Decision-making and Practice*, Police Research Series Paper 130, London: Home Office.

Race and the Criminal Justice System: an overview to the complete statistics 2003–2004 (2005), London: Criminal Justice System Race Unit.

Raine, J. and Walker, C. (2002) *The Impact of the Courts and the Administration of Justice of the Human Rights Act 1998*, London: Lord Chancellor's Department, Research Secretariat.

Ramsbotham, Sir D. (1997) *Women in Prison*, London: Home Office.

Rawls, J. (1972) *A Theory of Justice*, Oxford: Oxford University Press.

Rawls, J. (1972) *Political Liberalism, John Dewey Essays in Philosophy*, New York: Columbia University Press.

Rawls, J. (2001) *Justice as Fairness: A Restatement*, London: Harvard University Press.

Renton, D. (1975) *The Preparation of Legislation*, London: HMSO.

Restorative Justice: helping to meet local need (2004) London: Office for Criminal Justice Reform.

Review of the Crown Prosecution Service (The Glidewell Report) (1998) Cm 3960, London: HMSO.

Robertson, G. (1993) *Freedom, The Individual and The Law*, London: Penguin.

Royal Commission on Criminal Justice Report (1993), Cm 2263, London: HMSO.

Royal Commission on the Reform of the House of Lords, Report of the (2000) *A House for the Future*, Cm 4534, London: HMSO.

Sanders, A. (1993) 'Controlling the Discretion of the Individual Officer' in Reiner, R. and Spencer, S. (eds) *Accountable Policing*, London: Institute for Policy Research.

Sanders, A. and Bridge, L. (1982) 'Access to Legal Advice' in Walker, C. and Sturner, K. (eds) *Justice in Error*, London: Blackstone.

Sanders, A. *et al.* (1989) *Advice and Assistance at Police Stations and the 24 Hour Duty Solicitor Scheme*, London: Lord Chancellor's Department.

Schur, E. (1965) *Crimes Without Victims: Deviant Behaviour and Public Policy, Abortion, Homosexuality, Drug Addiction*, New York: Prentice Hall.

Skryme, Sir T. (1979) *The Changing Image of the Magistracy*, London: Macmillan (2nd edn, 1983).

Smith and Bailey: see Bailey, S. and Gunn, M. (2002).

Smith, A. *et al.* (1973) *Legal Problems and the Citizen*, London: Heinemann.

Smith, D. and Gray, J. (1983) *Police and People in London* (The Policy Studies Institute), Aldershot: Gower.

Smith, J.C. and Hogan, B. (2002) *Criminal Law*, London: Butterworths.

Stanko, E. (2000), *The Day to Count: A Snapshot of Domestic Violence in the UK*, London: Royal Holloway, University of London.

Stern, V. (1987) *Bricks of Shame: Britain's Prisons*, London: Penguin.

Summers, R. (1992) *Essays on the Nature of Law and Legal Reasoning*, Berlin: Duncker & Humblot.

Tata, C., T. Goriely, P. McCrone, *et al.* (2004) 'Does mode of delivery make a difference to criminal case outcomes and clients' satisfaction? The public defence solicitor experiment' [2004], *Criminal Law Review* 120.

Taylor, R. (1997) *Cautions, Court Proceedings and Sentencing in England and Wales 1996*, London: Home Office.

Thomas, D. (1970) *Principles of Sentencing: The Sentencing Policy of the Court of Appeal Criminal Division*, London: Heinemann.

Thomas, D., 'The Criminal Justice Act 2003: Custodial sentences' [2004], *Criminal Law Review* 702.

Tonry, M. (1996) *Sentencing Matters*, Oxford: Oxford University Press.

Twining, W. and Miers, D. (1991) *How To Do Things With Rules*, London: Weidenfeld & Nicolson.

Vennard, J. (1985) 'The Outcome of Contested Trials' in Moxon, D. (ed.) *Managing Criminal Justice*, London: HMSO.

Vennard, J. and Riley, D. (1988a) *Triable Either Way Cases: Crown Court or Magistrates' Court?*, London: HMSO.

Vennard, J. and Riley, D. (1988b) 'The use of peremptory challenge and stand by of jurors and their relationships with trial outcome', *Criminal Law Review*, 7, 31.

Vogt, G.S. and Wadham, J. (2002) *Deaths in Custody: Rights and Remedies*, London: Civil Liberties Trust.

Waldron, J. (1989) *The Law*, London: Routledge.

Walker, N. (1999) 'The end of an old song?', 149 *New Law Journal* 64.

Warnock, M. (1986) *Morality and the Law*, Cardiff: University College Cardiff.

Weber, M. (1979) *Economy and Society*, Berkeley: University of California Press.

White, P. and Power, I. (1998) *Revised Projections of Long Term Trends in the Prison Population to 2005*, London: Home Office.

White, P. and Woodbridge, J. (1998) *The Prison Population in 1997*, London: Home Office.

White, R. (1973) 'Lawyers and the Enforcement of Rights' in Morris, P., White, R. and Lewis, P. (eds) *Social Needs and Legal Action*, London: Martin Robertson.

Whittaker, C. and Mackie, A. (1997) *Enforcing Financial Penalties*, London: Home Office.

Williams, G. (1983) *Textbook of Criminal Law*, London: Stevens & Sons.

Willis, J. (1938) 'Statutory interpretation in a nutshell', 16, *Canadian Bar Review*, 1–27.

Wilson, W. (2003) *Criminal Law: Doctrine and Theory*, London: Pearson Education.

Women in Prison: A Thematic Review (1997), London: Home Office.

Wolfenden, J. (1957) 'Report of the Committee on Homosexual Offences and Prostitution', Cm 2471, London: HMSO.

Woodhead, Sir P. (1998) *The Prison Ombudsman's Annual Report*, London: Home Office.

Woolf, Lord Justice H. (1995) *Access to Justice: Interim Report to the Lord Chancellor on the Civil Justice System in England and Wales*, London: Lord Chancellor's Department.

Wootton, B. (1981) *Crime and the Criminal Law: Reflections of a Magistrate and Social Scientist*, Oxford: Clarendon Press.

Yarrow, S. (1997) *The Price of Success: Lawyers, Clients and Conditional Fees*, London: Policy Studies Institute.

Yearnshire, S. (1997) 'Analysis of cohort' in Bewley, S., Friend, J. and Mezey, G. (eds) *Violence Against Women*, London: RCOG Press.

Young, J. (1971) *The Drugtakers: The Social Meaning of Drug Use*, London: Paladin.

Young, S. (2005) 'Clementi: in practice', *New Law Journal*, 155, 45.

Your Right to Know (1997) Cm 3818, London: HMSO.

Zander, M. (1988) *A Matter of Justice*, Oxford: Oxford University Press.

Zander, M. (1998) 'The Government's plans on civil justice', *Modern Law Review*, 61, 382.

Zander, M. (1999) *The Law Making Process*, London: Butterworths.

Zander, M. (2000) 'The complaining juror', *New Law Journal*, 150, 723.

Zander, M. (2001) 'Should the legal profession be shaking in its boots?', *New Law Journal*, vol. 151, no 6975, p. 369.

Zander, M. (2005) 'The Prevention of Terrorism Act 2005', *New Law Journal*, 155, 438.

Zander, M. and Henderson, P. (1993) *Crown Court Study*, London: HMSO.

Glossary

Absolute discharge. When a court has found a person guilty it can order an *absolute discharge*. This will be done where the court believes that in the circumstances it is unnecessary to punish the person. It effectively means that no action is taken at all against the individual.

Actus reus. Comprises all the elements of a criminal offence other than the state of mind of the defendant.

Administrative law. The body of law which deals with the rights and duties of the state and the limits of its powers over individuals.

ADR. An abbreviation for 'alternative dispute resolution'. It refers to methods of resolving disputes outside the traditional court forum.

Adversarial system. A legal system which puts considerable emphasis on a public trial where the parties are able to present evidence orally and the judge merely plays the role of an arbiter. The adversarial system is frequently contrasted with an inquisitorial system.

Advisory, Conciliation and Arbitration Service. This body mediates in many industrial disputes and unfair dismissal cases.

Advocates General. These assist the judges in the European Court of Justice. They produce opinions on the cases assigned to them, indicating the issues raised and suggesting conclusions. Their opinions do not bind the judges but are frequently followed in practice.

Alternative dispute resolution. Methods of resolving disputes outside the traditional court forum.

Anti-social behaviour order. Section 1 of the Crime and Disorder Act 1998 provides that an anti-social behaviour order (ASBO) can be made against a person aged 10 or over who has acted in an anti-social manner and is likely to do so again. Anti-social behaviour is behaviour that is likely to cause harassment, alarm or distress to someone not in the same household. While the ASBO is obtained using civil procedures, breach of the ASBO can give rise to the criminal sanctions of a fine or imprisonment.

Appropriate adult. An adult who accompanies the young offender in the police station. They may be any responsible adult, including the young person's parent or a social worker.

Arbitrators. Individuals who hear arbitration cases. They may be lawyers or experts in the subject of the dispute.

Arraignment. The process whereby the accused is called to the Bar of the court to plead guilty or not guilty to the charges against him or her.

Bail. Bail may be granted to a person accused of an offence, convicted or under arrest. When a person is granted bail it means that they are released under a duty to attend a court or police station at a given time.

Bar Council. The governing body for barristers. It acts as a kind of trade union, safeguarding the interests of barristers, and also as a watchdog, regulating barristers' training and activities.

BarDIRECT. A scheme under which individuals and organizations, such as police forces and insurers, may be approved by the Bar Council to instruct barristers directly.

Bench. A term used to describe the judge or judges (including magistrates) who sit and hear a case.

Bill of Rights. A statement of the basic rights which a citizen can expect to enjoy.

Binding over to be of good behaviour. This order can be made against any person who has breached the peace. People who are bound over have to put up a sum of money and/or find someone else to do so; this sum will be forfeited if the undertaking is broken. The order usually lasts for a year.

Bye-laws. A form of delegated legislation made by local authorities, public and nationalized bodies.

Cab rank rule. Under the cab rank rule, barristers must accept any case which falls within their claimed area of specialization and for which a reasonable fee is offered, unless they have a prior engagement.

Case management. The court, and in particular the judge, is the active manager of the litigation.

Case stated. Under this procedure, a person who was a party to a case before the magistrates (or the Crown Court when it is hearing an appeal from the magistrates) may question the decision of the court on the ground that there was an error of law or the court had acted outside its jurisdiction. The party asks the court to state a case for the opinion of the High Court on the question of law or jurisdiction.

Caution. 1. A warning to an accused person administered on arrest or before police questioning. Since the abolition, by the Criminal Justice and Public Order Act 1994, of the right to silence, the correct wording is: 'You do not have to say anything. But it may harm your defence if you do not mention when questioned something which you later rely on in court. Anything you do say may be given in evidence.'

2. A formal warning given to an offender about what he or she has done, designed to make him or her see that he or she has done wrong and deter him or her from further offending. This process is used instead of proceeding with the prosecution.

Caution-plus. Sir Robin Auld has recommended that a system of caution-plus should be introduced. This would allow the prosecutor, with the consent of the offender, to impose a caution combined with a condition as to their future conduct where a minor offence is alleged to have been committed. Offenders would be brought before the court if they breached one of the conditions.

Certiorari. An order quashing an *ultra vires* decision.

Chambers. The offices of a barrister.

Claimant. The party who issues legal proceedings.

Class action. A claimant or small group of claimants bring an action for damages on behalf of a whole class of claimants.

Committal proceedings. An initial hearing in the magistrates' courts for triable either-way offences. They are designed to allow the magistrates to check that there is sufficient evidence to proceed to a full Crown Court trial and to filter weak cases.

Community sentence. This means a sentence of one or more community orders.

Conditional fee agreement. A lawyer agrees to take no fee or a reduced fee if he or she loses a case, and raises the fee by an agreed percentage if it is won, up to a maximum of double the usual fee.

Constitution. A set of rules and customs which detail a country's system of government; in most cases it will be a written document but in some countries, including Britain, the constitution cannot be found written down in one document and is known as an unwritten constitution.

Contingency fee. A fee payable to a lawyer (who has taken on a case on a 'no win, no fee' basis) in the event of him or her winning the case.

Convention. 1. A long-established tradition which tends to be followed, although it does not have the force of law.

2. A treaty with a foreign power.

Conveyancing. The legal process of transferring an interest in land.

Corporation aggregate. This term covers groups of people with a single legal personality (e.g. a company, university or local authority).

Corporation sole. This is a device which makes it possible to continue the official capacity of an individual beyond their lifetime or tenure of office; e.g. the Crown is a corporation sole; its legal personality continues while individual monarchs come and go.

Council on Tribunals. A body that was established following the 1957 Franks Report. It exercises an advisory role over the tribunal system. It has 10 to 15 members appointed by the Lord Chancellor.

Counsel's opinion. A barrister's advice.

CPS. An abbreviation for 'Crown Prosecution Service'. This institution brings criminal prosecutions on behalf of the state.

Cracked trial. A case in which public money and administration is wasted because, once the court room is booked and the parties ready to proceed with a full trial, the defendant pleads guilty, leaving no time to arrange for another case to slot into the court timetable.

Criminal Defence Service. This has replaced the old system of criminal legal aid. Through the Legal Services Commission, the Criminal Defence Service provides direct funding for the provision of criminal legal services, employs public defenders and pays for duty solicitor schemes.

Crown Prosecution Service. This institution brings criminal prosecutions on behalf of the state.

Curfew. Home detention curfews were introduced by the Crime and Disorder Act 1998. Released prisoners under a curfew are required to remain at a certain address at set times, during which period they will be subjected to electronic monitoring.

Custody officer. The police officer who has responsibility for the welfare of any individual being held in detention in the police station. One of the ways he or she does this is by maintaining a custody record.

Custody plus. Under a system of custody plus, an offender spends a maximum of three months in custody, and is then released and subjected to a minimum six months' post-release supervision in the community. A court can attach specific requirements to the sentence, based upon those available under a community sentence.

Custom. 'Such usage as has obtained the force of law' (**Tanistry Case**, 1608).

Deferred sentence. A court is allowed to delay passing a sentence for up to six months after conviction.

Delay defeats equities. Where a claimant takes an unreasonably long time to bring an action, equitable remedies will not be available.

Directives. A form of European legislation discussed on p. 75.

Disclosure of documents. The procedure whereby one party to an action provides the other party with a list of documents relating to the action which are or have been in his or her possession. The other party can then ask to see some or all of the documents.

Divisional Court. This is also known as the Queen's Bench Division and is a Division of the High Court. The major part of its work is handling those contract and tort cases which are unsuitable for the county courts. Its judges also hear certain criminal appeals and applications for judicial review.

Double jeopardy. In the past once a person had been tried and acquitted they could not be retried for the same offence, under the principle of double jeopardy. The application of this principle has been significantly reduced by the Criminal Justice Act 2003.

Draft Bill. A proposed piece of legislation.

Duty solicitors. Solicitors working under the duty solicitor schemes. They are available to give free legal advice at police stations and magistrates' courts.

Either-way cases. Criminal cases that can be tried either in the magistrates' court or in the Crown Court.

Ejusdem generis rule. General words which follow specific ones are taken to include only things of the same kind.

Enabling Act. An Act of Parliament which grants the power to make delegated legislation.

Equity. In law it is a term which applies to a specific set of legal principles which were developed by the Chancery Court and add to those provided in the common law.

Executive. The administrative arm of the state.

Expert witness. A person who is not a party to legal proceedings, but who provides expert evidence to the court.

Expressio unius est exclusio alterius. Express mention of one thing implies the exclusion of another.

Freemasonry. A secret society with an all-male membership. Among its stated aims is the mutual advancement of its members.

Habeas corpus. This is an ancient remedy which allows people detained to challenge the legality of their detention and, if successful, to get themselves quickly released.

Hereditary peers. These are members of the British aristocracy who inherit their title.

He who comes to equity must come with clean hands. This means that a claimant who has been in the wrong in some way will not be granted an equitable remedy.

He who seeks equity must do equity. Anyone who seeks equitable relief must be prepared to act fairly towards his or her opponent.

Indictable offences. These are the more serious offences, such as rape and murder. They can only be heard by the Crown Court. The indictment is a formal document containing the alleged offences against the accused, supported by brief facts.

Inquisitorial system. A legal system where the judge plays a dominant role in collecting evidence before the trial. The final trial is often just to rubber-stamp the investigating judge's findings.

Intermediate recidivist. An offender in his or her late twenties or early thirties with a criminal record dating back to childhood.

Judicial review. The courts undertake a review of the process that has been followed in making a decision and can make sure that the public authority had the power to make this decision.

Jury vetting. This consists of checking that the potential juror does not hold 'extremist' views which some feel would make them unsuitable for hearing a case. It is done by checking police, Special Branch and security service records.

Justice of the peace. An alternative name for lay magistrates.

Law centres. Offices which offer a free, non-means-tested legal service to people who live or work in their area.

Law Commission. A government body that considers possible reforms of the law.

Law Officers. They are the Attorney-General and the Solicitor-General.

Law Society. The solicitors' professional body.

Lawyer. This is a general term which covers both branches of the legal profession, namely barristers and solicitors, as well as many people with a legal qualification.

Leap-frog procedure. This is the procedure provided for in the Administration of Justice Act 1969, whereby an appeal can go directly from the High Court to the House of Lords, missing out the Court of Appeal.

Legal executive. A member of the Institute of Legal Executives, who frequently carries out legal work within a firm of solicitors or as an in-house lawyer.

Limited liability partnerships. These were created in 2001. Solicitors can choose to form a limited liability partnership. Under this type of partnership a partner's liability is limited to negligence for which he or she was personally responsible.

Lord Chancellor. A Government Minister who used to be responsible for the Lord Chancellor's Department.

Lord Chief Justice. He or she presides over the Criminal Division of the Court of Appeal.

Mandamus. An order requiring a particular thing to be done.

Master of the Rolls. He or she presides over the Civil Division of the Court of Appeal.

McKenzie friend. A litigant in person may take with him to the court or tribunal someone to advise him (a McKenzie friend), but that person may not usually address the court.

Means test. This looks at the financial position of the applicant for state funding.

Mediation. This is an alternative method of dispute resolution. A mediator is appointed to help the parties to a dispute reach an agreement which each considers acceptable.

Mens rea. Traditionally refers to the state of mind of the person committing the crime.

Natural law. A kind of higher law, to which we can turn for a basic moral code. Some, such as St Thomas Aquinas, see this higher law as coming from God, others see it simply as the basis of human society.

Obiter dicta. This is Latin and can be translated as 'things said by the way'. All the parts of the judgment which do not form part of the *ratio decidendi* of the case are called *obiter dicta*. This part of the judgment is merely persuasive and not binding.

Orders in Council. A form of delegated legislation made by Government in times of emergency. They are approved by the Privy Council and signed by the Queen.

Parenting order. A court order designed to help and support parents (or guardians) in addressing their child's anti-social behaviour.

Parliament. Consists of the House of Commons, the House of Lords and the monarch.

Per incuriam. Where a previous decision has been made in ignorance of a relevant law it is said to have been made *per incuriam*.

Pilot schemes. These are established to test in selected areas the impact of reforms that could subsequently be introduced more widely.

Plaintiff. This is the old term used to describe the person who issued legal proceedings. Following reforms introduced to civil litigation in 1999, the plaintiff is now known as the claimant.

Plea bargaining. This is the name given to negotiations between the prosecution and defence lawyers over the outcome of a case; e.g. where a defendant is choosing to plead not guilty, the prosecution may offer to reduce the charge to a similar offence with a smaller maximum sentence in return for the defendant pleading guilty to that offence.

Practice direction. An official announcement by the court laying down rules as to how it should function.

Pre-action protocol. A code of conduct for pre-trial proceedings.

Prohibition. An order prohibiting a body from acting unlawfully in the future; e.g. it can prohibit an inferior court or tribunal from starting or continuing proceedings which are, or threaten to be, outside their jurisdiction, or in breach of natural justice.

Public Bills. Proposals for a piece of legislation that have been prepared by the Cabinet.

Public defenders. Defence lawyers who are employed by the Legal Services Commission. They are based in regional offices, can provide the same services as lawyers in private practice and have to compete for work.

Puisne judges. High Court judges are also known as puisne judges (pronounced puny) meaning junior judges.

Pupillage. A one-year apprenticeship in which pupils assist a qualified barrister, who is known as their pupil master.

Queen's Bench Division. A Division of the High Court. The major part of its work is handling those contract and tort cases which are unsuitable for the county courts. Its judges also hear certain criminal appeals and applications for judicial review.

Queen's Counsel. Senior members of the barrister profession.

Ratio decidendi. This is Latin and can be translated as the 'reason for deciding'. The *ratio decidendi* of a judgment is the legal reasons on which the decision is based.

Remand. Detention prior to a conviction or sentencing where bail has been refused.

Restorative justice. Offenders are required to provide a remedy to their victims or the community at large.

Retribution. Retribution is concerned with recognizing that the criminal has done something wrong and with taking revenge on behalf of both the victim and society as a whole.

Rights of audience. The rights to carry out advocacy in front of a court.

Royal Assent. A procedure under which the monarch consents to the passing of legislation. It transforms a Bill into an Act of Parliament.

Royal Commission. These are established to study a particular area of law reform, usually as a result of criticism and concern about the area concerned.

Secret soundings. A process which involves civil servants in the Lord Chancellor's Department gathering information about potential candidates for judicial office over a period of time by making informal inquiries from leading barristers and judges.

Small claims track. This is a procedure used by the county courts to deal with claims under £5,000.

Solicitor advocates. Solicitors who have successfully completed the additional training required in order to exercise their rights of audience before the higher courts.

Sovereignty of Parliament. This has traditionally meant that the law which Parliament makes takes precedence over that from any other source, but this principle has been qualified by membership of the European Union.

Stand by. As members of the jury panel are called and before they are sworn in, the prosecution may ask for them to *stand by*, without giving any reasons for this. They will then not be able to sit on the jury.

Stare decisis. This is Latin and can be translated as 'let the decision stand'. Under this principle, once a decision has been made on how the law applies to a particular set of facts, similar facts in later cases should be treated in the same way.

Statutory charge. Where a person has received state funding for civil proceedings, if the costs recovered from the other party and the contributions made by the state-funded party do not cover the amount paid by the state, the difference can be recovered from the damages awarded by the court (subject to certain restrictions in matrimonial cases). Where the statutory charge applies, the state funding is more like a loan.

Stereotype. A presumption as to the characteristics of a group of people.

Stipendiary magistrates. These judges are now known as 'district judges (magistrates' court)'. They are professional judges who sit in the magistrates' court.

Summary offences. These are most minor crimes and are only triable summarily in the magistrates' courts. 'Summary' refers to the process of ordering the defendant to attend court by summons, a written order usually delivered by post, which is the most frequent procedure adopted in the magistrates' court.

Tariff system. The tariff sentencing system is based on treating like cases alike: people with similar backgrounds who commit similar offences in similar circumstances should receive similar sentences.

Ultra vires. This is Latin and can be translated as 'beyond the powers'. It refers to the situation where a public authority has overstepped their powers.

Veto. A power to block a decision.

Wednesbury principle. This principle, which was laid down in **Associated Picture Houses Ltd** *v* **Wednesbury Corporation**, is that a decision will be held to be outside a public body's power if it is so unreasonable that no reasonable public body could have reached it.

Woolf Report. The official name of the Woolf Report is *Access to Justice*, which was published in 1996. It is the report of the review of the civil courts which was chaired by Lord Woolf and was the basis for the reforms to the civil justice system that were introduced in 1999.

Youth court. Young offenders are usually tried in youth courts (formerly called juvenile courts), which are a branch of the magistrates' court. Youth courts must sit in a separate court room, where no ordinary court proceedings have been held for at least one hour. Strict restrictions are imposed as to who may attend the sittings of the court.

Zero tolerance. A concept that was developed in the USA during Ronald Reagan's time in office; it has come to mean that the law will be strictly enforced in order to reduce crime.

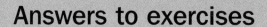

Answers to exercises

Chapter 1 Case law

Know your terms 1.1

1 *Stare decisis*: this is Latin and can be translated as 'let the decision stand'. Under this principle, once a decision has been made on how the law applies to a particular set of facts, similar facts in later cases should be treated in the same way.
2 *Ratio decidendi*: this is Latin and can be translated as the 'reason for deciding'. The *ratio decidendi* of a judgment is the legal reasons on which the decision is based.
3 *Obiter dicta*: this is Latin and can be translated as 'things said by the way'. All the parts of the judgment which do not form part of the *ratio decidendi* of the case are called *obiter dicta*.

Task 1.2

The judges in **In Re Pinochet** were Lord Browne-Wilkinson, Lord Goff, Lord Nolan, Lord Hope and Lord Hutton.

Quick quiz 1.3

1 Case law, Acts of Parliament, delegated legislation and legislation of the European Union.
2 1966.
3 Where the previous decision was made in ignorance of a relevant law; there are two previous conflicting decisions; there is a later, conflicting House of Lords' decision; and a proposition of law was assumed to exist by an earlier court and was not subject to argument or consideration by that court.
4 The High Court.

Quick quiz 1.4

1 When a decision of a lower court is overruled, the outcome of the decision remains the same. When it is reversed, the decision of the lower court is changed.
2 *Law's Empire.*
3 Critical theorists.
4 William Blackstone.

Task 1.5

1 In this context 'retrospectively' refers to the fact that judgments can have an effect on matters that occurred prior to the date that the decision was given.
2 See the first paragraph of the Practice Statement.
3 See the second paragraph of the Practice Statement.
4 See the third paragraph of the Practice Statement.

Chapter 2 Statute law

Task 2.2

A prohibition order prohibits a person from entering a place specified in the order for a maximum period of two years.

The explanatory notes state at paragraph 26 that: 'This Part of the Act provides for the extension of electronic monitoring. It creates a new disposal – an exclusion order – which can be used as a free-standing sentence or as a requirement of a community penalty. This order will require an offender to stay away from a certain place or places at certain times. Such monitoring is aimed at offenders who present a particular danger or nuisance to a particular victim or particular victims.'

Know your terms 2.3

1 *Hereditary peers* are members of the British aristocracy who inherit their title.
2 *Royal Assent* is when the monarch consents to the passing of legislation, transforming a Bill into an Act of Parliament.
3 *Public Bills* are proposals for a piece of legislation that have been prepared by the Cabinet.

Quick quiz 2.4

1 Green Paper.
2 Public Bill drafted.
3 First reading in the House of Commons.
4 Second reading in the House of Commons.
5 Committee stage in the House of Commons.
6 Report stage.
7 Third reading.
8 House of Lords considers the Public Bill.
9 Royal Assent.

Task 2.5

1 It prohibits the use of torture by the State.
2 The leader of the Conservative Party.
3 They do not have the power to strike down Acts of Parliament, but can only declare an Act to be incompatible with the European Convention.

Chapter 3 Statutory interpretation

Quick quiz 3.1

Any of the following cases could have been discussed:

Literal rule	See **Whitely** *v* **Chapell** (1868) and **Fisher** *v* **Bell** (1961) on p. 36
Golden rule	See **R** *v* **Allen** (1872), **Adler** *v* **George** (1964) and **Inco Europe Ltd** *v* **First Choice Distribution** (2000) on p. 37
Mischief rule	See **Smith** *v* **Hughes** (1960) and **Elliott** *v* **Grey** (1960) on p. 37

Quick quiz 3.2

1 The literal rule, the golden rule and the mischief rule.
2 The statute itself, rules of language and presumptions.
3 You could mention any of the following: the historical setting, dictionaries and textbooks, explanatory notes, reports that preceded the legislation, the Human Rights Act 1998 and *Hansard*.
4 The House of Lords ruled that *Hansard* could be consulted in order to determine the intention of Parliament when interpreting statutes.

Quick quiz 3.3

1 Dworkin thinks that the judges should favour the interpretation that allows the provision to sit most comfortably with the purpose of the rest of the law and with the principles and ideals of law and legality in general.
2 The article was called 'Statute Interpretation in a Nutshell'.
3 The case was concerned with Ken Livingstone's attempts to reduce the price of public transport in London. The case was of interest to Griffith because he thought it illustrated the way judges really make decisions.
4 Under the purposive approach to statutory interpretation, the judges seek to interpret statutes in ways that promote the general purpose of the legislation, even if this means paying less than usual regard to the actual wording of the statute.

Chapter 4 Delegated legislation

Task 4.1

1 The Data Protection Act 1998 (Commencement) Order 2000 can be found at:

http://www.hmso.gov.uk/si/si2000/20000183.htm

The power to make the Order was granted by ss. 67(2) and 75(3) of the Data Protection Act 1998.
2 The main provisions of the Data Protection Act 1998 came into force on 1 March 2000.

Know your terms 4.2

1 In a *judicial review* hearing the courts undertake a review of the process that has been followed in making a decision and can make sure that the public authority had the power to make this decision.
2 The term *ultra vires* is Latin and can be translated as 'beyond the powers'. It refers to the situation where a public authority has overstepped its powers.
3 *Bye-laws* are a form of delegated legislation made by local authorities, public and nationalized bodies.
4 *Orders in Council* are a form of delegated legislation made by Government in times of emergency. They are approved by the Privy Council and signed by the Queen.
5 An *enabling Act* is an Act of Parliament which grants the power to make delegated legislation.

Quick quiz 4.3

1 Statutory instruments, bye-laws and Orders in Council.
2 You could mention any of the following: insufficient parliamentary time, speed, technicality of the subject matter, need for local knowledge, flexibility and future needs.
3 Under the affirmative resolution procedure delegated legislation is laid before one or both Houses of Parliament and becomes law only if a motion approving it is passed within a specified time.
4 Procedural *ultra vires*, substantive *ultra vires* and unreasonableness.

Chapter 5 European law

Quick quiz 5.2

1 Twenty-five.
2 The Commission, the Council, the European Parliament and the European Court of Justice.
3 This is discussed on p. 71.
4 Unanimity, simple majority and qualified majority. This is discussed on p. 73.

Know your terms 5.3

1 The *Advocates General* assist the judges in the European Court of Justice. They produce opinions on the cases assigned to them, indicating the issues raised and suggesting conclusions. These do not bind the judges but are frequently followed in practice.
2 A *veto* is a power to block a decision. The European Parliament has a power of veto over the appointment of the Commission as a whole.
3 The *European Commission* is discussed on p. 68.
4 *Directives* are a form of European legislation discussed on p. 75.

Chapter 6 Law reform

Quick quiz 6.2

1 The case went to the House of Lords. The *ratio decidendi* of a case is the legal principle on which the decision was based. In this case the *ratio decidendi* was that a man could be criminally liable for the offence of rape where the victim was his wife.
2 Repeal, creation, consolidation and codification.
3 There are various pressure groups which you could have given as examples. Some examples are given in the text at pp. 84 5.
4 There is no right or wrong answer here. One of the reasons the Government was opposed to the campaign was that known paedophiles were likely to move and hide their new addresses making them a greater danger to children as their movements could not be monitored by the police and social services.

Quick quiz 6.5

1 1965.
2 This is discussed on pp. 90–1.
3 Criminal Law Revision Committee.
4 Lord Scarman.
5 These are discussed on pp. 95–6.

Chapter 7 The judiciary

Know your terms 7.1

1 The process of *secret soundings* involved civil servants in the Lord Chancellor's Department gathering information about potential candidates for judicial office over a period of time by making informal inquiries from leading barristers and judges.
2 The *Lord Chancellor* is discussed on pp. 103–5.
3 The *Master of the Rolls* presides over the Civil Division of the Court of Appeal.
4 The *Lord Chief Justice* presides over the Criminal Division of the Court of Appeal.

Task 7.2

1 No.
2 Horse hair.
3 No.

Quick quiz 7.3

1 The Criminal Division of the Court of Appeal.
2 The Minister for Constitutional Affairs, temporarily exercising the Lord Chancellor's powers.
3 The Queen on the advice of the Prime Minister, who in turn is advised by the Minister for Constitutional Affairs, temporarily exercising the Lord Chancellor's powers.
4 The Judicial Studies Board.
5 The doctrine of the separation of powers was first put forward by the eighteenth-century French political theorist, Montesquieu. This doctrine states that the only way to safeguard individual liberties is to ensure that the power of the state is divided between three separate and independent arms: the judiciary, the legislature and the executive. The idea is that each arm of the state should operate independently, so that each one is checked and balanced by the other two and none becomes all-powerful.

Quick quiz 7.4

1 Dismissal, discipline, resignation, retirement and removal.
2 The French political theorist, Montesquieu.
3 Sixty-six.
4 No.

Know your terms 7.5

1 The *executive* is the administrative arm of the state.
2 *Freemasonry* is a secret society with an all-male membership. Among its stated aims is the mutual advancement of its members.
3 The *Law Society* is the solicitors' professional body.
4 A *stereotype* is a presumption as to the characteristics of a group of people.

Chapter 8 The legal professions

Know your terms 8.1

1 The *Law Society* is the governing body of the solicitor profession.
2 *Conveyancing* is the legal process of transferring an interest in land.

3 *Rights of audience* are the rights to carry out advocacy in front of a court.

4 *Solicitor advocates* are solicitors who have successfully completed the additional training required in order to exercise their rights of audience before the higher courts.

Quick quiz 8.2

1 92,000.

2 They automatically acquire full rights of audience on becoming qualified, though they are only able to exercise these rights on completion of the necessary additional training.

3 98 per cent.

4 Consumer Complaints Service.

Task 8.3

1 The Office of Fair Trading has suggested that the rank of QC inflates the prices of barristers' services. The Bar Council argue that it is an important quality mark which directs the clients to experienced, specialist lawyers as required.

Know your terms 8.4

1 *Limited liability partnerships* were created in 2001. Solicitors can choose to form a limited liability partnership. Under this type of partnership a partner's liability is limited to negligence for which he or she was personally responsible.

2 The *Bar Council* is the governing body for barristers. It acts as a kind of trade union, safeguarding the interests of barristers, and also as a watchdog, regulating barristers' training and activities.

3 *Pupillage* is a one-year apprenticeship in which pupils assist a qualified barrister, who is known as their pupil master.

4 *Queen's Counsel* are senior members of the barrister profession.

Task 8.6

1 The person who uses the legal services.

2 Competition can ensure that professional fees are not higher than they need to be and that the professional rules do not unnecessarily inhibit efficiency.

3 Standards, integrity and concern for the client.

4 In trying to achieve a minor goal, something very valuable may be lost.

Chapter 9 The jury system

Quick quiz 9.1

1 No.

2 Libel and slander, malicious prosecution, false imprisonment and fraud.

3 18–70.

4 People who had been sentenced to prison or a young offenders' institute or its equivalent might have been disqualified from jury service, depending on how long the sentence was for and how recently it was made.

Quick quiz 9.2

1 See p. 164.

2 See p. 166.

3 Where a jury has been reduced to 10, then a majority of nine votes is required. For a full jury a majority of 10 is required.

4 See p. 167.

Task 9.3

1 Yes.

2 No.

Quick quiz 9.4

1 On the ground that the jury's decision had been perverse.

2 Where a person has been acquitted of an offence and someone is subsequently convicted of interfering with or intimidating jurors or witnesses in the case.

3 The matter has not yet been considered by the European Court of Human Rights, but Sir Robin Auld thought that the Convention right was probably not violated.

4 A trial in a magistrates' court.

Know your terms 9.5

1 *Jury vetting* consists of checking that the potential juror does not hold 'extremist' views which some feel would make him/her unsuitable for hearing a case. It is done by checking police, Special Branch and security service records.

2 As members of the jury panel are called and before they are sworn in, the prosecution may ask for them to *stand by*, without giving any reasons for this. They will then not be able to sit on the jury.

3 See pp. 162–3.

4 A summary offence is an offence that can only be tried in the magistrates' court.

Chapter 10 Magistrates

Quick quiz 10.1

1 The Lord Chancellor appoints lay magistrates in the name of the Crown.

2 The Local Advisory Committees interview candidates for the lay magistracy and make recommendations to the Lord Chancellor as to who should be appointed.

3 An applicant must be under 65 and live within 15 miles of the commission area for which he or she is appointed.

4 70.

Know your terms 10.2

1 *Stipendiary magistrates* are now known as 'district judges (magistrates' court)'. They are professional judges who sit in the magistrates' court.

2 The term *Justice of the Peace* is an alternative name for lay magistrates.

3 *The Bench* is the term used to describe the judge or judges (including magistrates) who sit and hear a case.

4 *Royal Commissions* are established to study a particular area of law reform, usually as a result of criticism and concern about the area concerned. They are discussed on p. 89.

Quick quiz: 10.4

1 See p. 188.
2 Three.
3 The primary function of the justices' clerk is to advise the lay magistrates on law and procedure. They are not supposed to take any part in the actual decision of the Bench.
4 See p. 193.

Chapter 11 Access to justice

Quick quiz 11.1

1 'Lumpers' were people of low income and low education levels. They were also frequently unemployed. They were unable to see any way out of their money and employment problems and therefore did absolutely nothing.
2 1949.
3 The six schemes were:
   ■ the legal advice and assistance scheme (known as the 'green form' scheme because of the paperwork used);
   ■ assistance by way of representation (ABWOR);
   ■ civil legal aid;
   ■ criminal legal aid;
   ■ duty solicitor schemes in police stations;
   ■ duty solicitor schemes for criminal cases in magistrates' courts.
4 The Legal Aid Board.

Quick quiz 11.2

1 1 April 2001.
2 The Legal Services Commission.
3 Community Legal Service Partnership.
4 The five categories are:
   ■ Legal Help
   ■ Legal Representation
   ■ Help at Court
   ■ Approved Family Help
   ■ Family Mediation.

Know your terms 11.3

1 See p. 215.
2 A *means test* looks at the financial position of the applicant for state funding.
3 The *Criminal Defence Service* has replaced the old system of criminal legal aid. Through the Legal Services Commission, the Criminal Defence Service provides direct funding for the provision of criminal legal services, employs public defenders and pays for duty solicitor schemes.
4 *Public defenders* are defence lawyers who are employed by the Legal Services Commission. They are based in regional offices, can provide the same services as lawyers in private practice and have to compete for work.

Task 11.5

1 A person being detained in a police station is in a very vulnerable position and access to a free lawyer aims to prevent miscarriages of justice. However, a minority of people detained in the police station are rich enough to pay for the services of a lawyer.
2 There might, for example, be cases which are particularly serious or where the detainee is particularly vulnerable (perhaps due to their age or disability) that make it particularly important that they see a lawyer.
3 Some defendants who turned up at court without a lawyer would have to represent themselves. They might not be able to express themselves clearly.
4 It may cause delay. Hearings may need to be postponed until a defendant has found a lawyer.
5 The number is likely to increase.

Quick quiz 11.6

1 See p. 219.
2 See p. 219.
3 The research found that many people felt that the legal system had given them a second-rate service. The research criticized the apparent lack of commitment and poor communication of some solicitors. There were still not enough solicitors and advisers specializing in areas like social security, housing, disability, discrimination, employment and immigration law.
4 See p. 222.

Know your terms 11.7

1 *Duty solicitors* work under the duty solicitor schemes. They are solicitors who are available to give free legal advice at police stations and magistrates' courts.
2 *Pilot schemes* are established to test in selected areas the impact of reforms that could subsequently be introduced more widely.
3 *Law centres* offer a free, non-means-tested legal service to people who live or work in their area.
4 Under a *conditional fee agreement* a lawyer can agree to take no fee or a reduced fee if he or she loses a case and to raise the fee by an agreed percentage if he/she wins, up to a maximum of double the usual fee.

Chapter 12 The police

Quick quiz 12.1

1 The Human Rights Act 1998.
2 Article 6.
3 The successful appeal of the Birmingham Six.
4 Lord Runciman.

Quick quiz 12.2

1 Police and Criminal Evidence Act 1984.
2 Criminal Justice and Public Order Act 1994.
3 They do not form part of the law and breach of these codes cannot be the ground for a legal action, but can give rise to disciplinary procedures.
4 No, at common law the police cannot physically detain a person without carrying out an arrest: **Kenlin *v* Gardiner** (1967).

Quick quiz 12.3

1 Section 1 of PACE.
2 Code of Practice A.
3 See pp. 246–7.
4 When a member of the public detains a person suspected of committing a crime.

Chapter 13 The criminal trial process

Quick quiz 13.1

1 Under s. 30 of PACE, an arrested person should normally be taken to the police station.
2 The police have to bring the person before a magistrates' court as soon as practicable: s. 46 of PACE.
3 Four days.
4 No. But a person's failure to answer questions may be used as evidence against him/her.

Quick quiz 13.2

1 The Royal Commission on Criminal Procedure 1981.
2 1985.
3 Yes, the neighbour can bring a private prosecution.
4 The Director of Public Prosecutions.

Know your terms 13.3

1 In an *inquisitorial system* the judge plays a dominant role in collecting evidence before the trial. The final trial is often just to rubber-stamp the investigating judge's findings.
2 The *custody officer* is the police officer who has responsibility for the welfare of any individual being held in detention in the police station. One of the ways he or she does this is by maintaining a custody record.
3 *Bail* may be granted to a person accused, convicted or under arrest for an offence. When a person is granted bail, it means that he or she is released under a duty to attend a court or police station at a given time.
4 *Remand* is a form of detention. A person is held on remand when he or she has been charged with a criminal offence but not yet convicted and sentenced for that offence and bail has been refused.

Task 13.4

Type of offence	Trial court
Summary	Magistrates' court
Triable either way	Magistrates' court or Crown Court
Indictable offence	Crown Court

Quick quiz 13.5

1 Summary offences, indictable offences and offences triable either way.
2 Adversarial.
3 The judges exercise tight control over the progress of a case through the criminal courts.
4 The Crown Court.

Task 13.7

1 81.8 per cent.
2 Fewer defendants are being convicted.
3 The percentage of cases being dismissed by the magistrates' court has remained unchanged.

Know your terms 13.8

1 *Indictable offences* are those offences heard by the Crown Court.
2 *Committal proceedings* are initial hearings in the magistrates' courts for triable either-way offences. They are designed to allow the magistrates to check that there is sufficient evidence to proceed to a full Crown Court trial and to filter weak cases.
3 *Plea bargaining* is the name given to negotiations between the prosecution and defence lawyers over the outcome of a case.
4 *Cracked trials* are those cases in which public money and administration is wasted because, once the court room is booked and the parties are ready to proceed with a full trial, the defendant pleads guilty, leaving no time to arrange for another case to slot into the court timetable.

Task 13.9

1 You could consider in particular the question of drug offences and offences committed by minors.
2 The appellate structure refers to the different courts where appeals can be heard.
3 The Human Rights Act 1998 which incorporated into national law the European Convention on Human Rights.

Chapter 14 Young offenders

Quick quiz 14.1

1 Ten.
2 In local authority accommodation.
3 A reprimand for a first offence, followed by a warning for a subsequent offence, then a charge on a third occasion.
4 There must be sufficient evidence; the young person must admit the crime; he/she must have no previous convictions and it is not in the public interest to bring a prosecution.

Task 14.2

1 A motoring offence.
3 46 per cent.

Quick quiz 14.3

1 The youth court.
2 Young persons can only be tried in a Crown Court if the offence with which they are charged is murder, manslaughter or causing death by dangerous driving, or if they are at least 14 years old and are likely if convicted to be detained under s. 90, PCC(S)A 2000 (this applies where they are charged with a very serious offence usually involving violence). They may also sometimes be tried in the Crown Court if there is a co-defendant in the case who is an adult.
3 Article 6 guaranteeing a right to a fair trial.
4 56 days.

Know your terms 14.4

1 *Remand* is detention prior to a conviction where bail has been refused.

2 Sir Robin Auld has recommended that a system of *caution-plus* should be introduced. This would allow the prosecutor with the consent of the offender to impose a caution combined with a condition as to the offender's future conduct where a minor offence is alleged to have been committed. Offenders would be brought before the court if they breached one of the conditions.

3 An *appropriate adult* is an adult who accompanies the young offender in the police station. This may be any responsible adult, including the young person's parent or a social worker.

4 *Zero tolerance* is a concept that was developed in the United States during Ronald Reagan's time in office, and has come to mean that the law will be strictly enforced in order to reduce crime.

Chapter 15 Sentencing

Quick quiz 15.1

1 Punishment, reduction of crime, reform and rehabilitation, protection of the public and reparation.

2 Criminals often act on impulse.

3 See p. 305.

4 The judge.

Task 15.2

1 Some parents felt that they had been forced to become unpaid jailers.

2 No.

3 The aim should be to make a real impact on crime figures and reoffending rates.

Quick quiz 15.3

1 Dr David Thomas.

2 Life imprisonment.

3 See p. 310.

4 See p. 313.

Quick quiz 15.4

1 See pp. 318–19.

2 £36,000.

3 75,000.

4 See p. 316.

Know your terms 15.5

1 *Retribution* is concerned with recognizing that the criminal has done something wrong and with taking revenge on behalf of both the victim and society as a whole.

2 An *intermediate recidivist* is an offender in his or her late twenties or early thirties with a criminal record dating back to their childhood (see p. 311).

3 When a court has found a person guilty it can order an *absolute discharge*. This will be done where the court believes that in the circumstances it is unnecessary to punish the person. It effectively means that no action is taken at all against the individual.

4 A *deferred sentence* allows the court to delay passing a sentence for up to six months after conviction.

Chapter 16 Sentencing young offenders

Task 16.1

1 People who are 21 years and over.
2 There could be a range of reasons for this, but one of the most important is that they are more likely to have already received a non-custodial sentence and subsequently reoffended, so that the court has now decided that a custodial sentence is appropriate.
3 People who are 21 years and over.

Quick quiz 16.2

1 Eighteen.
2 Under s. 90, PCC(S)A 2000 they are sentenced to be detained indefinitely, known as 'during Her Majesty's pleasure'.
3 Under a *detention and training order* a young person between the ages of 12 and 17 can be subjected to an order for between four and 24 months. The offender will spend half the sentence in detention and half under supervision.
4 A referral order.

Know your terms 16.3

1 See p. 342.
2 See p. 345.
3 See p. 344.
4 See p. 346.

Chapter 17 The civil justice system

Quick quiz 17.1

1 The burden of proof is usually on the claimant who must prove his/her case on the balance of probabilities.
2 The Courts and Legal Services Act 1990.
3 *Access to Justice*.
4 Queen's Bench Division, Family Division, Chancery Division.

Quick quiz 17.2

1 See p. 352.
2 26 April 1999.
3 The overriding objective is that the Civil Procedure Rules should enable the courts to deal with cases justly.
4 A claimant.

Task 17.3

1 Cases for a claim worth less than £1,000.
2 Cases for a claim worth more than £50,000.

Quick quiz 17.4

1 A claim form.
2 The county court.
3 Compliance with a pre-action protocol is not compulsory, but if a party unreasonably refuses to comply, then this can be taken into account when the court makes orders for costs.
4 The judge in court.

Know your terms 17.5

1 The *Queen's Bench Division* is a Division of the High Court. The major part of its work is handling those contract and tort cases which are unsuitable for the county courts. Its judges also hear certain criminal appeals and applications for judicial review.
2 The official name of the Woolf Report is *Access to Justice*, which was published in 1996. It is the report of the review of the civil courts which was chaired by Lord Woolf and was the basis for the reforms to the civil justice system that were introduced in 1999.
3 See p. 359.
4 See p. 360.

Know your terms 17.6

1 An *adversarial system* puts considerable emphasis on a public trial where the parties are able to present evidence orally and the judge merely plays the role of an arbiter. The adversarial system is frequently contrasted with an inquisitorial system.
2 See p. 363.
3 See p. 361.
4 See p. 363.

Task 17.7

1 Access to justice.
3 An interim report is a report which is published before the final report, and contains the provisional proposals which, following consultation, may be changed in the final report.
4 No, the government has adopted most of Lord Woolf's proposals.

Quick quiz 17.9

1 Small claims track, fast track and multi-track.
2 The small claims track.
3 See p. 371.
4 Case management tended to increase costs.

Chapter 18 Tribunals

Quick quiz 18.1

1 1957.
2 The Council on Tribunals.
3 Most tribunals consist of a legally trained chairperson and two lay people who have some particular expertise in the relevant subject area.
4 Full funding from the Legal Services Commission is available for only a small number of minor tribunals.

Know your terms 18.2

1 See p. 385.
2 The *Council on Tribunals* was established following the 1957 Franks Report. It exercises an advisory role over the tribunal system. It has 10 to 15 members appointed by the Lord Chancellor. For further details see p. 386.
3 The *Queen's Bench Division* is discussed on p. 8.
4 The *overriding objective* is discussed on p. 354.

Quick quiz 18.3

1 Sir Andrew Leggatt.
2 *Tribunals for Users: One System, One Service.*
3 The four aims were:
   - to make the 70 tribunals into one tribunal system;
   - to render the tribunals independent of their sponsoring departments by having them administered by one Tribunal Service;
   - to improve the training of chairpersons and members in the interpersonal skills particularly required by tribunals;
   - to enable unrepresented users to participate effectively and without apprehension in tribunal proceedings.
4 See p. 393.

Task 18.4

1 The Human Rights Act 1998 has incorporated the European Convention into national law. See p. 30.
2 The appeal courts.
3 A tribunal called the 'School Admissions Appeal Panel' exists to consider these disputes.
4 The Review concluded that the system was not coherent and recommended the establishment of a single Tribunal Service.

Chapter 19 Appeals

Quick quiz 19.1

1 Putting right any unjust or incorrect decision, whether caused by errors of fact, law or procedure and promoting a consistent development of the law.
2 Either the court that made the disputed decision, or the appellate court itself.
3 Three.
4 The Civil Division of the Court of Appeal.

Task 19.2

1 The House of Lords.
2 The Criminal Division.
3 Decreased.
4 The House of Lords' workload had remained the same until 2001 when it increased slightly. This increase has levelled out in recent years.

Quick quiz 19.3

1 The High Court.
2 The House of Lords.

3 1 per cent.

4 New evidence can be admitted if the Court of Appeal thinks it 'necessary or expedient in the interests of justice': Criminal Appeal Act 1968, s. 23(1).

Task 19.4

1 A stakeholder in this context is anyone with an interest in the service provided by the CCRC, with includes lawyers and convicts, and ultimately includes all members of the public.

2 The backlog in undecided cases.

3 An increase in the number of cases being referred to it and problems with recruiting staff.

Know your terms 19.5

1 See p. 400.

2 The *Divisional Court* is also known as the Queen's Bench Division and is discussed at p. 8.

3 See p. 406.

4 See p. 414.

Quick quiz 19.6

1 1995.

2 Where the court thinks the conviction is unsafe.

3 See p. 415.

4 The High Court.

Chapter 20 Alternative methods of dispute resolution

Know your terms 20.1

1 An *adversarial process* places an emphasis on a public trial where the parties are able to present evidence and question the evidence of the other parties. The judge plays only a limited role in the trial proceedings. This type of procedure is frequently contrasted with an inquisitorial system.

2 *Arbitrators* hear arbitration cases. They may be lawyers or experts in the subject of the dispute.

3 *ADR* stands for 'alternative methods of dispute resolution'.

4 *ACAS* stands for 'Advisory, Conciliation and Arbitration Service'. This body mediates in many industrial disputes and unfair dismissal cases.

Quick quiz 20.2

1 The Advisory, Conciliation and Arbitration Service (ACAS).

2 The Family Law Act 1996.

3 The Association of British Travel Agents (ABTA).

4 The Arbitration Act 1996.

Chapter 21 Elements of a crime

Quick quiz 21.1

1 To satisfy the 'but for' test it must be shown that but for the conduct of the accused the result of the offence would not have occurred as and when it did.

2 Under the 'thin skull' test, where the intervening cause is some existing weakness of the victim, the defendant must take the victim as he or she finds him.

3 The *ratio decidendi* of **R v Miller** was that people who are aware that they have done something which has endangered another's life or property, and do nothing to prevent the relevant harm from occurring, may be criminally liable, with the original act being treated as the *actus reus* of the crime.

4 Under a strict application of the law, a stranger might not owe a duty to a baby drowning in a puddle of water.

Know your terms 21.2

1 The *actus reus* comprises all the elements of the offence other than the state of mind of the defendant.

2 *Mens rea* traditionally refers to the state of mind of the person committing the crime.

3 *Cunningham* recklessness exists when a person foresees that the kind of harm that in fact occurred might occur, and went ahead anyway and took that risk.

4 Under the principle of *transferred malice*, if a person has the *mens rea* of a particular crime and does the *actus reus* of the crime, the person is guilty of the crime even though the *actus reus* may differ in some way from that intended. The *mens rea* is simply transferred to the new *actus reus*.

Quick quiz 21.3

1 A person who has direct intention wants to achieve a particular result. A person who has indirect intention does not want to achieve a particular result, but foresaw that result as a virtual certainty.

2 For **Cunningham** recklessness a person must simply have foreseen that a harm might occur. For indirect intention a person must have foreseen that a harm was virtually certain to occur.

3 **R v Woollin**.

4 No, motive is irrelevant to the *mens rea* issue.

Chapter 22 Strict liability in criminal law

Quick quiz 22.1

1 Strict liability offences are those offences which can be committed without *mens rea* regarding at least one aspect of the *actus reus*.

2 There is a presumption that *mens rea* is required.

3 Cause, possession and knowingly.

4 If strict liability applies, an accused cannot use the defence of mistake, even if the mistake was reasonable.

Know your terms 22.3

1 A *regulatory offence* is one in which no real moral issue is involved, and usually (though not always) one for which the maximum penalty is small.

2 A *stigma* is damage to a person's reputation.

3 A *Draft Bill* is a proposed piece of legislation. For further information see p. 25.

4 The *Law Commission* is a Government body that considers possible reforms of the law. For further information see p. 86.

Chapter 23 Non-fatal offences against the person

Know your terms 23.1

1 An *assault* consists of any act which makes the victim fear that unlawful force is about to be used against him or her.
2 A *battery* consists of the application of unlawful force on another.
3 In the case of **Miller** it was stated that *'actual bodily harm* includes hurt or injury calculated to interfere with health or comfort'.
4 In **Cunningham** it was stated that for the purpose of the 1861 Act *maliciously* means 'intentionally or recklessly' and 'reckless' is used in the **Cunningham** sense.

Quick quiz 23.2

1 Yes, words alone can constitute an assault.
2 The *mens rea* of assault is either intention or **Cunningham** recklessness. The defendant either must have intended to cause the victim to fear the infliction of immediate and unlawful force, or must have seen the risk that such fear would be created.
3 The *mens rea* of an assault occasioning actual bodily harm is the *mens rea* of an assault or battery.
4 The difference is that a higher level of *mens rea* is required for a s. 18 than for a s. 20 offence. The *actus reus* is identical.

Task 23.3

1 Violence that takes place in the home and the victim knows their aggressor well.
2 Yes.
3 People who are under 25.

Task 23.4

Intention is defined in Art. 14 of the Bill as:

(1) A person acts intentionally with respect to a result if –
(a) it is his purpose to cause it, or
(b) although it is not his purpose to cause it, he knows that it would occur in the ordinary course of events if he were to succeed in his purpose of causing some other result.

Task 23.5

1 'Court reports' are the reports on court cases in newspapers. 'Drama' is a reference to television programmes, such as *Ally McBeal* and *The Bill*.
2 'Unrepealed' means that the relevant parts of the Act have not been repealed and are still in force.
3 The law contained in a range of different sources is brought together in a single new Act.
4 The Government wants to introduce law that is robust, clear and well understood. The Government's aim is that the proposed new offences should enable violence to be dealt with effectively by the courts and that the law should be set out in clear terms and in plain, modern language.

Chapter 24 Negligence

Task 24.1

1 The House of Lords.
2 The case is also reported in the 1932 volume of the Appeal Cases Reports at p. 562.
3 Five judges heard the case. Their names were Lord Buckmaster, Lord Atkin, Lord Tomlin, Lord Thankerton and Lord Macmillan.
4 'Per LORD ATKIN' means 'Lord Atkin said that'.
5 Lord Buckmaster and Lord Tomlin gave dissenting judgments.
6 Lord Atkin's judgment.
7 In the Bible.
8 The appellant's action was successful and he was entitled to an award of damages.

Quick quiz 24.2

1 **Donoghue** *v* **Stevenson** (1932).
2 A duty of care, breach of that duty and damage resulting from the breach.
3 The neighbour principle lays down a basic test to determine whether a duty of care is owed. Lord Atkin stated in **Donoghue** *v* **Stevenson** that 'You must take reasonable care to avoid acts or omissions which you can reasonably foresee would be likely to injure your neighbour'. For these purposes my neighbours are 'persons who are so closely and directly affected by my act that I ought to have them in contemplation as being so affected when I am directing my mind to the acts or omissions which are called in question'.
4 **Murphy** *v* **Brentwood District Council** is likely to be followed as this case overruled **Anns** *v* **Merton London Borough**.

Quick quiz 24.3

1 A duty of care is breached when the defendant has fallen below the standard of behaviour expected in someone undertaking the activity concerned. The duty is breached if a person has not done what a reasonable person would have done in the circumstances to prevent harm.
2 You could have listed any of the following:
   - the special characteristics of the defendant;
   - the special characteristics of the claimant;
   - the magnitude of the risk;
   - how far it was practicable to prevent the risk;
   - any benefits that might be gained from taking the risk.
3 Yes. Thus, where the defendant is a child, the standard of care is that of an ordinarily careful and reasonable child of the same age: **Mullin** *v* **Richards**.
4 Following **Bolitho** *v* **City and Hackney Health Authority** the doctor must have behaved in a reasonable way, in that he or she had weighed up the risks and benefits of a course of treatment and had a logical basis for their choice of treatment.

Quick quiz 24.4

1 The 'but for' test asks whether the damage would not have occurred but for the breach of duty.
2 The **Wagon Mound (No. 1)**.
3 The current test for remoteness is whether the kind of damage suffered by the claimant was reasonably foreseeable at the time of the breach of duty.

4 Yes, liability will be imposed because so long as the type of damage sustained is reasonably foreseeable, it does not matter that it is in fact more serious than could reasonably have been foreseen.

Know your terms 24.5

1 A *novus actus interveniens* is Latin for a 'new intervening event'. It is the term used to describe intervening events which break the chain of causation.
2 *Res ipsa loquitur* is Latin for 'the facts speak for themselves'. This maxim can apply where the facts of the case are such that an injury could only have been caused by negligence. When the maxim applies the claimant does not have the burden of proving the existence of negligence.
3 An *objective test* is one which imposes the standards of the reasonable person, rather than the standards of the actual defendant.
4 *Contributory negligence* is a defence contained in the Law Reform (Contributory Negligence) Act 1945. Where the defence applies, damages can be reduced to take account of the fact that the fault was not entirely the defendant's.

Chapter 25 Remedies for torts

Quick quiz 25.1

1 Damages and an injunction.
2 The court seeks to put claimants in the position they would have been in if the tort had not been committed.
3 Examples include loss of earnings, medical expenses, damage to clothing and expenses incurred by a carer.
4 Damages for loss of amenity compensate a person where an injury has caused him/her to be unable to enjoy life to the same extent as before. It may include an inability to enjoy sport or any other pastime the claimant enjoyed before the injury, impairment of sight, hearing, touch, taste or smell, reduction in the chance of finding a marriage partner, and impairment of sexual activity or enjoyment.

Know your terms 25.2

1 Under the principle of *restitutio in integrum* an award of damages seeks to restore claimants to the position they would have been in if the tort had not been committed.
2 A *pecuniary loss* is one which can be calculated in financial terms, such as loss of earnings, and medical and other expenses.
3 A *loss of amenity* describes the situation where an injury results in the claimant being unable to enjoy life to the same extent as before.
4 *Interim damages* are an award of damages made prior to the final trial decision, where the defendant admits liability, and is only contesting the amount of damages claimed.

Quick quiz 25.3

1 Under the Supreme Court Act 1981 provisional damages can be awarded where there is a possibility that the injured person will, as a result of the tort, develop a serious disease, or serious physical or mental deterioration in the future.
2 Under the Supreme Court Act 1981 interim damages can be awarded before trial, where the defendant admits liability, and is only contesting the amount of damages claimed. The

defendant must also be insured, or be a public body, or have the resources to make an interim payment.

3 No, it is a matter for the parties to agree between themselves.

4 Set-offs include the tax that a person would have paid on an award for loss of earnings, sick pay and social security benefits.

Quick quiz 25.4

1 No, certain claims continue to exist which are discussed under the heading 'Fatal accidents' on p. 570.

2 Contemptuous damages, nominal damages, aggravated damages and exemplary damages.

3 Contemptuous damages are awarded where a court recognizes that the claimant's legal rights have technically been infringed, but disapproves of his or her conduct, and considers that the action should never have been brought.

4 Aggravated damages will be awarded where a defendant has behaved in such a way that the claimant has suffered more than would normally be expected in such a case.

Index